THE WORLD READERS
Series edited by Robin Kirk and Orin Starn, fou

THE ALASKA NATIVE READER
Edited by Maria *Shaa Tláa* Williams

THE BANGLADESH READER
Edited by Meghna Guhathakurta and Willem van Schendel

THE CZECH READER
Edited by Jan Bažant, Nina Bažantová, and Frances Starn

THE GHANA READER
Edited by Kwasi Konadu and Clifford Campbell

THE INDONESIA READER
Edited by Tineke Hellwig and Eric Tagliacozzo

THE OCEAN READER
Edited by Eric Paul Roorda

THE RUSSIA READER
Edited by Adele Barker and Bruce Grant

THE SOUTH AFRICA READER
Edited by Clifton Crais and Thomas V. McClendon

THE SRI LANKA READER
Edited by John Clifford Holt

The Ocean Reader

THE

OCEAN

READER

HISTORY, CULTURE, POLITICS

Eric Paul Roorda, editor

DUKE UNIVERSITY PRESS *Durham and London* 2020

Library of Congress Cataloging-in-Publication Data
Names: Roorda, Eric, editor.
Title: The ocean reader : history, culture, politics /
Eric Paul Roorda, editor.
Other titles: World readers.
Description: Durham : Duke University Press, 2020. |
Series: The world readers | Includes bibliographical
references and index.
Identifiers: LCCN 2019013468 (print)
LCCN 2019980730 (ebook)
ISBN 9781478006961 (paperback)
ISBN 9781478006008 (hardcover)
ISBN 9781478007456 (ebook)
Subjects: LCSH: Ocean. | Oceanography.
Classification: LCC GC21 .O266 2020 (print) | LCC GC21 (ebook) |
DDC 551.46—dc23
LC record available at https://lccn.loc.gov/2019013468
LC ebook record available at https://lccn.loc.gov/2019980730

Cover art: Surfing waves. © Michael Duva/The Image Bank.
Courtesy of the artist and Getty Images.

produced with a grant from
Hartford Foundation for Public Giving
publication of the global nation

To my brave companions of the Sea and of life:

My father, William Simon Roorda
My spouse, A. E. Dee Doyle
Our daughters, Alida Anna and Frances Elizabeth
My sister, Alida Kay "Leedee" Roorda Berryman
My brothers, Randall and Terence
And most of all, our beloved family matriarch,
Pearl Elaine Carpenter Roorda (1929–2005)

Contents

IV   Saltwater Hunt   121

V   Watery Highways   151

VI   Battlefields   203

A Note on *The Ocean Reader*

Most of the images in *The Ocean Reader* may be found in the Roorda/Doyle Collection. The collection gathers, preserves, and makes available online to the public images and other texts, mainly related to the Ocean and ships, the Dominican Republic, Cuba, and bananas, especially anything having to do with the United Fruit Company (UFCO).

A. E. Dee Doyle began the collection in 2005, while doing research on UFCO at the Munson Institute, when she began to collect ephemera related to the company's operations, beginning with a postcard of a "Great White Fleet" steamship. Doyle's subsequent UFCO acquisitions formed the foundation of the collection.

I also acquired items while pursuing my own research on the Dominican Republic and Cuba. Combining these with Dee's UFCO trove, the aggregate resembled a small archive. So we gave it a name and kept adding to it as we continued to work on our interrelated projects. Years later, the Roorda/Doyle Collection now contains thousands of items, the vast majority being images, including most of the illustrations from my previously published books: *The Dictator Next Door* (Duke University Press, 1998), *Cuba, America, and the Sea* (Mystic Seaport Press, 2005), *The Dominican Republic Reader* (Duke University Press, 2014), and *Twain at Sea: The Maritime Writings of Samuel Langhorne Clemens* (University Press of New England/University of Massachusetts Press, 2018).

The Roorda/Doyle Collection may be acessed at https://www.roorda-doyle.com.

Acknowledgments

The Ocean Reader originated with a graduate program called the Frank C. Munson Institute of American Maritime Studies, founded in 1955 at Mystic Seaport Museum. The anthology represents many aspects of the Munson Institute curriculum, which its faculty has shaped. The work of these scholars made this collection possible. Therefore, I am primarily grateful to the collective Munson Institute faculty, especially the codirector of the program, Glenn S. Gordinier.

I thank James T. Carlton, longtime director of the Williams College–Mystic Seaport Program, for my three great years as its postdoctoral fellow, and for his contributions to this anthology.

I am indebted to John B. Hattendorf, Ernest J. King Professor Emeritus at the U.S. Naval War College and former director of the Munson Institute. Thanks to the Munson Institute's other past faculty for building its strong foundation: former director Ben Labaree, William M. Fowler Jr., Jeffrey J. Safford, and the late Edward W. Sloan.

Among my Munson colleagues, I owe professional gratitude to W. Jeffrey Bolster for giving his time to the institute for a decade, and personal thanks for advising me in 1987 to apply to Long Island University's SEAmester program. Another Munson professor who merits my special thanks is Helen Rozwadowski, an energetic contributor to the Munson program, whose work on the Ocean's third dimension influenced this volume's contents, and whose erudition on the literature of the Ocean was key to assembling the "Suggestions for Further Reading."

Special thanks also to Marcus Rediker for giving his time to the Munson Institute and inspiring its participating scholars; for his many important books, which shaped this anthology's sections on piracy and the slave trade; and for providing the painting by Haitian master Frantz Zéphirin in the color plates.

The National Endowment for the Humanities generously funded Summer Institutes for college educators through the Munson Institute in 1996, 2006, 2010, 2012, 2014, 2016, and 2018, earning our lasting gratitude.

Mystic Seaport Museum graciously hosts the Munson Institute. Thanks to its helpful staff, especially President Steve White, Executive Vice President Susan Funk, Vice President of Collections Paul O'Pecko, Collections Access

Manager Maribeth Bielinski, Carol Mowrey, who also works in Collections Access and administers the Munson Institute's NEH Summer Institutes, and Associate Director of Institutional Advancement Claire Calabretta.

I am thankful for Bellarmine University in Louisville, Kentucky, which has been my academic home since 1996. The late Dr. Margaret H. Mahoney has my fond and undying respect and admiration. She was my loyal mentor until she retired in 2014, after fifty-five years of service at Bellarmine. Thanks to my congenial coworkers in the Department of History: Fedja Buric, Robert Pfaadt, and Timothy K. Welliver. I immensely appreciate the help of our administrative coordinator, Lora Roberts, and her student assistants, who were instrumental in preparing this manuscript.

The Ocean Reader reflects my time at sea, starting with SEAmester, led by C. Douglas Hardy, whom I thank for the experience of eighteen weeks on the Ocean, with its joys and terrors. For living to tell the tale, I thank Captain Bert Rogers of the *Spirit of Massachusetts*, now executive director of the American Sail Training Association. I've made forty voyages since then, totaling more than a year at sea, as a lecturer on cruise ships. Thank you Crystal, Cunard, Holland America, Princess, Regent Seven Seas, Royal Olympia, Seabourn, Silversea, and Viking.

Thank you to everyone who generously helped with permissions for the Reader's contents.

Thanks to Erin Grieb for the map.

Katrina Bercaw has my fond gratitude for kindly contributing photographs and excerpts from her journal of sailing around the world.

Friendly and generous help and encouragement from Deborah Byrd of EarthSky gave me a boost early in this effort—thanks, Deborah!

I thank the anonymous reviewers for offering useful advice and kind words.

Thanks to my advisors at Johns Hopkins, Louis Galambos and Franklin W. Knight Jr., and my mentor at William and Mary, Edward P. Crapol, for always supporting me.

Warm fuzzies to our friend and astrologist Julianne Johnson, a long-distance Ocean sailor, who is a magical touchstone for my family. (Pats for Pip!)

I am very proud of, and thankful for, my association with Duke University Press for more than two decades. I remember with gratitude and admiration the late Valerie Millholland. My editor, Miriam Angress, deserves sainthood for her patience and forbearance. I appreciate the editorial board's decision to publish this volume in the World Readers series. Duke provided the services of a legion of astute and energetic (and patient and forbearing) interns, who put in untold hours preparing this volume for publication. I thank each of them: Martin Caver, Peter Delgobbo, Natasha Derezinski-Choo, Manda Hufstedler, Camila Moreiras, Renee Michelle Ragin, Colleen Sharp, Tamar Malloy, and Whitney Wingate.

My survival depends on A. E. Dee Doyle, my life partner, editor, publicist, webmaster, computer consultant, and curator of our archive, the Roorda/Doyle Collection, source of most of this book's images. Dee's research on the United Fruit Company informed this book's treatment of the cruise industry. Moreover, she is the mother of our daughters, Alida and Frances, who are perfect in every way.

To end at the beginning, I owe an Ocean of gratitude to my parents, the late Pearl Elaine Carpenter Roorda (1929–2005) and the vigorous William Simon Roorda (born in 1923, the son and grandson of sailors). They inspired me to love Big Water, by providing my idyllic childhood summers on the shores of that inland sea Lake Huron.

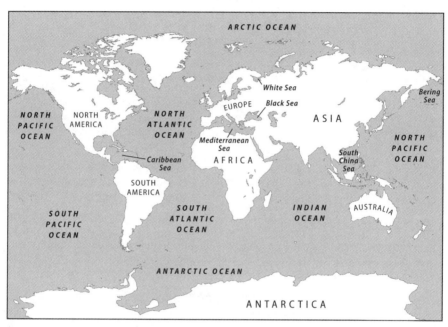

Five Oceans map.

Introduction

This volume of the World Readers series is devoted to the Ocean, which currently covers 71 percent of the world, a figure that is certain to rise along with sea level. The aqueous regions of the earth have been important throughout human history, politics, and culture, but never more so than now.

It has always been difficult for humans to think of the Ocean as a place. Those who have considered the watery majority of the planet on its own terms have often seen it as a changeless space, one without a history. Because the Ocean can't be plowed, paved, or shaped in ways the eye is able to discern, it has seemed to be a constant, while the land has changed drastically over the centuries. The fish and marine mammal populations of the Ocean have also seemed unchangeable, inexhaustible, and impervious to the onslaught of the harvesters. But such is not the case. As this collection emphasizes, the Ocean is changeable, and it has a history.

Terracentrism, a term that is rapidly gaining currency, refers to people's tendency to consider the world and human activity mainly in the context of the land and events that take place on land. This book aims to avoid that natural bias predominating among our terrestrial species and replace it with a steady focus on the Ocean and on events that take place offshore. Such an aquacentric perspective can be found in an increasing number of scholarly works, as the overarching importance of the watery parts of the world gains wider recognition. This awareness in turn contributes to a growing consensus that we need to take concerted action to avoid the devastating consequences of having ignored the Ocean for too long.

The Seven Seas is a mutable concept. In antiquity, the seven bodies of water in question were all really just embayments of the Mediterranean Sea, which itself is merely an embayment of the Atlantic Ocean. The Atlantic Ocean and the other bodies of water now designated as oceans on maps of the world constitute a relatively recent variation of the Seven Seas. In reality, there is only one interconnected global Ocean, with currents that exchange water widely among its different regions, with the same molecules of H_2O moving from one of today's seven Oceans to another, and then another, over the course of ageless and endless cycles of circulation.

There is one big Ocean, and while its regions have been conceptualized as separate bodies of water and named as different Oceans, the fact is, they are all connected, and seawater travels widely and endlessly across these artificial geographic markers. The largest of the regions is the Pacific Ocean, which is an expanse of 64 million square miles (about 165 million square kilometers [km]). It is difficult to grasp such enormous dimensions. By contrast, the landmass of Asia, the largest continent, is only about 17 million square miles (44 million square km), while North America covers just 9.5 million (24.6 million square km), of which the United States represents less than half, with 3.8 million square miles (9.8 million square km). The Atlantic Ocean is half the size of the Pacific, which is nearly ten times the size of the United States, at 32 million square miles (almost 83 million square km), while the Indian Ocean covers 28 million square miles (72.5 square km). The area of the Antarctic, or Southern, Ocean is less than 8 million square miles (20.7 million square km), and the smallest is the Arctic Ocean, with about 5.4 million (14 million square km).

The deepest place in the Ocean is in the Pacific, at the bottom of the Mariana Trench, a fissure in the seafloor some 1,580 miles (2,550 km) long and 43 miles (69 km) wide, which reaches more than 36,000 feet (nearly 11,000 meters [m]), more than 6.8 miles (about 11 km). The deepest Ocean generally is the Antarctic, which ranges from 13,100 to 16,400 feet (4,000–5,000 m) deep, while the average depth of the Indian Ocean is 12,762 feet (3,890 m). The Pacific Ocean averages more than 12,000 feet (3,600 m) deep, and the Atlantic, which reaches a depth of five miles (8 km) in the Puerto Rico Trench, averages nearly 11,000 feet (3,400 m). The shallowest is the Arctic Ocean, with an average depth of less than 3,500 feet (1,050 m), which allows the upwelling of nutrients from the seabed to take place, attracting whales and other sea animals to the northern latitudes.

The tectonic plates that make up the crust of the planet are most active around the Pacific Ocean, which is rimmed by subduction zones known as the Ring of Fire, a chain of submarine volcanoes and fault lines that make the Pacific the most volatile of the seas. Islands form and expand, as Hawai'i continues to do, with the most active volcano in the world pouring molten rock into the sea regularly, and they suddenly disintegrate, as Krakatoa did in 1883, when the largest explosion that has occurred in human history erased most of the island. Undersea earthquakes churn up epochal tsunamis around the Pacific basin, with the Japanese disaster of 2011 being both the most recent and the worst ever recorded.

The winds and waves that sweep over the Ocean are subject to circular patterns collectively known as the Coriolis effect, named for the French physicist Gaspard-Gustave de Coriolis (1792–1843), who first described the phenomenon in 1835. As a result of the earth's rotation, the air and water alike move in gyres, in both hemispheres, with the motion trending clockwise in the north and counterclockwise in the south. These predictable movements in the atmosphere go by names that have gained romantic connotations, such as the southeast and northeast trade winds, and the westerlies. Likewise, the enduring patterns that seawater follows in tandem with the winds have become fluid geographic references. The North and South Equatorial Currents, in both the Atlantic and Pacific Oceans, follow the storied line in opposite directions. The Canary Current brings cold water from the northern Atlantic to the latitude of its namesake islands, then feeds the North Equatorial Current, much like the California Current does in the Pacific Ocean. The chilly Peru Current, 100 miles wide, flows north in the Pacific Ocean, offering a highway for migrating sea life. Perhaps the most famous was the first to be identified, the Gulf Stream, which is equivalent to a thousand Mississippi Rivers gushing forth from the warm Gulf of Mexico and Caribbean Sea, skirting North America, making Bermuda balmy year-round, even when the coast of the Carolinas, 500 miles to the west, is frigid. The largest of them all is the Antarctic Circumpolar Current, or West Wind Drift, which flows clockwise around the frozen continent, a band of constantly moving seawater 13,000 miles (21,000 km) in circumference, with a volume equal to 100 times the combined capacity of all the rivers on the planet!

The Ocean Reader combines a present-day perspective with a broad approach and consciousness of future implications. It serves as an introduction to the multifaceted Ocean, which is an enormous and very complicated system. Humans interact with that system in many ways. They relentlessly hunt sea creatures, taking 90 million tons of fish from it annually. They use it as a highway, with 100,000 ships at sea right now. They study it, find inspiration in it, play on it, and fight over it.

This anthology samples a variety of approaches to understanding the sea, reflecting what might be called the new Ocean history. Kären Wigen introduced this reinvigorated field to the readers of the *American Historical Review* in a special issue called "Oceans of History" in June 2006. She said, "Maritime scholarship seems to have burst its bounds; across disciplines, the sea is swinging into view." Environmental science, social history, marine ecology, and other approaches have combined to transform the field of maritime studies.

The Ocean Reader includes many forgotten or overlooked gems of maritime writing, as well as previously unpublished selections from manuscript sources, from around the world. While the majority of the selections come from sources in English, and many have to do with topics touching on the United States, the balance of the entries come from non-English sources and have to do with other cultures and countries.

Ocean is capitalized in this book. This deviation from conventional style is intended to claim a formal name for that vast place within the realm of World History, as if it were a country or a continent. The stylebook spelling of "ocean" diminishes it as a geographic reference. To capitalize Ocean is to challenge the conventional wisdom that the seas can be taken for granted. They cannot.

The Ocean Reader is organized thematically into twelve parts. Each part consists of selections that range chronologically from the earliest applicable period to the most contemporary. The themes are, basically, as follows: tales of the Ocean's origin, ancient seafaring, exploration, fishing and whaling, warfare, piracy, transportation, survival, religious and artistic inspiration, recreation, marine science, and the dire present and future plight of the Ocean. These categories overlap and intertwine along manifold lines, to the extent that a large proportion of the entries could easily fit into more than one part. Each of the parts could stand alone as a book of its own, a thick volume, even a trilogy, or a series of books, for that matter, because the literature concerning each topic is so vast and rich. It has been an impossible task to choose the perfectly representative sample, one that could be printed as a manageable volume, from this Ocean of words.

However incomplete this Reader must be for that reason, the most important part is the last. It concerns the compounding environmental disasters taking place in the Ocean right now, which are mainly being ignored. Everyone should be aware of this information, because we all depend on the Ocean, which is in trouble.

I

Creation

Numerous religious traditions engage the Ocean, and some even center on it. This part samples from the wide variety of sacred texts that describe the origin of the sea or evoke it as a deity.

A wide variety of cultures through the ages and around the world have had in common earth-diver myths, in which a creator figure ventures to the bottom of the Ocean to bring up soil to create the first land. Such was the case among the Haida and Tlingit people, who inhabited the fertile rain forests blanketing the islands and coastline of southeastern Alaska, where they developed one of the most sophisticated Native American cultures in North America, second only to the México or Aztec civilization in its richness and complexity. In their cosmography, the original creature was Raven, who made the world from a small island and discovered five "earth surface people" in a clam he found on the shore. Similarly, the Wampanoag people of coastal New England believed in a land creator called We'tucks, or Maushop, and a powerful Ocean god named Paumpa'gussit. Several more examples are among the entries below, taken from the long list of cultures with briny tales of earth's origins.

Explanations for the origins of life on the planet in more recent centuries have come from scientists. They have developed numerous theories about how the Ocean formed, which seem as outlandish as the creation myths. One such notion is that comets and asteroids brought water to the earth, an idea greeted with understandable skepticism but that now seems to be supported by the evidence. However water came into being, the scientific consensus today is that for eons, a warm sea covered the earth, in which life originated. This scenario mirrors that of several religious narratives that explain how the world began, which are represented here as well.

The subject of part I is The Beginning, as understood by various religious traditions and scientific schools of thought. It sets the stage for this collection, which gains momentum toward The End.

The Egyptian Sea of Nun

Anonymous

The primordial sea in Egyptian cosmology was called Nun, or Nu, a watery chaos from which emerged Atum, the god of gods, who made everything else. Atum brought forth the land from Nun, then created Shu, the god of air, and Tefnut, the goddess of rain. Becoming curious about the sea, Shu and Tefnut ventured out onto the dark waters of Nun, where they became lost. But Atum sent the sun, in the form of the Eye of Ra, to find them, and when they returned, his tears of joy became the first human beings. The ancient Egyptians believed that Nun surrounded the dry land they inhabited and extended to the land of the dead, so that anyone who journeyed to the afterlife, such as the pharaohs, who had divine status, needed to cross it. Nun also took the form of the Ocean god, depicted as a bearded man with blue and green skin, the colors of the Mediterranean, sometimes shown holding a boat above his head.

Much of what is known today about ancient Egyptian cosmography and religion comes from hieroglyphics found on the walls of the Pyramid of King Wenis, or Unas, the last ruler of the Fifth Dynasty of the Old Kingdom. Known as the Pyramid Texts, they consist of 714 incantations called "utterances," carved and painted in Old Egyptian between 2400 and 2300 BCE, some of which were originally composed as early as 3000 BCE. These enigmatic lines are the oldest religious writings known to exist.

The first full translation of the Pyramid Texts was the work of Samuel A. B. Mercer (1880–1969), published in 1952. The following is his translation of Utterance 503, one of more than thirty incantations having to do with the oceanic Nun.

Utterance 503

> To say: The door of heaven is open, the door of earth is open,
> apertures of the [heavenly] windows are open,
> the steps of Nun are open,
> the steps of light are revealed
> by that one who endures always.
> I say this to myself when I ascend to heaven,
> that I may anoint myself with the best ointment and clothe myself
>   with the best linen,
> and seat myself upon [the throne] of "Truth which makes alive";

while my side is against the side of those gods who are in the north
    of the sky,
the imperishable stars, and I will not set,
the untiring [in swimming], and I will not tire [in swimming],
the one not drawn out of the water, and I will not be drawn out of
    the water.
If *Mnṯ.w* [a star?] is high, I will be high with him,
If *Mnṯ.w* hastens away, I will hasten away with him.

Babylon by the Sea

Anonymous

The creation tale of Mesopotamia, the ancient civilization that flourished between the Tigris and Euphrates Rivers in what is now Iraq 4,000 years ago, is called "Enuma Elish" after its first words. It was discovered in 1849, recorded on seven clay tablets, in the ruins of the Library of Ashurbanipal of ancient Nineveh, the present-day, war-torn city of Mosul. The tablets date to the seventh century BCE, telling a story first told a millennium or more before. According to the first tablet, the whole world began as water, with just two primordial deities: the god Apsu, who commanded freshwater, and the goddess Tiamat, who commanded seawater. The other tablets relate how other gods came into being from these two, preeminent among them Marduk, who led the second generation of deities in a bloody revolt against the first. Using a giant net, Marduk caught Tiamat and pulled her from the sea, then used two new winds he had devised, the hurricane and the tornado, to destroy her. He ripped the Ocean goddess's body in half, creating the land and the sky from the pieces. Marduk then created humankind from the blood of the god Kingu, another predecessor he murdered. Humans built the city of Babylon to honor Marduk, which became the center of Mesopotamia, with its Great Ziggurat, called the Tower of Babel in the Old Testament of the Bible.

The first lines from the first Tablet of Creation follow here, as translated by the eminent scholar Sir Ernest Alfred Wallis Budge (1857–1934) of the British Museum, which houses the original artifacts.

When the heavens above were yet unnamed,
And the name of the earth had not been recorded,
Apsu, the oldest of beings, their progenitor,
"Mummu" Tiamat, who bore each and all of them,
Their waters were merged into a single mass.
A field had not been measured, a marsh had not been searched out,
When of the gods none was shining,
A name had not been recorded, a fate had not been fixed,
The gods came into being in the midst of them.

Aphrodite Born from Sea Spray

Hesiod

The ancient Greeks believed that the Ocean encircled the land in a limitless river, and the Mediterranean Sea bisected the land. In their mythological worldview, the distant shores of the River Ocean were idyllic regions inhabited by peaceful populations, in contrast to the war-torn shores of their own Mediterranean.

The ancient Greeks ascribed their fates to a pantheon of capricious deities, each with powers to control certain aspects of the natural world and the human experience. The most powerful gods were the siblings known to the Greeks as Jupiter, Hades, and Poseidon, called Zeus, Pluto, and Neptune by the later Romans. They were the sons of Kronos, or Saturn, who had emasculated and deposed his own father Uranus to take his place as ruler of the world. Aphrodite, sex goddess of Greek mythology, sprang from the sea spray created when Kronos threw the severed genitals of Uranus into the Ocean. The alluring figure of Aphrodite, or Venus, represents the sensual nature of the sea. She is most famously depicted naked on a scallop shell, by mosaic artists in Pompeii and by the Renaissance master Sandro Botticelli. The Anacreontea, lyrics composed in the fifth century BCE, describes how Aphrodite came: "Roaming over the waves like sea-lettuce, moving her soft-skinned body in her voyage over the white calm sea, she pulls the breakers along her path." Seneca addressed Aphrodite this way in his Phaedra: *"Thou goddess, born of the cruel sea."*

The following selection is from the Theogony, *meaning "Birth of the Gods," written by the Greek poet Hesiod around 700 BCE. It is followed by the sixth poem of the thirty-three anonymous poems known as the* Homeric Hymns, *composed sometime between 700 and 500 BCE. It is one of three devoted to Aphrodite. The translations are the work of Hugh Gerard Evelyn-White (1884–1924), a prolific English author and translator who produced 146 works before his death at the age of forty.*

Hesiod, Theogony

Ouranos (the Sky) came, bringing on night and longing for love, and he lay about Gaia (the Earth) spreading himself full upon her. Then the son [Kronos] from his ambush stretched forth his left hand and in his right took the great long sickle with jagged teeth, and swiftly lopped off his own father's members and cast them away to fall behind him . . . and so soon as he had cut off

The Ocean-born Aphrodite, or Venus, has been the subject of countless canvases. This version of the goddess of love and beauty comes from an 1890s engraving of a painting by Paul-Jacques-Aimé Baudry (1828–86), *The Pearl and the Wave*, 1862. Engraving by Carey, published by Selmar Hess, New York. Courtesy of the Roorda/Doyle Collection.

the members with flint and cast them from the land into the surging sea, they were swept away over the main a long time: and a white foam spread around them from the immortal flesh, and in it there grew a maiden. First she drew near holy Kythera, and from there, afterwards, she came to sea-girt Kypros, and came forth an awful and lovely goddess, and grass grew up about her and beneath her shapely feet. Her gods and men call Aphrodite, and Aphrogeneia (the foam-born) because she grew amid the foam, and well-crowned (*eu-stephanos*), Kythereia because she reached Kythera, and Kyprogenes because she was born in billowy Kypros, and Philommedes (Genital-Loving) because she sprang from the members.[1] And with her went Eros (Love), and comely Himeros (Desire) followed her at her birth at the first and as she went into the assembly of the gods. This honour she has from the beginning, and this is the portion allotted to her amongst men and undying gods—the whisperings of maidens and smiles and deceits with sweet delight and love and graciousness.

Homeric Hymn 6, to Aphrodite

To Sea-set Kypros the moist breath of the western wind (Zephryos) wafted her [Aphrodite] over the waves of the loud-moaning sea in soft foam, and there the gold-filleted Horai (Seasons) welcomed her joyously. They clothed her with heavenly garments: on her head they put a fine, well-wrought crown of gold, and in her pierced ears they hung ornaments of orichalc and precious gold, and adorned her with golden necklaces over her soft neck and snow-white breasts, jewels which the gold-filleted Horai wear themselves whenever they go to their father's house to join the lovely dances of the gods.[2] And when they had fully decked her, they brought her to the gods, who welcomed her when they saw her, giving her their hands. Each one of them prayed that he might lead her home to be his wedded wife, so greatly were they amazed at the beauty of violet-crowned Kythereia.

Notes

1. Kythera is one of the Ionian islands of Greece, and Kypros is Cyprus, the large Mediterranean island.
2. Orichalcum was a yellow metal, perhaps brass or a brass-like alloy, that was highly valued in ancient Greece. The Horai were the goddesses of the seasons and of the movements of the constellations.

Izanagi and Izanami, Japanese Sea Gods

Ō no Yasumaro

The Kojiki is the oldest book written in Japanese, dating to the year 712 CE. The title means "Record of Ancient Things." The volume, compiled by scholars in the imperial court, includes works in a variety of literary genres, such as myths, legends, songs, historical narratives, anecdotes, word origins, and family trees, among others. The Kojiki was long considered to be a sacred text, but in the years since World War II it has come to be viewed as the foundational document of Japanese literature.

In the first two chapters of the Kojiki, "the Five Separate Heavenly Deities" and "the Seven Generations of the Age of the Gods" all emerge into existence from the primordial heavens and seas. At the time, the land was "young and like floating oil, [and] drifted about like a jellyfish." Chapter 3, which follows here, tells how they created the first island from the Ocean. Subsequent chapters tell of how they procreated in the human fashion to conceive and give birth to fourteen more islands and thirty-five additional deities. Basil Hart Chamberlain (1850–1935), one of the leading scholars of Japan in the late nineteenth century, who taught Japanese at Tokyo Imperial University, did the first English translation of the Kojiki in 1882, from which this excerpt is taken.

The Island of Onogoro

Hereupon all the Heavenly deities commanded the two deities His Augustness [Izanagi] the Male-Who-Invites and Her Augustness [Izanami] the Female-Who-Invites, ordering them to "make, consolidate, and give birth to this drifting land." Granting to them a heavenly jeweled spear, they thus deigned to charge them. So the two deities, standing upon the Floating Bridge of Heaven pushed down the jeweled spear and stirred with it, whereupon, when they had stirred the brine till it went curdle-curdle, and drew the spear up, the brine that dripped down from the end of the spear was piled up and became an island. This is the Island of Onogoro.

The Pacific Islanders' Angry Ocean God

George Grey

For thousands of years, the inhabitants of the far-flung archipelagoes of the South Pacific Ocean were more at home on the water than just about any population in human history. More than a thousand islands lie within the region, ranging from New Zealand in the south to Hawai'i in the north, and from the Solomon Islands in the west all the way to Easter Island in the east, including Fiji, the Marquesas, and the Society Islands, the most famous of which are Tahiti and Bora Bora. Beginning between 3,000 and 5,000 years ago, the Southeast Asian ancestors of today's Pacific Islanders navigated across enormous distances of saltwater to land on the shores of relative pinpricks of land, scattered across the forbidding expanse of the Ocean. The creation myth of the ancient islanders was shaped by their collective memories of arduous Ocean passages, and by their mid-Ocean environment, with its ferocious extremes. In the tale, the god of storms objected to how his divine brothers broke up the union of their parents, Heaven and Earth. The storm god took it out on the humans by stirring the Ocean god, Tangaroa, into a frenzy, which still happens regularly.

The island peoples, their similar cultures, and their homelands became known collectively as Polynesian, a term coined in 1756 by a French writer. "Polynesian" is falling into disuse, having been identified as an artifact of imperialist vocabulary by the people to whom it applies, who now prefer the term Pacific Islander. The version of celestial events recounted here comes from one of the most important figures in the history of New Zealand, Sir George Grey (1812–98), who was governor of the British colony twice, for a total of fifteen years, between 1845 and 1868. He compiled the myths of the Maori people of New Zealand and related Pacific Islanders in his 1855 book Polynesian Mythology and Ancient Traditional History of the New Zealand Race.

Children of Heaven and Earth

(KO NGA TAMA A RANGI—Tradition relating to the Origin of the Human Race)

MEN had but one pair of primitive ancestors; they sprang from the vast heaven that exists above us, and from the earth which lies beneath us. According to the traditions of our race, Rangi and Papa, or Heaven and Earth, were the source from which, in the beginning, all things originated. Darkness then rested upon the heaven and upon the earth, and they still both clave together, for they had not yet been rent apart; and the children they had begotten were ever thinking amongst themselves what might be the difference between darkness and light; they knew that beings had multiplied and increased, and yet light had never broken upon them, but it ever continued dark. Hence these sayings are found in our ancient religious services: "There was darkness from the first division of time, unto the tenth, to the hundredth, to the thousandth," that is, for a vast space of time; and these divisions of times were considered as beings, and were each termed "a Po"; and on their account there was as yet no world with its bright light, but darkness only for the beings which existed.

At last the beings who had been begotten by Heaven and Earth, worn out by the continued darkness, consulted amongst themselves, saying: "Let us now determine what we should do with Rangi and Papa, whether it would be better to slay them or to rend them apart." Then spoke Tu-matauenga, the fiercest of the children of Heaven and Earth: "It is well, let us slay them."

Then spake Tane-mahuta, the father of forests and of all things that inhabit them, or that are constructed from trees: "Nay, not so. It is better to rend them apart, and to let the heaven stand far above us, and the earth lie under our feet. Let the sky become as a stranger to us, but the earth remain close to us as our nursing mother."

The brothers all consented to this proposal, with the exception of Tawhiri-ma-tea, the father of winds and storms, and he, fearing that his kingdom was about to be overthrown, grieved greatly at the thought of his parents being torn apart. Five of the brothers willingly consented to the separation of their parents, but one of them would not agree to it.

Hence, also, these sayings of old are found in our prayers: "Darkness, darkness, light, light, the seeking, the searching, in chaos, in chaos"; these signified the way in which the offspring of heaven and earth sought for some mode of dealing with their parents, so that human beings might increase and live.

So, also, these sayings of old time. "The multitude, the length," signified the multitude of the thoughts of the children of Heaven and Earth, and the length of time they considered whether they should slay their parents, that human beings might be called into existence; for it was in this manner that they talked and consulted amongst themselves.

But at length their plans having been agreed on, lo, Rongo-ma-tane, the god and father of the cultivated food of man, rises up, that he may rend apart the heavens and the earth; he struggles, but he rends them not apart. Lo, next, Tangaroa, the god and father of fish and reptiles, rises up, that he may rend apart the heavens and the earth; he also struggles, but he rends them not apart. Lo, next, Haumia-tikitiki, the god and father of the food of man which springs without cultivation, rises up and struggles, but ineffectually. Lo, then, Tu-matauenga, the god and father of fierce human beings, rises up and struggles, but he, too, fails in his efforts. Then, at last, slowly uprises Tane-mahuta, the god and father of forests, of birds, and of insects, and he struggles with his parents; in vain he strives to rend them apart with his hands and arms. Lo, he pauses; his head is now firmly planted on his mother the earth, his feet he raises up and rests against his father the skies, he strains his back and limbs with mighty effort. Now are rent apart Rangi and Papa, and with cries and groans of woe they shriek aloud: "Wherefore slay you thus your parents? Why commit you so dreadful a crime as to slay us, as to rend your parents apart?" But Tane-mahuta pauses not, he regards not their shrieks and cries; far, far beneath him he presses down the earth; far, far above him he thrusts up the sky.

Hence these sayings of olden time: "It was the fierce thrusting of Tane which tore the heaven from the earth, so that they were rent apart, and darkness was made manifest, and so was the light."

No sooner was heaven rent from earth than the multitude of human beings were discovered whom they had begotten, and who had hitherto lain concealed between the bodies of Rangi and Papa.

Then, also, there arose in the breast of Tawhiri-ma-tea, the god and father of winds and storms, a fierce desire to wage war with his brothers, because they had rent apart their common parents. He from the first had refused to consent to his mother being torn from her lord and children; it was his brothers alone that wished for this separation, and desired that Papa-tu-a-nuku, or the Earth alone, should be left as a parent for them.

The god of hurricanes and storms dreads also that the world should become too fair and beautiful, so he rises, follows his mother to the realm above, and hurries to the sheltered hollows in the boundless skies; there he hides and clings, and nestling in this place of rest he consults long with his parent, and as the vast Heaven listens to the suggestions of Tawhiri-ma-tea, thoughts and plans are formed in his breast, and Tawhiri-ma-tea also understands what he should do. Then by himself and the vast Heaven were begotten his numerous brood, and they rapidly increased and grew. Tawhiri-ma-tea despatches one of them to the westward, and one to the southward, and one to the eastward, and one to the northward; and he gives corresponding names to himself and to his progeny the mighty winds.

He next sends forth fierce squalls, whirlwinds, dense clouds, massy clouds, dark clouds, gloomy thick clouds, fiery clouds, clouds which precede hurricanes, clouds of fiery black, clouds reflecting glowing red light, clouds wildly drifting from all quarters and wildly bursting, clouds of thunder storms, and clouds hurriedly flying. In the midst of these Tawhiri-ma-tea himself sweeps wildly on. Alas! alas! then rages the fierce hurricane; and whilst Tane-mahuta and his gigantic forests still stand, unconscious and unsuspecting, the blast of the breath of the mouth of Tawhiri-ma-tea smites them, the gigantic trees are snapt off right in the middle; alas! alas! they are rent to atoms, dashed to the earth, with boughs and branches torn and scattered, and lying on the earth, trees and branches all alike left for the insect, for the grub, and for loathsome rottenness.

From the forests and their inhabitants Tawhiri-ma-tea next swoops down upon the seas, and lashes in his wrath the ocean. Ah! ah! waves steep as cliffs arise, whose summits are so lofty that to look from them would make the beholder giddy; these soon eddy in whirlpools, and Tangaroa, the god of ocean, and father of all that dwell therein, flies affrighted through his seas; but before he fled, his children consulted together how they might secure their safety, for Tangaroa had begotten Punga, and he had begotten two children, Ika-tere, the father of fish, and Tu-te-wehiwehi, or Tu-te-wanawana, the father of reptiles.

When Tangaroa fled for safety to the ocean, then Tu-te-wehiwehi and Ika-tere, and their children, disputed together as to what they should do to escape from the storms, and Tu-te-wehiwehi and his party cried aloud: "Let us fly inland"; but Ika-tere and his party cried aloud: "Let us fly to the sea." Some would not obey one order, some would not obey the other, and they escaped in two parties: the party of Tu-te-wehiwehi, or the reptiles, hid themselves ashore; the party of Punga rushed to the sea. This is what, in our ancient religious services, is called the separation of Tawhiri-ma-tea.

Hence these traditions have been handed down: "Ika-tere, the father of things which inhabit water, cried aloud to Tu-te-wehiwehi: 'Ho, ho, let us all escape to the sea.'

"But Tu-te-wehiwehi shouted in answer: 'Nay, nay, let us rather fly inland.'

"Then Ika-tere warned him, saying: 'Fly inland, then; and the fate of you and your race will be, that when they catch you, before you are cooked, they will singe off your scales over a lighted wisp of dry fern.'

"But Tu-te-wehiwehi answered him, saying: 'Seek safety, then, in the sea; and the future fate of your race will be, that when they serve out little baskets of cooked vegetable food to each person, you will be laid upon the top of the food to give a relish to it.'

"Then without delay these two races of beings separated. The fish fled in confusion to the sea, the reptiles sought safety in the forests and scrub[land]s."

Tangaroa, enraged at some of his children deserting him, and, being sheltered by the god of the forests on dry land, has ever since waged war on his brother Tane, who, in return, has waged war against him.

Hence Tane supplies the offspring of his brother Tu-matauenga with canoes, with spears and with fish-hooks made from his trees, and with nets woven from his fibrous plants, that they may destroy the offspring of Tangaroa; whilst Tangaroa, in return, swallows up the offspring of Tane, overwhelming canoes with the surges of his sea, swallowing up the lands, trees, and houses that are swept off by floods, and ever wastes away, with his lapping waves, the shores that confine him, that the giants of the forests may be washed down and swept out into his boundless ocean, that he may then swallow up the insects, the young birds, and the various animals which inhabit them—all which things are recorded in the prayers which were offered to these gods.

Pele Loses Her Temper

Anonymous

The Hawaiian creation myth, called the Pele cycle, involves two sisters: Pele, goddess of fire, lightning, and volcanoes, and Nāmaka, goddess of the Ocean. Pele created the islands using volcanoes, but argued with her sister, who sent tidal waves to devastate Pele's lands. Since then, Nāmaka has perpetually besieged the archipelago with punishing surf.

Today, the Ocean is imposing its domination of earth again, inundating the margins of every landmass. Rising seas are already forcing people who live on islands in Alaskan waters, the South Pacific, and many other places to leave their homes, as encroaching saltwater threatens to erase them from the changing map.

Geologists tell a tale of earth's creation that is similar to the ancient Hawaiian Pele cycle. In their rendition, volcanoes rose from the seafloor over eons of spasmodic eruptions. These volcanic creators of new land are still busy all over the world, especially on Hawai'i, home to Kīlauea, the most active volcano of them all. Kīlauea continues to add to the Big Island, which gets bigger every time it disgorges lava in a stream that reaches the Ocean, where it becomes hard, black, dry land. The impressive eruption of Kīlauea in this photograph took place in 1925, almost a decade after the creation of Hawai'i Volcanoes National Park, which preserves its otherworldly landscape.

Mark Twain commented on the link between Hawaiian religion and volcanoes in his description of Kīlauea, which he visited in 1865, and wrote about in his 1872 book Roughing It: "All the natives are Christians, now, but many of them still desert to the Great Shark God for temporary succor in time of trouble. An irruption of the great volcano of Kilauea, or an earthquake, always brings a deal of latent loyalty to the Great Shark God to the surface. It is common report that the King, educated, cultivated and refined Christian gentleman as he undoubtedly is, still turns to the idols of his fathers for help when disaster threatens."

Missouri farm boy Earl "Dutch" Baldwin, who joined the US Navy and traveled the world in the late 1920s, bought this impressive photograph of the 1925 outburst of Kīlauea at a store in Honolulu, when his ship called there a short time later, and added it to his photograph album, where it took up a whole page by itself. Photographer unknown, from the Earl "Dutch" Baldwin Photograph Albums. Courtesy of the Roorda/Doyle Collection.

The Hindu Ocean Gods

Edward Washburn Hopkins

The Vedic religion, also called ancient Hinduism and Brahmaism, originated around 1,750 BCE in northern India. It is based on scriptures written in Sanskrit, organized into four compilations called the Vedas, which describe and relate the exploits of the devas, the pantheon of Vedic deities. Chief among these gods was Varuna, the god of water, the Ocean, the night sky (the stars were said to be his eyes), the dead, and the underworld. As Vedism developed into modern Hinduism, Varuna lost his exalted status in the pantheon of gods, first to Indra, then later to Vishnu and Shiva. But he is still recognized as the god of the western Ocean (while the eastern Ocean has become associated with the Ganges River) and is a symbol of strength and courage. In the rich iconography of Hinduism, Varuna often has four arms, rides on a giant sea monster called a Makara, and frequently wields a lasso and a Varunastra, a water weapon capable of taking the form of any weapon and of becoming a storm. The following description of Varuna is from a 1915 study titled Epic Mythology *by Edward Washburn Hopkins (1857–1932), a Yale professor who was the leading scholar of the Sanskrit language in the early twentieth century.*

Varuna and Ocean

Vestiges of his ancient glory and position remain to "king Varuna," who is armed with noose and thunderbolt . . . and once had a conch shell. A warrior in action is "like Varuna" and warriors are "children of Varuna" or "like sons of Varuna." The conch shell belongs to Varuna because he was born in ocean. . . .

All this, however, is no indication of Varuna's real epic position. He is no longer a heavenly god, no longer a god rivalling Indra, or having stars as eyes. He is lord of water, *Apampati, Salilendra, Jaladhipa, Jalesvara, Ambhasam raja, Varipa, Udakapati, Ambupati,* river-lord, *Saritampati,* and lord of the monsters of the deep . . . hence he is beryl-colored (*vaiduryavarna*), as well as white and also "cloud-dark" (*jaladharasyamo Varuno Yadasampatih*). The waters are medicinal, curative; hence Varuna is lord of the "constellation having a hundred medicines," and "the physician who performs the rite in honor of his ancestors under the asterism of Varuna would obtain success." . . . He is also *prac-*

etas, the "wise" god (water and wisdom are ever united), and perhaps as such is reckoned the father of the epic poet. Varuna is formally consecrated by the gods as lord of rivers and waters and told that his home shall be in Ocean, the home of *makaras*; that Ocean, the Lord of Rivers, shall be under his will. . . . There seems to be actually no difference felt here (though expressed) between Ocean and Varuna. . . . The home of Varuna is to be "always (*sada*) in Ocean"; and the final words can refer only to the tides of Ocean, though addressed to Varuna.

The heavenly world of Varuna is another reminiscence of his origin, but it does not offset the universal epic belief that his home is under the western waters, or in the waters under the earth, thought of as reaching westward rather than eastward, in contrast to Ocean whose wife is the Ganges. . . . The Ram[ayana] places the home of Varuna on the very peak of the western mountains in the general "district guarded by Varuna, who has a noose in hand."[1] Elsewhere he is represented as living in Ocean or as occupying both Ocean and the mountains. Both epics agree that his palace was made by Visvakarman, the gods['] artificer, and is bright or sunlike and white. . . . It is "undecaying," an epithet of Ocean, and has walls, gateways, etc., being surrounded by trees bearing jewels, where sing beautiful birds; it is neither too hot nor too cold.[2] Varuna, dressed in divine garments and gems sits there with Varum and about him are garlanded and perfumed *Adityas*, hosts of *Daityas*, *Danavas*, and *Nagas*, and the four oceans in person, rivers, lakes, the four personified directions, [the] *DiSas*, mountains (who converse), aquatic animals, *timi, timingila, makara, jhasa, kurma, graha*. . . .[3]

Ocean, *Sagara* (*Samudra*), is personified as subservient to Varuna. He is husband of Ganges, and is called *Aiksvaka Sagara*. . . . He persuades Rama to shoot the *Brahmastra* at the *Dasyus* and *Abhiras*, who had polluted his streams.[4] Agastya, son of Varuna, drinks up Ocean, to discover the *Kaleyas*.[5] King Sagara excavated Ocean's bed, hence Ocean is called Sagara. Sagara exhorted a mountain to rise and help Hanumat.[6] He injured his mother and apparently went to hell for this impiety. Dundubhi challenged him to fight but he was afraid.[7] Kartavirya attacked Ocean (Samudra).[8] Utathya also drank up Ocean. He was cursed several times, to have sharks, by Brhaspati, because his water was unfit for rinsing the god's mouth; and by Vadavamukha, the Mare's Mouth, to become salt, because he would not come to Mt. Meru when bidden to do so.[9] Till the divine Mare's Mouth drinks him up he will remain salt, the sweat of the divine being having given him his salt. Hence, it is said that a seer's wrath made Ocean salty.

Notes

1. The Ramayana is an epic poem of the fourth–fifth centuries BCE, consisting of 24,000 verses that fill seven volumes, recounting the deeds of Rama, an avatar of the preeminent

god, Vishnu. The Ramayana and the Mahabharata are considered the two great works of Hindu literature.

2. Visvakarman, the "maker of all," is the creator of the universe in Vedism, the forerunner of Brahma, the god of artisans and architects.

3. The Adityas are the twelve sun gods, one for each month of the year; the Daityas and the Danavas were races of giants, or Asuras, who competed with the more benign Devas for power; the Nagas were an ancient warrior tribe. Timi and Timingila were huge aquatic creatures capable of swallowing whales whole, described in the Hindu epic Mahabharata; Jhasa means huge fish or whale; Kurma was the second avatar of Vishnu, who is said to have "churned the milky Ocean"; the Graha are nine astrological figures that include the Sun, Moon, Mars, Mercury, Venus, Jupiter, Saturn, and the northern and southern lunar nodes.

4. Brahmastra was a devastating weapon created by Brahma, the deva of creation. Dasyus are superhuman enemies, and Abhiras are members of a tribe that plays a role in the Mahabharata.

5. Agastya was a saint and scholar extolled in the Vedas. The Kaleyas were a tribe of sea pirates.

6. Hanumat is a god and follower of Rama who plays a central role in the Ramayana.

7. Dundubhi is a particularly ferocious Asura, or giant.

8. Kartavirya was a legendary king.

9. Utathya was a sage, and Brhaspati was his younger brother. Vadavamukha is a god with a horse's head. Mount Meru was a legendary sacred mountain with five peaks.

The Finnish Sea Mother

Anonymous

The Kalevala *is the great literary epic of Finland. It consists of mythological tales that have been told for centuries, collected by Elias Lönnrot and first published in 1835. The epic takes the form of fifty poems, called runes, beginning with an account of how the daughter of the Sky descended to the Sea, where she created the land and gave birth to the first human, named Väinämöinen, whose name translates roughly to "stream pool." Väinämöinen is the hero of the* Kalevala. *In the epic's thirty-ninth poem, he and his brother embark on the first voyage by sea, in a magical boat with a crew of the first Finns, brought to life by the songs that Väinämöinen sings.*

The following version of the first rune, which describes creation, is the translation of William Forsell Kirby (1844–1912), an eminent entomologist and folklorist, who published it with the title Kalevala: Or the Land of Heroes, *in 1907.*

Rune I

I have often heard related,
And have heard the song recited,
How the nights closed ever lonely,
And the days were shining lonely.
Only born was Väinämöinen,
And revealed the bard immortal,
Sprung from the divine Creatrix,
Born of Ilmatar, his mother.[1]

Air's young daughter was a virgin,
Fairest daughter of Creation.
Long did she abide a virgin,
All the long days of her girlhood,
In the Air's own spacious mansions,
In those far extending regions.

Wearily the time passed ever.
And her life became a burden,

Dwelling evermore so lonely,
Always living as a maiden,
In the Air's own spacious mansions,
In those far-extending deserts.

After this the maid descending,
Sank upon the tossing billows,
On the open ocean's surface,
On the wide expanse of water.

Then a storm arose in fury,
From the East a mighty tempest,
And the sea was wildly foaming,
And the waves dashed ever higher.

Thus the tempest rocked the virgin,
And the billows drove the maiden,
O'er the ocean's azure surface,
On the crest of foaming billows,
Till the wind that blew around her,
And the sea woke life within her.

Then she bore her heavy burden,
And the pain it brought upon her,
Seven long centuries together,
Nine times longer than a lifetime.
Yet no child was fashioned from her,
And no offspring was perfected.
Thus she swam, the Water-Mother,
East she swam, and westward swam she,
Swam to north-west and to south-west,
And around in all directions,
In the sharpness of her torment,
In her body's fearful anguish;
Yet no child was fashioned from her,
And no offspring was perfected.

Then she fell to weeping gently,
And in words like these expressed her:
"O how wretched is my fortune,
Wandering thus, a child unhappy!
I have wandered far already,
And I dwell beneath the heaven,
By the tempest tossed for ever,
While the billows drive me onward.

O'er this wide expanse of water,
On the far-extending billows.

"Better were it had I tarried,
Virgin in aerial regions,
Then I should not drift for ever,
As the Mother of the Waters.
Here my life is cold and dreary,
Every moment now is painful,
Ever tossing on the billows,
Ever floating on the water . . ."

When the ninth year had passed over,
And the summer tenth was passing,
From the sea her head she lifted,
And her forehead she uplifted,
And she then began Creation,
And she brought the world to order,
On the open ocean's surface,
On the far extending waters.

Wheresoe'er her hand she pointed,
There she formed the jutting headlands;
Wheresoe'er her feet she rested,
There she formed the caves for fishes;
When she dived beneath the water,
There she formed the depths of ocean;
When towards the land she turned her,
There the level shores extended,
Where her feet to land extended,
Spots were formed for salmon-netting;
Where her head the land touched lightly,
There the curving bays extended.
Further from the land she floated,
And abode in open water,
And created rocks in ocean,
And the reefs that eyes behold not,
Where the ships are often shattered,
And the sailors' lives are ended.

Now the isles were formed already,
In the sea the rocks were planted;
Pillars of the sky established,
Lands and continents created;
Rocks engraved as though with figures,

And the hills were cleft with fissures.
Still unborn was Väinämöinen;
Still unborn, the bard immortal.

Väinämöinen, old and steadfast,
Rested in his mother's body
For the space of thirty summers,
And the sum of thirty winters,
Ever on the placid waters,
And upon the foaming billows . . .

[Ilmatar finally gives birth to Väinämöinen after a gestation lasting three decades, when he forces himself out of her womb, with the following result.—Ed.]

Headlong in the water falling,
With his hands the waves repelling,
Thus the man remained in ocean,
And the hero on the billows.

In the sea five years he sojourned,
Waited five years, waited six years,
Seven years also, even eight years,
On the surface of the ocean,
By a nameless promontory,
Near a barren, treeless country.

On the land his knees he planted,
And upon his arms he rested,
Rose that he might view the moonbeams,
And enjoy the pleasant sunlight,
See the Great Bear's stars above him,
And the shining stars in heaven.

Thus was ancient Väinämöinen,
He, the ever famous minstrel,
Born of the divine Creatrix,
Born of Ilmatar, his mother.

Note

1. Ilmatar means "female air."

The Sea-Creating, Rainbow-Loving Serpent God of Haiti

Joseph J. Williams

In the Haitian religion of Vodou, which derives from West African beliefs, the serpent god Damballa created the Ocean, then fell in love with and married the rainbow. The Cuban novelist Alejo Carpentier (1904–80) summarized the Haitian creation myth in a few sentences in The Kingdom of This World *(1949), a work of magical realism that evokes the era of the Haitian Revolution (1790–1804).*

> Long ago, the serpent spirit Danbala created the world. He used his 7,000 coils to form the stars and the planets in the heavens and to shape the hills and valleys on earth. He used lightning bolts to forge metals and make the sacred rocks and stones. When he shed his skin he created all the waters on the earth. And when the sun showed through mist settling on the plants and trees a rainbow was born. Her name was Ayida Wedo. Danbala loved her and made her his wife. They are still together today, the serpent and the rainbow. Danbala and Ayida Wedo.[1]

Carpentier visited Haiti in 1943 while researching his novel, and he drew from two influential published sources on the subject of Haitian religion. First was a book by the Haitian intellectual and diplomat Jean Price-Mars (1876–1969), whose history of the Haitian Revolution, called Ainsi parla l'oncle *(So spoke the uncle, 1928), argued that Vodou was deeply rooted in African religion. The second was by occultist and travel writer William Seabrook (1884–1945), who visited Haiti in 1928 and interviewed authorities on the subject, including Price-Mars, who later took issue with Seabrook's interpretation. The resulting publication,* The Magic Island *(1929), was a sensational account of worship practices that popularized the term "zombie" in the United States and led to a fascination for "Voodoo," as Vodou became known in English. Joseph J. Williams (1875–1950), a Jesuit priest and professor from Boston College, extensively quoted both Price-Mars and Seabrook in his scholarly study titled* Voodoos and Obeahs: Phases of West India Witchcraft *(1930), which emphasized ophiolatry, or snake worship, in Vodou, due to the central role of Damballa. The following selection from the book begins with references to the Ewe people in present-day Togo and Ghana; to Ardra, a name for the Fon Kingdom, lo-*

cated in what is now southern Benin and Togo; to the kingdom of Whydah, located in what is now Benin; and the powerful kingdom of Dahomey, which expanded at the expense of them all.

It is with good reason, then, that Colonel Ellis states: "In the southeastern portions of the Ewe territory, the python deity is worshipped, and this vodu cult, with its adoration of the snake god was carried to Haiti by slaves from Ardra and Whydah, where the faith still remains today. In 1724 the Dahomies invaded Ardra and subjugated it; three years later Whydah was conquered by the same foe. This period is beyond question that in which Haiti first received the vodu of the Africans. Thousands of Negroes from these serpent-worshipping tribes were at the time sold into slavery, and were carried across the Atlantic to the eastern island. They bore with them their cult of the snake. At the same period, Ewe-speaking slaves were taken to Louisiana. . . ."[2]

Richard F. Burton had already asserted positively: "I may observe that from the Slave-Coast 'Vodun' or Fetish we may derive the 'Vaudoux' or small green snake of the Haitian Negroes, so well known by the abominable orgies enacted before the (Vaudoux King and Queen) and the 'King Snake' is still revered at Sierra Leone. . . ."[3]

Despite his perfervid descriptions, Seabrook has much of real value and particularly as already noted in the second portion of his book. Thus for example: "Voodoo in Haiti is a profound and vitally alive religion. . . . Voodoo is primarily and basically a form of worship, and . . . its magic, its sorcery, its witchcraft (I am speaking technically now), is only a secondary, collateral, sometimes sinisterly twisted by-product of Voodoo as a faith." And "Voodoo is not a secret cult or society in the sense that Freemasonry or the Rosicrucian cult is secret; it is a religion, and secret only as Christianity was secret in the catacombs, through fear of persecution. Like every living religion it has its inner mysteries, but that is secretness in a different sense. It is a religion toward which whites generally have been either scoffers, spyers, or active enemies, and whose adherents, therefore, have been forced to practice secrecy, above all where whites were concerned. But there is no fixed rule of their religion pledging them to secrecy, and [Seabrook's informant] Maman Célie was abrogating nothing more than a protective custom when she gave me her confidence. . . ."

Again he says: "Although Damballa, the ancient African serpent god remains enthroned as its central figure, this Voodoo ceremony is not the old traditional ritual brought over from Africa, but rather a gradually formalized new ritual which sprang from the merging in earliest slave days of the African tradition with the Roman Catholic ritual, into which the slaves were all baptized by law, and whose teachings and ceremonials they willingly embraced, without any element of intended blasphemy or diabolism, incorporating modified parts of Catholic ritual—as for instance the vestments and

The Haitian *loa*, or god, who governs the Ocean is Agwé. He rules the sea creatures and plants, and is the patron of fishermen and sailors. Agwé has two wives: Erzulie, the goddess of love and beauty, and Mami Wata (or La Sirena), a mermaid goddess. Religious services for the Sovereign of the Seas must be held in boats, on the open Ocean. This sculpture of the deity depicts him with a crown and tentacles of hair, and with both human legs and a fish tail, aboard a vessel that is part sailboat, part sea serpent. Its round composition derives from its medium, which is the lid of a 55-gallon oil barrel. The inspiration to repurpose steel drums came first to Georges Liautaud, a former blacksmith in the village of Noailles, Haiti. Using the tools of his trade, Liautaud innovated an art form and has taught his techniques to many young, unemployed men from his village. There are now twelve artisan workshops in the area, providing livelihoods for 8,000 people. The subject matter of Haitian steel drum art is often sacred, depicting the main *loas* in the pantheon of Haitian Vodou. Several nonprofits market the artisans' work in galleries internationally and online. Jean Rony, *Agwé, Merman, Protector of Seafaring Men*, 2015, steel drum sculpture, designed by Casey Riddell and commissioned by itscactus.com. Courtesy of the Roorda/Doyle Collection. Photograph of sculpture courtesy of Joe Michael, photographer, Mystic Seaport Museum.

the processional—into their Voodoo ceremonials, just as they incorporated its Father, Son, Virgin, and saints in their pantheistic theology."

We rather suspect that the following passage is, partially at least, ascribable to Dr. Price-Mars from whom much of Seabrook's technical information was gathered. "The worship of the snake in Haiti," he declares, "is by no means so literal as commentators have supposed. It is true that on every *Petro* altar in Haiti there is a serpent symbol, sometimes painted on the wall, sometimes carved of wood and elevated on a staff.[4] It is true also that living snakes are regarded as sacred objects, not to be injured or molested. One of the commonest and handsomest is a harmless green tree snake which grows to three or four feet in length, but all snakes are held sacred. But the serpent is worshipped symbolically, and not because they believe he has any power of his own; he represents the great god Damballa. So far as I am aware no living serpent is kept 'in a box' or otherwise on any Voodoo altar today in Haiti. A negro friend has told me, however, of an Obeah ceremony which he had seen in Cuba in which a living snake was the central object.[5] He said that a large, non-poisonous snake was kept in a big earthern jar on an altar, that some ten or fifteen negroes made a sort of circular endless chain beginning and ending at the rim of the jar by lacing their arms around each other[']s shoulders: that the snake was then drawn from the jar and induced to crawl over their shoulders, making the circuit and returning to the jar. . . ."

Taking up the meaning of the word, Dr. Dorsainvil asserts: "Voodoo . . . is simply a generic term of the *fongbe* dialect. . . . It is the most important word of the dialect since it includes nearly the whole moral and religious life of the Fons and is the origin, or rather it is the invariable root, of an entire family of words.[6] What is the precise meaning of the word in *fongbe*? It designates the spirits, good or evil, subordinate to Mawu and, by extension, the statue of one of these spirits, or every object that symbolizes their cult or their power, protective or malevolent."[7] Again, "The most celebrated expression of the religion of the Voodoo is the cult of the serpent or of the adder Da, pronounced Dan, incarnating the spirit Dagbe, pronounced Dangbe." He is writing as a Frenchman. "The two principal sanctuaries of this cult were found in the sacred woods of Somorne near Allada and at Whydah.[8] Among us by contraction, the Dahoman expression Dangbe Allada has become the *loa* (a Congo word) Damballah, of which the symbol still remains an adder."

To our way of thinking, then, Voodoo as first found in Haiti was substantially the serpent worship of Whydah; and in the beginning at least, it was but slightly modified by local conditions.

As the children of the African "bush" were ruthlessly torn away from their native haunts, they naturally carried with them the practices and superstitions that served as cherished memories of the past, and thus introduced to their new surroundings the diverse forms of perverted worship or sorcery, as the case might be, and for a time at least clung to their own peculiar customs.

Those who had practiced Ophiolatry in Africa, had a great advantage over the rest. Seemingly they had not lost their deity after all. For the non-poisonous python was waiting their arrival in Haiti. It was the one familiar object to meet their gaze. It was the one connection with the past.

Notes

1. Alejo Carpentier, *The Kingdom of This World* (New York: Alfred A. Knopf, 1957), 36.
2. Alfred Burdon Ellis (1852–94) was a British Army officer who spent nearly his entire career in West Africa, beginning with service in the Ashanti War on the Gold Coast in 1873–74. The quotation is from an article he wrote for *Popular Science Monthly* in 1891, called "On Vodu-Worship."
3. Sir Richard Francis Burton (1821–90) was a British explorer, geographer, cartographer, soldier, diplomat, author, and translator, among many other professions, who was famous for his extensive travels in Africa, Asia, and the Americas. He is perhaps best remembered for his search for the source of the Nile between 1856 and 1860, and for his translation of the Arabian stories called *One Thousand and One Nights* (1885). The quotation is from his *A Mission to Gelele, King of Dahome* (1864), vol. 1, 98.
4. The gods, or *loas*, of Vodou fall into two categories, the more benevolent and potentially helpful Rada order, and the more sinister and potentially dangerous Petro order.
5. Obeah is another African-derived religious tradition, usually associated with Jamaica.
6. The Fon language was spoken by the Fon people in the former kingdom of Dahomey.
7. Justin Chrysostome Dorsainvil (1880–1942) was a Haitian physician, educator, and author who wrote several books on Vodou, including *Vaudou et Névrose* (Vodou and neurosis, 1913) and *Vaudou et Magie* (Vodou and magic, 1937). The passage is from *Une Explication Philologique du Vòdú* (A philological explanation of Vodou, Port-au-Prince, 1924), 14f. Mawu was the Dahoman creator goddess.
8. Allada, like Ardra, referred to the Fon kingdom; Allada is the name of a city in Benin today.

Did Comets Bring Water to Earth?

Kimberly M. Burtnyk

The theory that water was introduced to earth by comets has been proposed, accepted, debunked, and now revalidated. The following piece offers a concise synopsis of the competing theories of the Ocean's origin. It was posted in June 2012 on Earthsky.org, which began as the companion website of the internationally syndicated astronomy radio series EarthSky: A Clear Voice for Nature, *familiar to National Public Radio listeners since 1991. The radio show no longer broadcasts, but longtime* EarthSky *producer and host Deborah Byrd continues to edit the Earthsky.org website, which provides daily sky information and current science news, as well as podcasts and transcripts of reports on a range of cosmic topics, such as this one. This article at EarthSky.org is the work of freelance science journalist Kimberly M. Burtnyk.*

Astronomers have been arguing for some years about whether comets brought Earth its water. Then in 2011, an international team of astronomers using the Herschel Space Observatory to study Comet Hartley 2 (103P/ Hartley) published their results on the first comet confirmed to contain ocean-like water.

Besides life, the biggest thing that distinguishes the Earth from other planets in the solar system is the presence of copious amounts of liquid water. Water molecules have been found in nebulae in distant reaches of the galaxy, so water itself isn't uncommon in the universe. So it might be surprising to learn that no one really knows how all the water on Earth got here!

Over the years, four prominent theories explaining the origin of water on Earth have gained favor. In one, water-rich asteroids and meteorites impacted the infant Earth, distributing water across the planet by brute force. In another more serene process, the oceans formed when hydrogen and oxygen in the materials that made up the Earth (e.g., hydrocarbons and oxygen in iron oxides) combined chemically below the Earth's crust and emerged as volcanic steam that condensed and rained down on the surface. A more recent theory suggests that water molecules actually adhered to the surfaces of the interstellar dust grains that accreted to form the solar system. In that case, water accumulated simultaneously with the rest of the planet. And last, but not least, there are the comets.

For decades, the accepted wisdom had been that comets brought a large proportion of water to the primordial Earth. In spite of the seemingly logical connection between comets and oceans, there has been one serious problem with that theory: the composition of water thus far detected in comets has differed fundamentally from that of the Earth's oceans, so they couldn't possibly be a primary source. This problem was serious enough to threaten the comet source model altogether. Or at least it was until now.

Not All Water Is Created Equal

The composition problem that has dogged the comet model is rooted in the atomic structure of ocean water. It turns out that not all ocean water is made up of "regular" water (i.e., H_2O). About one out of every 3,200 water molecules in the ocean is a heavy water molecule made with deuterium—a hydrogen atom with an extra neutron. When this hydrogen isotope combines with oxygen to make water, it's actually about 10 percent heavier than the much more common form of water found everywhere around us on Earth.

Any theory of water transport to the Earth from space must account for this specific ratio of regular to heavy water molecules. This is why many researchers favor, for example, the asteroid impact model; scientists have verified that asteroids and some meteorites do contain the right ratio of heavy to regular water.

For comets to be a source of the Earth's ocean water, they too must contain just the right ratio of heavy to regular water. But until Comet Hartley 2, no comet had been found to meet this vital criterion.

In fact, the specific chemistry of comets was unknown until the 1980s, when the first direct measurements of comet ice were made on Halley's Comet and—years later—Comet Hyakutake. Unfortunately, these two comets contained twice as much heavy water than is found in water on Earth. That meant they, and comets like them, couldn't possibly be a source of ocean water. The comet model was sinking, fast.

But scientists weren't willing to give up. In 2000, scientists seized a rare opportunity to make another measurement of comet water when Comet LINEAR broke up as it approached the sun. While the right proportion of deuterium to hydrogen was not directly measured, other chemical tracers strongly suggested that deuterium was present in just the right amount required to explain ocean water composition.

For the next 10 years, the jury was still out on whether or not comets could contain the right amount of deuterium. Nowadays, thanks to Comet Hartley 2, it appears that comets are back in the game!

It is believed that comets like Hartley 2 and LINEAR, both of which originated in the Kuiper Belt near Jupiter's orbit, possess the appropriate amount of heavy water. Finding such comets is challenging since, over time, gravitational perturbations have depleted that source of comets. Comets Halley and Hyakutake did not originate in the same region, which explains their completely different chemical compositions.

Ted Bergin of the University of Michigan—a member of the team that discovered ocean-like water in Comet Hartley 2 in 2011—acknowledged that the result is based on a sample of one. He told EarthSky last fall:

"We really need to know if this comet is a representative member of the Kuiper Belt. It is one very important measurement but we need more to begin to put the pieces of this puzzle together. The results show that the amount of material out there that could have contributed to Earth's oceans is perhaps larger than we thought. What this adds to the story is that the reservoir of material that can potentially be brought to the Earth with the right 'kind' of water is much larger. This does not say that comets did bring water to the Earth but rather that they might."

While it is most likely that water came to Earth through a variety of processes, this latest finding reinvigorates the theory that comets may have contributed a lot more water to the Earth than was recently thought.

Now, as for the origin of comets themselves? That's a question for another rainy day.

Before the Great Extinctions

Jean-Bernard Caron

Earth was too hot to sustain bodies of water, but when the planet cooled, the rains came, forming the Ocean. The warm, globe-covering seas became a soup of life, which sustained the Cambrian Explosion of new organisms. The discovery and excavation of the Burgess Shale in the Canadian Rockies, which is 500 million years old, revealed the bizarre and abundant life forms that once existed in the vast waters of the Cambrian Period. Since the evolutionary surge reflected in the fossil record of the Burgess Shale, there have been five massive extinction events on earth. The extinction event that occurred about 252 million years ago, sometimes called the Great Dying, wiped out 96 percent of the species in the Ocean. The warming Ocean is again exhibiting signs of another such massive die-off of life forms, and in fact, the sixth great extinction may already be happening around us. The complex subject is clarified in various sections of the Burgess Shale website (http://burgess-shale.rom.on.ca), created by the Royal Ontario Museum and excerpted here.

The Cambrian Explosion

The "Cambrian Explosion" refers to the sudden appearance in the fossil record of complex animals with mineralized skeletal remains. It may represent the most important evolutionary event in the history of life on Earth.

The beginning of the explosion is generally placed about 542 million years ago, during the Cambrian Period at the start of the Palaeozoic Era (the same time the Ediacarans disappear from the fossil record). While the explosion was rapid in geological terms, it took place over millions of years—the Burgess Shale, at 505 million years old, records the tail end of the event. The explosion is particularly remarkable because all major animal body plans (each more or less corresponding to a distinctive Phylum—Mollusca and Chordata, for example) appeared during this time, changing the biosphere forever.

The Cambrian Explosion and the Origin of Modern Marine Ecosystems

The rapid appearance of a wide variety of animals—particularly bilaterians— led to the development of radical new ecological interactions such as preda-

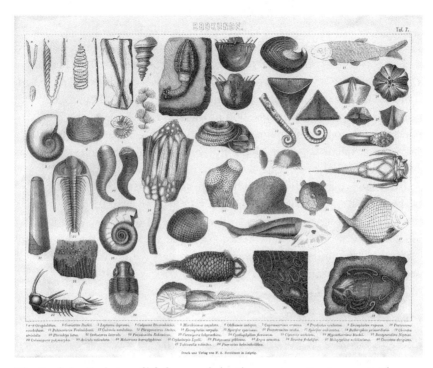

The Cambrian Explosion of life forms ended with a massive extinction event. The ancestors of the fossilized creatures shown here, from the Devonian Period, survived it but then fell victim to another great extinction, which ended that geologic epoch. Climate change and global warming suggest that earth may be poised for yet another catastrophic evolutionary winnowing. This selection of fossils was depicted in a wood engraving in one of the famed *Brockhaus Encyclopedia* series. Engraver unknown, from *Erdkunde* [Geography], edited by Bernhard von Cotta and Johann Müller, in *Bilder-Atlas: Ikonographische Encyklopädie der Wissenschaften und Künste*, 2nd ed., vol. 1 (Leipzig: F. A. Brockhaus, 1875). Courtesy of the Roorda/Doyle Collection.

tion. Consequently, ecosystems became much more complex than those of the Ediacaran. As the number and variety of organisms increased, they occupied a variety of new marine environments and habitats. Cambrian seas teemed with animals of various sizes, shapes, and ecologies; some lived on or in the sea floor (a benthic lifestyle), while others actively swam in the water column (nektonic).

The fundamental ecological structure of modern marine communities was firmly established during the Cambrian. By the end of the Period, some animals had also made the first temporary forays onto land, soon to be followed by plants. . . .

The Burgess Shale

The Burgess Shale is a scientific treasure trove. Usually, only the bones and shells of organisms tend to end up as fossils. But the Burgess Shale bestiary is almost exclusively composed of soft-bodied animals that in normal circumstances would stand no chance of being preserved. Given these exceptional fossils and the site's unique position at the tail end of one of the most important evolutionary events in life history—the rise of animals during the Cambrian Explosion—it is perhaps unsurprising that the Burgess Shale has attracted, and continues to attract, researchers from around the world.

Even though more than a hundred years have passed since the discovery of the main Burgess Shale site, field research continues to turn up new fossils, and many recent discoveries are waiting to be described. A number of previously-known species now need to be revised, thanks to the recovery of better fossil specimens, the development of innovative analytical techniques, or new interpretations. . . .

The Locality Today

The Burgess Shale refers to a fossil-rich locality on Fossil Ridge between Wapta Mountain and Mount Field, just a few kilometres north of the small town of Field, British Columbia. Charles Walcott coined the term to describe various fossiliferous rock layers with soft-bodied preservation that he found in 1909 and 1910 and excavated for several years thereafter.[1] The most important excavations were made within a two-metre-thick section representing a series of layers containing the most exquisitely preserved soft-bodied fossils. This section was named the "Phyllopod bed" by Walcott, in reference to the leaf-like structure of the appendages of certain abundant arthropods, including *Waptia*. Walcott excavated the Phyllopod bed for several years, leaving what is known today as the Walcott Quarry. This quarry has been expanded by subsequent excavations, in particular by the Geological Survey of Canada and the Royal Ontario Museum.

The Walcott Quarry remains the best-known Burgess Shale site, but is far from the only one. Among the 65,000 Burgess Shale specimens collected by Walcott (mostly from the Phyllopod bed) a few came from rocks about 22 metres higher on the slope. These layers were later excavated by Percy Raymond in 1930 and are now referred to as the Raymond Quarry.[2]

In summary, the different quarries of the Burgess Shale on Fossil Ridge represent various fossil assemblages within a body of shale roughly 100 metres thick, marking a history of fossil deposits covering about 200,000 years of the Cambrian Period. . . .

The Burgess Shale fossils are preserved in a type of sedimentary rock known as shale. Shale is a type of mudstone (or mudrock) that originally formed from deposits of fine mud, made mostly of clay minerals. The different fossil layers of the Burgess Shale represent different mud deposits, originally laid down in sheet-like horizontal beds ranging from a few millimetres up to several centimetres in thickness. These layers can still be seen today in the Burgess Shale.

Seafloor muds are transformed into shale (lithified) when they encounter increased temperature and pressure during their geological history. The mudstones of the Burgess Shale were exposed to even greater temperature and pressure during the formation of the Canadian Rocky Mountains.

During this process, the minerals (which have flat structures) gradually tend to align with each other, forming parallel layers. For shales (including the Burgess Shale), this results in rocks that tend to split into thin sheets. The presence of a fossil in the shale creates a zone of weakness between layers, so when the rock is broken open it is more likely to split along the plane containing the fossil, leaving parts of the fossil on each facing surface (as part and counterpart). . . .

The organisms whose remains are preserved in the Burgess Shale originally lived far off the coast of a land mass near the equator known to geologists as Laurentia (which would go on to form most of North America). Over the past half-billion years, plate tectonics has moved this parcel of land to its present location in the northern hemisphere. The same forces thrust the ancient seabed nearly three kilometres above sea level to form the Canadian Rockies. The last major uplift ended approximately 65 million years ago. Since then, the mountains have gradually been eroded away by wind, rain, rivers and ice, cutting deep valleys in the Canadian Rockies. This erosion eventually exposed the rocks containing the Burgess Shale fossils to the light of day for the first time in 500 million years.

Palaeoenvironmental Setting

Most of the creatures whose remains we find in the Burgess Shale lived in deeper (basinal) waters, making their homes on or in the sea floor or swimming above it. The local environment would have been calm—safely below the churning surface caused by storms or hurricanes. There were probably weak currents, allowing the many suspension feeders in the community to thrive. Most animals lived at the base of a large submarine cliff known as the Cathedral Escarpment. This formed at the outer edge of a wide, tropical platform of carbonate rock that may have extended as far as 400 kilometres (320 miles) from the shoreline.

At least twelve fossil localities have been discovered at the foot of the Escarpment along a 60-kilometre belt running roughly north-south. This suggests the Escarpment might have helped optimize conditions for a rich animal community to develop and be preserved as fossils. The Escarpment itself was about 200 metres (650 feet) high before mud and other sediments began to fill in the basin. The shape of the Escarpment may have channelled mudflows at its base, resulting in periodic deposits that enveloped and preserved the organisms living there. The presence of fossilized algae implies sunlight must have penetrated to the base of the Escarpment. As in today's marine environments, algae at the base of the food chain would have provided food for many other organisms. Periodically, the tranquil scene would be shattered by torrents of mud—burying living and dead organisms in a disorganized mass. This process continued for perhaps hundreds of thousands of years, with successive layers of sediment eventually filling the original basin.

Notes

1. The paleontologist Charles Doolittle Walcott (1850–1927) served as the fourth secretary of the Smithsonian Institution from 1907 to 1927.
2. Percy Raymond (1879–1952) was curator of paleontology at the Harvard University Museum of Comparative Zoology from 1912 to 1945.

II

Ancient Seas

People have been floating around for a very long time. By using rudimentary coracles, or "skinboats," constructed of branches and animal hides, or rafts made out of reeds, or dugout canoes fashioned from tree trunks, humans have crossed vast distances. Recent discoveries indicate that ancient seafaring folk went much farther, much earlier, than previous theories supposed. In fact, we now know that while *Homo sapiens* was still evolving in Africa, *Homo erectus* went to sea. Archaeological sites unearthed on the island of Crete reveal that our species' evolutionary ancestor, who evolved some 1.8 million years ago, navigated the Mediterranean Sea in considerable numbers. The sites date to some 130,000 years before the present, though the practice of getting around in some sort of boat could be even older.

Homo sapiens also took to the waves. The archaeological find of a single human finger bone in Saudi Arabia, announced in April 2018, showed that the first humans to migrate out of Africa left more than 80,000 years ago.[1] They they turned north for the Mediterranean coast and settled down. The second migration group crossed to the Arabian Peninsula and kept going, to India and on to Southeast Asia, then to Australia and the Americas. This part of the anthology surveys the vast, watery panorama of human migration.

Note

1. Sarah Givens, "88,000-Year-Old Finger Bone Pushes Back Human Migration Dates," *National Geographic*, April 9, 2018, https://news.nationalgeographic.com/2018/04/saudi-arabia -finger-human-migration-homo/.

The First Aussies

Fran Dorey

The ancient ancestors of Australia's aboriginal peoples were seafarers. They had to make their way across treacherous straits to the island continent, arriving at least 50,000 years ago, and possibly as long as 65,000 years ago. Archaeological discoveries in Australia have brought to light an abundant variety of evidence of this, changing our understanding of the timetable of early human migration, pushing it back thousands of years. These finds are the subject of this article, written in 2011 to accompany an exhibit at the Australia Museum in Sydney.

Origins of the First Australians

The viewpoints about the origins of these peoples are entangled with the wider debate regarding the origins of all modern humans. The two main viewpoints are:

THE "OUT OF AFRICA" MODEL

The most widely accepted viewpoint is that the first humans to colonise Australia came from a recent migration of *Homo sapiens* through South-east Asia. These people belonged to a single genetic lineage and were the descendants of a population that originated in Africa. The fossil evidence for the earliest Indigenous Australians does show a range of physical variation that would be expected in a single, geographically widespread population.

THE "MULTIREGIONAL" MODEL

Some scientists interpret the variation found in the fossil record of early Indigenous Australians as evidence that Australia was colonised by two separate genetic lineages of modern humans. One lineage was believed to have been the evolutionary descendants of Indonesian *Homo erectus* while the other lineage had evolved from Chinese *Homo erectus*. Modern Aboriginal people are the result of the assimilation of these two genetic lineages.

The Asian Connection

Modern humans had reached Asia by 70,000 years ago before moving down through South-east Asia and into Australia. However, *Homo sapiens* were not the first people to inhabit this region. An older species, *Homo erectus*, had already been in Asia for at least 1.5 million years. It is possible that these two species may have coexisted, as new dates for Indonesian *Homo erectus* suggest they may have survived there until as recently as 50,000 years ago. *Homo erectus* remains have never been found in Australia. . . .

Gateways into a New Continent

There has always been an ocean separating Asia and Australia. At times this distance was reduced but the earliest travellers still had to navigate across large stretches of water.

For much of its history Australia was joined to New Guinea, forming a landmass called Sahul. These countries were finally separated by rising sea levels about 8,000 years ago. Genetic evidence supports the close ties between these two countries—the Indigenous peoples from these regions are more closely related to each other than to anyone else in the world, suggesting a recent common ancestry.

There are a number of likely paths of migration across Asia and into Sahul. These are based on the shortest possible route and take into consideration the land bridges that would appear during times of low sea levels. However, travel may have also occurred when sea levels were high. High sea levels would have reduced the amount of usable land and increased the population pressure. During these times it may have been necessary to expand into new areas.

CHANGING SEA LEVELS

Changing sea levels have significantly affected the geography of South-east Asia and Australia and the migration patterns of prehistoric peoples. During times of low sea levels the travelling distance between Timor and Sahul would have been reduced to about 90 kilometres (56 miles).

Present sea levels are higher than they have been for most of the last million years. When water is locked up in the polar ice caps (known as an Ice Age) the sea level drops. When the climate becomes warmer, the ice melts and the sea level rises again.

THE ORIGINAL SEAFARERS

The settlement of Australia is the first unequivocal evidence of a major sea crossing and rates as one of the greatest achievements of early humans. However the motive and circumstances regarding the arrival of the first Australians is a matter for conjecture. It may have been a deliberate attempt to colonise new territory or an accident after being caught in monsoon winds.

The lack of preservation of any ancient boat means archaeologists will probably never know what kind of craft was used for the journey. None of the boats used by Aboriginal people in ancient times are suitable for major voyages. The most likely suggestion has been rafts made of bamboo, a material common in Asia.

THE EARLY OCCUPATION OF AUSTRALIA

The earliest dates for human occupation of Australia come from sites in the Northern Territory. The Malakunanja II rock shelter in Arnhem Land has been dated to around 55,000 years old and is currently gaining support as Australia's oldest site.

Over the last decade, a significant number of archaeological sites dated at more than 30,000 years old have been discovered. By this time all of Australia, including the arid centre and Tasmania, was occupied. The drowning of many coastal sites by rising sea levels has destroyed what would have been the earliest occupation sites.

The First Australians

Much of our knowledge about the earliest people in Australia comes from archaeology. The physical remains of human activity that have survived in the archaeological record are largely stone tools, rock art and ochre, shell middens and charcoal deposits and human skeletal remains. These all provide information on the tremendous length and complexity of Australian Aboriginal culture.

HUMAN REMAINS

The oldest Australian human fossil remains date to around 40,000 years ago—15,000 years after the earliest archaeological evidence of human occupation in Australia. Nothing is known about the physical appearance of the first humans to colonise Australia over 50,000 years ago. What is clear is that Aboriginal people living in Australia between 40,000 and 10,000 years ago had much larger bodies and more robust skeletons than they do today and showed a wide range of physical variation.

STONE TOOLS

Stone tools in Australia, as in other parts of the world, changed and developed through time. Some early types, such as wasted blades, core tools, large flake scrapers and split pebble choppers continue to be made and used right up to today.

About 6,000 years ago, new and specialised tools such as points, backed blades and thumbnail scrapers became common. Significant variation between the tool kits of different regions also appeared. Prototypes for this technology appeared earlier in Asia, suggesting this innovation was introduced into Australia.

The ground stone technique produces tools with a more durable and even edge, although not as sharp as a chipped tool. The oldest ground stone tools appear in Australia about 10,000 years before they appear in Europe, suggesting that early Australians were more technologically advanced in some of their tool manufacturing techniques than was traditionally thought.

ROCK ART

Rock art, including painted and carved forms, plays a significant role in Aboriginal culture and has survived in the archaeological record for over 30,000 years. In age and abundance Australian Aboriginal rock art is comparable to world-renowned European cave sites such as those at Lascaux in France and Altamira in Spain.

It is probable that rock art was part of the culture of the first Australians. Its exact purpose is unknown but it is likely that from the earliest times rock art would have formed part of religious ritual activity, as is common in modern hunter-gatherer societies.

OCHRE AND MINERAL PIGMENTS

Mineral pigments, such as ochre, provide the oldest evidence for human arrival in Australia. Used pigments have been found in the earliest occupation levels of many sites, with some pieces dated at about 55,000 years old. This suggests that art was practiced from the beginning of colonisation. Natural pigments were probably used for a range of purposes including burials, cave painting, decoration of objects and body art. Such usage still occurs today.

Ochre is an iron oxide found in a range of colours from yellow to red and brown. Red ochre is particularly important in many desert cultures due to the belief that it represents the blood of ancestral beings and can provide protection and strength. Ochre is used by grinding it into a powder and mixing it with a fluid, such as water, blood or saliva.

SHELL MIDDENS

Ancient Aboriginal people did not build permanent shelters and evidence of living sites comes from the remains of meals and cooking activities rather than actual buildings. Shell middens are the most obvious remains of meals and are useful because they provide insight into ancient Aboriginal diets and past environments and can also be radiocarbon dated to establish the age of a site.

Important Sites

COOBOOL CREEK

The Coobool Creek collection consists of the remains of 126 individuals excavated from a sand ridge at Coobool Crossing, New South Wales, in 1950. After their excavation, they became part of the University of Melbourne collection until they were returned to the Aboriginal community for reburial in 1985.

The remains date from 9,000 to 13,000 years old and are significant because of their large size when compared with Aboriginal people who appeared within the last 6,000 years. They are physically similar to Kow Swamp people with whom they shared the cultural practice of artificial cranial deformation.

KOW SWAMP

This ancient burial site in northern Victoria was excavated between 1968 and 1972. The human skeletons discovered here were extremely significant because they were accurately dated between 9,500 to 14,000 years ago and demonstrated substantial differences between ancient and more recent Aboriginal people.

The remains of over forty individuals have been found at Kow Swamp and include those of men, women and children. This burial site is one of the largest from this time period anywhere in the world. Many of the skeletons have a greater skeletal mass, more robust jaw structures and larger areas of muscle attachment than in contemporary Aboriginal men. The female skeletons from this region also show similar differences when compared with modern Aboriginal women. . . .

LAKE MUNGO

The oldest Australian human remains have been found at Lake Mungo in south-west New South Wales. This site was occupied from 45,000 to 20,000 years ago when it was part of the Willandra Lakes system. Lake Mungo has been devoid of water for the last 16,000 years and is now a desert. In the past, rainfall was higher and the lakes contained plenty of fish and shellfish, making them a valuable source of food for the people that occupied the area.

Key remains:

"Lake Mungo 1" (WLH 1). Discovered in 1969. At 26,000 years old, this is the most securely dated human burial in Australia and the earliest ritually cremated remains found anywhere in the world. The cremation process shrinks bone and has made the skeleton of this originally small-bodied woman even smaller. Dr Alan Thorne reconstructed the skull from over 300 fragments.

"Lake Mungo 3" (WLH 3). Discovered in 1974. Due to the poor preservation of the pelvis it is not clear if this specimen is a man or a woman. It was laid out for burial and covered in red ochre. There is some controversy over the date of this burial with ages ranging from 26,000 to 60,000 years old. A date closer to 40,000 years old is most probable.

COHUNA

A skull was found in 1925 at Cohuna, north-west Kow Swamp, Victoria, and is undated. However, the similarity between this skull and the Kow Swamp people suggests they are both from a similar time period. This skull's long, high, flat forehead reflects the characteristics of cranial deformation and its teeth and palate are larger than the current Australian average.

KEILOR

Evidence of human activity at Keilor dates back nearly 40,000 years. Stone flakes and charcoal deposits have been found in the lowest archaeological levels.

One of the key remains from this site was that of a 12,000 year old skull discovered in 1940. It is one of the earlier prehistoric Aboriginal remains found in Australia.

TALGAI

A cranium was discovered in 1884 on the Darling Downs, Queensland. It was the first Pleistocene human skull to be found in Australia. It is dated to between 9,000 and 11,000 years old.

When it was found, the skull was covered in calcium carbonate, which gave the skull a deformed appearance. After cleaning, it was discovered that this skull belonged to a boy of about 15 years of age, who had died as a result of a blow to the side of the head. Features of the skull, such as the teeth and jaws, are remarkably large, but do fit within the range of variation of the Australian Aboriginal population.

A New View of the Ainu

David H. Gremillion

In their far-flung travels across the Pacific Ocean, the Ainu people of the northern Japanese island of Hokkaido predated the Bering Land Bridge. The hirsute Ainu may have arrived in the Western Hemisphere 20,000 to 40,000 years before the migration of people from Siberia. The evidence for this theory is the subject of this selection, written by David H. Gremillion, an infectious disease specialist and professor in residence at Nippon Medical School in Tokyo.

Our current understanding of human migration derives from advances in four more or less integrated disciplines: archaeology, physical anthropology, DNA analysis and linguistics. In recent years progress has slowed as researchers enroll familiar tools to validate or reject what have become more or less entrenched theories. For archaeologists, it almost goes without saying that advances in seemingly unrelated disciplines have great potential for breaking "logjams" and producing new ideas. Such was the case in 2003 when population based data in microbiology demonstrated that an ancient human pathogen, *Helicobacter pylori*, carried a key to the timing and pathway of early human migration out of Africa.

A landmark article in *Science* by Falush and associates (2003) reported on strain variation in *Helicobacter pylori*, a chronic gastric pathogen. Using known mutation frequency as a "biological clock" they were able to match known patterns of human migration with the molecular clock approach. Spread of this chronic human pathogen accompanied the migration of their human host and not surprisingly, the oldest strains with the most mutations were in Africa. Prior to this validation by pathogen genetic analysis, the "out of Africa" theory rested primarily on conventional archaeological and anthropological evidence.

The "Ah Ha!" moment of insight occurred when rapid advances in microbial genetic analysis were used to validate existing theories. Our microbial "hitchhikers" carry with them the secrets of their past and by inference our past. Such leaps forward in science often occur when the insights from apparently disparate disciplines merge and provide validation for or discredit earlier theories.

Another rapidly developing body of knowledge is challenging rather than validating the orthodox understandings of human migration. Human T cell lymphotrophic virus 1 (HTLV-1) has been part of the human condition for thousands of years and has an epidemiology and migration suggesting that the populating of the North and South American continents began long before the trans-Siberian migrations.

Human Migration into the Americas

Archaeologists are perhaps all too familiar with the long debate over the pathways and timing of human migration into the Americas. Based on oxygen isotope records from deep-sea cores, during the last major stage of the Pleistocene epoch (10,000–50,000 years ago), a land bridge formed across what now is the Bering Strait. With Siberia and the Americas connected, conventional accounts suggest nomadic peoples tracked the big game herds that migrated to modern-day Alaska. From here, this group (or groups) subsequently traveled south and east across America through an ice-free corridor. For better and worse these findings have been substantiated by the discovery of several ancient American archaeological sites, including those at Clovis, New Mexico[,] in 1932. Dating these findings between 12,800 and 13,300 years BP the artifacts were deemed the remnants of the so-called "Clovis culture." The land bridge theory has gained further credence with recent scholarship into the human genome. A 2007 study examining the genome of indigenous people from North and South America and two Siberian groups found one unique genetic variant across all populations, suggesting Native Americans descended from a common ancestor. Furthermore, this study found increasing genetic variation radiating from the Bering Strait, correlating to a more recent migration.

While it is perhaps all but indisputable that land migration occurred over the Bering Strait, it is not conclusive that this path was the first or the only means of migration to the Americas. There are incongruities in the archaeological record when North and South America are compared. There are South American sites, including Monte Verde, which predate the North American Clovis remains by at least 1,000 years.[1] These findings lend support to what has been argued to be an earlier and faster maritime migration. Furthermore, excavations across the Americas, the most recent of which unearthed coprolites in the Paisley Caves of Oregon's Cascade Range, suggest the first Americans were a maritime culture.[2] Beyond the earlier absence of the ice-free corridor—an absence which makes an earlier land-based migration virtually impossible—one of the primary clues is diet.

The diet of these early Americans consisted of turtles, shellfish, and tubers, a stark contrast to the big game the group(s) associated with the Clovis culture tracked across the Bering Strait. Finally, while the genetic research presents interesting conclusions, it does not take into account the assimilation or destruction of people who may have pre-dated the genome of modern Native Americans. New observations in the field of retrovirology allow a different marker to weigh in on the possible existence of extinct proto-American cultures.[3]

Human T-lymphotropic virus I (HTLV-I) was the first retrovirus (HIV-like) to be isolated and has infected human beings for thousands of years. Recent research has identified important elements of HTLV-I molecular biology, epidemiology and pathogenesis. The southern Japanese island of Kyushu has a surprisingly high prevalence as do certain areas of sub-Saharan Africa, the Caribbean, and South America. In some communities of Japan, clusters with prevalence in the 30% range have been reported. The Ainu of the Japanese island of Hokkaido currently have a high prevalence and historically they were the ancient indigenous peoples of the Japanese archipelago. Most HTLV-I carriers remain asymptomatic, but infection can be associated with severe diseases of immunodeficiency. Recent characterization of mutations in the viral genome has allowed viral pedigrees to be traced back thousands of years using a mutational biological clock. The more highly mutated viruses are presumed to be the older because of a relative constancy of mutation over time.

Four major strains of HTLV exist worldwide and are currently endemic in Sub-Saharan Africa, Japan, and the Americas. All four strains, including their primate precursors, are present in Africa, suggesting HTLV originated there in its primate form, PTLV. In southern Japan more than 10% of the general population is infected with HTLV-Ia. This endemicity extends to antiquity, as HTLV-Ia has been detected in the Japanese subpopulations of Ainu and Ryukyuans, the putative descendants of Japan's original inhabitants. This strain is also present in the Caribbean and South America, providing hints of an ancient migration into the Americas.

Throughout the Americas, HTLV-Ia is found predominantly among African descendants and indigenous populations. It is endemic in the Caribbean, Colombia, and northern Brazil and, to a lesser extent, found in Peru, [and] Argentina but is rare in Central and North America. Some researchers have interpreted this data as consistent with the dissemination of HTLV-Ia to the New World through the African slave trade. Contrasting this theory, HTLV-I exists in aboriginal populations on both sides of the Bering Strait, suggesting an ancient introduction of the virus into the New World prior to the slave trade. Furthermore, in 2000, Sonoda and colleagues described an Andean mummy with ancient HTLV-Ia, suggesting a prehistoric introduction of the virus similar to that prevalent in the Ainu population. Their conclusions remain controversial and can be resolved only with additional fieldwork on new specimens.

CUSTOMS OF HOKKAIDO TRIBE　(4)　第二輯　北海道土人風俗

Analysis of human retroviruses provided evidence that people of the Ainu ethnic group of Hokkaido, the northernmost island of Japan, voyaged across the Pacific Ocean tens of thousands of years ago—long before the Bering Strait land bridge formed—in boats made of animal skins and/or dugout canoes. Millennia later, the Ainu people continued to employ similar construction methods, as seen in this 1920s postcard, *Customs of Hokkaido Tribe* (Osaka: Seiundo Printing Co., c. 1910). Courtesy of the Roorda/Doyle Collection.

HTLV-I is often transmitted from mother to child through breastfeeding. The infected infant carries the virus for their lifetime and passes the virion to their progeny through sexual intercourse or breastfeeding. Contemporary epidemiology now also includes transfusions of blood products, contaminated needles (including acupuncture) and IV drug abuse. The duration of breastfeeding can be a major factor in transmission rates that range between 15% and 25%. Vertical transmission from mother to child is a prominent and efficient mode of transmission and likely occurred in ancient human populations even when there was little risk of blood borne transmission. The HTLV-I is thus an ideal migration marker, serving as a kind of historical "GPS" that tags an individual and subsequent generations.

HTLV-I's high prevalence in the Caribbean and South America has been presumed to be due to the post-Columbian slave trade into the Americas from regions of high HTLV-I prevalence in Africa. New technology[,] however, allows identification of strains with greater precision. The strains found in South America and the Caribbean are more similar to the strains prevalent in ancient Japan. The Peruvian mummy further confirms that HTLV-I was present in the Americas thousands of years prior to the slave trade. Similarly, a cluster of Japanese type HTLV-I has been detected in a Coastal population of Amerindian natives in British Columbia, although the significance of this may not have been appreciated in 1995 when first reported.

These new findings may help explain the relative paucity of HTLV-I in the African American populations of Northern latitudes in the Americas and the concentration of ancient Japanese strains in the Caribbean and South America. Coastal migration of ancient Ainu into the Americas did not require the Bering land bridge and the "ice-free corridor." Archaeological evidence may be submerged off the coasts of Canada and Western America. If this migration occurred 20,000–40,000 years earlier than the Siberian migration, the human migrants would have found an impenetrable ice sheet that extended deep into the Americas to at least as far as Meadowcroft Rockshelter in Pennsylvania.[4] Lower sea levels would have allowed easier movement to the Caribbean islands which may have been connected. South America would have been predominantly free of glacial ice and the flow of migrants over thousands of years would have gravitated in that direction.

When the Bering land bridge opened and the ice-free corridor formed (circa 12,500 BP), Siberian Asian populations flowed along with the mega fauna into the northern USA latitudes, which by then were more habitable.

Certain findings from the more classic disciplines, which deal with human migration, begin to make more sense as we build a better picture of an earlier wave of coastal migrants to the Americas. Retrovirology adds to this big picture.

Conclusions

A rapidly accreting body of evidence suggests that human migration into the Americas occurred much earlier than previously thought. Two distinct waves of migration have been documented with the characteristics of each dictated by the timing of the last ice age. Coastal migration was favored at the peak of the ice age when sea levels were lower and abundant seafood was available. The ancient people of Japan were known to be excellent coastal seafarers but reluctant visitors to the open sea. Sea craft during that phase of human migration were more primitive and did not support open sea migration. Siberian migration became dominant after the receding of the ice sheet and these later migrants may have replaced or assimilated the earlier migrants.

Awareness of the broad spectrum of science advancement creates the possibility that new insights will occur when overlapping discoveries validate new theories. Overspecialization within a scientific discipline may be a handicap when it comes to the big questions of humanity. Whether as scientists, scholars, or professional field archaeologists, we are all well served by maintaining a broader view of advances in many fields. Such key advances which allow a great leap forward in our own fields of expertise might occur in an isolated and seemingly unrelated discipline, such as retrovirology.

Notes

1. The Monte Verde site in the Patagonia region of Chile is remarkably well preserved in the anaerobic environment of a peat bog.
2. The archaeological site at the four Paisley Caves in arid southern Oregon, carbon dated to about 14,300 BP, was first analyzed in the 1930s and yielded more evidence in new excavations begun in 2002, including coprolites, which are fossilized feces.
3. Retrovirology is the study of retroviruses, which replicate within cells through reverse transcription, whereby RNA produces DNA (not the other way around, which is normal), resulting in potentially persistent and dangerous infections, such as HIV, the human immunodeficiency virus.
4. Meadowcroft Rockshelter is an archaeological site near Pittsburgh.

The Surfing Chinchorro of Chile

Various Authors

The most persuasive theory explaining how humans were able to move so far, so fast, is called the Kelp Highway. Jon M. Erlandson and his colleagues coined the phrase in 2007, when they "proposed an ecological correlate to the Coastal Migration Theory, the Kelp Highway Hypothesis, suggesting that kelp forests and other North Pacific coastal ecosystems may have facilitated the peopling of the Americas."[1] An exhibit at the Museum of Natural and Cultural History at the University of Oregon detailed the idea. The researchers "noted that extensive and highly productive kelp forests from Japan to Baja California supported similar marine organisms: sea otters and other marine mammals, abalones, urchins, and other shellfish; numerous fish and seabirds; seaweeds and more. As the world warmed after 17,000 years ago, and Cordilleran ice retreated from the coastlines of northwestern North America, seafaring peoples could have traversed the Pacific Rim relatively rapidly, following a coastal route entirely at sea level, without major obstructions, and offering a diverse array of terrestrial and marine resources." The most compelling evidence of very ancient seafaring to the Americas is the amazingly well-preserved archaeological site called Monte Verde, in the remote Patagonia region far in the south of Chile, which is at least 12,500 years old, and perhaps even older.[2]

The Chinchorro people of Chile drew their sustenance from the sea. They lived along the coast of the Atacama Desert, the driest place on earth, and are known for their mummies, which have remained incredibly well preserved in the arid environment. The German archaeologist Max Uhle (1856–1944), famous for his work on pre-Hispanic Andean sites, excavated the first of the Chinchorro mummies in 1914, and nearly 300 more have come to light since then, often at construction sites. Radiocarbon dating has shown that most of them are between 5,000 and 7,000 years old, which predates the more famous mummies of Egypt. The tissue of the embalmed bodies has permitted analysis of the Chinchorro people's diet, revealing that fully 90 percent of what they ate came from the Ocean. Other funerary evidence shows that they ventured far out onto the Pacific Ocean on reed rafts, which are still used as surfboards in that region, where there are virtually no natural harbors, and big waves break constantly on the rocky beaches.

Pre-Hispanic Cultures in the Atacama Desert: A Pacific Coast Overview

VICTORIA CASTRO

Just as plants and animals were domesticated over millennia, so did the extraction of marine resources and the technologies to facilitate this activity change over time. It has been suggested that, from the earliest occupation until late pre-Hispanic times, groups living on the coast extracted marine resources. In the first [stage] they gained dominion over the shore, then followed the mastery of deeper waters, and finally they mastered larger areas. . . . Around 6,500 BPE the shell hook appears in these latitudes as a tool that revolutionized fishing. At this time, mackerel became a popular catch and the size of the fish caught increases. Around this time local inhabitants developed the ability to master the second dimension—the ocean depths. As the cold oscillation withdrew, populations of *choro* [mussel], the bivalve used to manufacture the shell hooks, also decreased dramatically and the people invented the cactus needle hook and, later on, the bone fishing hook. The expansion of the marine territory appears to have occurred during the late pre-Hispanic times, around the same time seagoing vessels were invented. This corresponds to the third dimension of appropriation in which a quantitative and qualitative improvement in the extraction of marine resources is observed. These coastal groups had access to open water fish such as the large tuna and Mahi Mahi, semi-abyssal fish such as conger eel and whales, which they used for different purposes. . . . The knowledge of the sea and its resources led to surprising levels of sophisticated expertise related to fishing. These groups had reed rafts, miniatures of which have been found deposited as grave goods and which were dated at around 1,735 BPE; another miniature figure found of a wooden raft has been dated at 1,190 BPE and came from a cemetery at Cáñamo, a site south of Iquique. Yet another figure represents a vessel known as a single-hulled canoe, which is made of a single piece of wood and has been found near Arica in cemeteries that also contained some Inca materials. This figure has been dated at around 500 BPE. The most remarkable water craft of all, however, was the sea lion raft, probably made on the coast of the Norte Chico or near Antofagasta [Peru]. These craft were still being made in the middle of the twentieth century. All of these vessels expanded the area of operation into the vast Pacific Ocean, increased mobility between fishing coves, made long distance voyages easier and enhanced expertise in the use of harpoons for hunting whales, as has been documented in the rock art paintings of El Médano.

The Chinchorro Culture: Hunters, Gatherers, and Fishers
of the Atacama Desert Coast

VIVIEN G. STANDEN AND BERNARDO T. ARRIAZA

The Chinchorro skillfully developed diverse and efficient instruments for hunting, fishing, and maritime harvest. They fished with hooks made out of thorns, *Choromytilus* [mussel] shells, and bone. To sink the hook, a stone sinker was tied to the fishing line. This technology allowed access to deep-sea fish, widening the exploitation of food resources. In funerary contexts, the fishhooks were associated mainly with women and infants, suggesting a connection between fishing activities and gender roles. . . .

Instruments for hunting activities included harpoons with detachable heads to capture marine mammals (especially sea lions) and fish. Harpoon tips had lithic [stone] points and attached bone hooks, which assisted in catching the prey. In funerary contexts, harpoons were found with adult men and women. Some bodies had harpoons tied to their hands, providing symbolic value to this artifact. For capturing seabirds they probably used *bolas*. . . .[3]

Paleodietary studies undertaken [in the 1990s] showed that 10% of the diet came from terrestrial animals, 80% from marine food and the remaining 10% was of vegetal origin [mainly seaweed].

Notes

1. Jon M. Erlandson, Michael H. Graham, Bruce J. Bourque, Debra Corbett, James A. Estes, and Robert S. Steneck, "The Kelp Highway Hypothesis: Marine Ecology, the Coastal Migration Theory, and the Peopling of the Americas," *Journal of Island and Coastal Archaeology* 2, no. 2 (2007): 161.

2. Kathleen Flanagan Rollins, "Monte Verde Mysteries," *Misfits and Heroes*, August 24, 2014, https://misfitsandheroes.wordpress.com/2014/08/24/monte-verde-mysteries/.

3. A weapon made up of two rocks connected by a rope, thrown at prey.

Canoes: The World's First—and Simplest, and Most Graceful—Boats

Eric Paul Roorda

Along with skin boats, or coracles, the first vessels that humans built to venture out onto the Ocean were boats fashioned from—that is, dug out of—tree trunks. "Canoe" comes from the language of the Taíno, the first New World people who fell victim to European conquerors.

Carbon dating analysis shows that the three oldest canoes ever found—one each in Europe, Asia, and Africa—are more than 8,000 years old. The Pesse Canoe, unearthed in a peat bog in the Netherlands in 1955, benefited from anaerobic conditions, which preserved its six-and-a-half-foot wooden hull. Archaeologists excavated another quite like it in Kuahuqiao, Zhejiang Province, in eastern China in 2010. In 1987, a Fulani cattle herdsman in Yobe State, Nigeria, discovered a dugout of similar vintage made from a teak tree. Excavated near the Komadugu Gana River and the village of Dufuna, it has become known as the Dufuna Canoe.

In Columbus's 1493 letter to Luis De Sant Angel describing his first encounter with the Americas, he wrote of enormous Taíno dugouts: "In these isles there are a great many canoes, something like rowing boats, of all sizes, and most of them are larger than an eighteen-oared galley. They are not so broad, as they are made of a single plank, but a galley could not keep up with them in rowing, because they go with incredible speed, and with these they row about among all these islands, which are innumerable, and carry on their commerce. I have seen some of these canoes with seventy and eighty men in them, and each had an oar."[1]

Roger Williams left the best description of dugout canoe construction, in his overlooked book A Key to the Language of America (1634), in a chapter called "Of the Sea": "Ob[servation]. I have seene a Native goe into the woods with his hatchet, carrying only a Basket of Corn with him, & stones to strike the fire[;] when he had feld his tree (being a chestnut) he made a little House or shed of the bark of it, he puts fire and followes the burning of it with fire, in the midst in many places: his corne he boyles and hath the Brook by him,

Dugout canoe construction was essentially the same for the 8,000-year-old Dufuna canoe as it was for every dugout built since then. This photograph captures four graceful examples of dugout canoe construction, somewhere on the coast of West Africa, sometime in the first half of the twentieth century. It is a real photo postcard, the product of a camera technology popular at that time, which allowed people to buy film that developed each of their photographs as a postcard. Therefore, every real photo postcard is unique, and only those that are sent in the mail and signed by the sender offer a clue to the identity of the photographer. In this case, the postcard is unused, so the photographer is unknown. Certain aspects of its printing indicate that it was taken c. 1940. Courtesy of the Roorda/Doyle Collection.

and sometimes angles for a little fish: but so hee continues burning and hewing untill he hath within ten or twelve dayes (lying there at his worke alone) finished, and (getting hands) lanched his Boate; with which hee ventures out to fish in the Ocean."[2]

Notes

1. Christopher Columbus, "The Letter of Columbus to Luis De Sant Angel Announcing His Discovery," in *American History Leaflets: Colonial and Constitutional, No. 1*, edited by Albert Bushnell Hart and Edward Channing (New York: A. Lovell, 1892), 5.
2. Roger Williams, *A Key to the Language of America* (1634; reprint, Providence, RI: Plantations Tercentenary Committee, 1936), 106–7.

Pacific Island Open Ocean Navigation

David H. Lewis

The Pacific Islanders developed techniques of navigation that allowed them to travel thousands of miles between small islands. They paid close attention to many clues to find their way: cloud formations, winds, waves (formed locally), swells (emanating from distant storms), the color of the water, the movements of seabirds, and, most importantly, stars. By observing the rise and fall of individual stars, constellations, and planets, the Pacific Island navigators plotted star courses that combined the paths of several heavenly bodies. They named the courses after the first star or constellation in the sequence, including as many as nine stars. The ancient navigators devised star compasses, also called sidereal compasses, with thirty-two points, all of them a separate star course. This complicated body of knowledge was virtually unknown to Westerners until David Henry Lewis (1917–2002) published his book We, the Navigators: The Ancient Art of Landfinding in the Pacific, *in 1972. Born in England, Lewis grew up in Rarotonga, where he developed an early interest in Pacific Island seafaring. After medical training in England, service in World War II, and a medical career in New Zealand, Lewis began a second life devoted to sailing. He built a catamaran like those used by the Pacific Islanders, named* Rehu Moana, *which means "Sea Spray" in the Maori language, and competed in the 1964 single-handed race across the Atlantic from England to the United States. Soon after, Lewis, his wife, and two daughters sailed the catamaran around the world, the first circumnavigation by a multihull boat. Lewis bought another boat in 1967, the* Isbjorn, *and received a grant from the Australian National University to sail it around the South Pacific studying the islanders' navigation methods, which he and his family did for several years. He based* We, the Navigators *on his research from those travels. In the text included here, the author refers extensively to the individual Pacific Islanders who shared their expertise with him and took him along on voyages to see firsthand how they, and their ancient ancestors, understood the Ocean.*

In 2016, the Disney film Moana *(Maori for "sea") brought the South Pacific islanders' ancient navigation methods to a global audience. The delightful animated movie is accurate in its depiction of the sidereal compass, the design and rigging of catamarans, and other historical details, doubtlessly due to Lewis's work, although he was not acknowledged in the credits. After all, his catamaran was named* Rehu Moana.

Reasons for Voyaging

We will now tentatively approach the problem of defining the role played by conscious navigation in interisland contact—remembering how complex and variable must have been the social history of the centuries before written records begin. Impossible as it is to re-create the world of a prehistoric voyager, failure to attempt a partial appreciation of his motives may lead to the assumption by default that they equated with our own—and the one certainty is that they did not. In suggesting certain attitudes on the part of the voyagers and dividing the voyages themselves into categories, I want to stress that both motives and categories were mixed and overlapping and, moreover, did not exactly correspond to the European terms we have perforce used to describe them. The maintenance of clan and kinship relations and obligations do not, for instance, fit into a European social mould. We will concentrate, then, on illustrative examples, considered in the light of the efficacy of indigenous navigation.

ADVENTURE

All over Oceania a wandering spirit persists to this day.[1] The approach to voyaging of Rafe and other present-day Tikopians, of Tevake, Hipour, and Iotiebata, shows that confidence at sea has in no way abated. There is no element of "conquering" the ocean in their attitude. Untold generations have studied the sea's moods, so that the navigators' knowledge, even when residual, has made it for them a familiar and friendly place. They are as much at ease and at home with the aquatic environment as the Australian Aboriginal is with his inland ecosystem.

Firth, in an evocative passage, writes of the Tikopians:

"Fired by the lust for adventure and the desire to see new lands canoe after canoe set out and ranged the seas. . . . Fear of storms and shipwreck leaves them undeterred, and the reference in an ancient song to the loss of a man at sea as a 'sweet burial' expresses very well the attitude of the Tikopia."

Examples abound from earlier times of this restless urge. There were the Raiateans (from the Tahiti group) who, according to Banks, went on "very long voyages, often remaining out from home several months, visiting in that time many different islands of which they repeated to us the names of near a hundred." In the twenties of the following century the missionary John Williams was told of the Raiatean chief Iouri, an "enterprising spirit, he determined to go in search of other countries"; and had navigated his *pahi* to Rarotonga, 600 miles away, and when he came home again, it "became an object of ambition with every adventurous chief to discover other lands." . . .

Similarly in the Fiji-Tonga-Samoa area we find mid-nineteenth-century Islanders making voyages of "600 or 800 or even 1,000 miles—being not in-

The South Pacific Islanders guided their sail-powered outrigger vessels, like the one seen in this picture, across vast distances between islands, using navigational methods unknown in other parts of the watery world. Artist unknown, *The Valley of Voona, Feejee [Fiji] Island*, steel engraving, in Captain Charles Wilkes, U.S.N., *Narrative of the United States Exploring Expedition during the Years 1838, 1839, 1840, 1841, 1842*, vol. 2 (Philadelphia: Lea and Blanchard, 1845). Courtesy of the Roorda/Doyle Collection.

frequently absent a year or two from home, wandering and gadding about from island to island, . . . Samoa, Fiji, and all the Friendly Islands [Tonga] . . . Wallis, Fortuna, Nieuafou, Nieutobutabu."

They were proud and arrogant, these Polynesians of an earlier day, and they stood much less in awe of Europeans than many accounts would lead us to believe. Vancouver mentions a young seaman who was so upset by the Marquesans jeering at him and pulling his hair that, hardly in accord with Royal Navy traditions, he burst into tears. Equally contemptuous were the 80 returned voyagers who tramped uninvited through Diaper's trade store in Vava'u (Tonga) appropriating trinkets for their fair companion. These youths and one "physically perfect[,] morally, very imperfect" young woman had been away in a large kalia on a year's cruise to outlying islands, mostly Samoa.

THE PRIDE OF NAVIGATORS

A proud self-respect permeates Carolinian voyaging to this day. Thus there are three sets of circumstances, according to Beiong, in which visitors to an island will feel shamed and in honour bound to put to sea at once regardless of storms or even certainty of disaster. These are:

Any suggestion that they are becoming a burden to feed.
Any injury to one of their number in a fight with no apology offered.
A decision by the captain that the weather is too bad for voyaging,
    followed by a local canoe putting out even to fish a little way offshore.

It would be more in keeping with the dignity of a Puluwat captain to beat 150 miles to windward for five days to Moen Island in Truk lagoon to obtain cigarettes than to wait a short time for the administrator's motor vessel (Hipour).

The return voyage of the respected navigator brothers Repunglug and Repunglap and their three companions between Satawal in the Carolines and Saipan in the Marianas in April/May 1970 has been referred to. One important motive for the enterprise seems to have been that they felt shamed by Hipour's exploit the previous year and a revival of voyaging between the archipelagos would both renew their prestige and enhance their skill. The star courses and auxiliary sailing directions had been given the Repung brothers over thirty years previously by their father, who had not himself been to Saipan. Neither brother had any acquaintance with Western seamanship or navigation. There was no memory on Satawal of the voyage having been made in the present century.

There were no charts aboard the 26-foot canoe, though in accordance with modern Carolinian custom, a boat compass was used for secondary orientation in the daytime. A "walkie talkie" set with a range of 10 miles was carried.

The first stage was to uninhabited West Fayu, 52 miles from Satawal, where favourable winds were awaited. The remaining 422 miles to Saipan were covered in under four days. On the return journey the canoe was set to leeward by a storm so the brothers decided to proceed direct to Satawal, omitting the call at West Fayu (this would have been more than 470 miles non stop). However, they first contacted by radio a party of Islanders who were on West Fayu, and these requested assistance in transporting the eight turtles they had caught. The travelers were guided two days before completing their journey to Satawal.

The following story was recounted as a specific illustration of the pride of navigators. A Woleai canoe, driven south by contrary winds, decided to try for Kapingamarangi atoll, which lies in total isolation midway between the Carolines proper and the Solomons, 465 miles south-east of Pulusuk. None of the crew had been there but they knew the star course and were fortunate enough to arrive safely. Now the Kapingamarangi language is a Polynesian one quite unlike the Micronesian tongues spoken in the rest of the Carolines, so the inhabitants' speech was incomprehensible. This tended to confirm the identity of the landfall but the voyagers were uncertain, and being trained navigators, they were too proud to inquire. Instead they kept their ears open, and after about a week, overheard children at play (fishermen in another version) mention the island's name. They thereupon set off home, their dignity unimpaired.

All the examples here given have been from the Carolines, because there voyaging attitudes persist almost in their entirety. Traditions from other parts of Oceania, however, while less detailed, leave little doubt that exactly the same attitude was held throughout Polynesia in former times.

RAIDING AND CONQUEST

Tongan Raids. There is no absolute division, of course, between raiding and exacting tribute or maintaining hegemony, especially since spheres of influence seem to have been even more tenuous and transitory in the Pacific than in land-based empires. The Tongans raided well beyond their normal contact sphere, especially to the Polynesian Outliers fringing Melanesia away to the north-west. The nearest Outliers to the mis-named "Friendly Islands" (Tonga) are Tikopia and its neighbor Anuta, 960 miles from Tongatapu and 550 from Fiji.

"It appears from the account of the Tucopians and Anutoans," wrote Dillon, "that in the days of their ancestors these islands were invaded by five large double canoes from Tongataboo, the crews of which committed dreadful outrages." Firth puts this (or a similar invasion) at eight generations ago—at 25 years to a generation, about 200 years.

Further to the westward still, on Nukapu, one of the Santa Cruz Reef Islands, traditions of Tongan raids are well remembered.

West-north-west another 200 miles, the story was repeated on the Outlier, Sikaiana. Towards the close of the seventeenth century or nine generations before the publication of the account, a large Samoan double canoe came to Sikaiana. Typically the Samoans were peaceful, but a big Tongan party who arrived in the time of the same ruling chief (Alima) were the reverse. Having ravaged the island, they left for Taumako, 240 miles on their way towards home. They were not destined to see Tonga again, however, for they had taken with them Semalu, Alima's son, who revealed their depredations on Sikaiana. The Taumakoans thereupon exterminated the Tongans with bows and arrows. The kidnapped chief's son eventually returned home.

There are several points of interest about this tradition. "Tonga" is a word denoting some southerly direction in most Polynesian dialects, but this and similar accounts invariably draw such a definite distinction between Tongans and Samoans, that the geographical Tonga is clearly meant. Then Taumako, unlike most of Polynesia, is an island where bows and arrows are used in warfare. An elderly Sikaianan, Teai, who is most unlikely to have had access to Woodford's article in *Oceania*, told me the same story in 1968, except that he said the events had occurred not nine but eleven generations ago, a discrepancy accounted for by the 62 years that passed since the original recording of the tradition. . . .

New Guinea Raids on the Carolines. The people of Sonsorol, Kodgube (Tobi), and Merir, Hipour told me, were in former times afraid of the west wind lest it bring down raiders from New Guinea upon them. These westernmost of the Carolines are well over 1,000 miles from Hipour's home island of Puluwat, yet he was substantially correct in his assertion. The westerners had indeed had ample occasion for apprehension, for numerous savage raids did take place over a period of many generations. It had, however, been southerly rather than westerly winds that had filled the sails of the raiders, who seem to have mostly come from the Jobi-Sarmi, Tarkur-Saar region of West Irian. The same authority points out that these are the only New Guineans to use the loom, which is characteristic of Micronesia.

These raids force us to reconsider the generally accepted opinion of Melanesians and New Guinea Panuans as essentially coastal sailors. For from Jobi-Sarmi in New Guinea to Sonsorol and Tobi in the Carolines is 600 miles. There is a possible staging point at Mepia Island (Pegun), but even this leaves an unbroken stretch of 360 miles culminating in a difficult landfall.

DEEP SEA FISHING

A drawing of a Tongan bonito fishing canoe (*tafa'anga*) made during Tasman's visit in 1643 is identical with present-day craft and shows the bonito roof in position behind the steersman, demonstrating the relative antiquity of this type of deep-sea fishing. There is evidence from Samoa of similar boats being carried aboard large double canoes. Stair, who saw the last surviving *va'a tele* (analogue of the *tongiaki*) in 1838, wrote of them making long fishing expeditions carrying on deck two *va'a alo*, which were 25–30-foot bonito canoes equivalent to the Tongan *tafa'anga*. On reaching the destination reef these were used for fishing, "the large canoe being reserved for crew and cargo."

There are similar Tongan stories of long-range ventures like that to a distant fishing ground near Niue called Aka, 250 miles from the Ha'apai group (Ve'ehala). Now the Samoan *va'a tele* and its Tongan counterpart, the *tongiaki*, were notorious for their clumsiness in bad weather. It seems likely that some of these seaworthy but unhandy vessels would be driven far afield by storms. Should they accidentally come upon unknown or forgotten islands, such ships with their trained navigator-captains would be more capable than most of returning home with accurate information as to the position of their discovery.

TRADING VOYAGES

We have touched already upon a special example of indigenous trade in Kau Moala's ill-fated load of sandalwood. The tribute voyages to Yap, considered below, were another. The long voyages from isolated Pukapuka to Samoa and other islands have also been mentioned. There is only soft rock on Pukapuka and the island's legends make it apparent that the procurement of stone from which adzes could be made was an important motive for voyaging and, in confirmation, a basaltic adze found in a grave was similar to Samoan types. This is a reminder of how imperative it was to supplement the resources of the stark atoll environment even at the cost of lengthy and hazardous journeys. Naturally other reasons for putting to sea operated on Pukapuka . . . the search for adventure, desire to see lands known of old, prestige, and the exiling of men who might disrupt the community.

There is no space for further examples. We can only mention the existence of the complex trading cycles that were, and still are, typical of Melanesia.

TRIBUTE AND EMPIRE: THE SPHERE OF YAP

Tongan and Tahitian spheres could well have been considered under this heading, but since Tongan control and raids overlap and the Tahitian world is discussed in the next chapter, we will confine ourselves here to this single example from Micronesia. The Gail district of the Carolinian island of Yap once exercised political and religious hegemony as far to the eastward as Puluwat. This is, its power extended more than 700 miles with gaps of as long as 290 miles between individual atolls. As well as regular tribute-bearing fleets from the eastward, west Carolinian canoes transported the great wheel-sized discs known as "stone money" from the south-west. These objects were quarried on Palau and taken across 230 miles of open sea to Yap. . . .

DELIBERATE RETURNS AFTER FORCED DRIFTS

There are a number of reports of such episodes which are deserving of notice. In the first place they reveal how blurred is the line that really divides the somewhat Eurocentric categories of purposeful and accidental voyages. In the second they emphasize the extent and complexity of interisland contact made possible by the widely known and extremely efficacious land-finding techniques. We will give two examples.

Returns after drifting from Carolines to Philippines. Not a few of the canoes that were storm-drifted to the Philippines from the Yap region made successful return voyages. As late as 1910 the *Deutsches Kolonialblatt* wrote of canoes being cast away to the Philippines from the Carolines and returning. There were old people who had "been five times to the Philippines and made their own way back home, against the prevailing east wind, despite strict German regulations to the contrary."

It might be supposed that such recent return voyagers owed their success to European geographical knowledge were it not for the fact that similar episodes were recorded by Spanish missionaries in the Philippines at a time when the Carolines were virtually a closed book to Westerners. In the early 1690s the Jesuit Fr. Paul Clain was told by a Carolinian castaway named Olit that "six natives from Eap [Yap] island had been stranded in the Philippines and then returned to Eap, and that the voyage had lasted 10 days." The distance is 700 miles. Since the episode occurred some time in the 1680s no European could have directed them; the sailing directions they used must have been exclusively their own.

A little later, in 1696, two canoes were driven to the Philippines. The survivors eventually set off for home again, though the outcome of their voyage is uncertain. What is significant is that it was these Carolinians who were eagerly questioned about their islands by the Spaniards and not the other way around. They listed thirty-two islands including "Saypen" (Saipan) in the Marianas, and a map was drawn from their statements that depicted even more islands. It is not surprising that many of the positions shown are inaccurate, since Carolinian star courses and geographical data are, as we saw, expressed in terms very different from static maps. What is abundantly clear is that the castaways' range, extending as it did 2000 miles east of the Philippines and embracing Saipan 500 miles to the north, far surpassed the sketchy knowledge of the Europeans.

Even more striking is the fact that the oldest of the party had once before been cast on the Philippines, on Mindanao, "where he had seen only infidels," and whence he had sailed back to his own islands. In this instance also no "borrowing" of Western information can possibly have occurred since the old man encountered no Europeans. His accomplishment was formidable in that his probable landfall targets would have been either Palau, 450 miles from Mindanao, or Yap, a full 700.

Returning Tuamotuan drifters. When Captain Beechey landed on the Tuamotuan atoll of Ahunui in 1826 he encountered thirty-one Polynesians who were busy repairing a double canoe "upwards of thirty feet long." They had been bound from Anaa in the Tuamotus towards Tahiti 200 miles to the westward, the craft perilously overloaded with forty-eight souls and three weeks' provisions. Near Mehetia, 145 miles along the route, they encountered a series of westerly gales. Only after seventeen had died did they fetch up on Vanavana, an uninhabited Tuamotuan island, 420 miles east-south-east of Anaa and about 520 from the spot near Mehetia whence they had been drifted. After recouping their strength they set out for home and had reached Ahanui 100 miles along the way when Beechey encountered them. The manner in which the Anaa navigator retained his orientation, enabling the castaways successfully to complete the first quarter of their homeward voyage, is typical enough. The unusual feature was their meeting with someone who could record the episode.

VOYAGES BY ONE-WAY EXILES

This type of exodus, a journey of no return deliberately undertaken towards some mythical or very ill-defined destination, is well documented. For instance in 1813 Captain Porter was told of big parties of such voluntary exiles being encouraged by the priests to leave the Marquesas for legendary "lands," and hundreds of people having so departed over the years. There are examples of like nature from other parts of Oceania, although less institutionalised than the Marquesan custom appears to have been.

A late eighteenth-century chief's son on the Polynesian island of Uvea, west of Samoa, was accidentally hurt during the construction of a canoe. Fearing the father's wrath, his companions decided to "leave for lands unknown." Rather surprisingly in the circumstances, the injured man elected to join them. The fugitives eventually came to an island in the Loyalty group off New Caledonia 1000 miles to the south-west, which was named "Uvea" after their homeland, a designation it bears to this day. Practically the same story is told on the Loyalty Islands Uvea as on the Polynesian one. . . .

ACCIDENTAL DRIFTS
The picture of interisland contact in Oceania as having been made up of a complex pattern of deliberate and accidental voyages (and ones that defy such easy classification) has been discussed earlier. However, since "pure" drifts shed little light on navigational questions, we have perforce concentrated on the more planned varieties of voyaging, and if a sense of proportion is to be maintained, we must recognise this lack of balance. . . .

Note

1. [Note in original.] This section could equally well have been entitled "curiosity," "wandering," or "exploring" and cannot be strictly separated from trading ventures, assertion of traditional authority, or even raiding.

The Earliest Seafarers in the Mediterranean and the Near East

George F. Bass

Large vessels with polyglot crews and cargoes of goods with origins ranging from the British Isles to Afghanistan plied the Mediterranean Sea and the Black Sea thousands of years ago.

The new underwater archaeology has allowed a survey of shipwrecks in the Ocean that was previously unimaginable. Increasingly accurate sonar and the development of undersea vessels with greater ranges and abilities have led to numerous dazzling discoveries. Robert Ballard has been a leader in this rapidly expanding field. He is best known for locating the wreck of the RMS Titanic, which sank in April 1912, in 12,500 feet (3,800 meters) of icy water, in the turbulent North Atlantic Ocean. His many finds around the world are repainting our picture of the maritime past; he now estimates that there are probably one million shipwrecks resting on the bottom. Partly accounting for this astounding figure is the revelation that there was a great deal more seafaring in ancient times than was previously considered possible. Ballard's ongoing work in the Black Sea has been particularly startling, depicting a very crowded Ocean during antiquity.[1]

George F. Bass, the father of modern nautical archaeology, detailed his astounding finds in a classic work briefly excerpted here, on the subject of the earliest seafaring in the waters near Egypt and Mesopotamia.

Long before there were shepherds or farmers in Greece, there were sailors. More than nine thousand years ago, when men still gained their livelihood by hunting and gathering food, these seafarers set out to explore the Aegean. They sailed south to the island of Melos and discovered obsidian, a hard volcanic stone which they fashioned into sharp-edged knives and scrapers. Blades of this glassy material, dating from the eighth millennium BC, have been found in the Franchthi Cave of the Peloponnese, appearing at the same time as large fish bones which offer additional evidence that men were turning to the sea. And Mesolithic settlers on Skyros could only have reached their destination by water. About a thousand years later, we know not from where, Neolithic farmers had arrived on the great islands of Crete and Cyprus.

Anyone who sails the Aegean today, even during the relatively calm summer months, can guess what terror sudden wind storms brought to these earliest sailors. But what their primitive craft were like, whether skin-covered boats or dug-out canoes or rafts of logs, we do not know. Modern technology may one day provide the means of locating their sunken remains beneath the sand and mud of the sea bed. Until that time we must turn to the great riverine centres of the Near East—to Mesopotamia and Egypt—for our impressions of the earliest boats.

The Nile, emptying through its Delta into the Mediterranean, and the Tigris and Euphrates, which flow jointly into the Persian Gulf, provided ample opportunity for fishermen and ferrymen to venture gradually out into the open sea. To meet conditions there, they would have to build larger and stronger ships.

FOURTH MILLENNIUM BC

A clay model of the oldest known sailing vessel was found in a grave at Eridu, in southern Mesopotamia. A vertical cylindrical socket, placed slightly toward one end of the boat, indicates where the mast was stepped, and holes piercing the gunwale may have been for stays. The broad, almost oval shape of the hull suggests that perhaps this was a skin-covered boat, like the round coracles (*quffas*) shown on later Assyrian reliefs.

The sailing skiff was from the 'Ubaid period, around 3500 BC. The succeeding Uruk period, covering most of the second half of the fourth millennium in Mesopotamia, saw the appearance of the earliest written records. Among the many pictograms scratched onto clay tablets is the representation of a vessel with the high prow and stern which were to become distinctive of Mesopotamian ships. Marked on the hull are pairs of lines, suggesting that it was built up of bundles of reeds lashed together, much like a boat from the same area represented on an eighth-century Assyrian relief.

Similar vessels appear on a pair of finely carved seal stones of the same Uruk period. Their high, in-curving prows and sterns, seemingly bent over and tied down, end in leafy patterns. This does not provide certain proof, however, that these hulls were made of reeds; Egyptian wooden ships of a later period long preserved an in-curving stern ending in a floral decoration, a legacy from the days when most Nilotic craft were made of papyrus bundles. In each of the carvings, a man sits at the stern, either paddling or steering, while another man stands in the bows holding ready a forked stick for punting or sounding the river bed.

The shapes of such high-prowed ships are so typical of Mesopotamia that when similar vessels appear in prehistoric Egyptian art, we now call[ed] them "foreign ships" from the East. Egyptian ships of the same time, scratched or painted on pottery, indeed seem quite different. One of the earliest, on a bowl of the Amratian period, shows the low, "sickle-shaped" hull which continues well into the historical period of Egypt. Paddles for propulsion may be seen near the prow, with an additional pair of paddles for steering near the stern. On deck are two hut-like cabins or shelters, and a tassel hanging from the prow may represent the line used in mooring the ship.

These low ships are best known from innumerable examples painted on pottery of the following, Gerzean, period towards the close of the fourth millennium in Egypt. The pictures are so stylized that some authorities have thought them to represent palisaded fortifications on land, like those used on the western frontier in America, and one scholar even suggested that they were pens for ostrich farms! Now they are generally accepted as low hulls with lines protruding downward to represent oars or paddles. On each a palm branch or sprig of vegetation at the bows shades the look-out's bench, and just below is a tassel-like mooring line. A pair of cabins are placed amidships with a space between them; no oars are usually represented immediately beneath this space, so it is possible that a gangway was situated here. Just by the cabins are one or two posts supporting the standards of various prehistoric *nomes*, or districts. A rare mast and sail, possibly of matting, is placed forward in one of the hulls, but strange shield-like devices on poles are drawn near some of the ships and these may represent removable masts and sails. Crew members are not shown.

A unique example of such ships is found painted on a tattered textile fragment from El-Gebelein in Upper Egypt. Double-cabins, bearded rowers (facing forward), and steersmen are clearly seen.

Both types of boats, the squared "Mesopotamian" and the slightly crescent-shaped "Egyptian," appear frequently as rock carvings in the Wadi Hammamat, a natural passage through the eastern Egyptian desert from the Nile to the Red Sea. As the carvings are found far from any water, we may guess that the artists recalled both ships of the Nile and ships that arrived from the Red Sea.

Note

1. Interview by Dan Davis, "The Crowded Sea of Antiquity: Black Sea Archaeology with Robert Ballard," *University of Texas News*, October 27, 2008, formerly available at http://news.utexas.edu/2008/10/27/shipwrecks.

III

Unknown Waters

This section includes a number of explorers, but not the usual suspects. These important navigators are mainly outside the canon of Western civilization's Age of Discovery, but the history of global oceanic exchange, which continues to the present day, is incomplete without the exploits of these less-heralded adventurers. Their travels collectively limned the full extent of the Ocean in all three of its dimensions, ranging to its farthest reaches on the surface, and descending to its deepest depths.

Chinese Voyages on the Indian Ocean

Zheng He

The great Ming dynasty admiral Zheng He (1371–1433), called Cheng Ho in this selection, is sometimes called the Chinese Columbus, but the label is a misnomer, because the seven voyages that Zheng He commanded between 1405 and 1433 were not missions of exploration and conquest, as were those of the famous Genoan. Long before Columbus sailed into the unknown waters west of Europe in 1492, Zheng He's Treasure Fleets traversed well-established trade routes in the Indian Ocean, ranging all the way to Calicut and Zanzibar, ports famous for spices. His ships dwarfed any of the vessels that Columbus commanded, with the largest of them, the bao chuan, or Treasure Ships, measuring an estimated 440 feet long and 180 feet wide, making them the largest wooden boats ever built, whereas the Santa María was barely 60 feet in length and 18 feet in the beam. The disproportion in the size of the respective Chinese and Spanish flotillas was even more marked, as Zheng He's journeys set out with an average of 250 ships, with the largest being an armada of 317 vessels, while the most ships Columbus ever commanded was seventeen, with about 1,000 men. Conversely, Zheng He's retinues averaged 27,000 sailors and soldiers.

Zheng He was born into the ethnic Bai community of Chinese Muslims living in southerly Yunnan Province. His father and grandfather had both traveled from their home in that faraway corner of Asia to complete the hajj to Mecca during their lifetimes. The newly established and vigorously expansive Ming dynasty brought Yunnan under its subjugation when Zheng was a boy. The invaders executed his father and castrated the young Zheng, then carried him away to join the court of the emperor, where only females and male eunuchs were permitted. Zheng He rose in the ranks of the advisor-level eunuchs who surrounded the imperial throne, then chose a favorable moment to support the rebellious Zhu Di, a pretender who seized power and became emperor with Zheng's backing. He decided to project his realm's sea power to the world, with the Treasure Fleets of Zheng He spreading news of the great Middle Kingdom across the Ocean to Indonesia, India, the Middle East, and East Africa. Zheng He engaged in diplomacy from a position of unprecedented strength, negotiated trade relationships, and accepted tribute in the form of zebras, giraffes, and other exotic creatures, which he took to Beijing for the amusement of the emperor. His voyages were not without conflict, including trouble with pirates based in Sumatra on his first voyage, and a brief war with a Sri Lankan king on his third voyage, but there was no *comparison between that level of violence and the European model, which inflicted carnage.*

Zheng He died during his seventh voyage, in 1433, and was buried at sea. In the years that followed, China turned away from the sea, prohibiting most seafaring activity and expunging Zheng He's accomplishments from the record. China soon declined from being the preeminent naval power in the world to a condition of such weakness that the enormous country was beset by resurgent piracy and Western incursions into its coastal waters, which would eventually lead to disaster in the nineteenth-century Opium Wars. Despite the imperial court's attempt to efface the national memory of Zheng He, evidence survived in the form of inscriptions written in stone on temple steles. Not discovered until 1935, the Chinese steles date to 1431, the year the last Treasure Fleet departed. Their inscriptions summarize Zheng He's first six yoyages.

Inscription on stone in the palace of the Celestial Spouse at the Liu-chia-chian in eastern Lu in memory of the intercourse with the barbarians.[1] In the sixth year of the Hsüan-te of the Ming Dynasty (1431) the cyclical year *hsin-hai*, the first day of (the second) spring (month) (March 14th) the principal envoys, the Grand Eunuch Cheng Ho and Wang Ching-hung, the assistant-envoys, the Grand Eunuchs Chu Liang, Chou Fu, Hung Pao and Yang Chen, and the Senior Lesser Eunuch Chang Ta have erected an inscription as follows:

The Majestic miraculous power of the goddess of the Celestial Spouse to whom by imperial command the title has been conferred of "Protector of the country defender of the people whose miraculous power manifestly answers [prayers] and whose vast benevolence saves universally," is widely spread over the great sea and her virtuous achievements have been recorded in a most honorable manner in the Bureau of Sacrificial Worship. From the time when we, Cheng Ho and his companions, at the beginning of the Yung-lo period received the Imperial commission as envoys to the barbarians up till now seven voyages have taken place and each time we have commanded several tens of thousands of government soldiers and more than a hundred ocean-going vessels. Starting from T'ai-ts'ang and taking the sea we have by way of the countries of Chan-ch'eng (Chapma), Hsien-lo (Siam) Kua-wa (Java), K'oichih (Cochin) and Ku-li (Calicut) reached Hul-lu-mo-ssu (Ormuz) and other countries of the western regions, more than 3,000 countries in all, traversing more than one hundred thousand *li* of immense water spaces and beholding waves (gaping like the mouths of) whales, rising up to heaven, immense and (succeeding each other) endlessly. Now there was a drizzle of thick fogs, now steep wind-swept waves and in all those inconstant changes of the aspect of the ocean our sails, loftily unfurled like clouds, day and night continued their course, rapid like that of a star. Save by trusting in the divine power, how could we have found a tranquil crossing? When once it happened that we were in danger, as soon as we had pronounced the name of the goddess, the answer (to prayer) followed (swiftly) like an echo: suddenly there was a magic lantern in the mast and as soon as the miraculous light appeared the danger was becalmed. Everyone in the fleet, set at rest, felt assured that there was nothing to fear. This is in general terms what the merit of the goddess has accomplished.

On the arriving in the outlying countries, those among the barbarian kings who were obstructing the "transforming influence" (of Chinese culture) and were disrespectful were captured alive, and brigands who gave themselves over to violence and plunder were exterminated. Consequently the sea route was purified and tranquilized and the natives, owing to this, were enabled quietly to pursue their avocations. All this due to the aid of the goddess.

Formerly we have already reported the merits of the goddess in a memorial and have requested of the throne that a palace be erected at Nanking on the bank of the Dragon River where sacrificial worship is forever to be continued. We have respectfully received an imperial commemorative composition in order to glorify the miraculous favors, thus bestowing the highest praise. However, wherever one goes there are places of residence for the miraculous power of the goddess. Thus the "temporary palace" at the Liu-chia-chiang, built many years ago, has been repaired by us each time we have come hither. In the winter of the fifth year of the Hsüan-te (1430), having once more received a commission as envoys to the barbarian countries, we have moored our ships at the foot of the shrine and the soldiers of the government army have respectfully and sincerely assisted at the rites and the sacrifices have been continuous. We have added new improvements to the building of the goddess, which vastly surpass the old established usage, and we have rebuilt the shrine of the "Younger Sister of the Ch'ü Mountain" behind the palace, and have replaced the statue of the goddess in the principal hall with a new beautiful statue. Officers and common soldiers all gladly hastened hither to worship and there were some who could not control themselves (with joy). Could this have been brought about otherwise than by the sense of gratitude for the merit of the goddess, felt in men's hearts? Therefore we have written in inscription on stone and have moreover recorded the years and months of our voyages both going and returning in order to make these known forever.

I. In the third year of Yung-lo (1405) commanding the fleet we have gone to Ku-li (Calicut) and other countries. At that time the pirate Ch'en Tsu-yi and his followers were assembled at San-fo-ch'I (Palembang) where they plundered the native merchants. We captured that leader alive and returned in the fifth year (1407).

II. In the fifth year of Yung-lo commanding the fleet we went to Kua-wa (Java), Ku-li (Calicut), K'o-chih (Cochin) and Hsien-lo (Siam). The kings of these countries all presented as tribute local products, and precious birds and (rare) animals. We returned in the seventh year (1409).

III. In the seventh year of Yung-lo we went [to] the countries (visited) before and took our route by the country of Hsi-lan-shan (Ceylon). Its king Ya-lieh-jo-nai-erh (Alagakkoñara) was guilty of a gross lack of respect and plotted against the fleet. Owing to the manifest answer (to prayer) of the divine power (the plot) was discovered and thereupon that king was captured alive. In the ninth year (1411) on our return he was presented (to the throne as a prisoner); subsequently he received the Imperial favor of returning to his own country.

IV. In the twelfth year of Yung-lo (1414), commanding the fleet, we went to Hu-lu-mo-ssu (Ormuz) and the other countries. In the country of Su-men-ta-la (Sumatra) the false king Su-kan-la (Sekandar) was marauding and invading his country. Its king had sent an envoy to the Palace Gates in order to lodge a complaint and to request assistance. Approaching with the official troops under our command we have exterminated and arrested (the rebels), and silently aided by the divine power we thereupon captured the false king alive. In the thirteenth year (1415), on our return he was presented (to the Emperor as a prisoner). In that year the king of the country of Man-la-chia (Malacca) came in person with his wife and sons to present tribute.

V. In the fifteenth year of Yung-lo (1417) commanding the fleet we visited the western regions. The country of Hu-lu-mo-ssu (Ormuz) presented lions, leopards with gold spots and the giraffe, as well as the long horned animal oryx. The country of Mu-ku-tu-shu (Mogadishu) presented zebras as well as lions. The country of Pu-la-wa (Brawa) presented camels, which run one thousand li as well as camel-birds (ostriches). The countries of Kua-wa (Java) and Ku-li (Calicut) presented the animal *mi-li-kao*.[2] All presented local products the like of which had never been heard of before and sent the maternal uncle or the younger brother (of the king) to present a letter of homage written on gold leaf as well as tribute.

VI. In the nineteenth year of Yung-lo (1421) commanding the fleet we conducted the ambassadors from Hu-lu-mo-ssu (Ormuz) and the other countries, who had been in attendance at the capital for a long time, back to their countries. The kings of all these countries presented local products as tributes even more abundantly than previously.

VII. In the fifth year of Hsüan-te (1430), starting once more for the barbarians['] countries in order to make known the imperial commands, the fleet has anchored at the foot of the shrine and recalling how previously we have on several occasions received the benefits of the protection of the divine intelligence we have hereupon inscribed a text on stone.

Notes

1. The Celestial Spouse is the Buddhist sea goddess and protector of seafarers, who is still worshipped and goes by many names across the wide range of her devotion, such as Ah Ma.
2. An illustration of this mysterious beast from the temple inscription resembles one of the few antelope species native to India, but there have never been antelopes in Java.

Arab Voyages on the Indian Ocean

Paul Lunde

At a time when European sailors did little more than hug the coastlines of the seas they navigated, Arab mariners crisscrossed the wide Indian Ocean, far from the sight of land, confident in their navigational knowledge and technology. These topics came together in the work of the brilliant Ahmad ibn Majid (1432–1500), who composed a multivolume treatise detailing the intricacies of celestial navigation, among many complicated subjects, long before such concepts were grasped by sailors in northern waters. The historian, translator, and Arabist Paul Lunde wrote the following article, which summarizes Ibn Majid's career and describes the navigational instruments that he and countless other mariners employed to traverse the vast Indian Ocean. Lunde, who grew up in Saudi Arabia, has translated and edited the writings of Ahmad ibn Fadlan, a tenth-century Arab traveler who journeyed all the way to central Russia, leaving an account of a Volga Viking chieftain's cremation in his burning longship.

And He it is who appointed the stars to you, that you might guide yourselves by them through the darkness of land and sea.

—Qur'an, Sura 6, verse 97

Ahmad ibn Majid was born in Oman, probably in 1432, the year Zheng He's junks docked at Jiddah. The last of his approximately 40 known compositions, a poem on the heavens, is dated 1500, the same year Pedro Álvares Cabral discovered Brazil on his way to India by way of the Cape of Good Hope—thus linking Europe, the New World, Africa and Asia in a single voyage. Ibn Majid must have died soon after that date, his life spanning the most critical century in the history of the ocean whose currents, winds, reefs, shoals, headlands, harbors, seamarks and stars he spent a lifetime studying.

His most important work was *Kitab al-Fawa'id fi Usul 'Ilm al-Bahr wa 'l-Qawa'id* (*Book of Useful Information on the Principles and Rules of Navigation*), written in 1490. It is an encyclopedia of navigational lore: the history and basic principles of navigation, lunar mansions, rhumb lines, the difference between coastal and open-sea sailing, the locations of ports from East Africa to Indonesia, star positions, accounts of the monsoon and other seasonal winds, typhoons and other topics for professional navigators. He drew from his own experience and that of his father, also a famous navigator, and the lore of generations of Indian Ocean sailors.

The *Book of Useful Information* deals not only with the monsoon system, but also with the finer details of local wind regimes. The prevailing winds in the Red Sea north of Jiddah were among the most difficult, Ibn Majid writes, because they blew from the north all year round. Normal practice was to sail to Jiddah and there either transfer cargo to smaller boats, whose pilots were experienced in the local conditions between Jiddah and Suez, or to send cargoes overland. Even to Jiddah, and to 'Aydhab on the Egyptian side, access was only possible during the northeast monsoon, between October and mid-March. Other specialized knowledge was needed to sail elsewhere: south of the Equator, for example, where the monsoons gave way to the trade winds. The China Sea too had its own wind regime. Only a lifetime of sailing could teach a *mu'allim*, or master navigator, the skills upon which the entire trading network depended.

By Ibn Majid's time, four major innovations—two of them from China—had improved ship design and navigation.

Around the year 1000, the Chinese developed the axial stern-post rudder. It replaced the long "steering oar," which was always awkward to handle and prone to snap in heavy seas. The hinged rudder with its tiller made sailing easier and safer, especially in bad weather. It was not until the 13th century, however, that it reached the Mediterranean, probably about the same time as the compass, or a little later.

From the Arabian tradition of seafaring came the lateen sail, which had long allowed Arab *dhows* and other ships to sail closer to the wind than their Mediterranean counterparts. By the mid-15th century, however, the Portuguese and Spanish had combined it with their own square-rigged tradition, and it proved essential to their successes in both Asia and the New World.

Navigation relied on the third and fourth innovations—"fingers" and the *kamal*, as well as the early compass—for fixing a position at sea and setting a course out of sight of land. Ahmad ibn Majid and his fellow navigators used the Pole Star, determining latitude by its height above the horizon. By keeping the Pole Star at the same height, one could sail east and west on the same latitude; that height could be measured by the number of arm's-length finger-widths between the horizon and the star. Cambay, for example, lay at a latitude at which the Pole Star lay eleven fingers' width above the horizon. (This method was more precise than it might seem: Each "finger" was divided into eight parts.)

Another method of measuring the Pole Star's height above the horizon was by using the *kamal*. The *kamal* was a small rectangle of wood attached to

Whether the ancient vessel called the dhow originated in Arabia or India, or both, is unknown, but their triangular lateen sails dotted the Indian Ocean for centuries. Dhows created a nexus of connections between societies in East Africa, the Arabian Peninsula, and the subcontinent of India, carrying on commerce and knitting together a global community of Muslims. One form is the felucca, which plied the Nile River, eastern Mediterranean, and Red Sea. In this Egyptian postcard, ten feluccas crowd through the Gezira Bridge, the first span across the Nile, built 1872. Artist unknown, *Groupe de barques à voiles passant la pont*, Cairo, Egypt, c. 1907–15. Courtesy of the Roorda/Doyle Collection.

a cord which was calibrated by knots along its length. Each knot represented the latitude of a particular port. The navigator held the cord in his teeth at a certain knot and held the *kamal* at eye level at the cord's full length, aligning the lower edge of the rectangular plaque with the horizon. When the upper edge intersected the Pole Star, the ship was on the latitude of the desired port. Distance east and west was measured by time, not in hours but in *zam*, three-

The early Portuguese voyages of exploration, trade, and colonization, such as those of Bartolomeu Dias (1450–1500), Pedro Cabral (1467–1520), and Vasco da Gama (c. 1460s–1524) to Brazil and the Indian Ocean, established a maritime empire. After the completion of the Torre de Belém (Tower of Bethlehem) on the Tagus River in 1519, every ship that left Lisbon sailed past it. Steel engraving by Edward Finden, based on a painting by Clarkson Stanfield, in *Finden's Landscape Illustrations to Mr. Murray's First Complete and Uniform Edition of the Life and Works of Lord Byron*, by William Brockedon (London: John Murray, 1832). Courtesy of the Roorda/Doyle Collection.

hour increments—the length of a watch on board—measured by the burning of a standardized stick of incense.

Portuguese navigators, on the other hand, found latitude by measuring the altitude of the sun, rather than the Pole Star, and estimated their easting and westing by dead reckoning. Under King Manuel, tables of the sun's declination were compiled for mariners, based on similar tables prepared by Arab scholars in the mid-13th century. When the first European printed work on navigation appeared in 1509, it contained a method of "raising the Pole Star" that almost certainly came from Indian Ocean navigators, for the East–West dialogue on this subject had begun almost immediately: In 1499, Vasco da Gama's pilot had a long conversation on navigation with the Gujarati pilot who led the Portuguese to Calicut. Similarly, the earliest European maps of the Indian Ocean give the position of ports in *pulgadas*—"fingers"—and the Chinese used this method as well.

The development of the compass derived from knowledge of the properties of the lodestone, whose ability to attract iron had been known since remote antiquity. The late Joseph Needham showed how Chinese diviners in the second century BC cast lodestone spoons to align north-south. From this came the invention of the magnetized needle, which Ibn Majid attributed to the mythological patron of Indian Ocean sailors, al-Khidr, who, according to legend, had guided Alexander the Great over land and sea.

The compass proper is also a Chinese invention. The earliest known mention of it occurs in 990, and a Chinese encyclopedia of 1135 describes one in the shape of a wooden fish with a piece of magnetite inside that was floated in a bowl. In 1242 an Arabic text describes a compass seen on a voyage from Syria to Alexandria that was in the shape of a hollow iron fish that similarly floated on water in a bowl.

Toward the end of the 13th century someone—probably an Italian—fixed the magnetized needle to a wind rose. This created the basic form of the compass we know today. Traditionally, the Mediterranean wind rose had sixteen points, but with the compass this developed into a 32-point rose, allowing, for the first time, very precise courses to be laid. It also made it possible to draw up the accurate marine charts known as *portulani*.

An indication of the esteem in which Ahmad ibn Majid was held in his day is that Arab tradition actually ascribes the invention of the compass to him. What he may in fact have done is introduce the housed standing compass affixed to its card.

So by Ahmad ibn Majid's time, technology and economic expansion joined to mark a definitive break with the era before the compass and the axial rudder. Times were changing in other ways too. The foundation of Malacca, the Chinese voyages and the rapid growth of Islamic powers in northern India, Indonesia and the Philippines were all creating new poles of attraction in the East. Small Islamic principalities were springing up in Malaya, Java and Sumatra, and their only links to the Islamic heartland were by sea. Islamic space was expanding eastward, and with it the frontiers of the Islamic economy. Ahmad ibn Majid's publication of the secrets of Indian Ocean navigation can be seen as one response to this expansion.

Vasco da Gama's epochal voyage around the Cape of Good Hope in 1498 has often been presented as the irruption of a dynamic, technologically advanced Western power into an essentially static and backward Asia. Yet the Mediterranean and Indian Ocean worlds in the late 15th century were both responding to common historical forces. When Vasco da Gama's ship landed in Calicut in 1499 and the two worlds met, it was the visitors from the West who were at an economic and cultural disadvantage, only partially offset by their superior weapons. The Zamorin of Calicut, when showed the gifts brought by the Portuguese—the little bells and beads and the rough cloth—concluded that the Portuguese came from a poor and backward country, and advised them that, next time, they should bring gold. This they did—but even that came not from Portugal, but from Africa.

"We have 32 rhumbs, and *tirfa*, and *zam*, and the measurement of stellar altitudes, but they have not. They cannot understand the way we navigate, but we can understand the way they do; we can use their system and sail in their ships. For the Indian Ocean is connected to the All-Encompassing Ocean, and we possess scientific books that give stellar altitudes, but they do not have a knowledge of stellar altitudes; they have no science and no books, only the compass and dead reckoning. . . . We can easily sail in their ships and upon their sea, so they have great respect for us and look up to us. They admit we have a better knowledge of the sea and navigation and the wisdom of the stars."

A Chart of the Wet Blue Yonder, 1512

Jan ze Stobnicy

This 1512 map by the Polish metaphysician Jan ze Stobnicy (1470–1539) is one of the first to show the Western Hemisphere. Drafted two decades after the Spanish under Christopher Columbus conquered the Taíno people on the island of Hispaniola, but before Hernán Cortes completed the conquest of the México (Aztec) civilization on the mainland, this map reflects the extent of geographic knowledge in Europe at the time. Cartographers of the time had come to understand that an enormous expanse of Ocean covered much, maybe most, of the globe. In this depiction, the Atlantic, on the right, and the Pacific, on the left, bordering China, predominate. But the land in between remained almost entirely unknown—it was "Terra Incognita," as the label on western South America says here. Hispaniola and Cuba appear disproportionately large. A stumpy Florida is discernible close by, and above it, a sliver of the vast, unimagined North American landmass.

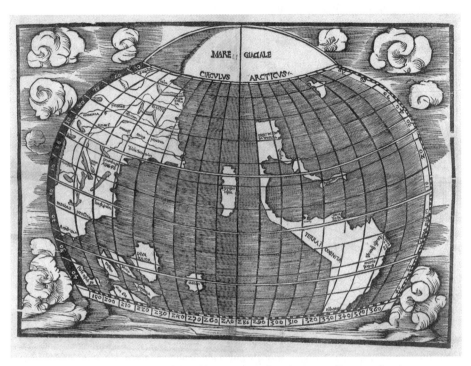

Jan ze Stobnicy's 1512 map is one of the oldest contained in the vast collection of early cartography at the John Carter Brown Library at Brown University. Jan ze Stobnicy, [Map of the Western Hemisphere] (Krakow: Florianum Unglerium, 1512). John Carter Brown Map Collection, File Name 15556, Call No. K12 5863i/2-SIZE. Courtesy of the John Carter Brown Library at Brown University.

No Welcome for Newcomers in New Zealand

Abel Janszoon Tasman

When the native Maori inhabitants opposed Abel Tasman's (1603–59) landing on the island he named New Zealand, he sailed away, becoming an exception to the bloody rule of European exploration.

In 1603, the year Tasman was born in the Dutch province of Groningen, the Dutch East Indies Company (known by its Dutch initials, VOC) established its first fortified trading factory on the island of Java, inaugurating the company's history of conquest, colonization, and commercial success in the Far East. Three decades later, when Tasman sailed to the Dutch East Indies for the first time, the major port in the region was Batavia, later Jakarta, which the VOC built on the Java coast in 1619. Tasman shipped as a common sailor to Batavia and then the island of Ambon, site of another VOC post. He rose to command of a ship named Mocha, serving two years in the lucrative trade in the Moluccas, or Spice Islands. Once, when the Mocha became separated from its fleet, Tasman sent crewmembers ashore for water, but the native people attacked and killed two of them. The VOC reprimanded Tasman for incaution and sent him back to Amsterdam as third mate. Given a second chance, Tasman sailed back to Batavia as captain of a ship named Engel (Angel), accompanied by his wife.

Tasman embarked next on his first voyage of exploration, which was the last voyage led by Matthijs Quast, who had previously reached Japan and China. The VOC ordered them to search for "certain rich auriferous and argentiferous islands," so Quast and Tasman set out into the North Pacific in two ships, spending months rarely sighting land, getting as far north as the Japanese island of Hokkaido (without seeing it) and eastward almost to the International Date Line. By the time they turned back and reached the VOC fort on the island of Taiwan, almost half of the men were dead of scurvy.

Tasman's best-known assignment was a voyage of discovery in search of the southern continent, Terra Australis, in 1642. In its instructions to Tasman prior to his departure, the VOC reminded him to expect conflict and told him what to do if it occurred. "Use great care . . . because it is apparent the Southlands are peopled with very rough wild people . . . [who] usually think that the people who appear so exceedingly strange and unexpected come only to take their lands. . . . You will prudently prevent all manner of insolence and all arbitrary action on the part of our men against the nations discovered, and take due care that no injury be done them in their houses, gardens, vessels or property, their wives, etc." Tasman chose a degree of latitude to plot his course that proved to be too far south to find Australia, but he did sight the island that was named Tasmania in 1856.

Tasman's ships first sailed west from Batavia, riding the prevailing winds almost all the way across the Indian Ocean, in order to take on provisions in bountiful Mauritius for his explorations into unknown waters. They spent several weeks there to accomplish that, and to make repairs to the ships, which were only a few years old but were already showing signs of decay in the extreme environment where they were deployed.

After leaving Mauritius, they sailed back to the east along 42 degrees south latitude, which put them on a course to miss Australia but to come across the future Tasmania, which they found to be uninhabited and uninviting. The waters of the Roaring Forties of latitude are notorious for their foul weather, which hit the Dutch ships in the form of "hollow Waves out of the S.W.," which made Tasman conclude incorrectly, "therefore from that Quarter no Land is to be expected." It would be two centuries before explorers proved the existence of Antarctica.

Continuing to the east, Tasman and his men were the first Europeans to see New Zealand, which he named for the Dutch coastal province of Zeeland. There, the Dutchmen and the native Maori people encountered one another. As narrated in the following selection, which comes from an English edition of Tasman's journal published in 1711, the meeting did not go well. No other Europeans reached New Zealand until James Cook nearly a century and a half later.

Tasman undertook a second attempt to find Australia in 1644, charting a good portion of its north coast, which he named New Holland. Tasman spent his last years as an envoy carrying company correspondence to Sumatra, Siam, and the Philippines, then retired in Batavia, one of the wealthiest men in the Dutch East Indies.

Abel Tasman has been taken to task for his lack of aggression. Captain Cook's hagiographic biographer J. C. Beaglehole concluded that he "was not a genius . . . not a great leader; he has left no legend." Other historians of the vaunted European Age of Discovery have said that he "stumbled" and "groped" along on his famous trek to Tasmania and New Zealand, and that he "lacked the determined curiosity of Cook." Still, those of a peace-loving bent may admire him for abstaining from the slaughter that his ships were capable of inflicting and instead simply sailing away.

"A Relation of a Voyage made towards the South *Terra Incognita*; extracted from the Journal of Captain *Abel Jansen Tasman*, by which not only a new Passage by Sea to the Southward of *Nova Hollandia*, *Vandemens Land*, etc., is discovered, and a vast space of Land and Sea incompassed and sailed round, but many considerable and instructive Observations concerning the Variation of the Magnetical Needle in Parts of the World almost Antipodes to us; and several other curious Remarks, concerning those Places and Peoples, are set forth. Not long since published in the *Low Dutch* by *Dirk Rembrantse*, and now in *English* from Dr. *Hook's* Collections."

In the Year 1642, Aug. 14. He set Sail with two Ships from *Batavia*, to wit, the Yacht *Heemskirk*, and the Fly-boat *Seahaen*;[1] and the 5th of September came to an Anchor at the Island of *Mauritius* 20 d. South Latitude, and 83 d. 48 m. Longit. . . .

December 13. Latitude S. 42 d. 10 m. Longitude 188 d. 28 m. N.E. var. 7 d. 30 m. they had Land in sight, which was very high and hilly, and which in the Charts is now called *New Zealand*; they went N. Eastwards along the Land as the Chart shewed it, till they anchored in a Bay, in S. Latitude 40 d. 50 m. Longitude 191 d. 41 m. N.E. variation 9 d. and that on the 18th of December. These Inhabitants were rough of voice, thick and gross made, they came not within a Stones cast on Board of us, and blew several times on an Instrument, which made a noise like a *Moorish* trumpet; in answer thereto we blew ours. Their Colour was between Brown and Yellow; they had black Hair, bound fast and tight upon the Crown of their Head, in the same manner as the *Japanese* have theirs behind their Head, and near as long and thick of Hair, upon which flood a great thick white Feather; their Clothes were of Mats, others of Cotton, but their Upper-parts were naked.

December 19. These Antipodes began to be somewhat bolder, and more free; so that they endeavored to begin a Truck or Merchandize with the Yacht, and began to come on Board; the Commander seeing this began to fear, lest they might be fallen upon, and sent his Boat or Prow with seven men to advertise them, that they should not trust these People too much; they went off from the Ship, and not having any Arms with them, were set upon by these Inhabitants, and three or four were killed, and the rest saved themselves by swimming: This they endeavored to revenge, but the Water going high, they were hindred; this Bay was by them, for this reason, named *Murderers Bay*, as it is marked in the Charts. From this Bay they went on E. and found the Land all round them; It seems a very good Land, fruitful, and well situated, but by reason of the bad Weather, and West Wind, they had a great deal of Trouble to get out. The 24th of December, because the Wind would not well suffer to go to the Northward, they not knowing if they should find any Passage to the North, and the Flood coming out of the S.E. they concluded to go back again into the Bay, and there seek a Passage; but the 26th the Wind better serving, they went away Northerly somewhat to the West. January 4, 1643, in S. Latitude 34 d. 35 m. Longit. 191 d. 9 m. N.E. variation 8 d. 40 m. they came to the N.W. Cape of this Land, and had hollow Waves out of the N.E. and therefore doubted not there must be a great sea in the N.E. whereupon they were glad, as having gotten a Passage. Here lay an Island which they named *Three Kings Island*, to which they went to refresh themselves, and being come near, they saw upon the Hill thirty or thirty five Men, being of tall Stature (as well as

"Murderer's Bay," an engraving from François Valentyn's 1726
journal, shows the clash when the Maori and Dutch worlds collided, after which the Dutch explorer Abel Tasman sailed away,
rather than exacting bloody revenge. By obeying instructions
from the Dutch East Indies Company not to use his cannons
on Maori dwellings, he became a rare exception to the rule that
violence accompanied European imperial expansion, which used
the Ocean as its medium. Francois Valentyn, *De Moordenaars Baay*,
engraving in *Oud en Nieuw Oost-Indiën*, vol. 3, part 2 (Dordrecht:
Joannes van Braam, 1726), after p. 50. Reprinted in a rotogra-
vure newspaper section, 1944. Courtesy of the Roorda/Doyle
Collection.

might be discerned from far) with Sticks or Clubs, who called to them with
harsh or loud Voices, but they could not understand them; and those Men,
when they walked, made very wide Paces or Steps. In turning about this Island there appeared very few Men, and they saw little or no cultivated Land,
but only found a fresh River, where our People intended to get fresh Water,
but by some unlucky Accident were prevented; whereupon it was resolved to
go with an Eastern Course to the Longitude of 220 d. and then Northward to
South Lat. of 17 d. and from thence Westward to the *Cocos* or *Horns Islands*,
first discovered by *William Scouten*;[2] and then, if not sooner, to recruit [return
home]; for they had indeed been upon *Anthony van Diemans Land*, but had

met with nothing; and upon *New Zealand* they had not so much as once been a-shore.

Notes

1. The *Heemskerck* (literally, Hometown Church) was a small "war yacht," heavily armed and fast, about 106 feet long and 24 feet wide, with 120 tons of interior space and a crew of seventy-five. The *Zeehaen* (literally, Seahen) was a small *fluyt*, built for carrying cargo, about 100 feet long and 20 feet wide, with a carrying capacity of 200 tons, and a complement of thirty-five men on board. Both ships were built at the VOC shipyard at Rapenburg in 1638–39, with the powerful *Heemskerck* sent as flagship and the tubby *Zeehaen* sent along to bring home the treasure they hoped to find.

2. In an attempt to evade the VOC's monopoly on the East Indies trade route around Africa, Willem Schouten (1567–1625) navigated to Java around the tip of South America in 1618, becoming the first mariner to round Cape Horn, which Schouten named for his hometown of Hoorn, in South Holland. The "Cocos and Horn Islands" referenced here are probably the archipelago now called the Schouten Islands, off the north coast of New Guinea.

The Oceanic Captain Kirk

William Reynolds

Gene Roddenberry (1921–91) based Star Trek *in part on the instructions given to US Navy Captain Charles Wilkes (1798–1877), whose five-year mission was to seek out new civilizations. The Wilkes Expedition was officially termed the Expedition of Discovery, spanning the globe from 1839 to 1844, laying claim to the Samoan Islands and laying waste to villages in Fiji, among many other things. The numerous scientists who went along gathered the first collection of specimens for the Smithsonian Institution. The expedition's Mr. Spock was James Dwight Dana (1813–95), a geologist, volcanologist, and zoologist, who pioneered the study of the origin of the continents and the Ocean and led the expedition's team of scientists.*

One important objective of the Wilkes mission was to prove the existence of Antarctica. Among the first people known to have seen Antarctica were the crew of a sloop named Hero, *less than 50 feet long, skippered by twenty-one-year-old Nathaniel Palmer (1799–1877) on an 1820 voyage in search of seals and sea lions to kill. The landmass they saw, now known as the Antarctic Peninsula, bears the name Palmer Land on old maps and globes. Twenty years later,* USS Peacock, *one of the smallest vessels of Wilkes's fleet, also sailed to Antarctica, confirming that the rumored landmass was indeed a continent.*

Lieutenant William Reynolds (1815–79), who was an officer aboard Peacock, *recounted his thrilling flirtation with disaster in the Antarctic Ocean, to his mother, whose reactions to reading it can only be imagined.*

U.S. Ship *Peacock*
Sydney, March 4th 1840

My dear Mother,
    . . . We left Sydney the day after Christmas and after rather a rough time for more than two weeks, we reached the barrier of Ice, having made *Maquarie Island* on our way.[1] *Ice bergs* we met with in Lat. 61° S and passed them daily until we arrived at the *field of Ice*, which prevented our farther progress South and sent us along its edge to the Westward. We separated from the Squadron while in the clear sea, but fell in with the

Vincennes and Brigs soon after we made the *barrier.*[2] We did not continue together, however, but parted, each to do our best, alone.

When we crossed the 60th degree of Latitude, we seemed to leave the stormy region behind us entirely. The weather was fair and mild and the Sea smooth; fog and sleet disappeared, and we had sunshine instead, which was gladly welcomed . . . confident that we should have the fame and the honor of finding *Land* where none had ever sought for it before; full of joy that we should accomplish this and so gain a name for us and for our country.

On, on we sailed for days with a fair breeze over almost a summer Sea and meeting with no signs of a *barrier* to cloud our fair expectations. At 12 o'clock on the 16th January, there *was not a particle of Ice to be seen from the mast head and we were nearly as far South as the Ship had gone last year:* the weather was quite clear and the excitement on board was intense. We were confident that we should eclipse all former navigators and leave but little for those who would come after us. Antarctic Stock was high! We were so elated at the prospect of such easy success that we could not restrain our feelings and we became quite extravagant, and almost wild.

We had no night—'twas broad daylight through the whole twenty four hours. We used no candles. The Sun *set in the East* about 10 ½ P.M. and rose again, close by where he disappeared, before 2 A.M. We shot birds at all hours and the *men read Pickwick* in the middle watch; the Doctor brought *his wife's bible* on deck every night at 12 o'clock and *read a chapter.*
. . .

A few days after turning to the Westward, we came to an opening in the Ice, which we entered though we scarcely thought it extended far to the Southward: we sailed along 30 miles ere we came to the head of it and were then enclosed on all sides, save the one small passage to the North, by immense fields of Ice. The long swell of the Ocean was shut off altogether, the water was smooth and motionless as an Inland Lake and lay like a vast mirror in its frosted frame. It was as a Bay marking far into the Land, but the boundaries *were not the green of Earth.* As we approached the end of the Bay, we fell in with innumerable pieces of floating Ice, broken off from the mass and drifting out into the Sea. Though the temperature was 21°, I spent more than one hour at the mast head for the sight from thence was grand, wild, strange beyond description: far as the eye could see, the Icy plains extended until they met the sky; the slightness of their elevation above the water, relieved in many places by towering Ice bergs of every form and hue and by immense Islands that arose like mountains from amidst the Desert of Ice; the whiteness of all this as dazzling and intense; unbroken, save by the glistening sheet of water where the Ship floated, idle, quiet and at rest.

I was alone on my airy perch; the hum of voices from the deck did not reach my ear for the tones of all were subdued and there was naught to disturb the solemn and almost awful stillness that hung over the frozen plains: the Ship ceased her groaning and the very second birds had gone from us; all that there was of life in the picture was beneath my feet, and *that* I heeded not. I thought there was no one but God near me and as I looked upon the mighty scene around which was neither Earth nor Sea, I was more impressed with the idea of His creative power and of the insignificance of man, than by any prospect that ever Earth afforded, or Sea assumed. *My feelings were new* and I enjoyed the hour far more than I can tell.

Once we thought we saw Land and as it happened I had been the first to discern the appearance, from the mast head: we neared it, and its high and broken sides and summit confirmed our conjectures. We were sure it was a portion of the Southern Continent and were elated beyond measure. We gave names to Points and Peaks and I stipulated for two, which were to be *Lancaster* and *Cornwall*, besides a *Cape Reynolds*.[3] Alas! We could not land upon it but it seemed to be an Island 1000 feet high or more. So it was frequently, though we were more than once deceived. Many circumstances prevented a close approach and the snowy mantle deceived us and kept us long in doubt and suspence.

On Thursday evening January 24th we were in another Bay and were strongly impressed with the belief that we were near Land and that some ridges that we saw were not all Ice, but Earth beneath. Two boats were sent away from the Ship for different purposes and the Lead line was put over the side. It was watched going down by eager eyes and when it brought up suddenly, there was almost a scream of delight: we had found the bottom at 350 fathoms—*mud* and *pebbles* came up on the lead and line and *then* we got a first sight of the Southern Land. Great was the joy and excitement throughout the Ship, for this was a certain indication that our belief was correct *this time*. We had "terra firma" in our grasp, as we thought, and the prize would be our own, poor, short sighted fools that we were! The boats were returning about this time and the crew were sent into the rigging to give three cheers for our luck; they did this with such a hearty good will that the old Ice rang out with sound.

All this bustle about the decks; below, some were playing shuffle board; on the gun deck, we were *rolling nine pins* (the Ship was so perfectly at rest) and on the Spar deck, the men were running away cheerily with the lead line to the music of the fiddle, occasionally bursting into the songs and hurrahs common among them when at any exciting work. When this was finished, all hands were called *to splice the main brace* and were a merry Ship.[4] Little did any one think of the change that a few short hours would bring about! I shall never give way to high wrought hopes again! When I have done so, disappointment was sure to come with a mountain's weight!

One of the Boats brought on board a mammoth penguin. A beautiful and kingly bird he was, but it was a bad day for him that the *Peacock* came to his haunts; he was cruelly put to death that his skin might be preserved for the satisfaction of those who are content to see the curious things of the world second hand.

The Sun set at 10 with all the splendor of a warmer clime, leaving a ruddy glow in the Horizon which vanished not, but chamelion like changed its hues from bright to brighter. 'Twas my middle watch and when I came on deck at 12, there was a deep peace all around; but a breath of air was stirring and the Ship was quiet and motionless as she would have been in *Speedwell dam*.[5] The Moon was bright in the Heavens, but she threw no light abroad: this eternal day puts her to shame and blots out the Stars altogether. The East was illuminated with those soft and blended tints that form the glory of an Italian sky at Eve and the reflection of these colours upon the Ice produced an effect, splendid, dazzling, grand beyond conception; the eye quailed at the sight and the imagination was utterly confounded. I felt that I was looking upon the painting of God! To heighten the scene, in the North and West the clouds were black and hung in gloomy contrast over the stainless field of Ice beneath them. Tell me no more of Earth[;] I have seen its fairest portions, but never have I looked upon so much vast, sublime and wondrous beauty as this rising and setting of the Sun presented in the midst of the Icy Sea.

The Captain came on deck in the greatest glee—35 large pebbles had been taken from the maw of the Penguin, another symptom that there was *Land* about.[6] Poor man! he was nearly beside himself with joy.

At 4 o'clock I turned in, dreading no evil and confident that we would succeed in finding the desired Land ere we were many days older—true! even in a few hours we came near to finding it, *but at the bottom of the Sea!*

At 8 o'clock, I found the Ship entered among the pieces of drift Ice; the Captain was trying to get near the barrier to determine whether the appearances of Land were real or false. At 8.40 it was evident we could go no farther with safety and that we had best get back into the clear water as speedily as possible. We were entirely surrounded by loose Ice; some pieces were much larger than the Ship and they were packed so closely together that we had no room to proceed or to manoeuvre in. Here and there small clear patches occurred, but these filled up and changed continually. In endeavouring to tack, the Ship got Sternboard and went Stern on to a huge lump of ice, splitting the rudder head and carrying away the wheel ropes. This shock sent her ahead, against all her sails, and it

HARPER'S WEEKLY.
JOURNAL OF CIVILIZATION.

Vol. XXXIV.—No. 1748.
Copyright, 1890, by Harper & Brothers.
All Rights Reserved.

NEW YORK, SATURDAY, JUNE 21, 1890.

TEN CENTS A COPY.
INCLUDING SUPPLEMENT.

AN OCEAN STEAMER AMONG ICEBERGS IN THE NORTH ATLANTIC.—Drawn by T. de Thulstrup.—[See Page 484.]

Many ships, most obscure, came to grief after collisions with icy floating mountains. The most famous example is the *Titanic*, which sank after sideswiping an iceberg on April 15, 1912. Sadly, if the ship had not steered to avoid the iceberg, but had
struck head-on, it would have stayed afloat; instead, the ice tore away iron plates
along the ship's hull as it steamed past, sending 1,514 of the liner's passengers and
crew to the bottom of the Atlantic Ocean. The cover of *Harper's Weekly* on June 21,
1890, featured an iceberg that could sink a ship, with a vessel in the background taking evasive action. Thure de Thulstrup, *An Ocean Steamer among Icebergs in the North
Atlantic*," engraving. Courtesy of the Roorda/Doyle Collection.

brought all hands on deck; but in another moment she gathered sternway once more and this time coming in contact with the same mass, the rudder was shattered and the head of it carried away entirely.

This was a terrible disaster alone: the Ship, with all her spars standing, her hull entire, her crew safe, was helpless as an infant—her *guiding power* was gone—but this was *merely* the *commencement* of our troubles. Our situation was evident at a glance; we must get clear of the Ice at once, *if we could?* repair the rudder, *if we could?* and get back to Sydney, *if we could?* All, or either of which, was problematical in the highest degree. We failed in the first attempt, *to get out!* Our own efforts could not succeed and we were most reluctantly obliged to run her farther into the Ice to reach a clear place that we noticed near a large Island of Ice.

We were obliged to steer the Ship by the Sails and of course her movements were awkward and slow: we could not avoid the Ice in our way and thumped heavily many times, carrying away part of the Fore foot and doing other damage. This was becoming too serious, the Ship could *not bear such shocks long.* It was really terrible to see her bearing down upon these masses and then feel her bring up, arrested at once by the mighty obstacles in her way; her whole frame quivered and shook and the poor craft groaned in her distress. *How* we watched her as she freed herself and more than once we thought spars and all would come down about our heads: *the danger was thickening fast.*

We now lowered the Boats and carried out Ice Anchors to the largest pieces, hoping to ride by them until we could hoist in the rudder: the sails were furled, but, vain hopes, the anchors would not hold; the wind freshened a little and, notwithstanding the exertions of the men to keep the Iron flues in their bed, we broke adrift and ere we could raise a hand to save ourselves, the Ship *went on to the Ice Island with a tremendous crash.* This Island was many miles in extent: from the mast heads, I could see over its flat top a long, long distance, but could not discern its termination. It rose from the Water, bluff as the sides of a house, the up[p]er edge projecting like the eaves and when we went under it, it towered above the mast head. It was the weakest part of the Ship's frame that came in contact with the mass, and the shock and crash and splintering of the riven spars and upper works was any thing but agreeable.

For *an instant, I thought that* the whole stern frame *must* be stove in and that a few moments would send us to the bottom. I thought any struggle for life would be in vain: to reach a piece of Ice would only be to linger in agony and suffer a more horrible death, and I settled in my mind with startling quickness *that it would be best to go down with the Ship.* . . .

The action was prompt, there was no time to lose, and sail was made with as much celerity and steadiness as if we were leaving a Harbour. The Ship moved, her head paid off from the danger, slowly but surely she reached ahead and *we were clear of the Island,* where to have struck again would have ensured our destruction. *Scarcely* had we got from under the pile, when *down came the overhanging ledge of snow,* flinging the foam it raised in the Sea upon our decks. *Mercy! a moment longer and it had crushed us.* I cannot tell you *how* I looked upon that Island as we were leaving it, by inches; there were the marks of the Ship's form and paint, and there, at its foot, were the tumbled heaps of snow that had so nearly overwhelmed us.

I had been almost immediately relieved from the apprehension of the Ship's sinking. The destruction had been great, but it was *only* the *upper* part of the Ship's frame, that was carried away, and *she was saved!* I shall never forget the look of the old craft as she lay beneath that ridge of Ice, trembling from the blow, and Ice, Ice piled up around her, so that we could see nothing else from the deck. The dark figures of the men and boats were the only relief to the dreary whiteness.

Now that we were freed from this peril, it was determined to struggle again for the clear Sea: 'twas about 11 A.M. We thumped, thumped until 3 in the afternoon, making but little progress and drifting to leeward all the while, with the Ice and the distance between us and the open Sea increased every moment from the quantity of floating pieces brought down by the wind. The men were kept incessantly at work, but all our efforts to get into places where the Ice was thinnest were of no avail; we were so jammed and the Ship so unmanageable that we missed every chance and became more and more involved. An hundred times we thought we should *surely succeed,* but the Ice crowded upon us the more and the Ship continued to strike as if she would knock herself to pieces. . . .

At 3 the wind died away and it came up *thick* and *blinding with snow.* We made fast again with Ice anchors and hoisted the rudder in. All of us were relieved to see *it* inboard, for oh! *how much depended on its being repaired!* The Carpenters went immediately to work upon it. Soon after, the breeze sprang up again, the anchors would not hold, and we made sail once more to try and force her out. It was the same thing over, with the same ill success; we became more and more remote shut in and chances for *getting out* seemed more remote than ever. To dwell at all upon our situation, while in a measure free from instant risk, afforded but little consolation: the Ship was so helpless without her rudder and it seemed as if we were striving against fate and would *never get clear:* allowing that we did escape the Ice, until we could get command of the Ship once more we could not choose our course; and after that *would* be accomplished, in the imperfect manner that was alone practicable, we had a long tract of stormy Sea to pass over ere we could reach our port. . . . *You good people* in your *quiet Home* can know but little of men's feelings in situations such as this and sure I am that I can tell you mine but very faintly.

We toiled, toiled on: *"never say die"* was the word. Even the Boys worked with all the ardour of Hercules, if not with his strength. Officers and all, there was no one idle, no one thought of rest. We used the Boats to plant the anchors for warping by and when we could use them no longer, the men went upon the Ice and crossing from piece to piece by planks laid over the chasms, transported the anchors to different positions; we had spars over the bows also, pushing with might and main. In this way, by 6 o'clock our exertion had brought us to within 100 yards of the open Sea, but we were wedged immoveable: we could neither advance nor recede and we had the cruel mortification of seeing the place of *comparative safety* so close at hand, and yet be in as much and more peril than we had experienced through the day. We *could all have walked* to the edge of the Ice, but the masses surrounding the Ship were so huge that all our thumping only did *her injury,* while it did not budge them an inch. *Now* was the time when the anxiety became *almost terrible!* Hitherto the weather, though thick, had not threatened. The wind had been moderate and there was but little swell; consequently the Ice had but little motion, not sufficient to throw *it* with any force against us: the *Ship* had been forced upon *it!* Now it seemed the tables were turned: Black clouds were gathering in the West; they were rolled and curled together in windy looking wreaths and they had all the appearance of *a coming storm.* I went up aloft and I fixed my gaze upon that portentous sky; I watched until I *saw its shadow coming over the water* and then I thought in sad earnest, *our time has come at last!*

Every one was watching those clouds: men and boys knew that in their shape hung our fate and *they were coming on like the angel of death.* Every rag was taken in and now, as we could do no more, we *silently awaited our chance.* The little breeze which had been blowing from another quarter died away entirely and that sort of breathless calm succeeded which is generally ominous of the wrath and tempest about to follow. *Now* you might see eye turn to eye, seeking for Hope or a glance of consolation; but even during this dreadful crisis, which thank God! was brief, there was no feeling *betrayed* that any one should be ashamed of. *With nothing to do,* you could read anxiety in many a face; you could tell of the trouble within by the quivering lips and the unsettled eye, but there was neither the voice of murmur or of fright; there was naught that could cast a stigma upon the manhood of the crew. Those who were timid kept their fears to themselves; if they needed the example of restraint and composure, it was set to them by the many who were made of firmer stuff.

Nearer and nearer came the funeral cloud; but suddenly its appearance changed! It spread wide and broke away! It lost its stormy aspect; the windy looking wreaths were dissolved in mist and thick snow! With *that change,* our sense of *present danger* passed away. We were relieved from the *fear of instant destruction!* It was evident to the eyes that had watched the progress of that cloud with so much anxiety that there need no longer be any apprehension of a storm. With the keenness of judgement common to seamen, every one knew *that the crisis had gone by* and that we might once more deem ourselves in comparative safety. The spell was broken! we breathed freely! the deep and joyful feelings of *that moment cannot be told!* . . .

Instead of a storm of wind from the cloud, we had a thick snow squall that almost blinded us and shut both Ice and Sea from our view. Presently a light breeze sprang up and sail was made once more. The Ice still came drifting down and, as before, when we had got the Ship nearly in a channel, it would close up and we had to try another and be again disappointed. In this way the time wore heavily and wearily away.

At 1 in the morning, we had been up 17 hours hard at work and as it was *labour in vain,* one watch's hammocks were piped down and the officers and crew, save the watch on deck, went below to sleep—if they could. I turned into my cot at once to make the best of a short *three* hours, for I had the morning watch to keep. . . . Those 3 hours in my cot were worse a thousand times than all the time on deck with real danger to look upon. I was glad when they were passed and got up very willingly to renew my watch. Just at this time, aided by a light breeze and a fortunate opening of the Ice, the Ship of her own accord slid into the clear water, free from the rough and cold embrace that had held her so long.

The weather was thick and chill and the wind light, but we managed to steer our disabled craft tolerably well, and without further accident reached the middle of the Bay we had entered with so much confidence and where our hopes had been raised so high. Towards 8 the mist cleared and all around us as far as we could see the Icy barrier extended, save one little corner left for us to creep out of.

My eyes were red and smarting from the loss of rest and I was fairly done over, half dead from anxiety and exertion. The Carpenters had worked all night upon the rudder and at 10 A.M. it was ready to be shipped. This was too important an operation not to be witnessed by everyone on board and so, foregoing the chance for sleep, we all assembled to see it completed. The precarious manoeuvre was accomplished with a seaman's ready skill and by 11 we were once more on our way, heading for the only passage that lead [sic] to the ocean. . . .

The evening was clear and mild, the sky rosy, the Ice no longer dangerous but reflecting a thousand tints, the Ship was manageable once more, and *all was different* from the same hour of the previous night. . . .

Notes

1. A long (almost 22 miles), narrow (about 3 miles) island halfway between New Zealand and Antarctica.
2. In addition to USS *Peacock*, a three-masted 650-ton sloop of war with twenty-two cannons, the Wilkes Expedition included the USS *Vincennes*, its flagship, also a sloop of war; the ship USS *Relief*; the brig *Porpoise*; and the schooners *Flying Fish* and *Sea Gull*.
3. Cape Lancaster, named for Reynolds's birthplace of Lancaster, Pennsylvania, and the Cornwall Peaks, named for the borough of Cornwall near Lancaster, are still on the map, as is Cape Reynolds.
4. "To splice the main brace" means to order a ration of alcohol as a reward.
5. Speedwell Forge Dam forms Speedwell Forge Lake, near Cornwall, Pennsylvania.
6. In naming the Hudson Mountains, Commander William Levereth Hudson left his name on the landscape of Antarctica as well.

A Half Mile Down

William Beebe

While exploration of the surface of the Ocean has been ongoing for thousands of years, the exploration of the deep sea is a relatively recent phenomenon. Early submarines were designed to be weapons, until Otis Barton (1899–1992) and William Beebe (1877–1962) pioneered one for scientific uses in the 1930s, enabling them to go deeper beneath the waves than anyone had done before, and to see there for the first time an astonishing and diverse environment, filled with fantastic creatures.

Will Beebe's first interest was ornithology. He became curator of birds at the Bronx Zoo in 1899, and wrote a four-volume treatise titled A Monograph of the Pheasants (1918–22). But then Beebe shifted his attention to the Ocean. He acquired a research vessel named the Arcturus, which he used to survey sea life, especially in the Galápagos Islands, and he began experimenting with using a diving helmet to observe creatures in their natural setting, rather than dragging them to the surface in nets, where they often arrived in a damaged state. He wrote about these experiences in Galápagos: World's End (1924), The Arcturus Adventure (1926), and Beneath Tropic Seas (1928). Beebe was a celebrity scientist during the Roaring Twenties, renowned for his globe trotting for the Bronx Zoo, for his popular books about foreign travels, and also for his love life. The news media covered his stormy divorce from his first wife, the author Blair Niles (who cowrote some of Beebe's works and went on to a successful career as a travel writer), and his high-society courtship of his second wife, the romance novelist Elswyth Thane, who was twenty-seven years old when she married the fifty-year-old Beebe aboard a wealthy friend's yacht in 1927.

In 1928, Beebe teamed with fellow New Yorker Otis Barton, a Harvard graduate who had devised a spherical diving compartment, to build what they called the bathysphere. In the early 1930s, Beebe and Barton made a series of record-breaking descents in the innovative submarine, reaching deeper than a half mile in 1934, which Beebe wrote about in his book Half Mile Down (1934). Barton starred in the 1938 Hollywood film version of the bathysphere dives, called Titans of the Deep. He later invented a submarine called the benthosphere, which he took to 4,500 feet by himself in 1949, breaking the record he set with Beebe in 1934.

Beebe's abridged accounts of a trial dive in the bathysphere in September 1932, which reached 2,200 feet, and his record-breaking descent to 3,028 feet in August 1934, in the waters near Bermuda, follow here.

The bathysphere was on deck at 12:50 P.M. which gave us only about a half hour to prepare for our descent in order to emerge before dark. Somehow or other this was done, and in spite of everyone seeming to be in everyone else's way we made a final survey of all instruments and apparatus and at 1:15 P.M. crawled painfully over the sharp-threaded bolts and curled up on opposite sides of the sphere. I arranged my instruments, flashes, and notebooks around me, tucking them away safely as a hen does her setting of disturbed eggs.

At last the door was lifted and clanged into place, and then came the terrific hammering home of the ten great nuts. The spectroscope and illuminometer were passed into the central four-inch hole, and with a last word, the wingbolt was quietly revolved home and the noise and air of the outside world shut off. Our oxygen began to send forth its life-giving stream, I called a Hello! through the halfmile of cable and we were off. . . . There was the never forgettable swash and flow of bubbles and foam over the glass, and then the splendid pale brilliance of the green upper layer of ocean. . . .

The signal came that all was ready, and I ordered our descent. The dimming of the light was more evident between the surface and fifty feet than anywhere else, for within this zone all the warm, red rays are absorbed and the remainder of the spectrum, with its dominance of green and blue, reflected a sense of chill through our eyes long before the thermometer had dropped a degree. For the first 200 feet we shifted and settled, and arranged our legs and instruments for the long period of incarceration. . . .

The cable was payed out so slowly and evenly that we had no sense of movement, either up or down. For example, at 275 feet it was with an effort that I mentioned such a common sight as an *aurelia* sun-jelly, until I realized that the record of one at this depth was a valuable and hitherto unknown fact. My hundreds of dives in a helmet had made familiar the sight of water outside the window, but there was nothing to make evident to eye or mind the quality of pressure. When at 1,000 feet a voice reminded me that there were twenty-three hundred tons of water pressing in on the bathysphere, and the window against which I had my face was withstanding six and one-half tons, it meant very little. I watched a delicate sea creature swimming slowly along and all sense of the terrific pressure was absent. So these things had to be intellectually admitted. The compensation was the perfect realization of where I was, which is far from being always the case when under temporarily unique conditions. . . .

At 500 feet we had an elaborate and careful rehearsal of light signals. These were of the greatest importance, for if anything should happen to our sole line of communication—the telephone wires—a single flickering of the light on deck would indicate at least that we were still alive, and a triple signal would cause us to be drawn up as rapidly as possible.

At 525 feet many siphonophores passed, and three, long, slender worms with elongated tentacles, others being just visible in the distance. At one time a maze of what looked like large ostracods came close to the glass but were probably pteropods. At 675 feet I saw my first school of *Argyropelecus* or silver hatchet-fish, which at once shows the imperfection of our trawling apparatus, as adults of this species have never been taken by us in these waters at a lesser depth than 1800 feet. At 700 feet we saw jellyfish of other than surface forms, and elongate fish were visible in the blackish blurred distance. Flying snails were seen jerking about in their characteristic way. A pair of dark-banded *Seriola*, or rudderfish, hung around for a minute or more. The sun went under a blanket of cloud at this moment and before it was announced through the telephone I knew it from the intensification of the blueness. Two more fish appeared at 800 feet and lights on their bodies were faintly visible for a moment. I now became aware of the presence of numerous invertebrates as my eyes became accustomed to the increasing gloom.

1,000 feet was reached at 2:37 P.M. with the light becoming ever more and more dim. Here we hung for a time until my eyes could get perfectly adapted to the blueblack gloom. Direct looking gave me sometimes less result than the oblique penumbra of vision—and I began to sense the passing of numberless little creatures. I watched pale gray beings only an inch or two in length come out of the darkness toward the window, puzzled over them for a moment and then knew them for *Cyclothones*, or roundmouth fishes, remembering them from two years ago. We took stock of the conditions in our little world. Barton found the door and oxygen valve in perfect shape, and the hose from the stuffing box showed not a drop of moisture. I flashed the light toward the windows and saw trickles of water coming from under the electric light screen. For a moment I had that peculiar feeling of momentary panic with which every honest explorer must admit familiarity, and then I saw that all the walls showed meandering trickles of moisture, and we knew that it was the normal condensation on the cold steel from the heat of our bodies. . . .

Our arrival at 1,426 feet was announced by loud whistles from the tugs floating far above our heads, celebrating our passing the lowest record of our dive in 1930. The first deep-sea eels appeared, slender, silvery creatures with long jaws and sharp teeth. A pair of them, swimming side by side, kept with us for 20 feet of depth, and siphonophores and a large ctenophore swept by close to my face. Our electric light now cast a strong beam showing as turquoise blue through the darkness. At 1,500 feet it revealed two large eels, which at once swam up out of the light. These showed no lights whatever on their bodies and were considerably more slender than those seen higher up. They were undoubtedly *Serrivomer*, or bronze sea eels. About this time word came down the wire that we were being broadcasted [nationally on NBC radio], but a moment later this was forgotten and not again remembered until we were reminded of its ending half an hour later. Sealed up as we were, the human mind utterly refused to conceive of anyone, except my assistant whose voice I constantly heard, being able to hear what I was saying. At 1,650 feet I recorded it as being as black as Hades. I was running out of reasonable similes. A school of brilliantly illuminated lanternfish with pale green lights swam past within three feet of my window, their lights being exceedingly bright.

A little after three o'clock, when we reached 1,700 feet, I hung there for a time and made as thorough a survey as possible. The most concentrated gazing showed no hint of blue left. All outside was black, black, black, and none of my instruments revealed the faintest glimmer to my eye. I had now attained one of the chief objects of this whole dive, namely, to get below the level of humanly visual light. I was beyond sunlight as far as the human eye could tell, and from here down, for two billion years there had been no day or night, no summer or winter, no passing of time until we came to record it. From here on, even if I went down six miles, to the bottom of Bartlett Deep [Cayman Trough], I would experience only differences in degree, not of kind. I could now prove without doubt whether continued observations from a window such as this would yield valuable scientific observations, or whether the attainment of these depths must be considered in the light of merely a stunt, breaking former records. The temperature outside was already ten degrees lower than that inside, and the pressure had increased to seven hundred and seventy pounds on each square inch. Two of the lanternfish with the pale green lights came close to the window and yard-long eels—several altogether—undulated past. Here I began to be inarticulate, for the amount of life evident from the dancing lights and its activity, the knowledge of the short time at my disposal, and the realization that most of the creatures at which I was looking were unnamed and had never been seen by any man were almost too much for any connected report or continued concentration.
. . .

At 1,750 feet six fish, each with a double line of lights down the side of the body, were in sight. They were most certainly *Melanostomiatid* dragonfish, but strain as I could, no evidence of barbel was visible. I again turned on the searchlight and they twisted and melted into the milky turquoise of the distant beam. The oxygen tank showed that we had now, at 3:11 P.M., breathed up half its contents. 1,800 and 1,900 feet were not blacker—that were impossible—but the complete dark seemed more tangible.

Not a ray of light illumined the inside of the bathysphere. Barton's voice seemed as unattached as that coming down the wire. Once when he unexpectedly threw on his pencil flash to examine the oxygen dial, I jumped as if the thin beam had been sound instead of light. At 1,825 feet coiled pteropods, almost certainly *Limacimiy* appeared by the dozen, clearly seen in our ray of light, and silver hatchet-fish, or *Argyropelecus*, of adult size were illumined by each other. They swam so closely together I could not judge of the amount of visibility which the lights of each individual fish would show. Their photophores appeared as pale blue and not purple as they appear in sunlight. A school of small lanternfish went past and their lights were not dimmed as they were higher up, but showed clearly even in the pale blue glare of the outer rim of the electric light path. A single large fish, which we estimated at four feet in length, went by at 1,850 feet, so rapidly that I got only a fleeting glimpse of many lights along a rather deep body. Once a school of large squids balanced near me, fulfilling my hope of two years ago. Their great eyes, each illumined with a circle of colored lights, stared in at me—those unbelievably intelligent yet reasonless eyes backed by no brain and set in a snail.

At 1,950 feet we got our first bad pitching. It was unexpected and I cut my lip and forehead against the window ledge and Barton struck his head against the door. This gave us the worst fright of the entire dive, and for a fraction of a minute, which seemed an exceedingly long time to us, it felt as if we had broken loose and were turning over. . . . When the darkness closed down on the path of the light again, I saw we were in the midst of a large number of shrimps and almost at once two large fish dashed into the midst of them, rolling them over and over, all these creatures and their actions silhouetted only in their own light. One at least of the fish had an isolated light, blue and pale reddish, which kept following it about, and I realized that this was a barbel light, whipping about as the fish turned. . . .

At 2,100 feet the bathysphere was rolling badly, considerable of the chemicals spilling off the racks and falling down on our heads. The remaining chemicals had to be constantly redistributed so that more surface could be exposed and their function of absorbing carbon dioxide and humidity could continue. . . .

Pteropods were close at hand and a host of unidentifiable organisms. I would focus on some one creature and just as its outlines began to be distinct on my retina, some brilliant, animated comet or constellation would rush across the small arc of my submarine heaven and every sense would be distracted, and my eyes would involuntarily shift to this new wonder. It is a marvel now to me that I was able to disentangle any definite facts on this first visit. I watched one gorgeous light as big as a ten-cent piece coming steadily toward me, until, without the slightest warning, it seemed to explode, so that I jerked my head backward away from the window. What happened was that the organism had struck against the outer surface of the glass and was stimulated to a hundred brilliant points instead of one. Instead of all these vanishing as does correspondingly excited phosphorescence at the surface, every light persisted strongly, as the creature writhed and twisted to the left, still glowing, and vanished without my being able to tell even its phylum. . . .

Nothing which I had seen at 1,400 feet in 1930, nor down to 1,700 feet on this occasion, prepared me in any way for this spectacular display of lights. . . .

My inarticulateness and over-enthusiastic utterances may well be excused on the grounds of sheer astonishment at the unexpected richness of display. Another thing too which was disconcerting as well as unexpected was the great activity of all the creatures except such as jellies and siphonophores. No wonder that but a meager haul results from our slow-drawn, silken nets when almost all the organisms which came within my range of vision showed ability to dart and twist and turn, their lights passing, crossing, and recrossing in bewildering mazes. While we hung in mid-ocean at our lowest level, of 2,200 feet, a fish poised just to the left of my window, its elongate outline distinct and its dark sides lighted from sources quite concealed from me. It was an effective example of indirect lighting, with the glare of the photophores turned inward. I saw it very clearly and knew it as something wholly different from any deep-sea fish which had yet been captured by man. It turned slowly head-on toward me, and every ray of illumination vanished, together with its outline and itself—it simply was not, yet I knew it had not swum away. . . .

Several minutes later, at 2,100 feet, I had the most exciting experience of the whole dive. Two fish went very slowly by, not more than six or eight feet away, each of which was at least six feet in length. They were of the general shape of large barracudas, but with shorter jaws which were kept wide open all the time I watched them. A single line of strong lights, pale bluish, was strung down the body. The usual second line was quite absent. The eyes were very large, even for the great length of the fish. The undershot jaw was armed with numerous fangs which were illumined either by mucus or indirect internal lights. Vertical fins well back were one of the characters which placed it among the sea-dragons, *Melanostomiatids*, and were clearly seen when the fish passed through the beam. There were two long tentacles, hanging down from the body, each tipped with a pair of separate, luminous bodies, the upper reddish, the lower one blue. These twitched and jerked along beneath the fish, one undoubtedly arising from the chin, and the other far back near the tail. I could see neither the stem of the tentacles nor any paired fins, although both were certainly present. This is the fish I subsequently named *Bathysphaera intacta*, the Untouchable Bathysphere Fish. . . .

I have seen and felt the heat of molten, blazing stone gushing out of the heart of our Earth; I have climbed three and a half miles up the Himalayas and floated in a plane still higher in the air, but nowhere have I felt so completely isolated as in this bathysphere, in the blackness of ocean's depths. I realized the unchanging age of my surroundings; we seemed like unborn embryos with unnumbered geological epochs to come before we should emerge to play our little parts in the unimportant shifts and changes of a few moments in human history. Man's recent period of strutting upon the surface of the earth would have to be multiplied half a million times to equal the duration of existence of this old ocean. . . .

We reached the surface and blazing sunlight, and crawled out, cramped and rather battered, but very happy, at 4:08 P.M. . . .

At 2,450 [feet, two years later,] a very large, dim, but not indistinct outline came into view for a fraction of a second, and at 2,500 a delicately illuminated ctenophore jelly throbbed past. Without warning, the large fish returned and this time I saw its complete, shadow-like contour as it passed through the farthest end of the beam. Twenty feet is the least possible estimate I can give to its full length, and it was deep in proportion. The whole fish was monochrome, and I could not see even an eye or a fin. For the majority of the "size-conscious" human race this marine monster would, I suppose, be the supreme sight of the expedition. In shape it was a deep oval, it swam without evident effort, and it did not return. That is all I can contribute, and while its unusual size so excited me that for several hundred feet I kept keenly on the lookout for hints of the same or other large fish, I soon forgot it in the (very literal) light of smaller, but more distinct and interesting organisms. What this great creature was I cannot say. A first, and most reasonable guess would be a small whale or blackfish. We know that whales have a special chemical adjustment of the blood which makes it possible for them to dive a mile or more, and come up without getting the "bends." So this paltry depth of 2,450 feet would be nothing for any similarly equipped cetacean. Or, less likely, it may have been a whale shark, which is known to reach a length of forty feet. Whatever it was, it appeared and vanished so unexpectedly and showed so dimly that it was quite unidentifiable except as a large, living creature. The next fish of unusual size was seen at 2,900 feet. It was less than three feet long, rather slender, with many small luminous spots on the body, and a relatively large, pale green, crescent-shaped light under the eye. Near it were five lanternfish, unlike all others I had seen. They swam so slowly that I made certain before they disappeared that they were of the genus *Lampadena*. At 11:12 A.M. we came to rest gently at 3,000 feet, and I knew that this was my ultimate floor; the cable on the winch was very near its end. A few days ago the water had appeared blacker at 2,500 feet than could be imagined, yet now to this same imagination it seemed to show as blacker than BLACK. It seemed as if all future nights in the upper world must be considered only relative degrees of twilight. I could never again use the word black with any conviction.

I looked out and watched an occasional passing light and for the first time I realized how completely lacking was the so-called phosphorescence with which we are familiar at the surface. There, whenever an ordinary fish passes, it becomes luminous by reflection from the lights of the myriads of the minute animals and plants floating in the water. Here each light is an individual thing, often under direct control of the owner. A gigantic fish could tear past the window, and if unillumined might never be seen.

My eyes became so dark adapted at these depths that there was no possibility of error; the jet blackness of the water was broken only by sparks and flashes and steadily glowing lamps of appreciable diameter, varied in color and of infinite variety as regards size and juxtaposition. But they were never dimmed or seen beyond or through any lesser mist or milky-way of organisms. The occasional, evanescent, defense clouds of shrimps hence stand out all the more strongly as unusual phenomena, and are quite apart from the present theme. If the surface light is emitted chiefly by *Noctiluca* and single-celled plants, the explanation of its abyssal absence is easy, for all surface forms of these groups have died out hundreds of feet overhead.

A second thing which occurred to me as I sat coiled in the bathysphere, more than half a mile down, was the failure of our powerful beam of light to attract organisms of any kind. Some fled at its appearance, others seemed wholly unconcerned, but not a single copepod or worm or fish gathered along its length or collected against the starboard window from which it poured.
. . .

Even in this extremity of blackness I sensed the purity of the water, its freedom from sediment and roiling; six miles from shore and a full mile from the bottom insured this. So there was no diffusion of light, no trails, no refraction. When sparks or larger lights moved they were as distinct as when they were motionless. But reflection was noticeable, as upon the eye or skin from a subocular or a lateral photophore, or upon my face when a shrimp exploded close in front.

Now and then I felt a slight vibration and an apparent slacking off of the cable. Word came that a cross swell had arisen, and when the full weight of bathysphere and cable came upon the winch, Captain Sylvester let out a few inches to ease the strain. There were only about a dozen turns of cable left upon the reel, and a full half of the drum showed its naked, wooden core. We were swinging at 3,028 feet, and, Would we come up? We would.

Walking on the Seafloor

Sylvia Earle

Following in the footsteps, or bubbles, of William Beebe came Sylvia Earle, who employed a new apparatus to breathe surface air while walking on the bottom of the Ocean. Her narrative of doing so forms part of her influential book, Sea Change: A Message of the Oceans, *from 1996. She gave this interview to the American Public Media program* On Being, *hosted by Krista Tippett, on June 7, 2012.*

MS. KRISTA TIPPETT, HOST: She's known affectionately by her fellow scientists as "Her Deepness." The oceanographer Sylvia Earle earned this nickname in 1979. That year, she became the first—and still the only—person to walk solo on the bottom of the world—on the ocean floor—under a quarter mile of water—600 pounds of pressure per square inch. She's watched humanity's enduring fascination with "outer space"; while she has delighted in "inner space"—the alien and increasingly endangered worlds beneath earth's waters. These frontiers, as Sylvia Earle points out, are our very life-support system. She takes us inside the knowledge she's gathered there in her 76 years. I'm Krista Tippett. This is *On Being*—from APM, American Public Media.

Sylvia Earle is a marine biologist and botanist, a National Geographic Explorer-in-Residence, and former Chief Scientist of the National Oceanic and Atmospheric Administration. In the course of her career, she has led more than 100 expeditions and logged thousands of hours underwater. In 1970, she led an historic team of all-female "aquanauts," as they were called, living for two weeks in an enclosed habitat on the ocean floor. When I interviewed her this year, she'd just returned from a dive in Panama. . . . I was very struck to read that a scuba, which was then called the Aqua-Lung, had just been invented, I guess, when you were beginning your graduate studies.

DR. EARLE: Yeah, I was lucky to be among the first to have a chance to try scuba in the United States. There were a couple of units that my major professor, Harold Humm, had secured. They really looked like the most appropriate for U.S. Navy divers with a big mouthpiece and just very basic tank regulator and a weight belt. I had two words of instruction: breathe naturally, over the side (laughter).

MS. TIPPETT: But what did that make possible? It sounds like that really opened a whole new world.

DR. EARLE: Oh, it did for me. It has for millions of people now. Now we have been able to see first of all that the ocean is alive. It's not just water, rocks, water, sand, whatever. It's a living system with every spoonful that you look at. We think of life in the sea in terms of fish and whales and coral reefs and the like, but most of the action is very small, microscopic and submicroscopic.

MS. TIPPETT: And that really was kind of new knowledge, I mean, in your lifetime.

DR. EARLE: I feel like a witness to—I am, to the greatest era of change on the planet as a whole. Anybody who's been around even for ten years is a part of this, but the longer you've been around, the more you've seen. The last half century in particular has been a time of revolutionary change. We didn't know the existence of those great mountain chains, hydrothermal vents, the existence of life in the deepest sea seven miles down. Nobody had been there. Not until 1960 was it possible for two men to make a descent to the deepest part of the sea.

MS. TIPPETT: You did a very remarkable thing also, one of those milestones, in 1979. This is, I think, at the time that people started to dub you "Her Deepness" (laughter). What a wonderful nickname to have. It was called the "JIM dive," and that's after the suit, I guess, that made that possible. Is that correct? JIM, J-i-m.

DR. EARLE: You know, Jim is the name of the first person willing to put that one-person diving system on going back to the late 1920s. Jim Jarrett, working with the designer, Joseph Peress, who came up with a way to build a diving suit made of metal. Most diving suits prior to that time were soft suits, so you felt the pressure. But the idea here was to develop something that a person could be inside a system at one atmosphere, no change in pressure from the surface, so no decompression was required.

The system had to be strong, of course, like a submarine, but also because it looked like an astronaut suit with arms and legs, Joseph Peress's breakthrough was to have joints that could move under pressure. But the idea that you had a personal submersible, a submarine that you could wear and walk around, protected from the pressure, was sort of revolutionary.

MS. TIPPETT: So you actually walked, were the first and still the only person to walk the ocean floor at 1,250 feet without a tether.

DR. EARLE: Back to the surface. There's a short line connecting me to my companion, that little submarine called the Star II. I rode down on the nose of that little submarine and then I walked off. But there's a line connecting the communication system from the submarine to me so we could talk and the submarine could talk to the surface, so we had this link back to those who were eager to know what's going on down there. There is a through-water communication system that worked for the sub, but not for me in the little suit.

MS. TIPPETT: So what was going on down there? I mean, what did you see when you looked around? When you looked up?

DR. EARLE: My first experiences going through the sunlit area and into what generally is known as the twilight zone, where sunlight fades and darkness begins to take over. It's like the deepest twilight or earliest dawn. You can see shapes, but not really distinct forms and this begins at about 500 feet. By the time you get down to 600 feet, 200 meters or so, it's really, really dark. It's like starlit circumstances. A thousand feet and below, it is truly dark, but still enough light penetrates clear ocean water in the middle of the day and that's when I made the dive, right about high noon in September. I could see shapes even at 400 meters, at 1,250 feet or so. That was exciting just to be able to realize that glow, that soft glow, was the sky above separated by 1,250 feet of water.

But the flash and sparkle and glow of bioluminescent creatures. There were corals that just grow in a single stretch, no branches, like giant bedsprings from the ocean floor. And when I touched them, little rings of blue fire pulsed all the way down from where I touched to the base of these spiraling creatures. They were taller than I; they're just beautiful creatures. They call them bamboo coral because they have joints that resemble the joints on a bamboo plant.

The submarine headlights were on, and I asked them to turn them off so that I could see the darkness and revel in the bioluminescence. It's that firefly kind of light, but also when the lights were on, I could see crabs that were attached to these large corals that grew on the sea floor. Some were pink, some were orange, some were yellow, some were black. They're just beautiful. It's a garden. It looks like a flower garden. And the red crabs were hanging onto these great sea-fan-like structures. They looked like shirts on the line. In that little bit of current, they were just, you know, slowly moving. There were eels that were wrapped around the base of the coral. It was just beautiful, really ethereal.

MS. TIPPETT: And you were down there for two hours?

DR. EARLE: On the bottom, two and a half hours, and I later spoke with an astronaut friend, Buzz Aldrin, and he said, "Well, that's about as long as we had to walk on the moon, two and a half hours." But what they did not have on the moon, Buzz Aldrin and Neil Armstrong and those who came later, they didn't have just this avalanche of life, this great diversity all around. Everywhere you looked, there were little fish with lights down the side. Of course, the corals themselves are alive. There were little burrows of creatures that were dwelling in the sediments on the sea floor. The water itself is like minestrone except all the little bits are alive.

MS. TIPPETT: And, you know, as I hear you talk about that and you made the connection with Buzz Aldrin, I was born in 1960, right? I still remember crowding around the television set with my family and everyone I knew was doing this, when men first walked on the moon. What you did was as remarkable, and it's not something that made such a sensation. I mean, I know you've talked and thought about this a lot, our fascination as human beings with outer space, when as you describe it, there's this inner space which is even less explored at this point.

DR. EARLE: And keeps us alive, oh, by the way (laughter).

MS. TIPPETT: And keeps us alive (laughter).

DR. EARLE: And it's changing. It's in trouble and that means we're in trouble, and we know so little about the ocean. Only about 5 percent has been seen, let alone explored. Anyone looking for new frontiers, think ocean because it's really important and it is there to be done. I mean, it's true on the land as well.

I had lunch once with Clare Boothe Luce, stateswoman, playwright, you know, just a remarkable human being. This question came up about why is it that people are so smitten with everything that goes up skyward and seem to neglect the ocean and this planet as a whole? This was at her home in Hawaii and there's some big puffy white clouds drifting by and blue sky. She said: "Well, my dear, it's actually simple. Heaven is in that direction and you know what's the other way." There is something to that. You know, people are uplifted and you think, oh, they're feeling really down. Our language reflects you're in over your head. I mean, that's not a good thing, right? Anyway, it's bizarre.

MS. TIPPETT: I mean, light is up and dark is down, but then what you discovered is—

DR. EARLE: There's heaven on earth. It just happens to be in the ocean. (laughter) . . .

MS. TIPPETT: Here're some lines you wrote, I believe, similar to how you described to me what it was like to walk on the bottom of the ocean. You said: "As I wandered to the area, the sub powering along behind, I concentrated on observing the corals, especially the bioluminescent spirals of bamboo. Why do they pulse with light? Why do they glow at night? How did they and their neighbors survive in the eternal night of the deep sea?" Are you still making discoveries, being surprised, you know, asking new questions like that?

DR. EARLE: Always, always. That's the joy of being a scientist and an explorer. You do what little children do: You ask questions like who, what, why, when, where, how? And you never stop and you never cease being surprised. You just never stop that sense of wonder. It is fantastic that life exists at all and I revel in just the joy of being out in some wild place or even in my own back yard. Just look at a leaf. It's an amazing thing what goes on in a leaf, and it happens all the time. And we can breathe because of it or because of photosynthesis that takes place there and in the sea. Knowing that, I think it's just impossible to be bored.

MS. TIPPETT: And you're still diving, aren't you?

DR. EARLE: Well, yeah. I breathe, so I can dive (laughter).

MS. TIPPETT: I mean, tell me where have you been recently? What would be an example of what you're doing now?

DR. EARLE: Well, a couple of weeks ago, I was on an expedition off the coast of Panama to a group of little islands called Coiba, beautiful little offshore islands, reefs, that have been unfortunately heavily exploited by fishing in recent times. I first went to Panama in 1965, and I go back to both coasts. Panama's one of those blessed nations that has two oceans, and the changes in just the sharks: You used to see sharks all over the place. Now you're lucky. I feel really so fortunate when I see a shark. It's a sign of health if you see a shark because the system has to be in pretty good shape to accommodate big predators. The site where the Tektite [underwater laboratory] operation took place in 1970, I was back last year. The reefs are simply gone. They're not there. The elkhorn and staghorn coral—it's like a meltdown. It's just rubble.

And the fish? The scientists who worked on the fish—I was mainly looking at the interactions between the seaweeds and the fish that tend to munch on the seaweeds, the parrotfish and the surgeonfish and the like. There were about a dozen variations on the theme of grouper, and I saw one variation on the theme of grouper when I went back and very few fish of any kind. It's just heartbreaking.

But the good news is, nature is resilient and places that have been protected in the last ten years show remarkable capacity to improve. That's why I'm so pleased to be able to have this interview, to tell people, look, it's not too late. The things that you can do, that all of us together can do to protect nature, to respect the trees, respect the fish, respect all forms of life and realize we're a part of the action.

Descent to the Deepest Deep

Jamie Condliffe

The deepest spot in the Ocean is the bottom of the Challenger Deep in the Mariana Trench, which is nearly 36,000 feet below sea level. The abyss was named for the HMS Challenger Expedition, 1873–76, which took the science of deep-sea exploration to new heights—or rather, depths. During its long, zig-zagging circumnavigation, the Challenger combined a team of scientists with a highly skilled crew to deploy the latest technology for sounding and otherwise measuring the Ocean.

More than a century later, on March 26, 2012, the famous film director and Ocean explorer James Cameron used revolutionary technology to go deeper than any human in history, reaching the bottom of the Challenger Deep. He accomplished the feat in a revolutionary submersible named Deepsea Challenger. *He launched the lime-green submarine from a ship named* Mermaid Sapphire, *and piloted it alone to a depth of more than 6.8 miles. The uniquely skilled Cameron then made a film about the experience called* James Cameron's Deepsea Challenge 3-D, *a synopsis of which appears on the Gizmodo website, included here. After being miles beneath the seas, the* Deepsea Challenger *caught fire in July 2015 on Interstate Highway 95, en route to its next adventure on the bed of a truck.*

Over the weekend, James Cameron successfully made it to the the bottom of the Mariana Trench—the deepest point on Earth. Bad. Ass.

But also: lucky, brave, well-prepared, and maybe a little bit daft: Any number of factors could have turned the the veteran explorer-slash-director's epic adventure into his last act.

The Mariana Trench is located in the western Pacific Ocean, to the east of the Mariana Islands. It's over 1,580 miles long, 43 miles wide on average, and at its deepest point—heroically known as Challenger Deep—it's an amazing 6.78 miles to the bottom. Almost 36,000 feet. Reaching those depths is incredibly dangerous, and James Cameron himself is alleged to have admitted that the mission offered "a lot of ways to die." So what could have gone wrong?

Implosion

The obvious, quickest, and most catastrophic route to failure. A weak spot in materials, a design flaw in the vehicle. Then, as the pressure increased—pop—the dive craft would have buckled. That doesn't mean drowning; it means James Cameron would have been squashed to death, with immense pressures of up to 15,750 psi turning his body into a James Cameron slurry.

Freezing

If the *Deepsea Challenger* had somehow gotten stuck at the bottom of the trench, Cameron would have been relying on his life support systems to keep him alive. In terms of resources, he had 60 hours of oxygen—but far less in the way of power for heating. With the water of the Mariana Trench being a fairly consistent 0°C, he would have died of hypothermia long before he ran out of air.

Fire

The sub was packed full of technology and gadgetry—all requiring electricity. There was also a vast amount of pure O_2 circulating around inside *Deepsea Challenger*. The tiniest of electrical faults or sparks, and that O_2 would have had a fire burning hard and fast. There was a small fire extinguisher on board—but it might not have stood up to something major.

Melting

Even though the Mariana Trench is cold, it's surrounded by hydrothermal vents—fissures in the Earth's surface from which geothermally heated water bursts, unannounced. Thing is, that water is incredibly hot—700°C to be precise. That's hot enough to melt the submarine's view port. Then Cameron would have had water issuing into his craft, driven by 15,750 psi of pressure. Game over.

Entanglement

Though you might not realize it, the sea bed—even the area surrounding the Mariana Trench—is littered with submarine communication cables. They're there to string together telecommunication systems around the globe, but also turn the bottom of the sea into an assault course for submariners. If Cameron had gotten tangled in one of those lines, he would've struggled to make it back to the surface.

Fortunately, Cameron was one lucky mother; he managed to make it down and back up without a hitch. Which is fortunate for us, because no doubt his footage from the alien-esque world of Challenger Deep is going to be freakin' amazing. Congratulations, James.

Rubber Duckies Navigate
the Northwest Passage

Eric Paul Roorda

Due to global warming, a new Northwest Passage is forming. It is a place that explorers of the past long imagined and sought, but which proved illusory—until now. Martin Frobisher (c. 1535–94) led three voyages seeking it. James Cook (1728–79) devoted much of his third and final exploration trying to find it, as did George Vancouver (1757–98) in his wake. Sir John Franklin (1786–1847) began his doomed expedition looking for the Northwest Passage in 1845 and was never heard from again. Several more expeditions trying to find out what happened to the Franklin Expedition came to grief over the decades. Finally, in 2014, a Canadian search team located Franklin's HMS Erebus *in the Queen Maud Gulf near O'Reilly Island. Two years later, another expedition from Canada found his HMS* Terror *near King William Island, on the bottom of Terror Bay (which would seem to have been the first place to look).*

In the meantime, the Norwegian explorer Roald Amundsen (1872–1928), who is best known as the first person to reach the South Pole, led six men through a kind of Northwest Passage in a small fishing boat on a 1903–6 expedition, but the route he took would never work for commercial traffic. Neither would the routes that the St. Roch *of the Royal Canadian Mounted Police charted, while becoming the first and still the only vessel to navigate the Arctic Ocean labyrinth in both directions, during a secret wartime mission from 1941 to 1943. But the new Northwest Passage that is taking shape across the formerly frozen waters of the Arctic Ocean will change shipping patterns, precipitate international conflicts, and alter the maritime environment profoundly and negatively.*

The harbinger of these changes is a misleadingly innocent symbol: the rubber duck.

A large flock of bath toys, including 7,200 iconic yellow duckies, like the rubber duckies made famous by Ernie of *Sesame Street*, went overboard from the Greek container ship *Ever Laurel* in the North Pacific Ocean on January 10, 1992. The ship was going from Hong Kong to Tacoma when it hit a storm in the notoriously tempestuous seas near the International Date Line south of the Aleutian Islands. The winds reached hurricane force, and the waves

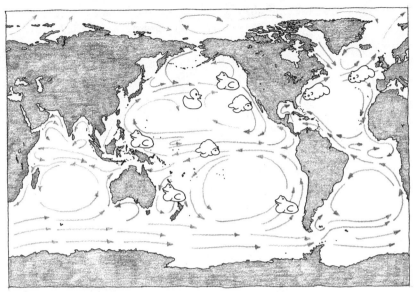

🐤 January 10, 1992: The *Ever Laurel* lost 28,800 bath toys at sea

🐤 Late 1992-1993: Toys are found in Alaska, Indonesia, Australia, and Chile

🐤 1995-1996: Toys are found in Hawaii and Washington State

🐤 2003: Toys are found in Maine and Scotland

Friendly Floatees World Tour, 1992–present? This cartographic collage depicts the many routes taken by toy ducks and other Friendly Floatees, showing all four Floatee varieties: yellow ducks, green frogs, blue turtles, and red beavers. Beachcombers, some of them dedicated Floatee fanatics, have retrieved thousands of the toys from the shorelines of five continents, but some of the original menagerie of 28,000 are still out there. Map by A. E-Dee Doyle. Courtesy of the cartographer.

mounted to 36 feet, slamming the giant vessel so violently that twelve containers broke loose and toppled from the deck. One of the lost containers ruptured somehow as a result, either striking the side of the *Ever Laurel* or colliding with another container, or both, during its fall. That single 40-foot-long box contained 28,800 plastic (not rubber) bath toys—yellow ducks, red beavers, blue turtles, and green frogs—packaged into 7,200 cardboard and cellophane cartons, each containing one each of the four different animals, labeled with the brand name Friendly Floatees. Freed into the saltwater, the packages gradually dissolved, releasing the enormous flotilla of Friendly Floatees to disperse on the Ocean.

After their escape, the rubber duckies, along with their less recognizable multicolored former shipmates, blazed watery trails for oceanographers to study, as they circulated with the North Pacific Gyre and often spun off to reach land or to find more distant seas. In the years since they went over-board, Floatees have washed up on Hawai'i, Alaska, the Pacific Northwest, the west coast of South America, and Australia. Some froze in Arctic ice. A small vanguard traversed the Northwest Passage, caught the North Atlantic Gyre, and arrived in Scotland and Newfoundland, among countless other places.

Many beachcombers collected the charismatic Friendly Floatees that came ashore and reported their finds to a website that oceanographer Curtis Ebbesmeyer established. He realized that the duckie data was a gift to his field, so he brought wide attention to the tale of the fugitive Floatees, to encourage people to look for them and inform him of new discoveries.

"We always knew that this gyre existed. But until the ducks came along, we didn't know how long it took to complete a circuit," said Ebbesmeyer. "It was like knowing that a planet is in the solar system but not being able to say how long it takes to orbit. Well, now we know exactly how long it takes: about three years."

About 2,000 of the toys continue to circle the North Pacific from Japan to Alaska and back via the equatorial current. They rarely come ashore now—the last reported find of a Friendly Floatee (a frog) came in August 2013—but it is certain that their story continues to the present day. Many are destined to add more plastic to the trash vortex called the Great Pacific Garbage Patch.

The exercise in creative cartography presented in the accompanying image depicts the four Floatees—beavers, frogs, turtles, and the famous duckies —and traces their far-flung travels since they became castaways.

IV

Saltwater Hunt

It is well known that fishing has always been one of the main reasons people have ventured out onto the Ocean. A discovery of fish traps on the floor of the Baltic Sea in 2012 showed that humans have been employing complicated techniques for luring and catching fish for at least 9,000 years. Archaeologists found this Stone Age fishing equipment off the coast of southern Sweden, in an area that was above sea level at the time, where the mouth of the Verke River was located then. Their discovery consisted of an arrangement of long sticks the width of a finger formed into a fence, which once would have been connected by ropes and driven into the riverbed, as a way to corral spawning species into nets near the riverbank. These devices would become known as weirs, and would be deployed with disastrous effect on rivers and along coastlines around the world, as this part shows. A complementary find by the divers, which points to another human behavior that would have deeply deleterious effects in the future, was an abundance of trash that the ancient fishing families threw into the river, the same river where their food lived.[1]

Fishing and whaling, unfortunately, have proven to be tragic pursuits. As in a tragedy, the history of these activities leads to an unhappy ending, which anyone who is paying attention can see coming well in advance. The belief that the unfathomable Ocean holds inexhaustible stocks of marine life went unquestioned by most people, except for those whose profession was hunting and harvesting the creatures themselves. Going back centuries, not decades, whalers and fishermen have repeated the same grim cycle of depleting one species after another, in regions of the Ocean ever more remote, with more and more effective equipment. The logs, journals, letters, and petitions of the individuals who caught the fish, whales, and seals recount the slaughter of the world's marine species over centuries. "Saltwater Hunt" samples from that long record of excessive, unsustainable hunting in the Ocean. In doing so, it continues the overall theme of negative change brought about by humankind's impact on the maritime environment, and, in particular, it foreshadows the last part of this volume, "The Endangered Ocean."

Note

1. "'World's Oldest Fishing Tools' in Swedish Waters," *The Local: Sweden's News in English,* June 6, 2012, http://www.thelocal.se/20120605/41256.

Basque Whaling in the North Atlantic Ocean

Alex Aguilar

The Basque people began whaling a thousand years ago, ranging far around the North Atlantic Ocean in their pursuit of the largest creatures on earth. The wreck of a large Spanish galleon, discovered in 1978 at the site of a Basque whaling settlement in Red Bay, on the southern coast of Labrador in Newfoundland, revealed the scale of the operation there in 1565, when the vessel sank carrying 1,000 barrels of whale oil. The movements of the Basque whalers have been known for a long time, but relatively recent research abstracted here shows that Basque whaling took a heavy toll on the North Atlantic right whale population, which went into decline. Even so, as subsequent entries document, the killing had scarcely begun.

Ancient Basque operations have been divided into three episodes according to the areas of exploitation. In the local fishery of the Bay of Biscay, *Eubalaena glacialis* [North Atlantic right whale] was the main target species, although *Physeter macrocephalus* [sperm whale] and other species might also have been harvested at least occasionally. Whaling seems to have appeared first in the French Basque country in the 11th century and later it spread gradually to the remaining areas but this should not be related to a reduction of stocks. A peak in the overall operations was probably reached around the 16th and 17th centuries but thereafter a decline in the fishery is evident. The catch rate per season was probably not very high but other factors such as the preference of the whalers for the calves would have had detrimental effects on the stock. The total removals are impossible to estimate but the present population in the Bay of Biscay must be negligible, since only a few records of this species have occurred during this century. Whaling in Newfoundland began during the 1530s and reached its maximum success at the end of the 16th century. *Eubalaena glacialis* probably represented the bulk of the catches, although *Balaena mysticetus* [bowhead whale] was also taken, especially from 1610, when the Basques moved further to the north due to the scarcity of whales in the initial whaling grounds. The average catch per boat is estimated at 12 whales or thereabouts and thus, the total harvest per season ranged from 300 to 500 whales. This means that about 25,000 to 40,000 whales might have been killed from 1530 to 1610, when the stock showed signs of depletion.

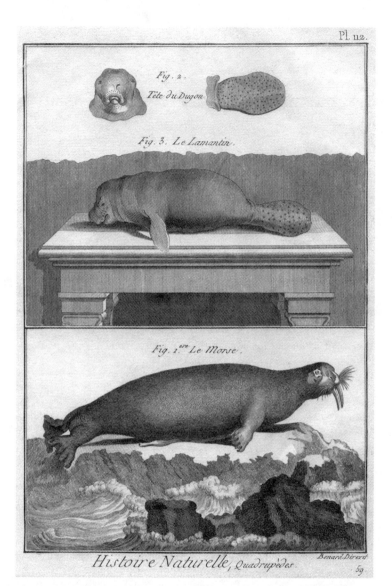

Pl. 112.

Fig. 2.
Tête du Dugon

Fig. 3. Le Lamantin.

Fig. 1.re Le Morse.

Bernard Direxit

Histoire Naturelle, Quadrupèdes.

59

Russian hunters killed every last Steller's sea cow. The largest member of the taxonomic order Sirenia, they grew up to thirty feet long and weighed up to eleven tons. When this picture of the related West Indian manatee was published in 1790, Steller's sea cow had been extinct for nearly fifty years. Later, New England sealers raided the rookeries of walruses, also pictured here, and fur seals, in the Atlantic, Pacific, Arctic, and Antarctic Oceans, depleting the pinniped population with such myopic efficiency that they put themselves out of business in a few decades. Bernard Direxit, *Le Lamantin* (The manatee) and *Le Morse* (The walrus), copper plate engravings, *Histoire Naturelle, Quadrupèdes*, in *Tableau encyclopédique et méthodique des trois regnes de la nature*, edited by Charles Joseph Panckoucke (Paris: Panckoucke, 1790). Courtesy of the Roorda/Doyle Collection.

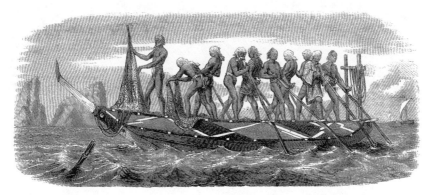

As shown in this *Illustrated London News* engraving, *A Japanese Whaling Boat*, November 19, 1864, Japanese whalers used boats with standing rowers to drive whales into their nets. Japanese dolphin hunters employ this technique with motorboats, herding pods to shore to kill en masse, a practice brought to light by the 2009 documentary *The Cove*, which ignited an international campaign to end the slaughter. Foreign opinion also decries Japanese whaling offshore, which targets larger species—sei and Bryde's whales—also hunted by whalers from Iceland, Norway, and South Korea. Courtesy of the Roorda/Doyle Collection.

Basque whaling on the Canadian grounds continued until the end of the 17th century. Little information is available for whaling operations in the northeastern North Atlantic, since most of the capital invested came from outside the Basque whaling community, and often they only acted as harpooners or sailors. Purely Spanish expeditions were only occasionally carried out, and they took place from the 15th to the middle of the 18th century. The target species in Ireland, Norway and Iceland was probably *E. glacialis*, but in North Greenland and Spitzbergen it was *B. mysticetus*. At the beginning of the 18th century, Spanish whaling operations, both in local and northern grounds, were in clear decline. Several companies, some of them with the support of the Crown, were created in order to carry on whaling in the northern seas, the Canary Islands and South America.

However, all the enterprises failed and, in 1797, the last overseas Spanish whaler was back in port.

The Tragedy of the Mackerel

George Brown Goode

Declining stocks of fish prompted the formation of the United States Fish Commission in 1871, a federal agency with a mission to study and report on the country's many different fisheries, with the aim of promoting and preserving all of them. The first US commissioner of fish and fisheries was Spencer F. Baird (1823–87), who was also the first curator of the Smithsonian Institution, which increased its collection of natural history specimens from 6,000 to more than 2 million during his tenure. The Smithsonian worked closely with the Fish Commission and shared key staff members who served both, such as Baird's chief collaborator, George Brown Goode (1851–96). Goode was an ichthyologist who split his time between doing research for the Fish Commission and designing exhibits for the Smithsonian, the most ambitious of them being for the Philadelphia Centennial Exposition in 1876. Goode headed the Fish Commission's research program from 1873 to 1887, producing annual reports that culminated in an exhaustive seven-volume survey titled The Fisheries and Fishery Industries of the United States *(Washington, DC, 1884–87). These unique publications have proven to be a goldmine for researchers in the field of marine environmental history.*

In his research, Goode discovered that the waters of the North Atlantic have been troubled for a very long time. Evidence came from the complaints of the fishermen themselves going back to early colonial times in North America, documented in the petitions they filed with their governments, asking that fish stocks be protected. They were particularly concerned about anadromous species, which have to ascend rivers and streams to spawn, making them vulnerable to being caught en masse in nets along the way. The portion of Goode's 1883 Materials for a History of the Mackerel Fishery *that follows illustrates this concern with specific reference to the increasingly beleaguered mackerel.*

Goode was fish commissioner for a year after Baird died in 1887 but stepped down to write a history of the first fifty years of the Smithsonian. He was working on that volume when he died suddenly of pneumonia at the age of forty-five, cutting short a career during which he had already published more than 100 works, was named a member of the National Academy of Sciences and the American Academy of Arts and Sciences, and received the Order of Isabel la Católica from the Queen Regent of Spain.

LAWS, PETITIONS, AND PROTESTS

Legislation in the seventeenth and eighteenth centuries. At an early day in the history of the United States a failure of the mackerel fishery was apprehended. The following notices of legislation, copies of laws, and newspaper extracts will serve to give an idea of the state of public opinion at different periods from 1600 to the present time:

1660. Early regulation of the mackerel fishery. The commissioners of the United Colonies recommended to the several general courts to regulate the mackerel fishery; conceiving that fish to be the most staple commodity of the country. Few, who have not investigated the subject, have at the present day an adequate conception of the importance of this branch of productive industry. (*Freeman's History, of Cape Cod*, Boston, 1862, vol. i, p. 239.)

1670. Prohibition of early mackerel fishing by laws of Plymouth Colony. "Wheras wee haue formerly seen Great Inconvenience of taking mackerell att unseasonable times wherby there encrease is greatly deminished and that it hath bine proposed to the Court of the Massachusetts that some course might be taken for preventing the same and that they have lately drawne vp an order about the same this Court doth enacte and order that henceforth noe makerell shall be caught except for spending while fresh before the first of July Annually on penaltie of the losse of the same the one halfe to the Informer and the other halfe to the use of the Collonie; and this order to take place from the 20th of this Instant June." (*Plymouth Colony Records*, vol. xi, 1623–1682. Laws, p. 228.)

1684. Prohibition of mackerel seining. "In 1680, Cornet Eobert Stetson, of Scituate, and Nathaniel Thomas, of Marshfield, hired the Cape fishery for bass and mackerel. In 1684, the court enacted a law 'prohibiting the seining of mackerel in any part of the colony'; and the same year leased the Cape fishery for bass and mackerel to Mr. William Clark for seven years, at £30 per annum. Subsequently to 1700, it is certain that the mackerel were very abundant in Massachusetts Bay. It was not uncommon for a vessel to take a thousand barrels in a season. The packing, as it is called, was chiefly done at Boston and Plymouth." (*Deane's History of Scituate, Mass.*)

1692. Repeal of prohibitory laws in Massachusetts. "And be it further enacted and declared, That the clause in the act, entitled 'An Act for the Regulating and Encouragement of Fishery,' that henceforth no mackeril shall be caught (except for spending whilst fresh), before the first of July annually, be and hereby is fully repealed and made void, anything therein to the contrary notwithstanding." [Passed February 8, 1692–93.] (*Acts and Resolves of the Province of Massachusetts Bay*, vol. 1, 1692–1714, p. 102.)

1692. An Act for the regulating and encouragement of fishery. "Upon consideration of great damage and scandal, that hath happened upon the account of pickled fish, although afterwards dried and hardly discoverable, to the great loss of many, and also an ill reputation on this province, and the fishery of it,—Be it therefore enacted by the Governor, Council and Representative, convened in General Court or Assembly, and it is enacted by the authority of the same, that no person or persons whatsoever, after the publication hereof, shall save or salt any sort of fish (that is intended to be dried) in cask or fattes, or any other way than what hath formerly and honestly been practised for the making of dry fish, on penalty of forfeiting all such fish so salted and pickled, whether it be green or drye; the one moiety thereof to the use of the poor of the town where the offence is committed, and the other moiety to the person that shall sue for the same. And it is further enacted by the authority aforesaid, that henceforth no mackrel shall be caught (except for spending whilst fresh) before the first of July annually; and no person or persons whatsoever, after the publication hereof, shall at any time or place within this province take, kill, or hale ashore any mackrel, with any sorts of nets or sa'ens whatsoever, on penalty of forfeiting all such mackrel so taken or haled ashore, and also all such nets or sa'ens which were so imployed; the one half thereof to their majesties towards the support of this their government, and the other half to him or them that shall inform and sue for the same. And all justices are hereby impowered, and required to grant their warrants for the seizing of the same and the aforesaid forfeitures, or the receiving of the like value in currant money of this province. [Passed November 26, 1692.] (*Acts and Resolves of the Province of Massachusetts Bay*. Vol. I. 1692–1714, p. 71. Province Laws, 1692–3. Chap. XXXII.) . . .

Protests against Gigging and Seining in the Present Century

1838–9. Protests against gigging. "The *Boston Journal* protests strongly against the barbarous method of taking mackerel called 'gigging,'[1] and urges that it is not only liable to censure on the score of humanity, but it is also impolitic, and that if this destructive method of fishing is generally continued a few years longer it will break up the fishery. We have for a year or two past entertained a similar opinion, and probably the complaints now so frequently made by the fishermen that, though mackerel are plenty, they 'will not bite,' is owing to the custom of 'gigging.' There is hardly anything which possesses life that has so little instinct as not to become very shy under such barbarous inflictions. It is obvious that all which are hooked in this manner are not taken on board; the gig frequently tears out, and thousands, millions of these fish are lacerated by these large hooks and afterwards die in the water." (*Newburyport Herald, Gloucester Telegraph,* 23 September 1838.)

The following protest appeared in the *Gloucester Telegraph*, Wednesday, 7 August 1839, it being a quotation from the *Salem Register*:

"All the mackerel men who arrive report the scarcity of this fish, and at the same time I notice an improvement in taking them with nets at Cape Cod and other places. If this speculation is allowed to go on without being checked or regulated by the government, will not these fish be as scarce on the coast as penguins are, which were so plenty before the Revolutionary war that our fishermen could take them with their gaffs? But during the war some mercenary and cruel individuals used to visit the islands on the eastern shore where were the haunts of these birds for breeding, and take them for the sake of the fat, which they procured, and then let the birds go. This proceeding finally destroyed the whole race. It is many years since I have seen or heard one except on the coast of Cape Horn. In 1692 the General Court passed an act prohibiting the taking of mackerel before the first day of July annually, under penalty of forfeiting the fish so taken. In 1702 this act was revived with additional penalties—besides forfeiting the fish and apparatus for taking, 20 shillings per barrel, and none to be taken with seines or nets."

"A Fisherman"

MARBLEHEAD, AUGUST 3, 1839

1870–1882. Protest against the purse-seine. Since the general adoption of the purse-seine no year has passed without a considerable amount of friction between fishermen using this engine of wholesale destruction in the capture of mackerel and menhaden and those engaged in fishing with other forms of apparatus. Petitions to Congress and State legislatures have been made from both sides, and in some instances laws have been passed by State legislatures prohibiting the use of menhaden seines within certain specified tracts of water, such as the Chesapeake Bay. These laws, while especially antagonistic to menhaden fishing, were aimed chiefly at the purse-seine as a means of capture, and would doubtless have been equally prohibitory of mackerel fishing with purse-seines had this been attempted within the limits. In 1878 a delegation of fishermen from Portland, Maine, and Gloucester, Massachusetts, visited Washington for the purpose of securing the passage of a law prohibiting the use of purse-seines in the mackerel fishery. In 1882 the clamors of shore fishermen, especially on the coast of New Jersey, led to the appointment of a committee of the United States Senate, which at the time of printing this report is engaged in taking testimony regarding the effect of the purse-seine upon the menhaden fishery, and incident among these men that the mackerel were to be used for the manufacture of oil and guano, but this has been denied by Capt. David T. Church and other representative men, who, reasonably enough, state that they could not afford to use so valuable a fish for this purpose, and who claim that they have an undoubted right to use their steamers in the capture of mackerel for sale fresh in the markets and for pickling. As a matter of record we reproduce the following paragraphs from an editorial in the *Cape Ann Advertiser*, July 14, 1882: "It is not a difficult

Herring, menhaden, and sprat all belong to the taxonomic family Clupeidae, which includes many species of oily schooling fish, including shad and sardines. For millennia, these types of fish created an enormous biomass in the Ocean. In recent centuries, humans have drastically thinned their numbers, hunting them for food, for use in fish oil as well as fish meal for fertilizer, and to use as bait for larger prey such as codfish. The oiliest fish were highly valued: menhaden in North America, and sprat in Europe. These scenes show each step in the process of trawling for sprat, or spratting. I. R. Wells and Charles Joseph Staniland, *Our Fishing Industries: Spratting*, engraving, *London Illustrated News*, August 18, 1883. Courtesy of the Roorda/Doyle Collection.

matter to anticipate the result if this class of steamers engage in this branch of the fisheries. There is no reason to doubt their ability to catch almost or quite as many mackerel as they have formerly caught menhaden. Several of them are large, capable of carrying 2,800 barrels of fish in bulk. These carry a double gang of men, and apparatus to correspond. During moderate weather, when mackerel generally school the best, and sailing vessels find it difficult to move, these steamers can play around the fleet of schooners, catch almost every fish that shows itself, and carry them away to be used, not for food fish as they were intended, but for oil and guano, to enrich a few men at the expense of many.

"If the steamers were to engage in the mackerel fishery, selling their catch for food, and were obliged to spend the requisite time for dressing them, which would debar them from an overcatch and carrying them to market, thus placing them on somewhat equal footing with the other fishermen, there could be no reasonable objection to their employment; but it certainly seems, in view of this startling innovation, that some decided action should be taken by 'the powers that be' to prevent the catch of mackerel for the purpose of manufacturing oil and guano. They are altogether too valuable for such a purpose, and the risk of breaking up the schools and driving them almost entirely from our waters, as has been the case with menhaden, is altogether too great.

"Unless some action is taken, and taken at once, and stringent laws enacted, we may confidently look forward to the destruction in a few years of one of the important industries of New England and the permanent and serious injury of large communities which now derive a considerable part of their support from the mackerel fishery."

Note

1. The method of capture called "gigging" here is undoubtedly gaffing, since a fish-gaff is even yet called a "gig" by some of our fishermen. [A gaff is a hook on the end of a pole used to snag fish when they rise to the bait thrown in the water; a gig is a shiny metallic lure on the end of a fishing line, which is dangled in the water from a fishing boat and attracts the fish to bite it, allowing them to be yanked on board.]

The Tragedy of the Menhaden

Genio C. Scott

One of the many threatened species that George Brown Goode assessed was Brevoortia tyrannus, the Atlantic menhaden, also called bunkers, mossbunkers, and pogies, which was the subject of his 1880 study, History of the Menhaden. *For centuries, an enormous biomass of menhaden migrated in giant schools annually along the Atlantic coast of North America, providing a key resource for Native American peoples and European colonists alike. The name "menhaden" partly derives from an Algonquian word that connotes fertilizer, which has long been the main use of the barely palatable fish. The Patuxet people of Cape Cod sowed menhaden together with corn, a technique that the famous Patuxet man named Tisquantum, better known as Squanto, is said to have shared with the Pilgrims. At the time, in the 1620s, incalculable numbers of menhaden thrived in the coastal waters, but by the mid-1800s, their stocks had plummeted, and were still falling fast.*

Genio Columbus Scott (1806–79) bemoaned the ongoing crisis of the menhaden in his thick tome Fishing in American Waters, *first published in 1869. Born in Ontario, New York, on the shores of the Great Lake of that name, Scott moved to New York City, where he became famous as a designer, illustrator, and purveyor of high fashion. He published both* The Monitor of Fashion *and* Scott's Report of Fashions, *which included his own stylized drawings, and he operated a retail establishment offering haute couture on Broadway, which was called simply* Fashions. *In the 1850s, Scott published colorful posters twice a year (which are now valuable collectibles) to illustrate the latest seasonal looks for men, from formal attire to natty outfits for fly fishermen. Scott might have used himself as the model for the latter, because fly-fishing for trout was in fact his personal passion. He produced 170 drawings for his compendium on fishing in American waters, which was an immediate success. Scott followed with a revised and expanded version in 1875, from which the following excerpt was taken.*

The Mossbunker or Menhaden

On salt-sea borders, sound, and bay,
The twinkling springtime sunbeams play,
And white with froth the billows shine
Where the mossbunkers lash the brine.

Mackerel and herring are pelagic fish, which migrate in large schools close to the surface of the Ocean, often in the same waters. Fishermen targeted both species, catching them from sailboats with seine nets. With marine engines, it became easier to take larger hauls onboard than muscle power could. These scenes show the herring fishery based in Yarmouth, England. Clockwise from upper left, they are "Towing Out the Boats," "Ferrying Across with the fish," "Signaling to the Boats to Enter the Harbor," "Curing the Herrings," "Ready for Packing," "Herring-Nets on the Denes [Beach at Southwold]," "Laid Up," "Packing," and in the center, "Hauling in the Nets." I. R. Wells and Charles Joseph Staniland, *Our Fishing Industries: The Yarmouth Herring Fishery*, engraving, *London Illustrated News*, May 19, 1883. Courtesy of the Roorda/Doyle Collection.

> Above them flocks of sea-gulls swing,
> Beneath the hungry bluefish spring.
> And, deadlier still, the surfmen strain
> The oars, and mesh them with the seine.

The menhaden is a white fish, with large scales of metallic lustre. It disports, during spring, summer, and autumn, off the coast and in the estuaries from Delaware to the Bay of Passamaquoddy [Maine]. It is from nine to twelve inches long, and in shape resembles a diminutive shad, though not so wide or thin for its length. It is a very oily fish, very bony, and therefore never eaten except by fishermen, who frequently salt it for winter use. Its flavor is like that of the shad. The principal estimate of value put upon the menhaden is for its quality as the best bait for attracting mackerel, striped bass, bluefish, and even such of the *Gadidae* as the haddock, and of the *Crustacea* as the lobster. It is either ground or chopped fine and cast upon the water to attract mackerel and other food-fishes to the hook, while it is the best bait for lobster-pots. The annual diminution in the numbers of mackerel taken within the past five years—as shown by the statistics—is justly attributable to the increase of the manufacture of menhaden oil. About five years since some person conceived the brilliant idea of making oil from menhaden by grinding them to a pulp, putting them under a press, and squeezing out the oil. He formed a company, which erected buildings, introduced machinery, and bought sailboats and nets. For a couple of years, while menhaden were so abundant as to be used for manure in some places along the coast, the menhaden oil companies made generous dividends; but no sooner did this fact become known among enterprising geniuses than nearly two hundred manufactories were put in operation, and the sails of menhaden boats enlivened Long Island Sound throughout its length and breadth, their flocks of white wings extending along the Atlantic shore for five hundred miles, as if striving with the numerous shoals of porpoises to see which could do the most harm to the fishing interest by robbing the fishermen of the greatest amount of bait.

But every year since the shoals of menhaden have decreased in number, so that while the fishermen begin to find the price of bait oppressive, some oil factories have been compelled to suspend operations. It may be a question worthy of attention by political economists and statesmen whether menhaden oil-manufactories should not be taxed out of existence for the injury they are causing to the public; for the oil companies offer inducements which attract fishermen from their legitimate calling, enhance the prices of most kinds of food-fishes, and thus injure the public. Laws which should adequately encourage by premiums the capture of the black porpoise and the puffer would greatly improve the coast fisheries. This course was deferred until the porpoises robbed some of the rivers of Ireland of their salmon, by watching in large shoals at the mouths of rivers when the salmon were returning to spawn. Already the black porpoise—the most injurious to food-fishes of all the mammal tribes—are becoming so numerous along the coast, and in the bays and estuaries, that the fishermen rightly consider them one of the principal causes of the annual decrease of striped bass and many other excellent fishes. The valuable oil of the porpoise would be a sufficient reward for its capture if the fishermen could be so encouraged as to induce them to decline catching menhaden for oil mills, and bring their forces to bear against the porpoise, the oil of which is the finest in the world for jewelers' use, and the lubrication of all machinery requiring a fine and pure article. By some such means as I have hinted at the shoals of food-fishes may be checked in their eastern migrations, and induced to forage in the waters of the United States, instead of settling beyond their limits.

The Perils of South Pacific Whaling

Nelson Cole Haley

When whales in the Atlantic Ocean had been hunted to scarcity by the whalers of many nations, the hunters pursued them into the Arctic Ocean. The next productive hunting ground was Spitsbergen, the Dutch term for both an archipelago and the archipelago's largest island, located between Scandinavia and Greenland, at approximately 75 degrees north latitude. Now called Svalbard, the islands are part of Norway. The Dutch explorer Willem Barentsz discovered Spitsbergen, which he believed was one large island, in 1596, and called the place Pointed Mountains. When news of what Barentsz had found spread around the whaling ports of the Netherlands, his countrymen rushed north to exploit the new resource, and in 1619 they established the first whaling station on the shore. The Dutch whalers did not enjoy their monopoly on Spitsbergen for long; soon there were whalers from other nations, especially Germany, joining them on the whale grounds. Inevitably, within a short time, the whale hunters depleted the Atlantic Ocean whale population—350 years ago! It would get worse.

The Charles W. Morgan is the last remaining wooden whale ship in the world, among the many thousands of such craft of many countries that once crisscrossed the Ocean, hunting the largest animals on earth. In thirty-seven voyages over eighty years, the Morgan plied the Atlantic, Pacific, and Indian Oceans, with large, international, multiethnic, polyglot crews on board to kill and process the whales. The Morgan retired in 1927 and became a museum ship at Mystic Seaport in 1941. With millions of visitors having been aboard since then, the ship has acquired a kind of iconic status, symbolizing as it does the strange, doomed industry of whaling. In 2014, having been completely restored, Charles W. Morgan defied all precedent and conventional logic by setting sail again, to return to the Ocean where it once caught whales.

By the time the Charles W. Morgan was first launched in 1841, which was near the height of nineteenth-century whaling, the species that was most highly prized, the awe-inspiring sperm whale, was scarce in the Atlantic Ocean, both North and South. Whale ships from the northeastern United States, most of them based in New Bedford, Massachusetts, had to sail to the Pacific Ocean, the Indian Ocean, and later all the way to the Arctic Ocean via the Bering Strait, on voyages lasting three to seven years, to fill their holds with whale oil. To do so, they employed essentially the same techniques and technology that whalers had used for 500 years. They approached the *enormous creatures in small rowboats, then stabbed them with harpoons attached to long ropes. After being harpooned, a whale would dive, or swim away, or attack the attackers, or a combination of all three responses, until it was exhausted, when the whalemen would approach to stab the mammal again, this time with a long lance, to kill it. That was often the most dangerous moment for the humans in the conflict, as the whale was most likely to wreck their boat when in its death throes.*

This bizarre and treacherous pursuit was the basis of a lucrative industry for decades, but like other sprawling enterprises on the seas that are now essentially extinct—like the menhaden fishery, for example—the whale fishery would be a footnote in history now, if not for Herman Melville (1819–91), who immortalized whaling as an existential symbol in Moby-Dick (1851). The quintessential description of a whale chase in the genre of nonfiction comes from the memoir of Nelson Cole Haley (1832–1900), who was seventeen years old in 1849, when he sailed aboard the Charles W. Morgan on a four-year voyage to the Pacific Ocean, in the following selection.

Stove In

When in about the Lat. of 50 South, Long. 1700 East, about a month after we left Rotuma [Island, near Fiji], all hands were made happy one morning, just as seven bells struck, by the pleasing sound from the masthead of "T-h-e-r-e s-h-e b-l-o-w-s!" The answer to the Captain's question of "Where away? And how far off?" being "Four points on the lee bow, two and a half miles off," the mainyard was hove aback, lines were placed in the boats, and all hands but those to keep ship went to a hurried breakfast, which was soon finished, and the boats lowered away.

The weather for the past two or three days had been squally. Squalls of wind and rain would blow for an hour at a time, with rain coming down in torrents, obscuring everything but a narrow circle of darkened waters half a mile around the ship. When the squall would pass over, the sun would shine out and the sky become quite clear until another squall forming would cover all up again, sometimes two or three hours apart, at other times not so long. It was in between two of these squalls that the whale we lowered for was sighted; and the weather continued so good that before another squall came on we caught sight of him again: a large lone bull whale, who no doubt had been driven off from a school of cows by one more vigorous than he.

Two large bull whales in one school of whales at the same time is unknown without they would be fighting, when the conquered one would leave instantly. They fight with terrific fury, using their jaws in rushing at each other, some thing like two men fencing with swords; and cases have been known of whales having their jaws twisted quite out of shape and sometimes broken entirely asunder. I have seen one or two instances of the first kind myself.

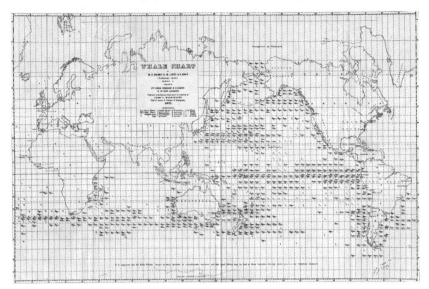

In August 1935, the United States Hydrographic Office reprinted Matthew Fontaine Maury's 1851 Whale Chart, depicting areas of the Ocean where the most whales had been killed. Maury noted that the Arctic Ocean was "Unexplored by Whalemen," and said of the Antarctic Ocean, "It is supposed that the Right Whales resort to these grounds in considerable numbers and that good fishing may be had in these latitudes during winter i.e. the Southern Summer." By 1935, whalers had virtually scoured the Arctic clean of whales, while the onslaught on whales in the Antarctic was just beginning. This particular chart seems to have been put to use, most likely on a whaleboat, as indicated by the multiple thumbtack piercings in the corners and the many spectral erasures of course routes to and from southern seas. Matthew Fontaine Maury, "Whale Chart," constructed by Lieutenants Leigh, Herndon & Fleming and passed Midshipman Jackson (Washington, DC: United States Naval Observatory, 1851). Courtesy of the Roorda/Doyle Collection. Large-scale, high-definition scan compliments of Paul O'Pecko, Mystic Seaport Museum.

Before the whale went down again, we had got so good a run of him that by the time the next squall cleared off we sighted him no great distance from our boat, and although drenched to the skin by the rain, we started for him with glee. As we were some two or three ship's lengths nearer to him when he broke water than any other boat, and square in after him, the chance was ours, and with our sail and oars we improved it for all it was worth.

The whale was heading to the leeward with the wind about four points on his quarter, and as there was a fresh breeze blowing, we shot up across the corner of his flukes with a free sheet, and when the boat's stern passed clear of his flukes a quick stroke with the steering oar caused the boat's head to shoot to windward (as it is always the rule to go on the lee side of a sperm whale when approaching to strike or lance). Bringing the boat's head within two or three feet of his side, I let him have the first iron, which I had been holding in my hand since ordered to stand up by the 2d Mate when crossing the whale's flukes. The second iron was planted into his huge body, no great distance from the first, a second after. Throwing overboard the coil of stray line, I turned around and commenced to roll up the sail.

This job was none too easy, as the whale, instead of sounding as is almost always the first thing they do when fastened to, took to running to the windward. . . .

As soon as the mast was out of the way, the 2d Mate took his place in the head of the boat and I went aft to the steering oar. By the time everything was straightened in the boat, we had run quite a distance away from the other boats and were as far to the windward as the ship, but some mile and a half ahead of her, the whale showing no signs of slacking his speed; so all we could do was to hold our line, trim boat and keep the water bailed out that now and then rolled over her sides and bows when she pitched into a larger sea than common.

This thing went on for an hour or more, when big dark masses of clouds could be seen to the windward, making up into a mess that denoted a squall of unusual severity and continuance. The ship saw it and took in her main-top gallant sail and flying jib.

Not much had been said out of the usual line by either the 2d Mate or myself up to this time, but now we both expressed ourselves in regard to the whale and the look of the weather. If the confounded whale would only give us a show to lance him, though, we did not care much about what might be in that impenetrable mass of black matter that was fast rolling down on our unprotected heads from the windward.

About the time the clouds had gathered overhead so thick that all signs of blue had vanished and the first pattering drops of rain began to hit us, the whale milled a little to the leeward; and by the time the full force of the squall was on us, he was running at the rate of ten knots an hour with the wind abaft the starboard beam. Keeping this course and speed for half an hour, he suddenly stopped and commenced to roll and tumble, snap his jaws and strike with his flukes. This was what we wanted, in one way, since now might be a chance to get a lance into him; whereas there would be none when he was running like he had been.

But of all the different views of whaling that it has been my lot to see, this beat them all. Here we were in the midst of a raging tempest, rain pouring down in torrents, the sea and wind combined in a roar that was accompanied now and then by the sound of the whale's flukes as he struck the water, after raising them fifteen or twenty feet above the surface, sending the foam flying in every direction when he brought them down in his rage.

All the world was lost to our view, a little space in the world of waters in which a battle was going on; a whaleboat with six men in it, a whale and a gale, each trying to win. We did not pay much heed to anything but the whale, and watching a chance the whale gave us, we sent the boat ahead and with a skilled aim the 2d Mate drove his lance deep into the life of the whale, and the thick blood that came pouring out from his spout hole told of our battle won. "Stern all! Stern all hard!" was the cry from both of us to the men, as the whale turned towards us with his head and just missed the boat with his wide-open jaw. Sterning off a safe distance from him, as he was tumbling about too much for us to do any fooling just then, we watched him in his struggles for a few minutes. Raising his head at last well out of water, he shot ahead and turned flukes.

"Look out for the line!" was the order from the 2d Mate to me. "He is going to sound."

"Aye, aye, sir," was my reply and at the same time I took an extra turn around the loggerhead and reached for a canvas nipper to shield my hands from burning by the friction of the line passing through them when grasping it to prevent its running any faster around the loggerhead in the stern of the boat than safety obliged.[1]

Down he went, dragging flake after flake out of the tub until more than one-half had rapidly disappeared;[2] I holding the line at times hard enough to pitch the head of the boat under water, and getting a sharp word of warning to be careful from the officer. Still the line ran out . . . to the last two flakes; about one hundred and eighty fathoms [1,080 feet] being gone of the two hundred and twenty that is the length of a whale line.

We commenced to look blue, as, if he took our line, we should have but little chance of ever seeing any more of him. We knew he had his death wound; and if he did not take our line, when he came again to the surface his life would be short. Just then the strain on the line slackened. This made our hearts rejoice, and when our officer gave the order "Haul line," every man faced around forward on his thwart, and with both hands pulled hard together and brought a little line back into the boat, gaining on it faster and faster as the whale approached the surface, which he now was doing. . . .

By the time he broke water, some three or four hundred feet from us, we had hauled into the boat about two-thirds of our line. . . . The whale was throwing out thick clots of blood by the barrelful at each spouting, and hardly moving through the water, and the boat shot towards him as fast as four men could haul the line.

When we had approached within a short distance of him, the 2d Mate, much to my astonishment, ordered the men to take the oars, and at the same time he told me: "Put the boat on the whale, so that I can lance him again." He and I had had so many bouts with each other that I hardly liked to say anything against any more orders he might give, but in this case I could not keep still, for our lives were to be placed in jeopardy very foolishly.

. . . The men had stopped pulling, no doubt at my great breach of discipline in asking him such a question, so the boat almost stopped.

This is one of the whales in the *Morgan*'s vicinity on its unlikely thirty-eighth voyage in 2014, a young humpback whale that played on the surface while the adults in the pod repeatedly dove deep to feed. Photograph by Frances E. Roorda, July 13, 2014. Courtesy of the photographer.

"Pull ahead!" he yelled at the top of his voice.

"Hold on a minute, Mr. Griffin, let me say a few words first," was my reply, and then as rapidly as possible I called his attention to the fact that the whale was about dead and would soon go into his flurry. Also, that though the worst part of the squall was over, nothing could be seen yet any great distance from the boat and the ship could not tell our position, as the whale had changed his course so much, from what it was when we were last seen by her, that if our boat should get stoven the chance of her finding the whale or us would be mighty slim when the weather cleared up again. "This is all I have to say in the matter, except, if you are bound to lance that whale, let me put the boat on his lee side, instead of going to him as we are now, heading on to windward of him."

The only answer he made to any of the reasons or requests made by me was that he did not think I was such a coward, and to put the boat on to the whale the way she was headed; the quicker I did it, the better.

Telling the men to pull ahead, I told him he would not find me far behind him in any danger that any reasonable man had to face. A few strokes of the oars, and the heave of the seas sent the boat on to the whale. He set his lance over its shoulder blade and, holding by the pole, thrust it up and down two or three times, and then sung out: "Stern all!"

The men did their level best to obey the order, but even with the 2d Mate assisting at the harpooner's oar when he saw the four men failed to stern off the whale, nothing more could be done than to get the boat a short distance away from him to the windward, and then be swept back by the next heavy sea. This happened three or four times, and the boat had worked aft on the whale quite a piece, when the whale, with a blow from his flukes, knocked the bottom half-out of her and tumbled us all into the water.

The 2d Mate, who could not swim a stroke, managed to be amongst the first to grasp hold of some part of the boat and so keep afloat; and before he had hardly got the salt water out of his mouth, he was giving orders for securing the oars and lashing them across the gunwales of the boat, to keep her from rolling over and over in the seaway, and drowning us all. He was a brick, in many ways, when a pinch came.

The situation we were now in was rather critical, to say the least, and how it would end would be hard to say. We had lashed the oars across the boat by pieces of small throat-seizing stuff fastened under each gunwale for just such an emergency as this, and so we kept the boat on her keel, thus affording us a good resting-place for our arms over the gunwales on each side.[3] Of course, our bodies and legs hung in the water, which would afford an easy meal for the sharks that abound in the sea in those Latitudes. Of these we felt somewhat nervous, but had hopes the whale would attract them by the blood from his carcass, that lay dead on the water some hundred yards away; for soon after he stove us, he had gone into his flurry and turned fin out.

Just before we took our bath, the clouds began to break, and an hour afterwards the sun was shining brightly. The wind went down to a light royal breeze and the sea in two hours was so smooth that it ceased to break over us. The last squall had been the most severe of any in the last twenty-four hours and seemed to have exhausted itself and brought good weather with it, much to our satisfaction in more ways than one. When the weather cleared,

The *Charles W. Morgan* embarked on its thirty-eighth voyage from May 17 to August 6, 2014. Along the way, the *Morgan* visited historic ports from New London, Connecticut, to New Bedford, Massachusetts (where it was built in 1841) and on to Boston. But the most significant port of call may have been Provincetown, Massachusetts, at the tip of Cape Cod. From there, the *Morgan* sailed to the nearby Stellwagen Bank National Marine Sanctuary, where it once again encountered whales, this time with peaceful intentions for the first time. This photograph was taken that day, from the Marine Sanctuary's research vessel, *Auk*. Photograph by David Arch, July 15, 2016. Courtesy of the photographer.

the ship could be seen some eight or ten miles away, but no signs of any boats to cheer us with hopes of relief. They had lost all run of us as well as the ship had, and when it cleared up they went to the ship and added their eyes to the others on board, in the vain effort to catch sight of our boat on the waste of waters. . . .[4]

We yelled, we shouted and laughed. Cold and sharks were nothing now to us. With blue lips and drawn faces some of the boys tried to make a joke, but it ended in a sob that was almost a fresh-water cry. When all doubt of their losing run of us had passed, we let the mast down for fear the boat might roll over and cause a tragedy.

The old ship came bowling along. Oh, how good she looked! To me she seemed the biggest spot on earth or ocean, and to once more tread her white decks would seem bliss indeed. Soon the white foam under her forefoot could be seen rolling and tumbling as she dashed her sharp bows into the seas that attempted to stop her on her mission of mercy; she in scorn smashing them into bubbles and suds that went dancing along her sides into the wake astern, with hissing sounds that might mean regret at their impotency.

When some half-mile from us, she hauled up her mainsail and laid the main-topsail to the mast, and lowered three boats, one of which went to the whale. (It was about a half-mile from us, we had drifted apart.) The other two boats came to us. One took us into it and the other commenced to clear the stoven boat of the oars and sail, to take it alongside the ship. The ship ran towards us as soon as they saw us leave the stoven boat, so we had but a short pull. When we arrived alongside, most of the boys had to be hauled on deck with a rope. Hot coffee was given us and we were sent below to change clothes, after which we turned in and had a rest for an hour or two, to set our blood in motion.

Notes

1. A loggerhead is a post in the stern around which the harpoon line is wound to add drag and slow it down as the whale dives.
2. To arrange a line in a coil is to flake it, and one loop in the coiled line is also called a flake.
3. The "throat-seizing stuff" consisted of short lengths of rope stored along the sides of the boat.
4. After the whale wrecked their boat around 10 A.M., the men clung to its wreckage for hours, watching the ship sail back and forth searching for them, approaching them and making their hopes rise, then turning away and making them despair. Sharks began to gather, one of them biting off the steering oar, and the sun began to set. Facing certain death if darkness fell before they could be found, the men took the risk of a capsize by rigging a sail, which finally caught the attention of their comrades on the distant whale ship.

The Collapse of Newfoundland Cod

Greenpeace

The Basques, pioneers of whaling, also fished for cod, which became the dominant spe-
cies in the economy of the Atlantic world. Salted codfish was the key commodity link-
ing Europe with the Americas and Africa. It was cod that made plantation agricul-
ture possible in the torrid zones of the New World, because it fed the enslaved workers
whose labor ran the system. The fishermen of many nations other than Basques also
chased the mighty cod, leading to disputes over the various shallow parts of the Ocean
where they proliferated, in particular the Grand Banks. Overfishing depleted the gar-
gantuan stocks there, until a moratorium imposed by the government of Canada in
1992 ended commercial fishing in the region. But it was too late. The codfish have
never come back. The sad tale is summarized on the website of Greenpeace, an activ-
ist organization dedicated to preserving the environment and protecting endangered
species, especially whales, for which Greenpeace is most famous.

In 1992, the collapse of the Newfoundland Grand Banks cod fishery in Canada
put 40,000 people out of work. The area, once renowned as the world's most
productive fishing grounds, was devastated by years of overfishing and in-
competent fisheries management. The environmental, social and economic
damages are still being paid for today.

On 1 July, 1992 Canada celebrated its 125th anniversary, but the then fisheries minister John Crosbie was not enjoying the party. He had just been
confronted by a crowd of hostile cod fishermen in Bay Bulls, a small community in Newfoundland. They had demanded to know why there were no
fish left in their waters, and what he was going to do about it. Crosbie angrily
responded, "There's no need to abuse me, I didn't take the fish from the God-
damn water."

The next day, under police protection, Crosbie announced a two-year
moratorium on cod fishing in St. John's, the Newfoundland capital. A mob of
angry fishermen had tried to force their way into the hotel ballroom where
he was making his speech, and Crosbie was forced to make a hasty retreat.

The Newfoundland Grand Banks were once renowned as the world's
most productive fishing grounds. The first European explorers described the
waters as being so full, one just had to lower a basket into the water and

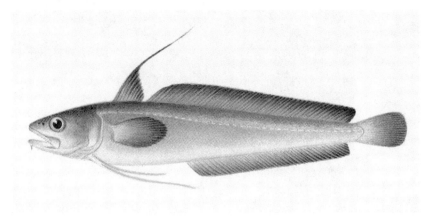

Just about every species of the taxonomic order Gadiformes is under lethal assault by human hunters. The red squirrel hake is a close relative of the very well-known cod and haddock, but the hake's flaky flesh makes it less desirable to cooks, and so the fish is unfamiliar in the US market. Illustration by Sherman Foote Denton (1856–1937), who worked with the US Fish Commission at the Smithsonian Institution, in *Annual Reports of the Forest, Fish, and Game Commissioner of the State of New York for 1904–1905–1906* (Albany, NY: J. B. Lyon Company, State Printers, 1907), after p. 220. Courtesy of the Roorda/Doyle Collection.

it would come up filled with cod. Up to the 1950s the bounty of the Grand Banks was enough to supply local small-scale fishing, as well as feed millions of harp seals.

But this happy picture was not to last. The Grand Banks fishery was destroyed by technological advances in fishing techniques in the 1950s and 60s. Small artisan fishing boats found themselves competing with trawlers modelled on the factory whaling ships that had devastated the last remaining whale populations.

The giant trawlers came from distant countries, attracted by the seemingly endless bounty of the fishery. Their huge nets took unprecedented amounts of fish, which they would quickly process and deep-freeze. The trawlers worked around the clock, in all but the very worst weather. In an hour they would haul up to 200 tonnes of fish; twice the amount a typical 16th century ship would catch in an entire season.

In 1968, the cod catch peaked at 800,000 tonnes. By 1975, the annual catch had fallen by more than 60 per cent. Catches of other fish species were also plummeting. In a desperate attempt to increase catches Canada extended its fishing limit for foreign vessels from 12 to 200 miles from the coast.

As cod catches declined, factory trawlers used ever more powerful sonar and satellite navigation to target what was left. This led to overall catches remaining steady throughout the 1980s. But traditional inshore fishermen noticed their catches declining. The government, most members of which

This photograph of a 950-pound halibut hangs on the wall of the
Potlatch Bar in Ketchikan, Alaska, which has been an anglers' wa-
tering hole for almost a century. A note on the back says Emmet
Woods of the fishing boat *Pelican* snagged the mammoth bottom
feeder in a net in 1956. In 2012, the largest specimen among the 113
halibut caught during the Ketchikan Halibut Derby weighed in at
a mere 147 pounds, with the smallest coming in at less than seven.
There has not been a Halibut Derby in Ketchikan since then. Photograph by Don Koenig, 1956. Courtesy of the photographer.

owned shares in industrial fishing companies, refused to listen to them, or to
the growing scientific warnings that cod was in crisis.

Politicians also feared that cutting the quota would lead to politically un-
acceptable job losses, but their short-term thinking led to catastrophe.

By 1992, when the cod catch was the lowest ever measured, the government was forced to close the fishery.

Seaweed is underrated. For many centuries, it has been integrally important to coastal communities worldwide. Whereas people hunt fish and marine mammals, seaweed is harvested, a task requiring skill and strength, usually done by women, as seen by the figure wearing long skirts in the bow of the boat in this image. Women still cultivate and harvest nori in contemporary Africa for Japanese restaurants, where, as sushi, it encircles raw tuna, swordfish, and other beleaguered macrofauna. Engraving by Charles Cousen, based on a painting by Colin Hunter, *Their Only Harvest*, 1879, in *The Art Journal* (London: J. S. Virtue and Co. Ltd., 1883). Courtesy of the Roorda/Doyle Collection.

In what may be the biggest single lay-off in history, the moratorium put 40,000 people out of work in 5 Canadian provinces, and required a several billion dollar relief package to be disbursed to coastal communities.

In 1993 the moratorium, initially put in place for two years, was extended indefinitely. It is still in place 14 years later. In 2003, the two main populations of Atlantic cod were added to Canada's list of endangered species. Recovery efforts are hampered by the trawling for other species that still goes on in the area, and which often leads to high levels of cod as bycatch.

The Death of Coral Reefs

Bob Stewart

The market for colorful aquarium fish and culinary delicacies has led to overfishing on the world's coral reefs, and sometimes has triggered their willful destruction. Pollution and Ocean acidification have teamed up to create the phenomenon called coral bleaching, which is ravaging the reefs as well. The coral heads in the waters of the Bahamas and the Caribbean Sea, the Philippines, and the islands of the South Pacific Ocean are all in danger. Their destruction eliminates the fishes' habitat, puts fishing families out of work, and undercuts the growth of scuba diving and ecotourism, which could provide alternative livelihoods in those impoverished places. Moreover, coral reefs are essential to the health of the Ocean. Their loss would compound the ongoing environmental crisis and make the planet much less beautiful.

Ten percent of the world's reefs have been completely destroyed. In the Philippines, where coral reef destruction is the worst, over 70% have been destroyed and only 5% can be said to be in good condition. What has happened to destroy so many reefs? Human population has become very large, and the earth is warming.

There are two different ways in which humans have contributed to the degradation of the Earth's coral reefs, indirectly and directly. Indirectly, we have destroyed their environment. Coral reefs can live only in very clear water. The large population centers near coasts have led to silting of reefs, pollution by nutrients that lead[s] to algal growth that smothers the coral, and overfishing that has led to an increase in the number of predators that eat corals.

Warming of the ocean causes corals to sicken and die. Even a rise of one degree in the average water temperature can hurt the coral. Due to global warming, 1998 was the hottest year in the last six centuries and 1998 was the worst year for coral. The most obvious sign that coral is sick is coral bleaching. That is when either the algae inside die, or the algae leave the coral. The algae are what give coral its color, so without the algae the coral has no color and the white of the limestone shell shines through the transparent coral bodies. People have been noticing coral bleaching since the turn of the century, but only since the 1980s has it gotten really bad.

The warmer water and more nutrients also encourages the growth of harmful algae on top of the coral, which kills it, because it blocks out the sun. Without the sun, the zooxanthellae cannot perform photosynthesis and so they die.[1] Without the zooxanthellae, the coral polyps die too. This algae is usually eaten by fish, but because of overfishing, there aren't enough fish left to eat all the algae. And the pollution we dump in the ocean is just what the algae needs to grow and be healthy, which means covering and eventually killing the coral reefs.

The direct way in which humans destroy coral reefs is by physically killing them. All over the world, but especially in the Philippines, divers catch the fish that live in and around coral reefs. They sell these fish to fancy restaurants in Asia and to fancy pet stores in the United States. This would be OK if the divers caught the fish carefully with nets and didn't hurt the reefs or take too many fish. But the divers want lots of fish and most of them are not very well trained at fish catching. Often they blow up a coral reef with explosives and then catch all the stunned fish swimming around. This completely destroys the reefs, killing the coral polyps that make it as well as many of the plants and animals that call it home. And the creatures that do survive are left homeless.

Another way that divers catch coral reef fish is with cyanide. Cyanide is a poison. The divers pour this poison on the reef, which stuns the fish and kills the coral. Then they rip open the reef with crowbars and catch the fish while they are too sick from the poison to swim away. This poison kills 90% of the fish that live in the reef and the reef is completely destroyed both by the poison and then by being ripped apart.

Note

1. Zooxanthellae are dinoflagellates, single-celled organisms with two whiplike appendages that allow them to swim. They are a major constituent element of plankton, and they teem in the vicinity of marine invertebrates such as coral, existing symbiotically with them.

V

Watery Highways

The Ocean is a low-friction medium through which to transport cargo and passengers. "Watery Highways" surveys some of the ways in which the Ocean has served as a highway.

The movement of goods across saltwater is a very ancient activity. Despite its multitude of risks, shipping goods by sea has always been less arduous, less dangerous, and less expensive than carrying them across land. Merchant marine sea lanes gradually spanned the globe, defying its most turbulent zones, in order to connect the continents commercially. Today, the dimensions of oceanic trade boggle the mind, from the capacity of individual container ships, which carry as much as an entire convoy of the freighters of the 1950s, to the number of ships at sea, which is about 100,000 en route to someplace or other at any given time.

For centuries, for millennia, travel by sea was dreadful and dangerous. But it evolved in a relatively short time to be luxurious. Beginning in the late 1800s, steamship accommodations came to rival any land-based luxury. The contrast between the experiences of these groups is jarring: the millions of enslaved African people who endured tortuous Atlantic Ocean crossings in chains; the millions of European immigrants who were "packed like bales of cotton" to come to the United States in the holds of the same ships used to export that commodity, as Herman Melville wrote in *Redburn* (1849), his memoir of the cotton trade; and the millions more who emigrated in relative comfort on transoceanic steamships in the half century bracketing 1900. And yet, despite these advancements, the urgency of emigration in a crisis-ridden world continues to drive desperate refugees to sea, embarking on dangerous, punishing voyages to reach more promising shores.

The Maritime Silk Road

Anonymous

The Maritime Silk Road led from the South China Sea across the Indian Ocean to the Persian Gulf and the Arabian Sea. This accounts for the fact that Theravada Buddhism is the dominant religion in Thailand. Coming directly from the cradle of that belief system in India, it is a more ancient form of Buddhism than Mahayana Buddhism, which spread on the Silk Road that everyone thinks about when the term is mentioned, the one across the Chinese deserts. Islam also spread on the Maritime Silk Road. Zheng He, the "Chinese Columbus," was a Muslim born far in the interior of China, whose father and grandfather were both hajji, men who completed the requisite pilgrimage to Mecca by sea. The 1987 discovery of the shipwreck named Nanhai No. 1 in the headwaters of the Pearl River west of Guangzhou, China, offers a new understanding of the Maritime Silk Road's antiquity and dimensions, which were much greater than had been thought. In a bold innovation in nautical archaeology and museum construction, the entire site of the shipwreck was raised inside a huge aquarium, along with the vessel and its cargo of Chinese trade goods. This allows the excavation of the artifacts to proceed inside the Guangdong Maritime Silk Road Museum, built to house the structure, with the entire process transparent to visitors as a giant exhibit.

The wreck of the *Nanhai No 1* was found in the western part of the mouth of the Pearl River (Zhu Jiang), the starting point of China's "Marine Silk Road." It once connected China with the Middle East and Europe. It takes its name from "Nanhai"—the South China Sea. The wreck is in exceptional condition. It is thought to contain 60,000 to 80,000 precious pieces of cargo, especially ceramics.

The wreck is currently still entirely covered by silt so that its location and shape had to be verified by [a] sub-bottom profiler. It was recovered in an exceptional exploit—a bottomless steel container was placed over the wreck site. The lower part of the container was sharpened and it was driven into the seabed by placing heavy concrete weights on the container. The surrounding area was then dug out, the container closed from below with steel sheets and the whole raised.

The Guangdong Maritime Silk Road Museum is at Hailing Island close to Yangjiang, a three-hour drive from Guangdong. The museum features an aquarium with the same water quality, temperature and environment as the spot in which the wreck was discovered. Archaeologists will now excavate the vessel inside the aquarium, thereby enabling visitors to observe underwater archaeological work in a museum environment.

The remains of the ancient vessel are expected to yield critical information on ancient Chinese ship building and navigation technologies. Its significance has been compared to the famous Chinese terracotta warriors discovered in Xian.

The *Nanhai No 1* museum is to become certainly one of the most important museums of underwater cultural heritage worldwide.

Navigating the Indian Ocean in the 1300s

Ibn Battuta

One of the principal reasons for people to go to sea was their faith in Islam. All devout Muslims must travel to Mecca to perform the hajj, the annual pilgrimage, at least once in their lives, provided they can afford it. Long before the European Age of Discovery, the sea lanes of the Indian Ocean and the Red Sea teemed with vessels bringing pilgrims from every corner of the vast world of Islam to Arabia. The practice dates at least to the time of the Prophet Muhammad (570–632), though tradition holds that worshippers have been making the trip since Abraham of the Old Testament. Long before long-distance travel became commonplace, Muslims undertook arduous journeys in large numbers from thousands of miles away to become hajji before their deaths.

That was why Ibn Battuta (1304–69) left his home in Morocco, to begin what turned out to be an epically peripatetic life of travel in and around the Mediterranean Sea, Red Sea, Arabian Sea, Persian Gulf, Indian Ocean, and South China Sea. Two hundred years before Vasco da Gama (c. 1460s–1524) arrived in Calicut, India, Ibn Battuta had been there en route to China, a place that Europeans knew next to nothing about, to serve in a diplomatic post. Along the way he was shipwrecked and robbed by pirates (familiar hazards of the Ocean), among many adventures. This globetrotting existence began when the call of Mecca drew him away from his seaside hometown of Tangier. After making it to Mecca for the first time, it seems he could not get enough of the experience. He completed the hajj six more times. Then he succumbed to acute wanderlust, beginning three decades of nearly perpetual motion. The fact that he was able to move with relative ease around the Red Sea, Arabian Sea, and Indian Ocean testifies to the advanced state of Islamic trading routes in the fourteenth century. The commercial pathways that Ibn Battuta came to know doubled as watery pilgrimage routes for the faithful, on their way to Mecca and Medina, to walk in the footsteps of the Prophet of Allah.

After finally settling down, Ibn Battuta wrote a book describing his long, strange trip, which filled four volumes. He titled it A Gift to Those Who Contemplate the Wonders and the Marvels of Travelling. *Today his epic is known simply as his* Rehla, *or* Travels. *The following selections from Ibn Battuta's* Rehla *are taken from his extensive sea travel, in this case down the eastern seaboard of India to the Maldive Islands. Battuta's account offers a unique view of the theory and practice of globe-trotting seaborne diplomacy in the Asian subcontinent seven centuries ago, which involved bringing along gifts to lubricate the process of establishing peaceful, and potentially very profitable, foreign relations with the strongmen of coastal India. Battuta's excursion to the Maldives, on the other hand, seemed driven more by his own intellectual curiosity than diplomacy.*

Chapter XV: Along the Malabar Coast

AN ACCOUNT OF OUR EMBARKATION

We embarked in a ship that belonged to the above-mentioned Ibrahim and was called *al-Jakur*. We accommodated seventy horses, which formed part of the presents, placing the rest together with the horses of our suite in the ship which belonged to the brother of the above-mentioned Ibrahim. . . . [He] gave us a ship in which we placed the horses of Zahir-ud-din, of Sumbul and of their comrades.[1] He fitted it out for us with water, provision and fodder and sent his son with us to accompany us on a ship named *al-'t'Kani*, which resembled a kind of *ghurāb* except that it was larger.[2] It carried sixty oars and at the time of war was covered with a roof so that the rowers should be struck neither by an arrow nor by a stone. I embarked on the *al-Jakur* on which were fifty archers and fifty Abbysinian warriors who are the lords of this sea; whenever one of them is on a ship the Hindu pirates and infidels avoid attacking it. After two days we arrived at the island of Bairam, which is uninhabited and is four miles distant from the mainland.[3] We landed there and drew water from a pond which was there. The reason why it is deserted is that the Muslims had attacked the infidels there and since then it has not been inhabited. . . .

Then we left Bairam and the following day we came to Gogo, a large city with spacious markets.[4] We cast anchor four miles from it because of the ebb-tide. I entered a boat with some of my comrades, while the tide was low in order to reach the town; but the boat ran into the mud when we were still about one mile from land. Thrown in the mud, however, I supported myself on two men of my suite. People inspired me with apprehensions about the possible return of the tide before my arrival in the city and I could not swim well. Nevertheless, I arrived at Gogo, visited its bazaar and saw a mosque which is ascribed to Khizr and Ilyās.[5] May peace be on them! There I performed the *maghrib* prayer and saw a group of the fakirs of the Haideri order along with their chief.[6] Then I returned to the ship. . . .

The raja of Fakanar is an infidel named Bas Deo, who has about thirty warships, the commander of which is a Muslim named Lilla.[7] The latter is a rogue, who carries on piracy and plunders the merchants' ships. When we cast anchor at Fakanar, its sultan sent us his son who remained on board as hostage. And we visited the sultan who entertained us handsomely for three days out of his regard for the emperor of India to fulfill his obligations and with a view to the profit which he wished to derive from trading with the passengers of our ships. It is the custom for every ship passing the town of Fakanar always to cast anchor there and to offer the ruler a present which is known as the "customs-tax." Whoever does not do that is pursued by the local ships and brought by force into the harbour. They impose on him double the tax and prevent him from travelling further as long as it suits them.

We left Fakanar, and after three days came to the city of Manjarur—a large city on a bay, called the bay of *'ad-Dumb*.[8] It is the largest bay in the Malabar country, and in this city most of the merchants from Fars and Yemen disembark. And there is an abundance of pepper and ginger there.[9]

SULTAN OF MANJARUR

He is one of the most powerful rulers of this country and his name is Ram Deo. In this city there are about four thousand Muslims, who inhabit a suburb of their own inside the jurisdiction of the city. There is fighting between them and the inhabitants of the city often, but the sultan intercedes since he has need of merchants. There is a *qazi* in Manjarur, an accomplished and beneficent man of the Shaf'ai cult named Badr-ud-din of Ma'bar who patronizes learning.[10] He came to us onboard the ship, and asked us to disembark at his town. "Not until the ruler sends his son to stay on board our ship," we replied. "The sultan of Fakanar did this because the Muslims in his town have no power. But as for us, the sultan fears us," he rejoined. Nevertheless, we refused to land until the sultan had sent his son. Consequently, he sent his son just like the other ruler. Then we disembarked and were treated with great respect and we stayed with them for three days. Then we started for the city of Hili, which we reached after two days.[11] It is an imposing city which has been well built and is situated on a large bay in which big ships enter; and it is to this city that the Chinese ships, which enter only this harbour and those of Quilon and Calicut, are bound. . . [12]

The China Sea is navigated only by the Chinese ships which I am going to describe now.

DESCRIPTION OF THE CHINESE SHIPS

The Chinese ships are of three kinds; the large are called junks, the singular being junk; the middle-sized are called *zau*, and the small *kakam*.

On each of the large ships there are anything from three to twelve sails, consisting of bamboo canes, which are woven like mats. They are never let down and are turned according to the direction in which the wind blows. When the ships are anchored the sails are left floating in the wind. On each of these ships there serve a thousand men, of whom six hundred are sailors and four hundred warriors. Amongst the latter there are archers, shield-bearers and cross-bow archers, that is, the people who shoot naphtha missiles. To each large ship three small ships are assigned—the *niefi*, the *palai* and the *rub'i*. These vessels are not built except in the town of Zaitun in China or in

Great China, that is, China of China.[13] And the way these ships are built is as follows: two wooden walls are built connected by extremely strong beams which are fastened throughout their length and breadth by means of thick nails. The length of such a nail is three cubits. When the two wooden walls are joined together by the beams the lower deck is built on them and these are launched into the sea. Then they complete the construction. The beams and wooden walls which jointly touch the water enable the people to descend to it and wash and satisfy their needs. By the aids of these beams there are oars which are as large as ships' masts, and at each one of these oars ten to fifteen men come together, and they row standing on their feet. Four decks are constructed on the ship which contains apartments, cabins and rooms for the use of the merchants; and a cabin in the ship contains apartments and lavatories and has a door which can be bolted by the occupant who may take with him his female slaves and women. Sometimes it so happens that a passenger is in the aforesaid residential quarters and nobody on board knows of him until he is met on arriving at a town. The sailors let their children live in these quarters and they sow greenery, vegetables and ginger in wooden tubs. The administrator of the ship holds a position like that of a great *amir*. When he lands, the archers and the Abyssinians march before him with lances and swords, kettledrums, horns, and trumpets. When he has reached his residence they plant their lances in the ground on both sides of his gate and continue to observe these ceremonies as long as he dwells there. There are Chinese who have many ships on which they send their employees to foreign countries and there are no richer people in the world than the Chinese. . . .

HOW WE UNDERTOOK THE JOURNEY TO CHINA
AND THE FATE OF THAT JOURNEY

When the time for the journey to China came, the raja Zamorin fitted out for us one of the thirteen junks which lay in the harbour of Calicut. The administrator of the junk was named Sulaiman and came from Safad in Syria.[14] I was acquainted with him and said to him, "I want a cabin for myself because of the female slaves, for it is my habit not to travel except along with them." He answered, "The Chinese merchants have hired the cabins for the return journey. My brother-in-law has a cabin which I should like to give you, but it has no lavatory; but perhaps it is possible to change it for another." I gave my men the necessary orders, and they loaded my luggage on the boat, and the male and female slaves boarded the junk. This happened on Thursday.

I remained on land to perform the Friday prayer and then to join them, while Malik Sumbul and Zahlr-ud-din boarded the boat with the presents. Then a servant of mine named Hilal came to me on Friday morning and said, "The cabin which we have taken on the junk is too small and unsuitable." I informed the captain of the ship who expressed his inability to help in the matter. "But would you prefer to be on the *kakam*," he asked. "On it,"

Throughout history, mariners on the Indian Ocean have plowed through "heavy weather en route to Bombay, India," the label on this photograph, taken in the early twentieth century. The clash between the ship and waves is described on the reverse as "taking them on the bow." Photographer unknown, real photo postcard, c. 1910–1930. Courtesy of the Roorda/Doyle Collection.

he added, "there are cabins to suit your choice." "Right," said I and gave my people the order. They brought my female slaves and goods on to the *kakam* and embarked on it before the Friday prayer. Usually the waves on this sea rise regularly after the prayer when nobody can embark. The other junks had already departed and the only one left was the one on which were the presents; and there was a junk whose owners had decided to stop for the winter at Fandarayna; then there was the above-mentioned *kakam*. We spent the night along the shore without being able to reach the *kakam* and the people on it could not come to us. Nothing had remained with me except a carpet on which to lay myself. The junk and the *kakam* were far out of the harbour by Saturday morning. The junk on which the passengers were bound for Fandarayna was shattered by the sea and broken, and some of them were drowned while some were saved. Among the survivors was a slave girl, who belonged to one of the merchants and was very dear to him. He desired to give ten gold dinars to one who might save her, and she had clung to a piece of wood at the back of the junk. One of the sailors of Hormuz heard her cry and saved her. But he declined to accept the dinars saying,

"I have done that only for the sake of Allah the exalted." At nightfall the sea shattered also the junk which contained the presents, and all who were on it died. In the morning we looked at the place where their corpses lay and I saw that Zahir-ud-din had broken his skull, and his brain had come out, and that a nail had penetrated one temple of Malik Sumbul and had come out at the other. We prayed over their corpses and buried them. Then I saw the heathen sultan of Calicut who wore a large piece of white cloth around his middle from the navel to the knees and on his head he wore a small turban. He was barefooted, and a servant held an umbrella over his head. A fire was lit before him on the coast, and his police officers belaboured the people so that they should not plunder what the sea had cast up. . . .

Chapter XVI: The Maldive Islands

I resolved to undertake a journey to the Maldive islands, of which I had heard a lot. Ten days after we had embarked at Calicut we reached the Maldive islands. These islands are to be reckoned as one of the wonders of the world. There are about two thousand of them of which a hundred or less form together a cluster round-shaped like a ring and have an entrance similar to a gate by which alone ships can enter. When a ship comes to one of these islands it is absolutely necessary for her to have a native pilot in order to be able to put in at the other islands under his direction. They are so close to one another that the tops of the palm trees in one island are visible from another when the ship is putting out to sea. And if the ship misses the direction of the islands she cannot reach them, and the wind drives her to M'abar or to Ceylon. All the inhabitants of these islands are Muslims—religious and upright people. . . .

It is the custom in these islands that when a ship puts in there, the *kandurir*, that is, small boats—the singular of the word is *kandura*—sail out to meet it. On these are inhabitants of the island who have with them betel and *karamba*, that is, green coconuts. And everyone offers these according to his choice to one of the passengers, who thereupon becomes his guest, and he takes his luggage to his house as if he were a relative of his. . . .

The inhabitants of these islands buy crockery, on being imported to them, in exchange for fowls so that a pot sells in their country for five or six fowls. The vessels take from these islands the fish, coconuts, waist-wrappers, and turbans made of cotton. And people take from there copper vessels which are abundant with the Maldivians as well as cowries and *qanbar*, that is, the fibrous covering of the coconut. This is tanned in pits on the shore, beaten with mallets and then spun by the women. Ropes are made from it which are used to bind the ships together and are exported to China, India and Yemen; these ropes are better than those made from hemp, and with these ropes the beams of the Indian and Yemenite ships are sewn together for the Indian Ocean has many rocks. If a ship nailed together with iron nails collides with rocks, it would surely be wrecked; but a ship whose beams are sewn together with ropes is made wet and is not shattered.

All transactions take place in this country by means of the cowrie, which is an animal picked from the sea and deposited in pits on the shore.[15] Its flesh disappears and only the white bone remains. . . . They are used for buying and selling. . . . They are sold to the inhabitants of Bengal for rice, because the cowries are also currency in Bengal, and also to the inhabitants of Yemen, who use these instead of sand as ballast in their ships. The cowrie is also the currency of the Sudanese in their country.

Notes

1. As a privileged envoy on his way to China, Ibn Battuta brought along many valuable gifts to aid his diplomacy there, and he received presents from authority figures along his route.
2. A galley-type warship of the Malabar Coast, with a long, pointed hull and square-rigged sails on two or three masts, in addition to oars; the term has evolved to *grab*.
3. Piram Island, in the Gulf of Khambhat, also called the Gulf of Cambay, which borders the modern state of Gujarat, India.
4. Gogo is now called Ghogha; it is located on the western shore of the Gulf of Khambhat and was an important port for the Arabian Sea until the nineteenth century.
5. In the Quran, Khizr, or Khidr, is a wise servant of God, described variously as a prophet, a messenger, and an angel. Ilyā is Arabic for the prophet Elijah.
6. The maghrib prayer, prayed just after sunset, is the fourth of five daily prayers performed by practicing Muslims. Fakirs are Islamic ascetics, similar to monks of other religions who take vows of poverty and chastity. The Haideri order refers to Shiʻa Muslims who observe rituals during the month of Muharram, to remember the martyrdom of Hussein ibn Ali, Muhammad's grandson, at the Battle of Karbala on October 10, 680. In the past, fakirs figured prominently in these events.
7. Fakanar is a reference to modern Barkur on the coast of Karnataka state, India.
8. Mangalore, in the Indian state of Karnataka, is still an important port on the Arabian Sea. It is located on an estuary, translated here as "bay," formed by the confluence of the Gurupura River, north of the city, and the Netravati River, south of it.
9. The province of Fars in Iran, on the Persian Gulf, is the historic cradle of Persian civilization.
10. In Shariʻa law, called here "the Shafʻai cult," a *qadi* is a judge whose roles include mediator, supervisor of public works, and guardian of orphans and other needful minors.
11. The port of Eli.
12. The ancient seaport of Quilon, now Kawlam, on the shore of the Laccadive Sea in the state of Kerala, India, was a trading center for a thousand years, going back to the Phoenicians, but was already in decline by the time Ibn Battuta visited. Nearby Calicut, also in Kerala, now the city of Kozhikode, was the major entrepôt on the west side of India in Ibn Battuta's time, until conquered by the Portuguese under Vasco da Gama in 1502.
13. Zaitun, an important stop on the Maritime Silk Road, is now the major commercial port of Quanzhou, on the Taiwan or Formosa Strait, in Fujian Province, People's Republic of China.
14. The inland city of Safed is now in northern Israel.
15. Cowry is the common name for certain marine gastropod mollusks—sea snails—within the taxonomical family Cypraeidae, which range in size, and inhabit shells that, when polished, have such a luster that the etymology of the word "porcelain" goes back to *porcellana*, the archaic Italian term for the cowry.

The Ocean: Bridge or Moat?

Benjamin W. Labaree

Does the Ocean facilitate travel or impede it? Is it a bridge or a moat? The classic essay on the issue comes from Benjamin Labaree, an eminent historian of maritime history, who founded the interdisciplinary and peripatetic Williams College–Mystic Seaport Maritime Studies Program in 1974. This essay, published as "The Atlantic Paradox," appeared in a collection to celebrate the career of Robert Greenhalgh Albion (1896–1983), a towering figure in maritime history, who was professor of oceanic history at Harvard University and founded the graduate-level Frank C. Munson Institute for American Maritime Studies at Mystic Seaport in 1955. Here are excerpts from Labaree's piece.

The Atlantic Ocean has played a paradoxical role throughout the history of North America. From the beginning it has been a barrier, a moat isolating the continent from Europe and Africa and giving specific meaning to the term "New World." Yet at the same time the Atlantic has been a bridge between the Old World and the New. Moat and bridge—two contradictory themes which together have woven into the American fabric a special theme—the maritime way of life. . . .

The Americans first affected by the fact of the Atlantic were of course the Indians. Lands into which they moved were vacant primarily because the Atlantic moat had prevented migrating Europeans from reaching America before them. More than that, the vastness of the ocean had isolated the Americas from the Old World in botanical and zoological terms as well. As Alfred W. Crosby has noted in his proactive work *The Columbian Exchange* [1976], even Columbus, who after all believed himself to be in another part of the known world, still remarked that "all of the trees were different from ours as day from night, and so the fruits, the herbage, the rocks, and all things." These variations proved very difficult to explain. It is not surprising that so many Europeans toyed with the heretical idea of multiple creation, a belief that both accepted and reinforced the concept that America had been from the beginning an island in the midst [of] an impassable sea. . . .

Behind their protective moat for thousands of years the native Americans developed their distinctive cultures free from the influence of Old World institutions—without feudalism, without manorial estates, without religious wars pitting one sect against another. The first Americans were in the view of Alfred Crosby "more different from the rest of mankind in 1492 than any other major group of humanity" except for Australian aborigines. Scientists have concluded from the preponderance of O-type blood among American natives that they also possessed a genetic uniformity unmatched by any other group of humans spread over such a large area.

But this cultural and biological isolation left Indians totally defenseless against European invaders who followed Columbus. No horse, no effective armor, no gunpowder. Far more significant, however, was the fact that the Atlantic moat had prevented the Indian from developing the defense he needed—immunity against major European diseases like influenza, measles, and especially smallpox. The New World was conquered not so much by the gun as by the microbe. To cite but a single example, within fifty years after the first Spaniards reached the island of Hispaniola its native population fell from about one million to around five hundred, almost entirely the result of devastating epidemics. . . .

For the English Puritans the remoteness of America created still another meaning, the idea of the New World as a sanctuary for God's chosen people. The fact that in English eyes North America was vacant strengthened the conviction that God had intended it to be their promised land, as Canaan had been for the Hebrews. While John Winthrop and other Puritan leaders watched what they considered the decay of English society during the 1620s, they concluded that the old country was marked for eternal punishment by a wrathful God. By the end of the decade a considerable number of Englishmen agreed with Winthrop that withdrawal to New England was their best hope for perpetuating God's purified church.

Immigration to America, however, meant a permanent commitment to the New World, for few people would cross the ocean merely to seek temporary refuge during hard times. Especially in the seventeenth century, when vessels were small and ocean passages a novelty, the idea of such a crossing terrified otherwise brave men and women. Those among the Puritans who may have minimized the sea's dangers before their crossing had good reason to alter their opinions afterward. Winthrop admitted to his wife in England that his fleet had "a longe and troublesome passage," although in his journal he wrote in more positive terms of his experience. Other accounts spoke of bad weather, illness among the passengers, and death to more than one-third of the cattle being transported. Some saw in the necessity of crossing the Atlantic a divine test of their faith, the successful fulfillment of which confirmed in their minds that God had indeed protected them en route. Winthrop, for instance, likened the undertaking to the crossing of the Red Sea by the Jews. Others referred to the North Atlantic as the Sinai desert. One observer concluded that God had made the passage stormy so that New England "might not be deserted by them at first entrance, which sure it would have been by many."

Another measure of [the] persistent impression made by the Atlantic crossing on New England Puritans was the continuing use of nautical references in the sermons of their ministers, most of whom had no contact with the sea before or after their own crossing. From his new pulpit deep in the Connecticut valley the Reverend Thomas Hooker warned his congregation of the "ship wrack" of heretical thought endangering its adherents "as a ship that is foundered in the midst of the main Ocean without sight of any succor, or hope of Relief." Such errors were "as violent and boisterous winds and raging waves, [which] force the Vessel out of the channel" and lift "it upon the shore and shelves where it set on ground, if not split." John Cotton cautioned those among his congregation who went to sea that their safety "lieth not on ropes or cables . . . , but in name and hand of the Lord." The minister of inland Concord likened the man who depended on good works for salvation to "a wave of the Sea, tossed and tumbled up and down and [who] finds no rest." "People will accept of a quiet harbor," suggested another minister, "rather than be afflicted with continual tossings in stormy seas." The Reverend Thomas Shepard suffered such a difficult crossing himself that the experience of having "stood many a week within six inches of death" marked his sermons for twenty years thereafter. The now familiar metaphor "ship of state" appeared in numerous Puritan political writings of the seventeenth century, to suggest that the political establishment was like a vessel that bore its people safely through the seas of anarchy. . . .

The crossing remained throughout the long era of immigration one of the most significant influences of the Atlantic on American life. Especially during the age of sail the course across the North Atlantic was fraught with danger. Prevailing winds and currents headed the westward voyagers much of the way; autumn hurricanes, winter gales, and springtime fogs limited the favorable season to a few short months. Even after steam replaced sail as the primary means of Atlantic navigation, the passage was sometimes dangerous and usually uncomfortable. But for the forty million immigrants to America an ocean crossing was the only way to reach the promised land. Few of them forgot the traumatic experience. Immigrant literature abounds with references to storms, shipwrecks, inedible food or none at all, arrogant captains and cruel sailors. The more impoverished the immigrant, the more helpless he was to protect himself and his family against these conditions. One vessel arrived in Philadelphia in 1805 with tales of the captain turning some of his passengers over to impressment gangs in England, then whipping and deliberately starving those who refused to go. In January 1868 the immigrant ship *Leibnitz* entered New York after a passage of about ten weeks, during which nearly 20 per cent of the original 554 German passengers on board had died. Upon inspection by the New York authorities the lower steerage was found to be so foul that their lanterns would hardly stay lighted. And for Africans forced to make the crossing on board the slave vessels of the eighteenth and early nineteenth centuries, conditions reached the very depths of inhumanity.

Year in and year out, disease, starvation, and shipwreck took a toll on from 10 to 20 per cent of all passengers, slave and free alike. Still more perished later from the effects of the ocean passage. In 1847, for instance, ten thousand immigrants died in Quebec shortly after their arrival in the New World. Death at sea was a frightening prospect. Wrote one Irishman:

> Ah, we thought we couldn't be worse off than we war [in Ireland] but now our sorrow we know the differ; for supposing we *war* dyin of starvation [at home], it would still not be dyin like a rotten sheep thrown into a pit; and the minit the breath is out of our bodies, flung into the sea to be eaten by them horrid sharks.

Toward the end of the nineteenth century some of the conditions had been ameliorated by the strict enforcement of sanitary regulations, but crossing the Atlantic still retained its grim moments. In 1879 Robert Louis Stevenson described what life was like in the steerage of a steamer during a storm on the North Atlantic:

> A more forlorn party, a more dismal circumstance, it would be hard to imagine. The motion here in the ship's nose was very violent; the uproar of the sea often overpoweringly loud. . . . The air was hot, but it struck a chill from its fetor. From all around in the dark bunks the scarcely human noises of the sick joined in a kind of farmyard chorus. . . . I heard a man run wild with terror, beseeching his friend for encouragement. "The ship is going down!" he cried with a thrill of agony. "The ship is going down."

. . . The impact of this experience on American life becomes even more apparent when one realizes that as recently as 1930 one out of every three American families included at least one parent who made the passage. Even now the third generation of the nation's last immigrant families vividly remembers grandparents telling of their trepidation at boarding the vessel that would take them across the ocean—an anxiety born not only from a fear of the sea itself but from the sense that they would probably never see their homeland again.

The differences between seaports and inland towns point to a more fundamental contrast that I have called the Atlantic paradox. We have already noted that for most Americans the Atlantic has been a moat cutting them off from the rest of the world. Paradoxically, however, for a small number of citizens living in seaports and other coastal communities, the sea has been a bridge to opportunity and to new and different experiences. Like most paradoxes, the juxtaposition of the Atlantic's roles as both moat and bridge has never been resolved for most Americans, nor is it ever likely to be. Yet it is precisely this paradox that has made the maritime way of life a subject of such enduring interest. *Because* millions of landbound Americans view the sea as an impassable moat, the lives of those who paradoxically use it as a bridge are that much more fascinating. For only in their lives can the Atlantic paradox find resolution.

The maritime way of life has intrigued landsmen for a number of reasons. For one, going to sea has always been an uncommon experience in this nation. Mariners, fishermen, and others who work on the sea have never comprised more than a small minority within the labor force. At the height of maritime enterprise in the mid-nineteenth century, fewer than 1 per cent of the work-force of ten millions went to sea for a living. Furthermore, seafaring has been one of the most dangerous of all occupations. Specific mortality figures are difficult to compile, but the experience of Gloucester's fishing fleet suggests the risks involved. In the twenty-two year period 1861–1882, almost two thousand Gloucester fishermen lost their lives at sea—an annual average of eighty-eight. This figure represents one fatality for every seventy fishermen of the port as of 1885. In contrast, another dangerous occupation, railroading, reached about half that rate at its worst, while still another high-risk endeavor, mining, proved even less devastating to its workers.

Yet another fascinating aspect of the mariners' way of life was how utterly different it was from anything experienced by those who worked ashore. The sailor committed himself totally to his vessel—he had no other existence for the duration of the voyage, no contact with family or friends, no privacy, no personal freedom. From the moment he stepped aboard he became part of a rigidly structured work-force under that most authoritarian of all bosses, the shipmaster. In contrast, a very large number of landsmen worked for themselves as farmers, small entrepreneurs, or skilled craftsmen, and self-employment remained a realizable dream for at least some of those who worked for others. And even the factory and other laborers had families and a degree of privacy. Except perhaps for the Gloucester doryman, virtually no mariner worked alone at sea; the success of his efforts indeed his very life depended on the skill and cooperation of others. This principle of interdependence was also reflected in the joint ownership of vessels and their cargoes, and in the public's awareness of their coming and going. In short, mariners were and remain rather special people among Americans because they constantly risk their lives to bridge the dreaded moat.

The sea voyage has always been an extremely popular theme in American literature and to a slightly lesser extent in American art as well. By reading about those who went down to the sea, landbound Americans could themselves vicariously bridge the moat. That basic ingredient of all good stories—conflict—is a dominant theme at sea and compels the reader to put himself

This twentieth-century photograph captures a four-masted lumber schooner, heavily laden with a deck load of wood, on the California coast. It has only a few feet of freeboard, but it will not sink: wooden boats carrying wooden cargo always float. Untitled photograph, Morton-Waters Co. Photographers, San Francisco, c. 1920s–1930s. Courtesy of the Roorda/Doyle Collection.

to the test, alongside the story's main characters. Furthermore, the sea is mysterious as well as dangerous, and the reader is transported into an environment totally different from the familiar land. "How I spurned that turnpike earth!" said Ishmael as he sailed for Nantucket, "that common highway all over dented with the marks of slavish heels and hoofs; and turned me to admire the magnanimity of the sea which will permit no records." [Herman Melville, *Moby-Dick*, chapter 1.]

The Atlantic, of course, is but one of the several seas upon which American mariners have sailed. While the Pacific and Indian oceans are more remote and are ringed by perhaps more exotic cultures, the Atlantic has borne the great majority of American coastal, fishing, and deepwater voyages. It remains the ocean that has most profoundly affected the history of America, both as a barrier separating us from our European past and as a bridge to that older world.

Surviving the Slave Ship

Olaudah Equiano

The enormity of the slave trade's depravity is difficult to confront, but to do so, one must turn to firsthand accounts, such as The Interesting Narrative of the Life of Olaudah Equiano, or Gustavus Vassa, the African. Written by Himself, *published in 1789. Born in what is now Sierra Leone, Equiano (1745–97), who was kidnapped as a child by slave raiders and carried to the coast in a bag, is among the most famous survivors of the Atlantic Ocean crossing known as the Middle Passage. An estimated 12 million African people endured the ordeal to reach the Americas over the course of centuries of suffering, while untold numbers died en route. The fact that Equiano wrote about the horrors he witnessed sets him apart, along with the fact that he went on to become a sailor, a free man, and an abolitionist. His unprecedented memoir and his personal activism helped abolitionism gain traction in the United Kingdom, leading to the Slave Trade Act of 1807, which outlawed the heinous practice.*

The first object which saluted my eyes when I arrived on the coast was the sea, and a slave ship, which was then riding at anchor, and waiting for its cargo. These filled me with astonishment, which was soon converted into terror when I was carried on board. I was immediately handled and tossed up to see if I were sound by some of the crew; and I was now persuaded that I had gotten into a world of bad spirits, and that they were going to kill me. Their complexions too differing so much from ours, their long hair, and the language they spoke, (which was very different from any I had ever heard) united to confirm me in this belief. Indeed such were the horrors of my views and fears at the moment, that, if ten thousand worlds had been my own, I would have freely parted with them all to have exchanged my condition with that of the meanest slave in my own country. When I looked round the ship too and saw a large furnace or copper boiling pot, and a multitude of black people of every description chained together, every one of their countenances expressing dejection and sorrow, I no longer doubted of my fate; and, quite overpowered with horror and anguish, I fell motionless on the deck and fainted. When I recovered a little I found some black people about me, who I believed were some of those who brought me on board, and had been receiving their pay; they talked to me in order to cheer me, but all in vain.

I asked them if we were not to be eaten by those white men with horrible looks, red faces, and loose hair. They told me I was not; and one of the crew brought me a small portion of spirituous liquor in a wine glass; but, being afraid of him, I would not take it out of his hand. One of the blacks therefore took it from him and gave it to me, and I took a little down my palate, which, instead of reviving me, as they thought it would, threw me into the greatest consternation at the strange feeling it produced, having never tasted any such liquor before.

Soon after this the blacks who brought me on board went off, and left me abandoned to despair. I now saw myself deprived of all chance of returning to my native country, or even the least glimpse of hope of gaining the shore, which I now considered as friendly; and I even wished for my former slavery in preference to my present situation, which was filled with horrors of every kind, still heightened by my ignorance of what I was to undergo. I was not long suffered to indulge my grief; I was soon put down under the decks, and there I received such a salutation in my nostrils as I had never experienced in my life: so that, with the loathsomeness of the stench, and crying together, I became so sick and low that I was not able to eat, nor had I the least desire to taste any thing. I now wished for the last friend, death, to relieve me; but soon, to my grief, two of the white men offered me eatables; and, on my refusing to eat, one of them held me fast by the hands, and laid me across I think the windlass, and tied my feet, while the other flogged me severely. I had never experienced any thing of this kind before; and although, not being used to the water, I naturally feared that element the first time I saw it, yet nevertheless, could I have got over the nettings, I would have jumped over the side, but I could not; and, besides, the crew used to watch us very closely who were not chained down to the decks, lest we should leap into the water: and I have seen some of these poor African prisoners most severely cut for attempting to do so, and hourly whipped for not eating. This indeed was often the case with myself. In a little time after, amongst the poor chained men, I found some of my own nation, which in a small degree gave ease to my mind. I inquired of these what was to be done with us; they gave me to understand we were to be carried to these white people's country to work for them. I then was a little revived, and thought, if it were no worse than working, my situation was not so desperate: but still I feared I should be put to death, the white people looked and acted, as I thought, in so savage a manner; for I had never seen among any people such instances of brutal cruelty; and this not only shewn towards us blacks, but also to some of the whites themselves. One white man in particular I saw, when we were permitted to be on deck, flogged so unmercifully with a large rope near the foremast, that he died in consequence of it; and they tossed him over the side as they would have done a brute. This made me fear these people the more; and I expected nothing less than to be treated in the same manner. I could not help

The Royal Navy's West Africa Squadron captured 1,600 slave ships and freed 150,000 of their enslaved passengers, effectively eliminating the transatlantic slave trade by 1860. But the slave trade continued in the Indian Ocean, controlled by Arab slave traders who transported captive Africans to India and the Middle East. Pirates cruised the same waters, attacking merchant ships. The HMS *Daphne*, a sloop of war, set out to suppress slave trading and piracy there in 1883. Over a span of ten days, the warship captured or destroyed eleven Arab dhows and three cutters, and rescued about 200 enslaved Africans. Engraver unknown, *The Cutter of HMS Daphne Capturing a Slave-Dhow off Brora*, in *London Illustrated News*, February 27, 1884. Courtesy of the Roorda/Doyle Collection.

expressing my fears and apprehensions to some of my countrymen: I asked them if these people had no country, but lived in this hollow place (the ship): they told me they did not, but came from a distant one. "Then," said I, "how comes it in all our country we never heard of them?" They told me because they lived so very far off. I then asked where were their women? had they any like themselves? I was told they had: "and why," said I, "do we not see them?" they answered, because they were left behind. I asked how the vessel could go? they told me they could not tell; but that there were cloths put upon the masts by the help of the ropes I saw, and then the vessel went on; and the white men had some spell or magic they put in the water when they liked in order to stop the vessel. I was exceedingly amazed at this account, and really thought they were spirits. I therefore wished much to be from amongst them, for I expected they would sacrifice me: but my wishes were vain; for we were so quartered that it was impossible for any of us to make our escape.

While we stayed on the coast I was mostly on deck; and one day, to my great astonishment, I saw one of these vessels coming in with the sails up. As soon as the whites saw it, they gave a great shout, at which we were amazed;

and the more so as the vessel appeared larger by approaching nearer. At last she came to an anchor in my sight, and when the anchor was let go I and my countrymen who saw it were lost in astonishment to observe the vessel stop; and were not convinced it was done by magic. Soon after this the other ship got her boats out, and they came on board of us, and the people of both ships seemed very glad to see each other. Several of the strangers also shook hands with us black people, and made motions with their hands, signifying I suppose we were to go to their country; but we did not understand them. At last, when the ship we were in had got in all her cargo, they made ready with many fearful noises, and we were all put under deck, so that we could not see how they managed the vessel.

But this disappointment was the least of my sorrow. The stench of the hold while we were on the coast was so intolerably loathsome, that it was dangerous to remain there for any time, and some of us had been permitted to stay on the deck for the fresh air; but now that the whole ship's cargo were confined together, it became absolutely pestilential. The closeness of the place, and the heat of the climate, added to the number in the ship, which was so crowded that each had scarcely room to turn himself, almost suffocated us. This produced copious perspirations, so that the air soon became unfit for respiration, from a variety of loathsome smells, and brought on a sickness among the slaves, of which many died, thus falling victims to the improvident avarice, as I may call it, of their purchasers. This wretched situation was again aggravated by the galling of the chains, now become insupportable; and the filth of the necessary tubs, into which the children often fell, and were almost suffocated. The shrieks of the women, and the groans of the dying, rendered the whole a scene of horror almost inconceivable. Happily perhaps for myself I was soon reduced so low here that it was thought necessary to keep me almost always on deck; and from my extreme youth I was not put in fetters. In this situation I expected every hour to share the fate of my companions, some of whom were almost daily brought upon deck at the point of death, which I began to hope would soon put an end to my miseries. Often did I think many of the inhabitants of the deep much more happy than myself. I envied them the freedom they enjoyed, and as often wished I could change my condition for theirs. Every circumstance I met with served only to render my state more painful, and heighten my apprehensions, and my opinion of the cruelty of the whites. One day they had taken a number of fishes; and when they had killed and satisfied themselves with as many as they thought fit, to our astonishment who were on the deck, rather than give any of them to us to eat as we expected, they tossed the remaining fish into the sea again, although we begged and prayed for some as well as we could, but in vain; and some of my countrymen, being pressed by hunger, took an opportunity, when they thought no one saw them, of trying to get a little privately; but they were discovered, and the attempt procured them some

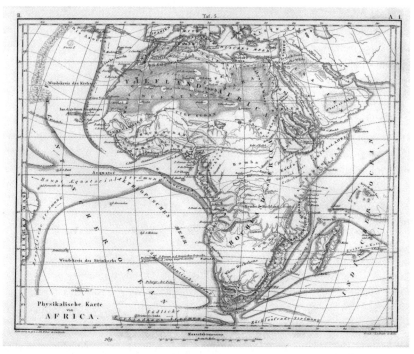

The Atlantic and Indian Ocean currents surrounding the continent of Africa were highways for many different kinds of trades, from the nefarious to the sacred. At the evil end of the spectrum was the transatlantic slave trade from Africa to the Americas, which lasted more than three centuries. Slave ships rode the South Atlantic Equatorial Current westward from the African coast, carrying their passengers to hellish futures. At the benevolent end of the spectrum is the hajj, the annual pilgrimage of Muslims to Mecca in Arabia, attracting untold millions of the faithful to embark on Ocean voyages to the land of the Prophet Muhammad. The watery route to reach Mecca was on the Indian Ocean North Equatorial Current. P. Weber, *Physikalische Karte von Afrika*, engraving designed by J. L. von Baehr, in *Atlas géographique, astronomique et historique, servant à l'intelligence de l'histoire ancienne, du moyen-âge et modern*, edited by Johann Georg Heck (Paris: Maillet, 1842), 269. Courtesy of the Roorda/Doyle Collection.

very severe floggings. One day, when we had a smooth sea and moderate wind, two of my wearied countrymen who were chained together (I was near them at the time), preferring death to such a life of misery, somehow made through the nettings and jumped into the sea: immediately another quite dejected fellow, who, on account of his illness, was suffered to be out of irons, also followed their example; and I believe many more would very soon have done the same if they had not been prevented by the ship's crew, who were instantly alarmed. Those of us that were the most active were in a moment put down under the deck, and there was such a noise and confusion amongst the people of the ship as I never heard before, to stop her, and get the boat out to go after the slaves. However two of the wretches were drowned, but they got the other, and afterwards flogged him unmercifully for thus attempting to prefer death to slavery. In this manner we continued to undergo more hardships than I can now relate, hardships which are inseparable from this accursed trade. Many a time we were near suffocation from the want of fresh air, which we were often without for whole days together. This, and the stench of the necessary tubs, carried off many.

During our passage I first saw flying fishes, which surprised me very much: they used frequently to fly across the ship, and many of them fell on the deck. I also now first saw the use of the quadrant; I had often with astonishment seen the mariners make observations with it, and I could not think what it meant. They at last took notice of my surprise; and one of them, willing to increase it, as well as to gratify my curiosity, made me one day look through it. The clouds appeared to me to be land, which disappeared as they passed along. This heightened my wonder; and I was now more persuaded than ever that I was in another world, and that every thing about me was magic. At last we came in sight of the island of Barbadoes, at which the whites on board gave a great shout, and made many signs of joy to us. We did not know what to think of this; but as the vessel drew nearer we plainly saw the harbour, and other ships of different kinds and sizes; and we soon anchored amongst them off Bridge Town. Many merchants and planters now came on board, though it was in the evening. They put us in separate parcels, and examined us attentively. They also made us jump, and pointed to the land, signifying we were to go there. We thought by this we should be eaten by these ugly men, as they appeared to us; and, when soon after we were all put down under the deck again, there was much dread and trembling among us, and nothing but bitter cries to be heard all the night from these apprehensions, insomuch that at last the white people got some old slaves from the land to pacify us. They told us we were not to be eaten, but to work, and were soon to go on land, where we should see many of our country people. This report eased us much; and sure enough, soon after we were landed, there came to us Africans of all languages.

Hating the China Trade

Frederick Law Olmsted

Frederick Law Olmsted (1822–1903), founder of modern landscape architecture, is best known for Manhattan's Central Park. Before he found his true calling, Olmsted tried out being a sailor, signing on at age twenty-one for a voyage to China, aboard an overloaded square-rigger named Ronaldson. *His 1843 letters to his parents and brother about that trip offer his eyewitness account of the China Trade. A catalyst of United States expansion into the Pacific, the China Trade took ships from New York to Whampoa Island, on the Pearl River near Canton, now Guangzhou, the only port in the Middle Kingdom open to foreign trade before the First Opium War (1839–42). Immediately prior to Olmsted's arrival there, the British Royal Navy had destroyed the Chinese fleet in that one-sided conflict, which led to the opening of six other ports in China, the cession of Hong Kong Island to the British Empire, the expansion of the China Trade, and the loss of Chinese sovereignty.*

If Olmsted's first experience on the Ocean had agreed with him, as was the case with so many of the writers represented in this volume, we might not have his many lovely public parks and campus quads to enjoy today. But he hated just about every minute of the ordeal and, after surviving his time at sea, and his four months in the miasmic environs of the Pearl River estuary, he devoted his life to the very terrestrial pursuit of landscape design. Parts of three hurried letters he wrote home follow here, the first sent from the Indonesian port of Anjer, on the island of Java; the second from Hong Kong; the third from Whampoa Island.

Ronaldson, Latitude 11°50' South, Longitude 106°10' East
August 6, 1843

Dear Parents,

Thinking it possible we may meet some homeward bound English or American Indiaman at Anjer, where we hope to arrive in course of a week, I take occasion to assure of our safety, for which I hope I am truly thankful to God who has preserved us through a long and perilous voyage. (It grieves me very much to tell you it has likewise been in many respects a disagreeable & unpleasant one, for I know [how] much it will pain you.)

We have not seen land since we left New York [on April 23] nor seen a human face out of our "floating (workhouse) castle." . . . Our barque was so loaded & crammed with freight that room for men [and] their effects—necessities of life, food, water, etc.—was scarce to be found. You will recollect remarking how our deck was lumbered up when we left. This has furnished us with a great deal of work, & in fact the loading her so deep & heavily has nearly proved our destruction altogether. Again, for want of room she was certain (say) as well provisioned as she might or I suppose otherwise would be. Instance, we were out of potatoes & all fresh fruit & put on an allowance of water the first month.

For nearly a month I suffered exceedingly from sea sickness. . . . I determined to be as contented as possible & although I think I have suffered as much or more as any one, I do think I am as & have generally been happier than any one else of the crew. But a more discontented, grumbling, growling set of mortals than our men are, you can not imagine. . . .

Left by seasickness so weak I could hardly stand, I was not able, had they wished, to do active duty for some time. I was set to filing rust, etc. . . . And we were in the latitude of the Cape of Good Hope [with] cold weather early in June, but we had thousands of miles of easting yet to make before we could double it, through the most boisterous seas. And now we began to experience the beautiful qualities of our wash tub. She is loaded so deep that most every sea washes over her. From that time to this we have not had a dry deck.

On fourth of July we were reefing topsails off "Cape of Good Hope." ("Off" some way to be sure for we were driven to near 40° South.) A few days after, we were shortening sail. I had furled the royal in the A.M.[1] In the P.M. Jacob (Braisted) was slapped off the lee fore-topgallant yard. (I was on the lee main-topgallant.) Most providentially he fell between the sail (outside) & the foretack. If he had wetted he would [have] been lost. (No stop.) Much to our surprise he has almost entirely recovered. The same night, we had the heaviest squall the captain or mate ever knew. The double reefed main-topsail was split to ribbons before we could close reef it, & the ship so nearly overwhelmed that they (officers) say if it had lasted with the same strength five minutes she would never have come up.[2] We were scudding under bare poles the rest of the gale.[3]

From that time to this we had a succession of gales, being under reefed topsails half the time. Allowance of water was three times shortened: the last off Cape, to three quarts including water for cooking—coffee often each one quart, dinner often another quart, so we have to go without it often.

9th August, "At Anchor off Anjer"

You cannot think how busy I have been since I wrote above. Having unexpected good run, we have not had time to prepare for port. All hands—most of the time getting up anchors &c, guns, gun gear, &c, &c, and continual shifting sails. Oh dear, I shouldn't think it possible to work so as I have.

About a month since, I had a stroke of Paralysis in my right arm, which for a time rendered it useless, but I have now recovered it sufficiently to go on duty again. Still, it [is] extremely weak & if it don't ache now! (dinner time.) The thumb & finger are yet numb, but not so much as they were.

It is hot here, dead calm & a burning sun.

We have had two or three on the sick list ever since we left.

All old Indiamen on board say this has been the worst voyage (for weather) they ever knew. . . .

September 5th, 1843, At anchor off Hong Kong

Dear Parents,

We arrived at this port day before yesterday, one hundred and thirty-two days from New York. . . .

We had a most remarkable passage through the "straits."[4] We had anticipated a very hard and dangerous time. There is a very beautiful clipper built English vessel now lying by us which was over three weeks getting through, anchoring every night. I think we were through in three *days*, and did not anchor once. The second night we were becalmed and all hands kept up some time, expecting to anchor. The magazine was opened, guns loaded with grape[shot], &c, for you know this sea ("Java Sea") is infested with Malay pirates, who *very* often attack vessels. But just as we were about to drop the kedge [anchor], a light breeze sprung up. It soon became strong & so favorable that we could lay our course. Sunday (twelfth, I think) P.M. land was made right ahead, and at dark we were almost enclosed by it. Before midnight we passed "Jasper" Island at the head of the ("Jasper" or "Gaspar") Straits & were in the China Sea.

The next morning I made three sail from the royal masthead. Before night we were near enough to see that they were "Malay Proas."[5] Our course was altered a little & next morning they were out of sight. We were now standing before the regular "monsoons"[6]—which gave us plenty of work. Thus at daylight we are "right before it" carrying lower, topmast, topgallant and *royal* stud'n sails on both sides.[7]

A dark cloud is seen rising on our larboard bow. Those that have a chance perhaps put on an oil[skin] jacket. The cloud rises small, or rather

The old China Trade depended on Macao. Foreign merchants stopped at the Portuguese island for permission to enter the Pearl River and reach Canton (Guangzhou), the only open port. Today, a new city on the mainland, Zhuhai (Pearl of the Sea) overshadows Macao. It is one of the Special Economic Zones accelerating China's economic rise since 1979. Goods are loaded in containerships made in and owned by China, and sailed by Chinese crews—a reversal of the system that Frederick Law Olmsted knew. A. H. Payne, *Macao*, steel engraving (London: E. T. Brain and Co., c. 1860s). Courtesy of the Roorda/Doyle Collection.

narrow, but long. Likely, we see a distant water spout (we *did* notice several.) The wind is perhaps subsiding. All hands on deck busy washing down, feeding the fowls, &c, & paying no attention to the weather, till: "Stand by fore-royal halyards!" Then we all knock off work & soon one is standing by the main royal & to'gallant & fore royal & to'gallant halyards.[8]

The squall strikes us. Everyone is wet through & those not "standing by" crowd under the lee of the rail. The old man [captain] comes out on deck having noticed the barometer. "Clup fry'l!" ("Clew up the fore royal.") "Haul down flying jib." "Clew up main-royal." "Lay aloft you b'ys & furl 'em." . . .

In ten or fifteen minutes (from commencement) the squall breaks. "Hoist the main-to'g'l't sail!" then the fore. The royals are loosed, sheeted home & hoisted up, flying jib set & gaff topsail. Then we have a bracing spell—or rather a squaring—for as the squall passes, the wind is coming on her quarter again; & one after another, the studdingsails are set.

Oh! This is the weather to kill sailors.

To John Hull Olmsted
Ronaldson, Whampoa Beach
September 28th, 1843

Dear Brother,

. . . Well, how do you like the *sea?* The sea. On the whole, I believe if I had been in some ships, with some officers, & some crews, & those not *very* uncommon and enjoyed the health I might have expected, I should not have been *agreeably* disappointed. *But*—my dear brother, I was not well when I came on board, I suffered most severely from seasickness, in the first place, and since the first of April, say, I don't think I have enjoyed twenty four hours of as good health *and strength* as for years previously. Though I had no regular severe illness, and was not off duty before our arrival, but very little, yet I don't think I ever felt the strength of spirit, that I had a year since. In the severe weather I had a pretty bad fall on the spars, with a heavy coil of manila [rope] to settle in & so on to the scuppers—which exposure & wet *rheumatized*—but I never lost a watch by it, though you may be sure that for some days I could not "fly round" aloft so handy as usual. This was a bore, but my general health in the worst weather was better than at any other time. Why so? Well I suppose—I'm pretty sure—it was because we had at that time "watch and watch."[9] If any one you know wishes to try his fortune on the deep, recommend his first enquiry when looking for a ship to be in regard to the time he is likely to have to rest and take care of himself.

Notes

1. The royals are the highest sails on the ship, and the topgallants are just below them, more than 100 feet above the deck. A tack is a corner of a sail, the farthest out on the narrow spars that hold the sails, making the tack the most perilous place to be for a sailor trying to furl them.
2. To reef is to partially furl a sail, using ropes sewn into the sail for that purpose, leaving less canvas to catch the wind. There are often three rows of these ropes, called reef points, on a large sail, allowing the crew to reduce canvas in three stages: reefed, double-reefed, and close-reefed.
3. With no sails set on any of the masts, a very unusual and extreme state for a vessel under sail. At the very least, a small trysail to keep the ship's bow into the wind would be set, if possible. The fact that it was impossible to set even such a sail indicates the severity of the squall.
4. The Gaspar Strait between the islands of Sumatra and Java, which separates the Indian Ocean and the Pacific Ocean's China Sea, has long been notorious for piracy, down to the present day.
5. Malaysian and Indonesian pirates alike favored *proas*, outrigger canoes about 30 feet long, sometimes armed with a long cannon in the bow.
6. Seasonal winds blowing across the Indian Ocean from the southwest, perfect for the purposes of sailing ships engaged in the China Trade.

7. Studding sails were set from small wooden booms, rigged as extensions on the ends of the yards, in order to display more canvas and catch more wind. Rigging the booms and setting these sails meant hard, dangerous work for the sailors. Olmsted wrote the next section of the letter in the technical language of sail handling, which people of his day spoke fluently, even those who were not sailors, but which is inscrutable to the average modern reader. In it, he described the constant, strenuous labor of hauling lines to adjust for minor changes in the wind, with the massive sail space afforded by having so many "stud'n sails deployed.

8. Halyards haul sails up or down from yards—haul yards—so to stand by them (get ready near them) means they are preparing to reduce sail quickly, by heaving the halyards and "clewing up" the sails.

9. A watch was a four-hour period of duty, and "watch and watch" meant serving four hours on, four hours off, around the clock, punctuated by calls of "All hands on deck!" to handle sail. Despite being a prescription for sleep deprivation, "standing watch and watch" was the norm on sailing ships well into the twentieth century.

About All Kinds of Ships

Mark Twain

Mark Twain (1835–1910) made several Ocean passages in his life.[1] His first was from San Francisco to Hawai'i in 1866, returning the following year aboard a square-rigged sailing ship that was becalmed for three weeks on the way. Later, he traveled to Europe through a North Atlantic storm on a noisy, nauseating, coal-powered steamship of the pioneering Cunard Line, which rescued survivors from the wreck of another vessel en route. Finally, he transited around the world on a quiet, comfortable German Lloyd Line diesel steamship that was state of the art for the 1890s. He reflected on his life experience on the Ocean in a delightful, comprehensive, but little-known essay called "About All Kinds of Ships" (1893). His humorous and remarkably perceptive observations include a description of the new technology of using water as ballast. As shall be seen, ballast water became the primary substrate for the deleterious transfer of invasive species around the globe, which threatens the balance of ecosystems worldwide.

The Modern Steamer and the Obsolete Steamer

We are victims of one common superstition—the superstition that we realize the changes that are daily taking place in the world because we read about them and know what they are. I should not have supposed that the modern ship could be a surprise to me, but it is. It seems to be as much of a surprise to me as it could have been if I had never read anything about it. I walk about this great vessel, the *Havel*, as she plows her way through the Atlantic, and every detail that comes under my eye brings up the miniature counterpart of it as it existed in the little ships I crossed the ocean in, fourteen, seventeen, eighteen, and twenty years ago.

In the *Havel* one can be in several respects more comfortable than he can be in the best hotels on the continent of Europe. For instance, she has several bath rooms, and they are as convenient and as nicely equipped as the bath rooms in a fine private house in America; whereas in the hotels of the continent one bath room is considered sufficient, and it is generally shabby and located in some out of the way corner of the house; moreover, you need to give notice so long beforehand that you get over wanting a bath by the time you get it. In the hotels there are a good many different kinds of noises, and they spoil sleep; in my room in the ship I hear no sounds. In the hotels they usually shut off the electric light at midnight; in the ship one may burn it in one's room all night.

In the steamer *Batavia*, twenty years ago, one candle, set in the bulkhead between two state-rooms, was there to light both rooms, but did not light either of them. It was extinguished at 11 at night, and so were all the saloon lamps except one or two, which were left burning to help the passenger see how to break his neck trying to get around in the dark. The passengers sat at table on long benches made of the hardest kind of wood; in the *Havel* one sits on a swivel chair with a cushioned back to it. In those old times the dinner bill of fare was always the same: a pint of some simple, homely soup or other, boiled codfish and potatoes, slab of boiled beef, stewed prunes for dessert— on Sundays "dog in a blanket," on Thursdays "plum duff." In the modern ship the menu is choice and elaborate, and is changed daily. In the old times dinner was a sad occasion; in our day a concealed orchestra enlivens it with charming music. In the old days the decks were always wet, in our day they are usually dry, for the promenade-deck is roofed over, and the sea seldom comes aboard. In a moderately disturbed sea, in the old days, a landsman could hardly keep his legs, but in such a sea in our day, the decks are as level as a table. In the old days the inside of a ship was the plainest and barrenest thing, and the most dismal and uncomfortable that ingenuity could devise; the modern ship is a marvel of rich and costly decoration and sumptuous appointment, and is equipped with every comfort and convenience that money can buy. The old ships had no place of assembly but the dining-room, the new ones have several spacious and beautiful drawing-rooms. The old ships offered the passenger no choice to smoke except in the place that was called the "fiddle." It was a repulsive den made of rough boards (full of cracks) and its office was to protect the main hatch. It was grimy and dirty; there were no seats; the only light was a lamp of the rancid-oil-and-rag kind; the place was very cold, and never dry, for the seas broke in through the cracks every little while and drenched the cavern thoroughly. In the modern ship there are three or four large smoking-rooms, and they have card tables and cushioned sofas, and are heated by steam and lighted by electricity. There are few European hotels with such smoking-rooms.

The former ships were built of wood, and had two or three water-tight compartments in the hold with doors in them which were often left open, particularly when the ship was going to hit a rock. The modern leviathan is built of steel, and the water-tight bulkheads have no doors in them; they divide the ship into nine or ten water-tight compartments and endow her with as many lives as a cat. Their complete efficiency was established by the happy results following the memorable accident to the *City of Paris* a year or two ago.[2]

One curious thing which is at once noticeable in the great modern ship is the absence of the hubbub, clatter, rush of feet, roaring of orders. That is all gone by. The elaborate maneuvers necessary in working the vessel into her dock are conducted without sound; one sees nothing of the processes, hears no commands. A Sabbath stillness and solemnity reign, in place of the turmoil and racket of the earlier days. The modern ship has a spacious bridge fenced chin-high with sail-cloth and floored with wooden gratings; and this bridge, with its fenced fore-and-aft annexes, could accommodate a seated audience of a hundred and fifty men. There are three steering equipments, each competent if the other should break. From the bridge the ship is steered, and also handled. The handling is not done by shout or whistle, but by signaling with patent automatic gongs. There are three tell-tales, with plainly lettered dials—for steering, handling the engines, and for communicating orders to the invisible mates who are conducting the landing of the ship or casting off. The officer who is astern is out of sight and too far away to hear trumpet calls; but the gongs near him tell him to haul in, pay out, make fast, let go, and so on; he hears, but the passengers do not, and so the ship seems to land herself without human help.

This great bridge is thirty or forty feet above the water, but the sea climbs up there sometimes; so there is another bridge twelve or fifteen feet higher still, for use in these emergencies. The force of water is a strange thing. It slips between one's fingers like air, but upon occasion it acts like a solid body and will bend a thin iron rod. In the *Havel* it has splintered a heavy oaken rail into broom-straws instead of merely breaking it in two as would have been the seemingly natural thing for it to do. At the time of the awful Johnstown disaster, according to the testimony of several witnesses, rocks were carried some distance on the surface of the stupendous torrent; and at St. Helena, many years ago, a vast sea-wave carried a battery of cannon forty feet up a steep slope and deposited the guns there in a row. But the water has done a still stranger thing, and it is one which is credibly vouched for. A marlin-spike is an implement about a foot long with tapers from its butt to the other extremity and ends in a sharp point. It is made of iron and is heavy. A wave came aboard a ship in a storm and raged aft, breast high, carrying a marlin-spike point-first with it, and with such lightning-like swiftness and force as to drive it three or four inches into a sailor's body and kill him.

In all ways the ocean greyhound of to-day is imposing and impressive to one who carries in his head no ship-pictures of a recent date. In bulk she comes near to rivaling the Ark; yet this monstrous mass of steel is driven five hundred miles through the waves in twenty-four hours. I remember the brag run of a steamer which I traveled in once on the Pacific—it was two hundred and nine miles in twenty-four hours; a year or so later I was a passenger in the excursion-tub *Quaker City*, and on one occasion in a level and glassy sea, it was claimed that she reeled off two hundred and eleven miles between noon

The transition from sail to steam eliminated the mortal danger of becoming becalmed on the Ocean. When they did not prove deadly, weeks with no wind were deathly boring, as Mark Twain kidded about in "About All Kinds of Ships." This photograph from the early twentieth century shows three square-rigged ships, probably whalers, with sails hanging limply. Photographer unknown, *Becalmed*, rotary photographic plate postcard, c. 1903–8. Courtesy of the Roorda/Doyle Collection.

and noon, but it was probably a campaign lie. That little steamer had seventy passengers, and a crew of forty men, and seemed a good deal of a bee-hive. But in this present ship we are living in a sort of solitude, these soft summer days, with sometimes a hundred passengers scattered about the spacious distances, and sometimes nobody in sight at all; yet, hidden in the vessel's bulk, there are (including crew), near eleven hundred people.

The stealthiest lines in the literature of the sea are these:

"Britannia needs no bulwark, no towers along the steep—

Her march is o'er the mountain wave, her home is on the deep!"

There it is. In those old times the little ships climbed over the waves and wallowed down into the trough on the other side; the giant ship of our day does not climb over the waves, but crushes her way through them. Her formidable weight and mass and impetus give her mastery over any but extraordinary storm-waves.

The ingenuity of man! I mean in this passing generation. To-day I found in the chart-room a frame of removable wooden slats on the wall, and on the slats was painted uninforming information like this:

Trim Tank. . . . . Empty
Double-Bottom No. 1. . . . Full
Double-Bottom No. 2. . . . Full
Double-Bottom No. 3. . . . Full
Double-Bottom No. 4. . . . Full

While I was trying to think out what kind of a game this might be and how a stranger might best go to work to beat it, a sailor came in an and pulled out the "Empty" end of the first slat and put it back with its reverse side to the front, marked "Full." He made some other change, I did not notice what. The slat-frame was soon explained. Its function was to indicate how the ballast in the ship was distributed. The striking thing was, that the ballast was water. I did not know that a ship had ever been ballasted with water. I merely read, some time or other, that such an experiment was to be tried. But that is the modern way: between the experimental trial of a new thing and its adoption, there is no wasted time, if the trial proves its value.

On the wall, near the slat-frame, there was an outline drawing of the ship, and this betrayed the fact that the vessel has twenty-two considerable lakes of water in her. These lakes are in her bottom; they are imprisoned between her real bottom and a false bottom. They are separated from each other, thwartships, by water-tight bulkheads, and separated down the middle by a bulkhead running from the bow four-fifths of the way to the stern. It is a chain of lakes four hundred feet long and five to seven feet deep. Fourteen of the lakes contain fresh water brought from shore, and the aggregate weight of it is four hundred tons. The rest of the lakes contain salt water—six hundred and eighteen tons. Upwards of a thousand tons of water, altogether.

Think how handy this ballast is. The ship leaves port with the lakes all full. As she lightens forward through consumption of coal, she loses trim—her head rises, her stern sinks down. Then they spill one of the sternward lakes into the sea, and the trim is restored. This can be repeated right along as occasion may require. Also, a lake at one end of the ship can be moved to the other end by pipes and steam pumps. When the sailor changed the slat-frame to-day, he was posting a transference of that kind. The seas had been increasing, and the vessel's head needed more weighting, to keep it from rising on the waves instead of plowing through them; therefore, twenty-five tons of water had been transferred to the bow from a lake situated well toward the stern.

A water compartment is kept either full or empty. The body of water must be compact, so that it cannot slosh around. A shifting ballast would not do, of course.

The modern ship is full of beautiful ingenuities, but it seems to me that this one is the king. I would rather be the originator of that idea than of any of the others. Perhaps the trim of a ship was never perfectly ordered and preserved until now. A vessel out of trim will not steer, her speed is maimed, she strains and labors in the seas. Poor creature, for six thousand years she has had no comfort until these latest days. For six thousand years she swam through the best and cheapest ballast in the world, the only perfect ballast, but she couldn't tell her master and he had not the wit to find it out for himself. It is odd to reflect that there is nearly as much water inside this ship as there is outside, yet there is no danger. . . .

It can be shown that the differences between that ship and the one I am writing these historical contributions in, are in several respects remarkable. Take the matter of decoration, for instance. I have been looking around again, yesterday and today, and have noted several details which I conceive to have been absent from Columbus's ship, or at least slurred over and not elaborated and perfected. I observe state-room doors three inches thick, of solid oak polished. I note companionway vestibules with walls, doors and ceilings paneled in polished hard woods, some light, some dark, all dainty and delicate joiner-work, and yet every joint compact and tight; with beautiful pictures inserted, composed of blue tiles—some of the pictures containing as many as sixty tiles—and the joinings of those tiles perfect. These are daring experiments. One would have said that the first time the ship went straining and laboring through a storm-tumbled sea those tiles would gape apart and drop out. That they have not done so is evidence that the joiner's art has advanced a good deal since the days when ships were so shaky that when a giant sea gave them a wrench the doors came unbolted. I find the walls of the dining-saloon upholstered with mellow pictures wrought in tapestry, and the ceiling aglow with pictures done in oil. In other places of assembly I find great panels filled with embossed Spanish leather, the figures rich with gilding and bronze. Everywhere I find sumptuous masses of color—color, color, color—color all about, color of every shade and tint and variety; and as a result, the ship is bright and cheery to the eye, and this cheeriness invades one's spirit and contents it. To fully appreciate the force and spiritual value of this radiant and opulent dream of color, one must stand outside at night in the pitch dark and the rain, and look through a port, and observe it in the lavish splendor of the electric lights. The old-time ships were dull, plain, graceless, gloomy, and horribly depressing. They compelled the blues; one could not escape the blues in them. The modern idea is right: to surround the passenger with conveniences, luxuries, and abundance of inspiring color. As a result, the ship is the pleasantest place one can be in, except, perhaps, one's home.

A Vanished Sentiment

One thing is gone, to return no more forever—the romance of the sea. Soft sentimentality about the sea has retired from the activities of this life, and is but a memory of the past, already remote and much faded. But within the recollection of men still living, it was in the breast of every individual; and the further any individual lived from salt water the more of it he kept in stock. It was as pervasive, as universal, as the atmosphere itself. The mere mention of the sea, the romantic sea, would make any company of people sentimental and mawkish at once. The great majority of the songs that were sung by the people of the back settlements had the melancholy wanderer for subject and his mouthings about the sea for refrain. Picnic parties paddling down a creek in a canoe when the twilight shadows were gathering, always sang

> Homeward bound, homeward bound
> From a foreign shore;

and this was also a favorite in the West with the passengers on sternwheel steamboats. There was another—

> My boat is by the shore
>   And my bark is on the sea,
> But before I go, Tom Moore,
>   Here's a double health to thee.

And this one, also—

> O, pilot, 'tis a fearful night,
> There's danger on the deep.

And this—

> A life on the ocean wave
>   And a home on the rolling deep,
> Where the scattered waters rave
>   And the winds their revels keep!

And this—

> A wet sheet and a flowing sea,
> And a wind that follows fair.

And this—

> My foot is on my gallant deck,
> Once more the rover is free!

These twelve women enjoy each other's company aboard a passenger ship on a sunny, windy day in March 1946. It is a spirited example of a popular photographic genre: group shots of happy people at sea. Several of them wear the uniform of the US Navy female auxiliary corps, called the WAVES (Women Accepted for Volunteer Emergency Service). Photographer unknown, 1946. Courtesy of the Roorda/Doyle Collection.

And the "Larboard Watch"—the person referred to below is at the masthead, or somewhere up there—

O, who can tell what joy he feels,
As o'er the foam his vessel reels,
And his tired eyelids slumb'ring fall,
He rouses at the welcome call
   Of "Larboard watch—ahoy!"

Yes, and there was forever and always some jackass-voiced person braying out—

Rocked in the cradle of the deep,
I lay me down in peace to sleep!

Other favorites had these suggestive titles: "The Storm at Sea"; "The Bird at Sea"; "The Sailor Boy's Dream"; "The Captive Pirate's Lament"; "We are far from Home on the Stormy Main"—and so on, and so on, the list is endless. Everybody on a farm lived chiefly amid the dangers of the deep in those days, in fancy.

But all that is gone, now. Not a vestige of it is left. The iron-clad, with her unsentimental aspect and frigid attention to business, banished romance from the war-marine, and the unsentimental steamer has banished it from the commercial marine. The dangers and uncertainties which made sea life romantic have disappeared and carried the poetic element along with them. In our day the passengers never sing sea-songs on board a ship, and the band never plays them. Pathetic songs about the wanderer in strange lands far from home, once so popular and contributing such fire and color to the imagination by reason of the rarity of that kind of wanderer, have lost their charm and fallen silent, because everybody is a wanderer in the far lands now, and the interest in that detail is dead. Nobody is worried about the wanderer; there are no perils of the sea for him, there are no uncertainties. He is safer in the ship than he would probably be at home, for there he is always liable to have to attend some friend's funeral and stand over the grave in the sleet, bareheaded—and that means pneumonia for him, if he gets his deserts; and the uncertainties of his voyage are reduced to whether he will arrive on the other side in the appointed afternoon, or have to wait till morning.

Notes

1. Eric Paul Roorda, *Twain At Sea: The Maritime Writings of Samuel Langhorne Clemens* (Hanover, NH: University Press of New England, 2018).
2. The ss *City of Paris* of the British Inman Line was launched in 1889 and set the record for fastest Atlantic Ocean crossing on its second voyage. In March 1890, en route to Liverpool, its propeller shaft broke, piercing the hull, but it did not sink and was towed to port.

Loving Cape Horn

Irving Johnson

The last bastion of commercial transportation under sail was the trade in bulk car-goes of Australian wheat and Chilean nitrates around Cape Horn, which lasted into the 1930s. The most vivid record remaining of this last vestige of the Great Age of Sail comes from Captain Irving Johnson (1905–91), who was born far from the Ocean, in Hadley, the Breadbasket of Massachusetts, but dreamed of going to sea. The farm boy avidly read the sea literature of Joseph Conrad and Jack London, and he would climb a utility pole that had rotted at the base, imagining it was a ship's mast during a storm, and sway back and forth on it. Determined to be prepared for anything when he had the chance to go aloft for real, he did headstands at the top of the unsteady pole! He got to sea and went around Cape Horn in 1929 aboard Peking, *one of the last huge, square-rigged windjammers, which is now a museum ship at South Street Seaport in New York. Johnson brought along a rudimentary movie camera, which he took with him everywhere, even going aloft with it during storms to film them. His unique footage proves that he witnessed two tremendous storms while rounding Cape Horn, which he described in his book* Round the Horn in a Square Rigger *(1932). Irving Johnson and his wife, Electa, went on to become revered figures in the sailing world. They circumnavigated the globe seven times with coeducational student crews aboard two brigs, both named* Yankee, *voyages that they wrote books about, and that* National Geographic *magazine covered closely, helping to establish sail training as an educational genre.*

Two Cape Horn Rip-Snorters

From latitude fifty on the east of South America to latitude fifty on the West is called "the Horn," and mariners always figure from these points the number of days around. The distance as we planned to sail, going south of the Strait of Magellan and well away from the coast, was nearly a thousand miles. We crossed latitude fifty in a dead calm without a ripple on the water.

Many giant white jelly fish were adrift that would each fill a five bushel basket, and that had tails fifteen feet long. I spent four hours on Monday, February 3rd, on the royal looking down into the clear, quiet water at the schools of jelly-fish, some of them blobs of pulp, white, yellow, or brown, and some of them like long, filmy rubber ropes.[1]

Cape Horn winds continued pretty tame in the first two days after we crossed the boundary, but I told the captain and Charlie at dinner that I wasn't going to give up wishing for a real rip-snorter before we got around.[2]

The water we were sailing through the next day looked as black as ink, although perfectly clear and clean. Rain squalls hovered around, and there was much pulling and hauling, and taking in and setting of sails because of the changeable winds. One riotous squall caught us with every stitch of canvas set. Six men heaved at the steering wheel to luff her before she should go over bottom side up.[3] Sails and yards came down on the run, but the scud soon passed.[4] In one calm spell the waves made a great slapping and plopping noise by jumping up two or three feet in points like pyramids. It gave me a queer feeling with other things so quiet, even though I knew perfectly well that it was caused simply by the meeting of opposing currents.

Thursday, about sixty miles east of Staten Island, the captain and mate got together and made a delicate wind-direction indicator of a feather, so they could tell where the wind was coming from. What a queer occupation off Cape Horn, the reputed home of all sorts of violent storms! It was colder now than at any time in the North Sea. . . .

Sunday, the 9th, the wish that I first made at the Giants Causeway came true.[5] A real storm got started that morning and gathered headway all day. "Mine eyes have seen the glory of the coming of the *wind*," but what I saw while the storm lasted can't be told in words. The log book showed a number twelve hurricane, long before the worst came. A tremendous sea had worked up that gave a show worth the whole trip. We were hove to and shortened down to the lower tops'ls and two stays'ls.

The blowing spray and flying spume turned the surface of the ocean white, except for faint grayish streaks, and the water around the ship as far away as I could see had the appearance of being blanketed with snow. Meanwhile the wind was roaring and screeching through the rigging with sounds as if a lot of savage beasts were fighting, threatening, and clawing up there.[6]

I always had wanted to see a big, heavy sail blow away in a hurricane, and now came my chance. The steel wires three quarters of an inch in diameter around the edge of the main lower tops'l broke with a noise that made me think some one had shot off a cannon. The canvas was the very heaviest made, and brand new, so it didn't all go at once, but banged and snapped making a racket like a machine gun. If anyone had told me canvas could make such a noise I would have said, "Tell that to the marines." . . .

At times water blew along the surface of the sea like a fog, and the wind was so fierce it couldn't be faced. While the captain and I were eating dinner there was such a jarring crash that felt and sounded like hitting a rock. The captain jumped up exclaiming, "Mine Gott! Ist der mast gone?"

On deck we found that a terrific wave had struck the port side of the ship, and the captain ordered the carpenter to sound the wells to see if she were leaking. In ten or fifteen minutes the carpenter returned and reported, "No water in the wells."

However, further inspection revealed that a whole section of the side of the ship, twenty feet across, was bent in, steel plates, frames, and all. Yet the only places that water was coming through the sides was where the sea had broken the glass in some portholes. The skipper said he never heard of a wave bending the side of such a ship before.

I thought I would go up to the main royal yard to see if I could hold on under such conditions. . . .

When I had gone about to the height of the upper tops'l yard, a sea smashed against the windward side of the ship and sent spray over my head. It takes some force to shoot water up that high against such a gale. Meanwhile the sun occasionally shone down on all the confusion and violence and made dainty rainbows in the flying scud.

As I neared the top of the mast I would stop whenever the ship rolled to windward, because I had such difficulty in pulling my feet back against the wind and getting them up to the next ratline. The air rushed past me at about one hundred and fifty miles an hour, making a horrible screeching howl such as I never had heard before.

The top of the mast swung in an arc fully three hundred feet at some of the rolls, and these rolls of forty-five degrees often were made in eleven seconds. . . .

I had demonstrated to myself that it was possible to hold on, and I went back down, got my movie camera, and returned to the mast-top. After tangling my arms and legs up in the ratlines to keep from blowing away, I took movies of the Cape Horn gray backs that went sweeping across the deck of the ship a hundred and seventy-five feet below me. That downlook onto the churning sea as it battered the old *Peking* and kept filling her decks with its writhing waters, was the grandest sight I ever had looked upon.

The water got into the ship everywhere, except the cargo hold, and a dozen boys were kept busy bailing out. Most of the sailors slept on the spare sails in the sail locker because their foc'sle was so filled with water. Such big seas came aboard that they couldn't open the foc'sle door, and the only way they could enter was by the skylight.

To go into the foc'sle half full of water during such a storm, with sea chests, bunk boards, and suit cases banging and crashing at each roll, was just looking for death. Down below deck the ship creaked as if she might break up at any minute.

In the night the steering cable that led to the midships wheel broke. The after wheel was stuck, and the spanker had to be set to keep the vessel up into the wind until the cable was fixed.[7]

At noon on Monday we had been driven back eighty-four miles since the previous noon. We took down what was left of the lower tops'l that blew out and set another in its place. . . .

One thing we lost in the storm was our shark's tail at the tip of the boom. "That was our fair weather charm," I said to Charlie, "and it's gone." . . .

A shark's tail is tough, and ours had been firmly spiked on. Besides, it was fifty feet above the water level, yet some wave must have reached it and given it an awful wallop, or it couldn't have been torn loose.

Monday night we had eight sails set, as there was far less wind and waves were smaller. Nevertheless there was wind enough to blow out the mizzen topmast stays'l when we tried to set it. All the crew were kept busy repairing the damage done by the storm. There was a snow-squall in the afternoon, and when it was over we had a snowball fight. Cape Horn snow doesn't fall in flakes, but in little pellets like hail. It is known as Cape Horn sugar. The thermometer registered a little above freezing, which is as cold as the dickens at sea.

We saw Cape Horn Tuesday night. It rises abruptly to a height of fourteen hundred feet so it can be seen forty miles on a clear day. We were lucky to see it at all, for most ships go around the Horn without getting a sight of land. This was the first we had seen since passing the Isle of Wight about two months before.

The wind was light and it shifted every hour or so. That kept us hauling sails up and down and bracing yards half the time. . . . Each watch that was off duty did what it could to clear up the mess the sea had made of their foc'sle.

There were head winds nearly all the time for several days, so that on Wednesday we were only ten miles from where we had been Sunday noon. The nights were very short and we had gone south so far that it was not really dark even at midnight. . . .

A peach of a storm came up during the night. It was even better than the one on Sunday! According to the captain, the wind scarcely ever blows any harder. Summer storms, he claimed, were shorter, but stronger, than those in winter. I'd swear to it that some of the waves looped up to a height well over the fifty feet which it is said scientific measurements prove to [be] the limit. We everlastingly rolled, jumped, wallowed, and dived.

The creakings of the ship under us at such a time conveyed a sense of suffering—as if she were in pain and anguish. To hear them after I had gotten into my bunk, made me feel like drawing the bedclothes over my head. I wanted to shut out not only those dismal creakings below deck, but the frightful wailing and snarling that came to my ears from the rigging.

In general, however, I had a good time getting thrills out of the storms. Every walloping big wave was a joy—I welcomed it. The wildness of the winds was glorious. There was charm in all the sights and sounds, and in the ever-varying motions of the vessel, the waves, and the clouds. A few weeks more battling in those savage waters at the Horn would have suited me.

But for the crew this was a dreary time of hardship. They were sore and glum, and the glory of the storms was lost on them. So far as my feeling was concerned the only time I found a little dull was between storms. . . .

There was nothing warm for breakfast, and only soup for dinner, but I couldn't blame the cooks. What surprised me was that they were able to make soup. Salt water was everywhere inside of the ship's living quarters. I stayed out on deck in the cold hour after hour just to watch the waves. No two were alike, and I always was wondering what the next one would do. It was while there that I saw the maintopmast stays'l leave us for parts unknown; and every half hour or so a big sea came aboard. Then, whatever else we did, our chief job was holding on.

Some months later we learned that when the *Peking* was going back round the Horn, one of these big waves washed five men overboard, leaving that many empty bunks.

It was calm for a while on the morning of the 15th, but the swell from the previous day's storm hadn't smoothed out and we rolled in fine style. The only time we were warm in the Cape Horn vicinity was when we were in bed, or after the exertion of taking in or setting a sail. . . .

Now fog shut down on us, and although there was no likelihood that any ship was within a thousand miles, our old fashioned foghorn had to be gotten into action. It was a portable chest with a copper funnel, and looked like a gramophone of the 90s. One of the crew, usually the dumbest man on board, because he was the one who could best be spared from other work, brought it up on the foc'sle, set it on the rail, and by turning a crank, kept it emitting a series of dismal, prolonged hoots. . . .

The next day we completed the rounding of Cape Horn—a nineteen days' voyage. Rather slow, but ships have been known to take two months. On the other hand, favoring winds make [it] possible in a minimum of a week. This was our first day of sunshine for [a] long time.

Notes

1. On the *Peking*, the royal sail and the royal yard where Johnson perched were about seventeen stories above the deck.
2. Captain Jüss had rounded Cape Horn 100 times in his long career; Charlie was the American friend who accompanied Johnson on the *Peking*. They went along as paying passengers who also did some work, but they were accommodated in the officers' quarters and fed at the captain's table.
3. Steering the ship toward the wind, in order to make the sails shake, or luff, makes it lose momentum.
4. The sailors hurried to take in canvas and lower the yards.
5. Johnson so badly wanted to experience a Cape Horn storm that before the voyage he

went to the Wishing Chair at the geologic formation in Northern Ireland called the Giant's Causeway and wished for one!

6. In his 1976 narration of the film he recorded, Johnson chose a more memorable metaphor, saying the screaming in the rigging sounded "like animals being tortured to death. Tortured! Tortured!"

7. The fore-and-aft-rigged spanker, farthest in the stern and nearest to the rudder, could aid the ship's steering but was not meant to steer it alone. The period when they were hurrying to fix the two broken helms, steering only with the spanker, must have been a long and anxious one for everyone aboard, because if the ship had turned sideways to the wind, it would have been overwhelmed by the seas and wrecked.

"Bitter Strength": The International "Coolie" Trade

The Chinese Cuba Commission

One of the largest maritime migrations was that of Chinese workers to other parts of the globe, which began in the mid-nineteenth century. The California gold rush attracted droves of hopeful Chinese men, who came to be known as "coolies," from the Cantonese ku li, meaning "bitter strength." Not all of those who left to find their fortune on Golden Mountain made it to the goldfields. A large number of them signed onto ships they thought were going to California, but that took them to the guano islands off the coast of Peru instead. There they faced a kind of slavery that usually ended only in death. Other workers from China moved around the British Empire, to India, Malaysia, and the Caribbean region, often working for a period of years before repatriating with their savings, as evoked by Joseph Conrad in his novel Typhoon *(1902), which is set on a steamship carrying hundreds of such laborers home. Large numbers of men from China labored aboard the ships of the salmon fishery in the North Pacific Ocean, staying below decks for weeks at a time in the waters off Alaska and the Pacific Northwest, preparing the fish for canning. Workers from India and their families who went abroad also carried the pejorative label of "coolies," most of them going to the colonies of Trinidad and Guyana as indentured laborers. Although the so-called coolie trade from China to the United States and Peru was outlawed in 1862, as the following report shows, it was going strong in the 1870s between Macao and Havana, where it became known as the "yellow trade." The document below comes from the investigation conducted by the Chinese Cuba Commission, published in English in 1876.*

In fact, the "coolie trade" in Chinese immigrant workers continued throughout the twentieth century, in a diminished and clandestine form. While most of that illicit transit seems to have gone on undetected, an exception to that rule was the wreck of the Golden Venture *on the night of June 6, 1993.*

The Golden Venture's *secret human cargo consisted of 286 Chinese immigrants (262 of them men) when the rusting freighter went aground off Fire Island near New York City. Ten of them drowned, six swam to the beach and sprinted into oblivion, and the rest were taken into custody. Reporter Mike Argento of the* York Daily Record *followed up on their fates twenty years later, and found that 14 juveniles had been released to court custody, 35 received political asylum, 55 were released on bond or paroled, two received artist's visas, 53 were paroled in February 1997 but not awarded legal status, and 111 were deported. Out of that group, Argento wrote, "it's believed that about half again have returned to the U.S. illegally."[1] Now a scuba-diving destination, the wreck of the* Golden Venture *is emblematic of human trafficking, which is an ongoing problem on the Ocean.*

All investigations of Chinese were conducted verbally and in person ourselves. The depositions show that eight tenths of the entire number declared that they had been kidnapped or decoyed; that the mortality during the voyage from wounds caused by blows, suicide and sickness proved to have exceeded ten percent; that on arrival in Havana they were sold into slavery,—a small proportion being disposed of to families and shops, whilst the large majority became the property of sugar planters; that the cruelty displayed towards those of the former class is great, and that it assumes in the case of those of the latter, proportions that are unendurable. . . .

The majority of the Chinese Coolies in Cuba sailed from Macao, Amoy [Xiamen], Swatow [Shantou] and Canton [Guangzhou]. They were mainly decoyed abroad, not legitimately induced to emigrate. . . .

The vessels—whether steamers or sailing vessels—which convey Chinese labourers to Cuba appertain to various nationalities, and in consequences are not subject to any uniform system of regulations.

Of the more than 140,000 Chinese who sailed for Cuba, more than 16,000 died during the voyage, a fact which is sufficient evidence of the absence of effective regulations.

The petition of Li Chao-ch'un and 165 others states, "when, quitting Macao, we proceeded to sea, we were confined in the hold below; some were even shut up in bamboo cages, or chained to iron posts, and a few were indiscriminately selected and flogged as a means of intimidating all others; whilst we cannot estimate the deaths that, in all, took place, from sickness, blows, hunger, thirst, or from suicide by leaping into the sea." . . .

Liu A-san deposes, "Twenty men cast themselves overboard." Chên A-sheng deposes, "on board 300 died from thirst." Chou Ch'êng deposes, "all of us who seemed strong were placed into irons." The deposition of Li A-te and one other states that the space for sleep allowed to each man measured only one *ch'ih* two *ts'un*. . . .[2]

Wu Yüeh deposes, "the treatment on board was bad and twenty men being afraid of the sea committed suicide." Chou Jun-shêng deposes, "one man who complained to the mate of the rottenness of the fish was almost beaten to death by the sailors by the order of the master." Wu A-'hu deposes, "suffering from sea-sickness I was unable to work, and was in consequence beaten by the mate." The deposition of Li Yu and 23 others testify to their each having witnessed one case of suicide by jumping overboard. The depositions of Huang A-pei and four others again testify to their severally witnessing one case of suicide. The deposition of Lung A-ch'uan and 29 others testify to their each having witnessed two cases of suicide by jumping overboard. The depositions of Wang Chêng-fu and six others testify to their each having witnessed three cases of suicide by jumping overboard. The depositions of Huang A-chang and four others again testify to the water and rice having been insufficient and to each having witnessed four cases of suicide by jumping overboard. The depositions of Lin A-ssu and two others testify to the cruelties each experienced, and to each having witnessed five cases of suicide by jumping overboard. Ts'ui An deposes, "I saw eight men tied and flogged with great severity, two of whom were also kept in irons until arrival in Havana." Li Hui deposes, "I saw one man, a native of Tungkwan, tied up and shot, and five others tied up and cast into the sea." Li Yü deposes, "the treatment on board was bad; two men were beaten to death." Ts'ui Têng-lin deposes, "two men threw themselves overboard and two hanged themselves." Lo A-fa deposes, "one man was beaten to death." Chao A-ling deposes, "the fresh water insufficient; three men were shot." Li Wên-ts'ai deposes, "the master intending to arrest five men who had been decoyed, and were discontented, in error seized and chained five others; upon this, the men whom he had desired to punish threw themselves into the sea." Li A-chieh deposes, "five men who rose at night to relieve themselves were shot by the sailors." Shi A-kou deposes, "the drinking of salt water caused much sickness, which was incurable." Wan A-fu deposes, "eight men jumped overboard. They did so because they had been decoyed and were dissatisfied." Hsieh Kuan-chieh deposes, "one man jumped overboard because he was constantly being beaten by the master and interpreter; moreover those who asked for water were beaten and many died of thirst." Tsêng A-tai deposes, "the interpreter was a Portuguese, and constantly kicked us." Ni A-huan deposes, "the mate constantly struck us with a thick rope." Hsieh Fa deposes, "I was chained to the bottom of the hold." The depositions of Lin A-ssu and one other state that they were not allowed on deck even for air. Ch'ên A-shun deposes, "two men committed suicide. On board a sailor wounded me with a knife and the scar is still visible. The master with a firearm wounded two men." Li Shun deposes, "water and rice were both insufficient. Two men were shot, and two jumped overboard." Li Hsin deposes, "two men who in want of rice created an outcry, were shot with a pistol." Ch'ên A-wei deposes, "many leaped overboard, on account of being forced to cut their queues; if we asked for water we were struck with an iron chain." . . . Huang A-fang deposes, "eleven men committed suicide. The day after I embarked we were all ordered on deck, and foot irons were attached to 173 physically strong men, besides 160 men stripped and flogged on their naked persons with rattan rods." Wang T'ing-kuei deposes, "24 men leaped overboard and two poisoned themselves with opium. They committed suicide because they had been decoyed and were unwilling to go abroad."

Lai A-shih deposes, "we all were being taken away against our will, and created an uproar. The master upon this directed the sailors to strike us with chains and eighty men were killed." . . . Liang A-yu deposes, "two insane men were struck to death by the carpenter." Lin Chin deposes, "thirty men committed suicide." Ts'ui Lan-fang deposes, "three men made an outcry, declaring that they would not go abroad; of these two were killed by firearms, and one was hanged." Tsêng A-shêng deposes, "the men who were decoyed did not wish to go abroad, and in consequence sixty were either shot by the master or committed suicide." Kuan A-hsiao deposes, "on account of smoking four men were flogged until they spat blood and died." Mo Shuang deposes, "four men committed suicide and the master shot three others." . . . Wên Ssu deposes, "one man on board committed suicide, and fifty men who were suspected of mutiny were placed in irons." Lo A-fa deposes, "on board two men committed suicide and two men were beaten to death." Pêng A-shêng deposes, "one man committed suicide by swallowing opium." Huang A-tou deposes, "before the vessel sailed five men who attempting to escape jumped overboard, were shot, and after departure 24 men were tied up, severely flogged, and kept in chains in the forepart of the vessel, of whom two committed suicide by jumping overboard."

Notes

1. Mike Argento, "Golden Venture Twenty Years Later Today: Many Lives Remain in Limbo," *York Daily Record*, June 6, 2013, https://www.ydr.com/story/archives/2013/05/31/golden-venture-20-years-later-many-lives-remain/74873348/.
2. The "Chinese foot," the *chi'h*, measures about 13 inches, or one-third of a meter; one *t'sun*, or *cun*, measures one and one-third inches, or one-thirtieth of a meter. The passengers had about 15 inches in which to fit the width of their bodies!

The Container Ship

Roz Hamlett

The complete transformation of cargo transport on the Ocean came with container-ization. The concept first went into action on D-Day, June 6, 1944, the Allied inva-sion of Normandy, which required many logistical innovations to bring off success-fully. Among these innovations was the practice of packing supplies into huge metal boxes—containers—that could be unloaded with comparative ease on the beaches of France, using vessels called landing ships, which could drive up onto the sand to dis-gorge their contents through giant doors in the bow, themselves an innovation neces-sitated by World War II. After the war, a trucking magnate named Malcom McLean (1913–2001) adapted container shipping for commercial purposes. Thinking inside the box, McLean purchased a surplus wartime oil tanker and converted it to carry the same metal containers that his semitrucks hauled across the landscape. Renamed the SS Ideal X, the vessel became the first container ship, inaugurating the practice of intermodal transport, which allows the same big boxes to move smoothly from ships to trucks to trains. The capacity of the futuristic-sounding Ideal X, first of the fleet of McLean's new Sea-Land Corporation, was fifty-eight containers, each twenty feet long, a measure now known as a TEU, or twenty-foot equivalent unit. Today, the largest container ships can handle 19,224 TEUs. These enormous vessels operate with a crew of only thirty or so, at most, and are able to unload their cargoes in less than a day, using huge cranes guided by a single individual. As a result, merchant sailors in the twenty-first century spend almost no time on land, unlike the days before con-tainer ships, when "break bulk" freighters carried cargoes stowed in barrels, bags, and wooden crates, which defied uniform stowage and required days or weeks to load and unload.

Sixty years ago this week, Malcom McLean, trucking mogul turned ship-ping magnate, tilted the shipping world on its axis when the 524-foot *Ideal X* cast off from Berth 24 at the foot of Marsh Street in Port Newark en route to Houston, Texas[,] carrying 58 containers on its maiden voyage.

To many in the shipping world, *Ideal X* signaled a sea change in the mari-time industry, putting into practice a powerful idea that had played at the back of McLean's mind since 1937[,] when he was the sole driver for his com-pany, McLean Trucking. McLean was a man born to set trends, not follow them. Had he not spent what seemed to be wasted hours idling at Hoboken, frustrated, waiting to unload his truckload of cotton bales and thinking there had to be a better way to load cargo aboard ships than piece by piece, containerization might not have turned out the same.

After *Ideal X* came the 450-foot *Gateway City*, which left Port Newark the following year on Oct. 4, 1957, the same day the Soviet Union launched Sputnik I, the world's first earth-orbiting satellite. The pioneering *Gateway City* carried more than three times the number of containers as the *Ideal X*. With her voyage came the awareness of a new normal in shipping: the era of modern containerization was underway. Containerships were transforming the industry by enabling more cargo to be placed on board and creating efficiencies, making shipping more profitable and opening up new global markets.

"I knew what was going on [in containerization] was revolutionary. That's why I wanted to be a part of it," said Charles Cushing, who was McLean's first full-time engineer at the Pan-Atlantic Steamship Company, eventually becoming Chief Naval Architect at McLean's Sea-Land Service.

The year before *Ideal X* sailed, McLean had sold his trucking company for $25 million and purchased Pan-Atlantic (which eventually became Sea-Land), and the Gulf Florida Terminal Company from Waterman Steamship Corporation, with the idea of using Pan-Atlantic's vessels and operating rights to carry containers.

McLean wanted the best people. To get them he conducted the shipping world's equivalent of the NBA lottery. He wanted only top picks, well-educated people who were still down to earth enough to mix it up with the truckers and pinch pennies with the best of them. Many were invited to Newark for an interview; a handful were chosen. Cushing went to work full-time for McLean in 1960.

"I was extremely lucky to get a job at Pan-Atlantic," Cushing recalled. "Malcom started out by putting truck bodies on ships. [Then] in 1957, he bought six old World War II break bulk cargo ships, gutted them and began putting cells in them to hold containers—The first cellular ship was the *Gateway City*. I was still a student at MIT in 1958, but I sailed on the *Gateway City* during a vacation."

After joining McLean at Pan-Atlantic, Cushing began working on the basic design features that became characteristic of modern containerships—stacks of containers in customized cells below deck and additional stacked containers atop each other as deck cargo.

McLean ran into fierce resistance in his effort to transform the industry. Venerable ocean-going steamship operators, particularly British companies, regarded McLean as an unwelcome maverick and considered containerization a marginal idea. They threatened distilleries in an effort to keep their product off the first containerships. However, J&B Scotch broke from the pack and was among Pan-Atlantic's first shipments across the Atlantic. Other distilleries would follow. By 1963, J&B Scotch was a huge hit in the U.S. and selling one million cases per year.

McLean persisted and expanded his shipping operations to Puerto Rico in 1958, to the West Coast via the Panama Canal in 1962, and north to Alaska that same year. In 1972, Sea-Land acquired eight new containerships able to reduce ocean crossings by a full day, the fastest merchant ships ever built. They could carry more than 1,000 containers compared to *Gateway City*'s 226 and the *Ideal X*'s 58. Ever-larger ships continue to this day with vessels able to carry 20,000 containers and more.

Cushing worked for McLean until 1968, before founding C.R. Cushing & Co., a naval architecture firm in New York City that has designed more than 250 vessels built in the U.S. and abroad, and completed some 3,000 projects. Cushing and other shipping industry leaders established the McLean Container Center at the Merchant Marine Academy at King's Point to preserve records, photographs, and other items documenting the history of containerization.

On the morning of McLean's funeral in 2001, container ships around the world blew their whistles in his honor. Cushing delivered the eulogy. A newspaper editorial stated that "McLean ranks next to Robert Fulton as the greatest revolutionary in the history of maritime trade." *Forbes Magazine* called him "one of the few men who changed the world."

VI

Battlefields

Fighting on the high seas has been going on for millennia. There have been countless bloody ways to contend for control of the Ocean, from the galleys that the Persians rafted together to form islands to the submarines that fought two world wars and the Cold War beneath the surface of the sea. Unlike major battles fought on land, however, the sites where pivotal naval clashes took place in the past remain mainly unmarked. "Battlefields" portrays war at sea in some of the many ways it has been fought, on a few of its countless watery battlefields.

The Epic Galley Battle of the Ancient Sea

Herodotus

Galleys were the first complex fighting platforms on the high seas. Trireme galleys, the dominant warships on the Mediterranean Sea in ancient times, had three banks of rowers, typically 170 of them among a crew of 200, and could reach speeds of more than nine miles per hour. At the epochal Battle of Salamis in 480 BCE, the galleys of the invading Persian fleet, estimated to be at least 300 and as many as 600 vessels, rafted together in the cramped waters near Athens, forming a virtual island of boats. They proved to be vulnerable to the more maneuverable Athenian galleys, 380 of them, which routed the Persian forces, destroying 200 to 300 of their ships, while losing only forty Greek craft. The victory turned back the Persian invasion of Greece. Herodotus (484–425 BCE) is still a familiar name, but his account of the Battle of Salamis in The History, book 8, though still compelling, has become undeservedly obscure. It demonstrates that seemingly overwhelming naval forces can be defeated by smaller, faster, more determined opponents, as would be seen again with the defeat of the hulking galleons of the Spanish Armada by the nimble English ships of Sir Francis Drake. It is a lesson that the US Navy has to remember in order to avert a similar disaster in its ambitious policing of the Persian Gulf and the Strait of Hormuz, where swift assaults by unconventional naval forces are a constant and real threat. The following excerpt is the translation of George Rawlinson (1812–1902), an Oxford University professor and theologian, whose older brother was Sir Henry Rawlinson, an eminent scholar of ancient Assyria.

Then Aristides entered the assembly, and spoke to the captains: he had come, he told them, from Egina, and had but barely escaped the blockading vessels—the Greek fleet was entirely inclosed by the ships of Xerxes—and he advised them to get themselves in readiness to resist the foe. Having said so much, he withdrew. And now another contest arose; for the greater part of the captains would not believe the tidings.[1]

But while they still doubted, a Tenian trireme, commanded by Panaetius the son of Sosimenes, deserted from the Persians and joined the Greeks, bringing full intelligence. For this reason the Tenians were inscribed upon the tripod at Delphi among those who overthrew the barbarians. With this ship, which deserted to their side at Salamis, and the Lemnian vessel which came over before at Artemisium, the Greek fleet was brought to the full number of 380 ships; otherwise it fell short by two of that amount.[2]

The Greeks now, not doubting what the Tenians told them, made ready for the coming fight. At the dawn of day, all the men-at-arms were assembled together, and speeches were made to them, of which the best was that of Themistocles; who throughout contrasted what was noble with what was base, and bade them, in all that came within the range of man's nature and constitution, always to make choice of the nobler part.[3] Having thus wound up his discourse, he told them to go at once on board their ships, which they accordingly did; and about this time the trireme, that had been sent to Egina for the Aeacidae, returned; whereupon the Greeks put to sea with all their fleet.[4]

The fleet had scarce left the land when they were attacked by the barbarians. At once most of the Greeks began to back water, and were about touching the shore, when Ameinias of Pallene, one of the Athenian captains, darted forth in front of the line, and charged a ship of the enemy.[5] The two vessels became entangled, and could not separate, whereupon the rest of the fleet came up to help Ameinias, and engaged with the Persians. Such is the account which the Athenians give of the way in which the battle began. . . . It is also reported, that a phantom in the form of a woman appeared to the Greeks, and, in a voice that was heard from end to end of the fleet, cheered them on to the fight; first, however, rebuking them, and saying, "Strange men, how long are ye going to back water?"

Against the Athenians, who held the western extremity of the line towards Eleusis, were placed the Phoenicians; against the Lacedaemonians, whose station was eastward towards the Piraeus, the Ionians.[6] Of these last a few only followed the advice of Themistocles, to fight backwardly; the greater number did far otherwise. . . .

Far the greater number of the Persian ships engaged in this battle were disabled, either by the Athenians or by the Eginetans. For as the Greeks fought in order and kept their line, while the barbarians were in confusion and had no plan in anything that they did, the issue of the battle could scarce be other than it was. Yet the Persians fought far more bravely here than at Euboea, and indeed surpassed themselves; each did his utmost through fear of Xerxes, for each thought that the king's eye was upon himself.

What part the several nations, whether Greek or barbarian, took in the combat, I am not able to say for certain; Artemisia, however, I know, distinguished herself in such a way as raised her even higher than she stood before in the esteem of the king.[7] For after confusion had spread throughout the whole of the king's fleet, and her ship was closely pursued by an Athenian trireme, she, having no way to fly, since in front of her were a number of friendly vessels, and she was nearest of all the Persians to the enemy, resolved

This image illustrates a variety of Mediterranean warships, differing in the number of rowers each could accommodate. The warships were used for peacetime sea fights, called Naumachia, originated by Julius Caesar and similar to the gladiator battles practiced in coliseums. Ships were built in the arena, which was then filled with water. The fighters were usually slaves and prisoners, and their mock engagements often resulted in dreadful slaughter on both sides. Naumachia vessels featured in the engraving include Phoenician, Roman, and Norman warships. Engraving by Henry Winkles, under the direction of Johann Georg Heck, in *Atlas géographique, astronomique et historique, servant à l'intelligence de l'histoire ancienne, du moyen-âge et modern*, edited by Johann Georg Heck (Paris: Maillet, 1842). Courtesy of the Roorda/Doyle Collection.

on a measure which in fact proved her safety. Pressed by the Athenian pursuer, she bore straight against one of the ships of her own party, a Calyndian, which had Damasithymus, the Calyndian king, himself on board.[8] I cannot say whether she had had any quarrel with the man while the fleet was at the Hellespont, or no—neither can I decide whether she of set purpose attacked his vessel, or whether it merely chanced that the Calyndian ship came in her way—but certain it is that she bore down upon his vessel and sank it, and that thereby she had the good fortune to procure herself a double advantage.[9] For the commander of the Athenian trireme, when he saw her bear down on one of the enemy's fleet, thought immediately that her vessel was a Greek, or else had deserted from the Persians, and was now fighting on the Greek side; he therefore gave up the chase, and turned away to attack others.

Thus in the first place she saved her life by the action, and was enabled to get clear off from the battle; while further, it fell out that in the very act of doing the king an injury she raised herself to a greater height than ever in his esteem. For as Xerxes beheld the fight, he remarked (it is said) the destruction of the vessel, whereupon the bystanders observed to him, "Seest thou, master, how well Artemisia fights, and how she has just sunk a ship of the enemy?" Then Xerxes asked if it were really Artemisia's doing; and they answered, "Certainly, for they knew her ensign" while all made sure that the sunken vessel belonged to the opposite side. Everything, it is said, conspired to prosper the queen; it was especially fortunate for her that not one of those on board the Calyndian ship survived to become her accuser. Xerxes, they say, in reply to the remarks made to him, observed, "My men have behaved like women, my women like men!"

There fell in this combat Ariabignes, one of the chief commanders of the fleet, who was son of Darius and brother of Xerxes; and with him perished a vast number of men of high repute, Persians, Medes, and allies.[10] Of the Greeks there died only a few; for, as they were able to swim, all those that were not slain outright by the enemy escaped from the sinking vessels and swam across to Salamis. But on the side of the barbarians more perished by drowning than in any other way, since they did not know how to swim. The great destruction took place when the ships which had been first engaged began to fly; for they who were stationed in the rear, anxious to display their valour before the eyes of the king, made every effort to force their way to the front, and thus became entangled with such of their own vessels as were retreating.

Notes

1. Aristides (530–468 BCE) was an Athenian statesman called the Just, who gained fame as a military commander at the Battle of Marathon (490 BCE). Aegina is a large island in the Saronic Gulf south of Salamis, which in ancient times was a rival to nearby Athens. Xerxes I (519–465 BCE), called Xerxes the Great, ruled the vast Achaemenid, or First Persian, Empire.
2. "Tenian" refers to the Greek island of Tinos in the southern Aegean Sea, and "Lemnian" refers to the Greek island of Lemnos in the northern Aegean, both of which were compelled to join the Persian invasion. Artemisium is a cape on the north end of the island of Euboea which was the site of a naval engagement fought simultaneously with the land battle of Thermopylae in late summer 480 BCE, a few months before the Battle of Salamis.
3. Themistocles (524–459), a populist political leader and general who increased Athenian naval power in the years leading up to the war with Persia, and was one of the commanders at the Battle of Marathon.
4. The Aeacidae were the inhabitants of Aegina, said to be the descendants of Aeacus, the island's mythological king.
5. Ameinias was the younger brother of the playwright Aeschylus and the hero of the Battle of Marathon. Pallene was a provincial town near Athens, now a district of the city called Pallini.
6. Eleusis is a town at the northern end of the Saronic Gulf, about eleven miles north-

west of Athens. Phoenicia was an ancient civilization centered on the eastern coast of the Mediterranean, around modern Lebanon, which was renowned for its wide-ranging maritime trade. Lacedaemonia refers to Laconia, the southernmost region of the Peloponnese Peninsula, of which Sparta was the capital. Piraeus is the port of Athens. Ionia was a Greek civilization established on the west coast of the Anatolian Peninsula, now modern Turkey, which the Achaemenid Empire conquered in 547 BCE. The Ionians' struggles to gain independence from Persia, assisted by the Athenians, provoked the Persian invasion of Greece in 480 BCE.

7. Artemisia I of Caria was the queen of Halicarnassus, a Greek city in the satrapy of Caria, within the Achaemenid Empire.

8. Calynda was another Greek city in the Achaemenid Empire's satrapy of Caria.

9. The Hellespont was the ancient name for the Dardanelles, the strait separating the Aegean Sea from the Sea of Marmara and the Black Sea, later the site of Constantinople/Istanbul.

10. The Medes were an Iranian people from the ancient civilization of Media, located in the northwestern part of modern Iran, who allied with the Persians.

The Crest of Islamic Sea Power

Matthew Merighi

The Battle of Preveza in 1538 represents the height of Islamic sea power. The story of how Hayreddin Barbarossa (1478–1546), regarded as a pirate in Christendom, led the Ottoman Empire's fleet to victory over the Holy League forces, was once central to the curriculum of college Western Civilization courses. It is less well known now but has taken on fresh significance since the resumption of another round of religious warfare in the eastern Mediterranean Sea in the twenty-first century. The victory for Ottoman arms has never been forgotten in Turkey, where it is still celebrated as Turkish Naval Forces Day every September 28.

In 1538, Christendom assembled one of the largest allied fleets in its history. Called the Holy League to honor its Papal sponsors, it numbered 157 ships and was drawn from many of the strongest maritime powers of the age, including Spain, the Papal States, Venice, and the Maltese Knights of St. John. This motley alliance had one goal: to defeat the fearsome fleet of the Ottoman Empire under the legendary pirate Hayreddin Barbarossa.

The Ottoman Empire was not always a maritime powerhouse. Until the mid 15th century, the Ottomans were best known for their dominant land forces[,] which they used to counter the land powers in their neighborhood. This all changed under the Sultan Mehmet II, who intentionally increased the size of the navy to fuel his wars of conquest and, specifically, to go after the greatest city in the medieval world.

In 1453, Mehmet II conducted his famous final siege of Constantinople. In order to fully surround the city, he needed to move naval forces into the Golden Horn. Unfortunately for him, the Byzantines used a traditional medieval anti-access/area-denial (A2AD) technology to keep out enemy navies; a massive chain lay across the entire expanse. To achieve his encirclement, Mehmet ordered his army to physically drag his ships out of the Bosphorus to the east of the city and, using logs as rollers, drag them across the northern landmass and deposit them in the western part of the Horn away from Byzantine forces. The move, though daring, was essential but not sufficient for the defeat of the city. Constantinople fell on 29 May 1453 only after the army breached the supposedly impregnable land walls to the west. Even when it played a crucial role in operations, the Ottoman navy played second fiddle to the army.

The mainline in the Ottoman navy for most of its history was the galley. For those unfamiliar, the galley was a warship first devised in the Classical era and first made famous in Greece, particularly in its roles in the Persian and Peloponessian Wars in the 300s BC It had two methods of propulsion: sail-power and oar-power. Sails provided the fastest and most efficient speed but, in times of bad weather or no wind, or when rapid movements were needed in close combat, oars provided a useful alternative. Oar-power, while useful, did have a significant drawback: it required a lot of manpower. The Ottomans, however, possessed the bureaucratic acumen to recruit these rowers through a sophisticated administrative and judicial apparatus that levied paid conscripts from provinces around the empire. They divided up recruitment between coastal and inland provinces, leveraging experienced mariners from the coastal levies for work in rigging and the non-maritime-minded levies from the inland provinces as rowers.

Although the 15th and 16th century century saw the rise of the high-sided, sail-powered galleass as a weapon of war, the galley remained a viable military technology throughout this entire period. The galley's capabilities were not useful on the Atlantic and other harsh ocean waters but, inside the confines of the Mediterranean, their utility was still as manifest in the 1500s as it was two thousand years earlier; weather was still unpredictable and the Mediterranean, although dangerous, was still not as violent as the deep ocean. Galleys had similar gunpowder armaments as their galleass competitors during this period, so they retained their lethality as well.

While the Ottomans were causing general mayhem for Christendom in the Eastern Mediterranean through the early sixteenth century, including the conquest of Venetian islands and the expulsion of the Knights of St. John from Rhodes, another Islamic force caused similar problems on the Western shores. Piracy was rife across the entire Mediterranean but those in the west were of a particularly brutal and effective breed. Chief among these brigands were the forces of the pirate brothers Uruj and Hayreddin.

While these two men were the scourges of the western Mediterranean, they were not natives to the region. The brothers lived and conducted piracy in the Aegean with the tacit backing of the brother of the man who would become Selim I, the ruling Sultan. Selim fought a brutal succession war against his brother but emerged victorious and had his brother executed in 1513. Sensing their mortal peril, the young brothers fled to safer waters in the west. They made a reputation for themselves there as ruthless raiders but also as folk heroes to the Islamic community when they used their fleets to smuggle Muslim refugees fleeing persecution in Spain. Their efforts were so successful that they amassed enough resources, both money and manpower, to conquer the city of Algiers in 1516, establishing themselves as the Sultans of

North Africa and converting one of the largest cities in the region into their own private pirate base. It is at this time that Hayreddin acquired his nickname Barbarossa (Red Beard) from European commentators.

Charles V of the Habsburg Empire, one of the greatest monarchs in European history, laid the foundations for the world's first global empire. . . . His personal motto, "Plus Ultra" (onwards and upwards) still graces the Spanish flag to this day.

Unfortunately for the brothers, 1516 also marked the accession of a new king in Spain: Charles V. Charles was a young, dynamic leader who wanted nothing more than to establish himself as the universal king of Christendom. He was expansionist minded and could not tolerate the existence of Barbarossa's raiding fleets in the south. He organized a counteroffensive which, with himself at the head, wrested control of Algiers and other cities from the brothers. Uruj himself died in 1518 while fighting the Spanish, leaving Barbarossa to salvage what he could. Salvation came from an unlikely source: Selim I.

Selim I and Barbarossa both needed each other. Barbarossa was desperate for assistance from whatever source he could find to keep his pirate business–turned–political empire alive. Selim I, meanwhile, was fighting against the Habsburgs in central Europe and needed to maintain as much pressure on Charles V as he could. Selim I also needed a stronger navy to secure lines of supply and communication between the Ottoman capital and the newly conquered province of Egypt.

Selim I's assistance to Barbarossa came with strings attached. Barbarossa lost his political independence but retained control of his territory. While Barbarossa retained OPCON ["operational control," a system of lower-echelon officers making decisions in their local areas] over his forces, they were placed under Ottoman jurisdiction, essentially the medieval equivalent of ADCON ["administrative control," an overarching command structure making top-down decisions]. Imperial inspectors would personally inspect each ship, determine their capabilities, and issue a formal letter authorizing them to operate in certain sectors and solely against targets of states at war with the Empire. Thus was the transition from pirate to a state-sponsored corsair. For those familiar with navy history, these corsairs were exactly the same as European privateers during this period.

The benefits of the partnership paid off quickly. With his newfound resources and top-cover, Barbarossa's forces were able to push back against the Habsburgs. In the East, Selim I died in 1522 and was replaced with his son Suleyman. Later known as "the Magnificent" and "the Lawgiver," Suleyman proved a valuable partner and patron for Barbarossa. Suleyman's forces in the East displaced the troublesome Knights of St. John from Rhodes in 1522, making them homeless for eight years until Charles V gave them the island of Malta in 1530. Recognizing Barbarossa's talents and feeling the pressure of

Charles V and the other naval superpower, Venice, Suleyman elevated Barbarossa to Admiral of the Ottoman Navy in 1533. In that same year, the Ottomans concluded a formal alliance with the Habsburgs' perennial European opponent, France.

Charles V was in a tough spot in 1537. Ottoman armies were invading through Hungary, his North Africa campaign was stalling, and he was embroiled in a brutal war against the Ottoman-allied French in Italy. The Reformation was in full swing, undermining his position as the champion of a Christendom united under Catholicism. His Venetian allies were entirely expelled from the Aegean thanks to Barbarossa's command of the Ottoman fleets in the Eastern Mediterranean. Charles was on the back foot and needed to find a way to put up organized resistance at sea. Using his position as the strongest Catholic monarch and the Holy Roman Emperor, Charles leveraged the Papal States to create a Holy League of naval powers to finally defeat the Ottomans once and for all. This League, founded in February 1538, was placed under the command of the Genoese pirate-turned-admiral Andrea Doria. Doria's forces trapped Barbarossa and his 122 ships in the narrow strip of water between the north and south halves of Greece, near the city of Preveza. Victory seemed assured.

The Battle of Preveza was a disaster for the Holy League. At the outset of the battle, unfavorable winds kept the League's fleet divided while the Ottoman galleys were still able to maneuver using oar power. Barbarossa, too, outfoxed Doria and seized the initiative despite the Ottomans' smaller numbers. In total, the League lost 49 ships while the Ottomans did not lose any. The defeat was so lopsided that the Venetians had to pursue a separate peace with the Ottomans in 1540 in which they had to surrender a number of their islands and pay large war reparations. Barbarossa became a rock star in the medieval naval community. Suleyman made him a permanent member of the Ottomans' governing council and [he] received fan mail from across Europe, including from the great English privateer Sir Francis Drake. The Eastern Mediterranean was transformed into the so-called Ottoman Lake which freed up additional resources to fight the Habsburgs in the West. The Ottomans, despite their humble beginnings, truly evolved from dragging ships across the land to become the strongest naval power in the Mediterranean.

Lessons Learned

1) BE A REALIST AND DO NOT TAKE THINGS PERSONALLY.
It would have been very easy for Selim I to get hung up on Barbarossa's connection to Selim's executed brother and ignore Barbarossa's plight in 1518; worse yet, Selim might have welcomed Charles' efforts against Barbarossa. Instead, Selim recognized a win-win opportunity and incorporated them into the Ottoman fold.

The same thinking goes for Suleyman's cooperation with Christian France. Without the French causing trouble for Charles V, Barbarossa might have faced even more ships at Preveza and failed to triumph. Realism wins the day.

2) MERITOCRACY IS THE BEST WAY TO SELECT COMMANDERS.
Just as Selim I could have easily overlooked Barbarossa's difficult position in 1518, Suleyman could have easily overlooked the corsair for the position of Admiral of the Navy in 1533. The historical precedent was for the governor of the Dardanelles province, with the largest armory and naval base in the Empire, to be the Admiral, but Suleyman took a chance and elevated the former pirate instead. This meant that the brilliant commander was in place for the Battle of Preveza whereas another commander might have failed to deliver a victory.

3) TECHNOLOGY IS NOT ENOUGH TO WIN. ALSO, OLD TECHNOLOGY
DOES NOT MEAN BAD TECHNOLOGY.
The victory at Preveza was only possible because the Ottomans used galleys rather than galleasses. Even though the initial design was pioneered millennia earlier, galley technology still had utility in the strategic game that the Ottomans played. Also, as Barbarossa's actions against Andrea Doria at Preveza demonstrated, a good commander plays a greater role in a battle's outcome than numbers or technology.

Elizabethan England's Plausibly Deniable War in the Pacific Ocean

Francis Pretty

The naval innovations of Sir Francis Drake (1540–96) had an enormous impact on warfare at sea. As a protégé of John Hawkins (1532–95), Drake began as an English sea dog, harassing the Spanish Empire in the Caribbean Sea. That region lay "beyond the Line," meaning the longitudinal boundary established by Pope Alexander VI in 1494, in the Papal Bull Inter Caetera *and the Treaty of Tordesillas between Spain and Portugal, which divided the New World between those two maritime powers, to the exclusion of up-and-comers like England, France, and the Netherlands. Rejecting the arrangement, Queen Elizabeth I of England authorized a covert, undeclared war "beyond the Line" against her former brother-in-law, King Philip II of Spain. Drake's circumnavigation of the world, from 1577 to 1580, was only the second in history, after the 1519–22 expedition led by Ferdinand Magellan (c. 1480–1521) and Juan Sebastián Elcano (1476–1526). Drake's voyage was part of the queen's shadow war. Undertaken to carry the conflict into waters on the other side of the world, the voyage resembled a long-distance covert action, with Queen Elizabeth I plausibly able to deny her complicity in such a far-flung raiding enterprise, though she knighted its leader upon his return. Drake's exploits and the queen's collaboration indicated the global scale of England's imperial ambition, even before its empire came into being.*

A state of open warfare between England and Spain followed in 1585, leading to Drake's 1588 defeat of the castle-like galleons of the Spanish Armada in the English Channel. In defeating the mammoth Spanish fleet, Drake used faster, more nimble "flyboats," which would presage future tactics, all the way up to the contemporary threat that the Iranian navy could deploy armed small craft to swarm the conventional warships of the US Navy in the Persian Gulf. Drake's around-the-world raid is not as well known as the watershed demise of the Spanish Armada but is deeply significant in its own right, demonstrating the devastating effect of hit-and-run tactics. This entry samples an unattributed 1742 book on Drake's voyage around the world, which seems to have been derived from the little-known account written by Drake's shipmate, Sir Francis Pretty, which appeared a century and a half earlier, though the later publication does not credit Sir Pretty.

The Famous Voyage of Sir Francis Drake, the First General
that ever sail'd round the whole GLOBE.

The 15th of *November* 1577, Sir *Francis Drake*, with a Fleet of five Ships and Barks, (in which were about 164 Persons) set sail from *Plymouth*, pretending a Voyage to *Alexandria*. . . .[1]

Before this Island they saw two Ships under Sail, one of which they took, and found to be a good Prize, well laded with Wines. The Admiral retain'd the Pilot, but discharged the Ship and the Men, giving them some Victuals, a Butt of Wine, and their wearing Clothes.

The same Night they came to the Island of *Fogho* [Fogo], or the burning Island, which is inhabited by *Portugueze*. . . . Here was no convenient Road for their Ships, the Sea being so deep, that there was no Possibility of fixing of an Anchor thereabouts.

Leaving these Islands, they drew towards the Line [equator], being sometimes becalm'd for a long Time together, and at others beaten with Tempests. They had continually great Plenty of Fish, as Dolphins [dorado or mahimahi], Bonito's and Flying Fishes, some of which dropp'd down into their Ships, and could not rise again, because their Wings wanted Moisture.

From the first Day of their Departure from the Islands of Cape *Verd*, they sail'd 54 Degrees without Sight of Land; and the first which they saw was the Coast of Brazil, in 33 Degr. of South. Lat. *April* 5. The barbarous People ashore having discovered the Ships, began to use their accustomed conjuring Ceremonies, in order to raise a Storm to torment them and sink their Ships. For this Purpose they made great Fires, and offered some Sacrifices to the Devil; but he was not able to serve them at that Time; the Wind and Seas being kept in good Order, by a Power superior to the Prince of the Air.[2]

They entered the great River of *Plate*, and into between 53 and 54 Fathom [318–24 feet, not quite 100 meters] of fresh Water; but finding no good Harbour there, they put out to Sea again. . . .[3]

The Natives came boldly and confidently about them, while they were working ashore; their Faces were painted, and their Apparel only a Covering of some Beasts Skin (with the Fur on) about their Wastes, and something wreath'd about their Heads. They had Bows an Ell long [the length from the elbow to the fingertips], but no more than two Arrows a-piece. They seem'd to be not altogether destitute of martial Discipline; as appear'd by the Method they observed in ordering and ranging their men. And they gave sufficient Proof of their Agility, by stealing the Admiral's Hat from his very Head; which was a brave Prize amongst them, one taking the Hat, and another the Gold Band that was in it, neither of which could ever be gotten again from them.

Having dispatched all Affairs in this Place, they set sail; and *June* the 20th they harbour'd at St. *Julian*, so call'd by *Magellanicus*. Here they saw the Gibbet, on which *Magellanicus* had formerly executed some of his mutinous Company. And here also did Admiral *Drake* execute one of his.

August the 17th, they left St. *Julian's* Port, and the 20th fell in with the Streight of *Magellan*, going into the *South Sea*. The 21st they entred the Streight, which they found to lie very intricate and crooked, with divers Turnings; by which Means, shifting about so often, the Wind would sometimes be against them, which made their Sailing very troublesome; and not only so, but dangerous too, especially if any sudden Blasts of Wind came. For tho' there be several good Harbours about, and fresh Water enough, yet the Sea is so deep, that there is no anchoring there, except in some very narrow River or Corner, or between the Rocks. There are vast Mountains covered [with] Snow, that spread along the Land on both Sides of the Streight, the Tops of which mount up in the Air to a prodigious Height, having two or three Regions of Clouds lying in order below them. The Streight is extremely cold, with Frost and Snow continually, yet do the Trees and Plants maintain a constant Verdure and Flourish, notwithstanding the Weather. . . .

Continuing their Course, they came *November* the 29th, to the Isle *Moha* [Mocha, off the coast of central Chile], where they cast Anchor, and the Admiral, with ten Men went ashore. The People that dwelt there, were such as the extreme cruelty of the *Spaniards* had forced from their own Habitations to this Island, to preserve their Lives and Liberties there. They carried it very civilly to the Admiral and his Men, bringing them Potatoes and two fat Sheep, promising further to bring them Water, for which they received some Presents. The next Day two Men went ashore with Barrels for Water, and the Natives having them at an Advantage, presently seized them, and, as 'tis probable, knock'd them on the Head. The Reason of this Outrage was, because they took them for *Spaniards*, whom they never spare when they fall into their Hands.

Continuing their Course for *Chili*, and drawing near the Coasts of it, they met an *Indian* in a Canoe, who mistaking them for *Spaniards*, told them, that at St. *Jago* [Santiago] there was a great *Spanish* Ship laden from *Peru*. The Admiral rewarding him for this intelligence, he conducted to the Place where the Ship was at Anchor, which was the Port *Val Parize* [Valparaíso], in 33 Degr. 40 Min. of South Lat. All the Men they had in her were no more than eight *Spaniards* and three Negroes; and they supposing the *English* to have been Friends, welcom'd them with the Beat of a Drum, and invited them to drink some *Chili* Wine with them. But they resolving to secure their Prize, and then drink afterwards, boarded the Ship, and laying all the *Spaniards* under Hatches, took Possession. One of the *Spaniards* seeing how they were served, desperately leap'd over-board, and swam to the Town of St. *Jago* to give them Notice of the *English's* coming; upon which all the Inhabitants quitted the town, and ran away; which they might quickly do, there not being about nine Households in the whold Town. The Admiral and his Men being entered, rifled the Town and the Chapel, taking out of it a Silver Chalice, two Cruets and an Altar-Cloth. They found in the Town also a good cargo of *Chili* Wine, and Boards of Cedar Wood; all which they carried to their Ships, intending the Boards for Firing, and with the Wine to drink the *Spaniards*['] Health. . . .[4]

From hence they came to a Port called *Tarapaxa* [Tarapacá, the region near the Chilean coastal city of Iquique]; where being landed, they found a *Spaniard* asleep upon the Shore, with thirteen Bars of Silver lying by him, which came to 4,000 *Spanish* Ducats; they did not think fit to disturb the *Spaniard's* Repose, but taking the Silver, they left him to his Nap. Not far from thence, going ashore for Water, they met a *Spaniard* and an *Indian*, driving eight *Peruvian* Sheep (which are as big as Asses) [llamas] laden with very fine Silver; every Sheep having two Leather-bags, (containing *50 lb.* Weight each) on his Back. They deliver'd the poor Animals from those irksome Burdens, and lodged the Bags in their own Ships. After which, the *Indian* and *Spaniards* were permitted to drive on.

They sail'd hence to *Arica*, which is in 18 Degr. 30 Min. South Lat. and in the Port found three small Barks, which being rifled, yielded them 57 Wedges of Silver. . . . They did not assault the Town, having not Strength enough for it. So that putting off to Sea again, they met with another little Bark laden with Linen Cloth, Part of which the Admiral took, and so let her go.

They came, *February* the 13th to *Lima*, which lies in 11 Degr. 50 Min. South Lat. and being entered the Haven, found there twelve Sail of Ship, lying fast at Anchor, with all their Sails down, without Watch or Guard, their secure Masters being all a drinking and carouzing ashore. Examining the Contents of these Ships, they found all full of Rials of Plate, good Store of Silks and Linnen; all of which Plate they carried to their own Ships, and good Part of the Silks and Linnen.

The Admiral had here Notice of another rich Ship named the *Cacafuego*, which was going towards *Paita*; which they pursuing thither, found her before their Arrival gone for *Panama*. . . .[5] But resolving still to proceed in the Pursuit of the *Cacafuego*, the Admiral, to encourage his Company, promised, That whoever first saw her, should have his Golden Chain for a Reward; which fell to the Share of Mr. *John Drake*, who first descried her about three a-clock. About six a-clock they came up with her, gave her three Shots, struck down her Mizen[mast], and boarded her.

They found her as rich and weighty as she was reported to be, having aboard her thirteen Chests full of Rials of Plate, 80 *lb.* Weight of Gold, a good Quantity of Jewels, and 26 Tons of Silver. The Place where this Prize was taken was called Cape *San Francisco*, about 150 Leagues from *Panama*. . . .

After this, having entirely ransack'd the *Cacafuego*, they cast her off; and continuing their Course to the West, they met a Ship laden with Linnen Cloth, *China* Dishes, and Silks of the same Country. The Owner of it was a

Spaniard there present; from whom the Admiral took a Faulcon wrought in massy Gold, with a great Emerald wrought in the Breast of it. Besides this, chusing what he lik'd of the Wares aboard this Vessel, and seizing the Pilot for his own Service, he turn'd the Ship going. This Pilot brought them to the Haven of *Guatulco* [somewhere in Mexico], the Town adjacent, which had but (as he said) fourteen *Spaniards* in it. Having therefore put to Shore, they marched directly into the Town, and so put up to the publick Hall of Justice; where they found the Court sitting, and a Judge ready to pass Sentence upon a Parcel of poor Negroes, that were accus'd of a Plot to fire the Town. But the Admiral's Coming chang'd the Scene of Affairs at the Court; for he being Judge himself, pass'd Sentence upon them all, both Judges and Criminals, to become his Prisoners; which Sentence was presently executed, and they all carried away to the Ships. . . .

And now the Admiral thinking he had in good Measure revenged both the publick Injuries of his Country, as well as his private Vengeance upon the *Spaniards*, began to deliberate upon the return home. . . .[6]

Notes

1. After a false start caused by stormy weather, Drake's fleet proceeded south to the island of Santiago in the Cape Verde archipelago.
2. Drake's fleet coasted south along a Brazilian shore where "the inhabitants seemed to be only some Herds of wild Deer," though they saw human footprints, "and those of a large Size too." Contenting themselves with killing "several Sea-Wolves, (which we call Seols) keeping them for Food," the Englishmen set sail for the future Argentina.
3. Drake found a better anchorage farther south, where the local people offered their own version of piratical behavior.
4. Drake lost fourteen men in battle with a superior force of Spanish cavalry while attempting to replenish his fresh water supply in Coquimbo, but his next foray ashore was far more peaceful.
5. The literal translation of *Cacafuego* is "shitfire"; Webster's dictionary modestly renders the word as "braggart."
6. Drake opted to continue west, traversing the Pacific and Indian Oceans, rounding the Cape of Good Hope, and completing the circumnavigation, returning to a hero's welcome in England.

The Iconic Tactic of the Age of Sail

Godfrey Basil Mundy

The Battle of Trafalgar in October 1805 is the most famous of the many battles fought during the wars between Great Britain and France. The hero of that clash, Lord Horatio Nelson (1758–1805), died in action aboard his flagship HMS Victory, *in a manner that was predictable (he wore his largest medals on his chest, presenting a perfect target for enemy sharpshooters) and picturesque (looking stoic and poised, martyr-like). Nelson became a towering figure in British naval history, both figuratively and literally, in the form of his iconic statue at the top of a column above Trafalgar Square in central London.* HMS Victory, *now a museum ship in Portsmouth, became the Royal Navy's most famous and longest-lived vessel. At the battle off Cape Trafalgar, near Cádiz and Gibraltar, Nelson defied the tactical conventions of the Great Age of Sail by ordering his line of warships to steer directly into the combined fleet of France and Spain, rather than sailing abreast of them to fire broadsides of all the cannons on one side of the ship, famously "crossing the T" and triggering a melee. The result was a complete debacle for the French and Spanish forces, which lost virtually all their ships either during the battle or in the hurricane that struck immediately afterward. Although the United Kingdom lost Nelson at Trafalgar, his unconventional T-crossing tactic there won the battle, which in turn ensured British naval supremacy, which led eventually to winning the Napoleonic Wars.*

But the first time that the T-crossing maneuver was used was twenty years earlier, at the Battle of the Saintes in April 1782. Fought in the waters off the small island group called Îles des Saintes or Les Saintes, near Guadeloupe, the Battle of the Saintes was the most significant battle ever contested in the Caribbean Sea. Victory at the Saintes turned back a French invasion of Jamaica and ensured Royal Navy control of the region, but few people now have ever heard of it. Also rarely mentioned now is the man who ordered the maneuver, the dashing Lord George Brydges Rodney (1718–92), who was already famous when Horatio was a pup. Rodney rose from humble means to become rear admiral at the age of forty-one, when Nelson was not yet one year old. Rodney fought in many famous battles during the War of the Austrian Succession (1740–48), the Seven Years' War (1756–63), and the American Revolution (1777–83), including the Moonlight Battle in 1780, when he captured a Spanish convoy near Cape St. Vincent in Portugal, and the seizure of the Caribbean island of Saint Eustatius

(Statia) from the Dutch in 1781. But he tarried there too long afterward, in order to capture unsuspecting ships coming to the rich smuggling port, and so he did not make it to Virginia in time to save the British Army from having to surrender at the Siege of Yorktown. Instead, the French admiral François Joseph Paul de Grasse (1732–88) seized the entrance to the Chesapeake Bay at the Battle of the Capes, September 5, 1781, preventing the British forces from being evacuated and allowing the landing of heavy French artillery. Using these cannons, the veteran French infantry, along with George Washington's ragtag Continental Army, besieged the British at Yorktown and forced their submission in October, which virtually ended the American Revolution.

Yet before that war formally ended with the Peace of Paris in 1783, Rodney had his greatest achievement in the crushing defeat of the French fleet at the Saintes, when the Royal Navy exacted a measure of revenge on de Grasse and his fleet. The account below comes from Rodney's adoring son-in-law, Major General Godfrey Basil Mundy, who extensively quoted the eyewitness account of ship's surgeon Sir Gilbert Blane (1749–1834), a Scottish physician who pioneered the use of lemon juice to combat scurvy. The passage begins with a reference to the controversy over Rodney's delay at Statia.

The grand scene of Rodney's glory was now fast approaching, when he was not only to crush and annihilate the mighty projects of the coalesced powers of France, Spain, &c., &c., but to triumph over the malice of his enemies at home, who, although they succeeded in depriving him of his command, could not rob him of his popularity, nor of his renown, the former of which he enjoyed, and was his consolation to the last hour of his existence; and the latter of which is inscribed, and will endure, in the annals of his country, until she shall be blotted from the list of nations.

The French fleet at this time assembled in Fort Royal Bay, Martinique, consisted of thirty-three sail of the line, and two ships of fifty guns, and in this fleet were embarked a large body of troops, viz. five thousand four hundred men, accompanied with a train of heavy cannon, and every other requisite for accomplishing the reduction of an island of such importance as Jamaica. In forming an idea of the number of ships and vessels which composed this fleet, the artillery and ammunition vessels, those destined to carry the baggage and tent equipage, and the trade for Hispaniola, are to be reckoned, forming altogether a very large convoy.

The design of the Comte de Grasse was to proceed with all the diligence in his power, to Hispaniola, where he was to join the forces under the Spanish Admiral, and whose united strength would have been so superior as to have bid defiance to any exertions of the British Admiral, whose situation was now full of danger and intense activity. Not only did the preservation of Jamaica, and the other West Indies islands, depend upon the successful exertion of the fleet under his command, but the interest of the British empire demanded that the enemy should be defeated, as nothing but the most complete and decisive victory could prevent the nation from falling into that degredation with which she was threatened. Not only were her power and pre-eminence at stake, but her existence as an independent nation, which she had to defend against enemies who were actuated by every motive of policy, ambition, and resentment. A most important crisis therefore was now approaching, and at no period of our history did there ever depend so much upon the issue of a naval combat.

The subjoined account of the operations of the British fleet, from the 8th to the 12th of April, is extracted from Sir Gilbert Blane's *Select Dissertations on Subjects of Medical Science*, a work replete with interest and information. The concluding narrative of the great battle of the 12th, written by the friend and companion of the Admiral, and who was by his side during the greater part of that glorious day, is an invaluable document. . . .

"On the morning of the 8th of April, a signal was made through the chain of frigates stationed between St. Lucie and Martinique, that the enemy's fleet had unmoored, and were proceeding to sea. Upon this the British fleet, at that moment in complete readiness, took up their anchors, and in little more than two hours were all under weigh, standing towards the enemy with all the sail they could crowd. It was the decided policy of the French commander not on any account to hazard a battle, the sole object of the expedition being that of joining a large sea and land force of the Spaniards then waiting at Cape François, in order to proceed against Jamaica with their joint armament, amounting to the overwhelming force of near fifty ships of the line, and twenty thousand land troops.

"This mighty and deep-laid scheme, so hostile to the best interests of the British nation, could no otherwise be disconcerted than by the discomfiture of the armament now rising into full view. In proportion to the momentousness of the object was the anxiety of our Commander-in-chief to overtake and attack the enemies of his country; and there has seldom occurred in the history of rival nations an occasion in which higher interests or a deeper stake in point of honour were to be contended for, than what presented itself at this moment. We gained so much upon them, that next morning the van and centre of our fleet, including the flag-ship, had got within cannon-shot of our enemy's rear, and a sharp cannonade ensued, which however proved partial and indecisive, from the falling of the wind, and from a great part of our fleet being becalmed under the high lands of Dominique. In the course of the two next days, the enemy, by dint of great efforts, kept far to windward, and would probably have made their escape had they not been brought down on the 11th to save one of their ships which had dropped to leeward, in consequence of being crippled by running foul of another ship in the night. By this casualty, we had the inexpressible pleasure, at daybreak, on the 12th, to dis-

This engraving depicts warfare during the Great Age of Sail. Upper panel, left to right: *Maneuvers by Schooners; Steamer of War Carrying Despatches*; and *Line of Battle*. Main composition: *Naval Battle*, resembling the Battle of the Saintes and the Battle of Trafalgar, with the Royal Navy fleet on the left crossing the T of the French fleet's line of battle. Engraving by Henry Winkles, under the direction of Johann Georg Heck, in *Atlas géographique, astronomique et historique, servant à l'intelligence de l'histoire ancienne, du moyen-âge et modern*, edited by Johann Georg Heck (Paris: Maillet, 1842). Courtesy of the Roorda/Doyle Collection.

cover that we were in a situation to weather a large part of the enemy's fleet, which was now reduced to thirty ships, two having been so much damaged by the action of the 9th, that they could not resume their place in the line, and one having been rendered inefficient by the accident above mentioned.

"The line of battle was formed in an incredibly short time, the officers of the fleet having acquired the utmost experience in naval evolutions in the course of the two last years' practice on this station.

"About half an hour before the engagement commenced, at breakfast on board of the *Formidable*, the company consisting of the Admiral, Sir Charles Douglas, captain of the fleet (an officer whose functions nearly correspond with those of the adjutant-general of an army), Captain Simmons, commander of the ship, Lord Cranstoun, a volunteer post captain, the admiral's secretary, and myself, the conversation naturally turned on the glorious prospects of the day; and Lord Cranstoun remarked, that if our fleet maintained its present relative position, steering the same course close hauled on the opposite tack to the enemy, we must necessarily pass through their line in running along, and closing with it in action.

"The Admiral visibly caught the idea, and no doubt decided in his own mind at that moment to attempt a manoeuvre at that time hitherto unpractised by him with the most complete success, setting the illustrious example in the ship which bore his own flag; for the signal for close action being thrown out, and adhered to in letter and spirit for about an hour, and after taking and returning the fire of one half of the French force, under one general blaze and peal of thunder along both lines, the *Formidable* broke through that of the enemy. In the act of doing so, we passed within pistol-shot of the *Glorieux*, of seventy-four guns, which was so roughly handled, that, being shorn of all her masts, bowsprit, and ensign staff, but with the white flag nailed to the stump of one of the masts, breathing defiance as it were in her last moments, became a motionless hulk, presenting a spectacle which struck our Admiral's fancy as not unlike the remains of a fallen hero, for, being an indefatigable reader of Homer, he exclaimed, that now was to be the contest for the body of Patroclus; but the contest was already at an end, for the enemy's fleet being separated, fell into confusion, a total rout ensued, and victory was no longer doubtful.[1]

"It was natural, at first sight, to attribute this success to the numerical superiority of our ships; but it was computed by Sir Charles Douglas (the most enlightened and scientific naval officer with whom I was ever acquainted), that the sum total of the weight of a broadside of the French fleet exceeded that of the British fleet by four thousand three hundred and ninety-six pounds; and although the number of our guns exceeded that of theirs by one hundred and fifty-six, their lower-deck batteries, in ships of seventy-four guns and upwards, the difference of the round of the two nations, are equal to our forty-two pounders, and gave the enemy the abovementioned preponderance of metal on the whole amount. The difference in the number of men was still more considerable; for besides that the French have a much greater complement of men to the same tonnage, they had the assistance of a large body of land forces.

"The only cause, therefore, that can be assigned for British superiority in this and in many other naval encounters, can be not other than the closeness of the action—an advantage, however, which, being mutual and equal, can be available only to that party which possesses the moral pre-eminence of undaunted courage, and the consequent physical superiority of a better sustained fire, and this was never more fully exemplified and proved than in the present instance.

"In breaking the line, the *Formidable* passed so near the *Glorieux*, that I could see the cannoniers throwing away their sponges and handspikes in order to save themselves by running below, while our guns were served with the utmost animation. Another advantage of close fight is, that more of the shot tell in this situation, though they are much less destructive both to ships and men; unless, according to the recommendation of Robins, a smaller charge of powder should be used in close action. Distant shot, in consequence of their momentum being spent, make large chasms in a ship's side, shivering whole planks, and causing innumerable splinters, more destructive to men than the ball itself; whereas a close shot cuts so clear, that it makes an orifice even less than its own diameter, and without producing splinters. The average proportion of wounded to killed is about three to one; but this ratio will vary according to the distance and the charge of powder."*

*"Comte de Grasse," said Rodney in a private letter to his family, "who is at this moment sitting in my stern gallery, tells me he thought his fleet superior to mine, and does so still, though I had two more in number; and I am of his opinion, as his was composed of large ships, and ten of mine were only sixty-fours."

Note

1. Patroclus was a Greek hero of the Trojan War, who led an amphibious assault against Troy, during which Hector killed him. Achilles, the Greek commander, fought to recover his body.

Captain Marryat's War

Frederick Marryat

Captain Frederick Marryat (1792–1848) was among the most popular authors in the world in the nineteenth century. Herman Melville and Mark Twain dropped his name in their writing, confident that Marryat was familiar to their readers. The Marryat Cycle of novels, the best known of which is Mr. Midshipman Easy, *initiated and largely defined the popular modern genre of swashbuckling maritime fiction, prefiguring the work of C. S. Forster, famous for the Horatio Hornblower series, and Patrick O'Brien, whose books about Captain "Lucky Jack" Aubrey and the surgeon/ spy Stephen Maturin were adapted in the 2003 film* Master and Commander: The Far Side of the World. *Even so, few people know Marryat's name today. Although presented as fiction, his descriptions of Napoleonic naval combat derived from his twenty years of personal experience in the Royal Navy.*

This selection comes from the novel Peter Simple *(1834), in which the title character's experience reflects Marryat's own, as he enlists as a jejune midshipman and rises in the ranks while learning from veterans. It includes a narrative of the Battle of Cape St. Vincent off the coast of Portugal, which took place on Valentine's Day, 1797, when Marryat was just five years old, but his description of it, delivered in the form of a yarn by a gnarled survivor, draws from the author's familiarity with naval warfare and his fluency in the language of seamen, and it reflects the cult of adoration that formed around the charismatic figure of Horatio, Lord Nelson.*

"Well, Mr. Simple, as I told you before, old Jervis started with all his fleet for Cape St. Vincent.[1] We lost one of our fleet—and a three-decker, too—the *St. George*; she took the ground, and was obliged to go back to Lisbon; but we soon afterwards were joined by five sail of the line, sent out from England, so that we mustered fifteen sail in all.[2] We had like to lose another of our mess, for d'ye see, the old *Culloden* and *Colossus* fell foul of each other, and the *Culloden* had the worst on it, but Troubridge, who commanded her, was not a man to shy his work, and ax to go in to refit, when there was a chance of meeting the enemy—so he patched her up somehow or another, and reported himself ready for action the very next day.[3] Ready for action he always was, that's sure enough, but whether his ship was in a fit state to go into action, is quite another thing. But as the sailors used to say in joking, he was a *true bridge*, and you might trust to him; which meant as much as to say, that he knew how to take his ship into action, and how to fight her when he was fairly in it. I think it was the next day that Cockburn joined us in the *Minerve*, and he brought Nelson along with him, with the intelligence that the [Spanish] Dons had chased him, and that the whole Spanish fleet was out in pursuit of us.[4] Well, Mr. Simple, you may guess we were not a little happy in the *Captain*, when Nelson joined us, as we knew that if we fell in with the Spaniards, our ship would cut a figure—and so she did, sure enough. That was on the morning of the 13th, and old Jervis made the signal to prepare for action, and keep close order, which means, to have your flying jib-boom in at the starn windows of the ship ahead of you; and we did keep close order, for a man might have walked right round from one ship to the other, either lee or weather line of the fleet.[5] I shan't forget that night, Mr. Simple, as long as I live and breathe. Every now and then we heard the signal guns of the Spanish fleet booming at a distance to windward of us, and you may guess how our hearts leaped at the sound, and how we watched with all our ears for the next gun that was fired, trying to make out their bearings and distance, as we assembled in little knots upon the booms and weather gangway. It was my middle watch, and I was signalman at the time, so of course I had no time to take a caulk [nap] if I was inclined. When my watch was over, I could not go down to my hammock, so I kept the morning watch too, as did most of the men on board: as for Nelson, he walked the deck the whole night, quite in a fever. At daylight it was thick and hazy weather, and we could not make them out; but about five bells, the old *Culloden*, who, if she had broke her nose, had not lost the use of her eyes, made the signal for a part of the Spanish fleet in sight. Old Jervis repeated the signal to prepare for action, but he might have saved the wear and tear of the bunting, for we were all ready, bulkheads [ship's interior walls] down, screens up, guns shotted, tackles rove, yards slung, powder filled, shot on deck, and fire out—and what's more, Mr. Simple, I'll be damned if we wer'n't all willing too. About six bells in the forenoon [11 A.M.], the fog and haze all cleared away at once, just like the rising of the foresail, that they lower down at the Portsmouth Theatre, and discovered the whole of the Spanish fleet. I counted them all. 'How many, Swinburne?' cries Nelson. 'Twenty-six sail, sir,' answered I. Nelson walked the quarterdeck backwards and forwards, rubbing his hands, and laughing to himself, and then he called for his glass, and went to the gangway with Captain Miller. 'Swinburne, keep a good look upon the admiral,' says he. 'Ay, ay, sir,' says I. Now, you see, Mr. Simple, twenty-six sail against fifteen were great odds upon paper; but we didn't think so, because we know'd the difference between the two fleets. There was our fifteen sail of the line all in apple-pie order, packed up as close as dominoes, and every man on board of them longing to come to the scratch; while there was their twenty-six, all *somehow nohow*, two lines here, and *no line* there, with a great gap of water in the middle of them. For this gap between their ships we all steered, with all the sail we could carry, because, d'ye see, Mr. Simple, by getting them on both sides of us, we had the advantage of fighting both broadsides, which is just as easy as fighting one, and makes shorter work of it. Just as it struck seven bells, Troubridge opened the ball, *setting* to half-a-dozen of the Spaniards, and making them *reel* 'Tom Collins,' whether or no. Bang-bang-bang, bang! Oh, Mr. Simple, it's a beautiful sight, to see the first guns fired, that are to bring on a general action. 'He's the luckiest dog, that Troubridge,' said Nelson, stamping with impatience. Our ships were soon hard at it, hammer and tongs, (my eyes, how they did pelt it in!) and old Sir John, in the *Victory*, smashed the cabin windows of the Spanish admiral, with such a hell of a raking broadside, that the fellow bore up as if the devil kicked him. Lord-a-mercy! you might have drove a Portsmouth waggon into his starn—the broadside of the *Victory* had made room enough. However, they were soon all smothered up in smoke, and we could not make out how things were going on—but we made a pretty good guess. Well, Mr. Simple, as they say at the play, that was act the first, scene the first; and now we had to make our appearance, and I'll leave you to judge, after I've told my tale, whether the old *Captain* wasn't principal performer, and *top sawyer* over them all. But stop a moment, I'll just look at the binnacle [ship's compass used for steering], for that young topman's nodding at the wheel.—I say, Mr. Smith, are you shutting your eyes to keep them warm, and letting the ship run half a point out of her course? Take care I don't send for another helmsman that's all, and give the reason why. You'll make a wry face upon six-water grog, to-morrow, at seven bells. Damn your eyes, keep them open—can't you?"

Swinburne, after this genteel admonition to the man at the wheel, re-seated himself and continued his narrative.

"All this while, Mr. Simple, we in the *Captain* had not fired a gun; but were ranging up as fast as we could to where the enemy lay in a heap. There were plenty to pick and choose from; and Nelson looked out sharp for a big one, as little boys do when they have to choose an apple: and, by the piper that played before Moses! it was a big one that he ordered the master to put him alongside of. She was a four-decker, called the *Santissima Trinidad*. We had to pass some whoppers, which would have satisfied any reasonable man; for there was the *San Josef*, and *Salvador del Mondo*, and *San Nicolas*; but nothing would suit Nelson but this four-decked ship; so we crossed the hawse of about six of them, and as soon as we were abreast of her, and at the word 'Fire!' every gun went off at once, slap into her, and the old *Captain* reeled at the discharge as if she was drunk.[6] I wish you'd only seen how we pitched it into this *Holy Trinity*; she was *holy* enough before we had done with her, riddled like a sieve, several of her ports knocked into one, and every scupper of her running blood and water. Not but what she stood to it as bold as brass,

We saw a boat full of negroes.

The youthful protagonist of Captain Frederick Marryat's *Peter Simple* leads an adventurous life. Voyaging to the Caribbean Sea, he endures a hurricane, staves off pirates, and survives a shipwreck by clinging to the mainmast with his shipmates. Local fishermen, out in their canoe to catch flying fish, rescue the seamen after many terrifying hours adrift. Geoffrey Walter Goss, "We saw a boat full of Negroes," illustration in *Peter Simple*, by Frederick Marryat, retold and edited by Constance M. Martin (London: Philip and Tacey Educational Publishers, Ltd., 1940), 38. Courtesy of Rosalind Goss and the Roorda/Doyle Collection.

and gave us nearly gun for gun, and made a very pretty general average in our ship's company. Many of the old captains went to kingdom come in that business, and many more were obliged to bear up for Greenwich Hospital.

"'Fire away, my lads—steady aim!' cries Nelson. 'Jump down there, Mr. Thomas; pass the word to reduce the cartridges, the shot go clean through her. Double shot the guns there, fore and aft.'

"So we were at it for about half-an-hour, when our guns became so hot from quick firing, that they bounced up to the beams overhead, tearing away their ringbolts, and snapping the breechings like rope yarns. By this time we were almost as much unrigged as if we had been two days paying off in Portsmouth harbour. The four-decker forged ahead, and Troubridge, in the jolly old *Culloden*, came between us and two other Spanish ships, who were playing into us. She was as fresh as a daisy, and gave them a dose which quite astonished them. They shook their ears, and fell astern, when the *Blenheim* laid hold of them, and mauled them so that they went astern again. But it was out of the frying-pan into the fire: for the *Orion*, *Prince George*, and one or two others, were coming up, and knocked the very guts out of them. I'll be damned if they forgot the 14th of April, and sarve them right, too. Wasn't a four-decker enough for any two-decker, without any more coming on us? and couldn't the beggars have matched themselves like gentlemen? Well, Mr. Simple, this gave us a minute or two to fetch our breath, let the guns cool, and repair damages, and swab the blood from the decks; but we lost our four-decker, for we could not get near her again."

"What odd names the Spaniards give to their ships, Swinburne!"

"Why, yes, they do; it would almost appear wicked to belabour the *Holy Trinity* as we did. But why they should call a four-decked ship the *Holy Trinity* I can't tell. Bill Saunders said that the fourth deck was for the Pope, who was as great a parsonage as the others: but I can't understand how that can be. Well, Mr. Simple, as I was head-signalman, I was perched on the poop, and didn't serve at a gun. I had to report all I could see, which was not much, the smoke was so thick; but now and then I could get a peep, as it were, through the holes in the blanket. Of course I was obliged to keep my eye as much as possible upon the admiral, not to make out his signals, for Commodore Nelson wouldn't thank me for that; I knew he hated a signal when in action, so I never took no notice of the bunting, but just watched to see what he was about. So while we are repairing damages, I'll just tell you what I saw of the rest of the fleet. As soon as old Jervis had done for the Spanish admiral, he hauled his wind on the larboard tack, and, followed by four or five other ships, weathered the Spanish line and joined Collingwood in the *Excellent*.[7] Then they all dashed through the line; the *Excellent* was the leading ship, and she first took the shine out of the *Salvador del Mondo*, and then left her to be picked up by the other ships, while she attacked a two-decker, who hauled down her colours—I forget her name just now. As soon as the *Victory* ran alongside of the *Salvador del Mondo*, down went her colours, and *Excellent* reasons had she for striking her flag. And now, Mr. Simple, the old *Captain* comes into play again. Having parted company with the four-decker, we had recommenced action with the *San Nicolas*, a Spanish eighty, and while we were hard at it, old Collingwood comes up in the *Excellent*. The *San Nicolas*, knowing that the *Excellent's* broadside would send her to old Nick, put her helm up to avoid being raked: in so doing, she fell foul of the *San Josef*, a Spanish three-decker, and we being all cut to pieces, and unmanageable—all of us indeed reeling about like drunken men—Nelson ordered his helm a starboard, and in a jiffy there we were, all three hugging each other, running in one another's guns, smashing our chain-plates, and poking our yard arms through each other's canvas.

"'All hands to board!' roared Nelson, leaping on the hammocks and waving his sword.

"'Hurrah! hurrah!' echoed through the decks, and up flew the men, like as angry bees out of a bee-hive. In a moment pikes, tomahawks, cutlasses, and pistols were seized (for it was quite unexpected, Mr. Simple), and our men poured into the eighty-gun ship, and in two minutes the decks were cleared, and all the Dons pitched below. I joined the boarders and was on the main-deck when Captain Miller came down, and cried out, 'On deck again immediately.' Up we went, and what do you think it was for, Mr. Simple? Why to board a second time; for Nelson having taken the two-decker, swore that he'd have the three-decker as well. So away we went again, clambering up her lofty sides how we could, and dropping down on her decks like hailstones. We all made for the quarter-deck, beat down every Spanish beggar that showed fight, and in five minutes more we had hauled down the colours of two of the finest ships in the Spanish navy. If that wasn't taking the shine out of the Dons, I should like to know what is. And didn't the old captains cheer and shake hands, as Commodore Nelson stood on the deck of the *San Josef*, and received the swords of the Spanish officers! There was enough of them to go right round the capstern, and plenty to spare. Now, Mr. Simple, what do you think of that for a spree?"

"Why, Swinburne, I can only say that I wish I had been there."

"So did every man in the fleet, Mr. Simple, I can tell you."

"But what became of the *Santissima Trinidad*?"

"Upon my word, she behaved one *deck* better than all the others. She held out against four of our ships for a long while, and then hauled down her colours, and no disgrace to her, considering what a precious hammering she had taken first. But the lee division of the Spanish weather fleet, if I may so call it, consisting of eleven sail of the line, came up to her assistance, and surrounded her, so that they got her off. Our ships were too much cut up to commence a new action, and the admiral made the signal to secure the prizes. The Spanish fleet then did what they should have done before—got into line; and we lost no time in doing the same. But we both had had fighting enough."

"But do you think, Swinburne, that the Spaniards fought well?"

"They'd have fought better, if they'd only have known how. There's no want of courage in the Dons, Mr. Simple, but they did not support each other. Only observe how Troubridge supported us. By God, Mr. Simple, he was the *real fellow*, and Nelson knew it well. He was Nelson's right-hand man; but you know there wasn't room for *two* Nelsons. Their ships engaged and held out well, it must be acknowledged, but why wer'n't they all in their proper berths? Had they kept close order of sailing, and had all fought as well as those who were captured, it would not have been a very easy matter for fifteen ships to gain a victory over twenty-six. That's long odds, even when backed by British seamen."

"Well, how did you separate?"

"Why, the next morning the Spaniards had the weather-gauge, so they had the option whether to fight or not. At one time they had half a mind, for they bore down to us; upon which we hauled our wind, to show them we were all ready to meet them, and then they thought better of it, and rounded-to again.[8] So as they wouldn't fight, and we didn't wish it, we parted company in the night; and two days afterwards we anchored, with our four prizes, in Lagos Bay. So now you have the whole of it, Mr. Simple, and I've talked till I'm quite hoarse. You havn't by chance another drop of the stuff left to clear my throat? It would be quite a charity."

"I think I have, Swinburne; and as you deserve it, I will go and fetch it."

Notes

1. Admiral Sir John Jervis (1735–1823) commanded the British fleet at the Battle of St. Vincent and was subsequently knighted as the Earl of St. Vincent for his actions.

2. A three-decker was a ship with three decks for cannons; a ship of the line usually had three decks, which accommodated at least seventy-four cannons, and often many more.

3. After leading the line at the Battle of St. Vincent, Sir Thomas Troubridge (1758–1807) went on to fight with Nelson at Tenerife and the Battle of the Nile in August 1798, rising to the rank of rear admiral.

4. Sir George Cockburn (1772–1853) is best known for capturing and burning the city of Washington, DC, in August 1814.

5. The flying jib boom is the part of the vessel that is furthest forward; it is the spar at the tip of the bowsprit, which is the pole at the front, or bow, of the ship, to which the forward-most sails, the jibs, are attached. The weather or windward side of a ship is toward the direction of the wind, while the lee or leeward side is the direction away from the wind. Being to windward of the enemy, or having "the weather gauge," was of paramount

importance in battles between sailing ships, because with it, they could attack with the momentum of the elements, which their opponent battled.

6. The hawser is the chain or cable that holds the anchor, and the hawse holes are in the bow of a ship; to cross the hawse means to sail past.

7. To haul wind is to reduce speed; larboard means left, the opposite of starboard. Baron Cuthbert Collingwood (1748–1810) fought with Nelson at several battles, rising to Vice Admiral.

8. To round to means to turn around.

World War I beneath the Waves

Edgar von Spiegel von und zu Peckelsheim

The excerpt here is from the 1916 best-selling book Kriegstagebuch *[war diary]* U-202, *by Captain Baron Edgar von Spiegel von und zu Peckelsheim, an active U-boat captain. It shows from a periscope's perspective that submarine attacks unleashed horrific chaos on any people (and animals) on board. Such terrible scenes unfolded more than 5,000 times during World War I, as U-boats sank that many merchant ships, along with more than 100 warships, killing some 15,000 people. The German Navy did so at a high cost, losing 217 of its 351 U-boats, with roughly 5,000 crew members entombed in them when they sank. The travesty of submarine warfare, branded as "unmanly" by President Woodrow Wilson in his War Message of April 1917, brought the United States into the Great War.*

The Sinking of the Transport

Soon the outline of a ship told us that ahead of us was a large steamer, steaming westward at high speed. The disappointment which we experienced at first was soon reversed when it was clearly shown that the fortunes of war had again sent a ship across our course which belonged to a hostile power. . . .

"The steamer's armed! Take a look, mate."

I stepped away from the sights of the periscope. "Can you see the gun mounted forward of the bridge?"

"Yes, certainly," he replied excitedly. "I can see it, and quite a large piece it is, too."

"Now take a look at her stern—right by the second mast—what do you notice there?"

"Thousand devils! Another cannon—at least a ten-centimeter gun. It's a transport, sure." . . .

Oh, what a glorious sensation is a U-boat attack! What a great understanding and cooperation between a U-boat and its crew—between dead matter and living beings! What a merging into a single being, of the nerves and spirit of an entire crew!

. . . I could clearly distinguish the various objects on board, and saw the giant steamer at a very short distance—how the captain was walking back

R. M. S. „Arabic"

When a German submarine sank the British Cunard Line's *Lusitania* in May 1915, it set the United States on a course to enter World War I. Three months later, a U-boat torpedoed the Royal Mail Steamship *Arabic* of the White Star Line, further propelling the country toward a declaration of war upon Germany in April 1917. Photographer unknown, postcard, c. 1902–15. Courtesy of the Roorda/Doyle Collection.

and forth on the bridge with a short pipe in his mouth, how the crew was scrubbing the forward deck. I saw with amazement—a shiver went through me—a long line of compartments of wood spread over the entire deck, out of which were sticking black and brown horse heads and necks.

Oh, great Scott! Horses! What a pity! Splendid animals!

"What has that to do with it?" I continually thought. War is war. And every horse less on the western front is to lessen England's defense. I have to admit, however, that the thought which had to come was disgusting, and I wish to make the story about it short.

Only a few degrees were lacking for the desired angle, and soon the steamer would get into the correct focus. It was passing us at the right distance, a few hundred meters.

"Torpedo ready!" I called down into the "Centrale" [control room].

It was the longed-for command. Every one on board held his breath. Now the steamer's bow cut the line of the periscope—now the deck, the bridge, the foremast—the funnel.

"Let go!"

A light trembling shook the boat—the torpedo was on its way. Woe, when it was loose!

There it was speeding, the murderous projectile, with an insane speed straight at its prey. I could accurately follow its path by the light wake it left in the water.

The fog of war is the general confusion that arises during a battle, caused literally
by fog and smoke, and figuratively by failed communication, flawed intelligence,
misguided orders, and the like. The Battle of Jutland is an example of the fog of war
at sea. The major naval clash of World War I took place on the west side of the Jutland
Peninsula from May 31 to June 1, 1916, in conditions of very poor visibility, produced by
a combination of natural fog banks, the smoke from incessant cannonades, and smoke
screens that ships intentionally laid to disguise their movements. After Jutland, navies
developed more efficient ways to produce and deploy screens of dense, black plumes.
This photograph shows US Navy ships deploying a smoke screen as part of fleet maneuvers in 1925. Photographer unknown, from the Earl "Dutch" Baldwin Photograph
Albums. Courtesy of the Roorda/Doyle Collection.

"Thirty seconds," counted the mate. . . .

"Twenty-two seconds!"

Now it must happen—the terrible thing!

I saw the ship's people on the bridge had discovered the wake, which was
leaving a slender stripe. How they pointed across the sea in terror; how the
captain, covering his face with his hands, resigned himself to what must
come. And next there was a terrific shaking so that all aboard the steamer
were tossed about and then, like a volcano, arose, majestic but fearful in its
beauty, a two-hundred meter high and fifty-meter wide pillar toward the sky.

"A full hit behind the second funnel!" I called down to the "Centrale."
Then they cut loose down there for joy. They were carried away by ecstasy
which welled out of their hearts, a joyous storm that ran through our entire
boat and up to me.

And over there?

Landlubber, still thy heart!

A terrible drama was being enacted on the hard-hit ship. It listed and sank
toward us.

From the tower I could observe all the decks. From all the hatches human beings forced their way out, fighting despairingly. Russian firemen, officers, sailors, soldiers, hostlers, the kitchen crew, all were running and calling for the boats. Panic stricken, they thronged about one another down the stairways, fighting for the life-boats, and among all were the rearing, snorting and kicking horses. The boats on the starboard deck could not be put into service, as they could not be swung clear because of the list of the careening steamer. All, therefore, thronged to the boats on the port side, which, in the haste and anguish, were lowered, some half empty; others were overcrowded. Those who were left aboard were wringing their hands in despair. They ran from bow to stern and back again from stern to bow in their terror, and then finally threw themselves into the sea in order to attempt to swim to the boats.

Then another explosion resounded, after which a hissing white wave of steam streamed out of all the ports. The hot steam set the horses crazy, and they were beside themselves with terror—I could see a splendid, dapple-grey horse with a long tail make a great leap over the ship's side and land in a life-boat, already overcrowded—but after that I could not endure the terrible spectacle any longer. Pulling down the periscope, we submerged into the deep.

The Far-Flung Battle of Midway

Office of Naval Intelligence

The Battle of Midway, fought in the North Pacific in early June 1942, was the most important naval battle of the twentieth century. It was only the second naval battle in history during which the opposing ships engaged in combat while out of sight of each other over the horizon, with the attacks being carried out by airplanes, the first having been the Battle of the Coral Sea one month before. At Midway, the Japanese attempt to seize that mid-Ocean island failed, turning the tide of war in the Pacific. The following account comes from military documents captured after Japan surrendered in September 1945, translated by the Office of Naval Intelligence, and published in 1947 as The Japanese Story of the Battle of Midway. *The sources show that the Japanese Imperial Navy command was uncertain of the damage it had inflicted at Pearl Harbor the previous December, that it badly underestimated US naval strength, and was completely wrong about the number of ships in the vicinity of the tiny atoll of Midway. Unknown to the Japanese, cryptanalysts working for US Pacific Fleet Intelligence had broken their code, so Admiral Chester Nimitz knew in advance that Admiral Isoroku Yamamoto intended to approach with his task force—with a nucleus of four aircraft carriers—from the north, at the latitude of the Stormy Forties usually avoided by mariners. But knowing that the ships were coming and finding them on the vast Ocean were two different things, and the fact that US airplanes spotted them in time determined the outcome of the battle, which was the sinking of all four Japanese aircraft carriers and their 248 warplanes, killing more than 3,000 sailors and pilots, a blow from which the Imperial Navy never recovered. The US Navy lost one of its three aircraft carriers and a destroyer, with just over 300 men killed in action. The captured documents presented here offer the Japanese analysis before the battle, a minute-by-minute account of the decisive day of battle on June 4, 1942, and an after-action report summarizing and putting a positive spin on the catastrophic defeat.*

Part I. Existing Conditions and Trends

I. GENERAL SITUATION OF THE ENEMY

Because of developments during the First Phase Operations, the enemy's outposts which he had relied on to be his first line of defense, collapsed one after another until he began to feel direct threats even to such areas as India, Australia, and Hawaii.[1] The enemy was exerting every pressure to stem this tide by stepping up his submarine strength in the waters controlled by us and by increasing his air strength in the Australia area. He employed these to carry on guerrilla type tactics. Task force thrusts were also made in the Western and Southwestern Pacific.

These seemed to indicate that the enemy was planning on more positive actions than heretofore.

Subsequent to the beating he received in the Coral Sea on 7–8 May, the enemy was temporarily subdued, but by the end of May—by the time the Fleet was about to sortie from Hashira Jima[2]—the enemy again began to show considerable life in all areas, particularly in the Australia area.

2. SITUATION IN THE MIDWAY AREA

Midway acts as a sentry for Hawaii. Its importance was further enhanced after the loss of Wake and it was apparent that the enemy was expediting the reinforcing of its defensive installations, its air base facilities, and other military installations as well as the personnel. . . .

Of the enemy's carriers, the *Ranger* was apparently in the Atlantic. According to some prisoners' statements, the *Lexington* had been sunk. There were others, however, who claimed that she was under repair on the West Coast.[3]

The *Enterprise* and the *Hornet* were definitely placed in the Pacific, but we could get no reliable information as to the whereabouts of the *Wasp*.

About six auxiliary carriers had been completed and there were indications that about half of this number were in the Pacific. However, they were known to be inferior in speed and could not be effectively employed for positive action. . . .

3. MOBILE FORCE COMMANDER'S ESTIMATE OF THE SITUATION

(a) Although the enemy lacks the will to fight, it is likely that he will counter attack if our occupation operations progress satisfactorily.

(b) The enemy conducts air reconnaissance mainly to the West and to the South but does not maintain a strict vigil to the Northwest or to the North.

(c) The enemy's patrol radius is about 500 miles.

(d) The enemy is not aware of our plans. (We were not discovered until early in the morning of the 5th at the earliest.)

(e) It is not believed that the enemy has any powerful unit, with carriers as its nucleus, in the vicinity.

(f) After attacking Midway by air and destroying the enemy's shore based air strength to facilitate our landing operations, we would still be able to destroy any enemy task force which may choose to counter attack.

(g) The enemy's attempt to counterattack with use of shore based aircraft could be neutralized by our cover fighters and AA [antiaircraft] fire. . . .

Part III. Description of the Operation . . .

The *Mobile Force* departed Hashira Jima at 0600 17 May. Maintaining strict anti-sub screen and a rigid radio silence, the force headed for the area to the northwest of Midway following course 1 as given in *Mobile Force* Secret OpOrd 35.

On 1 and 2 June, all ships were refueled.

Visibility steadily decreased from about 1000 2 June so that by 2300 on the 3d, all ships were being navigated blindly. No visual signals could be employed during this period. Since there seemed little likelihood of the fog's lifting, the radio was used as a last resort at 1030 on the 3d (long wave) to give change of course.

Shortly after this, the fog lifted somewhat, making visual signals barely possible. By the morning of the 4th visibility on the surface improved greatly, but there were scattered clouds overhead.

At 1640 the *Tone* reported sighting about 10 enemy planes bearing 260 degrees. Three fighters immediately took off from the *Akagi* in pursuit of these but they were unable to sight the enemy. There is some element of doubt in the reported sighting.

At about 2330 on the same day, the *Akagi* twice sighted what was thought to be enemy planes weaving in and out of the clouds. All hands were immediately ordered to battle stations. There is considerable doubt as to the reliability of this sighting.

At 0130 on the 5th, under command of flight officer of the *Hiryu*, Lieut. Tomonaga, Organization #5 composed of 36 ship-based fighters, 36 ship-based bombers, and 36 ship-based torpedo planes, took off to attack Midway. . . .[4]

From about 0230, two to three enemy flying boats maintained continuous contact with us.

Shortly after taking off, the attack unit was contacted by enemy flying boats. When about 30 miles short of the target on Midway, the above mentioned flying boats suddenly dropped illumination bombs over our attack plane units to attract overhead cover fighters.

Thereafter, while engaging in bitter air combats, bombs were dropped on military installations on Midway between about 0345 and 0410. Fires resulted. All but 2 ship-based fighters, 1 ship-based bomber and 3 ship-based torpedo planes returned to their carriers by about 0600.

After our attack unit had taken off, enemy flying boats maintained contact with us. At about 0400 the first enemy wave attacked. From then until about 0730, the enemy attacked almost continuously. We counter attacked with fighters and AA fire and were able to bring most of the attackers down by 0645. About 30 carrier-based bombers then attacked us resulting in fires

This US Navy photograph was captioned "Heavy anti-aircraft fire greets Japanese torpedo planes attacking U.S. Pacific Fleet forces during the battle of Midway June 4, 1942. Note the smoke from the enemy plane shot down to the right, the shrapnel bursts in the water and the fast-moving cruiser (left) and destroyer (right)." Taken by an unknown photographer, it went to the London Office of War Information, where it was "certified as passed by [the] SHAEF [Supreme HQ Allied Expeditionary Force] Censor," but was "not issued." Courtesy of the Roorda/Doyle Collection.

aboard the *Akagi*, *Kaga*, and *Soryu*, forcing them to fall behind and leaving only the *Hiryu* untouched. . . .

At about 0500, *Tone*'s #4 plane reported: "Sighted what appears to be the enemy composed of 10 (ships), bearing 10 degrees, distance 240 miles from Midway, on course 150 degrees, speed 20 knots (0428)." . . .

At 0530, *Tone*'s plane reported: "The enemy is accompanied by what appears to be a carrier in a position to the rear of the others (0520)." And again at about 0540: "Sight what appears to be 2 cruisers in position bearing 8 degrees, distance 250 miles from Midway; course, 150 degrees; speed 20 knots (0530)."

Thus, it was definitely established that enemy carriers were operating in the vicinity. The following dispatch was, therefore, sent to CinC *Combined Fleet*:

"(Info: CinC 2nd Fleet) At 0500, the enemy composed of 1 carrier, 5 cruisers, and 5 destroyers, was sighted in position bearing 10 degrees, distance 240 miles from Midway. We are heading for it." . . .

While we were engaged in this, the enemy struck. Communication facilities were knocked out of all damaged ships. There was little likelihood of the fires being extinguished in the immediate future. For these reasons, I decided to direct the operations from the *Nagara*, and transferred to her at 0830.

After our ships had been damaged, the commander of CarDiv 2 decided to carry out the attack against the enemy carrier sighted by *Tone*'s float recco plane. At 0758, *Hiryu*'s attack unit (6 fighters and 18 bombers) took off and carried out the attack. Direct hits by 5 #25 ordinary and 1 land bombs were scored on an *Enterprise* class carrier, inflicting serious damage to her (possibly sinking her).

Prior to this, at 0530, a type 13 experimental ship-based bomber from the *Soryu* was ordered to maintain contact with the enemy carrier but due to break-down in radio facilities, it was not known until the return of this plane that, in addition to the aforementioned, there was a task force which had as its nucleus a carrier of the *Enterprise* class and another of the *Hornet* class. This task force was operating in waters to the north of the other one.

With this information at hand, the *Hiryu* attack unit (4 fighters and 9 torpedo planes, supplemented by 2 fighters from the *Kaga* and 1 torpedo plane from the *Akagi*) was ordered to the attack. Three torpedo hits were scored on a carrier of the *Enterprise* class, seriously damaging her. Heavy damages were also inflicted on a heavy cruiser of the *San Francisco* class. . . .

At 1045, the enemy changed its course to 90 degrees and the opportunity for battle seemed to be close at hand. Somewhat later, *Tone*'s #4 plane reported: "The enemy is in position bearing 114 degrees, distance 110 miles from my position of 1230." From this it became evident that the enemy was trying to put distance between himself and us.

It was deemed that if under these conditions, the enemy chose to strike, we would be at a distinct disadvantage in that we would be unable to carry out a decisive battle.

We, therefore, turned about and proceeded westward, with the expectation of destroying the enemy in a night encounter. . . .

While thus laying plans for the night attack, the *Hiryu* also broke out in flames at 1405. That meant that while all four of our carriers had been lost, the enemy had at least one. Moreover, as long as we were in the operational radius of their shore-based air, we would be at a very distinct disadvantage.

By 1433, the enemy began to retreat to the east on course 70, speed 20 knots, which further reduced our hopes for a night engagement. However, we still were determined to carry it out. *Nagara*'s plane was ordered to prepare for a take-off and all the ships were ordered to assemble in the vicinity of the *Nagara*. . . .

At about this time the commander of the *Chikuma* made the following report: "This ship's #2 plane reports that at about 1530 he sighted 4 enemy carriers, 6 cruisers and 15 destroyers proceeding westward in a position about 30 miles east of the listing and burning enemy carrier."

This was the first inkling we had of the overwhelming superiority of the enemy's carrier strength. . . .

3. ACTUAL CONDITION OF THE ENEMY

(a) Actual conditions in the Midway area:

The enemy apparently anticipated our attack and had their attack planes and flying boats take off. They also concentrated about 50 fighters (all Grummans), and intercepted our first attack wave at a point approximately 30 miles short of our target. When we subjected these to fierce counterattacks, however, they were put on the defensive and engaged, for the most part, in evasive maneuvers. Our ship-based attack planes and bombers suffered no casualties from enemy interceptors while the greater part of their fighters were brought down by us. Results we obtained were 41 enemy ship-based fighters, 1 ship-based bomber and 1 float recco shot down. We lost 4 planes from the exceedingly hot enemy AA fire, so our total losses including 2 which were scuttled during air engagements, were 6 planes.

Twelve bomb hits were scored by us on two enemy runways with #80 land bombs, but these were insufficient to render them inoperational, since the large shore-based attack planes were very active subsequently. We are of the opinion that it is impractical to attempt to render such air fields as these inoperational through bombings. . . .

6. GENERAL SITUATION AT CONCLUSION OF OPERATIONS
AND THE COMMANDER'S ESTIMATE CONCERNING IT

Exceptional fighting was shown by all forces and all ships participating in this operation, and because of it, severe damages were inflicted on the enemy. At the same time, our losses numbered four carriers and the occupation of Midway was not carried out.

The enemy, however, having lost two of their powerful carriers and many of his air personnel, would undoubtedly be unable to effect any large-scale operation in the near future.[5] It is believed that the enemy will surely strike back at some time, and every precaution should be taken against this.

Through this operation, there are some vital lessons learned in aircraft carrier warfare, which should be kept alive. These include such items as the reinforcements of searches for the enemy, flexibility of assembling and dispersing, and the speedy take-offs of friendly aircraft when the enemy is sighted.

Notes

1. The First Phase began with the attack on Pearl Harbor on December 7, 1941, and included successful offensives to take the Philippines, Hong Kong, Singapore, and much more of Southeast Asia by April 1942.

2. The Battle of the Coral Sea, fought in that body of water between northeast Australia and New Guinea, is considered a strategic victory for Japan but a tactical win for the United States.

3. The *Lexington* had indeed been scuttled after taking heavy damage at the Battle of the Coral Sea, and the *Yorktown* nearly sank but was repaired hastily at Pearl Harbor, in time to play a major role at Midway, where it finally succumbed and sank, as well.

4. Perhaps because the International Date Line nearly bisects Midway Atoll, the dates employed in this report are one day later than standard accounts, which give June 4 as the climactic day of battle.

5. Actually only the *Yorktown* was lost.

The Barents Sea, Most Dangerous Waters of World War II

Jack Bowman

The most lethal success of submarine technology came during World War II. German "wolf packs" of U-boats devastated shipping on the North Atlantic Ocean during the early years of the Battle of the Atlantic, and the United States' submarine offensive in the Pacific Ocean swept the seas clear of Japanese ships of all kinds. But German submarines inflicted the greatest destruction in the Arctic Ocean against the Allied convoys bound for the Soviet Union. The highest US casualty percentages of the war did not occur among island-hopping marines in the Pacific Ocean or army soldiers storming the beaches on D-Day, but among merchant mariners on the Murmansk Run to the port of Archangel on the White Sea.

The journal of Engineering Petty Officer Jack Bowman (1907–88), aboard the corvette HMS *La Malouine in 1942, is a terse, grim account of the doomed convoy codenamed PQ-17, going to the bottom one by one in the dark waters around the Kola Peninsula. Despite being guarded by nearly twenty warships and two submarines, the convoy lost twenty-four of its thirty-five merchant ships to repeated attacks by nine Nazi submarines and nearly forty warplanes. Bowman himself did not have to be there. As a ferry operator on England's Lake Windermere, he had an exemption from the mass military draft that World War II necessitated in the United Kingdom, but he enlisted voluntarily in the Royal Navy in October 1940. He was not a habitual diarist, but for unknown reasons, he recorded his experiences on PQ-17, although it is unlikely that he anticipated the carnage he would witness. The first dozen PQ-numbered convoys had lost only one ship, and losses had been relatively light for the next four voyages to Archangel. But the German navy, recognizing the importance of the supply route for keeping the Soviet Union from collapsing, moved many more submarines and warplanes to the region prior to the seventeenth convoy. Winston Churchill called the disastrous fate of PQ-17 "one of the most melancholy naval episodes in the whole of the war," which was saying a great deal. Jack Bowman survived the ordeal and the rest of the war, and went back to running his ferryboat on Lake Windermere for the next three decades. He never again kept a journal and he rarely spoke of PQ-17.*

WEDNESDAY, JULY 1ST.

By now we are 70 degrees N, and on the bridge it is below freezing point. I have seen my first small iceberg, we were attacked all afternoon by subs, but no ship took any harm—the escort was too strong for them to enter. It was deafening in the engine room, depth charges going off everywhere. I thought many a time that everything was up. Standing by all the time with lifebelts on. My thoughts always with home.

THURSDAY, JULY 2ND.

Attacks started early again this morning by subs. It was reported that we had been spotted by a Focke-Wulf. This was bad, because later in the day we noticed three Dornier flying-boats shadowing us on our port beam.[1] They kept manoeuvering for position, and at 2000 pressed their attack home. We beat them off, our ship bringing one down in flames. We picked their rubber dinghy up. It was well packed with stores. Subs came on again for the rest of the night.

FRIDAY, JULY 3RD.

Spasmodic raids by aircraft, who are still flying on our port side. At the moment we are on the outer screen. The Admiralty have just sent a signal to say that the German fleet, *Hipper*, *Lutzo* [*Lutzow*], *Tirpitz* and *von Sheer* [*Admiral Scheer*] with escort of destroyers have left Narvik and Trondheim [Norway]. Icebergs are getting fairly big now. It is damned cold. 11.00pm.

SATURDAY, JULY 4TH. FATAL DAY.

German planes still making swoops at us, and shadowing. At 1800 suddenly the sky is black with bombers and the attack is on. It was a small hell let loose. As far as is known, all these were carrying tinfish [torpedo bombs]. One of the merchant ships, it must have been an oiler, sank within five seconds. Soon the sea was covered with boats and rafts and bodies. As far as I know, three ships were sunk and some abandoned, but later were boarded again. All this time neither cruisers, battleships, or aircraft from the carrier came to our assistance. I suppose they were looking for the German fleet. Later on the Admiralty signalled all destroyers to leave the convoy and try to engage the Germans. The convoy was to split up, every man for himself. We seemed to be in a very hopeless situation. Soon ships seemed to be racing in every direction. Our captain decided to go north. Two or three followed us.

SUNDAY, JULY 5TH.

By this morning we could get no further because of icefields. We are 15 degrees off the North Pole. What a sight! Icebergs as big as Orrest Head, all a lovely bluey-green, covered with arctic birds.[2] I think we have covered about 200 miles trying to get round these icefields. At 1600 another Admiralty signal. Two German battlewagons and eight destroyers were likely to intercept that night, or early morning. Imagine our feelings. By this time we were beginning to lose hope. Remember that we had never had our clothes off for a week, and nerves were becoming taut. I never lost hope myself, but felt very sorry for one of my stokers whose nerve has gone. I was prepared, if given the chance, to sell my life very dearly. My only regrets were those I loved at home. A fog set in and we must have lost the fleet.

MONDAY, JULY 6TH.

We have come to a big island, roughly the size of Britain. Its name is Nov[a] ya Zemlya, about 1,000 miles north of Archangel. We have found a bay and anchored. The place seems uninhabited, it is all snow and ice. I have heard that it is only open two months in the year. This voyage is becoming an adventure. Here we are, stuck in a bay, oil running short, food becoming rationed very thinly, and awfully cold. Several ships have come in tonight, including four American merchant ships laden with tanks and bombers, and a corvette with 70 survivors. I have not heard of *Dianella* since leaving Iceland, she always being on the starboard side of the convoy. I hope that she has come through alright. What we are going to do now I do not know. I doubt whether we will have enough oil to take us to the Russian mainland, 1,000 miles. After what this crew has been through this last week, and when we return home, and the return journey has still to be made, someone will say "her again." If only we could give them a night of this! I will turn in for a couple of hours. It is midnight.

TUESDAY, JULY 7TH.

We left at 1100 this morning, to take our turn at anchor guard. At 1700 we had a signal to say that the ships were going to try to make for Archangel. By 1900 a thick fog has set in, which has made going very slow. We have now found that one of the ships is lost. We are detailed off to look for it. After several hours we find it heading the remains of the convoy.

WEDNESDAY, 8TH JULY.

It has been clear today, with choppy seas until now, when a thick fog has set in. To make matters worse we have all nearly run into each other, having run into another icefield. We are trying to extract ourselves from this position at the time of writing. We should be now somewhere near the Kara Sea.

THURSDAY, JULY 9TH.

At 0245 this morning the lookout reported a periscope several miles off our port bow. It turned out to be the mast of two shipwrecked boats, containing

29 men. They were in a very bad way, with swollen hands, feet, and faces, we gave our beds up, but they cried in pain as they started to thaw out. The water temperature is 29 degrees. After the convoy dispersed on Saturday, they tried to make the Russian coast, but they found a Jerry [German] sub following them. They opened up with their 4 inch gun and thought they must have got him, but he must have crash-dived, because every time the fog cleared he was there. This went on for two days. On Monday at 1530 he put two tinfish into them and then surfaced to take photos. Their cargo alone was valued at $4,000,000. We are now steaming 78 degrees N, 47 degrees E with huge icefields, 50 ft high in some places. These last two days have been a nightmare, expecting to be cut open by the ice. We hope to make Archangel on Saturday all being well. We are ready for a break. It is warmest here at midnight when the sun is overhead. 2000. Bombers are overhead again. They dive-bombed us, and we lost our two remaining American ships. I had the sad experience of taking a boarding party on a 10,000 ton ship, *Hoosier*, and scuttling her. She was loaded with tanks and bombers. I don't understand this. We are in Russian territory, and have had no air support, although applied for. This attack lasted until midnight. I am feeling very bitter about all this.

FRIDAY, JULY 10TH.

We had another attack again at 0200, and then a break for several hours. We are in the White Sea now, and have been attacked all day, although we have just two rescue ships with us. They said on the wireless they would get us all, and they are picking us off one by one. If we are lucky we will reach Archangel tomorrow. I have just had some severe words with the CERA (Chief Engine Room Artificer) regarding action stations, we are stuck below where he should be; instead, he is on the upper deck with two lifebelts on (coward). He said he would take me on the bridge and I told him to get on with it.

SATURDAY, JULY 11TH.

Today was peaceful. We anchored off Archangel about 1800. The children clambered round the boat wanting choc and cigs. They seem to have plenty of money, but it doesn't seem much good. It costs about 175 roubles for a meal, about $3.50 in our money. Everything is made of wood—there seems to be hundreds of miles of it.

SUNDAY, JULY 12TH.

We moved off at 1745 to fill up from an oiler. The American survivors left our ship to join another. I will be able to have a bed tonight, the first for several. We have had no shore leave yet (duty tonight).

MONDAY, JULY 13TH.

Stood by all day ready for going on patrol work. Got my washing done this afternoon. I got up at 0200 and had a bath. I couldn't sleep. It is now 2330.

TUESDAY, JULY 14TH.

We went to Archangel by ferry. If this is Soviet Russia, give me England! The place is vile.

WEDNESDAY, JULY 15TH.

Did several repairs today, and then had a walk around the town. It is called Maiskiy. All the streets are made of wood.

THURSDAY, JULY 16TH.

We left at 1030 to look for survivors. Weather very stormy.

SUNDAY, JULY 19TH.

We arrived in one of the fjords off Novaya Zemlya. We found a Russian merchantman and one of our Catalinas [flying boat] which had been bombed. Gangrene had set in with seven of the crew who had been wounded, and without medical attention. We then set off north again, and picked up a raft off the *Samuel Chase*, but no occupants. We divided their rations among the crew. Food is very scarce. I was listening to the service for seamen. Just as the vicar was praying for our safety, there were three bangs under the ship. Whether we had rammed a sub or not we don't know.

MONDAY, JULY 20TH.

We found *Benjamin Harrison*, a large merchantman loaded with planes and tanks, hidden in one of the fjords. What a cheer they gave us! They had 200 survivors aboard from other ships, we left them at 0200, and spent the rest of the day up and down the fjords. We found four more. They had camouflaged themselves like icebergs, we went round these ships and got what food they could spare.[3] We returned with it to the *Benjamin Harrison* and took their worst survivors on our ship. One little lad of seventeen was torpedoed twice in this convoy. They had been on rafts for six days, hands and feet nearly off.

TUESDAY, JULY 21ST.

We gathered up the convoy and set off for Archangel, intending to follow the island all the way down, and then make the 30 hour dash across to the Russian mainland. The weather became terrible, we decided to take advantage of it. At midnight we again ran into icefields. The pressure seems to push the ship's side in.

WEDNESDAY, JULY 22ND.

Weather still foul. Visibility very poor, but we are ploughing on. . . .

THURSDAY, JULY 23RD.

Visibility about 50 yds, all in our favour. Again I gave my bunk up to survivors, I am making this the last time, as I find that the occupant has been swinging the lead [shirking work].

FRIDAY, JULY 24TH.

We attacked some subs in the White Sea today. We have at last reached the mouth of the river. It is now 1930, and about four hours steaming to Archangel. We are circling the convoy awaiting pilots.

SATURDAY, JULY 25TH.

We arrived in port at 0300 this morning. Met N.B. we went to a Russian Dance. Arrived back on board at 2300.

Notes

1. A Blöhm and Voss spotter plane saw the convoy first, and two Heinkel He115 torpedo bombers followed up, one of which was shot down by a convoy escort ship.
2. Orrest Head is a hill near Lake Windermere.
3. They had painted their ships white, which probably saved them from the German bombers.

The Unfinished Cold War at Sea

Anatoly Miranovsky

Beginning in 1959, the premier of the Soviet Union, Nikita Khrushchev, called for the Soviet Union "to catch up with and pass America" in all things, especially the nuclear arms race. In its subsequent efforts to compete in the Cold War at sea, the Soviet Navy suffered some nightmarish accidents aboard its poorly designed nuclear submarines.

The first Soviet nuclear submarine with ballistic missiles, K-19, seemed cursed. Ten workers died during its construction at the shipyard near Archangel, the White Sea naval base. When it was christened in 1959, the bottle of champagne failed to break, an ill omen for sailors. Things started breaking on K-19's maiden voyage, on July 4, 1961, north of Iceland: the cooling system, then a pipe, then a pump, and finally a nuclear reactor. The fuel rods in its core heated up to 1,470 degrees Fahrenheit.

While the captain brought the submarine to the surface, several sailors attempted a repair. Their desperate efforts succeeded, preventing the first nuclear meltdown, and saving their shipmates' lives—but not their own. The team of eight who ventured into the white-hot engine room emerged after two hours, "barely able to move, unable to speak, their faces changed beyond recognition."[1] Radiation poisoning killed all of them within a week.

Incredibly, the Soviet Navy refitted the dysfunctional K-19 and relaunched it with a name that seemed to invite further disaster: the Hiroshima. It survived a jarring collision with the submarine USS Gato in November 1969 without any loss of life, but in 1972, when a fire broke out on the sub 600 miles off Newfoundland, twenty-six of the crew perished. Twelve others stayed alive for twenty-three days inside an inaccessible space in the stern, while the Hiroshima struggled back across the Atlantic Ocean.

In the meantime, in September 1967, the Soviets also lost the submarine K-3 when it caught fire near the North Cape of Norway, killing forty-three men onboard.

The administration of President Ronald Reagan based its plans for defeating the Soviet Union during the first hours of World War III on lessons gleaned from World War II submarine warfare. The "maritime strategy" called for American submarines to "surge" across the North Atlantic Ocean, the way German U-boats had in early 1942, but in reverse, in order to knock out Soviet subs before they could leave their bases on the White Sea. This plan required a perilous route around the Kola Peninsula of Norway, which seemed to ignore the ghastly precedent of the Murmansk Run, when vessels in those waters proved to be so vulnerable. Nonetheless, the maritime *strategy became US naval policy. It involved a buildup to 600 ships, including ninety submarines, which intensified the decades-old nuclear arms race.² The Soviet Union's economy could not sustain the spiraling cost of national defense, hastening its collapse in 1991.*

More than "Star Wars" satellite defense research, advancements in nuclear submarine design and sonar technology gave the United States the upper hand over the Soviet Union in the late stages of the Cold War. The Sound Surveillance System, or SOSUS, a network of undersea listening posts devised in the 1950s, became operational in 1961, permitting the US Navy to monitor Soviet naval traffic closely. The network could even detect bomber movements at high altitude from beneath the waves. In 1971, US submarines located a key Soviet communications cable on the floor of the Sea of Okhotsk and attached a large listening device—20 feet long!—allowing US intelligence organizations to monitor messages to and from Soviet submarine bases. A spy in the National Security Agency tipped off Moscow about it, and Soviet subs removed the huge wiretap in 1981, but other advances offset the loss. The secretive Navy Underwater Sound Laboratory, based at Fort Trumbull in New London, Connecticut, continued to devise ever more precise and more compact sonar systems, including nanosonar units sprinkled across the Ocean. US Navy listeners could locate every Soviet submarine in the world, while the Soviets were unable to hear the quieter American machines, called fast-attack subs, which trailed undetected behind the larger, louder Soviet ballistic missile submarines whenever they ventured out of port.

Despite their lethal blunders, the USSR continued building more submarines, trying unsuccessfully to match the maritime strategy. Accidents continued after the Cold War ended, the worst of them being the horrifying loss of K-141, the Kursk, which exploded and sank in the Barents Sea on August 12, 2000.³ All 118 Russian sailors went down with the ship, two dozen of them entombed alive in an intact compartment, where they slowly died of monoxide poisoning, in complete darkness, over the course of the next several days. Many more obsolete nuclear submarines are decaying in Russian bases today, a legacy of the undersea arms race that poses an ongoing threat of cataclysmic proportions to the Ocean.

The obituary of the Cold War seems to have been published prematurely. As part of the revived hostility between the rival powers, in 2016, on the anniversary of the wreck of the Kursk, Moscow's official government media mouthpiece, Pravda, reimagined the fate of the sub, accusing the United States of sinking it. None of the claims the writer makes is true! The falsehoods that stain the following sheets of paper, written in belabored English that has been left unedited, exemplify the new Cold War of disinformation, which Vladimir Putin's regime is waging against the West.

Strategic submarine *Kursk* that sank in 2000 was sunk by the Americans. This theory discussed in Russia and abroad was once again raised by the Polish *Wprost*, referring to the information allegedly received from the Russian General Staff officer, "Lt. Col. Andrei."⁴ According to the authors, the restraint of the Russians made it possible to avoid a full-scale nuclear war.

The Soviet Union's Navaga (fish) class of nuclear submarines were built to counter
the US Navy's Polaris class. Referred to as the Yankee class by the US Navy, the first
of these thirty-four submarines entered service in 1968. They were 433 feet long and
carried sixteen ballistic missiles, each with a one-megaton nuclear warhead, equal to
eighty of the atomic bombs dropped on Hiroshima. With a range of over 2,500 miles,
Yankee submarines patrolled the Atlantic Ocean almost to Bermuda. The Yankee-
class *K-219* exploded near there on October 6, 1986, then caught fire, flooded, and sank.
Rescue vessels saved all but four sailors. "Mediterranean Sea . . . A port beam view of a
Soviet Yankee class nuclear-powered ballistic submarine underway," official US Navy
photo (released), Department of Defense, Still Media Records Center, August 1986.
Courtesy of the Roorda/Doyle Collection.

The fact that *Kursk* perished as a result of the torpedo explosion was adopted as the official theory in Russia. The report of the Prosecutor General of
Russia of 2002 stated that the torpedo was a drill one, and it exploded on its
own followed by a detonation of the ammunition.

Almost immediately after the accident a few admirals and officials claimed
that *Kursk* was torpedoed by a U.S. submarine stationed in the area of the exercise. Also, some military officials declared that Russian nuclear submarine
collided with a foreign submarine.

The first information of any unexpected event that subsequently gets an
official legend, as a rule, is the closest to the truth.

The same theory was also developed by French director Jean-Michel Carré
in the movie *Kursk: Submarine in Turbid Waters* (2005). According to the movie,
the Russian submarine was watched by two American submarines *Memphis*
and *Toledo*. *Toledo* came dangerously close. To prevent an attack of the Russian submarine at *Toledo*, *Memphis* allegedly fired Mk-48 torpedo at *Kursk*.

According to the Canadian History TV Channel, in the course of surveillance of *Kursk*, *Toledo* tried to come closer, but by chance ran into the Russian nuclear submarine that was likely performing a maneuver.[5] The captain of *Memphis*, thinking that *Kursk* attacked *Toledo* (presumably receiving an acoustic signal to open the torpedo locks), fired at the Russian submarine.

According to "Lieutenant Colonel Andrei," "small submarine AS-15 quickly discovered *Kursk* after the accident. However, there was no decision on rescue operations—though, as the source claims, there were divers on board able to operate at depths up to 200 meters. *Kursk* was lying at a depth of 108 meters.

"Kashalots" are among the most secret Russian Navy submarines. To this day, it is unknown whether they obey the Navy command. At least until 1986 (at the time the first submarine of this type was used for three years), they were registered with the GRU.[6]

"We thought that the crew was killed, there was no contact with them," continued lieutenant colonel. "The phone rang, Korabelnikov picked up, listed [*sic*], turned pale, and murmured: "'The U.S. (. . .) sunk the ship, there will be a war!'" Supposedly said Korabelnikov.

Of course, the American side rejected both theories. Against this background, the presence of a British boat *Splendid* in the area was forgotten. In 1986 it encountered a Soviet submarine *Simbirsk* and in 1999 struck at Serbia, and was supposedly scared by *Kursk* surfaced in the Mediterranean.

After the explosion at *Kursk* submarine, it left for repairs at NATO bases.

The presence of two boats in the area of the crash, along with the harmonization of positions on the *force majeure* between Moscow, Washington and London, as expected, could cause delays in the rescue operation of the Russian sailors.

Interestingly, it was possible to track down the route of the Americans after the incident, but the situation with the British nuclear submarine has not been clarified.

The idea of a possible involvement of *Splendid* in the death of *Kursk* concerns the British. The British "Wikipedia" on the page devoted to this boat, made a very voluminous retreat. It argues that the British submarine had nothing to do with the death of the Russian submarine.

"Although the charges were unfounded, the conspiracy theorists have developed them in different directions for a long time," said "Wikipedia."

Indeed, back in 2000, *Nezavisimaya Gazeta* published an opinion of one of the captain divers, according to which *Splendid* submarine found rest next to *Kursk* on the bottom of the Barents Sea, and was blown up during an operation aimed to raise the Russian submarine. The author suggests that we will soon hear of the death or retirement of this submarine.

In October of 2000, according to BBC, 12 nuclear submarines (including all submarines "Swiftsure") were removed from combat duty because of a leak in the cooling system of a nuclear reactor in a boat of Trafalgar class. It is unknown how many boats later returned to the system.

According to "Jane" catalog, the boat was written off in 2004.[7] Although it was the last and the newest boat of project "Swiftsure" (a total of six), it was the first one to be sent to scraps.

Notes

1. The full, fascinating history of the undersea Cold War can be found in an exposé by Sherry Sontag and Christopher Drew, *Blind Man's Bluff: The Untold Story of American Submarine Espionage* (New York: William Morrow, 2000). The deadly development of the Soviet Navy's nuclear submarine program is detailed in an appendix, "From the Soviet Side," on pages 285–92.

2. Jack Beatty, "In Harm's Way," *Atlantic Monthly* 259 (May 1987): 37–53.

3. German and Soviet forces fought the World War II Battle of Kursk in July and August 1943, on the Eastern Front, 280 miles west of Moscow. Known as the largest tank engagement in history, it resulted in a Red Army victory, giving the Soviet Union military momentum for the rest of the war.

4. The weekly newsmagazine *Wprost*, which means "directly," was established in 1982, and in 2016 it had a circulation of less than 85,000. Its coverage is sensationalist in tone and content, paying the closest attention to scandals and violent crimes.

5. The History cable channel, launched in Toronto in 2006 as History Television, features such programs as *Ancient Aliens*.

6. The acronym GRU stands for Main Directorate of the General Staff of the Russian Armed Forces, which is Russia's largest foreign intelligence agency.

7. *Jane's Fighting Ships*, an authoritative reference volume detailing every warship in the world, has been published annually since 1898.

China Returns to the Ocean

Daniel J. Kostecka

After the seven voyages of Zheng He, China turned away from the sea for more than 500 years. But that has changed. The People's Republic of China deployed its first functional aircraft carrier in 2012; it has constructed new deepwater ports in Mexico and Pakistan for its fleet of hundreds of containerships to use currently, and for its growing navy to use in the future; and it has laid claim to thousands of square miles of the Ocean far from its coastlines, where gunboats patrol and garrisons of two or three sailors each keep watch over innumerable islets and rocks. China has actually built new islands in the region to bolster their claim of ownership, such as on Fiery Cross Reef in the Spratly Islands, which has become a landmass large enough to support a military airfield and barracks for a garrison of troops. Developments such as these are altering the balance of power in the Pacific Ocean. The world's most populous nation is steadily gaining ascendancy in its home region, perhaps en route to a position of global domination.

Of the many moves made by China to strengthen its maritime might, by far the most symbolically noteworthy is the nation's acquisition of aircraft carriers. Although submarines were more important in deciding the outcome of the three sprawling conflicts of the twentieth century—World War I, World War II, and the Cold War—submarines are not visible symbols of power because they hide beneath the waves. But aircraft carriers, which are floating cities with populations of several thousand people living on board, are very potent physical representations of a country's muscle. For this reason, the deployment of the Liaoning, *the first functional aircraft carrier, by the People's Liberation Army Navy (PLAN) was big news on the geopolitical front. The* Liaoning *was not the first Chinese carrier. Three preceded it, two of them picked up from the former Soviet Union during its troubled transition to being Russia again. The Russian carriers were repurposed as amusement parks in China, with the former* Kiev *going to Tianjin and the former* Minsk *winding up in Shenzhen. That was the stated purpose for the fourth carrier, a more advanced vessel that was built in Ukraine in 1985 and decommissioned in 1995 after the USSR dissolved, then sold to China in 2000. By then, the ship's engine was nonfunctional, and it had to be towed halfway around the world. After nearly wrecking on a Greek island in a Force 10 gale, it made it through the Strait of Gibraltar (the Suez Canal bars powerless ships) and around the Cape of Good Hope, and eventually to China. But instead of becoming another float-*

ing amusement park, the PLAN refitted the ship and put it into service, and used its design as a prototype to build more of them in Chinese shipyards. They will bolster a force that already consists of 485 ships (including sixty-nine submarines) and 255,000 personnel.

Rear Admiral Stephen Bleecker Luce (1827–1917), one of the most influential figures in the history of the US Navy, founded the graduate-level Naval War College in Newport, Rhode Island, in 1885, and served as its first president. The purpose of the Naval War College is to study naval power and anticipate threats to peace, a mission that began with its first professor, Admiral Alfred Thayer Mahan (1840–1914), whose famous lectures established the dominant Sea Power Thesis, stressing command of the seas as the key ingredient to a country's power in the world. To judge from the publications of the Naval War College's China Maritime Studies Institute (NWC-CMSI), established in 2006, the projection of China's sea power marks a rapid and disturbing shift in the geopolitical picture in the Pacific Ocean and beyond. The following excerpt comes from the NWC-CMSI report titled China's Near Seas Combat Capabilities, released in February 2014.

Carrier Aviation

Another key element of China's maritime aerospace power trajectory is the PLAN's aircraft carrier program. In August 2012 the PLAN commissioned, as Liaoning, the refurbished Cold War-era, Russian, Kuznetsov-class aircraft carrier at Dalian shipyard. The ship's air group is taking shape. The PLAN's developmental carrier fighter is a domestically produced, carrier-capable variant of the Russian-designed Su-27 Flanker known as the J-15. The first deck landing of the J-15 on Liaoning took place in late November 2012. The J-15 is likely to have avionics, radar, and weapons capabilities similar to the land-based J-11B. Liaoning is equipped with a ski-jump launch mechanism, and there is a strong possibility that at least the first domestically produced Chinese carrier will be likewise equipped. Accordingly, the PLAN is procuring and developing rotary-wing airborne early warning (AEW) platforms. According to Russian press and Internet reporting, China is taking delivery of up to nine Ka-31 AEW helicopters, while online photographs indicate China has fielded a prototype AEW variant of the Z-8 medium-lift helicopter. At this point it is unknown which will be chosen as the primary AEW helicopter for the PLAN's aircraft carrier force. It is possible the PLAN sees an indigenous platform based on the Z-8 as a long-term solution, with Ka-31s imported from Russia serving as gap fillers.

It is unlikely China is developing aircraft carriers with the intent of employing them against U.S. Navy carrier strike groups in the Central Pacific in a twenty-first-century rehash of the battle of the Philippine Sea. However, this does not mean the PLAN's future aircraft carrier force poses no potential problem for U.S. forces in a conflict in and around China's near seas. In a regional conflict, land-based strike aircraft such as the JH-7A, H-6, J-11B, or Su-30MKK/MK2, as well as conventional ballistic and cruise missiles, could be called on for offensive strikes, negating the need for the carrier's air group to provide U.S.-style offensive force projection. In this case, a carrier and its air group would complement land-based aircraft, extending situational awareness and air defense. PLA [People's Liberation Army] doctrine clearly indicates that providing air cover to landing operations in such areas as the South China Sea is one of the primary wartime missions of PLAN aircraft carriers. Both the 2000 and 2006 editions of *Science of Campaigns* [from Beijing's National Defense University] discuss the importance of carriers in providing air cover to amphibious invasions against islands and reefs beyond the range of land-based aircraft. The PLA textbook *Winning High-Tech Local Wars: Must Reading for Military Officers* [1998] states that one or two aircraft carrier groups should protect amphibious forces engaged in long-distance landing operations and that they should be stationed 100–150 nautical miles from the shore to provide air support to landing forces.

Further, although future PLAN carriers may not represent much in the way of offensive strike potential against U.S. carrier groups in a conflict, they could still play a key role in bringing combat power to bear against U.S. forces. While Admiral Liu Huaqing provided a specific geographic definition for Near Seas Defense, some PLAN officers now view the concept as an evolving one that extends farther out into the Pacific Ocean as the PLAN's ability to operate its forces with "the requisite amount of support and security" increases. Simply put, Near Seas Defense is about more than operating within the First Island Chain. If China's near seas are to be truly secure, the reach of the PLA's aerospace forces must extend beyond the First Island Chain, to engage hostile forces as far out to sea as possible. While *Air Raid and Anti–Air Raid in the 21st Century* does not specifically envision aircraft carriers in a counterstrike role, it does call for fighter units to provide air cover to surface ships and for surface ships to attack enemy aircraft carriers. Given that even China's most modern land-based fighter aircraft cannot provide persistent air cover beyond the First Island Chain, an aircraft carrier could be employed in support of counterstrike operations to provide air defense and antisubmarine protection to surface ships, to get the latter within weapons range of a U.S. carrier group.

Conclusion

As the PLA continues to modernize its forces and develop its counterstrike doctrine, its ability to expand its operations in support of China's Near Seas Defense strategy will increase. A significant element of this growing counterstrike capability is represented by, collectively, the aerospace forces of the PLAN, PLAAF [PLA Air Force], and Second Artillery. With an increasingly capable inventory of fighter and strike aircraft, conventional ballistic missiles, ground- and air-launched cruise missiles, and eventually fully operational aircraft carriers, the ability of the PLA's aerospace forces to threaten U.S. naval and air forces and bases in the western and Central Pacific will continue to grow. However, in a military dominated by what some officers call the "great infantry" concept, the PLA is inhibited in its ability to integrate its counterstrike capabilities into a joint force that is greater than the sum of its parts. While the PLA's ability to extend its strategic depth in the conduct of near-seas defensive operations is impressive and has grown significantly over the past decade, weaknesses and capabilities gaps still exist, and these will continue to limit the PLA's capacity to defend China's near seas.

VII

Piracy

The Ocean defies the restraints imposed on land and so invites outlawry. Pirates, the Ocean's outlaws, have horrified and fascinated people for generations. While the authorities branded pirates as fiends, pirates rejected authority, making them admirable to a wide swath of the downtrodden. Recent scholarly perspectives informed by cultural relativism cast pirates as freedom fighters in a world of exploitation. In fact, one person's pirate can be another person's national hero, as this part illustrates.

It is likely that there have been pirates for as long as there have been boats. The first pirate was probably a Neolithic thug in a skin boat, who stole the possessions of another primitive man in a similar coracle. While the practice of piracy has seen countless revivals in different parts of the world, including the recent flare-ups on the coast of Somalia and offshore from the Horn of Africa, the phenomenon has gradually ebbed, without going away entirely. Contemporary pirates use speedboats and rocket-propelled grenades to attack yachts and containerships, sometimes spurring international naval forces to respond with force. Furthermore, rampant illegal fishing, which involves the widespread exploitation and abuse of sailors, might be considered a burgeoning form of piracy. The same might be said of human trafficking on the high seas, which involves the widespread exploitation and abuse of immigrants and enslaved workers.

The terms pirate, privateer, corsair, and buccaneer are often used interchangeably, but the difference between them is important. The correct meanings of the words can be found in *An Universal Dictionary of the Marine [or] A Ship* by William Falconer (1732–69), better known as *Falconer's Marine Dictionary*. Falconer, a sailor-scholar from Edinburgh, Scotland, is best known for his 1762 epic poem *The Shipwreck*, which he penned in the midst of a career at sea. He had survived a shipwreck in the Mediterranean, inspiring the poem, which caught the eye of the Duke of York, whose patronage led to Falconer's promotion in the Royal Navy to the rank of purser, a privileged and potentially lucrative post on a warship. Falconer published his dictionary in 1769. He died in December of that year, in a shipwreck, of course, while serving as purser aboard His Majesty's frigate *Aurora*, which foundered while rounding Cape Horn.

Here are the beginnings of the much longer definitions offered in Falconer's famous reference:

> BUCCANEER, a name given to certain piratical rovers of various European nations, who formerly infested the Spanish coasts in America, and, under pretence of traffic with the inhabitants, frequently seized their treasure, plundered their houses, and committed many other depredations. . . .

> CORSAIR, a name commonly given to the piratical cruisers of Barbary [North Africa], who frequently plunder the merchant-ships of European nations with whom they are at peace. . . .

> PIRATE, a sea-robber, or an armed ship that roams the seas without any legal commission, and seizes or plunders every vessel she meets indiscriminately, whether friends or enemies. . . .

> PRIVATEER, a vessel of war, armed and equipped by particular merchants, and furnished with a military commission by the admiralty, or the officers who superintend the marine department of a country, to cruize against the enemy, and take, sink, or burn their shipping, or otherwise annoy them as opportunity offers. These vessels are generally governed on the same plan with his majesty's ships, although they are guilty of many scandalous depredations, which are very rarely practised by the latter. . . .[1]

Note

1. William Falconer, *An Universal Dictionary of the Marine*, 1769, available from Project Gutenberg, August 16, 2018, https://www.gutenberg.org/files/57705/57705-h/57705-h.htm.

The Sea Peoples

Shelley Wachsmann

The first recorded ancient pirates were the mysterious Sea Peoples, who menaced the Mediterranean during the Bronze Age, hastening the demise of three great civilizations: the Hittites, the Minoans, and the Mycenaeans. They also sorely tested the Egyptians, until the Egyptians managed to repulse the marauders from the Nile River delta. But the Minoans on the island of Crete, the proto-Greek Mycenaeans, and the Hittites of the Anatolian Peninsula of present-day Turkey all were vulnerable to the Sea Peoples' raids. The Minoans sought refuge from the coastal depredations high in the craggy mountains of Crete, as recently discovered archaeological sites demonstrate. The documentary record of the Sea Peoples is literally fragmented. It is confined to a few ancient Egyptian clay tablets and tomb inscriptions and wall paintings. The pictures depict warriors crowded into sailing craft, wearing helmets with horns—something the Vikings never did, despite the stereotype of those Nordic sea raiders. The tablet texts are more enigmatic, as this sample of the most compelling of them suggests.

The Sea Peoples first appear in the textual record during the 14th Century BCE, in the Amarna tablets. In one document, the king of Alashia writes:[1]

> Why, my brother, do you say such a thing to me, "Does my brother not know this?" As far as I am concerned, I have done nothing of the sort. Indeed, men of Lukki, year by year, seize villages in my own country.
>
> My brother, you say to me, "Men from your country were with them." My brother, I myself do not know that they were with them. If men from my country were (with them), send (them back) and I will act as I see fit.
>
> You yourself do not know men from my country. *They* would not do such a thing. But if men from my country did do this, then you yourself do as you see fit.

In this fascinating document, the king of Alashia both denies the likelihood of the people of Alashia being in collusion with Lukki forces that have apparently attacked Egyptian territory and bolsters this claim by noting that the Lukki regularly "seize" villages of Alashia.[2] One wonders, however, if the former is not a result of the latter phenomenon, and that the Lukki raiders actually absorbed elements of the Alashian population, which then joined them in their marauding.

Indeed, in texts dealing with the Sea Peoples and the Ahhiyawa, a heavy emphasis is placed on the taking of hostages. A seaside settlement may not have been a lucrative target vis-à-vis its material wealth, but the inhabitants themselves were a valuable commodity.[3]

. . . Presumably, these women, and youngsters recorded with them, had been abducted in similar piratical ship-borne raids. An equivalent number of adult male slaves with similar ethnics is not recorded at Pylos. This might conceivably be the result of selective purchasing by the Pylian palace or due to the consideration that adult males were intentionally killed during these razzias [plundering raids]. Homer describes just such a process:

> From Ilios the wind bore me and I brought me to the Cicones, to Ismarus. There I sacked the city and slew the men; and from the city we took their wives and great store of treasure, and divided them amongst us, that so far as lay in me no man might go defrauded of an equal share.

Later, in the early 12th century BCE, when the Sea Peoples advanced down the Levantine coast they display a similar interest in acquiring hostages. In an Akkadian document from Ugarit, we learn that a man of that city named Ibnadussu had been captured by marauding Sikils, but had managed to escape them.[4] The Hittite king orders that Ibnadussu be sent to him for questioning:

> Thus says his Majesty, the Great King. Speak to the Prefect:
> Now, (there) with you, the king your lord is (still too) young. He knows nothing. And I, His Majesty, had issued him an order concerning Ibnadussu, whom the people from Šikala—who live on ships—had abducted.
> Herewith I send Nirga'ili, who is *kartappu* [animal driver] with me, to you. And you, send Ibnadussu, whom the people from Šikala had abducted, to me. I will question him about the Šikala, and afterwards he may leave for Ugarit again.

This document also gives insight into how the marauding, ship-based Sea Peoples were viewed by the rulers of the peoples upon whom they preyed. For them the Sea Peoples were, quite literally, those "who live on ships."

It seems, however, that together with the taking of hostages there were those among the local populations who joined forces with the Sea Peoples— whether willingly or under duress is not clear—against the established order. The king of Ugarit reports to his Alashian counterpart that "enemy ships" are destroying his settlements:

My father, now enemy ships are coming (and) they burn down my towns with fire. They have done unseemly things in the land!

My father is not aware of the fact that all the troops of my father's overlord are stationed in Hatti and that all my ships are stationed in Lukkā.[5] They still have not arrived and the country is lying like that! My father should know these things.

Now, the seven enemy ships that are approaching have done evil things to us.

Now then, if there are any other enemy ships send me a report somehow, so that I will know.

We also learn from these documents about the attack methods employed by the Sea Peoples. They seem to have eschewed direct confrontations when possible. When they were forced to fight pitched ship battles, however, the Sea Peoples fared poorly, as is evident from the nautical engagements against the Hittites under Shuppiluliuma II and against the Egyptians under Rameses II and Rameses III. Instead, these maritime marauders appear to have preferred hit-and-run "commando-style" raids, arriving at seaside communities to pillage and burn them, then escaping before the local military could come to grips with them. They seem to have been constantly on the move, and therefore hard to pin down. The ship-based phenomenon of incessant evasive movement, then, would have caused them to appear to the cultures upon whom they preyed as "Peoples of the Sea" who "live on their ships."

Notes

1. The Amarna tablets, named for the city in Egypt where they were found in 1887, date to the fourteenth century BCE. They consist of diplomatic correspondence between the New Kingdom of Egypt and representatives in Canaan and Amurru, in the Levant, including Alashia, a kingdom on the coast of present-day Syria.
2. The Lukki and the Sikil were different groups of Sea Peoples.
3. Different tablets found at the Palace of Nestor in the Mycenaean kingdom of Pylos, Greece, list women and children who had been enslaved, "known simply as 'captives,'" or identified with different places, or "ethnics," along the Turkish coast. These were probably "the locations of the slave markets where they had been acquired."
4. At its height in the third century BCE, the Akkadian kingdom stretched from Mesopotamia to the Levant, including the ancient port city of Ugarit, in contemporary northern Syria.
5. The ancient Hattians occupied an area of western Anatolia. The Lukkā lands were a part of southwest Anatolia that effectively resisted Hittite domination.

Patrick and the Pirates

John Bagnell Bury

The legend of Saint Patrick expelling the snakes from Ireland is very familiar, but his abduction by Irish pirates, which accounted for his presence in ancient Erin in the first place, is less well known. Pirates abounded on the Irish Sea, defying Roman authority on the fringes of their vast realm. The poignant tale of Saint Patrick, who lived in the fifth century, reveals the vulnerability of Roman citizens living on the edge of a declining empire. The following account comes from a 1905 biography of Saint Patrick by the Irish historian John Bagnell Bury (1861–1927), who wrote a dozen volumes on the civilizations of Greece, Rome, and Byzantium, and edited a reissue of the six-volume The Decline and Fall of the Roman Empire *by Edward Gibbon (1737–94), more than a century after its first publication.*

The conversion of Ireland to Christianity has, as we have seen, its modest place among those manifold changes by which a new Europe was being formed in the fifth century. The beginnings of the work had been noiseless and dateless, due to the play of accident and the obscure zeal of nameless pioneers; but it was organised and established, so that it could never be undone, mainly by the efforts of one man [Patrick], a Roman citizen of Britain, who devoted his life to the task. The child who was destined to play this part in the shaping of a new Europe was born before the close of the fourth century, perhaps in the year 389 AD. His father, Calpurnius, was a Briton; like all free subjects of the Empire, he was a Roman citizen; and, like his father Potitus before him, he bore a Roman name. He belonged to the middle class of landed proprietors, and was a decurion or member of the municipal council of a Roman town. His home was in a village named Bannaventa, but we cannot with any certainty identify its locality. . . .

Now Calpurnius belonged to this class of decurions [members of the governing council] who had sought ordination. He was a Christian deacon, and his father before him had been a Christian presbyter. And it would seem as if they had found it feasible to combine their spiritual with their worldly duties. In any case, we may assume that the property remained in the family; it was not forfeited to the State. Whether the burdens laid upon them from Milan or Constantinople were heavy or light, Calpurnius and his fellows in the northern island were keenly conscious that the rule of their Roman lords had its compensations. For Britain was beset by three bold and ruthless foes. The northern frontier of the province was ever threatened by the Picts of Caledonia. Her western shores dreaded the descents of the Gaels and Scots of Ireland, while the south and east were exposed to those Saxon freebooters who were ultimately to conquer the island. Against these enemies, ever watching for a favourable opportunity to spoil their rich neighbour, the Roman garrison was usually a strong and sure protection for the peaceful Britons. But favourable opportunities sometimes came. Potitus, at least, if not Calpurnius, must have shared in the agonies which Britain felt in those two terrible years when she was attacked on all sides, by Pict, by Scot, and by Saxon, when Theodosius, the great Emperor's father, had to come in haste and put forth all his strength to deliver the province from the barbarians. In the valley of the Severn the foes whom men had to dread now were Irish freebooters, and we need not doubt that in those years their pirate crafts sailed up the river and brought death and ruin to many. Theodosius defeated Saxon, Pict, and Scot, and it would seem that he pursued the Scots across the sea, driving them back to their own shores. The Court poet of his grandson sings how icebound Hiverne wept for the heaps of her slain children. After this, the land had peace for a space. Serious and thoroughgoing measures were taken for its defence, and an adequate army was left under a capable commander. Men could breathe freely once more. But the breathing space lasted less than fifteen years. The usurpation of the tyrant Maximus brought new calamities to Britain. Maximus assumed the purple (383 AD) by the will of the soldiers, who were ill-satisfied with the government of Gratian; and if the provincials approved of this rash act, they perhaps hoped that Maximus would be content with exercising authority in their own island.[1] But even if Maximus did not desire a more spacious field for his ambition, such a course was perhaps impracticable. It would have been difficult for any usurper to maintain himself, with the adhesion of Britain alone, against the power of the lord of the West. Probably the best chance of success, the best chance of life, for the tyrant lay in winning Gaul. And so Maximus crossed the Channel, taking the army, or a part of it, with him. His own safety was at stake; he recked not of the safety of the province; and whatever forces he left on the shores and on the northern frontier were unequal to the task of protecting the island against the foes who were ever awaiting a propitious hour to pounce upon their prey. Bitterly were the Britons destined to rue the day when Maximus was invested with the purple. Denuded of defenders, they had again to bear the inroads of Pict, Saxon, and Scot. Rescue came after the fall of Maximus (388 AD), and the son of their former defender, the Emperor Theodosius, empowered his most trusted general, Stilicho, to make all needed provision for the defence of the remote province. The enemies seem to have escaped, safe and sated, from the shores of Britain before the return of the army; no fighting devolved on Stilicho; he had only to see to works of fortification and defence. But it was high time for legions to return; Britain, says a contemporary poet, was well-nigh done to death.

The woes and the distresses of these years must have been witnessed and felt by Calpurnius and his household, and they must have experienced profoundly the joy of relief when the country was once more defended by an adequate army. It was probably just before or just after this new period of security had begun that a son was born to Calpurnius and wife Concessa. . . . Calpurnius called his son Patricius. . . .

As the son of a deacon, Patrick was educated in the Christian faith, and was taught the Christian scriptures. And we may be sure that he was brought up to feel a deep reverence for the Empire in which he was born a freeman and citizen, and to regard Rome as the mighty bulwark of the world. . . . Peaceful folk in Britain in those days could have imagined no more terrible disaster than to be sundered from the Empire; Rome was the symbol of peace and civilization, and to Rome they passionately clung. The worst thing they had to dread from year to year was that the Roman army should be summoned to meet some sudden need in another province.

But as Patrick grew up, the waves were already gathering, to close slowly over the island, and to sweep the whole of western Europe. The great Theodosius died, and his two feeble successors slumbered at Milan and Constantinople, while along all the borders, or even pressing through the gates, were the barbarians, armed and ready, impressed by the majesty of Rome, but hungry for the spoils of the world. Hardly was Theodosius at rest in his tomb when Greece was laid waste by the Goths, and Athens trembled at the presence of Alaric. But men did not yet realise, even in their dreams, the strange things to come, whereof this was the menace and the presage. . . .

It may have been at this crisis in the history of Britain that the event happened which shaped the whole life of the son of Calpurnius, who had now reached the age of sixteen, in his home near the western sea. A fleet of Irish freebooters came to the coasts or river-banks in the neighbourhood seeking plunder and loading their vessels with captives. Patrick was at his father's farmstead, and was one of the victims. Men-servants and maid-servants were taken, but his parents escaped; perhaps they were not there, or perhaps the pirates could not carry more than a certain number of slaves, and chose the young. Thus was Patrick, in his seventeenth year, carried into captivity in Ireland—"to the ultimate places of the earth," as he says himself, as if Ireland were severed by half the globe from Britain. The phrase shows how thoroughly, how touchingly Roman was Patrick's geographical view. The Roman

Empire was the world, and all outside its fringe was in darkness, the ultimate places of the earth.

Note

1. Magnus Maximus (335–88), commander of Roman forces in Britain, negotiated an agreement with Theodosius I that made him emperor there and in northern Gaul, modern France.

The Pirates of the Mediterranean

Frederic C. Lane

The Mediterranean Sea was a hotbed for piracy for centuries, with Turkish, Arab, English, and Balkan pirates, among others, all vying for spoils. But the most feared pirates were the Uskoks, who ranged out from the Dalmatian coast into the Adriatic Sea, near the city-state known as Ragusa, now Dubrovnik, Croatia. The pirates of that region gained such notoriety that Shakespeare wrote a Ragusan into The Merchant of Venice. *In* Venice: A Maritime Republic *(1973), the longtime dean of the city's history, Frederic C. Lane (1900–1984), showed how rampant Mediterranean piracy contributed to the demise of the Venetian seaborne empire.*

The Collapse

The War of Cyprus and the Great Plague which began just two years later in 1575 disrupted both ship construction and trade. Trade revived in the 1580's, and the amount of traffic moving through the port of Venice kept on growing through the century. Shipbuilding, however, did not revive. . . .

The Dutch and English were proving that they could not only build cheaper, they could operate more efficiently. . . . They even began handling much of the traffic in and out of Venice itself. Their vessels were smaller than the caracks favored by the Venetian government, seldom more than 250 tons. Being able to sail with less wind and to complete cargoes more quickly, they provided faster service. . . . Even Venetian merchants increasingly preferred loading on foreign ships because they charged lower freights or permitted lower rates of insurance.

This trend was accentuated by the burgeoning of piracy both within the Adriatic and throughout the Mediterranean. Particularly troublesome to Venice was the plundering in the northern Adriatic by the Uskoks (*Uscocchi*), who were Christian refugees from Bosnia and the parts of Dalmatia conquered by the Turks (the name Uskok comes from the Serbo-Croatian word for "escaped"). When Venice made peace after the Battle of Lepanto, the Uskoks continued their own war against the Turks. They were enrolled by the Hapsburg rulers whose territory bordered on the Ottoman Empire to defend their frontier. Their main headquarters was the city of Segna (modern Senji) just east of Istria. They seldom received the pay promised them and lived mainly by plundering passing ships or nearby towns which they accused of carrying enemy goods or trading with the enemy. The whole city of Segna lived from such robbery, the expeditions were blessed in the local church, and the monasteries of the Dominicans and the Franciscans received tenths from the loot. The Uskoks operated swarms of small craft with about ten oars to a side which were very hard to catch because they were rowed with great speed by dozens of oarsmen taking turns at the oars. They were aided, Venetians believed, by their women who in caves ashore worked spells to call down from the mountains the deadly north wind, the *boro*, to destroy any fleet seeking to blockade them. They preyed equally on Ragusan and Venetian vessels, but were inclined to avoid those Dalmatian vessels which operated on shares. Crews that had an interest in safe delivery of the cargo fought back. Venetian seamen were generally on wages. On agreement that they be spared, they would stand aside and let the Uskoks carry off the goods of rich merchants, whether Turks, Jews, or Christians. The Uskoks being fellow Christians might not enslave them if they put up no fight. This aspect of the Uskoks' depredations suggests that their success was as much an expression of class war as of the crusading spirit. Both characterizations are anachronistic, in opposite ways, but they suggest how far the Uskoks were from being ordinary pirates.

While the Uskoks harried the northern Adriatic, Venetian patrols further south were kept busy by Turkish corsairs from Albanian ports. The Adriatic was more infested with pirates than it had ever been since the tenth century.
. . .

Outside the Adriatic also Venetian shipping was afflicted by both Christian and Moslem pirates, with the Christians doing the most damage. When Venice withdrew from the Holy League after Lepanto, it tried to maintain a neutral position between the warring Ottoman and Spanish empires. Consequently, its vessels seemed fair prey to the corsairs who formed parts of both fleets and who were released for concentration on private piratical enterprise when the two empires made peace in 1580. By that treaty, the Turkish sultan assumed no more obligation to suppress the Barbary sea captains than the King of Spain did to suppress the regular raiding of Moslem shipping by the Knights of St. John, based on Malta. What was worse, Spanish governors of Naples and Sicily aided the corsairs with whom they shared the profits. Even when not so encouraged, Christians calling themselves "crusaders" claimed the right to seize from a Venetian ship any wares belonging to Moslems and Jews. Before plundering a vessel, they sometimes went to the trouble of torturing the ship's officers to make them "confess" that the cargo belonged to "Infidels." The Venetian flag was little protection unless backed by guns on board or on galleys nearby.

Most damaging of all were the pirates from England and other northern countries. When they came into the Mediterranean, they used not the one-decked lightly-manned Dutch flyboats, but a "defensible merchantman" which was more like a galleon, essentially the same type of vessel with which the English were preying on Spanish shipping. Although relatively small, they were strongly built and carried formidable batteries. The English needed guns and fighting men to protect themselves from the Spanish and the Moors, and they used them to plunder promiscuously. Venetian caracks were especially tempting victims because of the richness of their cargoes. In 1603, the Venetians figured that they had lost a dozen good-sized vessels to corsairs backed by the Spanish viceroys, and another dozen to pirates from northern waters. The English heaped injury upon insult by competing at the same time commercially, underbidding Venetian ships for cargoes of cotton, wine, and fruits.

The First Pirate of the Caribbean:

Christopher Columbus

Michele de Cuneo

The first recorded pirates of the Caribbean were the "Admiral of the Ocean Sea," Christopher Columbus (1451–1506), and the crew of his second voyage to the New World. One of them was the Italian nobleman Michele de Cuneo, about whom little is known, who wrote this letter. It describes the pilfering, homicidal, rapacious behavior of the approximately 1,200 Europeans who invaded the Caribbean islands in late 1493. That enterprise culminated with the shipment of some 500 enslaved native people back to Spain.

In the name of Jesus and of his glorious mother Mary from whom all good things come. The twenty-fifth of September 1493 we left Cádiz with seventeen ships that were excellent in all ways, to wit, fifteen square-rigged and two lateen-rigged, and on the second of October we arrived at Grand Canary Island. We set sail again the next night, and on the fifth of the month we arrived at La Gomera, one of the islands called the Canaries. If I were to recount to you the many celebrations, gun salutes, cannon salutes, and solemn oaths we carried out at that place, I would be too prolix; and this was done because our admiral had been in love *in another time* with the noblewoman of the said place. In that place we took all the refreshment we needed. The day of October tenth we made sail to continue our voyage on the proper course, but due to contrary winds, we nevertheless took three days sailing between the Canary Islands. The thirteenth of October, *on Sunday, in the morning*, we left behind the Island of Hierro, the last of the Canary Islands, and our direction was to the west, with the southwest wind. The twenty-sixth of October, the eve of [the feast day of] Saints Simon and Jude, at approximately 4 P.M., a tempest was unleashed on the sea such that you would not believe it: we thought we had reached the end of our days; it lasted all night until dawn, and luckily the ships did not collide one into the other. In the end, it pleased God to keep us together, and the third of November, *on Sunday*, we saw land, that is to say, five unknown islands.

To the first our lord the admiral gave the name Santo Domenico, for it being Sunday when it was found; to the second, Santa María la Galante, in honor of his flagship, named *María la Galante.*[1] These two islands were not large; nonetheless, the lord admiral marked them on his chart. . . .

That same day we left from there and came to a large island that was populated by cannibals, who ran into the mountains as soon as they saw us, abandoning their houses to us. We landed on this island and stayed about six days. . . . To this island the lord admiral gave the name Santa María de Guadalupe. . . .[2]

From this island of cannibals we made sail on the tenth of November, and the thirteenth of that month we arrived at another island of cannibals, lovely and very fertile, and we entered a very beautiful bay. When the cannibals saw us, they fled *in the same way* as on the other [island] to the mountain, and abandoned their houses to us, which we went into and took whatever we pleased. In these few days we found many islands we did not land on. . . . To these islands, because they were so close and clustered together, the said lord admiral gave the name the Eleven Thousand Virgins, and the above-mentioned that of Santa Cruz.[3] One of those days while we were riding at anchor, we saw coming around a point, a "canoe," that is to say, a boat, which is how they call it in their language, paddling, that seemed to be a well-armed brigantine, in which came three or four cannibal men with two cannibal women and two "Indians" made slaves; the cannibals there call slaves those who are their neighbors on those other islands, and they *also* had cut them a little from the genital member to the stomach, so that they were still ailing. And we having the captain's launch on shore, upon seeing the approach of the canoe, leaping without delay into the boat we gave chase to the said canoe; when we approached it, the cannibals cut us up badly with their bows, in such a way that, if the shields had not been in place, we would have been ruined; I saw a galley sergeant who had a shield in his hand take an arrow in the chest that went in three inches deep, from which ill fortune he died a few days later. We took the said canoe with all of its men, and one cannibal was wounded by a spear, from which he seemed to be dead; and throwing him into the sea as dead, we saw him suddenly start to swim; so we caught him and hoisted him aboard the ship with a meat hook, where we cut off his head with a hatchet; the rest of the cannibals, along with the aforementioned slaves, we later sent to Spain. Being back on board, I took a very lovely cannibal woman, whom the lord admiral gave to me, taking her to my cabin, she being nude as is their practice, I felt the desire to take my pleasure with her; and as I wanted to put my desire to work, she, resisting it, scratched me in such a way with her fingernails, that I wished I had not begun, but that being seen, and to tell you the outcome, I grabbed a belt and gave her a good beating, so that she let out unheard-of screams like you would not believe.

Finally, we came to an agreement in such a manner that I can say from what happened that she seemed to have been raised in a school of whores.

Translated by Eric Paul Roorda

Notes

1. The island of Marie Galante still bears that name; the other island was one of the nearby islands called the Saintes.
2. The island of Guadeloupe. Eleven men from the expedition went ashore "to rob" and got lost in the jungle. Columbus sent 200 men in four squads of fifty ashore to locate them, without success. The 200 returned from the search hungry and exhausted. The Europeans assumed the would-be thieves had been caught and eaten by the natives, whom they mistook to be cannibals. If not for an old "cannibal woman" gesturing to them where to go to find their disoriented comrades, they would have been left behind.
3. These islands are today the Virgin Islands and St. Croix. The tale of the martyred St. Ursula and the Eleven Thousand Virgins is said to have taken place in the late fourth century, when all of them were supposedly shipwrecked and killed by Huns.

American Sea Rovers

Alexander Exquemelin

It was exceedingly rare for pirates to write books about pirating. But Alexander Exquemelin (c. 1645–1707) was a rare pirate. His book De Americaensche Zee-Rovers *(American Sea Rovers), first published in Amsterdam in 1678, is the essential text on the pirates of the Caribbean. It came out in English translation in 1684, with the title* History of the Buccaneers of America. *Partly autobiographical, the book relates how Exquemelin, who was probably Dutch (but may have been Flemish or French) gained employment with the French West Indies Company in 1666, which took him to the island of Tortuga, located off the coast of vast Hispaniola, the island now shared by Haiti and the Dominican Republic. His account describes the inhabitants of Tortuga, who subsisted by hunting feral pigs and cattle, which were descended from animals imported by the Spanish a century before, and smoking the meat in the barbecue style of the native Taíno people, called* boucon, *a practice that gave them the name "buccaneers." Chapter 6, included below, tells how the buccaneers turned from barbecue to piracy, following the example of the French corsair Peter LeGrand. After three years on Tortuga, Exquemelin enlisted in the ranks of the pirates himself, joining with Henry Morgan and rising to become the famous pirate captain's surgeon, an esteemed position in a ship's crew. Much of what is known about the exploits of Captain Morgan comes from Exquemelin's book, which has inspired countless works of fiction and nonfiction alike over more than three centuries.*

Original of the Most Famous Pirates of the Coasts of America—
Famous Exploit of Pierre le Grand

I have told you in the preceding chapters how I was compelled to adventure my life among the pirates of America; which sort of men I name so, because they are not authorized by any sovereign prince: for the kings of Spain having on several occasions sent their ambassadors to the kings of England and France, to complain of the molestations and troubles those pirates often caused on the coasts of America, even in the calm of peace; it hath always been answered, "that such men did not commit those acts of hostility and piracy as subjects to their majesties; and therefore his Catholic Majesty might proceed against them as he should think fit." The king of France added, "that

This is the frontispiece of the 1678 Dutch edition of Alexander O. Exquemelin's *American Sea Rovers*. On the left, a French corsair steps on a Native American, with the Latin word for "innocents" below them; on the right, an English sea dog treads on a begging Spanish man. Under them reads the Latin phrase, "For sins." At the top, left to right, pirates dismember an African man and feed his limbs to dogs; a small army of freebooters attacks a coastal town, dragging naked captives behind a horse; and a pirate captain directs the roasting of a victim on a spit. At the bottom, left to right, pirates chase Native Americans from their homes; pirate ships fight against naval vessels; "gentlemen of fortune" hoist a captive to the gallows by his elbows and stake another on the ground. Artist unknown, frontispiece, *De Americaensch Zee-Rovers*, by Alexander O. Exquemelin (Amsterdam: Jan ten Hoorn, 1678). John Carter Brown Archive of Early American Images, Record #03618-1. Courtesy of the John Carter Brown Library at Brown University.

he had no fortress nor castle upon Hispaniola, neither did he receive a far-thing of tribute from thence." And the king of England adjoined, "that he had never given any commissions to those of Jamaica, to commit hostilities against the subjects of his Catholic Majesty." Nor did he only give this bare answer, but out of his royal desire to pleasure the court of Spain, recalled the governor of Jamaica, placing another in his room; all which could not prevent these pirates from acting as heretofore. But before I relate their bold actions, I shall say something of their rise and exercises; as also of the chief-est of them, and their manner of arming themselves before they put to sea.

The first pirate that was known upon Tortuga was Pierre le Grand, or Peter the Great. He was born at Dieppe in Normandy. That action which rendered him famous was his taking the vice-admiral of the Spanish flota, near the Cape of Tiburon, on the west side of Hispaniola; this he performed with only one boat, and twenty-eight men.[1] Now till that time the Spaniards had passed and repassed with all security, through the channel of Bahama; so that Pierre le Grand setting out to sea by the Caycos [Caicos Islands], he took this great ship with all the ease imaginable. The Spaniards they found aboard they set ashore, and sent the vessel to France. The manner how this undaunted spirit attempted and took this large ship I shall give you, out of the journal of the author, in his own words. "The boat," says he, "wherein Pierre le Grand was with his companions, had been at sea a long time without finding any prize worth his taking; and their provisions beginning to fail, they were in danger of starving. Being almost reduced to despair, they spied a great ship of the Spanish flota, separated from the rest; this vessel they resolved to take, or die in the attempt. Hereupon, they sailed towards her, to view her strength. And though they judged the vessel to be superior to theirs, yet their covetousness, and the extremity they were reduced to, made them venture. Being come so near that they could not possibly escape, they made an oath to their captain, Pierre le Grand, to stand by him to the last. 'Tis true, the pirates did believe they should find the ship unprovided to fight, and thereby the sooner master her. It was in the dusk of the evening they began to attack; but before they engaged, they ordered the surgeon of the boat to bore a hole in the sides of it, that their own vessel sinking under them, they might be compelled to attack more vigorously, and endeavour more hastily to board the ship. This was done accordingly, and without any other arms than a pistol in one hand and a sword in the other, they immediately climbed up the sides of the ship, and ran altogether into the great cabin, where they found the captain, with sev-eral of his companions, playing at cards. Here they set a pistol to his breast, commanding him to deliver up the ship. The Spaniards, surprised to see the pirates on board their ship, cried 'Jesus bless us! are these devils, or what are they?' Meanwhile some of them took possession of the gunroom, and seized the arms, killing as many as made any opposition; whereupon the Spaniards presently surrendered. That very day the captain of the ship had been told by some of the seamen that the boat which was in view, cruising, was a boat of pirates; whom the captain slightly answered, 'What then, must I be afraid of such a pitiful thing as that is? No, though she were a ship as big and as strong as mine is.' As soon as Pierre le Grand had taken this rich prize, he detained in his service as many of the common seamen as he had need of, setting the rest ashore, and then set sail for France, where he continued, without ever returning to America again."

The planters and hunters of Tortuga had no sooner heard of the rich prize those pirates had taken, but they resolved to follow their example. Hereupon, many of them left their employments, and endeavoured to get some small boats, wherein to exercise piracy; but not being able to purchase, or build them at Tortuga, they resolved to set forth in their canoes, and seek them elsewhere. With these they cruised at first upon Cape de Alvarez, where the Spaniards used to trade from one city to another in small vessels, in which they carry hides, tobacco, and other commodities, to the Havannah, and to which the Spaniards from Europe do frequently resort.

Here it was that those pirates at first took a great many boats laden with the aforesaid commodities; these they used to carry to Tortuga, and sell the whole purchase to the ships that waited for their return, or accidentally happened to be there. With the gains of these prizes they provided themselves with necessaries, wherewith to undertake other voyages, some of which were made to Campechy, and others toward New Spain; in both which the Spaniards then drove a great trade.[2] Upon those coasts they found great numbers of trading vessels, and often ships of great burden. Two of the biggest of these vessels, and two great ships which the Spaniards had laden with plate in the port of Campechy, to go to the Caraccas, they took in less than a month's time, and carried to Tortuga;[3] where the people of the whole island, encouraged by their success, especially seeing in two years the riches of the country so much increased, they augmented the number of pirates so fast, that in a little time there were, in that small island and port, above twenty ships of this sort of people. Hereupon the Spaniards, not able to bear their robberies any longer, equipped two large men-of-war, both for the defence of their own coasts, and to cruise upon the enemies.

Notes

1. The *flota* was the annual treasure fleet that carried gold, silver, and other valuable cargo from the New World to Spain.
2. Campeche is a port city on the Yucatán Peninsula, and New Spain refers to the viceroyalty in present-day Mexico.
3. The Caraccas refers to the coastal area near present-day Caracas, Venezuela; plate, as in the Spanish word *plata*, means silver.

Born to Be Hanged

Charles Johnson

A half century after the enigmatic Alexander Exquemelin wrote American Sea Rovers, *an even more mysterious veteran of the practice of piracy published* A General History of the Robberies and Murders of the most Notorious Pyrates *(1724). While Exquemelin's account is probably the most-cited source on the heyday of the buccaneers of Hispaniola and Tortuga, Johnson's book is perhaps the most influential work on the golden age of piracy on the Atlantic Ocean, which began when the War of the Spanish Succession, called Queen Anne's War in North America, ended in 1713, putting thousands of Royal Navy sailors out of work. Many of them became freebooters, continuing to target Spanish ships, but often attacking the vessels of other nations as well. An estimated 5,000 seamen opted to "go a-pyrating" at the time, motivated principally not by greed but by the desire to be free of shipboard abuse. Captain Johnson's book went through five printings in a decade, appearing in an expanded two-volume edition with the title* The History and Lives of All the Most Notorious Pirates, and their Crews *in 1735, by which time the golden age was over. Ever since, histories written about the pirates of that era have relied at least in part on the brief biographies of the most famous of them left by Captain Johnson, about whom virtually nothing is known, apart from the fact that he knew a great deal about piracy. It is likely that Captain Johnson was a pseudonym for someone who knew at least a few of the individuals he portrayed so vividly, and took part in at least some of the events about which he had such intimate knowledge.*

The following vignette illustrates the pirates' liberty-seeking impulses. It tells of a pirate crew with time on their hands, amusing themselves by playacting a spoof on coercive authority, which they had succeeded in eluding, at least for the moment.

Captain Anstis, and His Crew

Thomas Anstis shipped himself at *Providence* [Nassau, the Bahamas], in the Year 1718, aboard the *Buck* Sloop, and was one of the six that conspired together to get off with the vessel, along with *Howel Davis, Dennis Topping*, and *Walter Kennedy*, etc. I shall only observe, that this combination was the beginning of Captain *Roberts's* company, which afterwards proved so formidable, from whom *Anstis* separated the 18th of *April*, 1721, leaving his Commodore to pursue his adventures upon the Coasts of *Guinea*, whilst he returned to the *West Indies*, upon the same design.[1]

About the middle of *June*, he met with one Captain *Maiston*, between *Hispaniola* and *Jamaica*, bound to *New York*, from which he took all the wearing apparel, liquors and provisions, and six men. Afterwards he met with the *Irwin*, Captain *Ross* from *Cork*, on the Coast of *Martinico*, which ship had Colonel *Doyly* of *Montserrat* on board, and his Family, and 600 barrels of beef.

Afterwards they went into one of the Islands to clean [the barnacles and other fouling organisms from their ship's hull], and thence proceeding towards *Bermudas*, they met with a stout ship called the *Morning Star*, bound from *Guinea* to *Carolina*, which they kept for their own use. Just after, they took a ship from *Barbadoes* bound to *New England*, from whence taking her guns, they mounted the *Morning Star* with 32 pieces of cannon, and 100 men, appointing *John Fenn* Captain: For *Anstis* was so in love with his own vessel, she being a good sailor, he made it his choice to stay in her, and let *Fenn* have the other ship. Though they were not sufficiently strong, yet being most new men, they could not agree, but resolving to break up company, sent a Petition to His Majesty by a Merchant Ship, expecting her Return at *Cuba*.

Here they staid about nine months; but not having provisions for above two, they were obliged to take what the Island afforded; which is many sorts of fish, particularly turtle; though they eat not a bit of bread, nor flesh meat, during their being on the Island.

They passed their time here in dancing, and other diversions, agreeable to these sort of folks. Among the rest, they appointed a mock Court of Judicature, to try one another for Piracy, and he that was a Criminal one day, was made a Judge another. I shall never forget one of their Trials, which for the curiosity of it, I shall relate. The Judge got up into a tree, having a dirty tarpaulin over his shoulders for a robe, and a Thrum Cap upon his head, with a large pair of spectacles upon his nose, and a monkey bearing up his train, with abundance of Officers attending him, with crowbars and hand-spikes instead of wands and tip-staves in their hands.[2] Before whom the Criminals were brought out, making 1000 wry Faces; when the Attorney-General moved the Court, and said, "An't please your Lordship, and you Gentlemen of the Jury, this fellow before you is a sad dog, a sad, a sad dog, and I hope your Lordship will order him to be hanged out of the way; he has committed Piracy upon the High Seas; nay, my Lord, that's not all; this fellow, this sad dog before you, has out-rid a hundred storms, and you know, my Lord, *He that's born to be hanged, will never be drowned.* Nor is this all, he has been guilty of worse villany than this, and that is of drinking of small beer; and your Lordship knows, there was never a sober fellow but what was a rogue—My Lord, I should have said more, but your Lordship knows our rum is out, and how should a Man speak that has not drunk a dram to-day."

JUDGE: Harkee me, Sirrah—you ill-looked dog. What have you to say why you may not be tucked up, and set a-sun-drying like a scare-crow? Are you Guilty, or not?

PRISONER: Not Guilty, an't please your Worship.

JUDGE: Not Guilty! say so again, and I will have you hanged without any Trial.

PRISONER: An't please your Worship's Honour, my Lord, I am as honest a fellow as ever went between stem and stern of a ship, and can hand, reef, steer, and clap two ends of a rope together, as well as e'er a He that ever crossed Salt-water; but I was taken by one *George Bradley* (the name of the Judge) a notorious Pirate, and a sad rogue as ever was hanged, and he forced me, an't please your Honour.

JUDGE: Answer me, Sirrah—how will you be tried?

PRISONER: By God and my country.

JUDGE: The Devil you will. . . . Then, Gentlemen of the Jury, we have nothing to do but to proceed to Judgment.

ATTORNEY-GENERAL: Right, my Lord; for if the fellow should be suffered to speak, he might clear himself; and that, you know, is an affront to the Court.

PRISONER: Pray, my Lord, I hope your Lordship will consider.

JUDGE: Consider! How dare you talk of considering! Sirrah, Sirrah, I have never considered in all my life. I'll make it Treason to consider.

PRISONER: But I hope your Lordship will hear reason.

JUDGE: What have we to do with Reason? I would have you to know, Sirrah, we do not sit here to hear Reason—we go according to Law. Is our dinner ready?

ATTORNEY-GENERAL: Yes, my Lord.

JUDGE: Then harkee you rascal at the Bar, hear me, Sirrah, hear me.— You must be hanged for three reasons: *First*, because it is not fit that I should sit as Judge, and no-body to be hang'd: *Secondly*, You must be hang'd because you have a damn'd hanging Look: *Thirdly*, You must be hanged, because I am hungry. There's Law for you, ye dog; take him away, Gaoler.

By this we may see how these fellows can jest upon things, the thoughts of which should make them tremble.

Notes

1. The renowned Black Bart, Bartholomew Roberts (1682–1722), was the most successful pirate of the golden age, whose crews took more than 300 ships in three years. Roberts dressed the part of the stereotypical pirate, according to Captain Johnson, who devoted the longest chapter in his book to Roberts. He wore a crimson coat, gold chain necklace, and a feather in his hat. He died in a battle with a Royal Navy ship.

2. A thrum cap is a kind of shaggy-looking, wig-like hat that sailors knitted together from raw wool and bits of string.

The Dutch Pirate Admiral: Piet Hein

Jan Pieter Heije

The iconic English admiral Sir Francis Drake, whose round-the-world raid was the subject of an entry in part VI, personified the double-sided nature of piracy. That fact is most wittily and succinctly captured in the lyrics of "When You're a Professional Pirate," a song from Muppet Treasure Island *(1996), the most hilarious and perceptive adaptation of Robert Louis Stevenson's classic 1883 novel about pirates in the Caribbean. Long John Silver, played by Tim Curry, sings the number:*

> *Now take Sir Francis Drake, the Spanish all despise him,*
> *but to the British, he's a hero, and they idolize him!*
> *It's how you look at buccaneers that makes us bad or good.*
> *I see us as the members of a noble brotherhood!*

England was not alone in having a great naval hero who was defined as a pirate by the empire against which he and his nation fought. The citizens of the Netherlands and China, among other nations, also revere such figures. Dutch and Chinese pirate/ heroes are the subjects of this and the following selection.

Dutch rebels went to sea to fight against the imperial rule of Spain over the Low Countries during the Eighty Years' War (1568–1648), which ultimately gained independence for the United Provinces. They adopted the name Water Beggars, proudly appropriating a pejorative description of them uttered by the hated Spanish governor. The most famous of these Dutch pirates, as they were seen from the perspective of Madrid, was Piet Pieterszoon Hein (1577–1629), who spent four years enslaved in a Spanish galley. Gaining his freedom, Hein became the most successful pirate of his age and a national hero for the nascent Netherlands. His greatest triumph was capturing the entire Spanish treasure fleet as it departed from Havana, Cuba, in 1628, which yielded a fabulous lode of gold and silver. The deed was memorialized in a children's ditty composed in 1844 by Jan Pieter Heije (1809–76), which generations of proud Hollanders have sung. It is still familiar in the Netherlands today.

A Song of Triumph about the Silver Fleet

Have you heard about the Silver Fleet?
The Silver Fleet from Spain [Spanje]?
They had so many Spanish coins on board,
Little apples of the Orange [Oranje].[1]

CHORUS

Piet Hein, Piet Hein, Piet Hein his name is tiny,
His many deeds were great, his many deeds were great,
He has taken the Silver Fleet, He has taken the Silver Fleet!

Piet Hein was never heard to say a single reckless word:
Well, well, you boys of Orange!
On Spanish ships, here and there, come, climb aboard,
And roll to me the coins of Spain!

Don't the boys, like cats, climb up into the rig
And don't they fight like the lion?
They shamed the Spaniards with a beating so big
Back in Spain they heard them cryin'.

If there came again now such a Silver Fleet,
Say, would you behave the same way?
Or out of range would you soon retreat
And safe in your hammock stay?

Well, blood that's Dutch,
Of courage, that blood has much!
We may not be large, we may be petite,
But we would still win a Silver Fleet!
But we would still win a Silver Fleet!

Translated by Eric Paul Roorda and William S. Roorda

Note

1. The House of Orange is the royal family of the Netherlands, and orange is the national color. In Dutch, *oranje* rhymes with España and anything with the diminutive suffix *je*, but in English, "orange" rhymes with nothing.

The Chinese Pirate Admiral: Koxinga

Koxinga

The Ming Dynasty naval commander Koxinga (1624–62) earned his sobriquet of "pirate chief" in the West for expelling the Dutch from Taiwan in 1662. But in a familiar twist of cultural relativity, he is a national hero in the Republic of China, the People's Republic of China, and Japan, where he was born. He was the son of a Japanese woman and a Chinese pirate named Zheng Zhilong, who had taken refuge in Nagasaki Prefecture. His father would soon be the most powerful individual in the coastal waters of China, with a thousand ships under his control between the Yangtze and Pearl Rivers. After capturing the port of Amoy in his native Fujian Province, Zheng relocated his family to China when his son, who was named Zheng Sen, was seven years old. While the boy grew up on the coast of the Strait of Taiwan, his father's influence continued to grow, until the Ming dynasty relinquished naval command to him.

In 1644, Manchurian forces invaded China and seized Beijing, where the emperor hanged himself in the Forbidden City. The new emperor came to power with the key support of Zheng Zhilong, and afterward he conferred the title of Koxinga (which means Lord of the Imperial Surname) on the admiral's son. The next year, the emperor ignored Zheng's advice, which had been to consolidate his forces in coastal enclaves, under the guns of his massive fleet, and instead ordered a ground offensive against the Manchurians, who had reached Nanjing. Disaster ensued for the Chinese, resulting in the death of another emperor, by either suicide or starvation, in 1646. At that point, Zheng Zhilong switched sides, accepting the offer dangled by the first emperor of the Qing, or Manchu, dynasty, to accept a commission in his navy. But his son Koxinga decided to remain loyal to the doomed Ming dynasty, whose latest emperor swore resistance to the Qing. Burning the robes he wore as a Confucian scholar, Koxinga became a military man, leading the losing fight against the Qing usurpers on land and sea for the next fifteen years, until there was no Ming dynasty left to defend. The last Ming emperor fled southwest, away from the Ocean, pursued by the Manchurians, who captured and beheaded him. Koxinga solidified his hold on China's coastal waters, but the Qing rulers ordered the mainland coast to be depopulated, leaving him nowhere to go, except the island of Taiwan.

Koxinga's greatest victory was his invasion of Taiwan, where the Dutch East Indies Company (VOC) had established a trading post, named Castle Zeelandia, in 1624.

His turncoat father is said to have facilitated the original arrangement, which had endured for almost four decades prior to Koxinga's arrival. The appearance of his vast armada of ships, more than 1,100 in number, astonished the occupants of the fortress. One of them wrote, "On the morning of 30th April 1661 there was a very thick fog. . . . As soon as the fog had lifted we perceived such a fleet of ships, Chinese junks lying in the sea . . . such that we could not even estimate their numbers, let alone count them. There were so many masts that it was as if a thick wood had appeared. We beheld this sight as if overcome with astonishment, for no one, not even the Governor himself, could have expected this, and no one knew whether they had come as friend or enemy." The following selection is the ultimatum that Koxinga sent in response to the Dutch governor's polite inquiry into the nature of his business there. The brave governor rejected the admiral's ultimatum, triggering the sanguinary nine-month Siege of Formosa, which ended when the Dutch surrendered. Koxinga granted them liberal terms of capitulation, permitting them to sail away with much of their wealth, but he executed his interpreter, a Dutch missionary, for not convincing his compatriots to give up sooner. Koxinga soon consolidated his control of Taiwan, declared himself to be the last Ming dynasty emperor, then died. There are a dozen different versions of his death. Some accounts say he died of rage at news that the Spanish had expelled people of Chinese ethnicity from the Philippines. Others say he caught a cold.

Koxinga's legend took shape soon after his death in 1662. The greatest dramatist in the history of Japanese theater, Chikamatsu Monzaemon (1653–1725), wrote the classic puppet play The Battles of Coxinga, first performed in Yokohama in 1715, which portrays him as a hero, not a pirate. In the late twentieth century, Koxinga gained status in the People's Republic of China as a symbol of opposition to foreign domination. Since the 1980s, a monumental statue of Koxinga has towered over Gulangyu (Drumbeat Island) in the harbor of Xiamen, formerly the port of Amoy, which was once Koxinga's headquarters. Later, Xiamen came under Western domination as a treaty port yielded for the use of foreigners by the decrepit Qing dynasty, and now it is one of the coastal Special Economic Zones that drive the Chinese export economy.

Translation of the Letter sent by Heer Pompoan to Heer Frederick Coyett, Governor in Tayouan; Teybingh, Syautoo, Teysiankon, Koxsin sends this letter to the Governor Coyett in Tayouan[1]

You Dutch, scarcely a hundred in number, how can you war against us, who are so mighty? Surely you must be wandering out of your senses and deprived of reason.

I, Pompoan, declare that it is the will of God that all things live and be preserved from destruction. I am therefore disposed that you people remain alive; it is for this reason that I have sent you my letters at various times. You should consider well, as a matter of the greatest importance, the preservation from harm of your wives, your children, and all your possessions.

I send to you my mandarin, Sanquae by name, and in addition the preacher

Chinese pirates and fishermen used the same watercraft, in the same waters. "The *Mon Lei* is a Foochow [Fuzhou] fisher junk," reads the reverse of this postcard, "designed like the pirate craft of the China Coast for 1,000 years past. 50 ft. long, 16 ft. beam and 5 ft. draft, the ship is of teak throughout. Her name means Bon Voyage." *Mon Lei*—also translated as "ten thousand miles," "infinity," and "good luck"—was built in Hong Kong before 1920. A quintet of adventurous Englishmen purchased it, sailing it across the Pacific Ocean and through the Panama Canal to the East Coast of the United States in 1939–40. Robert Ripley of "Believe It or Not" fame purchased it in 1946, to entertain guests on Long Island Sound. The junk has spent time exhibited at Mystic Seaport, and still plies the seas. Photographer unknown, postcard, c. 1940s. Courtesy of the Roorda/Doyle Collection.

Hambroeck, the interpreters Ouhincko and Joucko, to greet the Governor and to ask your surrender on such conditions as hereafter follow: consider them well, you people.[2]

First: If you hand over the fortress before my artillery has displayed its might against it, I shall treat you in the same way I treated the Commandant of Fort Provintia and his people; if you desire anything and request it, you will receive it in the same way.[3] I tell the truth and shall not deceive you.

Furthermore: Even when my artillery has already displayed its might, I shall order cease fire at once if the Governor, together with some other persons of great and small degree, raise the white flag, come out to me, and ask for peace. That should be sufficient for you to have confidence in my words. When high and low commanders come out to welcome me with their wives and children, I shall at once order all my artillery to be silenced. When I am made aware that you seriously mean peace, I shall give the Governor and his men such additional proofs that they will trust me all the more.

One other word: When you will have made peace, your soldiers must march out immediately. I shall despatch some of my troops inside to guard the fort and the houses within, and to establish order, so that your property will not be made the less by the least blade of grass or hair. I shall also give permission for some male and female slaves to remain within these houses to look after them. I shall also permit those of you who want to live at Saccam (Provintia) or Tayouan, either at your own homes or at the homes of others, to do so, and you may take then all the money and goods you possess there.

Still another word: It is the Chinese custom to grant everything which is requested save possession of the fortress; we place much importance on that. All other things that you people want you may have, but you will not have the two days time to salvage your goods and march out with them that the people at Saccam had. You will not have this time because you have delayed, while the people of Saccam surrendered before they tasted our gunfire. But if you people wait so long that you desire peace only when our guns have opened breeches in your walls, you will not have a single hour's respite, but will have to march out at once.

Furthermore: I realize that since the Dutch have come here from so great a distance to carry on trade it is their duty and obligation to do whatever they can to preserve their fortress. This devotion pleases me, and I see no guilt or misdeed in it; I hope that you will not be afraid for that cause.

When I say something the whole world has confidence in me, and knows that I shall keep my word. I am inclined neither to lie nor deceive. Preserve this letter, all you Hollanders. Everything in it is just and certain.

The point has been reached where we can take or save your lives. You must therefore decide at once. To let your thoughts wander is to long after death. Mr. Coyett has indicated to this writer that he does not understand Chinese, and I have thus often written him letters which he has not comprehended. Now I send a letter to him with interpreters who have read and translated the same. Valentyn has had it written in Dutch so that nothing will be left to be desired. You people must understand my intentions.

Translated by J. Valentyn 24th May 1661, to the best of my capability.

Notes

1. Born in Sweden, Heer (Sir) Frederick Coyett (1615–87) was a high-ranking administrator for the VOC who served in Nagasaki, Japan, before becoming governor in Formosa (Tayouan here) in 1656. Koxinga had many monikers, including Heer Pompoan, Teybingh, Syautoo, Teysiankon, and Koxsin.
2. Koxinga captured the Dutch missionary Antonius Hambroeck (1607–61) and his family, forced him to be his interpreter during the Siege of Formosa, then executed him when the Dutch governor refused to surrender.
3. Prior to enveloping Fort Zeelandia, Koxinga's forces captured the smaller VOC factory called Fort Provintia and spared the garrison.

Song of the Pirate

José de Espronceda

In the early nineteenth century, despite flare-ups of piracy in the Caribbean and the waters of Southeast Asia, the pirates of the past came to be romanticized in Western culture, as exemplified in this paean by the Romantic Spanish poet José de Espronceda (1808–42). Espronceda resisted authority at the age of fifteen, when he joined a conspiracy against King Ferdinand VII. Found out, Espronceda was incarcerated in a monastery, then sent into exile. He spent a decade abroad, living in Portugal, England, France, Belgium, and the Netherlands, then returned to Spain to involve himself once more in radical politics. He finally broke with his native nation and went to the Dutch East Indies, where he died. His rebellious, picaresque existence inclined him to idealize the figure of the pirate, which he extolled in his most famous poem.

With ten cannons per broadside,
Wind astern and sails filling
Not cutting through the sea, but flying,
A full-rigged brigantine:
A pirate ship that's called
The *Feared*, for her ferocity,
Known all across the sea
From shore to shore and in between.

The moon on ocean's surface shines,
In the canvas moans the breeze,
And raises gently on the seas
Wavelets of silver and of blue;
And the pirate captain,
Singing happily on the poop,
Asia on one side, on the other Europe
And there in front of him Istanbul.

"Sail onward, my sailboat,
Without fear,
Of any enemy afloat,
Neither tempest, neither treasure

To turn you from the course you measure,
Nor your valor to domineer.

> "Twenty prizes
> We've made ours
> Despite the powers
> Of the Brit,
> A hundred nations
> Have surrendered
> Laid their standard
> At my feet."

CHORUS

> "It is my ship that's my treasure lode,
> And my only God is Liberty,
> Force and the wind are my legal code,
> My only homeland is the sea."

"There they go to ferocious war,
Monarchs so blind,
Over palm-sized bits of land more:
But out here I can take for mine
All that embarks upon the brine,
No one's laws do I have to mind.

> "And there is no beach,
>   Of any manner,
> Nor a banner,
> Nation's splendor,
> Beyond the reach
> Of my behest,
> And in every chest
> I strike terror.

CHORUS

"To hear the hail 'Here comes a ship!'
   Is to view
It veer and try in vain to slip
Away, by any means to flee:
For I'm the king of the sea,
And my fury is terror true.

"From the prizes
I distribute
All the loot

Equally:
Unless I want
For my share
A woman fair
All for me.

CHORUS

"I'm sentenced to the death penalty!
    At that I laughed:
Good luck has not abandoned me,
And the one who condemned me to die,
I will hang from a yardarm high,
Perhaps on his own craft.

"And if I falter,
What's life to live?
Except to give
Freely, scoff
To wear the halter,
Yoke of the slave.
Like me, be brave!
I shook it off.

CHORUS
"My favorite melodies
    Are North Wind howls;
The racket of the timpanis
Of letting go the anchor,
Of the black seas'
Bellow and roar,
And my cannons' thundering growls.

"And through the thunder
Through the violent wail
Of the screaming gale
Through the commotion,
I just slumber
Pacified,
Lullabied
By the ocean."

CHORUS

Translated by Eric Paul Roorda

Somali Pirates Attack a Cruise Ship

Eric Paul Roorda

Attacking big ships in little boats is by definition an audacious undertaking. Among the many daring exploits of the pirates of Somalia during their twenty-year heyday, perhaps the most audacious occurred in November 2005, when they attacked a cruise ship. It was a very close call, much closer than was reported at the time.

When the sun rose over the Indian Ocean on November 5, 2005, an unusual sight drew the attention of two pairs of wakeful eyes aboard the cruise ship *Seabourn Spirit* that were gazing out to sea that morning. Other eyes were awake but focused on the duties involved in operating a floating hotel: preparing breakfast, setting up room service, getting ready to clean rooms, oiling machinery, and umpteen other tasks. But on the navigation bridge, a sailor serving as lookout and the officer of the dawn watch saw two small boats approaching. This was odd, because the ship was seventy miles from the nearest land. Had this been anywhere in the world except off the Horn of Africa, this oddity would have raised curiosity, not alarm. But the cruise ship was en route from Egypt to Kenya; the motorboats now racing toward *Seabourn Spirit* carried ten pirates.

Back on the coast of Somalia, in many sleepy port towns, the sun rose on another day of desperation for the population. Not long ago, fishing had not only provided a livelihood for the people who lived there, it had permeated their culture. Dawn after dawn, century after century, men and boys had set out in skiffs to harvest the Ocean, never depleting the abundant stocks of fish by using their traditional nets. But then huge fishing boats arrived from distant European and Asian nations, employing modern technologies that swept the seas clear of finny prey in less than a lifetime, leaving the Somali citizenry without an economy. Moreover, it left lifelong fishermen without a reason for being, with no incentive to push their boats into the surf, but with many reasons to despise the interlopers who came from afar.

It was a handful of these angry former fishermen who decided to make a dramatic and dangerous career transition. They took to piracy, employing the same motorized launches that had previously taken them to the fishing grounds.

This image shows the sort of watercraft used by pirates around the Horn of Africa. Becalmed merchant ships were at the mercy of swarms of canoes like these, each crowded with armed men who attacked and often commandeered the much larger vessels. (Pirates did the same thing in the Caribbean, the Adriatic, the Sunda Strait, the South China Sea, and many other hotbeds of lawless high seas predation.) Visible across the water is a row of sturdier hulls, capable of going far out to sea to trade, which were easily adapted for piracy. Today's pirates of Somalia use both crafts, with commercial trawlers as mother ships, and aluminum launches with outboard motors instead of canoes. *Boats of Soudan*, photogravure from *All Round the World: An Illustrated Record of Voyages, Travels and Adventures in All Parts of the Globe*, vol. 3, edited by W. F. Ainsworth (New York: Selmar Hess, 1894), 190. Courtesy of the Roorda/Doyle Collection.

Piracy in the waters near the Horn of Africa was nothing new. The area teemed with trade during antiquity, and pirates there became a problem for the Roman Empire. To ward off pirates and protect their trading routes through the Red Sea to rich ports in East Africa, the Romans established a naval base at Aden in 106 BCE. In later centuries, the Ottoman Empire and the Portuguese Empire alike had trouble suppressing Somali corsairs, who preyed on the merchant vessels of both. In the late 1500s, Somali pirates teamed with an Ottoman navy to expel the Portuguese from several of their colonial footholds in Africa, such as Mombasa, Kenya. But the Portuguese navy responded in force, reasserted their control, consolidated the region under their rule, and suppressed piracy.

Piracy off the Horn of Africa returned in the late twentieth century and caught the world's attention in the early twenty-first century. Somali pirates gained international notoriety in April 2009, when a small group of them carried out the brazen but doomed seizure of the *Maersk Alabama*. The ensuing hostage standoff held the world's attention as it unfolded in real time over the course of five tense days. The 2013 film *Captain Phillips*, starring Tom Hanks in the title role, brought the attention of an enormous audience of moviegoers to the new piracy, by dramatizing the *Maersk Alabama* saga in a commercially and critically successful way.

But the movie only hinted at the underlying reasons for piracy in the vicinity of the Horn of Africa. The main cause was illegal overfishing by foreign trawlers in the sovereign waters of Somalia. This unfair competition denied the local men their traditional livelihood as fishermen. Some of them, unable to feed their families from the scarce catches they could eke out of the Ocean, lashed out at the foreign fishermen and their boats—after all, stealing fish is itself a form of piracy. The Somali fishermen began to seize the trawlers, holding the vessels and their crews for ransom, and in so doing, they themselves became pirates. But the parent companies of fishing operations proved to care little for the trifling investments represented by rusty fishing boats and their exploited crews, and they either did not pay up much or failed to pay up at all.

So the out-of-work fishermen became the pirates of Somalia, broadening their operations, adapting new tactics, strengthening their arsenals, and targeting much larger, far more lucrative prey, such as container ships. Working from a mother ship (often a captured trawler), which had the engines and the fuel capacity needed to reach the commercial shipping lanes, the pirates went offshore looking for targets. Spotting one, they deployed small speedboats to swarm the prize, trying to stop it with automatic rifles and rocket-propelled grenades, and trying to board it using grappling hooks and aluminum ladders. Most ships got away, using an array of countermeasures to repulse boarders: speeding up and steering an evasive course; aiming sound cannons or LRADs (long-range acoustic devices) at them; and hitting them with high-pressure fire hoses. In the rare event that a pirate attack worked, the gleeful boarding party would take their prize into one of the Somali ports where the pirates held sway, to begin negotiating ransom for the ship and crew.

But to attack a cruise ship was a step beyond. *Seabourn Spirit*, however, is one of the smallest cruise ships in the world, a ship of Carnival Corporation's elite, all-inclusive Yachts of Seabourn cruise line, and a tempting target. It has a passenger capacity of only 208 well-heeled passengers, and only 115 guests were aboard when it attracted the attention of the Somali pirates as dawn broke on November 5, 2005. They saw *Seabourn Spirit* as a potential goldmine.

When the two speedboats neared *Seabourn Spirit*, the masked men aboard them opened fire with machine guns and rocket-propelled grenades. At least one of the grenades struck the ship, exploding against the window of a state-

The diminutive cruise ship *Seabourn Spirit*, only 440 feet long, glides past the Castle of St. Peter the Liberator in Bodrum, Turkey, in July 2007. Eighteen months before, the *Seabourn Spirit* had presented a tempting prize for pirates off the coast of Somalia, who attacked the ship. Photograph by A. E. Doyle, July 3, 2007. Courtesy of the photographer.

room, showering the room with glass shards, and terrifying the couple who had been asleep inside, according to a *Seabourn Spirit* security officer, who narrated the event to this writer aboard the vessel in June 2007. The crew herded the passengers into an interior space, as the pirates peppered the ship with bullets.

Seabourn Spirit proceeded to follow the protocol for ships under attack by pirates in small craft: it made a quick turn, accelerated, blasted its sound guns, and zigzagged away at its maximum velocity, leaving the cockleshells full of pirates in their wake. They returned to port like the fishermen they used to be, with nothing to tell but a tale of the whopper that got away.

After *Seabourn Spirit's* close call, Queen Elizabeth II honored the ship's security and safety officer, Michael Groves, and master-at-arms, Som Bahadur Gurung, who sustained minor injuries from grenade shrapnel, calling them "very courageous."

Even so, Groves filed suit for negligence against Carnival Corporation, according to the blog *Cruise Critic*. In his suit, he claimed that *Seabourn Spirit* was in "blatant violation" of regulations of the UK's Department for Transport, among others, to stay at least 170 miles off the piracy-plagued coast of Somalia.

After the well-publicized *Maersk Alabama* event, an international naval consortium led by the United States initiated patrols to regain command of the vital sea lanes that skirt the Horn of Africa, effectively suppressing Somali piracy. In all of 2017, the International Maritime Bureau's Piracy Reporting Centre recorded only three pirate attacks off the Horn of Africa, only one of them successful: the hijacking of a humble dhow with a crew of twenty, whom the pirates released, keeping the boat.

But nothing has been done to address the crisis of disastrous overfishing, of which Somali piracy was a simply a symptom.

VIII

Shipwrecks and Castaways

The open Ocean is like a vast desert, a place offering no potable water, where the wakes of passing ships disappear like footprints erased from sand by wind. The inshore Ocean is jungle-like, where rocks, reefs, shoals, rip currents, breaking surf, and dense fogs can be as impenetrable and dangerous as the thorniest rainforest, full of poisonous creatures. And at any given moment, somewhere in the world, the Ocean is a maelstrom. The kinds of potential chaos that can occur have in common their ability to sink ships: gales, cyclones, mountainous waves, waterspouts, torrents of rain, snowstorms, every other kind of freezing precipitation . . . the list goes on.

Right now, about 100,000 ships are active on the Ocean. If present trends continue, an estimated 1,600 of them will go missing in the next decade, an average of one shipwreck every day and a half, taken without a trace by the voracious sea. For instance, in October 2015 the US-flagged cargo ship *El Faro* sank with all thirty-three crew members, after setting out from Jacksonville, Florida, for Puerto Rico, into the brewing Hurricane Joaquín. On February 15, 2016, the Indonesian tanker KM *Azula* sank in the Arafura Sea off Papua, Indonesia, taking thirteen of its crew with it. Eleven sailors perished on October 13, 2017, when the bulk carrier *Emerald Star* from Hong Kong capsized north of the Philippines. Enormous waves formed rapidly off the island of Phuket, Thailand, on July 5, 2018, sinking the excursion vessel *Phoenix* and drowning 56 of the 104 people on it. On March 12, 2019, twelve of the fourteen men aboard the Chinese trawler *Zhedaiyu 020611* went down with the ship in the Yellow Sea, after colliding with an iron ore carrier running between Port Hedland, Australia, and Shanghai. Virtually every month of every year, the Ocean's casualty count continues to mount.

Rogue waves of freakish immensity claim many victims on the high seas. One grim example was the Cypriot cargo ship *Cemfjord*, which capsized in the North Sea off northern Scotland in January 2015. Bound from Denmark to the United Kingdom loaded with a million pounds of concrete, the vessel encountered an immense example of the Merry Men of Mey, a standing-wave phenomenon that occurs in the busy, treacherous Pentland Firth when gale winds coincide with an ebb tide. The stricken freighter remained afloat afterward, with only its bow projecting straight up out of the water, entombing its eight-man crew.

Such huge swells were once thought to be the stuff of old sailors' exaggerated yarns, despite the clear-headed testimony of many mariners who survived them, such as Joshua Slocum, whose account of a "great wave" that came out of nowhere and swamped his sloop appears in part X of this Reader. Today, the internet abounds with videos of waves that look like towering cliffs of water, providing abundant evidence to support centuries of oral tradition. In fact, the most massive rogue waves can be seen from space, as satellite photography revealed in 2004.

Survivors of shipwrecks confront the manifold menace of the Ocean. The extreme limits of human endurance have been defined at sea by individuals who often are not the strongest physically, but who prove to be the most determined, the most spirited, and ultimately the most life-loving of humans.

"Shipwrecks and Castaways" offers some of the most compelling episodes of people surviving the extreme conditions of the Ocean.

Shipwrecked by Worms, Saved by Canoe:

The Last Voyage of Columbus

Diego Méndez

Though less than an inch long, shipworms terrorized mariners for centuries. Teredo
navalis *is a species of saltwater clam that looks like a worm, which tunnels into the
hulls of wooden vessels and renders them unseaworthy. The fourth and final voyage
that Christopher Columbus undertook to the Americas ended prematurely in 1503, because shipworms devoured his three caravels, reducing their keels to something resembling waterlogged Swiss cheese. The admiral and his men—230 of them—spent the
next six months marooned on the island of Jamaica. The expedition was rescued only
because Diego Méndez de Segura (1475–1536) and seven companions went for help,
setting out on a desperate voyage by canoe from present-day Cape Morant, Jamaica,
to a point on the south coast of Hispaniola, a distance of about 120 miles across the
Caribbean Sea's turbulent Jamaica Channel.*

*Diego Méndez was probably born in Zamora, Spain, but like Columbus before
him, he went to Portugal as a young man and found a patron there. While Columbus
received the support of his father-in-law, a governor in the Madeira Islands, Méndez
became the protégé of the count of Penamacor, who took the teen to sea with him on
several voyages. In 1492, Méndez accompanied the count to Barcelona, where they
remained the following year, when Columbus returned to that city from his first voyage to report to King Ferdinand and Queen Isabella, whose court was in residence at
the time. The count of Penamacor died in Barcelona in 1494, and sometime thereafter
Méndez found a new patron in Columbus. In 1502, Méndez shipped out on the admiral's last trip to the New World in the position of* escribano mayor del armada
(head scribe of the fleet), a kind of personal secretary to the commander himself.

*After the ill-fated fourth voyage of Columbus, Méndez returned to Spain and re-
ceived knighthood from King Ferdinand for his intrepid rescue voyage by canoe. He
went back to Santo Domingo in 1509, as secretary and accountant for the second admiral of the Ocean seas, Christopher Columbus's son Diego. He later received a generous*
repartimiento, *a grant of land along with the people on it, and in 1522 he gained promotion to his dream job, becoming the* alguacil mayor *(chief sheriff) of Hispaniola.
He retired to Spain near the end of his life. Before he died in 1536, Méndez narrated
his version of the harrowing final voyage of Columbus in a codicil to his last will,*

which was not published until 1825 and is rarely referenced today. In the account, he so exclusively credited himself that he did not mention by name Bartolomé Flisco, the Spanish shipmate who went with him on his canoe crossing, and he failed to include the fact that nearly all of the six native men who paddled their boat died of thirst and exhaustion before the end of the ordeal. The codicil appears next, in its entirety.

On the last day of April, in the year fifteen hundred and three, we left Veragua,[1] with three ships, intending to make our passage homeward to Spain, but as the ships were all pierced and eaten by the teredo, we could not keep them above water; we abandoned one of them after we had proceeded thirty leagues; the two which remained were even in a worse condition than that, so that all the hands were not sufficient with the use of pumps and kettles and pans to draw off the water that came through the holes made by the worms. In this state, with the utmost toil and danger, we sailed for thirty-five days, thinking to reach Spain, and at the end of this we arrived at the lowest point of the island of Cuba, at the province of Homo, where the city of Trinidad now stands, so that we were 300 leagues farther from Spain than when we left Veragua for the purpose of proceeding thither; and this, as I have said, with the vessels in very bad condition, unfit to encounter the sea, and our provisions nearly gone. It pleased God that we were enabled to reach the island of Jamaica, where we drove the two ships on shore, and made of them two cabins thatched with straw, in which we took up our dwelling, not however without considerable danger from the natives, who were not yet subdued, and who might easily set fire to our habitation in the night, in spite of the greatest watchfulness. It was there that I gave out the last ration of biscuit and wine; I then took a sword in my hand, three men only accompanying me, and advanced into the island; for no one else dared go to seek food for the admiral and those who were with him. It pleased God that I found some people who were very gentle and did us no harm, but received us cheerfully, and gave us food with hearty goodwill. I then made a stipulation with the Indians, who lived in a village called Aguacadiba, and with their cacique [chief], to hunt and fish to supply the admiral every day with a sufficient quantity of provisions, which they were to bring to the ships, where I promised there should be a person ready to pay them in blue beads, combs and knives, hawks'-bells and fishhooks, and other such articles which we had with us for that purpose. With this understanding, I dispatched one of the Spaniards whom I had brought with me to the admiral, in order that he might send a person to pay for the provisions and secure their being sent. From thence I went to another village, at three leagues' distance from the former, and made a similar agreement with the natives and their cacique, and then dispatched another Spaniard to the admiral, begging him to send another person with a similar object to this village. After this I went further on, and came to a great cacique named Huareo, living in a place that is now called Melilla, thirteen leagues from where the ships lay. He received me very well; he gave me plenty to eat, and ordered all his subjects to bring together in the course of three days a great quantity of provisions, which they did, and laid them before him, whereupon I paid him for them to his full satisfaction. I stipulated with him that they should furnish constant supply, and engaged that there should be a person appointed to pay them; having made this arrangement, I sent the other Spaniard to the admiral with the provisions they had given me, and then begged the cacique to allow me two Indians to go with me to the extremity of the island, one to carry the hammock in which I slept, and the other carrying the food.

In this manner I journeyed eastward to the end of the island, and came to a cacique who was named Ameyro, with whom I entered into close friendship. I gave him my name and took his, which among these people is regarded as a pledge of brotherly attachment. I bought of him a very good canoe, and gave him in exchange an excellent brass helmet that I carried in a bag, a frock, and one of the two shirts that I had with me; I then put out to sea in this canoe, in search of the place that I had left, the cacique having given me six Indians to assist in guiding the canoe. When I reached the spot to which I had dispatched the provisions, I found there the Spaniards whom the admiral had sent, and I loaded them with the victuals that I had brought with me, and went myself to the admiral, who gave me a very cordial reception. He was not satisfied with seeing and embracing me, but asked me respecting everything that had occurred in the voyage, and offered up thanks to God for having delivered me in safety from so barbarous a people. The men rejoiced greatly at my arrival, for there was not a loaf left in the ships when I returned to them with the means of allaying their hunger; this, and every day after that, the Indians came to the ships loaded with provisions from the place where I had made the agreements; so that there was enough for the 230 people who were with the admiral. Ten days after this, the admiral called me aside, and spoke to me of the great peril he was in, addressing me as follows: "Diego Méndez, my son, not one of those whom I have here with me has any idea of the great danger in which we stand except myself and you; for we are but few in number, and these wild Indians are numerous and very fickle and capricious: and whenever they may take it into their heads to come and burn us in our two ships, which we have made straw-thatched cabins, they may easily do so by setting fire to them on the land side, and so destroy us all.[2] The arrangement that you have made with them for the supply of food, to which they agreed with such goodwill, may soon prove disagreeable to them; and it would not be surprising if, on the morrow, they were not to bring us anything at all: in such case we are not in a position to take it by main force, but shall be compelled to accede to their terms. I have thought of a remedy, if you consider it advisable; which is, that someone should go out in the canoe that you have purchased, and make his way in it to Española, to purchase a vessel with which we may escape from the extremely dangerous position in which we now are. Tell me your opinion." To which I answered, "My lord, I distinctly see the danger in which we stand, which is much greater than would be readily imagined. With respect to the passage from this island to Española in so small a vessel as a canoe, I look upon it not merely as difficult, but impossible; for I know not who would venture to encounter so terrific a danger as to cross a gulf of forty leagues of sea, and among islands where the sea is most impetuous, and scarcely ever at rest." His lordship did not agree with the opinion that I expressed, but adduced strong arguments to show that I was the person to undertake the enterprise. To which I replied, "My lord, I have many times put my life in danger to save yours, and the lives of all those who are with you, and God has marvelously preserved me: in consequence of this, there have not been wanting murmurers who have said that your lordship entrusts every honorable undertaking to me, while there are others among them who would perform them as well as I. My opinion is, therefore, that your lordship would do well to summon all the men, and lay this business before them, to see if, among them all, there is one who will volunteer to undertake it, which I certainly doubt; and if all refuse, I will risk my life in your service, as I have done many times already."

On the following day his lordship caused all the men to appear together before him, and then opened the matter to them in the same manner as he had done to me. When they heard it they were all silent, until some said that it was out of the question to speak of such a thing; for it was impossible, in so small a craft, to cross a boisterous and perilous gulf of forty leagues' breadth, and to pass between those two islands, where very strong vessels had been lost in going to make discoveries, not being able to encounter the force and fury of the currents. I then arose, and said, "My lord, I have but one life, and I am willing to hazard it in the service of your lordship, and for the welfare of all those who are here with us; for I trust in God, that in consideration of the motive which actuates me, he will give me deliverance, as he has already done on many other occasions." When the admiral heard my determination, he arose and embraced me and, kissing me on the cheek, said, "Well did I know that there was no one here but yourself who would dare to undertake this enterprise: I trust in God, our Lord, that you will come out of it victoriously, as you have done in the others which you have undertaken." On the following day I drew my canoe on to the shore; fixed a false keel on it, and pitched and greased it; I then nailed some boards upon the poop and prow, to prevent the sea from coming in, as it was liable to do from the lowness of the gunwales; I also fixed a mast in it, set up a sail, and laid in the necessary provisions for myself, one Spaniard, and six Indians, making eight in all, which was as many as the canoe would hold. I then bade farewell to his lordship, and all the others, and proceeded along the coast of Jamaica, up to the extremity of the island, which was thirty-five leagues from the point whence we started. Even this distance was not traversed without considerable toil and danger; for on the passage I was taken prisoner by some Indian pirates, from whom God delivered me in a marvelous manner. When we had reached the end of the island, and were remaining there in the hope of the sea becoming sufficiently calm to allow us to continue our voyage across it, many of the natives collected together with the determination of killing me, and seizing the canoe with its contents, and they cast lots for my life, to see which of them should carry their design into execution. As soon as I became aware of their project, I betook myself secretly to my canoe, which I had left at three leagues distance from where I then was, and set sail for the spot where the admiral was staying, and reached it after an interval of fifteen days from my departure. I related to him all that had happened, and how God had miraculously rescued me from the hands of those savages. His lordship was very joyful at my arrival, and asked me if I would recommence my voyage; I replied that I would, if I might be allowed to take some men, to be with me at the extremity of the island until I should find a fair opportunity of putting to sea to prosecute my voyage. The admiral gave me seventy men, and with them his brother [Bartholomew] the *adelantado*, to stay with me until I put to sea, and to remain there for three days after my departure; with this arrangement I returned to the extremity of the island and waited there four days. Finding the sea become calm I parted from the rest of the men with much mutual sorrow; I then commended myself to God and our Lady of Antigua, and was at sea five days and four nights without laying down the oar from my hand, but continued steering the canoe while my companions paddled. It pleased God that at the end of five days I reached the Island of Española at Cape San Miguel, having been two days without eating or drinking, for our provisions were exhausted. I brought my canoe up to a very beautiful part of the coast, to which many of the natives soon came, and brought with them many articles of food, so that I remained there two days to take rest. I took six Indians from this place, and leaving those that I had brought with me, I put off to sea again, moving along the coast of Española, for it was a 130 leagues from the spot where I landed to the city of San Domingo, where the governor dwelt, who was the Commander de Lares. When I had proceeded eighty leagues along the coast of the island (not without great toil and danger, for that part of the island was not yet brought into subjugation), I reached the province of Azoa [Azua], which is twenty-four leagues from San Domingo, and there I learned from the commander, Gallego, that the governor was gone out to subdue the province of Xuragoa [Jaragua], which was at fifty leagues' distance. When I heard this I left my canoe and took the road for Xuragoa, where I found the governor, who kept me with him seven months, until he had burned and hanged eighty-four caciques, lords of vassals, and with them Nacaona [Anacaona], the sovereign mistress of the island, to whom all rendered service and obedience.[3] When that expedition was finished I went on foot to San Domingo, a distance of seventy leagues, and waited in expectation of the arrival of ships from Spain, it being now more than a year since any had come. In this interval it pleased God that three ships arrived, one of which I bought, and loaded it with provisions, bread, wine, meat, hogs, sheep, and fruit, and dispatched it to the place where the admiral was staying, in order that he might come over in it with all his people to San Domingo, and from thence sail for Spain. I myself went on in advance with the two other ships, in order to give an account to the king and queen of all that had occurred in this voyage.

Translated by Eric Paul Roorda

Notes

1. The coast of Central America in present-day Nicaragua, Costa Rica, and Panama.
2. Columbus was no stranger to shipwrecks by 1503, so he may have had a sense of déjà vu when he drove his vessels onto the beach to live in them. The largest vessel among the three he commanded on his first voyage across the Atlantic Ocean, the famous *Santa María*, came to grief on Christmas Day, 1492, when it slid onto a sandbar off the north coast of Hispaniola on a quiet night, then came apart as the tide receded and the waves sprang up. He built a fort from the shipwreck's salvaged timbers for the crew to occupy, but after he left, his men angered the local people, who killed all of them by the time Columbus returned the following year. Their fate was undoubtedly in his mind when he told Méndez that the native Jamaicans would murder them, if they remained for long.
3. The native people of Hispaniola, the Taíno, organized the island into five chiefdoms, among them Jaragua. The Spanish under Governor Nicolás de Ovando (1439–1511) conquered Jaragua and executed the celebrated Queen Anacaona (1474–1504).

The Unparalleled Sufferings of John Jea

John Jea

Born in what is now Nigeria, John Jea (1773–?) survived the Middle Passage across the Atlantic Ocean from Africa to North America at the age of two. He endured a childhood of slavery in New York, then gained his freedom, and, like many free blacks at the time, went to sea for a living. Jea's career at sea took him all around the Atlantic world, as far as Buenos Aires, Argentina, which gave him the opportunity to preach of his religious faith to others. In his autobiography, The Life, History and Unparalleled Sufferings of John Jea, the African Preacher, *published in Portsea, England, in 1811, he described a disastrous passage that he lived to write about, during which the ship was struck by lightning, becalmed in the Gulf of Mexico for a full seven weeks, and then finally rescued. He eventually left the life of a sailor to become a full-time preacher, and in 1805 established a congregation of believers of color in the bustling seaport of Portsmouth, England, that was probably the first majority non-white church in the United Kingdom. Even so, nothing is known of his life after 1817.*

It pleased God to put it into my mind to cross the Atlantic main; and I embarked on board of a ship for that purpose. The name of the ship was the *Superb* of Boston, and the captain's name was ABLE STOVEY, with whom I agreed to sail for seventeen dollars per month. I was quite unacquainted with the sea, and was very much pleased in going on board the vessel; but the case was soon altered, for the first day I went on board to work, the captain and the men asked me if I came on board to work. I told them yes. They asked me where my clothes were. I said I had them on my back. They asked me if that was all I had. I told them I thought I had sufficient, for I was not certain of staying longer than one day; for if I did not like it I would not stay out the month; for I thought that a person going to sea, could go one day and return the next.

During this time the vessel had got under weigh, and was sailing through the river, which was very pleasant, until we got outside of the light-house, when the ship began to roll about very much, which greatly terrified me. The captain coming to me, said, "How do you come on?" I told him that I was tired, and that I wanted to get home. . . . The captain seeing how I was, bade me go below, for the men had some cold beef for supper, and that I should rest myself. When I was going below, I looked at the man at the helm with an evil eye, thinking he made the ship to go on one side on purpose to frighten me the more; but before I got down to the hold I fell down, by the vessel rolling, and all the men sung out, "Hollo, there is a horse down": and they laughing at me so, made me the more afraid and terrified, and after I had got down into the hold, I was afraid the ship would fall, and I strove to keep her up by pushing, and holding fast by different parts of the ship, and when the waves came dashing against the sides of the ship, I thought they were sea lions, and was afraid they would beat a hole through the ship's side and would come in and devour me; when day-light appeared, I was very much tired and fatigued, for I had been holding and trying to keep the ship upright all the night; in the morning I asked the sailors why they did not keep the ship upright, and one of the men said, pointing to another, "That is the man that makes the ship go on one side." This they said in their scoffing way, to deride me. Having been about eight or ten days at sea, I found out what it was, in some measure. The weather was very boisterous, the sea running very high, and thundering and lightning very much; the reason of which was, I believe, because they so ill-used and abused me, and swore they would throw me overboard, or beat me so that I should jump overboard. When they saw me praying to God, they called me by way of derision, a Jonah, because I prayed to God to calm the tempestuous weather. On the contrary, they were making game of the works of the Lord, and said that the old man had fine fire works, for it gave them light to go up on the yards to furl the sails; but to their great terror, after they had furled the sails, it pleased the Lord to send his lightning and thunder directly, which killed two men on the spot. One of them was burnt like a cinder, his clothes were totally consumed, not so much as a bit of a handkerchief nor any thing else being left. His name was George Begann, about thirty-six years of age. The other's name was James Cash, about twenty-five years of age: his body was entirely burnt up, not a single bit of it was to be seen, nothing but the cinders of his clothes, one of his shoes, his knife, his gold ring, and his key.

Seven more were wounded, some in their backs, and others in different parts of their bodies: and appeared to be dead for about ten or fifteen minutes.

At the time this dreadful carnage happened, I was standing about seven or eight feet, from them; my eye-sight was taken from me for four or five minutes, but my soul gave glory to God for what was done. When I recovered my sight I saw the captain standing in the cabin gangway, and the cabin-boy and three passengers behind him, lamenting greatly, [w]ringing their hands, and plucking their hair; the captain crying out, "O! my men, we are all lost!" I then took the boldness to speak unto him, and said, "Why do you cry and lament? You see that your ship is not hurt, and that the Lord has been pleased to spare your life; and what the Lord has done is right."

A short time after we had survived this awful scene, the captain ex-

This rendering of a small vessel in a big storm is reminiscent of the travails of John Jea. It is the work of John Sell Cotman (1782–1842), one of the leading artists of the English Norwich School, who specialized in maritime subjects. Halftone print (1897) of Cotman's painting *A Galiot in a Gale* (undated). Courtesy of the Roorda/Doyle Collection.

claimed, "O! my men, my men, the ship is on fire!" On hearing this, the men that were able to move, were roused to take off the hatches, to see where the fire was. But, blessed be God, the ship was not on fire, for it was part of the men's clothes who were consumed, which had got down into the hold, and was burning, which caused a very great smoke; for the sailors stood round the main-mast (excepting four who were at the helm) which was the most materially injured; that part of the cargo which was near the main-mast, consisting of tobacco and staves for casks, was nearly all consumed, but the ship sustained no damage whatever.

The captain and ship's crew were very much terrified when they saw the power of God in killing and wounding the men, and destroying the cargo; which judgments were sent on them, "Because they rebelled against the words of God, and contemned the counsel of the Most High: Therefore he brought down their heart with labour; they fell down, and there was none to help. . . ." Psalm 107 . . .

We had not been more than a fortnight at sea, after the first deliverance from the thunder and lightning, when we were visited by most dreadful whirlwinds and hurricanes, which dismasted the ship, and made her almost a wreck. We were forty-two days in the Gulph of Mexico, without receiving any assistance whatever; during three weeks of which we had not any dry clothes to put on, not one of us, and we were obliged to eat our victuals raw, for the weather was so very boisterous, that we could not light a fire; we were also put on short allowance, both of victuals and water, for we did not know how long it would be before we should meet with any deliverance. The quantity of provisions and water we were allowed was, half a pound of raw beef or pork, a biscuit and a half, and half a pint of water, for four and twenty hours. During this dreadful tempest, the snow and rain descended rapidly, which we caught, and put into casks, and of this we were only allowed the same quantity as of the good water.

My dear reader, consider what great distress we must have been in at this time, when the ship was tossed and rolled about in such a dreadful manner and expecting every moment that the ship would be staved in pieces, by the furiousness of the raging sea. Yea, this also terrified me, as well as the rest of the men, when it first began, and I entreated the Lord God Almighty to have mercy on us, that we might once more, by his grace and by the aid of his Spirit, arrive at our desired port; for our hearts were faint within us, and our spirits within us were famishing, that it caused every man on board to be earnestly inclined to call upon the Lord for deliverance; for they now believed that the Lord had sent this distress upon them, that they might earnestly desire the word of God, for the Scriptures saith, "Behold, the days come, saith the Lord God, that I will send a famine in the land, not a famine of bread, nor a thirst for water, but of hearing the words of the Lord: And they shall wander from sea to sea, and from the north even to the east, they shall run to and fro to seek the word of the Lord, and shall not find it. In that day shall the fair virgins and young men faint for thirst." Amos viii 11–13. Thus was our hearts faint within us, and we sought for the words of God's promise, unto us wretched miserable sinners, that "In the time of trouble he would deliver us"; and I have every reason to believe that the Lord did hear our feeble breathings, for we perished not, but at the end of forty-two days, we saw a sail making towards us, and afterwards another, which both came to our assistance.

Thus, blessed be God, our feeble breathings were heard, when we cried unto God with a sincere heart, he delivered us out of this distress, for these two vessels supplied us with provisions and water, and spars, whereby we were able to make jury-masts, so that we were enabled to gain the state of Merelian [Maryland?], in Virginia, which is not far from Baltimore, there we remained until our ship was repaired, and after that, we set sail for England, our destined port being London.

Pandora's Box

Peter Heywood

The mutineers of the Bounty *cast off Captain William Bligh and eighteen loyal members of his crew in an open boat just 23 feet long. The group undertook a passage of 3,500 nautical miles to the Dutch East Indies. They limited their daily ration to an ounce of bread and a quarter pint of water. The iron-willed Bligh maintained his place in the stern, steering the launch throughout the ordeal. After six weeks, they made it to a Dutch post on the island of Timor, completing one of the most astounding feats of Ocean survival of all time. Bligh's voyage is relatively well known, dramatized in books and movies such as* The Bounty *(1984), starring Anthony Hopkins as Bligh and the newly discovered Mel Gibson as Fletcher Christian.*

But almost unknown are the travails of the loyal sailors left behind in HMS Bounty. *Bligh ordered them to stay aboard rather than further overload his launch, and they had to accompany the mutineers back to Tahiti, where they remained "to wait patiently for the arrival of a ship," in the words of midshipman Peter Heywood (1772–1831). In the meantime, Bligh made his miraculous way all the way back to England, where he impugned the loyalty of all the men who had not been with him in the open boat, including Peter Heywood, accusing them of being complicit in the mutiny. So when* HMS *Pandora, sent to find them, arrived in Tahiti nearly a year later, it was not the moment of deliverance that those who had stayed there expected. Instead, the ship's captain ordered them to be arrested and crammed naked into a compartment below decks that became infamous as "Pandora's Box."*

After his own miraculous survival and return to England, Heywood faced a court-martial, at which he denounced Bligh as a tyrant and redeemed Fletcher Christian's reputation. The court acquitted Heywood, who went on to become a captain. Heywood's portrayal of Bligh as the villain and Christian as the tragic hero is the one that has endured in popular culture, with "Captain Bligh" now synonymous with the boss from hell. Heywood wrote to his mother about his misadventures. This letter best summarizes his sufferings.

Whilst we remained there [in Tahiti] we were used by our Friends (the Natives) with a Friendship, Generosity, & Humanity almost unparallelled, being such as never was equalled by the People of any civilized Nations, to the

Disgrace of all Christians.—We had some few Battles with the Enemies of the People we resided with, but I was always protected by a never failing Providence.—To be brief—living there till the latter end of March 1791, on the 26th. HMS *Pandora* arrived, & had scarce come to an Anchor when my Messmate & I went aboard & made ourselves known & the Manner of our being upon the Island known to Captain Edwards the Commander; and knowing from one of the Natives who had been off in a Canoe that our former Messmate Mr. Hayward (now promoted to the rank of Lieut.) was on board, we asked for him, supposing he might prove our assertions;—but he [(]like all Worldlings when raised a little in Life) received us very coolly, & pretended Ignorance of our Affairs; yet formerly he & I were bound in brotherly Friendship—But!—so that Appearances being so much against us, we were ordered in Irons & looked upon—infernal Words!—as piratical Villains! & treated in the most indignant Manner. . . .

Twelve more of the People who were at 'Taheite having delivered themselves up, there was a sort of Prison built upon the after Part of the quarter Deck, into which we were all put in close Confinement with both Legs & both Hands in Irons & were treated with great rigour, not being allowed ever to get out of this Place; & being obliged to eat, drink, sleep, & obey the Calls of Nature here, you may form some Idea of the disagreeable Situation I must have been in, (unable to help myself, being deprived of the Use of both my Legs & Hands) but by no Means adequate to the reality—such as I am unable to represent.

On May 9th, we left 'Taheite & proceeded to the friendly Isles & cruized about six Weeks to the Northward & in the Neighbourhood of these Islands in search of the *Bounty* but without success—in which Time we were so unfortunate as to lose a small Cutter & five Hands;—& having discovered several Islands, at one of these, parted Company with the Schooner which was built by our (the *Bounty*'s) people at 'Taheite (& taken as a Tender by Captain Edwards) in which was an Officer & eight or nine Hands, she was given up for lost.

From the friendly Islands we steered to the Westward, & about the Beginning of August got in among the reefs of New Holland to endeavour at the Discovery of a Passage through; but it was not effected, for the *Pandora*, ever unlucky, Aug 29, 1791 & as it were devoted by Heaven to Destruction, on the 29th of August at ½ past 7 oClock in the Morning was driven by a Current upon a Patch of a reef, upon which; as there was a heavy Surf—she was soon almost bulged to Pieces; but having thrown all the Guns on one side over board, & the Tide flowing at the same Time, she beat over the reef into a Bason encircled by the reef, & brought up in 14 or 15 Fathom—but was so much damaged while she was on the reef, that imagining she wou'd go to Pieces every Moment, we had wrenched ourselves out of Irons, & applied to the

Captain to have Mercy on us & suffer us to have a Chance for our Lives;—but it was all in Vain, & he was even so inhuman as to order us all to be put in Irons again, tho' the Ship was expected to go down every Moment, being scarce able to keep her under with all the Pumps at Work:—In this miserable Situation, with an expected Death before our Eyes, without the least Hope of relief & in the most trying State of Suspense we spent the Night, the Ship being by the Hand of Providence kept up till Morning, in which Time the Boats had all been prepared—& as the Captain & Officers were coming upon the Poop or Roof of the Prison to abandon ship, the Water being then up to the Coamings of the Hatchways, we again implored his Mercy, upon which he sent the Corporal & an Armourer down to let some of us out of Irons, when three only were suffered to go up, & the Scuttle being then clapped on & the Master at Arms upon it, the Armourer had only Time to let two People out of Irons (the rest letting themselves out except three, two of whom *went down with them on their Hands* & the third was picked up) when she began to heel over to Port so much that the Master at Arms sliding over board & leaving the Scuttle vacant, every one tried to get up, & *I* was the last out but *three*;— the Water was then pouring in at the Bulk-head Scuttles;—yet I got out & was scarce in the Water when I saw nothing above it but the Crosstrees & nothing around me but a scene of the greatest Distress.—I took a Plank (being stark naked) & swam towards an Island about three Miles off!—but was picked up on my Passage by one of the Boats.

When we got ashore to the small sandy Key, we found there were thirty four Men drowned[,] four being prisoners (one of whom was my Messmate) & ten of us & eighty nine of the *Pandora*'s saved.—When a Survey was made of what Provisions had been saved, it was two or three Bags of Bread & two or three Breakers of Water & a little Wine, so we subsisted three Days upon two Wine Glasses of Water and two Ounces of Bread per Day.

On September the 1st we left the Island & on the 16th arrived at Coupang in the Island Timor;—having been on short Allowance eighteen Days.—We were put in Confinement in the Castle, & remained till October; & on the 5th. went on board a Dutch Ship bound for Batavia—At Night weighed & set Sail, & after a very tedious & dangerous Passage, the Ship being twice near drove ashore & so very leaky as scarce to be kept above Water with both Pumps constantly going, on the 30th anchored at Samorong on the Isle of Java where we unexpectedly found the Schooner I mentioned parting Company with.

On Monday 7th anchored here at Batavia.—I send this by the first ship which is to sail in about a Week by one of the *Pandora*'s Men.—We are to follow in a Week after & expect to be in England in seven Months.—Tho' I have been eight Months in close Confinement in a hot Climate, I have kept my Health in a most surprising Manner, without the least Indisposition, &

am still perfectly well in every respect, Mind as well as Body; but without a Friend & only a shirt & pair of Trowsers to put on & carry me Home.— Yet with all this, I have a contented Mind, entirely resigned to the Will of Providence, which Conduct alone enables me to soar above the reach of Unhappiness.

The Real Moby-Dick

Owen Chase

The Narrative of the Most Extraordinary and Distressing Shipwreck of the Whale-Ship Essex *(1821), by Owen Chase (1797–1869), inspired Herman Melville to write* Moby-Dick *(1851) and provided much of the information for Nathaniel Phil-brick's prize-winning book* In the Heart of the Sea *(2000), which Ron Howard pro-duced and directed as a feature film in 2015. It stands on its own merits as one of the most hair-raising accounts of death and survival ever written.*

On November 20th, 1820, a male sperm whale, apparently attempting to protect his pod of females and calves from attacks by the Essex, *attacked the whaleship itself, not once, but twice. The second time the whale attacked, it slammed into the* Essex *at what Chase estimated was six knots (6.95 mph), then dove under the doomed vessel and swam away. This "sudden, most mysterious, and overwhelming calamity" left the crew of the* Essex *in a desperate situation.*

The Essex *had capsized but remained afloat long enough to allow the crew to retrieve a scanty supply of provisions and tools. Then it sank, and the twenty men in their three whaleboats set sail for South America, rather than steering the more logical course toward the Pacific Islands, because they were afraid of cannibals. In-credibly, just over a week after the sperm whale sank the* Essex, *in a violent storm at night, a second whale attacked, this time apparently a killer whale, nearly sinking one of the three whaleboats.*

For most of the next two weeks, the boats battled heavy weather, occasionally be-coming separated, only to reunite, to everyone's mutual relief. Then the boats became becalmed, drifting day after day under the relentless sun, from December 11 until December 16, when they found momentary relief from an unexpected source.

On December 20, the boats came upon a large, uninhabited island, now known to be Henderson Island, located little more than 100 miles from the inhabited Pitcairn Island. After days of searching, they found the water supply they desperately needed. Filling their casks, they set to sea once more on December 27, leaving behind three men who had chosen to take their chances by remaining, hoping to be rescued. Two weeks after leaving Henderson Island, the first member of the crew died. On January 12, the boats became separated in a violent storm.

On the night of January 18, whales spouted and surfaced near Chase's leaky boat, terrifying the five traumatized men. The first of them died on January 20, and his body was put overboard. For the rest of January and into early February, they endured shifting winds and periods of no winds at all, managing to stay alive on an ounce and a half of bread per day.

On February 8, Isaac Cole died, and his shipmates decided to devour him, beginning with his thirst-quenching heart. The next day, what remained of Cole's body showed signs of decomposing, so Chase and his shipmates cooked it in pieces to preserve it. They subsisted on this grim fare for most of the next week, conserving their remaining bread. They started eating the bread again on February 15, and on February 18, ninety days after their ordeal began, they had two days of miniscule portions left, and were still three miles from the nearest land.

After becoming separated from Chase's boat, the other two boats continued in tandem. One boat ran out of provisions two days later, and the other boat, which the captain commanded, exhausted its meager supplies within another week. At that point, the second man to die succumbed to his hunger and thirst. His shipmates decided to devour him to survive. Even so, three more of them died in the next week. On January 28, the first boat, with three men left aboard, separated from the captain's boat, never to be seen again. When the four men in the remaining boat ran out of human remains to eat on the first day of February, they opted to draw lots to determine which of them would be killed and eaten next, and who would pull the trigger. The captain's cousin, with the portentous name of Owen Coffin, lost the draw. He was seventeen years old, and the captain had promised his mother he would look after him during the long whaling voyage. The young man's close friend lost the second draw, and proceeded to shoot him. The other three men left in the boat consumed Coffin over the next ten days, when another of them died, leaving Coffin's captain cousin and his former friend another supply of meat. A whale ship spotted the pair close to the coast of Chile and rescued them on February 23, 1821, ninety-five days after the Essex sank. They were conscious, but utterly unaware of their surroundings, lying in the bottom of the whaleboat, gnawing human bones.

The three men who chose Henderson Island made the best choice, being rescued in early April, albeit close to starvation.

Incredibly, all eight of the survivors of the twenty-man crew of the whale ship Essex returned to make their living on the Ocean. One of them died there, drowning in a Caribbean hurricane.

On the 20th of November [1820] (cruising in latitude 0°40' S. longitude 71.19°0' W.), a shoal of whales was discovered off the lee bow. The weather at this time was extremely fine and clear, and it was about 8 o'clock in the morning, that the man at the masthead gave the usual cry of, "There she blows." The ship was immediately put away, and we ran down in the direction for them. When we had got within half a mile of the place where they were observed, all our boats were lowered down, manned, and we started in pursuit of them. . . . When I arrived at the spot where we calculated they were, nothing was at first to be seen. We lay on our oars in anxious expectation of discovering them come up somewhere near us. Presently one rose, and spouted a short distance ahead of my boat; I made all speed towards it, came up with, and struck it; feeling the harpoon in him, he threw himself, in an agony, over towards the boat (which at that time was up alongside of him), and giving a severe blow with his tail, struck the boat near the edge of the water, amidships, and stove a hole in her. I immediately took up the boat hatchet, and cut the line, to disengage the boat from the whale, which by this time was running off with great velocity. I succeeded in getting clear of him, with the loss of the harpoon and line; and finding the water to pour fast in the boat. I hastily stuffed three or four of our jackets in the hole, ordered one man to keep constantly bailing, and the rest to pull immediately for the ship; we succeeded in keeping the boat free, and shortly gained the ship. The captain and the second mate, in the other two boats, kept up the pursuit, and soon struck another whale. They being at this time a considerable distance to leeward, I went forward, braced around the mainyard, and put the ship off in a direction for them. . . .

I observed a very large spermaceti whale, as well as I could judge, about eighty-five feet in length; he broke water about twenty rods off our weather-bow, and was lying quietly, with his head in a direction for the ship. He spouted two or three times, and then disappeared. In less than two or three seconds he came up again, about the length of the ship off, and made directly for us, at the rate of about three knots. The ship was then going with about the same velocity. His appearance and attitude gave us at first no alarm; but while I stood watching his movements, and observing him but a ship's length off, coming down for us with great celerity, I involuntarily ordered the boy at the helm to put it hard up; intending to sheer off and avoid him. The words were scarcely out of my mouth, before he came down upon us with full speed, and struck the ship with his head, just forward of the fore-chains; he gave us such an appalling and tremendous jar, as nearly threw us all on our faces. The ship brought up as suddenly and violently as if she had struck a rock and trembled for a few seconds like a leaf. We looked at each other with perfect amazement, deprived almost of the power of speech. Many minutes elapsed before we were able to realize the dreadful accident; during which time he passed under the ship, grazing her keel as he went along, came up underside of her to leeward, and lay on the top of the water (apparently stunned with the violence of the blow), for the space of a minute; he then suddenly started off, in a direction to leeward. . . . I of course [gradually] concluded that he had stove a hole in the ship, and that it would be necessary to set the pumps going. Accordingly they were rigged, but had not been in operation more than one minute, before I perceived the head of the ship to be gradually settling down in the water; I then ordered the signal to be set for the other boats, which scarcely had I dispatched, before I again discovered the whale, apparently in convulsions, on the top of the water, about one hundred rods to leeward. He was enveloped in the foam of the sea, that his continual and violent thrashing about in the water had created around him, and I could distinctly see him smite his jaws together, as if distracted with rage and fury. He remained a short time in this situation, and then started off with great velocity, across the bows of the ship, to windward. By this time the ship had settled down a considerable distance in the water, and I gave her up as lost. . . .

Not a moment, however, was to be lost in endeavouring to provide for the extremity to which it was now certain we were reduced. We were more than a thousand miles from the nearest land, and with nothing but a light open boat, as the resource of safety for myself and companions. I ordered the men to cease pumping, and every one to provide for himself, seizing a hatchet at the same time, I cut away the lashings of the spare boat, which lay bottom up, across two spars directly over the quarter deck, and cried out to those near me, to take her as she came down. They did so accordingly, and bore her on their shoulders as far as the waist of the ship. The steward had in the mean time gone down into the cabin twice, and saved two quadrants, two practical navigators, and the captain's trunk and mine; all which were hastily thrown into the boat, as she lay on the deck, with the two compasses which I snatched from the binnacle. He attempted to descend again; but the water by this time had rushed in, and he returned without being able to effect his purpose. By the time we had got the boat to the waist, the ship had filled with water, and was going down on her beam-ends: we shoved our boat as quickly as possible from the plank-shear into the water, all hands jumping in her at the same time, and launched off clear of the ship. We were scarcely two boat's lengths distant from her, when she fell over to windward, and settled down in the water. Amazement and despair now wholly took possession of us. We contemplated the frightful situation the ship lay in, and thought with horror upon the sudden and dreadful calamity that had overtaken us. We looked upon each other, as if to gather some consolatory sensation from an interchange of sentiments, but every countenance was marked with the paleness of despair. Not a word was spoken for several minutes by any of us; all appeared to be bound in a spell of stupid consternation; and from the time we were first attacked by the whale, to the period of the fall of the ship, and of our leaving her in the boat, more than ten minutes could not certainly have elapsed! . . . Gracious God! What a picture of distress and suffering now presented itself to my imagination. The crew of the ship were saved, consisting of twenty human souls. All that remained to conduct these twenty beings through the stormy terrors of the ocean, perhaps many thousand miles, were three open light boats. . . .

We lay at this time in our boat, about two ship's lengths off from the wreck, in perfect silence, calmly contemplating her situation, and absorbed in our own melancholy reflections, when the other boats were discovered rowing up to us. They had but shortly before discovered that some accident had befallen us, but of the nature of which they were entirely ignorant. The sudden and mysterious disappearance of the ship was first discovered by the boat-steerer in the captain's boat, and with a horror-struck countenance and voice, he suddenly exclaimed, "Oh, my God! Where is the Ship?" Their operations upon this were instantly suspended, and a general cry of horror and despair burst from the lips of every man, as their looks were directed for her, in vain, over every part of the ocean. They immediately made all haste towards us. The captain's boat was the first that reached us. He stopped about a boat's length off, but had no power to utter a single syllable: he was so completely overpowered with the spectacle before him, that he sat down in his boat, pale and speechless. I could scarcely recognize his countenance, he appeared to be so much altered, awed, and overcome, with the oppression of his feelings, and the dreadful reality that lay before him. He was in a short time however enabled to address the inquiry to me, "My God, Mr. Chase, what is the matter?" I answered, "We have been stove by a whale . . ."

Our allowance of water, which in the commencement, merely served to administer to the positive demands of nature, became now to be insufficient; and we began to experience violent thirst, from the consumption of the provisions that had been wet with the salt water, and dried in the sun; of these we were obliged to eat first, to prevent their spoiling; and we could not, nay, we did not dare, to make any encroachments on our stock of water. Our determination was, to suffer as long as human patience and endurance would hold out, having only in view, the relief that would be afforded us, when the quantity of wet provisions should be exhausted. Our extreme sufferings here first commenced. The privation of water is justly ranked among the most dreadful of the miseries of our life; the violence of raving thirst has no parallel in the catalogue of human calamities. . . .

In vain was every expedient tried to relieve the raging fever of the throat by drinking salt water, and holding small quantities of it in the mouth, until, by that means, the thirst was increased to such a degree, as even to drive us to despairing, and vain relief from our own urine. Our sufferings during these calm days almost succeeded human belief. The hot rays of the sun beat down upon us to such a degree, as to oblige us to hang over the gunwale of the boat, into the sea, to cool our weak and fainting bodies. This expedient afforded us, however, a grateful relief, and was productive of a discovery of infinite importance to us. No sooner had one of us got on the outside of the gunwale than he immediately observed the bottom of the boat to be covered with a species of small clam, which, upon being tasted, proved a most delicious and agreeable food. This was no sooner announced to us, than we commenced to tear them off and eat them, for a few minutes, like a set of gluttons; and, after having satisfied the immediate craving of the stomach, we gathered large quantities and laid them up in the boat; but hunger came upon us again in less than half an hour afterwards within which time they

In this view of "the struggle for life" after a shipwreck, there is no altruism. The strongest men in an overcrowded lifeboat throw the weakest into the waves. They force four women and a man over the side, and at the apex of the composition, a child is flung in the air. Another child and an old man are in the sea nearby. The brutes fight among themselves, one with a knife, another using an oar as a club. Blind Fate steers the craft, while in the bow, a figure with an incongruous smile may represent Charon, ferryman of the dead across the River Styx to Hades. Richard Bong, *Der Kampf ums Dasein [The Struggle for Life]*, wood engraving based on a painting by Henry-Eugéne Delacroix, *Lutte pour la vie, naufrage [The fight for life, shipwreck]*, c. 1890s, in *Moderne Kunst* (Berlin: Richard Bong, 1900). Courtesy of the Roorda/Doyle Collection.

had all disappeared. Upon attempting to get in again, we found ourselves so weak as to require each other's assistance; indeed, had it not been for three of our crew, who could not swim, and who did not, therefore, get overboard, I know not by what means we should have been able to have resumed our situations in the boat. . . .

On the 15th of January, at night, a very large shark was observed swimming about us in a most ravenous manner, making attempts every now and then upon different parts of the boat, as if he would devour the very wood with hunger; he came several times and snapped at the steering oar, and even the stern-post. We tried in vain to stab him with a lance, but were so weak as not to be able to make any impression upon his hard skin; he was so much larger than an ordinary one, and manifested such a fearless malignity, as to make us afraid of him; and our utmost efforts, which were at first directed to kill him for prey, became in the end self-defense. Baffled however in all his hungry attempts upon us, he shortly made off. . . .

Our sufferings were now drawing to a close; a terrible death appeared shortly to await us; hunger became violent and outrageous, and we prepared for a speedy release from our troubles; our speech and reason were both considerably impaired, and we were reduced to be at this time, certainly the most helpless and wretched of the whole human race. Isaac Cole, one of our crew, had the day before this, in a fit of despair, thrown himself down in the boat, and was determined there calmly to wait for death. It was obvious that he had no chance; all was dark he said in his mind, not a single ray of hope was left for him to dwell upon; and it was folly and madness to be struggling against what appeared so palpably to be our fixed and settled destiny. I remonstrated with him as effectually as the weakness both of my body and understanding would allow of; and what I said appeared for a moment to have a considerable effect: he made a powerful and sudden effort, half rose up, crawled forward and hoisted the jib, and firmly and loudly cried that he would not give up; that he would live as long as the rest of us—but alas! this effort was but the hectic fever of the moment, and he shortly again relapsed into a state of melancholy and despair. This day (8 February) his reason was attacked, and he became about 9 o'clock in the morning a most miserable spectacle of madness: he spoke coherently about every thing, calling loudly for a napkin and water, and then lying stupidly and senselessly down in the boat again, would close his hollow eyes, as if in death. About 10 o'clock, we suddenly perceived that he became speechless; we got him as well as we were able upon a board, placed on one of the seats of the boat, and covering him up with some old clothes, left him to his fate. He lay in the greatest pain and apparent misery, groaning piteously until four o'clock, when he died, in the most horrid and frightful convulsions I ever witnessed. We kept his corpse all night, and in the morning my two companions began as of course to make preparations to dispose of it in the sea; when after reflecting on the subject all night, I addressed them on the painful subject of keeping the body for food!! Our provisions could not possibly last us beyond three days, within which time it was not in any degree probable that we should find relief from our present sufferings, and that hunger would at last drive us to the necessity of casting lots. It was without any objection agreed to, and we set to work as fast as we were able to prepare it so as to prevent its spoiling. We separated his limbs from his body, and cut all the flesh from the bones; after which, we opened the body, took out the heart, and then closed it again—sewed it up as decently as we could, and committed it to the sea. We now first commenced to satisfy the immediate craving of nature from the heart, which we eagerly devoured, and then eat sparingly of a few pieces of the flesh; after which, we hung up the remainder, cut in thin strips about the boat, to dry in the sun: we made a fire and roasted some of it, to serve us during the next day. In this manner did we dispose of our fellow-sufferer; the painful recollection of which, brings to mind at this moment, some of the most disagreeable and revolting ideas that it is capable of conceiving. We knew not then, to whose lot it would fall next, either to die or be shot, and eaten like the poor wretch we had just dispatched. . . .

At about seven o'clock this morning, while I was lying asleep, my companion who was steering, suddenly and loudly called out, "There's a Sail!" I know not what was the first movement I made upon hearing such an unexpected cry: the earliest of my recollections are, that immediately I stood up, gazing in a state of abstraction and ecstasy upon the blessed vision of a vessel about seven miles off from us; she was standing in the same direction with us, and the only sensation I felt at the moment was, that of a violent and unaccountable impulse to fly directly towards her. I do not believe it is possible to form a just conception of the pure, strong feelings, and the unmingled emotions of joy and gratitude, that took possession of my mind on this occasion: the boy, too, took a sudden and animated start from his despondency, and stood up to witness the probable instrument of his salvation. Our only fear was now, that she would not discover us, or that we might not be able to intercept her course: we, however, put our boat immediately, as well as we were able, in a direction to cut her off; and found, to our great joy, that we sailed faster than she did. Upon observing us, she shortened sail, and allowed us to come up to her. The captain hailed us and asked who we were. I told him we were from a wreck, and he cried out immediately for us to come alongside the ship. I made an effort to assist myself along to the side, for the purpose of getting up, but strength failed me altogether, and I found it impossible to move a step further without help. We must have formed at that moment, in the eyes of the captain and his crew, a most deplorable and affecting picture of suffering and misery. Our cadaverous countenances, sunken eyes, and bones just starting through our skin, with the ragged remnants of clothes stuck about our sun-burnt bodies, must have produced an appearance to him affecting and revolting in the highest degree.

The sailors commenced to remove us from our boat, and we were taken to the cabin, and comfortably provided for in every respect. In a few minutes we were permitted to taste of a little thin food, made from tapiocha, and in a few days with prudent management, we were considerably recruited.

The Castaway

Herman Melville

It is possible that Herman Melville (1819–91) would have become a great writer without going to sea. A different career choice might have led him to write a classic about digging canals or working in a factory. When he had to take a boring office job, he produced "Bartleby, the Scrivener" (1853), the first lampoon of mind-numbing work and dysfunctional workplaces, which initiated a thriving genre in literature, film, and television. Melville's "Bartleby" influenced Joseph Heller, author of Catch-22 (1961) and Something Happened (1974); Matt Groening, cartoonist of Work Is Hell and creator of the TV series The Simpsons and Futurama; and Mike Judge, writer and director of the "Bartleby" adaptation Office Space (1999). Instead, Melville spent years as a sailor, later brilliantly capturing the experience.

The voyage he began to the Pacific Ocean in January 1841, which kept him away from home until October 1844, and made possible his commercially successful first novels, Typee (1846) and Omoo (1847). These adventures in Tahiti, Moorea, and the Marquesas Islands made him into a literary celebrity. Melville's whaling years also set the stage for his monumental Moby-Dick (1851), which ironically destroyed his career as an author when reviewers panned it, but which later secured his reputation as one of the great writers of all time, when it gained fresh appreciation in the 1920s.

Today, Moby-Dick has a cult following that seems only to grow. On August 1, Melville's birthday, Moby-Dick Marathons take place at many sites, where participants take turns reading the novel aloud for about twenty-four hours, nonstop from start to finish, all 136 chapters and 206,052 words of it! The first of these events took place at Mystic Seaport Museum, aboard the Charles W. Morgan, the last wooden whaleship, in 1986; since then other Moby-Dick Marathons have been inaugurated in New York City, San Francisco, and New Bedford, Massachusetts.

Moby-Dick includes a chapter that penetrates the psychological trauma of being lost at sea. "The Castaway" reflects the existential terror of being alone on the Ocean.

It was but some few days after encountering the Frenchman, that a most significant event befell the most insignificant of the Pequod's crew; an event most lamentable; and which ended in providing the sometimes madly merry and predestinated craft with a living and ever accompanying prophecy of whatever shattered sequel might prove her own.

Now, in the whale ship, it is not every one that goes in the boats. Some few hands are reserved called shipkeepers, whose province it is to work the vessel while the boats are pursuing the whale. As a general thing, these ship-keepers are as hardy fellows as the men comprising the boats' crews. But if there happen to be an unduly slender, clumsy, or timorous wight in the ship, that wight is certain to be made a ship-keeper.[1] It was so in the Pequod with the little negro Pippin by nick-name, Pip by abbreviation. Poor Pip! ye have heard of him before; ye must remember his tambourine on that dramatic midnight, so gloomy-jolly.[2]

It came to pass that . . . Stubb's after-oarsman chanced so to sprain his hand, as for a time to become quite maimed; and, temporarily, Pip was put into his place.

The first time Stubb lowered with him, Pip evinced much nervousness; but happily, for that time, escaped close contact with the whale; and there-fore came off not altogether discreditably; though Stubb observing him, took care, afterwards, to exhort him to cherish his courageousness to the utmost, for he might often find it needful.

Now upon the second lowering, the boat paddled upon the whale; and as the fish received the darted iron, it gave its customary rap, which happened, in this instance, to be right under poor Pip's seat. The involuntary consterna-tion of the moment caused him to leap, paddle in hand, out of the boat; and in such a way, that part of the slack whale line coming against his chest, he breasted it overboard with him, so as to become entangled in it, when at last plumping into the water. That instant the stricken whale started on a fierce run, the line swiftly straightened; and presto! poor Pip came all foaming up to the chocks of the boat, remorselessly dragged there by the line, which had taken several turns around his chest and neck.

Tashtego stood in the bows. He was full of the fire of the hunt. He hated Pip for a poltroon.[3] Snatching the boat-knife from its sheath, he suspended its sharp edge over the line, and turning towards Stubb, exclaimed inter-rogatively, "Cut?" Meantime Pip's blue, choked face plainly looked, Do, for God's sake! All passed in a flash. In less than half a minute, this entire thing happened.

"Damn him, cut!" roared Stubb; and so the whale was lost and Pip was saved.

So soon as he recovered himself, the poor little negro was assailed by yells and execrations from the crew. Tranquilly permitting these irregular cursings to evaporate, Stubb then in a plain, business-like, but still half hu-morous manner, cursed Pip officially; and that done, unofficially gave him much wholesome advice. The substance was, Never jump from a boat, Pip, except—but all the rest was indefinite, as the soundest advice ever is. Now, in general, Stick to the boat, is your true motto in whaling; but cases will sometimes happen when Leap from the boat, is still better. Moreover, as if perceiving at last that if he should give undiluted conscientious advice to Pip, he would be leaving him too wide a margin to jump in for the future; Stubb suddenly dropped all advice, and concluded with a peremptory command "Stick to the boat, Pip, or by the Lord, I won't pick you up if you jump; mind that. We can't afford to lose whales by the likes of you; a whale would sell for thirty times what you would, Pip, in Alabama. Bear that in mind, and don't jump any more." Hereby perhaps Stubb indirectly hinted, that though man loved his fellow, yet man is a money-making animal, which propensity too often interferes with his benevolence.

But we are all in the hands of the Gods; and Pip jumped again. It was under very similar circumstances to the first performance; but this time he did not breast out the line; and hence, when the whale started to run, Pip was left behind on the sea, like a hurried traveller's trunk. Alas! Stubb was but too true to his word. It was a beautiful, bounteous, blue day! the spangled sea calm and cool, and flatly stretching away, all round, to the horizon, like gold-beater's skin hammered out to the extremest. Bobbing up and down in that sea, Pip's ebon head showed like a head of cloves. No boat-knife was lifted when he fell so rapidly astern. Stubb's inexorable back was turned upon him; and the whale was winged. In three minutes, a whole mile of shoreless ocean was between Pip and Stubb. Out from the centre of the sea, poor Pip turned his crisp, curling, black head to the sun, another lonely castaway, though the loftiest and the brightest.

Now, in calm weather, to swim in the open ocean is as easy to the practised swimmer as to ride in a spring-carriage ashore. But the awful lonesomeness is intolerable. The intense concentration of self in the middle of such a heartless immensity, my God! who can tell it? Mark, how when sailors in a dead calm bathe in the open sea—mark how closely they hug their ship and only coast along her sides.

But had Stubb really abandoned the poor little negro to his fate? No; he did not mean to, at least. Because there were two boats in his wake, and he supposed, no doubt, that they would of course come up to Pip very quickly, and pick him up; though, indeed, such considerations towards oarsmen jeopardized through their own timidity, is not always manifested by the hunters in all similar instances; and such instances not unfrequently occur; almost invariably in the fishery, a coward, so called, is marked with the same ruthless detestation peculiar to military navies and armies.

But it so happened, that those boats, without seeing Pip, suddenly spying whales close to them on one side, turned, and gave chase; and Stubb's boat was now so far away, and he and all his crew so intent upon his fish, that Pip's ringed horizon began to expand around him miserably. By the merest chance the ship itself at last rescued him; but from that hour the little negro went about the deck an idiot; such, at least, they said he was. The sea had leeringly kept his finite body up, but drowned the infinite of his soul. Not drowned entirely, though. Rather carried down alive to wondrous depths, where strange shapes of the unwarped primal world glided to and fro before his passive eyes; and the miser-merman, Wisdom, revealed his hoarded heaps; and among the joyous, heartless, ever-juvenile eternities, Pip saw the multitudinous, God-omnipresent, coral insects, that out of the firmament of waters heaved the colossal orbs. He saw God's foot upon the treadle of the loom, and spoke it; and therefore his shipmates called him mad. So man's insanity is heaven's sense; and wandering from all mortal reason, man comes at last to that celestial thought, which, to reason, is absurd and frantic; and weal or woe, feels then uncompromised, indifferent as his God.

For the rest blame not Stubb too hardly. The thing is common in that fishery; and in the sequel of the narrative, it will then be seen what like abandonment befell myself.

Notes

1. A wight is a person who is usually unfortunate in some way.
2. The allusion is to the night when Captain Ahab had his crew take an oath to pursue the White Whale.
3. Complete coward.

Just Keep Rowing . . . !

William Hale

Howard Blackburn of Nova Scotia fished on the Grand Banks aboard a schooner out of Gloucester, Massachusetts. Or rather, he fished from a small dory, one of a stack of such lightweight rowboats carried by the schooner. Dorymen were vulnerable to being separated from the mother ship when fog rolled in or storms blew up, which is what happened to Blackburn in January 1883, when he was twenty-three years old. While his dory mate literally curled up and died, Blackburn rowed and bailed for five straight days, with frozen, mittenless hands, and no food or water, to reach the wintry coast of Newfoundland. He survived the record-long row, but lost all of his fingers and toes to frostbite. He wrote about it immediately afterward, in a book he titled Fearful Experience of a Gloucester Halibut Fisherman, Astray in a Dory in a Gale Off the Newfoundland Coast in Mid-Winter *(1883). The account sampled below, published more than a decade later, was the work of William Hale, a physician who moved to Gloucester and became active in its famed fishing community. Hale wrote books about maritime subjects in his spare time, with titles such as* Dauntless Viking, Dory-mates, *and* Recreations: Swimming and Motoring. *The admiring tone of his book about Howard Blackburn, subtitled* Hero and Fisherman, *reflects the status that his subject had achieved.*

Perhaps more astounding than Blackburn's feat of survival is the fact that sixteen years later, the fingerless Blackburn sailed alone across the Atlantic Ocean. He is only the third person known to have done that, after Alfred "Centennial" Johnson in 1876 and Joshua Slocum in 1898, just one year before Blackburn's crossing to England, which took sixty-two days. Blackburn did it again in 1901, reaching Portugal in a 25-foot sloop in just thirty-nine days.

"A Story of Suffering and Heroism"

The morning of January 25, 1883, found the schooner *Grace L. Fears,* of Gloucester, Mass., lying at anchor on Burgeo Bank, some 30 miles from the southwest coast of Newfoundland. She had ventured thus far north, at this inclement season, in pursuit of halibut; and her crew had started out in their dories from the vessel's side to haul their trawls, which had previously been set. In one of the boats were Howard Blackburn and Thomas Welch, both young men of vigorous constitutions, their frames well knit, and their muscles toughened by constant labor and exposure, while their long familiarity with danger had rendered them almost insensible to fear—indeed, brave to a fault, as one must be who follows the hazardous occupation. When they left the vessel's side it was calm and just beginning to snow. Soon after, a light breeze sprang up from the southeast and rapidly augmented in force; while the snow fell thicker and faster, shutting the little dory and its occupants within a narrow circle, beyond which nothing could be seen. . . .[1]

In the meantime the wind changed, in a squall, from the southeast to the northwest, bringing the dory to leeward [downwind] of the vessel, and what was even worse, confusing the men as to the direction in which the schooner bore from them. After getting their trawl they pulled to windward [upwind] and tried to find the vessel, but failed. No bell nor horn nor other sound could be heard, and at last the fishermen, worn out from their labors, finding it required all their strength just to hold their own against the fast increasing wind, anchored the boat. Here they lay for about three hours,—until after dark—when the snow cleared off, and they saw the glimmer of the schooner's riding-light to windward. The anchor was pulled up and a desperate attempt made to reach the vessel. But though they rowed as only those can row who know that they struggle for life, all efforts proved fruitless; for the surging waves and increasing gale were too much even for the stout muscles of the two strong and determined men to make their way against. The anchor was thrown out, but the wind blew so hard that the boat did not fetch up, but drove slowly to leeward. For a time after the dory had anchored, as she rose to the crest of the waves, the drifting fishermen caught glimpses of the torch-light, which their more fortunate shipmates on board the vessel kept burning through the night. . . .

The imagination can scarcely picture, and words are inadequate to describe, the terrible struggle and fight for life which followed the failure to reach the vessel. All through the long hours of that dreary winter's night it required the utmost exertion and vigilance to prevent the little boat from being swamped by the rushing and breaking waves. In spite of all that could be done, the dory was often nearly filled, while the bitter cold of the biting blast, not only benumbed and pierced to the very marrow the unfortunate men, but covered with ice all portions of the boat that were not immersed. All of the fish were thrown overboard to lighten the dory.

The gray light of the following morning brought no comfort with it. The vessel was nowhere to be seen, nothing but the wild, snow-laden clouds overhead and the cruel sea around. . . .[2]

"Unfortunate Loss"

While rigging the drag or floating-anchor, Blackburn had the great misfortune to lose his mittens overboard. . . . His hands did not feel cold then, and the first he knew that they were freezing, was when Welch said: "Look how white your hands are getting, Howard! They are freezing!" Such a loss was irreparable, and the incurable suffering and ill-fortune which followed may be ascribed, in great measure, to this unhappy accident. Nothing but some warm covering, such as he had lost, could prevent his hands from freezing, and soon his fingers, stiffening in the icy grasp of the biting frost, warned the unfortunate but brave man that he must fight for his life against frightful odds. . . .

The dreadful nature of the situation was fully comprehended by Blackburn who, finding that he was fast losing control of his stiffening hands, grasped the oars, and squeezing his fingers into a curved position around the handles, allowed them to freeze in this shape, so that when the hour of trial came, he could be able to hold the oars and thus have some chance for rowing, upon which chance he knew his life depended. . . .

"Welch, Discouraged, Succumbs and Dies"

Blackburn's dory-mate, Welch, had been very hopeful up to this time; he believed they might be picked up by some passing vessel. By speaking encouragingly of the chances, he had sought to inspire his companion with hope, and, in anticipation of the much-to-be-wished-for-event, tried to make the best of the awful situation in which they were placed. One of the gamest of men, he would say, every little while, "This can't last long; we will soon be picked up." But a vessel could have passed to windward within a few dory-lengths of the unfortunate men and they not have seen her, for the wind was so sharp they could not look to windward. . . .

It was now Welch's turn to bail, but in reply to Blackburn's urgent request that he should jump quick to the work, he said that he could not see. Awful as was the fate this confession presaged, no time could be lost to think of it. Therefore, Blackburn bailed out the boat as well as he could with his bruised and frozen hands, which he had previously protected as much as possible by winding around them his socks that he had stripped from his feet. Knowing that Welch would have a better chance for life if he took some exercise, Blackburn, after freeing the boat, told him that he (Welch) must try to do his part, saying, "Tom, this won't do! You will have to do your part. Yours hands are not frozen and beaten to pieces, like mine," showing him his right hand, with all one side and the little finger nearly beaten off from pounding ice. But he has always been sorry he showed him his hand, as the freezing man gave up all hope at once, and replied in a despairing tone, "Howard, what is the use? We can't live until morning and might as well go first as last."

. . . The paralyzing effect of the bitter cold soon began to show itself in a new and horrible manner on the ill-fated Welch; his mind wandered, and he kept thrusting his feet over the sides of the boat. These symptoms on the part of Welch convinced Blackburn that his companion could not live. . . . It was exceedingly rough at this time, and the weary and half-frozen, but undaunted Blackburn, was constantly aroused and compelled to bail out the dory, which oftentimes his utmost endeavors scarcely sufficed to keep afloat.

His situation was rendered all the more disheartening by the moaning of his suffering companion, who constantly begged, in a most piteous tone, for water. On being told there was none, he asked Blackburn for a piece of ice from the boat's side, but after he had tasted of the nauseating morsel, he threw it away.

After this the dying man repeated in an audible tone, what sounded like a prayer, and twice he called Blackburn by name.

Between five and six o'clock—as nearly as could be estimated—Welch seemed to be suffering terrible agony; he moaned in a most piteous and doleful manner. This was, probably, the last struggle of the departing spirit; for when, a few minutes later, Blackburn got up to bail out the dory, he heard no sound from his companion, got no reply to his call; and going to the bow, he found that the soul had fled, and naught remained but the stark, stiff and frozen corpse—horrible enough to see and touch under any circumstances, but under such as these, with nothing but the dark night, the fierce and hungry waves, the cruel, pitiless blast—the Great and Merciful One above alone knows the terrible thoughts that were suggested to the survivor, by this distressing episode. The dead man was placed in the stern, and Blackburn made an attempt to get on one of his mittens, which he had taken from the corpse, but the frozen hands were so much swollen and distorted that he could not use this most necessary covering.

"Left Alone, Blackburn Makes a Desperate Fight for Life"

. . . The curling, breaking waves seemed just ready to engulf the little dory, which was half-loaded with water, and over which the spray was flying and forming into ice, as she bravely struggled to mount the crests of the rushing seas. The lion-hearted Blackburn stood in the middle of the boat, which he was busily engaged in freeing from the water with a huge bailer, improvised from a trawl-keg by breaking in one head. The frozen form of Welch lay in the stern; while the white forms of the tireless sea-gulls, outlined against the murky sky, were the only living witnesses to as gloomy a scene as the eye ever rested upon, and as brave a fight for life as has ever been recorded on the pages of history.

The 1871 North Pole expedition of the American steamship *Polaris* set a record by reaching beyond 89 degrees latitude before having to turn back. On the return, nineteen members of the crew became separated from the ship and floated on an ice cake for six months, traversing 1,800 miles before being rescued. Engraver unknown, *On the Ice-Cake, "Too Small for a Hut,"* from *The Polaris Expedition*, by William H. Cunnington (Philadelphia: Philadelphia Book Company, 1873), 627. Courtesy of the Roorda/Doyle Collection.

The long deferred light of another day came at last, and, the wind having moderated somewhat, the drag, which had done such good service, was hauled in, and Blackburn started to pull for land, fully determined to persevere while he had sufficient strength to row. His only hope of reaching the shore lay in the two oars, that, luckily, had not been swept away when the others were washed out of the boat. The wisdom of having allowed his hands to freeze in a curved position was now apparent, for, though there was no feeling in the stiffened fingers, he was able to grasp the oars with sufficient firmness to row. But the friction of the oar-handles wore away the skin and flesh, which crumbled from the inside of his unprotected hands like powder.

He rowed all that day, till night. That afternoon he had seen land; but as night drew on, and the land was still far away, he threw out the drag. It blew quite hard all night, but the dory did not ship any water. It was very cold, too, and in order to keep awake and alive, he had to take a position back to the wind, and, with his arms around a thwart, keep working backward and forward all night. Had he fallen asleep, he would have been frozen stiff in fifteen minutes.

We can easily imagine what a thrill of joy warmed the chilled blood of the weary Blackburn, when, early the next day he saw, looming in the distance, the high, barren hills of the Newfoundland coast. At first the land was rather indistinct, but the dory was headed for it, and soon the rugged outlines of the bleak snow-covered hills could be more clearly seen against the wintry sky, the sight giving new life, hope and comfort to the brave man struggling at the oars. All day long, hungry, thirsty, and suffering, he clung to the oars, pulling steadily toward the high land, which, as night fell on the scene, was still a long way off. During the day the wind decreased very materially, and when it grew dark, Blackburn, exhausted and sadly in need of rest, fearing he might lose his oars if he kept on, again hove to, and throwing out a drag, let his boat drift till Sunday morning.

The blessed light of the early day, beaming upon the land, now plainly in sight; the quiet stillness of the unruffled sea—for it was calm—and the rise in temperature which followed the decrease in the wind, inspired the now hopeful man, on this memorable Sabbath morning, to renewed exertion to a determined effort to reach the shore.

We confess that we cannot repress a shudder as we think of the flesh crumbling slowly from the frozen hands which clung with the grasp of despair, hour after hour, to the oars, until at last—2 P.M.—the River Rocks, the first mile-stone on this lonely route, were passed, while the land, seven miles further off, was reached at sunset.

No harbor could be seen at first, only the craggy, steep sides of the towering cliffs, that looked almost as uninviting as the dreary waste of waters left behind. Finally he got into the tide-rip at the mouth of a river, and just inside the headland, on his left, he saw a house. . . .

Notes

1. The young men continued to work pulling halibut to the surface and filling their small boat with the massive flatfish, ignoring the worsening weather, choosing to take this risk rather than returning to the schooner, perhaps to be accused of cowardice.
2. Blackburn and Welch miscalculated and began rowing to the east, into the wind, when in fact the closest land was north, while the tide ran to the south. As a result, their course was parallel to the coast. The boat filling dangerously deep with water, they fashioned a drag anchor from a wooden tub usually used to hold the fishing line—called a trawl keg—and an iron winch usually used to haul the line—called a hurdy-gurdy—which they attached to a rope and put over the stern. The contraption floated just below the surface, keeping the bow into the wind, and giving them a chance to bail.

Life of Poon

Anonymous

The best-selling novel Life of Pi *(2001) by Yann Martel, adapted as a film in 2012, movingly told the fictional tale of a young man shipwrecked and adrift on the Pacific Ocean for 277 days. But the actual record for endurance on a life raft is held by Poon Lim (1918–91), who spent 133 days adrift on the Atlantic Ocean during World War II. Poon Lim was a steward aboard the British merchant ship* SS Benlomond, *bound from New York to Brazil in November 1942, when a German submarine torpedoed it 750 miles off the coast of South America. Immediately after feeling the impact, Poon strapped on a life preserver and jumped into the water, then swam clear of the ship before the boilers exploded upon contact with seawater. After two hours of swimming around the area where the* Benlomond *had gone down, he came upon a life raft stocked with a modicum of supplies, as did Piscine Patel in* Life of Pi, *except without the zoo animals. Naked and alone in a cockleshell eight feet square, he was the only survivor among fifty-four passengers and crew. Poon Lim managed to catch fish, the occasional seabird, and rainwater to keep body in the proximity of soul. In a direct parallel with the novel, he lost much of his supply of canned food and water when a storm swamped his boat. In the imagined tale of Pi, he is able to net a big mahimahi. In the true story of Poon, he hooked a shark, hauled it thrashing and biting aboard his tiny craft, and beat it to death with a half-empty water jug containing the last of his supply. He cut open the shark using a knife he had fashioned from a tin can, and thirstily drank the blood from its liver. Then he dried the shark's fins, preparing a culinary delicacy on his home island of Hainan, the "Hawai'i of China." Finally, fishermen encountered him near the coast of Brazil. He was in good enough condition to walk onto shore under his own power, but he spent a month in the hospital recovering from the ordeal. His fifteen minutes of fame came in a British Pathé newsreel segment, which actually lasted only fifty seconds, then flickered out quickly amid the enormities of World War II, when thousands of people found themselves clinging to wreckage, life, and hope, after the sinking of the ships they were aboard. But no one (except the fictional Pi) has eclipsed Poon's record of survival on a life raft. This is the transcript of the brief newsreel.*

The arrival in Britain of the amazing Mr. Poon Lim. To all intents and purposes, Mr. Poon Lim is a dapper little Chinese one might meet anywhere.

Poon Lim built a replica of his raft at the request of the US Navy, which used it in survival training exercises. US Navy photo from *National Geographic Yearbook 1945* (Washington, DC: National Geographic Society), 632.

But now let's tell you something. He is a twenty-five-year old merchant seaman who, after his ship had been torpedoed, lived for 133 days on a raft in the South Atlantic, over four months adrift in midocean. Now you know why they had a big reception waiting for him up north, when he came to receive the congratulations and admiration of everyone. The natural outcome of this is Poon Lim's visit to Buckingham Palace to receive the British Empire Medal from the king. Not until he had told his story to His Majesty would he recount his amazing experience to the press.

Transcribed by Eric Paul Roorda

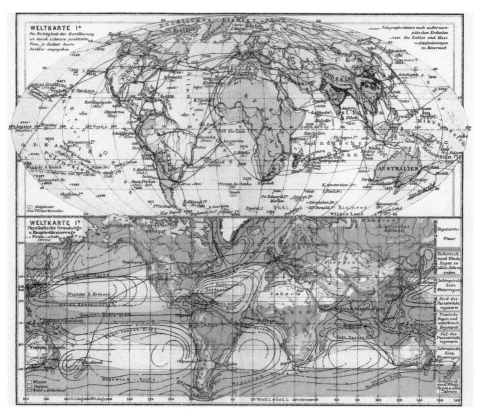

This is a page from a 1931 German pocket atlas. The upper map shows telegraph cables laid on the seafloor since 1866, when the megaship *Great Eastern* completed the first permanently successful link across the Atlantic Ocean. The lower map shows the whirlpool effects called gyres in the Ocean basins, which spin clockwise in the Northern Hemisphere and counterclockwise in the Southern. It also shows the major sea lanes, the preferred routes for ships. Cartographer unknown, *Weltkarte*, from *Taschen-Atlas* (Gotha, Germany: Justus Perthes, 1931). Courtesy of the Roorda/Doyle Collection.

The Great Wave off Kanagawa, seen in this 1830 print by the Japanese master Katsushika Hokusai, is often confused with a tsunami. In fact, the composition depicts storm waves, which are far more common. Tsunami waves, generated by subsea earthquakes, rise in huge masses of water and surge onto the land without breakers, unlike the whitecaps seen here. Hokusai's mountainous waves near Yokohama mirror the famous snow-capped Mount Fuji in the distance. The sacred peak resembles another cresting wave to challenge the men in their frail fishing craft, struggling to survive the tempest. Katsushika Hokusai, *Kanagawa-oki nami ura*, color woodblock print, c. 1829–33. From the Metropolitan Museum of Art, accession number JP1847.

(facing)
The effect of watching waves break has long captivated a certain sort of person. Painters and photographers have attempted to freeze the motion—the perpetual dynamism—of the Ocean. This composition is formed by eight postcards from the early twentieth century. Arranged in complementary pairs, they form a collage at the center of an ambient painting and show multiple, subtly different attempts to capture agitated saltwater in two dimensions. The image on the top left, captioned "Breaking Waves in the Moonlight, Ocean Grove, N.J.," is a nocturne; beside it, "Surf during Storm, Atlantic Ocean, Atlantic City, N.J.," captures the eerie darkness of a daytime tempest and shows spindrift: when high winds whip the crests of waves into sheets of

airborne spray. One row below, "Surf after a Storm, Pleasant View, R.I." (left) combines the blue skies and mountainous waves that follow a serious squall. Next to it, a comber crashes ashore in "By the Bounding Main." The third pair has similar compositions and subjects—"A Breaker on the Atlantic Ocean" and "The Storm on the Atlantic Ocean"—in which flocks of seabirds are hurrying past. The bottom pair shares the caption "Ocean Spray" and a focus on flying spume. The blue and green paint strokes that surround the postcards extend and blend patterns of sea and sky, just as the colors and shapes of waves and clouds so often merge on the horizon. Eric Paul Roorda, *Storm Waves Spray Breakers Surf,* acrylic paint and vintage postcards on canvas, 2018. Courtesy of the Roorda/Doyle Collection.

Marcus Rediker writes: "*The Slave Ship Brooks* originated in a long conversation I had with Frantz Zéphirin. We talked at length about his interest in Haitian history. When I returned to the artist's makeshift studio two days later, he had almost finished the painting. Alluding to the famous British abolitionist image of the *Brooks*, originally drawn in 1788 to evoke the horror of the slave trade for the reading public, Zéphirin creates a dungeon ship, out of which peer haunting red eyes. The artist renders the European crew as animals: the imperial alligator captain holds the deed to the land on which the enslaved will work. The first mate is Death incarnate. The Vodou deity of the sea, Agoue, announces the arrival of a shipload of new souls. On the sail of his boat in the background is his judgment: 'We are in a lot of trouble.' Chained to the outside of the vessel as food for the sharks is a group of rebellious slaves, the neckplate of each showing a different African ethnicity, the message being, 'from many, one.' Two of the enslaved, at right Toussaint Louverture (1742–1803) and at left Boukman Dutty (?–1791), break free of their chains, gesturing hopefully ahead to the Haitian Revolution they will lead." Frantz Zéphirin, *The Slave Ship Brooks*, 2007. Caption written for this volume by Marcus Rediker. Image courtesy of Frantz Zéphirin and Marcus Rediker (collection of Marcus Rediker).

This evocation of the nightmarish moment when a ship slips beneath the waves is the work of E. R. Kullberg, who chose the figure of a stoic officer as the focus of his composition. Color print, 1921, with border drawn by Franklin Booth, from *Nineteen Twenty One's Lucky Bag: The Annual of the Regiment of Midshipmen* (Annapolis, MD: United States Naval Academy, 1921), 6. Courtesy of the Roorda/Doyle Collection.

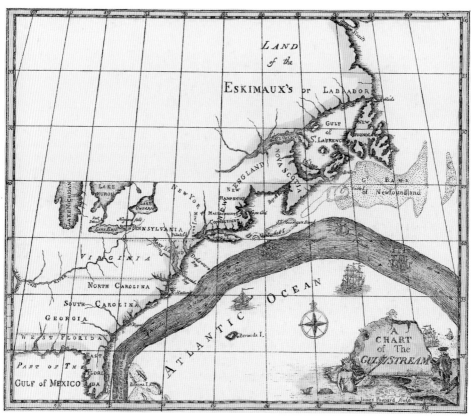

Benjamin Franklin's original rendering of the Gulf Stream, equal to 1,000 Mississippi Rivers in volume, was still considered useful more than a century after he drew it. This colored reprint of *The Gulf Stream According to Benjamin Franklin, 1770* was included in the 1891 United States Coast and Geodetic Survey. Engraving by James Poupard. Courtesy of the Roorda/Doyle Collection.

In the foreground of this *Yachting* magazine cover (May 1939) are two fishermen in sou'wester hats and foul weather gear, sailing a schooner like those clustered on the Grand Banks to fish for cod, shown in the lower left. In the background is a luxury motor yacht. They pass close to each other in the painting, but, figuratively speaking, they are worlds apart. Cover illustration by R. Verrier, c. 1939. Courtesy of *Yachting* magazine and the Roorda/Doyle Collection.

This single *Bizarro* comic by Dan Piraro from 2009 is worth a thousand words about the depletion of the Ocean's fish. Reprinted by permission of Dan Piraro.

The surfing prodigy Montgomery "Buttons" Kaluhiokalani personified the creative joy of that ancient water sport, as this still from a video attests. Born in 1959 to a native Hawaiian mother and an African American father from the mainland, he adopted his maternal surname and the Hawaiian Island culture. His grandmother nicknamed him Buttons for his tight curls; his corona of hair became one of his trademarks. He began surfing at age nine and quickly made a name for himself; he finished second at the US Surfing Championships at age fifteen, and at twenty, he won the 1979 Sunkist Pro in Malibu, California. Kaluhiokalani's unique surfing style made him famous. Using the split-rail stringer surfboard shown here, he emulated the moves of the skateboarders he saw in movies, and other surfers emulated him. The adrenaline-fueled lifestyle of surfers led many of them into drug use. Buttons Kaluhiokalani struggled with drug dependency for much of his life, derailing his career. He died of lung cancer in 2013 at the age of fifty-four, leaving a legacy summed up in his entry in *The Encyclopedia of Surfing*: "Loose and jiving . . . one of the sport's most naturally gifted riders . . . Kaluhiokalani was spontaneous and innovative, stringing together turns, cutbacks, tuberides, tailslides, and 360s with offhanded genius."

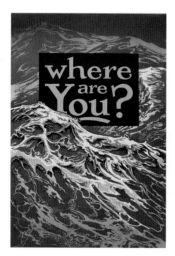

Ericka Walker turns a subversive, twenty-first-century lens on twentieth-century war propaganda themes using historically accurate lithography techniques. Walker's unsettling works offer a marked contrast to their wartime antecedents, whose purpose was to persuade reflexively and uncritically. *Where are You?* is one of two lithographs in a set from 2014 (along with "Career," which depicts a surfacing submarine and "Your career path begins"), which evoke the risk and terror of the human dimension of sea power. Lithograph from erickawalker.com. https://flatbedpress.com/collections/ericka-walker. Courtesy of the artist.

A Three-Hour Tour Becomes
a Four-Month Ordeal

Anonymous

The theme song of the popular 1960s TV sitcom Gilligan's Island *made famous the ominous phrase "a three-hour tour, a three-hour tour. . . ." Viewers of a certain age remember the poor SS* Minnow, *which set out from Honolulu for a charter of that duration, only to be hit by a storm and go aground on an "uncharted isle." Something like that happened in real life to Richard Van Pham. He set out from Long Beach, California, in his small sailboat with the intent of being out about three hours, only to run into a storm that disabled the engine, dismasted the vessel, and knocked out the radio. Van Pham ended up drifting helplessly on the Pacific Ocean for the next four months. A US Customs Service drug enforcement airplane finally spotted him, and summoned the closest US Navy vessel to rescue him. The guided-missile frigate* McClusky *found Van Pham drifting 300 miles off the coast of Costa Rica, a full 2,500 miles from his home port in southern California. He was cooking a cormorant for lunch on his grill, over a fire he made from bits of the sailboat's wooden trim, which had become his culinary practice. He was thoroughly discombobulated by that time, initially refusing assistance except to ask if the* McClusky *could spare him a new mast. Members of the* McClusky's *crew had to persuade the disoriented sailor, who thought he was nearing Hawai'i, to leave his rusty, shrouded vessel, which by then looked like a miniature* Flying Dutchman. *He was devastated that the huge frigate, more than 450 feet long, was unable to tow his dilapidated boat, named the* Sea Breeze, *which he lived aboard at a marina in Long Beach. He could not bear to watch as his home was burned and sunk to keep it from becoming a navigational hazard. News reports in the immediate aftermath of his rescue and follow-ups in the subsequent months suggest that Richard Van Pham, like Melville's Pip and countless other survivors of long ordeals on the Ocean, was transformed by the experience. The shipboard account of what transpired on September 17, 2002, when the* McClusky *rescued Richard Van Pham, follows.*

ABOARD USS *MCCLUSKY*, At Sea (NNS)—A calm but firm voice crackled across the ship's primary command and control circuit, "*McClusky* this is Alfa-Bravo, request you investigate suspected sailboat in distress in your area."

As the helmsman swung the ship around toward the sailboat's reported position, the rest of the crew sprang into action, manning the ship's boat and scouring the horizon for the stricken vessel.

The ship had a Search and Rescue (SAR) operation on its hands, the first of its deployment. A SAR mission means that a fellow mariner is in need of aid, may be injured, or, possibly worse.

In this instance a sailboat had been spotted by a U.S. Navy P-3C "Orion" long-range surveillance aircraft that earlier had been working in tandem with *McClusky*. Now, the mission had changed. Someone's life was at stake.

With the ship traveling at maximum speed, the ship's commanding officer, Cmdr. Gary R. Parriott, addressed the crew, notifying them of the new mission and the need to get to the sailboat quickly and to be prepared to render all necessary assistance. Within an hour the ship arrived on scene.

Standing just outside the boat's small cabin, the man broke into a wide grin; Mr. Richard Van Pham—adrift at sea for nearly four months—had at last been rescued.

A native of Vietnam, Pham fled that country and its protracted war in the early 70s. He made it to the United States and for 26 years lived in the Los Angeles area, working small jobs and earning just enough money to support a spartan lifestyle aboard his small boat.

He kept the boat at a marina in the Long Beach area. An avid mariner, he frequently sailed long distances for the sheer pleasure of getting away from it all.

This past June he had planned on a simple day sail from Long Beach to Catalina. As he had not planned on a lengthy voyage he did not take much. And he did not bother to tell anyone, save possibly a friend at the marina, that he was going away.

It is not known exactly what happened that day in June 2002. But this much Pham was later able to relate.

At some point during his ill-fated journey, the wind came up—suddenly and much stronger than he had anticipated. His [outboard motor failed and his] mast and sails began to groan under the strain of the sudden gale.

He attempted to alter course back to Long Beach but in so doing catastrophe struck—his mast broke in two. With no other means of propulsion, little food and an inoperative radio, Pham was in very deep trouble.

For days he drifted at the mercy of the ocean currents, hoping to happen upon a rescuer. For days he experienced disappointment, at the lack of contact with another boat; anger, at himself for getting into this predicament; and fear, at what lay ahead.

As the days turned into a week and then two weeks and more, Pham ran out of food. It was then that his previous ocean sailing experience and his lifelong close association with the ocean saved his life. He collected rainwater;

With large seabirds lined up on its bowsprit, Richard Van Pham's powerless sailboat, a forlorn speck on the vast Pacific Ocean, reaches the end of its accidentally record-setting voyage, which lasted four months instead of the intended three hours. US Navy photograph, 2002 (released), 020917-N-0000X-012.

stayed indoors [in] the boat's cabin during the hottest part of the day, and, most impressively, fished and caught sea turtles and gulls to eat.

Weeks then turned into months. Without any family to report him missing he continued to drift, alone at sea. Finally, after close to four months on the high seas, Pham saw the sleek hull of a Navy frigate making its way toward him. He was rescued.

Onboard *McClusky* the Damage Control Assistant, Ensign Matthew Chesnik, and his leading Chief, Chief Damage Controlman David Britton readied the ship's Rescue and Assistance Team. The ship slowed to a halt and launched its small boat.

The crew, including boat officer Lt. J. G. Charlie Collins, readied themselves. They did not know what to expect. The ship's Surface Combat Action Team, led by Chief Fire Controlman (sw) Scott Lee, manned their topside guns—just in case.

The boat approached Pham's small craft gingerly. The first thing noticeable was the vessel's mast—broken and lashed to the side. There was a makeshift sail, tattered and full of holes that was doing little good capturing the wind.

As the ship rolled with the waves, the revealed hull was covered in barnacles; brown rust streaked the vessel's sides. As *McClusky*'s boat neared the sailboat, the crew could see birds—dozens of them—sitting all over the boat.

"It seemed like if there was a spare space of freeboard, the birds were on it," said Collins. Continuing to close, the crew was surprised to see California registration markings on the boat's hull.

As the boat crew approached, a wispy little man in tattered jeans, a torn shirt and a longish beard appeared topside and began jumping up and down.

A quick inspection of the boat revealed no other passengers. Pham was brought aboard and transferred to *McClusky*.

Once onboard he received a thorough check up from the ship's Independent Duty Corpsman. He was in remarkably good shape.

After several days *McClusky* made a regularly scheduled port call to Guatemala. Pham was put ashore and transferred to the American Embassy personnel for further transfer back to the marina he calls home in Long Beach, Calif.

Before he left, however, the crew extended their hand in generosity once more, presenting him with $800 they had collected to help him start a new life.

IX

Inspiration

See the way the deep sea diver falls into the mermaid's arms . . .

—They Might Be Giants (John Flansburgh and John Linnell), "Erase" (2015)

There is an undeniable enchantment about the Ocean, just as there is a menace to it that also cannot be denied. The two are related.

Because it can be terrifying, the Oean is sublime, and because it is sublime, it has long been a source of inspiration for sentimental and spiritual souls. As the Ocean is conducive to religious feelings and creative urges, this part brings together a few representations of each.

The Asian Sea Goddess

Eric Paul Roorda

To judge from the number of worshippers worldwide—some 200 million in about twenty-six countries—and the number of temples—more than 5,000, at last count— the Asian goddess of the Ocean, who is recognized from Singapore to San Francisco, is among the most inspiring religious figures in the world. The charismatic deity, who came into being as an infant girl, is known by different names across the broad geographic range of her devotion. Her fame spread with the Treasure Fleet voyages of Zheng He, who credited her with his success, and it shows no signs of diminishing.

Lin Mo Niang—her name means "silent girl," because she did not cry at birth —was growing up on Meizhou Island, in Fujian Province, China, on the Strait of Formosa, when she began to demonstrate special gifts. At the age of four, while praying to a statue of the bodhisattva Guanyin at a Buddhist temple, she suddenly acquired the second sight from the goddess, allowing her to predict certain future events. When she was fifteen, a sea dragon reared up from the inshore waters of Meizhou Island and presented Lin Mo with a bronze disk. After receiving the gift, she could foretell foul weather. This power, now the commonplace profession of meteorologists, was completely novel during the tenth-century Song dynasty, when Lin Mo Niang lived. Once the local mariners put their faith in her forecasts, they faced fewer perils in their dangerous profession, staying onshore when she sounded her alarm. The future goddess grew famous while she was still a teen.

Once, when she was at home with her mother, Lin Mo sensed that her father and brother, fishing in their boat, were sinking in a sudden gale. She went into a trance and appeared beside them. First she saved her brother, guiding him to shore, then returned to bring her father to safety. But her mother, seeing Lin Mo in a seemingly lifeless state at home, gave the girl a shake, breaking her trance, and unwittingly drowning her husband. After that traumatic experience, Lin Mo redoubled her efforts to assist other shipwreck victims. Then, at the age of twenty-eight, she informed her mother and the rest of her family that it was time for her to go. As they and their neighbors watched in amazement, she climbed the mountain near their village, and, reaching the top, she ascended in a rainbow apotheosis.

This image of the A-Ma Temple, titled *The Landing Place at Macao*, came off the presses of William Collins, Sons of Glasgow, in 1858. Courtesy of the Roorda/Doyle Collection.

Lin Mo continued to save sailors after her stylish exit, appearing to them in the sky wearing brilliant red raiment. That is how she earned the title Tianfei, or Princess of Heaven. After repeated miraculous rescues over the course of centuries, the Qing dynasty emperor Kangxi promoted her to Tin Hau, or Empress of Heaven.

Joining the Buddhist pantheon, Lin Mo Niang became a favorite for families who draw their living from the sea, Ocean travelers, and, more recently, people who seek their recreation on saltwater. She acquired several new names in the far-flung places where people pray to her. In her native China and in Taiwan, they call her Mazu, which can mean mother, grandmother, or maternal ancestor. In her home province of Fujian, her devotees use the endearment Mazupo, roughly Grandma Mazu. Farther south, in Cantonese-speaking Hong Kong, the prayerful employ her title Tin Hau, while across the Pearl River estuary on the peninsula of Macau, the polyglot population evoke her as A-Ma, which is a Portuguese mash-up of both Tin Hau and Mazu. Other monikers include Shennü, meaning "divine woman," and Tongxian Lingnü, or "worthy and efficient lady."

By whatever name she is known, the Asian sea goddess attracts the adoration of the coastal Buddhists of Japan, Okinawa, Thailand, Vietnam, Malaysia, Singapore, Borneo, Melbourne (site of an enormous Mazu temple), and San Francisco. The Taiwanese seem to worship her the most, having built more than 1,000 temples dedicated to her, and hosting the most ambitious eight-day pilgrimage at the time of her birth festival, celebrated on March 23 on the Chinese lunar calendar, which falls between mid-April and mid-May on today's. The pilgrimage, performed by thousands annually, goes from one Mazu temple to the oldest Mazu temple on the island and back, covering a distance of 160 miles. Twenty temples in her honor stand on her little home island of Meizhou, where the women comb their hair into the shape of boats during the Mazu festival. Seventy more Mazu temples are located in mainland Fujian. Ninety shrines to Tin Hau can be found in Hong Kong, none more sacred than Fat Tong Mun Tin Hau Old Temple in Joss House Bay, located at the water's edge. That makes it a particularly good spot for mariners of all stripes—from working watermen to wealthy yachters—to perform *bai sun* to the goddess, asking for her protection during their voyages. They approach the temple in their vessels, then execute three figure eights within a few hundred yards of it, while making offerings of roast pork, cabbage, and fruit. Other offerings to Tin Hau are brightly colored treats in the shape of sea creatures fashioned from flour, mushrooms, and tree fungi: crabs, sharks, sea stars, different kinds of fish, and stingrays, among many other species. Towering over all the other tributes to the sea goddess, the Mazu statue erected in 2012 in Tianjin, the port of Beijing, measures 139 feet in height.

But out of the thousands of Asian sea goddess temples, the sea's-edge shrine in São Lourenço, Macau, called simply the A-Ma Temple, is perhaps the most revered. Completed in 1488, it stood out as a landmark when Portuguese mariners arrived in the 1500s and landed nearby. They are said to have asked the fishermen on the shore the name of the place, and they, thinking the question referred to the temple, replied, "Maa-gok" or "The Pavilion of the Mother," which is a name derived from Mazu. The sailors actually wanted to learn what the land itself was called, and so the peninsula became known as Macau, their mispronunciation of Maa-gok. The A-Ma Temple of Macau gained the status of a UNESCO World Heritage site in 2005.

The Hajj by Sea

Hadji Khan and Wilfrid Sparroy

For most of its history the hajj, the annual pilgrimage of devout Muslims to Mecca in Saudi Arabia, took place mainly on the Ocean. The religion of Islam spread so far, so fast that large numbers of the faithful had to travel great distances to complete the trip, and making it by ship was the only viable option. Yet despite the global nature and vast scale of the hajj, for centuries non-Muslims knew little about it. The only available reports came from a few European adventurers who disguised themselves to enter Mecca, which is forbidden to nonbelievers, most famously Sir Richard Francis Burton (1821–90). The first full account of the hajj came in 1902, when a Muslim correspondent for the London Morning Post *took part and wrote a series of columns about his journey, published as a book called* With the Pilgrims to Mecca *(1905). The author is obscure aside from his surname, Khan, and his pen name, Haji Raz, or Mystery Haji.*

On my arrival at Marseilles I booked a berth on board the steamer *Rewa*, belonging to the British India Steam Navigation Company, as it proved to be the only one that would enable me to reach Port Said and to proceed thence to Suez by rail in time to catch the connection by boat to Jiddah.

I shall neither tax the reader's patience nor trespass on my space by relating the trivial incidents of a voyage that presented little of interest to a travel-worn mind. It will be enough to say that the wind, which was as fair as one could desire till we reached the Straits of Messina, was bent afterward on making another and an angrier sea. The discomfort of the passengers, most of whom were Britains bound for India, was betrayed by their seclusion from the open air. The nearer we approached the East, the more kindly grew the elements, until, on the seventh day, about seven o'clock in the morning, Port Said hove in sight. An hour later I had packed my kit and was ready for a hearty landing. Steaming slowly into the canal we passed the pier, which was still in course of construction, saluted the statue of de Lesseps, and raised a shout of surprise on counting not less than five Russian warships before we reached our moorings.[1] . . . Not one single British man-of-war was to be seen. I had my breakfast at eight, after which I bade farewell to the captain and my travelling companions, going ashore in one of the boats that surrounded our steamer.

Two trains start from Port Said to Suez every day, one in the forenoon and one in the evening. . . . On my bidding good-bye to the dragoman I had engaged, he assured me that he was far too devout a Muslim to fleece so pious a pilgrim as myself, and he would not accept a centime more than five francs for the boat, the carriage, and his special services. It was from him that I first heard of the outbreak of cholera in Arabia—a report that was unfortunately confirmed at Suez, whither I journeyed in the discomfort of a dust-storm and a hot easterly wind. . . .

First, I bought a deep crimson fez with a black tassel and a straw lining.[2] Though it looked both cool and fanciful, and was therefore pleasing to my Oriental eye, I am not certain that a turban would not have been more in keeping with the complete Arab suit which I subsequently purchased. This consisted of a thin linen shirt, a pair of trousers, and two long and graceful robes. . . .

On donning this picturesque attire I returned to the Hôtel d'Orient by way of the narrow and filthy bazaars, where my attention was attracted by a band of dancers who were drawing together a crowd of sightseers of every nationality. While one man was cutting capers in the skin of a Polar bear, a second, tambourine in hand, powdered his face to imitate a European, while a third, got up in the guise of a Negro, played with a lively monkey in chains, and three dancing girls with huge artificial moles on their faces completed the company. . . .

Next morning I came across a blind Arabian priest patiently waiting on the landing-stage for the departure of the steamer, and in the evening he was still in the self-same spot, kneeling on his prayer-rug and singing aloud the verses of the Kurán in a deep original Arab melody, rosary in hand. His young son was kneeling by his side, listening with downcast eyes to the never-ceasing chants of his father, to say nothing of the saddening elegies of the Arabian traditionalists. Like most of the singers of the East, who pour out their rhapsodies all day long in an ever-flowing torrent of melody, he was extremely monotonous, and so I sought to stem the current of his song by entering into conversation with him. On hearing from me that he would be obliged to descend into the hell of a Turkish quarantine and to remain five days before he could ascend into the pilgrim's paradise of Mecca, a look of keen distress swept like a cloud over his enraptured countenance. Rising from his feet, he raised his sightless eyes, saying: "God, if it pleases Him, will provide me with a swift means of transport to His city. We shall meet again." So confident was his tone that my own misgivings yielded to the hope that I should yet overcome the difficulty of the quarantine. And soon after I was informed that all the first-class passengers on board the last pilgrim boat would be allowed to proceed to their destination without let or hindrance, but the unfortunate deck passengers would have to conform to the regulations. Never was privilege of wealth and curse of poverty brought home to the hearts of the weary in a more convincing fashion. The next best thing to being wealthy, I told myself, is to have the prerogatives of wealth thrust upon one.

Having had my passport *viséd*, I booked a berth and went on board the Khedivieh steamer, which completed the distance between Suez and Jiddah —some six hundred and forty-five nautical miles—in about eighty hours.[3] At ordinary times these steamers are simply employed for mail service, one of them leaving Suez for Jiddah every week—generally on Thursday—and another leaving Jiddah for Suez on the same day. Though they practically belong to a British syndicate, they go under the name of Khedivieh steamers. The captain and chief officers are English, whereas the crew are Egyptians and Lascars.[4] During the pilgrimage steamers run frequently between the two ports, and in the year 1902 not less than two hundred thousand pilgrims, I was told, had landed at Jiddah, the majority of whom embarked at Suez. Among these numbers must be reckoned the eighty thousand Russian subjects from the Caucasus and Central Asia, who, for the first time since they came under the Russian rule, had been granted the privilege of undertaking the ancient pilgrimage. Rumour credited them with being the main cause of the cholera that year. If only the half of what I heard about them were true their pollution would still beggar description.

The cruise in the Red Sea is not so interesting as that in the Mediterranean. Save an occasional ragged rock rising from the yellow waters, or a flight of white birds over the steamer, nothing was to be seen from hour to hour.

When we sighted the port of Jiddah . . . we were told to put on our ihrám, or sacred habit, before entering the holy territory on our way to Mecca. As a preliminary, I removed my Arabian costume, washed my hands, up to the elbow, and my feet, up to the knees; I afterwards shaved the upper lip, leaving the fresh-grown, unsightly beard to its own fate. Then, having performed the prescribed ablution of the head, I expressed, with the tongue of my heart, the earnest desire to cast off the garb of unrighteousness and pride and to put on the winding-sheet of humility and of passive obedience to God's will. . . .

Now, my ihrám, which I had bought at Suez, consisted of two thin woollen wrappers and a pair of sandals. One wrapper was tied about the middle and allowed to fall all round to the ankles, while the other was thrown over the shoulders, leaving the head and the forearms bare. Both wrappers were spotlessly white, and had neither seam nor hem. The sandal was a kind of shoe, consisting of a sole fastened to the foot by means of a tie which passed between the large toe and the first toe of the foot; it left uncovered both the instep and the heel. This sacred habit was worn by all pilgrims during the four days preceding the Hájj Day. While they have it on they must neither hunt nor fowl, though they are allowed to fish—a doubtful privilege in a dry land.

Notes

1. Ferdinand de Lesseps (1805–94) was the principal builder of the Suez Canal, which opened in 1869, linking the Mediterranean and Red Seas, and shortening the distance to India by thousands of miles.
2. Reaching Suez, the Mystery Haji outfitted himself in local garb to replace his Western suit.
3. The khedive was the viceroy of that region of the vast Ottoman Empire, with its capital at Constantinople.
4. "Lascar" was the generic term for sailors from any of the nations of the Indian subcontinent and Southeast Asia.

Durr Freedley's "Saints of the Sea"

Anonymous

The Seamen's Church Institute Memorial Chapel in Newport, Rhode Island, is a hidden gem of Art Deco design. It is the work of Durr Freedley (1888–1938), who painted its elaborate murals, which depict more than fifty Catholic saints associated with the Ocean, in 1933. Freedley came from landlocked Indianapolis to study art history at Harvard University and, after graduation, went to New York City to take a job at the Metropolitan Museum of Art, rising to become head of the Department of Decorative Art in six years. He enlisted in the army when the United States entered World War I and was sent overseas to perform an assignment appropriate to his talents: he became the director of camouflage painting for aircraft. After the war, Freedley stayed in Europe to pursue a successful career as a portraitist, living in Rome and then in Paris throughout the 1920s, where he gained a reputation for both his likenesses and for his interior designs. Moving to the wealthy enclave of Newport in 1930, he continued painting and designing. His commissions during that period included the murals for Trinity Church in New York City and the design and execution of the Memorial Chapel at the Seamen's Church Institute, a charity founded in 1919 to help mariners in need, housed in a handsome brick building on the waterfront, which many of the city's well-heeled citizens supported. The Memorial Chapel was Freedley's last major work completed before his sudden death in 1938. Soon after, a memorial exhibition of Freedley's artwork was held at the John Herron Art Museum in his native Indianapolis, which included his preliminary drawings for the Memorial Chapel murals, now in the collection of the Newport Art Museum. The next selection comes from the catalog of that exhibit.

The Memorial Chapel

The Chapel of the Seamen's Church Institute of Newport is for Seafarers. It depicts saints long associated with the Sea. For centuries these symbols of faith have been venerated and called upon by mariners in need. . . .

The Chapel is thought of as a quayside, looking out upon the Seven Seas of the world. The altar, set at one end, is hung with an embellished sail-cloth held by nautical knots—the models for which were made by sailors at the Newport Training Station. . . .

Most of the saints described in the guide to Durr Freedley's detailed mural may be discerned in the three photographs reproduced in this selection. The first one depicts the four apostles to the right of the altar. Photograph by A. E. Doyle, July 2016. Courtesy of A. E. Doyle. Used by permission of the Seamen's Church Institute, Newport, Rhode Island.

S. Michael's name means "Like Unto God." . . . He is the Guide and Protector of all seamen. To him are dedicated rocky islands and coastal promontories throughout the world serving as lighthouses and sailing marks for a thousand years.

Beside each of these archangels stands a saint, who exercised in life the same gifts as his angelic counterpart. By S. Michael is S. Nicholas of Bari—Patron of all sailors everywhere, of gifts and giving, and of our Christmas Seasons; guardian of boys; and friend of happy marriages. He protects merchants against robbers and against shipwreck. One of his many miracles was the restoration to life of a sailor who fell from the rigging of a ship on which S. Nicholas was traveling to the Holy Land. S. Nicholas' symbols are: anchor, book, and three bags of gold representing dowries he gave secretly to poor girls that they might be happily married.

By S. Raphael stands S. Christopher with the infant Christ on his shoulder. S. Christopher protects all travelers by land. He was humble, but of great strength—and a giant of a man. . . . A symbol of S. Christopher is often placed near the prow of ships and is carried by travelers throughout the world.

Beginning at the right of the window nearest the Altar, the panel contains four figures of the apostles. First, S. Andrew, a fisherman himself, and prime Patron of all Fishermen, shown with book, net, and the Cross on which he was martyred. Second: S. Peter, his brother, Prince of the Apostles, likewise a fisherman, and Protector of Fishmongers. S. Peter has a net; with him are the Keys to the Kingdom of Heaven—given to him to bind and to loose; the shell is the kind called Bishop's Miter—placed here as a symbol of S. Peter's Episcopate. Third, S. Paul, called "Paul the Traveler," in armor and with sword. Fourth, S. Mark, Protector against Sudden Death. S. Mark who is Patron of Venice was venerated through her vast maritime life. Here, he holds the mast of a galley and is accompanied by the winged lion (his symbol as Evangelist) and also seal of Venice. Mrs. Post was born and christened in Venice.

Above these four male figures in smaller scale are shown S. Malo of Brittany, after whom the great fishing port on the English Channel is named. He is in a boat with S. Brendan of Ireland, whose voyage across the Atlantic to the Promised Land of the Saints, afterwards called "St. Brendan's Island," is based on a legendary voyage to America long before the Norsemen. S. Brendan sailed for seven years among the marvelous islands of the unknown Western Ocean, where, in the icy regions of the North, he came upon a rock arising from the Sea. There sat Judas Iscariot, who was allowed an hour a year away from the fires of Hell, that he might cool himself in the Sea. Next, S. Alexis at his rope-walk—a Bishop and patron of Rope-Makers. Next, S. Ephraem Syrus, a patron of Sail-Makers, depicted at his task. He disapproved of improper literature and would glue together pages of bad books; a glue pot and volumes are associated with him.

On the back wall of the Chapel next to the window is S. James the Great. In Spain he is called S. James of Santiago de Compostella. His shrine there attracted countless pilgrims throughout Christian history. Here, he is a youth in his pilgrim's garb with staff, scrip, and scallop shell; he is being welcomed to shelter and rest by S. Julian Hospitaller, a knight and huntsman, who serves poor travelers and gives them hospitality. Over them is S. Dominic, a protector of drowning, rain storms, and wetting, in the garb of the order which he founded and with his attribute of the lily. Behind him is Father Noah in his Ark welcoming home the Dove.

Next, on a double throne are seated, side by side, S. Erasmus of Gaeta and S. Elmo. They lived nearly 1,000 years apart, but are often associated with each other and are always venerated by sailors of the Mediterranean. Beside S. Erasmus is the Capstan which was the instrument of his martyrdom. S. Elmo holds in one hand his attribute of an anchor and in the other, two blue lights called "S. Elmo's Fire." These sometimes mysteriously appear at the masthead and yardarms of ships. Sailors think of them as the lights of passing souls; they have lately been seen off Block Island. S. Elmo in Spain is called S. Peter Gonzalez.

Next stands St. Martin of Tours, a warrior and patron of good fellowship and jovial meetings. He is armed, and has half of his famous coat; he had given the other half to a beggar.

S. Augustine, the Doctor of Grace, kneels beside S. Martin. Once, walking

The second photo shows the back wall described in the guide. Photograph by A. E. Doyle, July 2016. Courtesy of A. E. Doyle. Used by permission of the Seamen's Church Institute, Newport, Rhode Island.

by the Sea and troubled with doubts, he came upon a strange child digging a hole in the sand. Pointing to this hole, the child told Augustine that it was useless to try to pour all the waters of the Sea into this hole—as to arrive by reason alone at the fullness of Christian faith. S. Augustine's life and work mature after this; his influence is present today.

Next, S. Anthony of Padua, a companion to S. Francis—preaching to the fishes, who listen to him more responsively than his human audiences. He is a protector against Fire.

Next to him is S. Cornelius, the Centurion, a Roman Captain, to whom the military Chapel at Governor's Island [in New York Harbor] is dedicated. Christ said to him: "Verily, I say unto you, I have not found so great faith, no, not in Israel. Go thy way; and as soon as thou hast believed, so be it done unto thee."

The small figures at the top are S. Columba, surnamed "The Apostle of Caledonia," who made an historic voyage in a wicker boat or coracle to the Island of Iona. Above him is S. Ramon of Penaforte who sailed away on a stone using his cloak as a sail to prove to the tyrannous King of Aragon the power of a holy man convinced of his own righteousness.

Next are three caravels sailing the Sea containing S. Ursula and her virgin companions starting off on their momentous voyage up the river Rhine to Rome and back to martyrdom.

The third photo is the east wall. Photograph by A. E. Doyle, July 2016. Courtesy of A. E. Doyle. Used by permission of the Seamen's Church Institute, Newport, Rhode Island.

Next comes S. Patrick, setting out to evangelize the infidels of Ireland. Although captured by pirates and cast upon a desert island he escaped bringing glory to himself and his adopted land. Here he drives the snakes from Ireland into the Sea. (And they never returned!)

Above him is S. Cuthbert of Lindisfarne, an early patron to English sailors. He quelled tempests and storms, praying by the shore while sea otters would attend and serve him.

On the east wall of the Chapel, on the right of the door stands young S. Leonard, deacon, whose name means "Brave as a Lion." Guardian of all prisoners and captives, he bears their chains and fetters.

Next, S. Roch, a great French pilgrim and traveler—protector of prisoners and persons threatened by contagion. Although he was imprisoned and suffered, his dog kept him alive by the daily offering of bread.

Above these two, the small figures represent S. John de Matha, who spent his life among the galley slaves and captives of the Barbary Pirates. He founded an order, The Trinitarians, whose chief purpose was to ransom or free victims of pirates. With him in the boat is S. Vincent de Paul, royal almoner of the Galleys of France and benefactor of the galley slaves of the 17th century. Riding with them is S. Swithin, an English holy man, whose name alone kept water spouts from destroying medieval barks. When his relics were enshrined in his church, torrents of rain hindered the ceremony; hence: the popular superstition about rain on that day and his association with downpours.

Among the larger figures next to the lighthouse and beacon stands S. Louis of France, who led the Crusaders across the Mediterranean to the Holy Land. He founded the Order of the Ship and is shown with this insignia on the shoulder of his cape; his costume is that of a crusader. He is in conversation with S. Clement, whose martyrdom was to be cast into the Black Sea with an anchor around his neck. However, his resting place beneath the waves became a place of healing and the center of ancient legend. . . .

The other small figures in this panel are next to Prince Henry the Navigator and proceeding to the left: S. Eulalia, patron saint of Barcelona and of sailors in the West Mediterranean, sitting by the pilot's wheel of a ship. Beside her stands S. Phocas. Though his symbol was a gardener's spade, he particularly watched over the sailor's mess; a mess fund on ships collected for the poor was called the "Meal of S. Phocas."

Beside S. Phocas sits S. Gertrude, also a patroness of travelers, who is said to harbor souls on the first night of their three days' journey to Heaven. She also protects against rats and mice and keeps ships from being overrun by them. An Abbess, she carries a crosier with a mouse running up it, and in her other hand is S. Gertrude's Cup, which old travelers pledged to her before beginning a journey.

On the next island stands S. Vincent, holding his ship and attended by the two crows who guided it on its last voyage; the headland, Cape S. Vincent, named after him, is the western-most point of Europe. On the island sits S. Zeno of Verona, a patron of anglers.

Below in the space between S. Clement and S. Denis is a boat of famous sea voyagers. Enemies of the faith set an open boat—without oars or sail—adrift on the Mediterranean with the three Marys, S. Martha and Sarah and their Black servant, together with S. Lazarus—brother of Martha, and S. Joseph of Arimathea, or S. Maximin. They suffered greatly but eventually drifted to the shores of France where they spread the Christian Faith. Their landing place today is called the "Three Marys of the Sea." One of the churches there is dedicated to Sarah, the Egyptian. Gypsies still come every year to worship at their shrine. Below this boat is Jonah escaping from the whale.

The design of the floor suggests the bottom of the Sea and is inlaid with sea shells and sea weed. In the center is a compass of good qualities: Duty, Faith, Honor, Obedience, Love, Hope, Courage, and Charity. Over this is the anchor, which is the device of the Seamen's Church Institute.

The cornice bears the verses from Psalm 107:

> They that go down to the Sea in ships, and occupy their business
>   in great waters;
> These men see the words of the Lord and His wonders in the deep.
> For He maketh the storms to cease so that the waves thereof are still.
> Then are they glad because they are at rest, and so he bringeth them
>   unto their desired haven.

Missionary to Micronesia

Hiram Bingham

Missionaries were among the first European explorers, and long after the unknown waters had been reconnoitered, the tradition of going to sea to save souls continued. One ambitious example of religious zeal on the Ocean was the career of Reverend Hiram Bingham Jr. (1831–1908), whose father was the leader of the first missionary group to the Hawaiian Islands in 1820. Born in Hawai'i, the younger Bingham devoted his life to carrying Christianity beyond his native archipelago, all the way to the South Pacific islands. The self-described Missionary to Micronesia took up collections to build a ship for his South Pacific ministry. He called this vessel Morning Star, *and his 1866 memoir of her voyaging is titled* Story of the Morning Star. *It is excerpted here, along with a passage from his 1883 sequel, which tells the fate of the inspirational ship. Bingham's son, Senator Hiram Bingham III, gained fame for discovering Machu Picchu. The tiny islands that Bingham's* Morning Star *traversed are now the places on earth that are most threatened by the rising level of the Ocean.*

Her Voyage around Cape Horn

On the evening of November 30th, 1856, a farewell meeting was held in Park Street Church, Boston, at which Captain Moore and his crew were present. Both he and myself were to receive our "instructions," as to where we were to go, and what we were to do. The house was crowded with the friends of the little vessel, who wished to hear what would be said to us.

The first day of winter was cold; but many Christian friends met on board our missionary packet, to bid her and her company "God speed!" It was not, however, till the next day that she spread her white sails for the long voyage. With deep interest we watched the forms of loved ones, as they stood on the wharves, sending after us their best wishes. When should we see their faces again? Though it was a tender hour, it was a happy one. We thought it a great privilege to be permitted to go to the heathen in such a vessel. Oh, how many prayers were offered by Jesus' little lambs for her preservation!

We sailed beautifully out of Boston harbor; but, not long after, a dreadful storm came upon us. The *Morning Star* was forced to anchor under the lee of Cape Cod, off Provincetown; and so were two other vessels, one on each side of her. The wind shifted during the night; and the next morning we saw our two neighbors high up on the shore, amid the breakers. But God had taken care of us, and the *Morning Star* held fast, and was all safe! There we lay for three days, till a steamer from Boston came to our assistance; and, having towed us around the Cape, she left us to go on our way over the stormy Atlantic.

When we reached the South Atlantic, we found that our fore-yard was sprung; and so we put into Rio [de] Janeiro for repairs. The harbor was very beautiful, and we enjoyed the visit, to which the nice oranges and bananas added not a little. On the 24th of February, we passed Cape Horn, where we encountered another severe gale. But God helped us, and in a few days we had passed the stormy Cape, where vessels are often detained for weeks.

Soon after entering the Pacific, we felt that the Holy Spirit was with us; and ere we reached the Sandwich Islands, we hoped that some of our company had given their hearts to the Saviour. Our carpenter had been very profane during the early part of the voyage, and, when reasoned with, he thought he could not help swearing. But when he determined to become a Christian, he strove hard and successfully against this great sin. Sometimes he would haul in a rope that might be accidentally dragging in the sea, without being told to do it. And when some of his companions wondered at this, he replied that the vessel belonged to Jesus, and he wished to help take care of it, even if he was not commanded by the officer to do what he knew he ought to do. It made us happy to think that God had blessed the little vessel on her first voyage.

On the 20th of April, 1857, we had our first view of the snow-capped mountains of Hawaii, distant more than a hundred miles. The sunrise was beautiful, the clouds being tinged with a gorgeous crimson, and everything seemed to be in harmony with the feelings of joy which we experienced, when, at about six o'clock, as I was sweeping the western horizon with my glass, the majestic Mauna Kea was distinctly seen! Many hours did we spend that day on deck, awed by the stupendous pile which, so far away from us, was piercing the clouds.

We passed Hawaii on our left; and the next morning had Maui and Molokai in full view. As we coasted along the shore of the latter, we were charmed with the numerous cascades which rushed down the rocky precipices near the sea.

I shall not soon forget the first sight of Oahu, the island of my birth, with its rugged mountains, cocoa-nut groves, little villages, and, last of all, the beautiful harbor of Honolulu. Many years had rolled away since I had left it, then a mere boy. As we neared the land, a small schooner passed us, and her captain, standing upon her rail, shouted, "Welcome to the *Morning Star!*" And then from the crowd of natives on her deck there went up a round of cheers, which seemed to come from full hearts. These people were very glad to see the *Morning Star*, of which they had heard so much, and toward the building of which many of their children had given their money. The captain who welcomed us was a brother of Dr. Gulick, of Micronesia; and he is now the principal of a Girls' Boarding School at Waialua, Oahu. He came on board with Mr. Bond, and the watermelon, cocoa-nuts, potatoes, sweet and Irish, which they gave us, were a great luxury, after we had been so many months upon the deep. We had not been long at Honolulu, when the good people wished to give the *Morning Star* a new flag. At the time it was presented, thousands assembled near the vessel on the wharf; speeches were made, songs were sung, and great joy was expressed in what the children had done. Amid the shouts of the people, the new flag was hoisted to the mast-head by Captain Moore. . . .

She Sets Out for Micronesia

By the 7th of August the *Morning Star* was ready to start for Micronesia. A farewell meeting was held on board; missionaries, foreigners, and natives crowding her deck. We were commended to the kind care of our heavenly Father, with prayer, both in English and Hawaiian; the "Missionary Hymn" was sung; the benediction was pronounced; the moorings of our little vessel were cast off, and our long voyage of more than twenty thousand miles was resumed, after a pleasant visit of three months, among a people so recently converted from heathenism.

We touched twice at Kauai, one of the Hawaiian Islands, and held pleasant meetings on shore. All were delighted to see us, and to contribute something for our comfort. But this last of Christian lands that we were to see for many years, faded at length in the distance. And yet, as we were wafted farther and farther from the friends we loved, our joy only increased; for we thought, "Soon we shall be proclaiming the love of Christ to those who are sitting in darkness."

After we had been fourteen days without the sight of land, the good chronometer which the Sunday-School children of Essex Street Church, Boston, had given to the *Morning Star*, told us that we were nearing Uderik [Utirik Atoll], one of the Marshall Islands. Oh, how eager I was to catch my first glimpse of a Micronesian island! And do you not think that I was very happy to be the first one to see the cocoa-nut tree tops just rising out of the ocean? With a burst of joy I shouted, "Land ho!" And instantly the word was taken up by almost all on board, till the fishes around us might have wondered at a sound so new and strange.

We passed near enough to see with the naked eye several specks upon the beach. These, the spy-glass showed us, were human beings. Gladly would we have stopped to tell them of our errand; but we were obliged to pass them by; and even to this day no missionary has landed there. Poor people! Do you not pity them? Perhaps the new vessel will bear the "glad tidings" to them.

Two days later we passed so near Mentschikoff Island that we could see the men, women, and children upon the beach. Some of them waved their mats to us, and we in turn waved our handkerchiefs to them.

It was not long before several of them pushed off in a *proa* to visit us. They were strange-looking men; and the strangest thing about them was the pair of ear-rings which they wore. Only think of having a hole in the lower part of one's ear, large enough to put a man's arm through! . . .

Her Visit to Kusaie

Though it was only three hundred and fifty miles from Mentschikoff Island to Kusaie, we were ten days in making the passage, owing to head-winds and calms.[1] Much of Micronesia is in the "doldrums," as the sailors call the low latitudes; and often, while passing from one island to another, our patience was sorely tried by fitful breezes, ocean-currents, and the torrid sun.

On the 8th of September we dropped anchor in one of the beautiful harbors of Kusaie. What a feast to our weary eyes was this gem of the Pacific,— so green, so romantic, so lovely! All about us there rose abruptly hills and mountains, covered to their very summits with the densest verdure. Beneath cocoa-nut and bread-fruit and banana and banyan trees nestled the picturesque dwellings of the natives. Here and there a light canoe passed rapidly along, bearing the rich, spontaneous fruits which had only to be gathered as they were needed. Snow-white birds sailed gracefully along, at a dizzy height, toward the dark mountain-sides. . . .

Her Visit to Ebon

Ebon is one of the Marshall Islands, all of which are coral reefs. . . .

The Marshall Islanders are bold navigators, and frequently set out in their *proas*, without any compass, for small islands distant a hundred miles. Sometimes they get adrift, however, and wander about over the ocean for weeks, before they find a landing-place.

It was in this way that the party of which I have spoken in another place, drifted to Kusaie, in a starving condition, and fully expecting to be put to death. But they were treated kindly, and permitted to return to their homes in peace. God had commanded the winds to take them to that distant island, that they might see what the missionaries were doing, and so be ready to welcome them. Some of these were among the people whom we met, as I have said, when sailing from Kusaie to Apaiang.[2] We had heard much of their barbarity; for they had made a covenant of death, and had resolved that every white man who should set his foot upon their island, should be killed! Only a little while before, indeed, a vessel had been seized by them, and all the crew slain.

And now, as we saw one large *proa* suddenly shoot out from the lagoon, and then another and another, (in spite of the roughness of the sea,) we began to fear lest our little vessel might be seized also. What then was our sense of relief, when, as Dr. Pierson addressed the first *proa* that reached us in the language of Ebon, the man who was steering recognized him, and exclaimed, repeatedly, and with great joy, "*Doketur!* (Doctor) *Doketur! Mitchinari!* (missionary) *Mitchinari!*" All in the canoe became highly excited, laughing most joyously. The news soon spread like wildfire among the fleet of seventeen *proas*. Some of the natives soon boarded us, and when they learned that Dr. Pierson was expecting to return in the course of one or two "moons," they were greatly delighted. . . .

Her Yearly Visits

The annual return of the *Morning Star* was always looked forward to with great interest. It would be difficult to say who of the missionaries wished to see her most; but I can assure my young readers that some of the most joyous days of my life were those on which she hove in sight.

The heathen children soon learned how we felt, when the time of her arrival drew near. As soon as a sail was seen in the distant horizon, a shout of "Te ro!" ("Sail ho!") was set up. Our waiting ears were not long in catching the sound, and immediately we sprang for the spy-glass. With almost breathless suspense it was directed to the far-off vessel. For a moment everybody kept still. If the "white flag" was seen at the mast-head, we were sure that she was coming; and shouts of joy, the clapping of hands, and happy faces, gave indications of the hearty welcome we were ready to give her. A large white flag, with the word WELCOME upon it, was speedily flung to the breeze from a pole tied to the top of a lofty cocoa-nut tree; and the missionaries' wives made haste to prepare shore-comforts for the weary voyagers.

From the 1883 Sequel

The little ship kept on her way prosperously until October 18, 1869. That day, having finished her Micronesian work for the year, she left Kusaie for Honolulu. Messrs. Snow and Sturges were on board for their return to America, and all were in buoyant spirits. At evening prayer they joyfully sang "Homeward Bound," but the Captain found when he went on deck after supper that the *Star* had been working in towards the island and was dangerously near the reef. She had got into a strong current. Boats were lowered and began towing her off shore. An anchor was let go in twenty fathoms of water and held her till a severe squall came up. Preparations had been made to slip the cable, in case the wind should favor, and try to shoot out clear of the reef with the fore and aft sails. But in trying to effect this after the squall, instead of shooting ahead, she only sagged off and soon struck the reef, broadside on. The surf was heavy, the shore rocky, and all hope for the vessel was gone.

The missionaries and all on board got safely to land in a boat, though with great peril of their lives; they also saved some of their effects and the ship's chronometers and charts. After a long month of waiting, they took passage in the *Annie Porter* and reached Honolulu, February 8, 1870.

Notes

1. Mentschikoff Island is in the Marshall Islands; Kusaie, in the Caroline Islands, is now called Kosrae.
2. A coral reef of Kirabati in the Northern Gilbert Islands.

The Voyage

Johann Wolfgang von Goethe

As the paragon of the German literary style called Sturm und Drang [storm and stress], it is fitting that Johann Wolfgang von Goethe (1749–1832), best known for Faust, *should compose an imaginative evocation of a stormy passage on the ocean, without having been to sea. Twelve years after writing this poem, "Seefahrt" (1776), Goethe traveled to Sicily and Venice during a long trip to Italy, when he had the chance to experience what he previously could only imagine.*

Long days and nights remained my laden ship;
Favorable winds we awaited, seated with trusted friends,
They drank to my patience and spirit,
In the harbor.

And they were doubly impatient;
They wished us well, a speedy journey,
Bon Voyage to you; Good fortune
Awaits out there in the world for you,
Upon homecoming, in our arms,
Love and praise will be yours.

And early next morning there was commotion,
And the sailors awoke us with shouts of joy,
Everything came alive, everything lived, moved,
With the first fair wind to cross the deck.

And the sails bloom in the breeze
And the sun entices with fiery love;
The sails fill, and the high clouds fill,
All friends on shore sing joyous songs
To us, in a state of ecstasy
Imagining the happiness of travel, as on the morning of departure,
As on the first high starry nights.

But God-sent shifting winds drive
Him to leeward from his plotted course,

This artistic evocation of the Ocean's inspiration references many poetic figures. The Greek muse of love poems, Erato, with her ancient lute, or cithara, touches the young man on his dreamy head. His gaze is on Aphrodite, who rises from a wave in front of him, while her minions, among them Cupid, luxuriate in the wavelets near the beach. Farther out, Poseidon drives a team of four *hippokampoi*, who have the head, torso, and front legs of a horse and a fish's tail. Apollo drives his chariot across the sun, and Icarus falls to his death. Three mermaids rise from the surf. One of them points at Arion, Dionysiac poet, who was kidnapped by pirates and rescued by a dolphin. Sea lions and seals surround Zeus. Engraver unknown, photogravure print based on a painting by Jean-Léon Gérôme, *The Poet's Dream* (1885) (New York: Cassell Publishing Co., 1892). Courtesy of the Roorda/Doyle Collection.

> And he seems as if he would give up,
> But subtly he strives to outwit them,
> True to his goal, even though he leans away.
>
> But out of the damp and gray distance
> The softly strolling storm announces itself
> Presses the bird down to the water,
> Presses down the swelling hearts of men;
> And it comes. Before its bristling havoc
> The sailors wisely strike the sails,
> Within the anguished orb, the sport of
> Wind and waves.
>
> And on that shore opposite stand
> Friends and lovers, trembling on solid ground;
> Oh, why did he not remain here!
> Oh, the storm! Driven off course from fortune!

Shall the good die this way?
Oh, he might, oh, he could! Gods!

Yet he stands manfully at the helm:
Wind and waves play with the ship,
But not with his heart, wind and waves.
Masterfully he looks upon the furious deep
And, shipwrecked or run aground, he trusts
His Gods.

Translated by Eric Paul Roorda

The Northern Seas

William Howitt

The English author William Howitt (1792–1879) was married to the poet Mary Howitt (1799–1881), who wrote more than one hundred books. This poem is from Mary's 1838 collection Sketches of Natural History, *which has a fairy-tale air. Though the two were authors in their own right, they collaborated on occasion. Mary seems to have written every other poem in this collection, as "The Northern Seas" is the only poem attributed to William in the entire book. Mary's most beloved work is "The Spider and the Fly," an 1829 poem that Lewis Carroll lampooned in* Alice's Adventures in Wonderland *(1865) as the "Lobster Quadrille." She was a devotee of all things Scandinavian and a translator of Swedish and Danish literature, most notably Hans Christian Andersen.*

Up! Up! let us a voyage take;
Why sit we here at ease?
Find us a vessel tight and snug
Bound for the northern seas.

I long to see the northern lights
With their rushing splendours fly,
Like living things with flaming wings,
Wide o'er the wondrous sky.

I long to see those icebergs vast
With heads all crowned with snow,
Whose green roots sleep in the awful deep
Two hundred fathoms low.

I long to hear the thundering crash
Of their terrific fall,
And the echoes from a thousand cliffs
Like lonely voices call.

There shall we see the fierce white bear
The sleepy seals aground,
And the spouting whales that to and fro
Sail with a dreary sound.

And while the unsetting sun shines on
Through the still heavens' deep blue,
We'll traverse the azure waves, the herds
Of the dread sea-horse to view.

We'll pass the shores of solemn pine
Where wolves and black bears prowl;
And away to the rocky isles of mist,
To rouse the northern fowl.

And there in the wastes of the silent sky
With the silent earth below,
We shall see far off to his lonely rock
The lonely eagle go.

Then softly, softly will we tread
By inland streams, to see
Where the pelican of the silent North
Sits there silently.

The World below the Brine

Walt Whitman

Long Islander Walt Whitman (1819–92), no stranger to Atlantic Ocean beaches, wrote this reverie on marine life and included it in the 1860 edition of his greatest work, Leaves of Grass.

The world below the brine,
Forests at the bottom of the sea, the branches and leaves,
Sea-lettuce, vast lichens, strange flowers and seeds, the thick tangle,
    openings, and pink turf,
Different colors, pale gray and green, purple, white, and gold, the play of
    light through the water,
Dumb swimmers there among the rocks, coral, gluten, grass, rushes,
    and the aliment of the swimmers,
Sluggish existences grazing there suspended, or slowly crawling close to
    the bottom,
The sperm-whale at the surface blowing air and spray, or disporting
    with his flukes,
The leaden-eyed shark, the walrus, the turtle, the hairy sea-leopard, and
    the sting-ray,
Passions there, wars, pursuits, tribes, sight in those ocean-depths,
    breathing that thick-breathing air, as so many do,
The change thence to the sight here, and to the subtle air breathed by
    beings like us who walk this sphere,
The change onward from ours to that of beings who walk other spheres.

Far Off-Shore

Herman Melville

Many years after leaving the sea and taking a safe, if stultifying, office job, Herman Melville (1819–91) kept thinking of the Ocean. In 1881, at the age of sixty-one, he wrote this brief, enigmatic poem about something he had seen at the age of nineteen, on his first sea voyage, a scene that had apparently haunted him for four decades.

Look, the raft, a signal flying,
Thin—a shred;
None upon the lashed spars lying,
Quick or dead.

Cries the sea-fowl, hovering over,
"Crew, the crew?"
And the billow, reckless, rover,
Sweeps anew!

The Ninth Wave

Ivan Aivazovsky

Ivan Aivazovsky (also Aiwasowski) (1817–1900) is widely regarded as one of the greatest Russian painters of all time; his most famous work is The Ninth Wave. *The title refers to the widely held belief that waves come in sets of nine, each one larger than the last. The six shipwrecked sailors in Aivazovsky's composition are clinging to a large section of a broken mast, as they ride out the successively taller and more treacherous waves that threaten to sweep them from their precarious perch—one of them is already in the water, trying to clamber back up, while also keeping a seemingly unconscious shipmate from falling off. But if the desperate group can endure the ninth wave, a comparative break will follow, and there is a chance for a happy ending. Barely visible against the mist and rising sun is the bowsprit and topsails of an approaching ship, which the castaways can see; two of them can be seen mustering their strength to wave at their potential savior, in a frantic attempt to signal it.*

The original of Ivan Aivazovsky's masterpiece, *Dyevyatiy val* (1850), hangs in the Hermitage Museum in Saint Petersburg, Russia. This wood engraving of the work, with its title translated into German as *Die Neunte Welle*, was published in *Moderne Kunst* (Modern art; Berlin: Richard Bong, 1900). Courtesy of the Roorda/Doyle Collection.

Sea Pictures

Edward Elgar

Everyone recognizes "Pomp and Circumstance" (1901), played when graduating students parade in their mortarboards and gowns, which is one enduring legacy of the English composer Edward Elgar (1857–1934), who is also known for the Enigma Variations *(1899). At the same time Elgar was working on his two most famous pieces, he was also setting to music a cycle of five poems, which he called* Sea Pictures. *Sung by a contralto accompanied by piano and orchestra, the composition is lush and hauntingly evocative of the Ocean. The celebrated diva Clara Butt gave the debut performances of* Sea Pictures *dressed as a mermaid, at the Norfolk and Norwich Festival and in London, in October 1899.*

The first poem in Elgar's Sea Pictures *is the work of the English poet Roden Berkeley Wriothesley Noël (1834–1894), who was a member of the Cambridge Apostles literary society while he was a student at that famous university. His collection of poignant poems about the loss of his son Eric at age five,* A Little Child's Monument *(1881), was his best-known publication.*

Alice Roberts, the future Lady Caroline Alice Elgar (1848–1920), was born in India, the daughter of the model Major-General Sir Henry Gee Roberts (1800–1860), who was knighted for his role in suppressing the Indian Rebellion of 1857. She studied geology, spoke four languages, published poetry and a two-volume novel, and played the piano. She outraged her elite family by marrying her piano teacher, Edward Elgar, because he was "below her station," Roman Catholic, and eight years younger than she was at the age of forty-one. Not only was she disinherited, she sacrificed her own creative endeavors to assist her husband, promoting his work, managing his business affairs, even preparing scores for his performances, marking the pages for the individual players. Partly through her efforts, her husband received the same royal recognition her father had, with conferral of knighthood in 1904, making her Lady Elgar. A poem of hers set in the fantastical island of Capri, in the Tyrrhenian Sea near the Bay of Naples, is the second in her husband's Sea Pictures *cycle.*

Elizabeth Barrett Browning (1806–61), one of the leading poets of Victorian England, composed the third poem of Sea Pictures *in 1839, sixty years before Elgar interpreted it in his musical composition.*

The most lasting effort of the widely published Richard Garnett (1835–1906) was

The Twilight of the Gods *(1888), a collection of short stories considered to be a seminal classic in the genre of literary fantasy. The fourth* Sea Pictures *poem was his.*

Adam Lindsay Gordon (1833–70), known more for his equestrian accomplishments than his poetry, was born in the Azores Islands and spent his earliest years on the island of Madeira, then moved to England and on to Australia. He was influenced by witnessing the shipwreck of the passenger steamship Admella, *one of the worst disasters in Australian history, which unfolded over a full horrific week in August 1859. Carrying 113 people, the* Admella *hit a reef along its Adelaide-to-Melbourne route, within sight of land, but out of reach of rescue. The survivors clung to the disintegrating hull, which broke into three pieces, battered by the surf. They died one by one as numerous attempts to save them failed, until the weather finally abated. A total of twenty-four passengers and crew lived to tell the tale, while Adam Lindsay Gordon attempted to immortalize the event with his poem "The Ride from the Wreck," inspired by the wintry trip that the local lighthouse keeper made to Adelaide, raising the alarm about the stranded* Admella. *Gordon gained fame and made his living as a steeplechase rider in Melbourne, but he died as the result of a bad fall in a race in 1870. The jockey wrote "The Swimmer," the last poem of* Sea Pictures.

Sea Slumber Song

RODEN BERKELEY WRIOTHESLEY NOËL

Sea-birds are asleep,
The world forgets to weep,
Sea murmurs her soft slumber-song
On the shadowy sand
Of this elfin land;

"I, the Mother mild,
Hush thee, O my child,
Forget the voices wild!
Hush thee, O my child,
Hush thee

Isles in elfin light
Dream, the rocks and caves,
Lull'd by whispering waves,
Veil their marbles
Veil their marbles bright,
Foam glimmers faintly white
Upon the shelly sand
Of this elfin land;

Sea-sound, like violins,
To slumber woos and wins,

I murmur my soft slumber-song,
My slumber-song,
Leave woes, and wails, and sins,

Ocean's shadowy might
Breathes good-night,
Good-night . . .
Leave woes, and wails, and sins,
Good-night . . . Good-night . . .
Good-night . . .
Good-night . . .
Good-night . . . Good-night . . ."

In Haven (Capri)

CAROLINE ALICE ELGAR

Closely let me hold thy hand,
Storms are sweeping sea and land;
Love alone will stand.
Closely cling, for waves beat fast,
Foam-flakes cloud the hurrying blast;
Love alone will last.
Kiss my lips, and softly say:
"Joy, sea-swept, may fade to-day;
Love alone will stay."

Sabbath Morning at Sea

ELIZABETH BARRETT BROWNING

The ship went on with solemn face;
  To meet the darkness on the deep,
    The solemn ship went onward.
I bowed down weary in the place;
  For parting tears and present sleep
    Had weighed mine eyelids downward.

The new sight, the new wondrous sight!
  The waters around me, turbulent,
    The skies, impassive o'er me,
Calm in a moonless, sunless light,
  As glorified by even the intent
    Of holding the day glory!

Love me, sweet friends, this Sabbath day.
  The sea sings round me while ye roll
    Afar the hymn, unaltered,
And kneel, where once I knelt to pray,
  And bless me deeper in your soul
    Because your voice has faltered.

And though this sabbath comes to me
  Without the stolèd minister,
    And chanting congregation,
God's Spirit shall give comfort. He
  Who brooded soft on waters drear,
    Creator on creation.

He shall assist me to look higher,
  Where keep the saints, with harp and song,
    An endless sabbath morning,
    And, on that sea commixed with fire,
Oft drop their eyelids raised too long
    To the full Godhead's burning.

Where Corals Lie

RICHARD GARNETT

  The deeps have music soft and low
  When winds awake the airy spry,
  It lures me, lures me on to go
  And see the land where corals lie.
  The land, the land, where corals lie.

  By mount and mead, by lawn and rill,
  When night is deep, and moon is high,
  That music seeks and finds me still,
  And tells me where the corals lie.
  And tells me where the corals lie.

  Yes, press my eyelids close, 'tis well,
  Yes, press my eyelids close, 'tis well,
  But far the rapid fancies fly
  To rolling worlds of wave and shell,
  And all the land where corals lie.

  Thy lips are like a sunset glow,
  Thy smile is like a morning sky,
  Yet leave me, leave me, let me go

And see the land where corals lie.
The land, the land, where corals lie

Swimmer

ADAM LINDSEY GORDON

With short, sharp, violent lights made vivid,
    To southward far as the sight can roam;
Only the swirl of the surges livid,
    The seas that climb and the surfs that comb.
Only the crag and the cliff to nor'ward,
the rocks receding, and reefs flung forward,
waifs wrecked seaward and wasted shoreward
    On shallows sheeted with flaming foam.

A grim, grey coast and a seaboard ghastly,
    And shores trod seldom by feet of men—
Where the battered hull and the broken mast lie,
    They have lain embedded these long years ten.
Love! *Love!* when we wander'd here together,
Hand in hand! Hand in hand through the sparkling weather,
From the heights and hollows of fern and heather,
    God surely loved us a little then.

The skies were fairer and shores were firmer—
    The blue sea over the bright sand rolled;
Babble and prattle, and ripple and murmur,
    Sheen of silver and glamour of gold—
    Sheen of silver and glamour of gold—
And the sunset bath'd in the gulf to lend her
A garland of pinks and of purples tender,
A tinge of the sun-god's rosy splendour,
    A tithe of his glories manifold
Man's works are graven, cunning, and skillful
    On earth, where his tabernacles are;
But the sea is wanton, the sea is willful,
    And who shall mend her and who shall mar?
Shall we carve success or record disaster
On the bosom of her heaving alabaster?
Will her purple pulse beat fainter or faster
    For fallen sparrow or fallen star?

I would that with sleepy, soft embraces
    The sea would fold me—would find me rest,

In luminous shades of her secret places,
   In depths where her marvels are manifest;
So the earth beneath her should not discover
My hidden couch—nor the heaven above her—
As a strong love shielding a weary lover,
   I would have her shield me with shining breast.

When light in the realms of space lay hidden,
   When life was yet in the womb of time,
Ere flesh was fettered to fruits forbidden,
   And souls were wedded to care and crime,
Was the course foreshaped for the future spirit—
A burden of folly, a void of merit—
That would fain the wisdom of stars inherit,
   And cannot fathom the seas sublime?

Under the sea or the soil (what matter?
   The sea and the soil are under the sun),
As in the former days in the latter
   The sleeping or waking is known of none.
Surely the sleeper shall not awaken
To griefs forgotten or joys forsaken,
For the price of all things given and taken,
   The sum of all things done and undone.

Shall we count offences or coin excuses,
   Or weigh with scales the soul of a man,
Whom a strong hand binds and a sure hand looses,
   Whose light is a spark and his life a span?
The seed he sowed or the soil he cumbered,
The time he served or the space he slumbered;
Will it profit a man when his days are numbered,
   Or his deeds since the days of his life began?

One, glad because of the light, saith, "Shall not
   The righteous Judge of all the earth do right,
For behold the sparrows on the house-tops fall not
   Save as seemeth to Him good in His sight?"
And this man's joy shall have no abiding
Through lights departing and lives dividing,
He is soon as one in the darkness hiding,
   One loving darkness rather than light.

A little season of love and laughter,
   Of light and life, and pleasure and pain,

And a horror of outer darkness after,
   And dust returneth to dust again.
Then the lesser life shall be as the greater,
And the lover of life shall join the hater,
And the one thing cometh sooner or later,
   And no one knoweth the loss or gain.

Love of my life! we had lights in season—
   Hard to part from, harder to keep—
We had strength to labour and souls to reason,
   And seed to scatter and fruits to reap.
Though time estranges and fate disperses,
We have *had* our loves and our loving-mercies;
Though the gifts of the light in the end are curses,
   Yet bides the gift of the darkness—sleep!

See! girt with tempest and winged with thunder,
   And clad with lightning and shod with sleet,
The strong winds treading the swift waves sunder
   The flying rollers with frothy feet.
One gleam like a bloodshot sword-blade swims on
The skyline, staining the green gulf crimson,
A death stroke fiercely dealt by a dim sun,
   That strikes through his stormy winding-sheet.

Oh! brave white horses! you gather and gallop,
   The storm sprite loosens the gusty reins;
Oh! brave white horses! you gather and gallop,
   The storm sprite loosens the gusty reins;
Now the stoutest ship were the frailest shallop
   In your hollow backs, on your high arched manes.
I would ride as never man has ridden
In your sleepy, swirling surges hidden,
I would ride as never man has ridden
To gulfs foreshadowed through straits forbidden,
   Where no light wearies and no love wanes,
   No love, where no love, no love wanes.

Voyage to Montevideo

Dino Campana

The deeply disturbed Italian poet Dino Campana (1885–1932) was incarcerated as a lu-
natic when he was twenty-one years old. His parents arranged his release and booked
his passage to South America to live with relatives in 1906, an experience he inter-
preted in the visionary verse of his only collection of poems, Canti Orfici *(Orphic*
songs), which he self-published in 1914. Like Vincent Van Gogh (1853–90), Campana
was unable to sell his work during his lifetime, was regarded as insane, and died in
obscurity; but he gained critical acclaim and public recognition after his death. His
hallucinatory poem about crossing the Atlantic Ocean appears here in translation.

I saw from the bridge of the ship
The hills of Spain
Vanish, in the green
Inside the twilight concealing the brown earth
Like a melody:
Lonely girl from a scene unknown
Like a melody
Blue, on the shore of the hills a violet still trembling . . .
The sky-blue evening languished on the sea:
And the golden silences from time to time took wing
Crossed over slowly in a royal blue . . .
Distant tints of various colors
From even more distant silences!
The golden birds crossed the sky-blue evening: the ship
Blindly crossing beating into the darkness
With our shipwrecked hearts
Beating into the darkness the sky-blue wings on the Ocean.
But one day
The grave matrons of Spain came aboard the ship
With turbid and angelic eyes
With wombs pregnant with vertigo. When
In a deep bay of an equatorial island
In a bay more tranquil and deeper than the night sky

We saw arise from the enchanted light
A white city somnolent
At the feet of the highest peaks of spent volcanoes[1]
In the turbid air of the Equator: until
After many shouts and many shadows from the land unknown,
After many chain-rattlings and much burning fervor
We left the equatorial city
Toward the restless night-time sea.
Onward we went and went for days and days: the ships
Somber with sails slapping in the warm slow breath of passing wind:
Very close to us on the quarterdeck there appeared a small bronze
Girl of the new breed,
Glowing eyes and clothing blowing in the wind!
Savage at the close of day there appeared
A coastline savage over the endless ocean:
And I saw like dizzied horses the dunes that melted
Into the boundless prairies
Deserted without human dwelling
And we turned shunning the dunes that appeared
On the sea yellow with the wonderful abundance of the river
Of the coastal capital of the new continent.[2]
Limpid fresh and electric was the light
Of the evening and the high houses seemed deserted
Yonder on the pirate sea
Of an abandoned city
Between the yellow sea and the dunes . . .

Translated by Eric Paul Roorda

Notes

1. Probably Santa Cruz de Tenerife in the Canary Islands, located at 18 degrees north latitude, where ships en route from Europe to southern South America were likely to call.
2. The River Plate is one hundred muddy miles wide at its mouth, on the north bank of which Montevideo, Uruguay, is located.

The Ballad of the Seawater

Federico García Lorca

The Spanish poet and playwright Federico García Lorca (1898–1936) wrote this poem in 1921, but he did not stray far from his home in Granada until 1929, when, at age thirty-one, he crossed the Atlantic Ocean to the United States aboard the grand RMS Olympic, *sister ship to the famous, ill-fated RMS* Titanic. *He returned to Spain the next year, only to die mysteriously in the Spanish Civil War, murdered by loyalists on his way home to Granada. His body has never been found, as if he had been lost at sea.*

The sea
smiles from afar.
Teeth of foam,
lips of sky.
What do you sell, oh turbid youth
with bosom in the wind?
I sell, sir, the water
of the seas.
What do you carry, oh black youth,
mixed with your blood?
I carry, sir, the water
Of the seas.
These salty tears
where do they come from, mother?
I weep, sir, the water
of the seas.
Dear heart, and this grave
bitterness, from where is it born?
Very bitter the water
of the seas!
The sea
smiles from afar.
Teeth of spray,
lips of sky.

Translated by Eric Paul Roorda

X

Recreation

In the modern era, the Ocean has become a recreational space, which it never really was for most of human history. In less than two centuries, many areas of the sea have turned into playgrounds, where people take part in many entertaining diversions that their ancestors knew nothing about or would not have considered. These fun things include recreational deep-sea fishing; boating for pleasure, such as racing; sailing long distances to pursue adventure and entertainment; skin diving using watertight masks and snorkels; spearfishing while skin diving; going on cruises; the list goes on. The exception to the rule that saltwater recreation is of relatively recent vintage is surfing, which is an ancient activity in the South Pacific, most famously in the Hawaiian Islands, but which did not become popular elsewhere until the twentieth century. The selections in "Recreation" represent these pursuits.

In the mid-nineteenth century, elite yacht owners on both sides of the Atlantic Ocean looked to the sea for amusement. The American variant of this wealthy class transitioned between their estates in Newport, Rhode Island, and their brownstones in Manhattan seasonally aboard palatial vessels, which professional crews and officers handled, while the owner and his family and guests relaxed. These ultrarich members of the New York Yacht Club also raced their yachts, watching from shore or from a moored observer boat to view the action, as their professional crews put their beautiful, purpose-built racing yachts through their paces.

Soon, middle-class boating enthusiasts got in on the action by sailing and racing their own small boats, with friends as crew members. Originating at the Corinthian Yacht Club in Marblehead, Massachusetts, this sail-it-yourself ethic, which caught on quickly and spread widely, became known as the Corinthian Movement. It might be seen as the start of a long-range development dubbed the "democratization of boating," which accelerated with the advent of automobiles, boat trailers, and outboard motors. These innovations put recreational boating within the budgetary means of millions of Americans and made it possible for families residing miles from the Ocean to hitch up their sailboats or runabouts and drive to the seashore, there to launch their boats (which often became like beloved members of the family, like a longtime pet) and get out on the water. So also began the phenomenon of the backyard boat, now a ubiquitous sight around the country.

According to the National Marine Manufacturing Association, there were 11.9 million registered recreational small craft in the United States in 2016 (down from more than 13 million before the recession of 2008), and that year, 87 million adult Americans messed about in boats, equal to 36 percent of all grown-ups in the country; untold numbers of minors went with them.

Although people have been sailing around the world for centuries, not until barely a century ago did anyone think of sailing around the world for fun. But now, sailing around the world at a leisurely pace is the goal of a large community of cruisers who spend their lives at sea—usually their second lives, as a majority of these free spirits seem to have cast off some previous career or identity. There are no statistics to estimate how many people annually complete their globe-spanning voyages, which typically require several years, but on the website Cruiserforum, when a sailor named Schoonerdog posted an inquiry in 2010 asking other members of the cruiser community how many of them finish their trips around the world every year, Estarzinger replied first, writing, "Probably more than you would guess . . . very roughly 200/300 boats/year. You can figure that by looking at the traffic through the 'choke points' on the main routes." Other participants in the exchange—slomotion, Capt Douglas, SaltyMonkey—found no reason to dispute that estimate.

Sailing around the world alone was not accomplished until 1898 and re-mained a rare feat for decades thereafter. But now it is a common, albeit an extreme, sporting event. The nonstop, single-handed Vendée Globe sailboat race, known as the Everest of the seas, is held every four years. It began in 1989 with thirteen competitors, seven of them finishing the circumnaviga-tion, the winner doing it in 109 days, 8 hours, 48 minutes, and 50 seconds. Twenty sailors entered the 2012 edition, with eleven crossing the finish line, the winner completing the trip in a record 78 days, 2 hours, 16 minutes, and 40 seconds. The largest Vendée Globe ever, with thirty skippers entered to race, finished in 2017. In January 2019, skipper Jean-Luc Van Den Heede, seventy-three years old, won the associated Golden Globe race in 212 days, the first of only five finishers out of the eighteen who began the stormy circumnaviga-tion. The last competitor completed the race in late June, 2019, nearly a year after starting the race.

For many people, the best reason to embark on a boat is to jump off it with a bathing suit, mask, and snorkel, or a wetsuit and scuba tanks, to marvel at underwater sights like coral reefs and shipwrecks. The Diving Equipment and Marketing Association website estimates that there are 2.7 to 3.5 million active scuba divers in the United States, and perhaps as many as 6 million in the world. The same organization pegs the number of American snorkelers at about 11 million, with approximately 20 million worldwide.

But the original saltwater sport was surfing, which is more popular now than ever. The International Surfing Association calculates that 1,736,000 Americans surf at least once a year and estimates the global population of board riders to number 20 million people. Surfing, then, is the fitting first subject for the following selections on Ocean recreation.

Surfing: A Royal Sport

Jack London

Swimming has to be the most ancient form of recreation on the water, but surfing may be a close second. Surfing was unknown outside of the South Pacific islands until the voyages of Captain James Cook, when the argonaut Englishmen observed the practice during their visits to various islands. Joseph Banks (1743–1820), the great naturalist who accompanied Cook on his first voyage, recorded the first written description of surfing in 1769, when he watched the local people in Matavai, Tahiti, enjoying themselves that way. Cook left an account of the sport in his journal upon his return to Tahiti in 1777, and his talented artist, John Weber, drew the first sketch of a surfboard and wrote the first report of Hawaiian surfing when Cook reached what he named the Sandwich Islands in 1778.

Mark Twain tried disastrously to surf in Hawai‘i in 1866 and wrote about the experience hilariously in Roughing It *(1872), but surfing remained mainly obscure until Jack London (1876–1916) sailed to Hawai‘i, tried out a surfboard, and sang its praises in writing after his return to the United States. London became famous for what specialists in his work call "the dog books," set during the 1898 Yukon gold rush, which he experienced himself, including* The Call of the Wild *(1903) and* White Fang *(1906). But he also wrote Ocean literature, especially* The Sea Wolf *(1904), based on his experience on a seal-hunting expedition in the North Pacific. The maritime writings of the adventure-seeking London include his nonfiction account of a transpacific voyage he made with his wife, Charmian, and a few others in 1907, titled* The Cruise of the Snark *(1911). London himself built the Snark, a 45-foot single-masted sailboat, which he navigated from San Francisco to Australia, visiting Hawai‘i en route. During his stay there, London saw Hawaiian islanders surfing, which he wrote about in the chapter titled "A Royal Sport," the beginning of which follows here. The rest of the chapter describes his attempts to master the art of surfing himself, with some success, but at the cost of debilitating sunburn. Upon his return to California, London published a version of the chapter in a magazine, first popularizing the sport of surfing in the United States, where millions of beachgoers have avidly practiced it in the century since.*

That is what it is, a royal sport for the natural kings of earth. The grass grows right down to the water at Waikiki Beach, and within fifty feet of the ever-

The first recreational activity that humans sought in saltwater probably was not swimming, but simply wading and lolling around in the shallows. The couples in this 1903 postcard, captioned "Oh, what bliss!," recline in the evening surf. Courtesy of the Roorda/Doyle Collection.

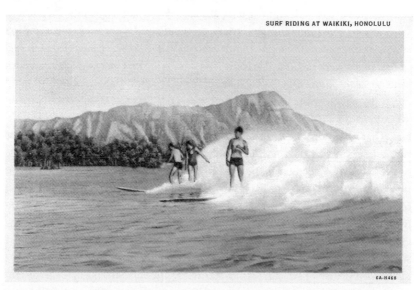

This image of a woman and two men surfing in Hawai'i dates to the 1930s, but it is an age-old scene. Hawaiians and other South Pacific Islanders have been riding boards in the breakers for centuries, if not millennia. *Surf Riding in Waikiki, Honolulu*, unused linen postcard, 1936. Courtesy of the Roorda/Doyle Collection.

lasting sea. The trees also grow down to the salty edge of things, and one sits in their shade and looks seaward at a majestic surf thundering in on the beach to one's very feet. Half a mile out, where is the reef, the white-headed combers thrust suddenly skyward out of the placid turquoise-blue and come rolling in to shore. One after another they come, a mile long, with smoking crests, the white battalions of the infinite army of the sea. And one sits and listens to the perpetual roar, and watches the unending procession, and feels tiny and fragile before this tremendous force expressing itself in fury and foam and sound. Indeed, one feels microscopically small, and the thought that one may wrestle with this sea raises in one's imagination a thrill of apprehension, almost of fear. Why, they are a mile long, these bull-mouthed monsters, and they weigh a thousand tons, and they charge in to shore faster than a man can run. What chance? No chance at all, is the verdict of the shrinking ego; and one sits, and looks, and listens, and thinks the grass and the shade are a pretty good place in which to be.

And suddenly, out there where a big smoker lifts skyward, rising like a sea-god from out of the welter of spume and churning white, on the giddy, toppling, overhanging and downfalling, precarious crest appears the dark head of a man. Swiftly he rises through the rushing white. His black shoulders, his chest, his loins, his limbs—all is abruptly projected on one's vision. Where but the moment before was only the wide desolation and invincible roar, is now a man, erect, full-statured, not struggling frantically in that wild movement, not buried and crushed and buffeted by those mighty monsters, but standing above them all, calm and superb, poised on the giddy summit, his feet buried in the churning foam, the salt smoke rising to his knees, and all the rest of him in the free air and flashing sunlight, and he is flying through the air, flying forward, flying fast as the surge on which he stands. He is a Mercury—a brown Mercury. His heels are winged, and in them is the swiftness of the sea. In truth, from out of the sea he has leaped upon the back of the sea, and he is riding the sea that roars and bellows and cannot shake him from its back. But no frantic outreaching and balancing is his. He is impassive, motionless as a statue carved suddenly by some miracle out of the sea's depth from which he rose. And straight on toward shore he flies on his winged heels and the white crest of the breaker. There is a wild burst of foam, a long tumultuous rushing sound as the breaker falls futile and spent on the beach at your feet; and there, at your feet steps calmly ashore a Kanaka, burnt, golden and brown by the tropic sun. Several minutes ago he was a speck a quarter of a mile away. He has "bitted the bull-mouthed breaker" and ridden it in, and the pride in the feat shows in the carriage of his magnificent body as he glances for a moment carelessly at you who sit in the shade of the shore. He is a Kanaka—and more, he is a man, a member of the kingly species that has mastered matter and the brutes and lorded it over creation.

And one sits and thinks of Tristram's last wrestle with the sea on that fatal morning; and one thinks further, to the fact that that Kanaka has done what Tristram never did, and that he knows a joy of the sea that Tristram never knew. And still further one thinks. It is all very well, sitting here in cool shade of the beach, but you are a man, one of the kingly species, and what that Kanaka can do, you can do yourself. Go to. Strip off your clothes that are a nuisance in this mellow clime. Get in and wrestle with the sea; wing your heels with the skill and power that reside in you; bite the sea's breakers, master them, and ride upon their backs as a king should.

And that is how it came about that I tackled surf-riding.

By the Sea, by the Sea . . .

Harold R. Atteridge

Bathers in the shallow inshore waters of the Ocean often wade out as far as they can, drawn by the horizon in one direction and fascinated by the view back on the increasingly distant beach. The women in this image have come for vacation to the coastal resort complex, a bathing club, on the North Sea island of Norderney.

Bathing or beach clubs became a global phenomenon around the turn of the twentieth century. Their architecture was often palatial or fortress-like. Club amenities varied by their location; for instance, bathing clubs in Havana had shark-proof sea fencing, while those on the North Sea had cabanas on wheels that could be hauled to a sheltered area when storms descended.

The titles of hit songs during the heyday of sheet music reflect the impulse to find fun in the Ocean. A few examples are "Bobbin' Up and Down" (1913), "Sit Down! You're Rocking the Boat" (1914), and the most famous and enduring of them all, "By the Beautiful Sea" (1914). In that song, Harold R. Atteridge's lyrics describe how Joe and Jane loved to drive in his Ford to the beach and cavort in the surf:

> Joe and Jane were always together,
> Said Joe to Jane "I love Summer weather,
> So let's go to the beautiful sea,
> Follow along, say you're with me!"

> By the sea, by the sea, by the beautiful sea,
> You and I, you and I, oh! how happy we'll be.
> When each wave comes a-rolling in,
> We will duck or swim.
> And we'll float and fool around the water,
> Over and under, and then up for air—[1]

The sheet music for Harry Carroll's catchy tune had a colorful cover closely resembling the image here. It features a dozen young women in dress-like Victorian bathing suits and stockings, dancing in the saltwater shallows, while one of them strums a stringed instrument. Distant buoys indicate the lifeguarded swimming area, but two ladies have swum beyond it, toward the horizon, where two sailboats heel over in the breeze.

The women here have come for vacation to the coastal resort complex on the North Sea island of Nordenay. Robert Bong, *Szene von Damenbadestrand in Norderney* [Scene of the ladies' bathing beach in Norderney], engraving from *Moderne Kunst* (Berlin: Richard Bong, 1905). Courtesy of the Roorda/Doyle Collection.

Note

1. Harold R. Atteridge, "By the Beautiful Sea" (New York: Shapiro, Bernstein and Co., 1914).

The Compleat Angler

Izaak Walton

Unlike fishing for sustenance and as a livelihood, fishing for recreation is an entirely different pursuit. Leisurely angling has been a contemplative and engaging pastime for centuries. The verb "to angle" derives from the German noun Angel, meaning a fishing pole and line, and originated in the 1400s. Izaak Walton (1594–1683), an English ironmonger, extolled the joys of fishing for pleasure in his classic book The Compleat Angler, or The Contemplative Man's Recreation. Walton became intellectually and spiritually engrossed in the pastoral pursuit of fish, and in 1644, nearing the age of fifty, he retired from the iron business and devoted the last four decades of his life to fishing. He practiced different kinds of fishing, discussed fishing with educated people all around England, and, most of all, wrote about fishing. Walton first published The Compleat Angler in 1653, and he continued adding to it over the years, while also writing poetry and a series of biographies, with expanded editions coming out in 1655, 1661, 1668, and finally 1676. Although the treatise was not the first on the subject—The Secrets of Angling by John Dennys, which Walton quoted, preceded it by more than forty years—it became the best-known work on recreational fishing.

"Angling" generally pertains to fishing in rivers and streams, and Walton devoted most of his book to those environments, making his preference clear in "The Angler's Song":

> I care not, I, to fish in seas,
> Fresh rivers best my mind do please,
> Whose sweet calm course I contemplate,
> And seek in life to imitate:
> In civil bounds I fain would keep,
> And for my past offences weep.

But in the twenty-first century, deep-sea fishing, also called sport fishing and big-game fishing, is one of the largest sectors of what has become an industry based on recreational fishing. Deep-sea fishing takes anglers up to 100 miles from the "sweet calm" of inland waters and employs large, powerful boats, in the range of 35–40 feet, equipped with heavy-duty gear and tackle, capable of reeling in tarpon, swordfish, and other trophy species weighing many hundreds of pounds. With scores of manufac-

turers of Ocean-going fishing boats and everything that goes aboard them, and thou-
sands of fishing charter operations clustered at seaside tourism destinations around
the world, deep-sea angling has become an industry in its own right.

In this passage from the outset of the book, Walton evoked the diversity of animal
species in the Ocean, with the humorous absurdity that makes his writing amusing to
read, then cited religious, historical, literary, and legal justifications for fishing, with
his characteristic erudition.

And as concerning fish, in that psalm, wherein, for height of poetry and wonders, the prophet David seems even to exceed himself, how doth he there ex-
press himself in choice metaphors, even to the amazement of a contemplative
reader, concerning the sea, the rivers, and the fish therein contained![1] And
the great naturalist Pliny says, "That nature's great and wonderful power is
more demonstrated in the sea than on the land." And this may appear, by the
numerous and various creatures inhabiting both in and about that element;
as to the readers of Gesner, Rondeletius, Pliny, Ausonius, Aristotle, and others, may be demonstrated.[2] But I will sweeten this discourse also out of a
contemplation in divine Du Bartas, who says:[3]

> God quickened in the sea, and in the rivers,
> So many fishes of so many features,
> That in the waters we may see all creatures,
> Even all that on the earth are to be found,
> As if the world were in deep waters drown'd.
> For seas—as well as skies—have Sun, Moon, Stars
> As well as air—Swallows, Rooks, and Stares;
> As well as earth—Vines, Roses, Nettles, Melons,
> Mushrooms, Pinks, Gilliflowers, and many millions
> Of other plants, more rare, more strange than these,
> As very fishes, living in the seas;
> As also Rams, Calves, Horses, Hares, and Hogs,
> Wolves, Urchins, Lions, Elephants, and Dogs;
> Yea, Men and Maids, and, which I most admire,
> The mitred Bishop and the cowled Friar:
> Of which, examples, but a few years since,
> Were shown the Norway and Polonian prince.

These seem to be wonders; but have had so many confirmations from men
of learning and credit, that you need not doubt them. Nor are the number,
nor the various shapes, of fishes more strange, or more fit for contemplation,
than their different natures, inclinations, and actions; concerning which, I
shall beg your patient ear a little longer.

The Cuttle-fish will cast a long gut out of her throat, which, like as an
Angler doth his line, she sendeth forth, and pulleth in again at her pleasure,

Deep-sea fishing was the rage in Florida in the 1920s, when the coastal tourism industry developed. These 1922 photographs promise "paradise for fishermen." *Finny Fighters That Test the Skill of Anglers* shows a charter boat captain and three fishermen posing with their "array of captured sailfish, groupers, amber-jacks and mackerel at Long Key." Below are "big tarpon, or silver king, regarded by anglers as the finest American game fishes," because "they fight furiously when hooked, with all the frenzy of the wild horse when he first feels the lasso." Photographs courtesy of Hamilton Wright and *Forest and Stream* (photographer unknown), previously published in the *New York Times*, 1923. Courtesy of the Roorda/Doyle Collection.

according as she sees some little fish come near to her; and the Cuttle-fish, being then hid in the gravel, lets the smaller fish nibble and bite the end of it; at which time she, by little and little, draws the smaller fish so near to her, that she may leap upon her, and then catches and devours her: and for this reason some have called this fish the Sea-angler.

And there is a fish called a Hermit, that at a certain age gets into a dead fish's shell, and, like a hermit, dwells there alone, studying the wind and weather and so turns her shell, that she makes it defend her from the injuries that they would bring upon her.

There is also a fish called by Ælian the Adonis, or Darling of the Sea; so called, because it is a loving and innocent fish, a fish that hurts nothing that hath life, and is at peace with all the numerous inhabitants of that vast watery element; and truly, I think most Anglers are so disposed to most of mankind. . . .[4]

And for the lawfulness of fishing: it may very well be maintained by our Saviour's bidding St. Peter cast his hook into the water and catch a fish, for money to pay tribute to Caesar. And let me tell you, that Angling is of high esteem, and of much use in other nations. He that reads the Voyages of Ferdinand Mendez Pinto, shall find that there he declares to have found a king and several priests a-fishing.[5] And he that reads Plutarch, shall find, that Angling was not contemptible in the days of Mark Antony and Cleopatra, and that they, in the midst of their wonderful glory, used Angling as a principal recreation.[6] And let me tell you, that in the Scripture, Angling is always taken in the best sense; and that though hunting may be sometimes so taken, yet it is but seldom to be so understood. And let me add this more: he that views the ancient Ecclesiastical Canons, shall find hunting to be forbidden to Churchmen, as being a turbulent, toilsome, perplexing recreation; and shall find Angling allowed to clergymen, as being a harmless recreation, a recreation that invites them to contemplation and quietness.

Notes

1. Psalm 107 of the Bible's Old Testament.
2. Pliny the Elder (23–79) was a Roman naval officer and naturalist who composed an encyclopedia, *Naturalis Historia* (Natural history), which includes a section on the Ocean that is excerpted later in this volume. Conrad Gesner (1516–65) was a Swiss naturalist and physician who wrote the first work of zoology, *Historiae animalium*, published in five volumes between 1551 and 1558. Rondeletius, or Guillaume Rondelet (1507–56), was a French naturalist and professor of medicine who wrote an exhaustive study of marine animals, *Libri de piscibus marinis* (Book of Ocean fish), published in Latin in 1554, and in French in 1558 with the title *L'histoire entière des poissons* (The complete history of fish), which remained the standard work on the subject for two centuries. Decimus Magnus Ausonius (310–395) was a Roman poet whose best-known work is a paean to the Moselle River; Aristotle (384–322 BCE),

the great Greek philosopher, described some 117 species in compiling the first taxonomy of fish and differentiated fish from marine mammals.

3. Guillaume de Salluste Du Bartas (1544–90), a French Huguenot from Gascony, was a poet and physician in the court of King Henri de Navarre, whose verse was well known across Europe in the late sixteenth and seventeenth centuries.

4. Ælian, or Claudius Aelianus (175–235), was a Roman author and teacher who compiled the seventeen-volume *De natura animalium* (On the characteristics of animals).

5. Ferdinand Mendez Pinto, or Fernão Mendes Pinto (1509–83), was a Portuguese explorer who recorded his travels in his 1614 memoir, *Peregrinação* (Peregrination).

6. Plutarch (46–120) was a Greek author who wrote on a wide variety of subjects, including *De sollertia animalium* (On the cleverness of animals), which addresses fish.

Women and Children Next:
The Family Goes to Sea

Anna Brassey

A once-famous travel writer who is now virtually forgotten, Lady Anna Brassey (1839–87) was the rare nineteenth-century woman who took to the Ocean for fun, sailing wherever her whims dictated aboard elegant yachts. In 1860, Anna Allnutt married Thomas Brassey, a member of Parliament from Hastings, England, who later became an earl, making Anna a baroness. The couple went to sea in 1869 with their three children: six, four, and barely one year old. They sailed from England to Gibraltar and toured the Mediterranean Sea aboard the yacht Meteor, *which Anna wrote about in her first book,* The Flight of the "Meteor" *(1869). The Brasseys crossed the North Atlantic Ocean in the yacht* Eothen *in 1872, which Anna chronicled in* A Cruise in the "Eothen" *(1872). They became even more ambitious in 1876, when they undertook the first circumnavigation of the world in a private yacht, with their children, who ranged in age from Allnutt at thirteen years to Marie ("Baby") at sixteen months.*

They embarked in their new yacht, Sunbeam, *a three-masted topsail schooner with a steam engine, a white hull 159 feet long, 9,000 square feet of sail, and a crew of thirty-five, including officers, sailors, cooks, stewards, maids, and a doctor. The trip took eleven months. Anna Brassey kept a diary about all of it, which she published in 1878 as a nearly 500-page book titled* A Voyage in the Yacht "Sunbeam," Our Home on the Ocean for Eleven Months, *which quickly became a best-seller, going through several editions in English and translation into five other languages. The book made Lady Brassey an international celebrity. She followed with other well-received travelogues, such as* In the Trades, the Tropics, and the Roaring Forties: 14,000 Miles in the "Sunbeam" *in 1883. She died at the height of her fame, succumbing to malaria aboard her beloved* Sunbeam *en route to Mauritius in 1887, and was buried at sea in the Indian Ocean. Her final publication,* The Last Voyage, to India and Australia, of the "Sunbeam," *appeared posthumously. Seventy volumes of her photographs are in the collection of the Huntington Library in California, and the figurehead of her* Sunbeam *is exhibited at the National Maritime Museum in Greenwich.*

We were forty-three on board, all told. . . . We had with us, besides, two dogs, three birds, and a charming Persian kitten belonging to the baby. The kitten soon disappeared, and it was feared she must have gone overboard down the hawse pipe. . . .

[*Saturday, July 8th.*]—About ten o'clock we got under way, but lay-to for breakfast. We then had a regular beat of it down Channel—everybody being ill. We formed a melancholy-looking little row down the lee side of the ship, though I must say that we were quite as cheery as might have been expected under the circumstances. It was bright and sunny overhead, which made things more bearable. . . .

[*Monday, July 10th.*]—The thirty extra tons of spare sails, spars, and provisions, the fifteen tons of water, and the eighty-four tons of coal, made a great difference in our buoyancy, and the sea came popping in and out at the most unexpected places; much to the delight of the children, who, with bare feet and legs, and armed with mops and sponges, waged mimic war against the intruder and against each other, singing and dancing to their hearts' content. This amusement was occasionally interrupted by a heavier roll than usual, sending them all into the lee scuppers, sousing them from head to foot, and necessitating a thorough change of clothing, despite their urgent protest that seawater never hurt anybody.

After our five o'clock dinner, however, we very nearly met with a most serious accident. We were all sitting or standing about the stern of the vessel, admiring the magnificent dark blue billows following us, with their curling white crests, mountains high. Each wave, as it approached, appeared as if it must overwhelm us, instead of which, it rushed grandly by, rolling and shaking us from stem to stern, and sending fountains of spray on board. Tom was looking at the stern compass, Allnutt being close to him. Mr. Bingham and Mr. Freer were smoking, half-way between the quarter-deck and the after-companion, where Captain Brown, Dr. Potter, Muriel, and I, were standing. Captain Lecky, seated on a large coil of rope, placed on the box of the rudder, was spinning Mabelle a yarn. A new hand was steering, and just at the moment when an unusually big wave overtook us, he unfortunately allowed the vessel to broach-to a little. In a second the sea came pouring over the stern, above Allnutt's head. The boy was nearly washed overboard, but he managed to catch hold of the rail, and, with great presence of mind, stuck his knees into the bulwarks. Kindred, our boatswain, seeing his danger, rushed forward to save him, but was knocked down by the return wave, from which he emerged gasping. The coil of the rope on which Captain Lecky and Mabelle were seated was completely floated by the sea. Providentially, however, he had taken a double turn round his wrist with a reefing point, and, throwing his other arm round Mabelle, held on like grim death; otherwise nothing could have saved them. She was perfectly self-possessed, and only said quietly, "Hold on, Captain Lecky, hold on!" to which he replied, "All right."

The Brassey family's circumnavigation of the world by sail in 1876–77 almost ended horribly before it had begun, when "an unusually big wave" surprised them, sweeping the deck, taking two of their children nearly overboard. Illustration based on a drawing by A. Y. Bingham, in Lady [Anna] Brassey, *A Voyage in the Yacht "Sunbeam": Our Home on the Ocean for Eleven Months* (Chicago: J. W. Henry, 1890), 5. Courtesy of the Roorda/Doyle Collection.

I asked her afterwards if she thought she was going overboard, and she answered, "I did not think at all, mamma, but felt sure we were gone." Captain Lecky, being accustomed to very large ships, had not in the least realized how near we were to the water in our little vessel, and was proportionately taken by surprise. All the rest of the party were drenched, with the exception of Muriel, whom Captain Brown held high above the water in his arms, and who lost no time in remarking in the midst of the general confusion, "I'm not at all wet, I'm not." Happily, the children don't know what fear is. The maids, however, were very frightened, as some of the sea had got down into the nursery, and the skylights had to be screwed down. Our studding-sail boom, too, broke with a loud crack when the ship broached-to, and the jaws of the fore-boom gave way.

Soon after this adventure we all went to bed, full of thankfulness that it had ended as well as it did; but, alas! Not, so far as I was concerned, to rest in peace. In about two hours I was awakened by a tremendous weight of water suddenly descending upon me and flooding the bed. I immediately sprang out, only to find myself in another pool on the floor. It was pitch dark, and I could not think what had happened; so I rushed on deck, and found that, the weather having moderated a little, some kind sailor, knowing my love of fresh air, had opened the skylight rather too soon; and one of the angry waves had popped on board, deluging the cabin. . . .

Tuesday, August 8th.—We crossed the line [equator] at daylight.

This event caused much fun and excitement, both in cabin and forecastle. The conventional hair was put across the field of the telescope for the unsophisticated "really to see the line," and many firmly believed they did see it, and discussed its appearance at some length. Jim Allen, one of our tallest sailors, and coxswain of the gig, dressed in blue, with long oakum wig and beard, gilt paper crown and trident, and fish impaled in one hand, was seated on a gun-carriage, and made a capital Father Neptune. Our somewhat portly engineer, Mr. Rowbotham, with fur-trimmed dressing-gown and cap, and bent form, leaning on a stick, his face partially concealed by a long gray beard, and a large bandbox of pills on one arm, made an equally good doctor to his Marine Majesty, while the part of Mrs. Trident was ably filled by one of the youngest sailors, dressed in some of the maids' clothes.

Soon afterwards we saw an enormous shoal of grampuses, large black fish, about 25 feet in length, something between a dolphin and a whale, with the very ugliest jaws, or rather snouts, imaginable. They are of a predatory and ferocious disposition, attacking not only sharks, dolphins, and porpoises, but even whales, more than twice their own size. We also passed through enormous quantities of flying fish, no doubt driven to the surface by dolphins and bonitos. They were much larger and stronger in the wing than any we have hitherto seen.

Lulu's puppies, born yesterday, have been respectively named Butterfly (who survived her birth only an hour), Poseidon, Aphrodite, Amphitrite, and Thetis—names suggested by their birthplace on the ocean close to his Marine Majesty's supposed equatorial palace. . . .

Sunday, August 13th.—Sailing in the tropics is really very delightful! When going to the westward, there is almost always, at this season of the year, a favorable breeze, and the weather is generally either quite fair or moderately so. . . .

The wind dropped at about 10 P.M., and we had an unpleasant amount of roll during the night, sails flapping, spars creaking, and booms swinging as if they would pull the masts out of the vessel.

Monday, August 14th.—This morning we saw a small schooner ahead, and thinking from her maneuvers that she wished to speak us, we made our number and ran towards her. We soon found out, however, that she was a whaler, in chase of two large grampuses. She had two men on the lookout in the cross-trees, in a sort of iron cage; and though she was of much smaller

For centuries, sailors have made much of the moment they crossed the equator (called the Line) for the first time. Any first-timers, or "Slimy Pollywogs," were made to assemble as the equator approached. At the moment of crossing, cross-dressing crewmembers appeared, costumed as King Neptune (Roman god of the Ocean), Her Highness Amphitrite (wife of Poseidon, Greek god of the Ocean), and their court of mermaids. "Wogs" were roughly shaved, covered with tar and spoiled food, and made to kiss a dead fish. The initiates were baptized, sometimes overboard. On cruise ships today, jello and whipped cream take the place of tar, and the swimming pool is the baptismal font, but the fish-kissing remains. Afterward, they are referred to as "Honorable Shellbacks." Seaman Earl "Dutch" Baldwin snapped these photographs, which he titled *Crossing the Equator Ceremony,* USS *Seattle,* in 1925. From the Earl "Dutch" Baldwin Photograph Albums. Courtesy of the Roorda/Doyle Collection.

tonnage than the *Sunbeam*, she carried five big boats, one of which, full of men, was ready to be lowered into the water the instant they had approached sufficiently near the whale or grampus. The seas used formerly to abound with whalers, but they are now much less numerous, the seasons having been bad of late. . . .

Tuesday, October 10th.—In the early morning, when we resumed our voyage, the weather was still fine; but a few light clouds were here and there visible, and an icy wind, sweeping down from the mountains, made it appear very cold, though the thermometer—which averages, I think, 40° to 50° all the year round—was not really low. The line of perpetual snow commences here at an elevation of from 2,500 to 3,500 feet only, which adds greatly to the beauty of the scene; and as it is now early spring the snow is still unmelted 500 feet, and even less, from the shore. The stupendous glaciers run right down into the sea, and immense masses of ice, sometimes larger than the ship, are continually breaking off, with a noise like thunder, and falling into the water, sending huge waves across to the opposite shore, and sometimes completely blocking up the channels. Some of these glaciers, composed entirely of blue and green ice and the purest snow, are fifteen and twenty miles in length. They are by far the finest we have, any of us, ever seen; and even those of Norway and Switzerland sink into comparative insignificance beside them. The mountains here are not so high as those of Europe, but they really appear more lofty, as their entire surface, from the water's edge to the extreme summit, is clearly visible. At this end of the Straits [of Magellan] they terminate in peaks, resembling Gothic spires, carved in the purest snow; truly "virgin peaks," on which the eye of man has but seldom rested, and which his foot has never touched. They are generally veiled in clouds of snow, mist, and driving rain, and it is quite the exception to see them as distinctly as we now do. . . .

The numerous floating icebergs added greatly to the exquisite beauty of the scene. Some loomed high as mountains, while others had melted into the most fanciful and fairy-like shapes—huge swans, full-rigged ships, schooners under full sail, and a hundred other fantastic forms and devices. The children were in ecstasies at the sight of them. . . .

Wednesday, November 15th.—Pleasant as we have found life at sea in the South Pacific hitherto, it is, I fear, monotonous to read about, and I dare say you will find it difficult to realize how quickly the days fly past, and how sorry we are when each one comes to an end. I am afraid they are among those things which do not repeat themselves. At any rate, they afford a golden opportunity for reading, such as we are not likely to have again often, if ever, in our busy lives; and Tom and I are endeavoring to make the best use of it by getting through as many of the seven hundred volumes we brought with us as possible.

Saturday, November 18th.—The days are so much alike that it is difficult to find anything special to say about them. They fly so quickly that I was surprised to be reminded by the usual singing-practice this afternoon that another week had gone by. . . .

Thursday, November 23rd.—After lunch, Tom had me hoisted up to the foretop-masthead in a "boatswain's chair," which is simply a small plank, suspended by ropes at the four corners, and used by the men to sit on when they scrape the masts. I was very carefully secured with a rope tied round my petticoats, and, knocking against the various ropes on my way, was then gently hoisted up to what seemed at first a giddy height; but when I once got accustomed to the smallness of the seat, the airiness of my perch, and the increased roll of the vessel, I found my position by no means an unpleasant one. Tom climbed up the rigging and joined me shortly afterwards. From our elevated post we could see plainly the formation of the island, and the lagune [lagoon] in the center, encircled by a band of coral, in some places white, bare, and narrow, in others wide and covered with palm-trees and rich vegetation;[1] it was moreover possible to understand better the theory of the formation of these coral islands. I was so happy up aloft that I did not care to descend; and it was almost as interesting to observe what a strange and disproportioned appearance everything and everybody on board the yacht presented from my novel position, as it was to examine the island we were passing. The two younger children and the dogs took the greatest interest in my aërial expedition, and never ceased calling to me and barking, until I was once more let down safely into their midst. . . .

Friday, December 22nd.—At 6:30 A.M. we made the island of Hawaii, rather too much to leeward, as we had been carried by the strong current at least eighteen miles out of our course. We were therefore obliged to beat up to windward, in the course of which operation we passed a large bark running before the wind—the first ship we had seen since leaving Tahiti—and also a fine whale, blowing close to us. . . .

It was a clear afternoon. The mountains, Mauna Kea and Mauna Loa, could be plainly seen from top to bottom, their giant crests rising nearly 14,000 feet above our heads, their tree and fern clad slopes seamed with deep gulches or ravines, down each of which a fertilizing river ran into the sea. Inside the reef, the white coral shore, on which the waves seemed too lazy to break, is fringed with a belt of coconut palms, amongst which, as well as on the hill-sides, the little white houses are prettily dotted. All are surrounded by gardens, so full of flowers that the bright patches of color were plainly visible even from the deck of the yacht. . . .

Sunday, January 14th.—I was on deck at 4 A.M. The Southern Cross, the Great Bear, and the North Star were shining with a brilliancy that eclipsed all the other stars.

During the day the wind freshened to a squally gale. Sometimes we were going ten, sometimes thirteen, and sometimes fifteen knots through the water, knocking about a good deal all the while. Service was an impossibility; cooking and eating, indeed, were matters of difficulty. It rained heavily and the seas came over the deck continually. . . .

Monday, January 15th.—I woke once or twice in the night, and felt exactly as if I were being pulled backwards through the water by my hair. We were rushing and tearing along at such a pace, against a head-sea, that it almost took one's breath away. But at noon, we were rewarded for all discomfort by finding that we had run 298 sea, or 343 land miles, in 24 hours, and that between 8:14 yesterday and 8:15 to-day we had made 302 knots, or 347 land miles—nearly 350 miles in the 24 hours—under very snug canvas, and through a heavy sea. The wind still continued fair and fresh, but the sea was much quieter, and we all felt comparatively comfortable. More sails were set during the afternoon. Some albatrosses and long-tailed tropic birds were seen hovering about us. The moon begins to give a good light now, and we found it very pleasant on deck this evening.

Wednesday, January 17th.—It was a fine warm morning, and we got the children on deck for the first time for ten days. . . .

Sunday, January 28th.—It is finer, but bitterly cold. Several of my tropical birds are already dead. The little pig from Harpe Island, and the Hawaiian geese, look very wretched, in spite of all my precautions. . . .

The decks were very slippery, and as we kept rolling about a good deal there were some nasty falls among the passengers. We had a splendid though stormy sunset, which did not belie its promise, for the wind shortly afterwards became stiffer and stronger, until at last we had two reefs down, and were tumbling about in all directions, as we rushed through the water. The dining-tables tilted till they could go no further, and then paused to go back again; but not quickly enough, for the glasses began to walk up-hill and go over the edge in the most extraordinary manner. On deck the night looked brilliant but rather terrible. The full moon made it as light as day, and illuminated the fountains of spray blown from the waves by which we were surrounded. Without her heavy jibboom, and with her canvas well reefed down, the *Sunbeam* rode through it all, dipping her head into the sea, shivering from stem to stern, and then giving herself a shake, preparatory to a fresh start, just like a playful water-bird emerging from a prolonged dive.

At midnight a tremendous sea struck her, and for a minute you could not see the yacht at all, as she was completely enveloped in spray and foam. Tom said it was just like being behind the falls of Niagara, with the water coming over you from every quarter at once. It was only loose stuff, however, for not a green sea did she take on board the whole night through. Our old engineer, who has been with us for so long, made up his mind that we struck on a rock, and woke up all the servants and told them to go on deck. I never felt anything like it before, and the shock sent half of us out of our beds.

Thursday, February 15th.—I wonder if anybody who has not experienced it can realize the stupefying, helpless sensation of being roused up from a sound sleep, in the middle of the night, on board ship, by the cry of "Fire!" and finding one's self enveloped in a smoke so dense as to render everything invisible.

At 2.30 A.M. I was awakened by a great noise and loud cry of "The ship is on fire!" followed by Mr. Bingham rushing into our cabin to arouse us. At first I could hardly realize where we were, or what was happening, as I was half stupid with chloral, pain, and smoke, which was issuing from each side of the staircase in dense volumes. My first thought was for the children, but I found they had not been forgotten. Rolled up in blankets, they were already in transit to the deck-house. In the meantime Mr. Bingham had drenched the flames with every available jug of water, and Tom had roused the crew, and made them screw the hose on to the pump. They were afraid to open the hatches, to discover where the fire was, until the hose and *extincteurs* were ready to work, as they did not know whether or not the hold was on fire, and the whole ship might burst into a blaze the moment the air was admitted. Allen soon appeared with an *extincteur* on his back, and the mate with the hose. Then the cupboard in Mr. Bingham's room was opened, and burning cloaks, dresses, boxes of curios, portmanteaus, &c., were hauled out, and, by a chain of men, sent on deck, where they were drenched with seawater or thrown overboard. Moving these things caused the flames to increase in vigor, and the *extincteur* was used freely, and with the greatest success. It is an invaluable invention, especially for a yacht, where there are so many holes and corners which it would be impossible to reach by ordinary means. All this time the smoke was pouring in volumes from the cupboard on the other side, and from under the nursery fireplace. The floors were pulled up, and the partitions were pulled down, until at last the flames were got under. The holds were next examined. No damage had been done there; but the cabin floor was completely burned through, and the lead from the nursery fireplace was running about, melted by the heat.

The explanation of the cause of the fire is very simple. Being a bitterly cold night, a roaring fire had been made up in the nursery, but about half-past ten the servants thought it looked rather dangerous and raked it out. The ashpan was not large enough, however, to hold the hot embers, which soon made the tiles red-hot. The woodwork caught fire, and had been smoldering for hours, when the nurse fortunately woke and discovered the state of affairs. She tried to rouse the other maids, but they were stupefied with the smoke, and so she rushed off at once to the doctor and Mr. Bingham. The former seized a child under each arm, wrapped them in blankets, and carried them off to the deck-house, Mabelle and the maids following, with more blankets and rugs, hastily snatched up. The children were as good as possible. They never cried nor made the least fuss, but composed themselves in the deck-house to sleep for the remainder of the night, as if it were all a matter if course. When I went to see them, little Muriel remarked, "If the yacht is on fire, mamma, had not Baby and I better get our ulsters, and go with Emma in the boat to the hotel, to be out of the way?" It is the third time in their short lives that they have been picked out of bed in the middle of the night and carried off in blankets away from a fire, so I suppose they are getting quite used to it. . . .

Friday, April 13th.—One of our large pigs took it into his head to jump overboard to-day. The helm was put round as quickly as possible, but the most anxious spying could not discover any trace of poor piggy's whereabouts; so we proceeded on our original course for a few minutes, when suddenly, to our great astonishment, we saw him alongside, having been nearly run down, but still gallantly swimming along. The dinghy was lowered and two men sent in pursuit. They had, however, no easy task before them, for as soon as they approached, piggy swam away faster than they could row, and bit and fought most furiously when they tried to get him into the boat. It was a good half-hour's work before he was secured, yet when he arrived he did not appear to be in the least exhausted by his long swim, but bit and barked at everybody so furiously that he was condemned to death, to prevent the possibility of further accidents. It is quite clear from the foregoing incident that some pigs can swim, and swim very well too, without cutting their own throats in the process. . . .

Sunday, April 22nd.— . . . The gale freshened, the screw was raised, the yacht pitched and rolled, and we were obliged to put her off her course and under sail before night fell. The spray came over the decks, and there was a strong wind dead ahead. We all felt cold and miserable, though the thermometer still registered 75°. The poor monkeys and parrots looked most wretched and unhappy, and had to be packed away as speedily as possible. Nine monkeys in an empty wine case seemed very happy and cuddled together for warmth, but the two larger and more aristocratic members of the party required a box to themselves. The gazelle had a little tent pitched for him specially in a sheltered corner, and the birds were all stowed away and battened over in the smoking fiddle. Dinner was rather a lame pretense, and it was not long before we all retired, and certainly no one wished to take his or her mattress on deck to-night. It is the first night I have slept in a bed on board the yacht for many weeks, and a very disturbed night it was, for the waves ran high, and we have lately been sailing so steadily over smooth seas, that we did not know what to make of this.

Tuesday, May 15th.—This was a somewhat sad day, many of our pets dying from the effects of the cold wind or from accidents. The steward's mockingbird from Siam, which talked like a Christian and followed him about like a dog, died of acute bronchitis early this morning; and his monkey, the most weird little creature, with the affectionate ways of a human friend, died in the afternoon, of inflammation and congestion of the lungs. Two other monkeys and several birds also expired in the course of the day.

This evening "Beau Brummel," the little pig I brought from Bow Island, in the South Pacific, died of a broken spine, as the doctor, who made a post-mortem examination in each case, discovered. A spar must have dropped upon poor piggy accidentally whilst he was running about on deck, though of course no one knew anything about it. I am very sorry; for though I must confess he was somewhat greedy and pig-like in his habits, he was extremely amusing in his ways. He ran about and went to sleep with the pugs, just like one of themselves. Besides, I do not think any one else in England could have boasted of a pig given to them by a South Sea Island chief. Probably "Beau Brummel" was a lineal descendant of the pigs Captain Cook took out in the "Endeavor."

The bodies were all placed together in a neat little box and committed to the deep at sunset, a few tears being shed over the departed pets, especially by the children. . . .

Wednesday, May 16th.—At 3 A.M. I was called to see the light on Europa Point, and staid on deck to watch the day dawn and the rising of the sun. It was not, however, a very agreeable morning; the Levanter was blowing, the signal station was enveloped in mist, the tops of the mountains of Africa were scarcely discernible above the clouds, and Ceuta and Ape's Hill [Mons Abylla] were invisible. Algeciras and San Roque gleamed white on the opposite shore of the bay, while the dear old Rock [of Gibraltar] itself looked fresher and cleaner than usual, exhaling a most delicious perfume of flowers. As the sun rose, the twittering of the birds in the Alameda sounded most homelike and delightful. . . .

Note

1. One of the coral atolls of the Tuamotu Archipelago of French Polynesia, near Tahiti.

The First Solo Circumnavigation

Joshua Slocum

The first person to undertake a solo circumnavigation of the world was Joshua Slocum (1844–1909), who had more than three decades of experience on the Ocean. Born in Nova Scotia, he went to sea at the age of sixteen, crossing the wild North Atlantic from Halifax to Dublin. Then he sailed to China by way of Cape Horn and spent the next twenty years in Pacific waters. He rose to be the captain of a series of square-rigged ships based in San Francisco, plying trade routes to Australia, Indonesia, and Japan, then became the owner and master of a 90-foot schooner, which he operated on the West Coast of North America and Hawai'i. His family often accompanied him, including on a voyage to New England around Cape Horn in 1884, and an 1887 trip to Brazil that ended in a shipwreck. Stranded with his wife and two of his sons, Slocum built a 35-foot vessel from pieces salvaged from the wrecked ship, which he termed a "canoe," and sailed it back to the United States, a distance of 5,500 miles, in fifty-five days. Approaching the age of fifty and finding jobs at sea difficult to get, Slocum spent a year rebuilding an old oyster sloop that a friend had given him, which had been sitting in a field for years, named Spray. *When he was finished, he tried his hand at commercial fishing, but he had no success during a season of baiting hooks. Soon, the urge to "get to sea in earnest" became overwhelming for the very salty Slocum, and he "resolved on a voyage around the world" simply for the diversion it would provide. That is, he challenged the Ocean for fun. He did so in the single-masted* Spray, *which was not quite 37 feet long and barely 14 feet wide. He embarked from Newport, Rhode Island, on April 24, 1895, logging the first of more than 46,000 miles. His cheerful account of his odyssey,* Sailing Alone around the World *(1900), offers many vignettes about the Ocean's perils, many of them mentioned in the excerpts chosen here, but also its allure, including Slocum's conclusion that the sea makes you young.*

My ship passed in safety Bahia Blanca [White Bay], also the Gulf of St. Matias and the mighty Gulf of St. George [all on the southern coast of Argentina]. Hoping that she might go clear of the destructive tide-races, the dread of big craft or little along this coast, I gave all the capes a berth of about fifty miles, for these dangers extend many miles from the land. But where the sloop avoided one danger she encountered another. For, one day, well off the Patagonian coast, while the sloop was reaching under short sail, a tremen-

403

dous wave, the culmination, it seemed, of many waves, rolled down upon her in a storm, roaring as it came. I had only a moment to get all sail down and myself up on the peak halliards, out of danger, when I saw the mighty crest towering masthead-high above me. The mountain of water submerged my vessel. She shook in every timber and reeled under the weight of the sea, but rose quickly out of it, and rode grandly over the rollers that followed. It may have been a minute that from my hold in the rigging I could see no part of the *Spray*'s hull. Perhaps it was even less time than that, but it seemed a long while, for under great excitement one lives fast, and in a few seconds one may think a great deal of one's past life. Not only did the past, with electric speed, flash before me, but I had time while in my hazardous position for resolutions for the future that would take a long time to fulfill. The first one was, I remember, that if the *Spray* came through this danger I would dedicate my best energies to building a larger ship on her lines, which I hope yet to do. Other promises, less easily kept, I should have made under protest. However, the incident, which filled me with fear, was only one more test of the *Spray*'s seaworthiness. It reassured me against rude Cape Horn.

From the time the great wave swept over the *Spray* until she reached Cape Virgins [on the north side of the entrance to the Strait of Magellan] nothing occurred to move a pulse and set blood in motion. On the contrary, the weather became fine and the sea smooth and life tranquil. The phenomenon of mirage frequently occurred. An albatross sitting on the water one day loomed up like a large ship; two fur-seals asleep on the surface of the sea appeared like great whales, and a bank of haze I could have sworn was high land. The kaleidescope then changed, and on the following day I sailed in a world peopled by dwarfs.

On February 11 the *Spray* rounded Cape Virgins and entered the Strait of Magellan. The scene was again real and gloomy; the wind, northeast, and blowing a gale, sent feather-white spume along the coast; such a sea ran as would swamp an ill-appointed ship. As the sloop neared the entrance to the strait I observed that two great tide-races made ahead, one very close to the point of the land and one farther offshore. Between the two, in a sort of channel, through combers, went the *Spray* with close-reefed sails. But a rolling sea followed her a long way in, and a fierce current swept around the cape against her; but this she stemmed, and was soon chirruping under the lee of Cape Virgins and running every minute into smoother water. However, long trailing kelp from sunken rocks waved forebodingly under her keel, and the wreck of a great steamship smashed on the beach abreast gave a gloomy aspect to the scene.

I was not to be let off easy. The Virgins would collect tribute even from the *Spray* passing their promontory. Fitful rain-squalls from the northwest followed the northeast gale. I reefed the sloop's sails, and sitting in the cabin to rest my eyes, I was so strongly impressed with what in all nature I might expect that as I dozed the very air I breathed seemed to warn me of danger. My senses heard *"Spray ahoy!"* shouted in warning. I sprang to the deck, wondering who could be there that knew the *Spray* so well as to call out her name passing in the dark; for it was now the blackest of nights all around, except away in the southwest, where the old familiar white arch, the terror of Cape Horn, rapidly pushed up by a southwest gale. I had only a moment to douse sail and lash all solid when it struck like a shot from a cannon, and for the first half-hour it was something to be remembered by way of a gale. For thirty hours it kept on blowing hard. The sloop could carry no more than a three-reefed mainsail and forestaysail; with these she held on stoutly and was not blown out of the strait. In the height of the squalls in this gale she doused all sail, and this occurred often enough.

After this gale followed only a smart breeze, and the *Spray*, passing through the narrows without mishap, cast anchor at Sandy Point on February 14, 1896. . . .[1]

To be alone forty-three days would seem a long time, but in reality, even here, winged moments flew lightly by, and instead of my hauling in for Nukahiva, which I could have made as well as not, I kept on for Samoa, where I wished to make my next landing. This occupied twenty-nine days more, making seventy-two days in all. I was not distressed in any way during that time. There was no end of companionship; the very coral reefs kept me company, or gave me no time to feel lonely, which is the same thing, and there were many of them now in my course to Samoa.

First among the incidents of the voyage from Juan Fernandez to Samoa (which were not many) was a narrow escape from collision with a great whale that was absent-mindedly plowing the ocean at night while I was below. The noise from his startled snort and the commotion he made in the sea, as he turned to clear my vessel, brought me on deck in time to catch a wetting from the water he threw up with his flukes. The monster was apparently frightened. He headed quickly for the east; I kept on going west. Soon another whale passed, evidently a companion, following in its wake. I saw no more on this part of the voyage, nor did I wish to.

Hungry sharks came about the vessel often when she neared islands or coral reefs. I own to a satisfaction in shooting them as one would a tiger. Sharks, after all, are the tigers of the sea. Nothing is more dreadful to the mind of a sailor, I think, than a possible encounter with a hungry shark. . . .

To the Keeling Cocos Islands was now only 550 miles; but even in this short run it was necessary to be extremely careful in keeping a true course else I would miss the atoll.[2]

On the 12th [of July, 1898], some hundred miles southwest of Christmas Island, I saw anti-trade clouds flying up from the southwest very high over the regular winds, which weakened now for a few days, while a swell heavier than usual set in also from the southwest. A winter gale was going on in the direction of the Cape of Good Hope. Accordingly, I steered higher to windward, allowing twenty miles a day while this went on, for change of current; and it was not too much, for on that course I made the Keeling Islands right ahead. The first unmistakable sign of the land was a visit one morning from a white tern that fluttered very knowingly about the vessel, and then took itself off westward with a businesslike air in its wing. The tern is called by the islanders the "pilot of Keeling Cocos." Farther on I came among a great number of birds fishing, and fighting over whatever they caught. My reckoning was up, and springing aloft, I saw from half-way up the mast cocoanut-trees standing out of the water ahead. I expected to see this; still, it thrilled me as an electric shock might have done. I slid down the mast, trembling under the strangest sensations; and not able to resist the impulse, I sat on deck and gave way to my emotions. To folks in a parlor on shore this may seem weak indeed, but I am telling the story of a voyage alone. . . .[3]

On May 18, 1898, is written large in the *Spray*'s log-book: "To-night, in latitude 7 degrees 13' N., for the first time in nearly three years I see the north star." The *Spray* on the day following logged one hundred and forty-seven miles. To this I add thirty-five miles for current sweeping her onward. On the 20th of May, about sunset, the island of Tobago, off the Orinoco, came into view, bearing west by north, distant twenty-two miles. The *Spray* was drawing rapidly toward her home destination. Later at night, while running free along the coast of Tobago, the wind still blowing fresh, I was startled by the sudden flash of breakers on the port bow and not far off. I luffed instantly offshore, and then tacked, heading in for the island. Finding myself, shortly after, close in with the land, I tacked again offshore, but without much altering the bearings of the danger. Sail whichever way I would, it seemed clear that if the sloop weathered the rocks at all it would be a close shave, and I watched with anxiety, while beating against the current, always losing ground. So the matter stood hour after hour, while I watched the flashes of light thrown up as regularly as the beats of the long ocean swells, and always they seemed just a little nearer. It was evidently a coral reef—of this I had not the slightest doubt—and a bad reef at that. Worse still, there might be other reefs ahead forming a bight into which the current would sweep me, and where I should be hemmed in and finally wrecked. I had not sailed these waters since a lad, and lamented the day I had allowed on board the goat that ate my chart. I taxed my memory of sea lore, of wrecks on sunken reefs, and of pirates harbored among coral reefs where other ships might not come, but nothing that I could think of applied to the island of Tobago, save the one wreck of Robinson Crusoe's ship in the fiction, and that gave me little information about reefs. I remembered only that in Crusoe's case he kept his powder dry. "But there she booms again," I cried, "and how close the flash is now! Almost aboard was that last breaker! But you'll go by, *Spray*, old girl! 'Tis abeam now! One surge more! and oh, one more like that will clear your ribs and keel!" And I slapped her on the transom, proud of her last noble effort to leap clear of the danger, when a wave greater than the rest threw her higher than before, and, behold, from the crest of it was revealed at once all there was of the reef. I fell back in a coil of rope, speechless and amazed, not distressed, but rejoiced. Aladdin's lamp! My fisherman's own lantern! It was the great revolving light on the island of Trinidad, thirty miles away, throwing flashes over the waves, which had deceived me! The orb of the light was now dipping on the horizon, and how glorious was the sight of it! But, dear Father Neptune, as I live, after a long life at sea, and much among corals, I would have made a solemn declaration to that reef! Through all the rest of the night I saw imaginary reefs, and not knowing what moment the sloop might fetch up on a real one, I tacked off and on till daylight, as nearly as possible in the same track, all for the want of a chart. . . .

The *Spray* was booming joyously along for home now, making her usual good time, when of a sudden she struck the horse latitudes, and her sail flapped limp in a calm. I had almost forgotten this calm belt, or had come to regard it as a myth. I now found it real, however, and difficult to cross. This was as it should have been, for, after all of the dangers of the sea, the dust-storm on the coast of Africa, the "rain of blood" in Australia, and the war risk when nearing home, a natural experience would have been missing had the calm of the horse latitudes been left out. Anyhow, a philosophical turn of thought now was not amiss, else one's patience would have given out almost at the harbor entrance. The term of her probation was eight days. Evening after evening during this time I read by the light of a candle on deck. There was no wind at all, and the sea became smooth and monotonous. For three days I saw a full-rigged ship on the horizon, also becalmed.

Sargasso, scattered over the sea in bunches, or trailed curiously along down the wind in narrow lanes, now gathered together in great fields, strange sea-animals, little and big, swimming in and out, the most curious among them being a tiny seahorse which I captured and brought home preserved in a bottle. But on the 18th of June a gale began to blow from the southwest, and the sargasso was dispersed again in windrows and lanes.

On this day there was soon wind enough and to spare. The same might have been said of the sea. The *Spray* was in the midst of the turbulent Gulf Stream itself. She was jumping like a porpoise over the uneasy waves. As if to make up for lost time, she seemed to touch only the high places. Under a sudden shock and strain her rigging began to give out. First the main-sheet strap was carried away, and then the peak halyard-block broke from the gaff. It was time to reef and refit, and so when "all hands" came on deck I went about doing that.

The 19th of June [1898] was fine, but on the morning of the 20th another gale was blowing, accompanied by cross-seas that tumbled about and shook things up with great confusion. Just as I was thinking about taking in sail the jibstay broke at the masthead, and fell, jib and all, into the sea. It gave me the strangest sensation to see the bellying sail fall, and where it had been suddenly to see only space. However, I was at the bows, with presence of mind to gather it in on the first wave that rolled up, before it was torn or trailed under the sloop's bottom. I found by the amount of work done in three minutes' or less time that I had by no means grown stiff-jointed on the voyage; anyhow, scurvy had not set in, and being now within a few degrees of home, I might complete the voyage, I thought, without the aid of a doctor. Yes, my health was still good, and I could skip about the decks in a lively manner, but could I climb? The great King Neptune tested me severely at this time, for the stay being gone, the mast itself switched about like a reed, and was not easy to climb; but a gun-tackle purchase was got up, and the stay set taut from the masthead, for I had spare blocks and rope on board with which to rig it, and the jib, with a reef in it, was soon pulling again like a "sodger" for home. Had the *Spray*'s mast not been well stepped, however, it would have been "John Walker" when the stay broke. Good work in the building of my vessel stood me always in good stead. . . .

The experiences of the voyage of the *Spray*, reaching over three years, had been to me like reading a book, and one that was more and more interesting as I turned the pages, till I had come now to the last page of all, and the one more interesting than any of the rest.

When daylight came I saw that the sea had changed color from dark green to light. I threw the lead and got soundings in thirteen fathoms. I made the land soon after, some miles east of Fire Island, and sailing thence before a pleasant breeze along the coast, made for Newport. The weather after the furious gale was remarkably fine. The *Spray* rounded Montauk Point early in the afternoon; Point Judith was abeam at dark; she fetched in at Beavertail next. Sailing on, she had one more danger to pass—Newport harbor was mined.[4] The *Spray* hugged the rocks along where neither friend nor foe could come if drawing much water, and where she would not disturb the guardship in the channel. It was close work, but it was safe enough so long as she hugged the rocks close, and not the mines. Flitting by a low point abreast of the guard-ship, the dear old *Dexter*, which I knew well, some one on board of her sang out, "There goes a craft!" I threw up a light at once and heard the hail, "*Spray*, ahoy!" It was the voice of a friend, and I knew that a friend would not fire on the *Spray*. I eased off the main-sheet now, and the *Spray* swung off for the beacon-lights of the inner harbor. At last she reached port in safety, and there at 1 A.M. on June 27, 1898, cast anchor, after the cruise of more than forty-six thousand miles round the world, during an absence of three years and two months, with two days over for coming up.

Was the crew well? Was I not? I had profited in many ways by the voyage. I had even gained flesh, and actually weighed a pound more than when I sailed from Boston. As for aging, why, the dial of my life was turned back till my friends all said, "Slocum is young again." And so I was, at least ten years younger than the day I felled the first tree for the construction of the *Spray*.

Notes

1. After an adventurous passage through the Strait of Magellan, Slocum visited Juan Fernández Island, made famous because Alexander Selkirk, the real-life Robinson Crusoe, was marooned there. Then he began the long crossing of the South Pacific, and after six week of sailing through all sorts of sea states, he reached Nuku Hiva in the Marquesas Islands.
2. The Keeling Cocos Islands are two low-lying coral atolls in the Indian Ocean, halfway between Australia and Sri Lanka, that are just over five square miles in area, making them a difficult navigational target.
3. It took Slocum nearly a year to complete his crossing of the Indian Ocean via Mauritius, round the Cape of Good Hope, and traverse the South Atlantic Ocean by way of St. Helena Island and Ascension Island, finally to reenter the North Atlantic. That is where this excerpt picks up.
4. Newport, site of several important naval facilities, was mined as a precaution during the Spanish-American War being fought with Spain in Cuba in 1898.

The Cruise

G. B. Barrows

The cruise industry began with banana boats. The Boston Fruit Company, which became the monopoly called United Fruit, marketed the concept of pleasure cruising to the Caribbean in the 1890s. The steamships going to Jamaica for bananas to bring north had no southbound cargo, until the company added passenger accommodations. The practice of going to sea for fun had been confined to a salty subset of the elite, but United Fruit's Great White Fleet, as it came to be known, made it affordable for a wider range of people to visit tropical locales. The company innovated air conditioning to keep the bananas fresh below decks and piped the cool air into the cabins and public spaces to keep the passengers comfortable. Business increased through the first three decades of the twentieth century, reaching its height in the 1920s, when Caribbean cruises to rum-producing islands, unburdened by Prohibition, were all the rage.

The Depression and World War II ended that heyday. In the 1970s, the cruise industry rose again, with mass-capacity vessels. When the second coming of the cruise industry began to gain momentum in 1970, about half a million passengers went on a cruise. Twenty years later, the number was 4.5 million worldwide, and twenty years after that, in 2010, it was 14.3 million. In 2017, according to Cruise Industry Overview 2018, *published by the Florida-Caribbean Cruise Association, a record 25.8 million people went on a cruise.*

It all started modestly in the 1890s, on ships like the SS *Belvidere of the Boston Fruit Company, steaming between Boston and Jamaica. A young woman from Massachusetts, one G. B. Barrows, boarded the* Belvidere *in March 1898 for a cruise to Jamaica. She followed the tourist itinerary when she got there, from Port Antonio over the mountains to Spanish Town and Kingston. This shore excursion, with its souvenir shopping, mirrors the experience of today's cruise passengers. Other common experiences that link Miss Barrows's cruise in 1898 with everyone going to sea on a cruise ship today include bonding with fellow passengers, enduring motion sickness in heavy weather, and glorying in the lovely sights at sea, such as sunrises, sunny afternoons, sunsets, and moonlight.*

Miss Barrows apparently loved her Caribbean cruise. For the rest of her life, she carefully preserved the papery ephemera of her trip. She cut out a United Fruit magazine advertisement that reminded her of the view from the veranda of her Port An-

tonio hotel (included as an illustration here). And she preserved a four-leaf clover, tucked inside her complimentary map of Jamaica from the ship. This lucky charm may have helped her get home safely after a stormy passage in April 1898. Less than two months later, on May 25, 1898, the Belvidere wrecked near Cape Maisi, the easternmost point of Cuba, on its way from Port Morant back to Boston.

16 March 1898

Boat office—photos of scenery—Left the wharf at 1. Tug-Barque *Herbert Fuller* at wharf. Chatham, Cape Cod, East-land. Sat outside till too cold, then in Music room of boat. Dinner at 6—assigned seats—then to state-room—a little rising water and went to bed, slept fairly well, only looked out once. Slept with open door-hasps—window a port-hole. Wash-bowls fold up—ledges in tables.

Thursday—Up bright to breakfast, rising bile—& kept flat and slept. Went on deck and sat aft with the Montreal lady—chat with Capt. A. (saw ship & steamer). Water around my chair and spray sent me in, I lay till lunch. I was the only woman at the table. Went to my berth and slept a while. Was one of *five* at dinner—not much appetite. Took an orange and crackers to my room—very rough. A little more "bile" & "turned in." "Terrible" rough night. Called the waiter to take down my cloak & umbrella, as they swung out two feet, etc. The orange very good in the night.

Friday—Tired and sore, and a very lame back. Stewardess encouraged me to keep up my good record and I went to breakfast. No longer "oiled" and a good appetite. Rested awhile, & went on deck. Miss Coffin appeared. I stayed till lunch. One lady at lunch. "Sargasso sea." Port[uguese] man o' wars. Saw vessel.

P.M. On deck till dinner & Miss C. went down. After, had a nap before going to bed—a calm smooth night. Rested well—ate orange at 12. Looked out at five to see Watling's Island & got up at 6:30.[1]

Sat. 19 Sunshine and beautiful. Every body out. Sea glassy very early—quite smooth all the A.M. but a swell that hindered writing—A poor night.

Sunday A heavy swell all day. A day of rest. Saw a steamer, a bird lighted on the boat, saw flying fish. Passed Crooked Fortune and Castle Is.

P.M. Had a nap in music room. Fine sunset at sea. Sat up till 10 with Mr. and Mrs. Whitcomb to see Cuba light on Cape Maysi [Maisí].

Changed to thinner underwear.

Monday [March 21]—Heavy swell and tumbled out of steamer chair—got named of the passengers "now you see me." Sighted Jamaica about 10—fine scenery—mountains and tropical vegetation. Arrived at 11. U.S. [Navy] ships *Cincinnatti* [sic] out by the lighthouse at Folly Point—*Castine* and *Wilmington* inside. Health officer came out—crowds of colored people on wharf—customs officer. Took to hotel through main street of stores looking like blacksmith shops. Fine situation of Litchfield House had rooms on first floor, detached dining room with branch of mango tree. Lunched—visited[,] wrote letter home.

After dinner on verandah. Search lights and signals on warships. Fire flies—crickets—A Jamaican woman's remark, "mile away the eagle scream'd."

Tuesday 22—Breakfast after 7—Tom had carriage & mules at 8[;] such a drive! Capt. Baker's Philip driver—variety of plants and trees. Market women with loads on head, hat on top. Water carriers—thatched cabins—many children—rags. Fine views of sea & surf. . . . Back at 12. Lunch—naval officers. A chat with Capt. Chester of the *Cincinnatti*. . . . Eve on the verandah—boy with mongoose—searchlights turned on red.

Wednesday—Not up early and the team waited for breakfast. Drove to Golden Vale, road full of market women. Basket on head, yams, etc. Push carts of bananas. Burros with panniers, well dressed woman and child on panniers. . . .

After return, . . . Tom called that the warship steamers were going out . . . shooters on the Navy Is. range. . . .

Watched a strange steamer coming in after 9 P.M. Proved to be a Norwegian, coming for a fruit freighter. (mosquitoes)

Thurs. 24—Up in season. Started for Hope Bay (10 miles) at 7. The drive a continual delight, along the seashore, surf, colored water. . . . Picturesque ruins of old waterworks on sugar plantation—another by the water side in a cove where vessels went up. Stone walls built in slavery times on both sides of the road, crossed with vines. Joseph's coat—ferns, &c—coolie child. Saw women washing clothes in a ravine. Hope Bay—B. F. Co.'s wharf very attentive wharfings [items awaiting shipment]—bags of cocoa-nuts, barrels of fish in storehouse—took a stroll along the seashore, gathered shells, pebbles, flowers, &c.[2]

Got back to P[ort] A[ntonio] before lunch.

P.M. Loafed on the verandah. . . .

Friday After breakfast went to the top of the house with Miss Brazil, the housekeeper.

Wanted to visit the schools at the old "barracks." . . .

Sat. 26 . . . Decided to go to the Market. . . . The market a busy scene. Bought lime, nutmegs. . . . Went to the Boat Office for ticket then we all went back in the boat across the harbor. . . .

Eve. As usual on the verandah. Watched the light on the *Bermuda*[,] the condemned filibuster that lay just across the channel. . . .[3] I hope never to forget the view from the verandah.

Sunday— . . . Went to the Wesleyan Church. Colored preacher—fair German deacon. . . .

P.M. Began to attempt to pack. . . . Worked till dismayed.

Eve. Verandah. Back to my room and worked, sewed and packed till 2 A.M. . . .

Monday 28. Was waked at quarter to five. Breakfast . . . third-class car. Passengers of all conditions, colors, & sizes & chickens! A diversified ride along the sea shore. Fine views of sea and mountains. 24 tunnels in 30 miles. Left the sea at Annotta Bay & the cars at "Bog Walk." A "haggle" for carriages but went in two. . . .[4]

Spent the evening in the reading room and verandah towards the sea— Saw the *Southern Cross* from my window. . . .

Tuesday 29. A woman with oranges at my door early—I got up in fine spirits.

Looked over pictures and curiosities and saw a boatload of large turtles.

Went to breakfast. Waited for a small spoon, then went to get my own & reported it. After breakfast we went shopping, with the Helmbolds ("from upland")—Nathan's Bee Hive—bought bandanna belt & Self Help full of curiosities—Victoria Market—Bought large basket & "lots of things."[5] Went back to dinner & intended to rest but the Helmbolds had engaged carriages to go to Hope Gardens[,] a fine place with all the plants of Jamaica. Hurried back expecting the boat to leave at 5. A dusty ride thro[ugh] Kingston streets. Broken glass bottles [on] top of jail walls, customs fences—Boat left at 7.

Women loaded the bananas, singing.

Met Mrs. Du Fresne nee Annie Heston of Portland and family. Mr. & Mrs. Ashton & the boat full.

Kept on deck till after we got to Morant Bay—bananas brought out on lighters—After ten went below before the boat started—Slept not very soundly till waked by women singing at Port Morant. Dressed & went out on the wharf—Women carried coal in baskets on their heads, weighing 60–70 lbs. Lazy men—"Turned in" again.

Wednesday 30—Waked in good season and went to breakfast—ought not to have taken coffee. Rather rough & lay down—one very sudden & heavy plunge of the boat. Slept & on waking found my dress wet & water dropping from above. The sudden start caused the loss of my breakfast. Slept again— tried to dress for lunch, but had to lie down. The stewardess encouraged me not to "break my second" & I "braced up" and went to lunch—Went up stairs & stayed on deck till dinner—also in the eve. Obliged to have a room-mate, as well as a pan to catch the water. Sat awhile with Mrs. Du Fresne.

Thurs. 31 (Stuart's birthday)

The water abated a little. Got up to see the sun rise. I went in again till bell time. Several persons not yet visible. Day passed quietly. A heavy "roll" at lunch. Threw dishes off the table.

Eve. Beautiful moonlight, I sat on deck till after nine.

Friday April 1—Put on thicker dress. On deck after breakfast & played checkers with Mrs. Wilcox—Found our fan palm leaves, but the rain drove us in before we secured them & they were lost. Miss Coffin *succumbed*. All the women below but Mrs. Parsons & myself & we stayed in the "music room"— a rainy afternoon but rather smooth.

Stayed up till nine—Mr. Fender.

Saturday—Overhauled my box & changed underwear—room leaking again, but not badly—my room-mate kept her berth—Mrs. & Miss Coffin got on deck.

Eve—In music room. Dr. Dunham. Cloudy all day. Three vessels & a Steamer that caused some excitement.

Sunday—A very rough day. Mrs. Parsons & myself were the only women up stairs. Read some, but sometimes hard work to keep one's seat—no comfortable chairs but steamer. A snow squall showed change of latitude.

Monday—Up early to see land. Delayed after making Boston harbor, waiting for Health Officer. Took oath to Customs officer & baggage[,] 6 or 8 packages! Landed—Stuart Mary and Ezra waiting for me. E. and I rode up to Chandler, & walked to 17. Glad to be on land again—all tired out by Sunday's roughness.

Notes

1. It is now called San Salvador Island in the Bahamas, famed as the site of Columbus's landfall in the New World in 1492.
2. Her budget notes record that she also acquired "3 bottles liquors" that day, for one dollar.
3. The USS *Maine* had exploded in Havana Harbor less than a month before Miss Barrows left for Jamaica. The US Navy warships in Port Antonio were on alert because of the resulting Spanish-American War, which stemmed from the ongoing Cuban Revolution of 1895. Vessels attempting to run guns and mercenaries to the island, called filibusters, were seized by US Navy patrols during the prelude to full intervention in April 1898.
4. After paying her exorbitant $1.08 admission to take the Bog Walk to see the waterfall there (it was the most she would pay for anything, aside from hotel bills), and visiting Spanish Town, Miss Barrows reboarded the train (for 28 cents) and reached Kingston in the late afternoon.
5. The log of expenses that Miss Barrows kept shows that she bought a starfish, a calabash, a "fern album," a necklace, napkin rings, a carved coconut, two photographs, and a selection of fresh produce: star apples, mangoes, pineapples, and yams.

The Compleat Goggler

Guy Gilpatric

Guy Gilpatric (1896–1950) was best known as the author of the hilarious, best-selling *Mr. Glencannon series, which followed Scottish chief engineer Colin Glencannon on his voyages aboard the tramp steamer* Inchcliffe Castle. *First serialized in the Sat-urday Evening Post, the Glencannon stories filled eight volumes and were a televi-sion series for thirty-nine episodes in 1959. But Gilpatric created much more than the scheming, tippling Mr. Glencannon, who was well known to 1940s readers. He published* Action in the North Atlantic *in 1943, about U-boats sinking US merchant ships. Warner Brothers made a movie of it starring Humphrey Bogart, which was nominated for Best Original Story at the 1944 Academy Awards.*

Gilpatric had personal experience with warfare, having been a pilot during World War I. Aviation—especially aviator goggles—led to his life's passions: skin diving and spearfishing. Gilpatric essentially invented both pursuits, by caulking his goggles to make them waterproof, fashioning the first dive mask. Like Izaak Walton before him, Gilpatric shared his knowledge of diving and spearfishing, which he gained through years of experience on the French Riviera, in his book The Compleat Goggler. *First published in 1934, the primer's full title spoofs Izaak Walton:* The Compleat Gog-gler, Being the First and Only Exhaustive Treatise On the Art of GOGGLE FISHING, That most Noble and Excellent Sport Perfected and Popularized by Guy Gilpatric in the Mediterranean Sea, though Long Practiced Elsewhere by Other BENIGHTED SAVAGES: Setting Forth the Proper Manner of Making the GOGGLES, SPEARS and Other Needful GADGETS Together with Descriptions of the Many Marvels Witnessed Upon the BOTTOM OF THE SEA and Fully Exposing the Author's Cunning Methods of Swimming, Diving & SPEARING FISH & OCTOPI. *The book found a fresh audience in 1957, when the newly founded* Skin Diver *magazine released a special printing for subscribers.*

By then, Gilpatric had inspired a wave of enthusiasm for dive masks and fish-ing spears. Jacques Cousteau was the most famous person who took up the sport, while living in the Riviera in the early 1930s. The next step after goggling was to add a breathing tube to begin snorkeling, and the step after that was to add tanks of compressed air for scuba diving, which revolutionized the undersea experience for recreational divers.

This excerpt comes from "Genesis," the first chapter of The Compleat Goggler, *which describes the first time that a member of our dry-footed species saw the world of fish as a fish does. This amusing and self-effacing testament to ingenuity, persistence, and wonderment offers the full-throated Gilpatric, with his echoes of Mark Twain. As the first person to strap a dive mask to his face and enter submarine environs with the independence of a marine mammal, limited only by his lung capacity, not by visual distortion, Gilpatrick effused about what that is like, in a way that resonates with anyone who has followed his example. Considering that since he wrote this passage, untold millions of people have delighted in the sense of underwater flight that he brilliantly captured, it is astounding that Guy Gilpatric is not a household name, like Jacques Cousteau, the man he inspired.*

The first thing you need, to be a successful goggle fisher, is a body of good clear water. Personally I use the Mediterranean Sea and there is still plenty of room in it, but parts of the Atlantic, the Pacific, the Mexican Gulf and the Caribbean will do just as well, and I know of many lakes and streams which would provide grand goggling. Next you need a pair of watertight goggles. I made my first pair myself from an old pair of flying goggles, plugging up the ventilating holes with putty and painting over it. . . .

My idea, originally, was merely to study the submarine scenery and vegetation, which in the clear warm water of this Riviera region I believed would be worth seeing. Accordingly, one day, I shoved off from shore on an innocent sight-seeing trip. I had ridden in the glass-bottomed boats of Catalina and Bermuda and used waterscope boxes in the Gulf of Mexico, but I was unprepared for the breathtaking sensation of free flight which swimming with goggles gave me. It wasn't at all like flying in a plane, where you are conscious of being borne by something tangible; there was a nightmare quality to this sensation as in a dream of falling, and in that instant I knew how Icarus felt when his wings melted off. I jerked my head out of water and looked around to reassure myself. The bottom was fifteen feet below me, now, but every pebble and blade of grass was distinct as though there were only air between. The light was a soft bluish-green—even, restful, and somehow wholly appropriate to the aching silence which lay upon those gently waving meadows and fields of flowers. On the pinnacle of a rock like a little mountain I saw a dwarf palm tree. I swam down to study it. I touched its trunk and—zip!—the feathery foliage vanished as quickly as the flame of a blown candle. I came up for air, a portion of which I used in vowing to get the explanation of this flummery. I swam along on the surface until I found another palm tree. This one I sneaked up on (or rather, down to) stealthily. I reached forward, touched the leaves and—they weren't! But this time it hadn't fooled me. The trunk had simply sucked the leaves inside itself. If my finger had been an anchovy or other small fish, it might have been sucked in with them, there to be consumed for the nourishment of the confounded plant. I have since learned that this was the *Spirographis Spallanzanii*, not a plant at all, but an animal;[1] but I decided right then and there that it is as foolhardy to go picking flowers on the sea bottom as it is in front of the cop in a public park.

Soaring on my way above hills and valleys upon which grew blossoms snowy white and flaming red, I came to a great submerged rock from one side of which projected a wide shelf. I could see small fish flashing in and out along its edges, and went down to have a look at them. The underside of the shelf, though only ten or twelve feet below the surface, was fifty feet above the bottom. It was heavily grown with weeds. Anchovies and sardines—thousands of them—were swimming around eating this foliage. But—I rubbed my goggles—they were swimming on their backs! Had I discovered a new species? At first I couldn't believe what I saw; then a larger fish happened along and he, too, was swimming on his back. I dove right under the ledge, where it was dark and cold, and shoo-ed the whole crowd out. As soon as they left the shadow and saw the sunlight above them, they turned right side up and went their ways like any self-respecting fish. Now those fish did not have to turn on their backs in order to eat weeds on the ceiling, for fish can eat in any reasonable position as well as in several which I might call scandalous. No, those fish were not aware that they were on their backs. They thought that the ceiling was the floor; they didn't know up from down, being in practically the same fix as the old-time aviators who, lacking instruments for flying in clouds and fog, used to lose all sense of direction and turn upside down without realizing it until loose objects, such as bottles, commenced falling upwards out of the cockpit. My discovery that sardines and anchovies can swim on their backs is fraught with significance and I have no doubt that after the publication of this book I will be the recipient of appropriate decorations and degrees from scientific organizations the world over.

Feeling pretty pleased with myself, I swam around to the other side of the rock. This face of it went down sheer until its base was lost in deep blue gloom. I had the sensation of flying in the chasm of a New York street. Below me I saw vague forms moving—fish, they were, and whoppers. I watched them for a long time as they lazed about in stately grace or poised in rumination, fearing that my slightest move would startle them. But presently a couple came up to within fifteen feet of me and seemed to be giving me the once-over. I thought I'd return the compliment. Swimming down as close to them as I dared, I hovered in suspense which they didn't seem to share. They were big fat dorades; I was so close that I could see the gold bands on their blue foreheads but I didn't hope that they'd let me come closer. I needed air and started upward. Suddenly, I found myself staring into the eyes of what looked like a German U-boat—a three-foot loup in a fine state of indignation, his dorsal fin jutting up like the bristles of a bulldog.[2] Without stopping to think, I cut loose my right and pasted him square on the jaw. I heard a whirring sound like that of wings as Mr. Loup departed under force of draught.

I came to the surface, gulped some air, and pondered on the sorry state to which I had fallen in being unable to knock out a three-foot fish. No use kidding myself, that blow wouldn't have bruised a stewed oyster. My knuckles were bleeding but this merely meant I'd scratched them on the little needles along the edge of his gill. I filled my lungs, swam down a way and indulged in some experimental shadow boxing. I soon found the trouble. Being full of air and therefore lighter than the water I walloped, the faster I shoved myself away from what I was aiming to hit. Also, I was using a lot of energy in resisting my tendency to float up to the surface. I blew out my air, sank down further, and uncorked a couple of rights and lefts. Now, I felt that my blows really had a little steam behind them. My body being heavier than water, my punches had something to react against.

I was feeling pretty tired, and I noticed that the skin on my fingers was shrivelled from being in the water too long. As I swam toward the beach, I thought of what I'd learned—namely, that some fish are not afraid of swimmers, and that to exert power under water you have to empty your lungs. It occurred to me that in these discoveries might lie the basis of a new sport. Still, I didn't feel that socking fish in the jaw was quite the way to do things, so I determined to buy a new spear.

When I reached the beach, I found that I had been swimming for two hours and a half. It had seemed like twenty minutes.

My first spear was a trident with piano wire teeth forged into barbs. The handle—it was the handle of a hay-rake—was six-feet-six-inches long. The head being light, the weapon floated with the business end about a foot under water and the handle exposed.

I thought that my best bet would be to work in fairly shallow water, so I scouted along parallel to the beach in a depth of eight to ten feet. Pretty soon I spotted a school of slim, stream-lined mullets—fish rather like trout and running from a foot to two feet in length. They were milling around on the bottom, eating, their sides flashing silver through the cloud of sand which their fins fanned up. Before I could get down to them, they spotted me and darted away. I followed on the surface, waiting for them to commence feeding again. They circled around at a good safe distance, watching me. Apparently they didn't care for the view, for with the skitter of tails, they beat it. A second school of them acted the same way. Now this was discouraging. The loup and the dorades of the day before had not behaved thus, so I concluded that fish are more wary in the shallows than in the depths. Diving is their instinctive means of escape, and when this avenue is closed to them, they won't take chances. . . .[3]

Inventors have envisioned breathing underwater since at least 1500, when Leonardo da Vinci sketched plans for a leather diving suit with breathing tubes. Henry Fleuss patented the first underwater rebreather in 1878, which scrubbed a diver's exhalations of CO_2, allowing submersions up to three hours long, and was employed to rescue trapped miners. Even more versatile was the rebreather that Sir Robert Davis invented in 1910, which saved the lives of sailors on sinking submarines. Rebreathers, which reuse the same supply of air, are complicated closed-circuit designs, not easily adapted for recreational purposes. The breakthrough came in 1943, when Jacques Cousteau and Émile Gagnan invented the aqualung, which used tanks of compressed oxygen. It was a "self-contained underwater breathing apparatus," or scuba. Recreational scuba diving boomed after World War II, and popular culture featured diving, as in Cousteau's best-seller *The Silent World*, TV series like *Flipper*, and racy dime novels such as *The Case of the Naked Diver*. This photograph of a scuba diver in the Adriatic Sea was taken in the 1960s with the first widely available underwater camera, the Calypso Shot. Photographer unknown, c. 1960s. Courtesy of the Roorda/Doyle Collection.

Next day I put to sea with a spear which would have held a walrus. I had learned that when a fish is eating in deep water he could be scragged, and I planned to wait around until meal time. But suddenly, perhaps ten feet under and a little ahead of me, I saw a gray fish with dark tiger-stripes. He was coming in a straight line, evidently intending to pass under me. This, I thought, would be like wing shooting. I sank to meet him. Our paths crossed just as he came within range. I lunged and caught him fair and square. This fellow, a mourme, was only a little over a foot long, but he raised a great ruction.[4] Fearing that he would pull himself off the barbs, I took him clear to the bottom and jammed him good and hard against the sand.

Well, my return to the beach with that mourme saw my stock rise considerably in Juan-les-Pins.[5] People had been kidding me in five or six languages about my expeditions with goggles and spear, but now they allowed as how maybe, *peut-être, quiza* and *vielleicht*, the thing was a pretty good sport. Next day, when I brought in a two-foot sargue and a dorade measuring twenty-six inches and weighing between six and seven pounds, a considerable portion of the summer population sprouted spears and goggles and started after the game in a big way.[6]

Notes

1. *Spirographis spallanzanii* is a species of polychaete worms known as Mediterranean fan-worms and feather duster worms that resemble their name. They are now regarded as an invasive species in many parts of the world, having spread from the Mediterranean and northeastern Atlantic in recent decades to reach Africa, South America, and Australia.

2. *Loup de mer* is the French name for *Dicentrarchus labrax*, the European or Mediterranean sea bass, also known as bronzino and robalo, a species of Ocean fish that can grow to be more than 3 feet long and weigh more than 30 pounds.

3. After several failed attempts to adapt a spear for underwater use, and to develop a technique to employ it, Gilpatric figured it out.

4. "Mourme" is the French name for striped bream, one of many species in the family Sparidae, which are called by many names, including porgies, in North America. They can reach 2 feet in length, and weigh more than 5 pounds.

5. Juan-les-Pins is a resort in the Antibes area of the French Mediterranean coast.

6. "Sargue" is another kind of bream, the white seabream, also called sargo, which also can reach 2 feet in length and weigh more than 5 pounds; dorade, also known as gilt-head bream, can grow to be more than 2 feet long and weigh nearly 40 pounds.

Round the World! Journal of a Sailing Voyage—from a Teen's Point of View

Katrina Bercaw

The Bercaw family, aboard their boat Natasha, *followed in the wake of the Brassey family aboard their* Sunbeam, *and of Irving Johnson, of Cape Horn fame, with his spouse, Elexa, and their children, aboard their famous* Yankee. *All of these families went around the world under sail.*

James Bercaw served as first mate with the Johnsons on one of the Yankee's seven circumnavigations, an experience that shaped his life and that of his spouse, Gretchen, and their children, as he determined to devote four years of the family's collective life to going around the world a second time. The odyssey shaped the futures of the three younger Bercaws. The eldest, Mary K (captured in this piece often reading Moby-Dick to her siblings and parents), went on to be a professor, write several books on Herman Melville, and serve as president of the Melville Society. The youngest, Sean (depicted here ingeniously rigging an extra sail to go a bit faster in light winds), became a sea captain and commanded a long list of historic sailing vessels. These days, he commands supply ships to Antarctica. The author, the middle child, spent her life finding many ways to answer the question she asked herself in her journal: "How can we share this beauty we live in with those less fortunate?" Most recently, Katrina Bercaw does so by teaching English as a second language to eager and appreciative adult immigrants in New London, Connecticut.

In October 1971, my family, the Bercaws, set sail on a world voyage (for context, Nixon was president in the U.S. at the time). Our boat was the 38-foot ketch *Natasha*. My dad was a marine technician, and my mom a nurse. Important skills! I was age 15 to 19; since we traveled about 5 miles per hour, it took three and a half years. My brother was 10 and my sister 16 when we left Santa Barbara, CA. We were the crew. We did the equivalent of homeschooling— we were avid readers, and had put together a good library. We learned languages, did celestial navigation, converted money to many currencies in our heads, learned about history, politics, commerce, ecology and geography. We used 24-hour time. We didn't have a refrigerator, but carried six months' supply of canned and dry goods, and got eggs and fresh produce in the markets.

We took seawater baths with buckets. Our longest passage was 29 days at sea. Our worst noon-to-noon run was 12 miles. Our best was 165.

Journal Excerpts

12.27.1971   Leaving Acapulco on our way to the Galápagos! Up early to get *Natasha* ready to sail. Topped our fuel and water tanks. Off to the market for produce and bread. Washed the fruit. Upped anchor. I steered out of the bay in a good wind. Beautiful sunset—it's our first night in a long time without neon lights.

12.28.1971   No land in sight. Southern Cross sighted by the dawn watch. Saw a big sea turtle sunning. The ocean looks huge.

12.29.1971   No wind. Sick crew members. Washed my hair in a bucket of saltwater.

12.30.1971   Crew are on the mend. I'm feeling super-healthy—I washed the head and made lunch.

12.31.1971   Beautiful on watch at 0300. I sang, thought, adjusted sails, looked after the sick ones and generally had a ball until 0600. It's three lunar months since we left home on October 3. Stood 1600–2000 watch by myself.

1.2.1972   We're in "squall country." It's wet outside and stuffy below. All the bunks but mine have leaks over them. Mary K and I sang Christmas carols on night watch. . . .

1.25.1972   Academy Bay, Galápagos Islands: I started the day frying shark steaks for breakfast. They were a little strong, but tasty. When Sean, Daddy and I were returning from a *panadería* [bakery] excursion, we saw our first *penguin*! It swam, zoom!, a few feet from us. It's Daddy's first in 21 years [he was here on the *Yankee* in 1951]. Goat meat for supper. After supper we went ashore for a *fresh*-water shower! It was in a tiny wooden building. The water wasn't heated, but was almost lukewarm. The mirror was fantastic; it's the first time I've combed my hair in front of one in months. The water was brackish, and by the time we were done smelled an awful lot of sulphur. Mosquitoes whining all night.

1.28.1972   Daphne Major Island. To the beach at 0530 where we found a turtle laying her eggs! The sun came up as she used her hind flippers to scoop sand over them. She was in a hurry, and seemed to be greatly relieved when she slipped back into the water.

1.29.1972   Conway Bay. Flamingos! Amazing to see them wild. I made pressure cooker bread (our kerosene oven wasn't working).

1.30.1972   Eden Island. Had a hard hike. Thick tree, thorn bush and cactus cover over rough lava and chasms. Mangroves and salt lagoons thrown in as extra obstacles. I began making up songs, noting that we were crazy to go on in such terrain. Didn't get much response. Mommy and Daddy called from

Katrina and Sean tie a reef in the mainsail on the squall-filled voyage from the Galápagos Islands to Pitcairn Island, home of the mutineers of HMS *Bounty* fame. Photograph by James Bercaw, c. 1972. Courtesy of Katrina Bercaw.

the skiff [rowboat], and we didn't have to walk all the way back. They were a beautiful sight.

1.31.1972   Sombrero Chino. We made pallets and slept ashore with friends from another boat. Full moon. Few bugs. Our first night ashore in an age!

2.29.1972   Floreana Island. Fried papaya for breakfast—my second attempt and it came out much better. Ashore early and hiked to Black Beach. The biggest bull sea lions I've ever seen. I wore my saddle shoes which are sturdy, but I got two blisters.

En Route to Pitcairn Island

3.4.1972   We're out of the Galápagos world [after nine weeks!] and into a new one—that of a long passage. All morning long Mommy and I did laundry. And laundry. And laundry! We washed it in saltwater, but rinsed in a bucket of fresh water we'd brought through the surf. At the high noon sun sight, we'd gone 60 miles in 17 hours.

3.5.1972   No wind. Daddy built us a shady "play house" with the awning. Funny—when we lived in a house, us kids built a canvas play boat! At 1600 we had swim call. Kept a lookout, but no sign of a shark. Mommy did a church service. I listened to Mary K read *Johnny Tremain* to Sean. Twenty-four-hour run: 77 miles.

3.7.1972   Practicing Spanish with Sean. A little laundry. Daddy checked

Morning watch at sea: Mary K steers while Katrina takes a sight with the ship's sextant and Gretchen does a load of laundry. Photograph by Jay Bercaw, c. 1971–75. Courtesy of Katrina Bercaw.

the batteries. We almost never use electricity now! We eat supper outside before dark and go to bed. It's neat!

3.10.1972   We had a wind squall and roared along beautifully for over an hour. It was a great squall because the wind and rain were separate, which made it easier to collect rainwater. I stood in the galley and filled bowls, pitchers, pans and canteens. I put the plug in the sink, filled it with fresh water and washed my face. That evening, Daddy tuned in Voice of America for the news. Then Mary K read us *Moby-Dick*, about the first lowering. They got caught in a squall, too, lost in it, in a longboat in the night. We're not so bad off, huh?

3.12.1972   Windy, lumpy and gray. We saw two birds: a sooty tern and a shearwater.

3.19.1972   Sunday. One hundred and eighteen miles noon to noon. I really miss a house these days: stove, oven, refrigerator, fresh dairy products and steady working space. But I love our big, clean beautiful bathtub. It's relaxing to throw bucketful after bucketful of cool water on myself, and even better to jump in. The days of calm when we swim in water thousands of fathoms deep are fabulous. . . .

Pitcairn Island, Home of [Descendants of] the Bounty Mutineers (1789)
and Their Tahitian Wives

4.1.1972   At 1015 we sighted Pitcairn. I'm super-jazzed, dancing around. Yippee! I've been reading about the island, but I'm still not sure what it will be like. Will we get baths and sleep in beds? Do they have refrigerators? I can't picture it at all.

4.6.1972   We got to stay with islanders: Sean and Mom with Jacob and Mavis Warren [the last name comes from a sailor shipwrecked on the island a few generations ago], Mary K and I with Warren and Millie Christian. They do have refrigerators, which are lovely. They've got porcelain wood-burning stoves. Everyone has an outhouse. They also have cockroaches, which I hate, and ants, which are easier to get used to. There are five girls almost my age: Julie, Brenda, Glenda, Carol, and Janet. When Olive invited me in for tea, I had my first breadfruit. Lots of neighbors came in, sat down, and took a project they were working on out of their basket. Soon they were all talking merrily.

4.9.1972   . . . I didn't enjoy their dances much at first. I was embarrassed and everything I did felt forced. But the Pitcairn teens kept calling me to the floor and giving encouragement. I got used to it. Shorts are the best thing to dance in.

4.27.1972   We left Pitcairn on a calm, windless day. It's now the eleventh day at sea, and the wind has still not come up. Plus we have an adverse current, so our daily runs are most discouraging. We haven't gotten much exercise for a long time, so our energy levels are down. I'm reading *Citizen Hearst*, *A Tree Grows in Brooklyn*, and a scuba diving manual.

Palmerston Atoll, South Pacific

7.28.1972   At 1000 Daddy sighted Palmerston. We arrived at 1500. Native men in a 16-foot longboat came aboard and told us where to anchor. They stayed an hour, then us kids went ashore with them. When a Korean fishing boat came in, the locals brought out a live pig, chickens, bush beer (moonshine) and fruit to trade for flour, rice and sugar. Twenty-two-year-old Tu became our guide. I liked how she'd strung shells to decorate her house. She made us juice from a commercial powder I wouldn't recommend. We met many of the 70 islanders. Everyone has the last name Marsters, and they're all related. Local produce includes coconuts, papayas, breadfruit, and taro. There are some banana trees, but they need to make special plots of less salty, richer soil to grow them. The islanders eat chickens, tropic birds, and a small black bird, lots of fish, some tinned meat. It got dark while we ate and we worried about getting back to *Natasha* because it was a very complicated pass through the reef. It turned out they thought we'd sleep ashore! But they did take us home once the moon came up.

7.30.1972   Tu's cousin Teipo gave me some tuna he'd deep-fried. Delicious! Then I wandered around taking pictures. We ate a big lunch at Tu's, including cooked "uto"—the center of a ripe coconut. Interesting texture. Tu fanned the food using big leaves to keep the flies away. It felt like Egypt days! . . .

Indonesia

8.31.1973   Through Roti Strait under full sail toward Koepang, Timor, Indonesia. Fair current, wind on the beam. Saw a jillion dhow-type Indonesian boats. They're double-ended and wide, with lateen-rigged sails. Trade wind clouds scudded about; the sun shone with vigor. Anchored among local boats; there are no other yachts at Koepang. Boats sailed to and from the anchorage all day, some to island homes, others off for night fishing, others coming in for a day's shopping in the "city."

9.2.1973   People are friendly, and the school kids know a few English phrases. We're slowly learning a few words of Indonesian. Mom and Sean went with an Indonesian lady doctor, Nafsiah, to see the hospital. Mary K and I set off hiking. Shouts of "Hello, Mister" deluge us and everyone asks, "Where are you going?" We answer, "Walking." A million kids pose for photos. At the house of Antonia we had a lovely coconut drink. Stayed for an hour, which was a little difficult with no English. Mom and Sean came down the road and we all had lunch at the doctor's: meat and veggies in peanut sauce, papaya flowers, fried pork. Nona and Pua came to the boat, and we entertained them with checkers, my photo album, and Galápagos books. When they left, we were ready to collapse, but then Mary K made chocolate fondue for dinner! . . .

Indian Ocean

10.19.1973   Ran 154 miles under reefed main, mizzen and jib. Twenty-five-hour day. Rough, squally, but felt at peace with my surroundings. Took a morning sun sight. Daddy took sailing photos, got spray on the camera but got good ones. Then, on #36, he found the roll had not gone through. Frustrating!

10.20.1973   Read on my 02–0500 watch. Very rolly without main [without the mainsail set, the ship rolled back and forth uncomfortably]. 0545 flush of dawn in east. 0800 rice with sweetened condensed milk and fruit cocktail. Mmmm! Read *Pitcairn's Island* by Nordoff and Hall. It's as captivating as their other two, but so tragic. Did laundry. Worked out two sun sights.

10.21.1973   Self-discipline collapsed and I read much of the day. Weather rough, gray and dreary. *Natasha's* company was lifeless, my forward bunk damp, and all was uninspiring.

10.25.1973   Good dinner and tea. Just after dusk, "Bang!" We were suddenly flying through a tempest—surfing and making 7 knots without the main. Safety belts in cockpit and a line rigged to guide us to the wheel.

10.26.1973   Tremendous speed. Much calmer. Arrived at Rodrigues, a French island. Peace Corps worker Maurice guided us through narrow channel into the harbor. Went in his Land Rover to his house, where about 30 people of all ages were hard at work finishing a volleyball net! Dad spliced an eye in each corner. The next day we saw them playing.

10.28.1973   Maurice invited us to a dance. When Kurt and Mommy said they'd accompany us, we reluctantly decided to go. Crazy us! It was the most fun, heartwarming evening ever! Met Joseph, Eddy, Henry, Christian, and sailors off a visiting supply ship.

11.1.1973   Rodrigues is growing ever smaller on the horizon. We got home from the dance about 0115 this morning, but were up at 0600 to prepare for sea. Set genoa and whisker pole for wing and wing. Going great, but feel very sad to leave our new friends. That's the worst part of this voyage: we make friends, then leave them.

Passage to Durban, South Africa

11.22.1973   Up 0910. Mom and Sean had put last year's Thanksgiving poster up—a nice surprise! Rough seas, very little wind. Too proud to use the engine, so we had *all* our sails set: main, mizzen, genoa, mizzen staysail, and Sean rigged an inner jib to the pulpit. If there had been wind, we'd have been flying. As it was, we moved at about 3 knots. Hot day. Wrote letters. Thanksgiving dinner was Stovetop Stuffing with cabbage in lieu of celery, canned turkey, cranberry jelly, and sultana loaf cake. Tea on deck. Mary K and I read each other's letters, sharing but skeptical. This trip has made us a lot closer than we used to be, but still. . . .

Thoughts on *Natasha* at sea: Cooking at sea is a nice challenge. For the most part, I don't mind the boat being closed up to stay dry. I love my bunk forward because it is all mine, has character, and it's so small. I love the tininess of boat living, so every inch can be memorized. Everything else in our life is changing, so we especially enjoy routine. An action done twice gives a feeling of continuity. The comments section in *Natasha*'s log will one day bring memories. For example: *Hot, hot. Rolly. SSB threw bottle overboard with note and a ceremony. We're really moving! Chilly. Wave below! Changed jib to genny. La lune est joli.*

12.1.1973   Hove-to under storm jib. 1100 sighted Africa, just five miles away! Got our location from a ship via UHF radio: Umhlonga Rocks. Beat against 20–35 knot wind. Heeled hard over. Wet below. Raining and cold. Safety belts and full foul weather gear. We could see cars zooming on a highway and fancy houses—how odd to look at civilization as we were in the midst of battling nature. Exhilarating! Lights at dusk were lovely. Arrived at 2200, exhausted but with a sense of satisfaction from crossing the Indian Ocean without mishap.

12.2.1973   Hot, fresh showers! Lunch ashore with ice cream!! Eighteen yachts in, many of whom we'd met in other ports. . . .

South Atlantic Ocean

3.11.1974   Stars on the 02 to 05 watch, plus clouds, moon, Venus. On the 12–1600 watch, hand-sewing, cleaning, bath, sun sight. Mary K reading *The Odyssey* to Sean (and us all!).

3.12.1974   Wing 'n wing [with sails deployed to port and starboard, like wings, with a following wind]. Halfway from Cape Town to Barbados. Love listening to gurgling of water passing the hull. Pondering: How can we share this beauty we live in with those less fortunate?

3.15.1974   Quiet, pleasant night watch. Stars and moon. Writing a book report on Anya Seton's *Green Darkness*. Did a moon sight at Mom's suggestion— it's a lot harder to work out and plot, but she helped me and it was fun. Mom and Sean did laundry.

3.17.1974   Sunday and St. Patrick's Day. Twenty-five-hour day. Canned bacon for breakfast! Sean planned a church service. Really well done, family receptive. I accompanied the songs on guitar—I'm getting there with it! Readings from *The Prophet*, *Little Book of Prayers*, Homer. Sighted a ship. Green peas and artichoke hearts made dinner special.

3.18.1974   Rain squalls and flukey winds all night. Cold out, hot in. Miserable doldrums. Collected eight gallons of rainwater in a squall. Saw storm petrels, sooty terns, boobies, and a tuna jumping. Spotted a Portuguese man o' war with lacy pink edging his glimmering jellied bubble. Yuck—reminds me of when Sean got stung off of Mexico. Saw fifty pilot whales traveling east!

3.19.1974   More squalls but now a steady wind. Noon to noon 124 miles. Mom collecting water. Sean and I made popcorn! Exhilarating squall with 25 kn. of wind and solid sheets of water. Afterward, set fishing line since dinner wasn't planned. No luck though.

4.1.1974   Approaching Barbados. On 02–05 watch there was a long string of lights, many more than I expected. Turbulent seas as we went over "the shallows," then wind and seas calmed as we got at last into the lee. At 0015, Sean turned the binnacle light off, surprising Daddy who muttered distractedly that it was acting up. Sean giggled and finally yelled, "April fools!" When Daddy woke Mary K and I at 0200 for watch, he said it was very wet on deck and to wear our slickers. April fools again! Slept 0515 to 0750, when the chain went out with a roar in 35 feet of water in Bridgetown, Barbados. Passage complete. Sean made oatmeal, we neatened up below and had the skiff ready to launch by the time Customs officials came to clear us in. We kids fended off the heavy pilot boat with its eight Barbadian men to keep it from bashing the side of *Natasha*. Once cleared, into town for our mail [we only got it every three months or so]. Many packages and letters! Great! But every piece had a 2.5 cent fee leveled on it. Cost us about $2, which seemed like a lot. . . .

After the Caribbean and Bermuda, We Sailed Up to Gloucester MA,
Then South to the Chesapeake and Down Through the Inland Waterway
to Florida, and Finally Out to the Bahamas

12.22.1974   Discussion over breakfast about where to spend Christmas. Decided to stay in Georgetown harbor [Bahamas]. Lashed a Christmas tree in place and decorated it with cute things we had made. Took turns wrapping presents and sailing our skiff. Twenty-knot sou'easter blowing.

   12.25.1974   Christmas Day—our fourth this voyage! Santa Claus had filled the stockings. Put bacon and tea on and began opening gifts. I got an ornament, egret postcard, bikini underwear, and treacle candy from Santa, plus a scrimshaw necklace from Mary K and a leather bracelet from Sean. Ashore, we kids all played in the sand with Sean's new Tonka trucks, then walked into town for conch fritters. . . .

Through the Panama Canal

1.29.1975   Up 0515, skiff aboard, four 150-foot dock lines on deck. At 0600 we called by radio about our overdue advisor. Now he will come at 11:30! "Robby" finally arrived, wearing a black suit, tie, and hard-soled shoes. We made it to the lock at Miraflores by 1300. Monkey's fists [the large knot at the end of a mooring line that allows it to be thrown to an approaching ship] fell over the boom. I grabbed one and tied it to my port aft line. The others did theirs, and the huge doors closed. All secure as water started to bubble then surge in. Took up the slack. Then to the next lock—the handlers walked with us to the middle chamber. Up another 30 feet. Then into the third chamber, all going smoothly. Climbed to the spreaders [at the top of the mast] to take photos. Set sail to traverse the 48 miles of Gatun Lake. Doused sail for Gaillard Cut as dusk fell. At Pedro Miguel locks (it was now evening but well-lit), monkey fists again came down to attach the dock lines. Smooth descent— and suddenly we were back in the Pacific Ocean, where we started! . . .

At Sea, Puntarenas, Costa Rica, to Acapulco, Mexico

3.4.1975   Dunes in sight. Windy, then calm. Mary K saw sea snakes. As dark fell, we could see the lights of 35 fishing boats. Fresh-caught Spanish mackerel for dinner—crisp and meaty. 2330 Porpoises in weird phosphorescent glows made sudden spots of light, not streaks but splotches. Thinking: Many stateside acquaintances won't be able to grasp it all, the idea or meaning of our voyage. For us, everything is about to change: Mom's planning full-time work; I'll be a live-in babysitter; Mary K is going to be a camp counselor at Mystic Seaport; Sean's summer plans are uncertain. The next six months will bring many changes.

3.8.1975   Up 0715. Cliffs of Bahía de Acapulco and huge cross of Las Brisas. Sun shining on steep hillsides piled with houses, villas, and restaurants. The beaches have skyscraper hotels. Gave three cheers as we crossed a line of foam and "closed the circle" of our voyage. We had officially circumnavigated the globe.

Final Sea Passage, Cabo San Lucas to Santa Barbara

3.17.1975   St. Patrick's Day. Wore green, of course. Pilot whales! Chubby and big. Saw birds: phalaropes, boobies, a tropic bird. Frustrating progress—just 42 miles in 24 hours. Tempers frayed. But, while chatting with MK on deck, we were startled by three sea creatures (possibly pilot whales) bejeweled with huge diamonds of phosphorescence. Really beautiful.

3.19.1975   Fifty porpoises at dawn. I heard their squeaking in my bunk! We ran to the bowsprit to watch. Later, Mary K made creampuffs with chocolate frosting and read us more *Moby-Dick*.

3.23.1975   Noon to noon 65 miles. Good fair wind for a few hours, then nothing, then headwind again. Sea life! Pilot whales with bulbous foreheads: first four, then eight, then 24. A marlin who leaped ten times. At dusk, manta rays jumping! In every direction, five feet across, clearing the water. Boy, were we excited. Dinner on deck. All stayed for the sunset and lingered as the sky darkened.

3.31.1975   Noon to noon 64 miles. One ship, sharks, turtle, green flash at sunset. Too little space at chart table, arguing. Ravioli for dinner. Saw California kelp.

4.1.1975   April Fool's Day: Daddy told us it was raining. Sean put our bunkboards up. We honor our routines! Gorgeous day. Little sign of life except on *Natasha*. Wouldn't trade our vibrant life.

4.2.1972   Almost a gale at 0630. Bent on storm jib. It moderated some and we set jib and mizzen. Head seas and chop. Now anxious to arrive, but head winds and adverse current delay us.

4.3.1975   Noon to noon 64 miles. Contented day of comradeship. Engine on to help make time while seas were calm. Made bread. Sewed on deck and chatted with Sean about how to display our curios. Took pictures of crew in funny cold-weather regalia. Dad pulled up vivid red 2-inch crabs in a bucket from some floating kelp. A big joy now is realizing how unusual the trip is, comparing our adventures to those of other Americans. Feeling happy.

The democratization of boating, brought about by companies such as Owens Boats, introduced small sail- and motorboats that middle-class families could afford. Owens started in 1924 as a family-run custom boatbuilding business in Maryland, delivering about twenty wooden vessels a year. In 1936, the family adapted the mass-production techniques of the automobile industry to boatbuilding. Owens constructed 2,500 landing craft during World War II, then produced wooden motorboats for the postwar pleasure market that are now considered watercraft classics. In 1957, Owens introduced the fiberglass Flagship line, like the model pictured here. Flagship boats offered "A new world of pleasure," according to this postcard that the Owens Company supplied to its distributors to help them attract prospective buyers. The card's reverse explained that fiberglass craft were lighter and more affordable, and required less maintenance than wooden boats. Runabouts like the Owens Flagship series fit nicely on boat trailers, which autos could easily haul, allowing suburbanites to stow them in the backyard or driveway. When the weekend came, average families like the happy trio shown in the photo could get out on the water, just as rich people had been doing for decades. The postcard text concluded a Flagship boat was like the "family 'Home Afloat.' . . . Own one for as little as the price of a second car!" Photographer unknown, postcard, Owens Manufacturing Co., c. 1950s. Courtesy of the Roorda/Doyle Collection.

4.5.1975   Noon to noon 43 miles. Near fishing boats and little islands. Occasional seals, porpoises, kelp, shearwaters, cormorant and seagull flocks. Engine. Laundry. Cold out all day. Heated fresh water and took turns sponge bathing. At 1330 hauled in a 37-inch yellowfin tuna! Pressure-cooked it in two batches since there was so much. We eat dinner below now for warmth.

4.6.1975   Cruising near land, but slowly. Fifty miles in 24 hours. Creamed tuna on Chinese noodles. Phosphorescent and chilly out, eerie.

4.7.1975   Hove to. Rough, boat active, discouraged about progress. Mary K cheered us with jokes and spaghetti.

4.8.1975   Underway at 0545, just making our desired course. Noon to noon 12 miles. Yuck! Head current is a trial. Bread wouldn't rise in our chilly boat.

4.9.1975   Noon to noon 95 miles! That was a help.

4.11.1975   We're ready for a break in this foul weather! Things as usual aboard, various projects and moods. Finally sighted the harbor light just before dawn.

My log stops there . . . because we arrived in California, back where we started from.

Round the world! There is much in that sound to inspire proud feelings; but whereto does all that circumnavigation conduct? Only through numberless perils to the very point whence we started, where those that we left behind secure, were all the time before us.

—Herman Melville, "The Albatross," in *Moby-Dick*

XI

Laboratory

The Ocean sciences constitute a vast field of inquiry with a complex set of languages beyond the comprehension of the average individual. This part discusses, in layman's language, how the Ocean has functioned as a laboratory down through the centuries. It assembles accounts of a few milestone moments from the history of science at sea and combines them with selections of nature writing that illuminate some of the same aspects of the Ocean that researchers pursue. New scientific advances continue at a rapid pace. For instance, the most remote places on earth, which are found on the deepest seafloor, have begun to yield their secrets relatively recently.

The Pliny Deep

Pliny the Elder

Pliny the Elder (23–79 CE) was a Roman soldier and sailor, whose career took him from his birthplace near Verona, Italy, to Germany, Belgium, Africa, and Spain, as he rose in the ranks to become a powerful procurator, the military governor of an imperial province. Pliny was a dedicated scholar, naturalist, and author, who read voraciously, noted his observations voluminously, and wrote tirelessly about seemingly everything under the sun. He enjoyed his greatest freedom to study and compose in the last years of his life, during the reign of his personal friend the Emperor Vespasian (9–79 CE), who had emerged victorious in a power struggle to succeed the repressive Emperor Nero. It was at that time, around 77 CE, that Pliny wrote about the wonders of the sea and other salty topics in his encyclopedic Naturalis Historiae *(Of natural history). The work filled thirty-seven books and is the only one of Pliny's many writings to survive. His nephew, the author, lawyer, and magistrate known as Pliny the Younger (61–113 CE), left an account of Pliny the Elder's death on August 25, 79, when he became the most famous victim of the eruption of Mount Vesuvius, which destroyed the cities of Pompeii and Herculaneum.*

Chapter 101: Wonders of the Sea

All seas are purified at the full moon; some also at stated periods. At Messina and Mylæ a refuse matter, like dung, is cast up on the shore, whence originated the story of the oxen of the Sun having had their stable at that place.[1] To what has been said above (not to omit anything with which I am acquainted) Aristotle adds, that no animal dies except when the tide is ebbing. The observation has been often made on the ocean of Gaul; but it has only been found true with respect to man. . . .

Chapter 104: Why the Sea Is Salt

Hence it is that the widely diffused sea is impregnated with the flavour of salt, in consequence of what is sweet and mild being evaporated from it, which the force of fire easily accomplishes; while all the more acrid and thick matter is left behind; on which account the water of the sea is less salt, at some depth

435

than at the surface. And this is a more true cause of the acrid flavour, than that the sea is the continued perspiration of the land, or that the greater part of the dry vapour is mixed with it, or that the nature of the earth is such that it impregnates the waters, and, as it were, medicates them. Among the prodigies which have occurred, there is one which happened when Dionysius, the tyrant of Sicily, was expelled from his kingdom; that, for the space of one day, the water in the harbour became sweet. . . .

The moon, on the contrary [to the sun], is said to be a feminine and delicate planet, and also nocturnal; also that it resolves humours and draws them out, but does not carry them off. It is manifest that the carcases of wild beasts are rendered putrid by its beams, that, during sleep, it draws up the accumulated torpor into the head, that it melts ice, and relaxes all things by its moistening spirit. Thus the changes of nature compensate each other, and are always adequate to their destined purpose; some of them congealing the elements of the stars and others dissolving them. The moon is said to be fed by fresh, and the sun by salt water.

Chapter 105: Where the Sea Is the Deepest

Fabianus informs us that the greatest depth of the sea is 15 *stadia* [almost 2 miles].[2] We learn from others that in . . . the Depths of the Euxine [Black Sea], about 300 *stadia* from the main land, the sea is immensely deep, no bottom having been found.

Notes

1. Messina is the name of a city and province located in Sicily, on the Strait of Messina, which separates the island from the mainland of Italy; Mylæ refers to Milazzo, a coastal city in the province of Messina.
2. Aristotle referred to Fabianus, but nothing more is known of the ancient naturalist.

Leonardo's Notes on the Ocean

Leonardo da Vinci

The polymath genius of the Italian Renaissance Leonardo da Vinci (1452–1519) was curious about everything. He filled many volumes with notes, diagrams, and drawings documenting his observations, analyses, and conclusions, on topics spanning the known (and unknown) world, including the Ocean. On the pages Leonardo filled on the subject of the sea, he surmised (very wrongly) that more of the earth is dry land than is covered by water. He debunked Pliny's explanation of why seawater is salty with his own wildly inaccurate theory (which does, however, show his rudimentary understanding of inorganic chemistry), and he reflected on wave action, among other inquiries. Leonardo's astounding notebooks found a global audience in 1883, with the publication of a two-volume edition translated and edited by Jean Paul Richter (1763–1825), an eminent German art historian, which is the version excerpted here.

The Beginning of the Book on Water

Sea is the name given to that water which is wide and deep, in which the waters have not much motion.

Of the Surface of the Water in Relation to the Globe

The centres of the sphere of water are two, one universal and common to all water, the other particular. The universal one is that which is common to all waters not in motion, which exist in great quantities. As canals, ditches, ponds, fountains, wells, dead rivers, lakes, stagnant pools and seas, which, although they are at various levels, have each in itself the limits of their superficies [surfaces] equally distant from the centre of the earth, such as lakes placed at the tops of high mountains; as the lake near Pietra Pana and the lake of the Sybil near Norcia;[1] and all the lakes that give rise to great rivers, as the Ticino from Lago Maggiore, the Adda from the lake of Como, the Mincio from the lake of Garda, the Rhine from the lakes of Constance and of Chur, and from the lake of Lucerne, like the Tigris which passes through Asia Minor carrying with it the waters of three lakes, one above the other at different heights of which the highest is Munace, the middle one Pallas, and the lowest Triton; the Nile again flows from three very high lakes in Ethiopia.

Of the Centre of the Ocean

The centre of the sphere of waters is the true centre of the globe of our world, which is composed of water and earth, having the shape of a sphere. But, if you want to find the centre of the element of the earth, this is placed at a point equidistant from the surface of the ocean, and not equidistant from the surface of the earth; for it is evident that this globe of earth has nowhere any perfect rotundity, excepting in places where the sea is, or marshes or other still waters. And every part of the earth that rises above the water is farther from the centre.

Of the Sea Which Changes the Weight of the Earth

The shells, oysters, and other similar animals, which originate in sea-mud, bear witness to the changes of the earth round the centre of our elements. This is proved thus: Great rivers always run turbid, being coloured by the earth, which is stirred by the friction of their waters at the bottom and on their shores; and this wearing disturbs the face of the strata made by the layers of shells, which lie on the surface of the marine mud, and which were produced there when the salt waters covered them; and these strata were covered over again from time to time, with mud of various thickness, or carried down to the sea by the rivers and floods of more or less extent; and thus these layers of mud became raised to such a height, that they came up from the bottom to the air. At the present time these bottoms are so high that they form hills or high mountains, and the rivers, which wear away the sides of these mountains, uncover the strata of these shells, and thus the softened side of the earth continually rises and the antipodes sink closer to the centre of the earth, and the ancient bottoms of the seas have become mountain ridges.

Let the earth make whatever changes it may in its weight, the surface of the sphere of waters can never vary in its equal distance from the centre of the world.

Of the Proportion of the Mass of Water to That of the Earth

WHETHER THE EARTH IS LESS THAN THE WATER
Some assert that it is true that the earth, which is not covered by water is much less than that covered by water. But considering the size of 7,000 miles in diameter which is that of this earth, we may conclude the water to be of small depth.

Of the Earth

The great elevations of the peaks of the mountains above the sphere of the water may have resulted from this that: a very large portion of the earth which was filled with water that is to say the vast cavern inside the earth may have fallen in a vast part of its vault towards the centre of the earth, being pierced by means of the course of the springs which continually wear away the place where they pass.

It is of necessity that there should be more water than land, and the visible portion of the sea does not show this; so that there must be a great deal of water inside the earth, besides that which rises into the lower air and which flows through rivers and springs.

On the Ocean

Refutation of Pliny's theory as to the saltness of the sea.

WHY WATER IS SALT

Pliny says in his second book, chapter 103, that the water of the sea is salt because the heat of the sun dries up the moisture and drinks it up; and this gives to the wide stretching sea the savour of salt. But this cannot be admitted, because if the saltness of the sea were caused by the heat of the sun, there can be no doubt that lakes, pools and marshes would be so much the more salt, as their waters have less motion and are of less depth; but experience shows us, on the contrary, that these lakes have their waters quite free from salt. Again it is stated by Pliny in the same chapter that this saltness might originate, because all the sweet and subtle portions which the heat attracts easily being taken away, the more bitter and coarser part will remain, and thus the water on the surface is fresher than at the bottom; but this is contradicted by the same reason given above, which is, that the same thing would happen in marshes and other waters, which are dried up by the heat. Again, it has been said that the saltness of the sea is the sweat of the earth; to this it may be answered that all the springs of water which penetrate through the earth, would then be salt. But the conclusion is, that the saltness of the sea must proceed from the many springs of water which, as they penetrate into the earth, find mines of salt and these they dissolve in part, and carry with them to the ocean and the other seas, whence the clouds, the begetters of rivers, never carry it up. And the sea would be salter in our times than ever it was at any time; and if the adversary were to say that in infinite time the sea would dry up or congeal into salt, to this I answer that this salt is restored to the earth by the setting free of that part of the earth which rises out of the sea with the salt it has acquired, and the rivers return it to the earth under the sea.

For the third and last reason we will say that salt is in all created things;

and this we learn from water passed over the ashes and cinders of burnt things; and the urine of every animal, and the superfluities issuing from their bodies, and the earth into which all things are converted by corruption.

But,—to put it better,—given that the world is everlasting, it must be admitted that its population will also be eternal; hence the human species has eternally been and would be consumers of salt; and if all the mass of the earth were to be turned into salt, it would not suffice for all human food; whence we are forced to admit, either that the species of salt must be everlasting like the world, or that it dies and is born again like the men who devour it. But as experience teaches us that it does not die, as is evident by fire, which does not consume it, and by water which becomes salt in proportion to the quantity dissolved in it,—and when it is evaporated the salt always remains in the original quantity—it must pass through the bodies of men either in the urine or the sweat or other excretions where it is found again; and as much salt is thus got rid of as is carried every year into towns; therefore salt is dug in places where there is urine. Sea hogs and sea winds are salt.

We will say that the rains which penetrate the earth are what is under the foundations of cities with their inhabitants, and are what restore through the internal passages of the earth the saltness taken from the sea; and that the change in the place of the sea, which has been over all the mountains, caused it to be left there in the mines found in those mountains, &c.

The characteristics of sea water.

The waters of the salt sea are fresh at the greatest depths.

THAT THE OCEAN DOES NOT PENETRATE UNDER THE EARTH

The ocean does not penetrate under the earth, and this we learn from the many and various springs of fresh water which, in many parts of the ocean make their way up from the bottom to the surface. The same thing is farther proved by wells dug beyond the distance of a mile from the said ocean, which fill with fresh water; and this happens because the fresh water is lighter than salt water and consequently more penetrating.

Which weighs most, water when frozen or when not frozen?

FRESH WATER PENETRATES MORE AGAINST SALT WATER
THAN SALT WATER AGAINST FRESH WATER

That fresh water penetrates more against salt water, than salt water against fresh is proved by a thin cloth dry and old, hanging with the two opposite ends equally low in the two different waters, the surfaces of which are at an equal level; and it will then be seen how much higher the fresh water will rise in this piece of linen than the salt; by so much is the fresh lighter than the salt. . . .

A wave of the sea always breaks in front of its base, and that portion of the crest will then be lowest which before was highest.

That the shores of the sea constantly acquire more soil towards the middle of the sea; that the rocks and promontories of the sea are constantly being ruined and worn away; that the Mediterranean seas will in time discover their bottom to the air, and all that will be left will be the channel of the greatest river that enters it; and this will run to the ocean and pour its waters into that with those of all the rivers that are its tributaries.

Note

1. Pietra Pana is a mountain near Florence; the lake of the Sybil is Lake Vico in the province of Lazio, Italy; Norchia (Norcia) was an Etruscan city near Viterbo.

The Discovery of the Gulf Stream

Benjamin Franklin

The Gulf Stream is a current of warm water the size of a thousand Mississippi Rivers. It flows even faster than the Big Muddy does, moving at 4 miles per hour from the Gulf of Mexico through the Strait of Florida, then north along the western fringe of the Atlantic Ocean. It surrounds Bermuda, making the island's climate suitable for its eponymous shorts year-round. When the residents of coastal North Carolina face freezing winter storms, the people in Bermuda, 500 miles east on the same latitude, enjoy its famous beaches and golf courses. The tepid Gulf Stream slows down as it goes farther north, then it veers east to the British Isles, where snow rarely falls, as a result of its moderating proximity. By the time the Gulf Stream reaches its northernmost latitude, it sinks somewhat, mitigating its effect on the Arctic climate. But global warming hinders that submersion of warm water, which instead stays on the surface of the Ocean, accelerating the melting of Arctic Ocean ice.

Benjamin Franklin (1706–90) documented the existence of the Gulf Stream for the first time during his many Atlantic passages, as seen in these conclusions, which he published in 1786 in the Transactions of the American Philosophical Society.

Vessels are sometimes retarded, and sometimes forwarded in their voyages, by currents at sea, which are often not perceived. About the year 1769 or 70, there was an application made by the board of customs at Boston, to the lords of the treasury in London, complaining that the packets between Falmouth and New York, were generally a fortnight longer in their passages, than merchant ships from London to Rhode Island, and proposing that for the future they should be ordered to Rhode Island instead of New York. Being then concerned in the management of the American post-office, I happened to be consulted on the occasion; and it appearing strange to me that there should be such a difference between two places, scarce a day's run asunder, especially when the merchant ships are generally deeper laden, and more weakly manned than the packets, and had from London the whole length of the river and channel to run before they left the land of England, while the packets had only to go from Falmouth, I could not but think the fact misunderstood or misrepresented. There happened then to be in London, a Nantucket sea-captain of my acquaintance, to whom I communicated the affair. He told me he believed the fact might be true; but the difference was owing to this, that the Rhode Island captains were acquainted with the gulf stream, which those of English packets were not. We are all acquainted with that stream, says he, because in our pursuit of whales, which keep near the sides of it, but are not to be met with in it, we run down along the sides, and frequently cross it to change our side: and in crossing it have sometimes met and spoke with the packets, who were in the middle of it, and stemming it. We have informed them that they were stemming a current, that was against them to the value of three miles an hour; and advised them to cross it and get out of it; but they were too wise to be counselled by simple American fishermen. When the winds are but light, he added, they are carried back by the current more than they are forwarded by the wind: and if the wind be good, the subtraction of 70 miles a day from their course is of some importance. I then observed that it was a pity no notice was taken of this current upon the charts, and requested him to mark it out for me, which he readily complied with, adding directions for avoiding it in sailing from Europe to North America. I procured it to be engraved by order from the general post-office, on the old chart of the Atlantic, at Mount and Page's, Tower-hill; and copies were sent down to Falmouth for the captains of the packets, who slighted it however; but it is since printed in France, of which edition I hereto annex a copy.

This stream is probably generated by the great accumulation of water on the eastern coast of America between the tropics, by the trade winds which constantly blow here. It is known that a large piece of water ten miles broad and generally only three feet deep, has by a strong wind had its waters driven to one side and sustained so as to become six feet deep, while the windward side was laid dry. This may give some idea of the quantity heaped up on the American coast, and the reason of its running down in a strong current through the islands into the bay of Mexico, and from thence issuing through the gulph of Florida, and proceeding along the coast to the banks of New-foundland, where it turns off towards and runs down through the Western islands. Having since crossed this stream several times in passing between America and Europe, I have been attentive to sundry circumstances relating to it, by which to know when one is in it; and besides the gulph weed with which it is interspersed, I find that it is always warmer than the sea on each side of it, and that it does not sparkle in the night: I annex hereto the observations made with the thermometer in two voyages, and possibly may add a third. It will appear from them, that the thermometer may be an useful instrument to a navigator, since currents coming from the northward into southern seas, will probably be found colder than the water of those seas, as the currents from southern seas into northern are found warmer. And it is not to be wondered that so vast a body of deep warm water, several leagues wide, coming from between the tropics and issuing out of the gulph in to the northern seas, should retain its warmth longer than the twenty or thirty days

Benjamin Franklin realized that locating and publicizing the Gulf Stream would benefit mariners, merchants, and passengers, making voyages both shorter and safer. A century and a half after Franklin drew his 1770 chart of the Gulf Stream (see color plate), hotel entrepreneurs in Florida decided that publicizing "the Magic of the Gulf Stream" would be similarly beneficial for vacationers, and for themselves. This advertisement, published by the Florida East Coast Hotel Association in the November 1926 issue of *Travel* magazine, depicts the recently completed highway skirting the shore of the Atlantic Ocean, as well as new, palatial seaside hotels in cities from ancient Saint Augustine to the tourist boomtowns of Palm Beach and Miami. The enormous facilities—the Royal Poinciana Hotel in Palm Beach was the largest wooden building in the world—sprouted along the East Florida Railroad, which was founded by Henry Flagler, financier of all the resorts on this map. Miniature graphic references in the advertisement's design illustrate Floridian recreation: polo, golf, tennis, sailing, swimming, sport fishing, and tea dances under the palm trees. Today, only two of the original sprawling structures remain, both in Saint Augustine. In their place, miles of high-rise hotels, apartment buildings, and condominium towers line the beach—and over the horizon is the mighty saltwater river of the Gulf Stream. Courtesy of the Roorda/Doyle Collection.

444

required to its passing the banks of Newfoundland. The quantity is too great, and it is too deep to be suddenly cooled by passing under a cooler air. The air immediately over it, however, may receive so much warmth from it as to be rarified and rise, being rendered lighter than the air on each side of the stream; hence those airs must flow in to supply the place of the rising warm air, and meeting with each other, form those tornados and warm spouts frequently met with, and seen near and over the stream; and as the vapour from a cup of tea in a warm room, and the breath of an animal in the same room, are hardly visible, but become sensible immediately when out in the cold air, so the vapour from the gulph stream, in warm latitudes is scarcely visible, but when it comes into the cool air from Newfoundland, it is condensed into the fogs, for which those parts are so remarkable.

The power of wind to raise water above its common level in the sea, is known to us in America, by the high tides occasioned in all our sea ports when a strong northeaster blows against the gulph stream.

The conclusion from these remarks is, that a vessel from Europe to North America may shorten her passage by avoiding to stem the stream, in which the thermometer will be very useful; and a vessel from America to Europe may do the same by the same means of keeping in it. It may often have happened accidentally, that voyages have been shortened by these circumstances. It is well to have the command of them.

Celestial Navigation for the People

Nathaniel Ingersoll Bowditch

The genius mathematician Nathaniel Bowditch (1773–1838) devoted his life to celestial navigation, using the deck of a merchant ship as his observatory. He devised a simplified approach to the notoriously complicated skill of finding latitude and longitude by measuring the positions of the sun, moon, and stars, putting it into use during five long Ocean voyages in less than a decade. Near the end of his career at sea, Bowditch disseminated his invaluable system in the indispensable handbook The New American Practical Navigator. *The volume became an essential tool for navigators from the moment it was first published in 1802. Bowditch became an insurance company president, but he continued to revise his encyclopedic reference work until his death in 1838. His son Nathaniel Ingersoll Bowditch took over editing and publishing subsequent editions of the book until 1866, when the government deemed it to be so important that the United States Hydrographic Office bought the copyright. The government has kept* Bowditch, *as the book has been known to generations of sailors, in print to the present day, with regularly updated editions; it is still up to date and available, free of charge, on a .gov website. Nathaniel Ingersoll Bowditch wrote two biographies of his father, one for juvenile readers, and one for a general audience, which provides the following portrait of the most influential navigator of all time.*

Dr. Bowditch began life with the same pursuits which his ancestors had followed for so many generations. Between the years 1795 and 1804, he made five voyages, performing the first in the capacity of clerk, and the three next in that of supercargo, all under the command of Captain Henry Prince, of Salem.[1] On his fifth and last voyage, he acted as both master and supercargo. He sailed upon the first of these voyages, January 11, 1795, in the ship *Henry*, bound to the Isle of Bourbon, and was absent exactly one year.[2] His three next voyages were in the ship *Astrea*, which sailed, in 1796, for Lisbon, Madeira, and Manilla, and arrived at Salem in May, 1797; and again in August, 1798, sailed for Cadiz, thence to the Mediterranean, loaded at Alicant, and arrived at Salem in April, 1799; and in July, 1799, sailed from Boston to Batavia and Manilla, and returned in September, 1800; and his fifth voyage was in the *Putnam*, which sailed from Beverly, November 21, 1802, bound for Sumatra, and arrived at Salem December 25, 1803.

He has related that, upon the first of these voyages, he carried out, as an adventure, a small box of shoes, which article proved on his arrival at the Isle of Bourbon to be in great demand. He sold them for about three times the first cost, and having made an advantageous investment of the proceeds, he returned home quite elated, and feeling that the fickle goddess had smiled upon him more propitiously than she ever had done upon any mortal before.

Of his second voyage, Captain Prince relates, that one day, when dining at the table of the American consul at Madeira, "his supercargo laid down his knife and fork, and, after squeezing the tips of his fingers for two minutes," gave to the lady of the house an answer to an intricate question which she had proposed; to the great astonishment of her clerk, who, after a long calculation, had succeeded in solving it, and "who exclaimed that he did not believe there was another man on the island who could have done it in two hours."

During his third voyage, on the passage from Cadiz to Alicant, they were chased by a French privateer; but, being well armed and manned, they determined on resistance. The duty assigned to Dr. Bowditch was that of handing up the powder upon deck. And in the midst of the preparations, the captain looked into the cabin, where he was no less surprised than amused at finding his supercargo quietly seated by his keg of powder, and busily occupied, as usual, with his slate and pencil. He said to him, "I suppose you could now make your will," to which he smilingly assented. He did in fact give to his eldest son his instructions in regard to his last will, with the like calmness and composure, when there was not only an apparent danger, but an absolute certainty, of the near approach of death.

Upon his arrival at Manilla, during his fourth voyage, the captain, being asked how he contrived to find his way, in the face of a north-east monsoon, by mere dead-reckoning, replied, "that he had a crew of twelve men, every one of whom could take and work a lunar observation as well, for all practical purposes, as Sir Isaac Newton himself, were he alive." During this conversation, Dr. Bowditch sat as modest as a maid, saying not a word, but holding his slate pencil in his mouth; while another person remarked, that "there was more knowledge of navigation on board that ship than there ever was in all the vessels that have floated in Manilla Bay." . . .

In his last voyage, Dr. Bowditch arrived off the coast in mid-winter, and in the height of a violent north-east snow-storm. He had been unable to get an observation for a day or two, and felt very anxious and uneasy at the dangerous situation of the vessel. At the close of the afternoon of December 25, he came on deck, and took the whole management of the ship into his own hands. Feeling very confident where the vessel was, he kept his eyes directed towards the light on Baker's Island, at the entrance of Salem harbor. Fortunately, in the interval between two gusts of wind, the fall of snow became less dense than before, and he thus obtained a glimpse of the light of which he was in search. It was seen by but one other person, and in the next instant all was again impenetrable darkness. Confirmed, however, in his previous convictions, he now kept on the same course, entered the harbor, and finally anchored in safety. He immediately went on shore, and the owners were very much alarmed at his sudden appearance on such a tempestuous night, and at first could hardly be persuaded that he had not been wrecked. . . .

But the long intervals of leisure which a sailor's life afforded, he chiefly devoted to his favorite study, pursuing with unremitting zeal those researches in which he had already made such progress, notwithstanding the interruptions and embarrassments of his earlier days. Here, with only the sea around him, and the sky above him, protected alike from all the intruding cares and engrossing pleasures of life, he especially delighted to hold converse with the master-spirits who had attempted to explain the mysteries of the visible universe, and the laws by which the great energies of nature are guided and controlled. M. Lacroix mentioned to one of the sons of Dr. Bowditch, that from him he had received several corrections and notices of errata in his works, which our navigator had discovered during these long India voyages.[3] And in the ship in which he sailed were witnessed not merely the labors and vigils of the solitary student, but the teachings of the kind and generous instructer [sic], anxious and eager to impart to others the knowledge which he had himself acquired. "He loved study himself," says Captain Prince, "and he loved to see others study. He was always fond of teaching others. He would do any thing if any one would show a disposition to learn. Hence," he adds, "all was harmony on board; all had a zeal for study; all were ambitious to learn." On one occasion, two sailors were zealously disputing, in the hearing of the captain and supercargo, respecting sines and cosines. The result of his teaching, in enabling the whole crew of twelve men to work a lunar observation, has been before stated. Every one of those twelve sailors subsequently attained, at least, the rank of first or second officer of a ship. It was a circumstance highly in favor of a seaman, that he had sailed with Dr. Bowditch, and was often sufficient to secure his promotion. Connected with much testimony of this sort, is that of the uniform affability and kindness of manner displayed by Dr. Bowditch in his intercourse with all on board, which were especially calculated to increase the self-respect of the sailor, and inspire him with a due sense of his own powers, and of the importance of his occupation. In a letter from an officer in the United States navy, who sailed twice in the *Astrea* with Dr. Bowditch, at first as a cabin boy, and who died a few months after the friend of whom he speaks, the writer states some of the above particulars respecting Dr. Bowditch, and adds that "his kindness and attention to the poor sea-sick cabin boy are to this hour uppermost in my memory, and will be so when his logarithms and lunar observations are remembered no more." . . .

The following is the account of his habits when at sea, given by one who was his companion during several voyages. "His practice was to rise at a very early hour in the morning, and pursue his studies till breakfast, immediately after which he walked rapidly for about half an hour, and then went below to his studies till half past eleven o'clock, when he returned and walked till the hour at which he commenced his meridian observations. Then came the dinner, after which he was engaged in his studies till five o'clock; then he walked till tea time, and after tea was at his studies till nine in the evening. From this hour till half past ten, he appeared to have banished all thoughts of study, and, while walking at his usual quick pace, he would converse in the most lively manner, giving us useful information, intermixed with amusing anecdotes and an occasional hearty laugh. He thus made the time delightful to the officers who walked with him. Whenever the heavenly bodies were in distance to get the longitude, night or day, he was sure to make his observations once, and frequently twice, in every twenty-four hours, always preferring to make them by the moon and stars, as less fatiguing to his eyes. He was often seen on deck at other times, walking, apparently in deep thought, when it was well understood by all on board that he was not to be disturbed, as we supposed he was solving some difficult problem; and when he darted below, the conclusion was that he had got the idea. If he were in the fore part of the ship when the idea came to him, he would actually run to the cabin, and his countenance would give the expression that he had found a prize." Another correspondent states that sometimes, when he wished to pursue his studies without disturbing those in the cabin by introducing a candle or lamp, he has seen him standing in the companion-way with his slate and pencil, working out some problem, at eleven o'clock at night, by the aid only of the binnacle lamp.[4]

Such was Dr. Bowditch's seafaring life, not wasted in ennui or idle reveries, but every moment of it devoted to the improvement alike of his own mind and character, and those of every individual in the little world around him.

Notes

1. A supercargo supervised the cargo, with no physical labor expected of him. Usually, the sailors resented the supercargo for the privileged position he held.
2. The former name of Reunión Island, in the Indian Ocean east of Madagascar.
3. Perhaps the French topographer Marie-Nicolas Chrestien de Lacroix (1754–1836). The polyglot Bowditch's command of French, facilitated by his grasp of Latin, was excellent, and he also acquired Spanish, German, and Dutch.
4. The companionway is the set of stairs down to the cabin. The binnacle is the compass, kept illuminated at night so that the helmsman can steer the vessel on its course.

The Ocean and the Atmosphere

Matthew Fontaine Maury

For someone known as the Pathfinder of the Seas, who is sometimes called the Father of Modern Oceanography, Matthew Fontaine Maury (1806–71) spent very little time on the Ocean. He spent thirty-five years in the US Navy, but a leg injury that he sustained early in his career prevented him from extensive shipboard service. Instead, he devoted his time to gathering information from mariners concerning every aspect of the Ocean, immersing himself not only in oceanography but also in astronomy and meteorology, and rose to be the superintendent of the US Naval Observatory. Maury furthered Benjamin Franklin's work on the Gulf Stream by locating it precisely, among many other areas of useful inquiry. He made his findings available in 1852 in the form of the portable Wind and Current Chart of the North Atlantic, *which allowed navigators to use to their advantage the collective experience that he had assembled and analyzed, by charting the most efficient routes and reducing the duration (thereby increasing the safety) of their voyages. Maury compiled his extensive data in the seminal study he titled* The Physical Geography of the Sea, *first published in 1855. When the American Civil War broke out, Maury resigned his US Navy commission out of loyalty to his native Virginia and volunteered his expertise to the navy of the Confederate States. During the war, he deviated from his life's work of analyzing and disseminating oceanographic information and devoted himself to the business of killing. He developed an "electric torpedo" that prefigured modern mines, and which destroyed twenty-seven Union vessels. Secretary of the Navy Gideon Welles stated that mines "cost the Union more vessels than all other causes combined." Maury's stature in the Confederate military was so high that his larger-than-life statue can be found today, along with those of Robert E. Lee and Thomas "Stonewall" Jackson, on Monument Avenue in Richmond, Virginia.*

The Equatorial Cloud-Ring

Seafaring people have, as if by common consent, divided the ocean off into regions, and characterized them according to the winds; e.g., there are the "trade-wind regions," the "variables," the "horse latitudes," the "doldrums," &c. The "horse latitudes" are the belts of calms and light airs which border the Polar edge of the northeast trades. They were so called from the circumstance that vessels formerly bound from New England to the West Indies, with a deck load of horses, were often so delayed in this calm belt of Cancer, that, for the want of water for their animals, they were compelled to throw a portion of them overboard.

The "equatorial doldrums" is another of these calm places. Besides being a region of calms and baffling winds, it is a region noted for its rains and clouds, which make it one of the most oppressive and disagreeable places at sea. The emigrant ships from Europe for Australia have to cross it. They are often baffled in it for two or three weeks; then the children and the passengers who are of delicate health suffer most. It is a frightful graveyard on the way-side to that golden land.

A vessel bound into the southern hemisphere from Europe or America, after clearing the region of variable winds and crossing the "horse latitudes," enters the northeast trades. Here the mariner finds the sky sometimes mottled with clouds, but for the most part clear. Here, too, he finds his barometer rising and falling under the ebb and flow of a regular atmospherical tide, which gives a high and low barometer every day with such regularity that the time of day within a few minutes may be told by it. The rise and fall of this tide, measured by the barometer, amounts to about one tenth (0.1) of an inch, and it occurs daily and everywhere between the tropics; the maximum about 10h. 30m. A.M., the minimum between 4h. and 5h. P.M., with a second maximum and minimum about 10 P.M. and 5 A.M. The diurnal variation of the needle changes also with the turning of these invisible tides. Continuing his course toward the equinoctial line, he observes his thermometer to rise higher and higher as he approaches it; at last, entering the region of equatorial calms and rains, he feels the weather to become singularly close and oppressive; he discovers here that the elasticity of feeling which he breathed from the tradewind air has forsaken him; he has entered the doldrums, and is under the "cloud-ring." Escaping from this gloomy region, and entering the southeast trades beyond, his spirits revive, and he turns to his log-book to see what changes are recorded there. He is surprised to find that, notwithstanding the oppressive weather of the rainy latitudes, both his thermometer and barometer stood, while in them, lower than in the clear weather on either side of them; that just before entering and just before leaving the rainy parallels, the mercury of the thermometer and barometer invariably stands higher than it does when within them, even though they include the equator. In crossing the equatorial doldrums he has passed a ring of clouds that encircles the earth. . . .

One need not go to sea to perceive the grand work which the clouds perform in collecting moisture from the crystal vaults of the sky, in sprinkling it upon the fields, and making the hills glad with showers of rain. Winter and summer, "the clouds drop fatness upon the earth." This part of their office is obvious to all, and I do not propose to consider it now. But the sailor at

Among Matthew Fontaine Maury's voluminous findings on Ocean currents, prevailing winds, weather, whale migration, and sea-lanes, his work on tides was also of great help to seafarers. By consulting Maury's tide charts, seafarers could time their departures and arrivals depending on whether they wanted to find the tide rising, as pictured in this postcard, or on the ebb. Photographer unknown, *Tide Rising*, rotary photographic plate postcard, c. 1909. Courtesy of the Roorda/Doyle Collection.

sea observes phenomena and witnesses operations in the terrestrial economy which tell him that, in the beautiful and exquisite adjustments of the grand machinery of the atmosphere, the clouds have other important offices to perform besides those merely of dispensing showers, of producing the rains, and of weaving mantles of snow for the protection of our fields in winter. As important as are these offices, the philosophical mariner, as he changes his sky, is reminded that the clouds have commandments to fulfill, which, though less obvious, are not therefore the less benign in their influences, or the less worthy of his notice. He beholds them at work in moderating the extremes of heat and cold, and in mitigating climates. At one time they spread themselves out; they cover the earth as with a mantle; they prevent radiation from its crust, and keep it warm. At another time, they interpose between it and the sun; they screen it from his scorching rays, and protect the tender plants from his heat, the land from the drought; or, like a garment, they overshadow

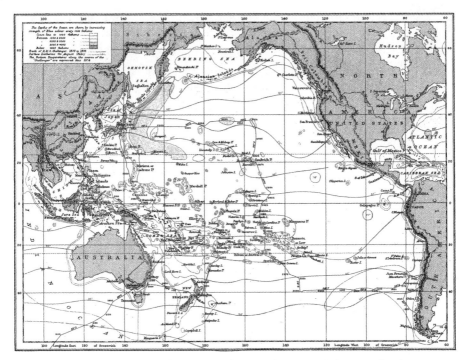

In 1871, the Royal Society of London chartered the warship HMS *Challenger*, refitted it as a floating laboratory, and dispatched it to explore and study the Ocean. *Challenger* took soundings for the first time in the deep Ocean, discovering on March 23, 1875, the deepest canyon in the Ocean floor, the Mariana Trench, at 8,184 meters. In the twenty-first century, submersibles recorded depths to nearly 11,000 meters nearby. The *Challenger* expedition covered 80,500 miles, identified more than 4,000 previously unknown species, and collected data, making possible charts like this one. The black line represents its route, showing depths in fathoms (the Mariana Islands being the most notable), in shading (the darker, the deeper), and temperature at the bottom. The curving lines are isotherms, which have the same average temperature at a given time. W. and A. K. Johnston, "Pacific Ocean," from *Encyclopedia Britannica*, 9th ed., vol. 18, edited by William Robertson Smith (London: A & C Black, 1878), plate 3. Courtesy of the Roorda/Doyle Collection.

the sea, defending its waters from the intense forces of evaporation. Having performed these offices for one place, they are evaporated and given up to the sunbeam and the winds again, to be borne on their wings away to other places which stand in need of like offices. Familiar with clouds and sunshine, the storm and the calm, and all the phenomena which find expression in the physical geography of the sea, the right-minded mariner, as he contemplates "the cloud without rain," ceases to regard it as an empty thing; he perceives that it performs many important offices; he regards it as a great moderator of heat and cold—as a "compensation" in the atmospherical mechanism which makes the performance of the grand machine perfect.

Marvelous are the offices and wonderful is the constitution of the atmosphere. Indeed, I know of no subject more fit for profitable thought on the part of the truth-loving, knowledge seeking student, be he seaman or landsman, than that afforded by the atmosphere and its offices. Of all parts of the physical machinery, of all the contrivances in the mechanism of the universe, the atmosphere, with its offices and its adaptations, appears to me to be the most wonderful, sublime, and beautiful. In its construction, the perfection of knowledge is involved.

Hurrah for the Dredge!

Edward Forbes

A nineteenth-century fad for Ocean science in the UK and the US brought droves of middle-class citizens to the seashore, where they combed the beaches and the rocky intertidal zones, collecting marine specimens. The more ambitious and adventurous among them set out in small boats, dragging dredges to catch bottom-dwelling life forms.

At the same time, professional naturalists who were interested in sea creatures— soon to be known as marine biologists—employed the same methods to advance their infant discipline. Prominent among these early practitioners was Edward Forbes (1815–54), from the Isle of Man, who received his education at the University of Edinburgh and later became a professor there. Forbes wrote his first book, History of the British Starfishes *(1841), based on findings from his hours of far-flung dredging, which he carried out with the help of fishermen, whose assistance and watercraft he hired for the purpose. He celebrated the challenges and triumphs of dredging in the lyrics to "The Dredging Song," which he set to a popular tune of the time and presented at a meeting of the British Society of naturalists in 1839.*

Forbes went on to serve as a naturalist for the Royal Navy, on a surveying voyage in the Mediterranean Sea aboard the HMS *Beacon, leading to a book on its mollusks and jellyfish. His magnum opus was* The Natural History of the European Seas *(1859), with a frontispiece in the form of a cartoon he drew, showing someone in a rowboat towing a dredge while, far below, gargantuan specimens of snails, fish, and jellyfish laughingly elude the contraption's open mouth. His contention that the seafloor in depths below 1,800 feet is mainly barren has been abundantly disproven, as subsequent entries in this volume demonstrate.*

Despite decades of dedicated dragging of the Ocean with dredges and nets, marine scientists failed to find the most abundant vertebrate in saltwater, the bristlemouth fish, until 2015. That's when the existence of this vast biomass briefly made news. The tiny fish had been hiding in plain sight the whole time, the perfect size to elude the multitude of nets deployed to find sea life. But when scientists finally found the bristlemouth fish, their sheer numbers astounded the experts. The low estimate is about 24 billion, but it is entirely likely that there are actually trillions of these organisms, thriving undetected in the vast, abyssal spaces of the deep Ocean.

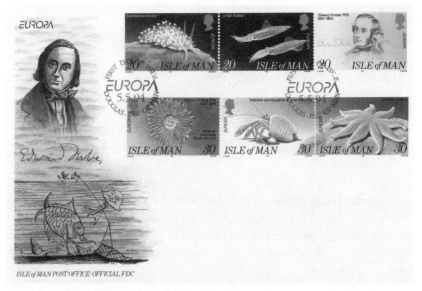

To celebrate Edward Forbes "as possibly the most eminent Manx scientist ever," the Isle of Man released a series of commemorative stamps in 1994. They featured five of the discoveries he made as "the father of British dredging," and "the father of British oceanography." The species included a cloak anemone, a purple sunstar, a sea slug, and the squid *Loligi forbesii*, named for him. Jennifer Toombs, Edward Forbes First Day Cover, Isle of Man Post Office, 1994. Contains public sector information licensed under the Open Government License v3.0. Courtesy of the Roorda/Doyle Collection.

Hurrah for the dredge, with its iron edge,
And its mystical triangle,
And its hided net with meshes set
Odd fishes to entangle!
The ship may move through the wave above,
'Mid scenes exciting wonder,
But braver sights the dredge delights
As it roveth the waters under.

CHORUS

Then a-dredging we will go, wise boys!
Then a-dredging we will go!

Down in the deep, where the mermen sleep,
Our gallant dredge is sinking,
Each finny shape in a precious scrape
Will find itself in a twinkling!
They may twirl and twist, and writhe as they wist,
And break themselves into sections,

But up they all, at the dredge's call,
Must come to fill collections.

The creatures strange the sea that range,
Though mighty in their stations,
To the dredge must yield the briny field
Of their loves and depredations.
The crab so bold, like a knight of old,
In scaly armour plated,
And the slimy snail, with a shell on his tail,
And the star-fish—radiated.

Return of the Fossil Fish

J. L. B. Smith

The biggest news in the field of zoology in the twentieth century was the astounding rediscovery of the ancient fish called the coelacanth, known only through bizarre fossils, in the waters off South Africa in 1938. The ichthyologist who confirmed the identity of the creature, J. L. B. Smith (1897–1968), spent years searching for new species, with the aid of Marjorie Courtenay-Latimer (1917–2004), curator of the East London Museum in Eastern Cape, South Africa, the nation's pioneer institution of natural history. Smith and Courtenay-Latimer enlisted fishermen to collect scientific specimens, asking them to preserve their unwanted, unmarketable bycatch from their trawling, for the experts to examine. The result of this collaboration was the unexpected find of a "living fossil," which Smith called "Old Fourlegs" and described in a book titled The Search beneath the Sea: The Story of the Coelacanth *(1956). Thirteen years later, a second specimen was caught in the Comoro Islands, finally giving Smith a chance to see one himself.*

So here we have the picture of the Coelacanths. This remarkable type appeared more than 300 million years ago, and has gone on, virtually unchanged as such things go, until the present time. In that long time countless other types of fishy creatures evolved, flourished, and vanished, many of them types that may have seemed more suited for survival than our old Coelacanth, but he has outlived them all. He goes plodding steadily on, his needs few and simple, and he will quite likely still be there when many of these "active modern types," which are supposed to have driven him to the depths, will be gone and long forgotten. He reminds one of a solitary, tough old man, asking favours of none. Old man Coelacanth. Degenerate? Never!

From the start Miss Latimer wisely concentrated on building up exhibits representative of the life of the area served by the Museum, and this she carried out with characteristic energy and enthusiasm. As Miss Latimer realised that angling is the chief sport and hobby in that area, she got the commercial fishing firms to collaborate, and especially from Messrs. Irvin and Johnson's branch at East London received a constant stream of valuable marine specimens which were mounted and exhibited at the Museum. She wisely made personal contact with the officers and crews of the trawlers, and infected them with some of her own enthusiasm, so that they watched for unusual specimens of all kinds from the trawl, many of which were kept and brought to port. It became the custom to pile up the "rubbish" so that she could scratch through it, and indeed she found many treasures that way.

It was therefore with no sense of anything unusual that Miss Latimer received a telephone message from the manager of Irvin and Johnson at East London in the late morning of the 22nd December 1938, to say that a trawler had brought in a pile of fish for her to examine. She called a taxi and with Enoch the native assistant of the Museum went down to the wharf some miles off. When she got there the captain had already left the ship, but one of the deck-hands took her to the pile of fish they had put aside, mostly sharks. Those she already knew and had got previously, but then, almost hidden, she noticed a large heavily scaled blue fish, and as a peculiar fin and the colour attracted her attention, she had the fish pulled out. It was a peculiar creature, like nothing she had ever seen before, and she stared at it in puzzlement for some time and examined its mouth and fins.

She asked the old trawlerman if he had ever seen one before, but he replied that in his thirty years at sea in that work he had certainly never seen any fish of that type, and he pointed out that the fins were like arms, it looked almost like a big lizard. Miss Latimer thought it looked something like a Lung-fish, but in any case decided that it was obviously something rare which it would certainly be advisable to keep. The trawlerman said it was a lovely blue when taken from the water, but was a vicious brute, snapping its jaws fiercely. They had all been struck by its unusual appearance, for none of them had seen anything like it before, so they had called Captain Goosen to look at it, and when he touched the body, it heaved itself up suddenly, snapping its jaws viciously and had nearly caught his hand in its formidable fang-lined mouth. The captain ordered the crew to put it on one side so that Miss Latimer could see it, for by then he had decided to go straight in to port.

The fish was 5 feet long and heavy. As a matter of interest Miss Latimer got them to weigh it; 127 lb. It was a scorching hot day and the fish had a smell— all fish have on hot days—but the Coelacanth has one all its own, as we came to know only too well. According to Miss Latimer, she had very considerable difficulty in persuading the taximan to consent to having the fish in his taxi at all, even though she had brought along old bags to put on the floor on which to rest any fish. The taximan was so reluctant that he stood aloof and distant while she and a native struggled and wrestled to get the creature into the vehicle. One may sympathise with that taximan, while smiling at the incongruity of refusing to transport what was the most valuable zoological specimen in the world, though none of them knew it at that time.

On the side of the lagoon at Knysna, some miles from the sea, we have a house with a laboratory, where I do not only considerable general angling but carry out regular and periodic investigations on the extraordinarily rich and

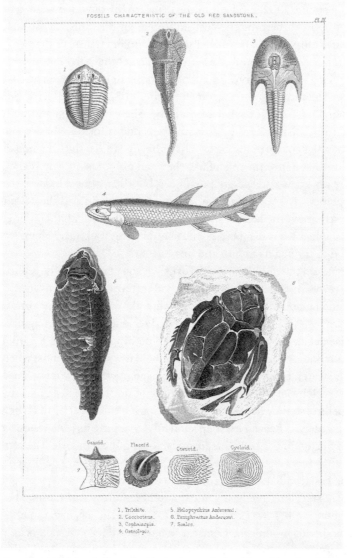

1. Trilobite.   5. Holoptychius Andersoni.
2. Coccosteus.   6. Pamphractus Andersoni.
3. Cephalaspis.   7. Scales.
4. Osteolepis.

Outcroppings of rock from the Devonian period are found in a band from northern North America, Greenland, the British Isles, and Norway. Formed between about 350 and 400 million years ago, the Old Red Limestone includes fossils of many vanished species, such as the trilobite on the upper left. The fish in the engraving's center is an *Osteolepis*, or "bone scale," of about eight inches, one of the many species of the Sarcopterygii (which means "flesh fin"), commonly known as lobefin fish. A far more massive lobefin fish, which was a relative of the little *Osteolepis*, was the coelacanth. Engraver unknown, *Fossils Characteristic of the Old Red Sandstone*, from *The Pictorial History of Scotland: From the Roman Invasion to the Close of the Jacobite Rebellion, A.D. 79–1746*, vol. 1, edited by James Taylor (London: J. S. Virtue, 1859), after p. xxvi. Courtesy of the Roorda/Doyle Collection.

varied fish-life of this large estuary. It is an exceedingly interesting body of water, with many unique characters.

In December 1938 we had gone from Grahamstown to Knysna. I had been unwell, and was not fully recovered even in the New Year. About midday on the 3rd January 1939 a friend brought us a large batch of mail matter from the town, very much of a Christmas–New Year accumulation, and this was sorted out between us, each settling down to his or her letters. Mine were the usual mixture of examination results and queries, and numbers about fishes. One was from the East London Museum, in Miss Latimer's well-known hand, the first page very much the usual form, asking for assistance in classification. Then I turned the page and saw the sketch, at which I stared and stared, at first in puzzlement, for I did not know any fish of our own or indeed of any seas like that; it looked more like a lizard. And then a bomb seemed to burst in my brain, and beyond that sketch and the paper of the letter I was looking at a series of fishy creatures that flashed up as on a screen, fishes no longer here, fishes that had lived in dim past ages gone, and of which only often fragmentary remains in rocks are known. I told myself sternly not to be a fool, but there was something about that sketch that seized on my imagination and told me that this was something very far beyond the usual run of fishes in our seas. It was as if my common sense were waging a battle with my perception, and I kept on staring at that sketch, trying to read into it perhaps more than it held. In this surge of violent thoughts and reactions, the world about me had ceased to exist, until I heard my name called, it seemed from far away, then suddenly again, close by, and more urgently, and loudly. ... There was my wife, staring at me from across the table with deep concern on her face, as was also her mother across at the corner; both were looking at me intently. I found to my surprise that I was standing. My wife tells that she was engrossed in a letter when suddenly she felt that something was wrong, and looking up saw me on my feet, staring at a letter in my hand. The light was behind me and she could see a fish-like drawing through the thin paper. "What on earth is the matter?" she said, and I came back to the present. Looking again at the letter and sketch I said slowly, "This is from Miss Latimer, and unless I am quite off the rails she has got something that is really startling. Don't think me mad, but I believe there is a good chance that it is a type of fish generally thought to have been extinct for many millions of years." My wife says that she did wonder if I had got a touch of the sun, for she knew that I usually weighed every word, and this was quite the most extraordinary thing she had ever heard from my lips.

XII

The Endangered Ocean

This part is a troubling news flash. The fish are disappearing, species are shifting around wildly, water temperatures and sea levels are rising, and humanity is threatened. The End?

Alarming signs of crisis in the Ocean can be seen in the form of exhausted walruses and starving seabirds. The mammals are unable to find floating sea ice in the rapidly warming Pacific Ocean to clamber up on and have no choice but to haul themselves onto the beaches of far northern Alaska or drown. The birds, many of them species of awk-like murres, come ashore in California, "some shrunken to little more than feather and bone," according to a four-sentence *New York Times* notice published on September 26, 2015. Murres dive deep to feed on small schooling fish, squid, crustaceans, amphipods, or just about anything in the water column, typically going 100–200 feet down, but murres reaching nearly 600 feet have been reported. Because they are so omnivorous and range so widely, these birds are a marker species to gauge the food supply. What canaries were to the coal miners, murres are to Ocean scientists. Skyrocketing mortality due to malnutrition in this species is a truly ominous sign, among many that have come to light very recently.

The Pacific Ocean faces a combination of warming factors, with a warning sign of the consequent disasters coming in October 2015 in a form that was impossible to ignore: Hurricane Patricia. That storm, the largest cyclonic event in recorded history, resulted from three different sources of heat, each of which is dangerous by itself, but which are much worse together. First, there is the naturally occurring Pacific Decadal Oscillation, which swings between cool phases—such as the past fifteen years or so, which have been termed a "warming hiatus" by climate scientists—and warmer phases, another of which seems to be commencing. Second, there is the unprecedented and unpredictable influence of global warming generated by humans. Finally, an unusually powerful El Niño event was brewing in those troubled waters at the time, peaking in 2016.

The most seriously affected areas so far include a mass of water near the coast of California that is being called the Blob, which is four degrees warmer on the Fahrenheit scale than the rest of the Pacific Ocean. Warm seawater leads to explosions in the algae population called blooms, which render the area uninhabitable for fish, and which produce such an enormous volume of toxins that shellfish and crabs along the coast become deathly poisonous to people. Another victim of higher water temperature is coral, which has been bleaching out and dying globally at an accelerated rate in the twenty-first century, with the reefs near Hawai'i hit the hardest. The repercussions of a more tepid Pacific Ocean are felt far away from the sea, not just in the western United States, which is getting hotter and drier and catching on fire more often because of the changes, but as far away as Indonesia, where there have also been catastrophic wildfires, and Australia, where drought conditions are severe, which is also true of California.

The warmer air and water are rapidly melting the ice sheets near both poles. For instance, the liquefaction of the Greenland Ice Sheet is happening with astonishing speed in the form of new rivers carving through the ice. In July 2019, an intense heat wave brought the highest temperatures ever recorded to northern Europe, then moved over Greenland, unleashing a massive melting event. A similar scenario had unfolded in 2012, but core samples of Greenland ice show that only two such meltdowns have taken place before—in 1889, and around the year 1200! The water contained in that ice sheet alone is enough to raise the level of the Ocean by twenty full feet. Meanwhile, chunks of Antarctic ice sheet the size of Rhode Island are breaking off regularly, to drift north and slowly become more Ocean. A vision of the world's coastal and island civilizations when the ice is gone brings to mind the legend of Atlantis.

In the midst of these manifold dislocations, humans must not despair, which accomplishes nothing. They must act, while keeping a better future in view. Deep-sea researcher and activist Sylvia Earle's Mission Blue program identifies "hope spots," areas of the Ocean that have not been extensively altered yet, such as the Galápagos Islands, in order to protect them and build on them to restore the health of the Ocean. Her succinct and prophetic article, "The Sweet Spot in Time: Why the Ocean Matters to Everyone, Everywhere," in the *Virginia Quarterly* (fall 2012) summarizes the dangers this blue planet faces, but it also indicates timely ways to avert disaster.

Goodbye, Plankton

William Beebe

William Beebe, inventor of the bathysphere, wrote a moving meditation on plankton, the foundation of the Ocean's food web, in his 1926 book The Arcturus Adventure. *The Ocean's plankton biomass is rapidly disappearing, due to rising water temperatures and the acidification of seawater, threatening a collapse of the marine environment. During the summer of 2015, an unprecedented number of baleen whales—those that filter plankton through bristly wands of keratin in their mouth—came in close along the coast of California to feed, where a dense cloud of krill had gone seeking refuge from the warming mid–Pacific Ocean, crowding into the narrow band of cooler water near the land. This phenomenon provided a feast for the cetacean community, and was good for whale watchers, but more alarmingly, it was an omen that the Ocean is quickly becoming uninhabitable for the most basic (and therefore the most important) sea creatures, upon whom all the others depend.*

The celebrity status of Will Beebe, once a tabloid mash-up of Captain Nemo and Indiana Jones, is a thing of the past, forgotten by our amnesiac popular culture. His standing in the history of science seems slippery. Moreover, his greatness as a writer of unequaled range has never been recognized. In Beebe's first selection in this reader, we heard his voice as explorer, going beyond; as poet, reporting lyrically; and as cinematographer, directing his camera to zoom in and pan out. In the following passage, Beebe begins as a philosopher might, then pivots to the quantitatively evidentiary discourse of his true calling as a scientist. Beebe closes spiritually, evoking the connectivity of all species in life's great tangle, and prophetically, with intimations of a great disturbance at the base of that pyramidal labyrinth.

Flotsam and Jetsam

If heat is the mother of all life then water is surely its father. We came from the water, we are still absolutely dependent upon it, two-thirds of our entire body is nothing but water. In our physical frame we carry with us many aquatic memories, water-logged characters which point to distant amphibious or submarine ancestors. The mark of the sea is upon us though our home may be in the heart of a continent.

The simplest of beings are inhabitants of water—mere droplets of movement, hesitant on the threshold of life, as yet neither quite plants nor animals. In comparison, a forming crystal may seem a great advance, a restless oil globule suggests a sentient organism. But the droplet of life can afford to rest motionless. It treasures in its minute nucleus a something possessed by neither crystal nor globule.

It would almost seem as if water, especially sea water, had some slumbering force within itself, a dormant sympathy for organic life which needed merely the slightest stimulus to awaken and to take its share in dynamic animation. A suspended cobweb vivifying the air about it into complex activities would be no more of a marvel than the jellyfish which moves through the sea and is itself the very essence of water. Dry it, and there remain neither bone nor tendons, disturbed organs nor traces of blood, but only the faintest of glistening films, which disintegrates and blows away with the first breath of air. Yet imbued with its ninety and nine parts of salt water, it moves and contracts and throws its poisoned darts, it swallows and digests, and dimly sees and feels, it produces eggs and strews them like chaff as it slowly vibrates on its course. Yet so evanescent is it that it seems like some organic mirage. The eye often misses it altogether, looking straight on and through its being, and finally locating it by its shadow. The earth-wide basins of liquid gently sustain and capably support the host of beings who experience life and death among the waves. In countless ways each tiny creature is ministered to, and given his chance to fight upward toward the unknown case-to-come which seems the sole object of the existing of these lives.

Important as water is to all higher creatures, its actual astounding percentage in tissues and organs is more and more completely concealed from view. But always we perceive new, unexpected qualities. And when unusual demands are made they too are granted. Creeping upon the mud and coral are myriads of shellfish whose flesh would tempt every passing fish. So when their need cries aloud for protection, the Father of Life comes to their aid. By some strange, secret alchemy they draw from the transparent water the hardest and most durable of walls, and encase themselves in shells of lime, and marvellous architecture and splendor of pattern and pigment.

In the course of past time, fishes of the sea covered themselves with scales of shining silver and developed four important fins—prophecies of wonderful legs and arms and feet and hands, if one could only have known. But in those times the Great Father of Waters was in no fear about the desertion of his children. Fishes leaped from the waves and even learned to skim through the air on outstretched fins. But they always plopped back exhausted. And when other creatures insisted on clambering out on mud-banks and flipping themselves along, the great breakers merely chased them and good-naturedly rolled and tumbled them back again into the green frothy water. And the ocean in those days swept round and partly over the half dried land,

and the sound of the storm waves vibrated uselessly around the headlands and through the valleys, for there were no ears to hear.

By the time the first little monkey climbed down a swaying vine for his evening's drink, the dominion of the sea had become lost in the past. The earth was galloped over and burrowed into by myriads of beings; trees were perched on and bored through; the air hummed and whistled with wings and webs and leaping forms. So completely a thing of the past had the sea life become that many creatures had gone back to it as to quite a new element. Their old, old aquatic memories helped them not at all, and the penguins had to re-stiffen their feathers into scales, and to encase their wings in immobile mittens cut after the fashion of sharks' fins. And the seals ceased the running about upon the land and became completely readapted to a sea life.

So let us return, at least mentally, to the Sea, for there is no happening on land which cannot there be duplicated and often bettered. But to appreciate these similarities to the full, one must become amphibious. As well live in Kansas or Switzerland and know the ocean only in the encyclopedia volume MUN to ODE, as sit in a deck chair and watch it pass or scan its waves with binoculars. To such a watcher no real secret is ever confided—he thinks in terms of waves and swells, and his eye is held by the horizon beyond which is the dry earth for which he longs. But to the aquatic devotee, the oceanic fan, surprise after surprise is vouchsafed, for to him the three elements are not phenomena wholly apart.

We are grateful to the dry land for standing room, to the air for the breath of life. But any glance askance at the watery depths is but a pitiful or a comic gesture when we remember that 85% of our brain is water, and much more akin to salt than to fresh. To be sure we cannot drink salt water and live, but when necessary it is an admirable temporary substitute for blood itself, whereas sweet water would be a fair poison in our veins. Take the man who shudders at the thought of the ocean's depths, and put him in the midst of a tropical desert at breathless noon, or make him frosted with the winds which caress Kinchinjunga, and his lungs cry out for their need of oxygen—and his natal earth will seem quite as inimical as the great waves of mid-ocean or the black liquid depths.[1]

For countless voyages I have hung over the bow of passenger steamers in midocean, making of myself a figurehead of sorts, straining my eyes downward to watch the living creatures which whirled into sight and swept past. Dolphins, flying-fish, tunny, an occasional shark—these are familiar to all who have ever glanced over the bow. But the rays of the slanting sun striking obliquely into the smooth surface often revealed a myriad, myriad of motes—more like aquatic dust than individual organisms, which filled the water from the very surface to as deep as the eye could penetrate.

Toward sunset these would vanish in the increasing dimness, and finally the bow would cut its way through an opaque, oxidized liquid, as unlike water as tar to glass. The moon overhead which showed in the waning day as a crescent of cloud, now cuts through the darkness like a sliver of gold. So the minute sea life becomes, in the dark, redoubly visible, and the ship ploughs a deep furrow through miles of star dust—phosphorescence which will fill the last imaginative human being as full of wonder and awe as it did the first who ever ventured out to sea.

As I have elsewhere explained, the floating oceanic life is known as plankton—indicating the helplessness of these wanderers, drifting about at the direction of the winds and currents.[2] Even vaguely to estimate the abundance or numbers of these powdery clouds of animals of the ocean is to attempt a Herculean task, second only to numbering the sands of the shore or the proverbial hairs of our head. One dark, moonless evening I put out a silk surface net the mouth of which was round, and about a metre or a yard in diameter. At the farther end of the net a quart preserve jar was tied to receive and hold any small creatures which might be caught as the net was drawn slowly along the surface of the water. This was done at the speed of two knots and kept up for the duration of one hour. When drawn in, the net sagged heavily and we poured out an overflowing mass of pink rich jelly into a white flat tray. This I weighed carefully and then took, as exactly as possible, a one-hundred-and-fiftieth portion. I began to go over this but soon became discouraged, and again divided it and set to work on one sixth of the fraction on which I had first started. After many hours of eye-straining and counting under the microscope, I conservatively estimated my 1/150 part of the hour's plankton haul as follows:

Feathery copepods—Candace-like	7,920
Bright blue copepods—Pontella-like	71,400
Other Copepods—Calanus-like, pink	139,320
Bivalve crustacean—Ostracod-like	4,920
Short-eyed shrimps	720
Siphonophores	14,400
Helix snails	8,800
Purple Ianthina snails	13,440
Egg masses of snails	1,080
Free eggs, various	5,280
Arrow-like flying snails	2,520
Nautilus-like flying snails	240
Oyster-like flying snails	960
	271,080

If we multiply this by one hundred and fifty we get forty million, six hundred and sixty-two thousand individuals. Please remember that this is a very conservative estimate of only a few of the more easily counted groups in one small haul of an hour's duration, and the magnitude of the life of the sea will begin to dawn upon our minds. Twelve hours later—in full daylight—I repeated the haul as closely as possible and, instead of forty million, I captured about one thousand individuals of the corresponding groups. So although plankton is an involuntary horizontal wanderer, yet vertically it has more perfect control, and having developed its own system of lighting it will have nothing of the sun or even of moonlight, and remains well below reach of the stronger rays.

My own interest in plankton is wholly that of trying to disentangle the lives of some of the small people—to put myself in their places by day and night, but I feel that I must establish their importance in the minds of more practical and farseeing readers. Realize then, that even for our human race, the universe of plankton is of vital importance. The surface-loving copepods are commonly and correctly known as "whale food," and they are also the most important food of many fishes. Only at the surface can vegetable life exist and develop, changing sunlight into edible materials, and in plankton diatoms and other plants affording satisfactory aquatic fodder to the small grazing animals about them. They thus start the ball of life rolling, which does not cease until it includes the possibility of continued existence for whales and food fishes, while, in the future, the whole human race may come to depend upon this larder of ocean.

Notes

1. Kanchenjunga, between Nepal and India, is the third-tallest mountain in the world.
2. The root of "plankton" is the Greek word *planktos*, which means "wandering."

Ocean Acidification

National Oceanic and Atmospheric Administration

The rapidly rising acidification of seawater is one of the gravest threats to the Ocean—if not the most serious of them all—but is also among those that are least recognized by the general public. At least for now. Scientists with organizations such as NOAA—the National Oceanic and Atmospheric Administration of the US Department of Commerce—are doing everything within their limited power to bring this potentially disastrous development to light, such as the following report posted on the NOAA website. As the deep-sea explorer Robert Ballard pointed out in his TED talk in 2008, the annual budget of the celebrated National Air and Space Administration (NASA) to explore outer space is 1,600 times greater than NOAA's yearly budget to study the all-important Ocean. This single fact is emblematic of the wide imbalance in priorities in our terracentric species. We face extinction if the Ocean turns into an acidic soup, yet hardly anyone realizes it—yet.

A pH unit is a measure of acidity ranging from 0–14. The lower the value, the more acidic the environment. Becoming more acidic is a relative shift in pH to a lower value.

The Chemistry

When carbon dioxide (CO_2) is absorbed by seawater, chemical reactions occur that reduce seawater pH, carbonate ion concentration, and saturation states of biologically important calcium carbonate minerals. These chemical reactions are termed "ocean acidification" or "OA" for short. Calcium carbonate minerals are the building blocks for the skeletons and shells of many marine organisms. In areas where most life now congregates in the ocean, the seawater is supersaturated with respect to calcium carbonate minerals. This means there are abundant building blocks for calcifying organisms to build their skeletons and shells. However, continued ocean acidification is causing many parts of the ocean to become undersaturated with these minerals, which is likely to affect the ability of some organisms to produce and maintain their shells.

Since the beginning of the Industrial Revolution, the pH of surface ocean waters has fallen by 0.1 pH units. Since the pH scale, like the Richter scale, is logarithmic, this change represents approximately a 30 percent increase in acidity. Future predictions indicate that the oceans will continue to absorb carbon dioxide and become even more acidic. Estimates of future carbon dioxide levels, based on business as usual emission scenarios, indicate that by the end of this century the surface waters of the ocean could be nearly 150 percent more acidic, resulting in a pH that the oceans haven't experienced for more than 20 million years.

The Biological Impacts

Ocean acidification is expected to impact ocean species to varying degrees. Photosynthetic algae and seagrasses may benefit from higher CO_2 conditions in the ocean, as they require CO_2 to live just like plants on land. On the other hand, studies have shown that a more acidic environment has a dramatic effect on some calcifying species, including oysters, clams, sea urchins, shallow water corals, deep sea corals, and calcareous plankton. When shelled organisms are at risk, the entire food web may also be at risk. Today, more than a billion people worldwide rely on food from the ocean as their primary source of protein. Many jobs and economies in the U.S. and around the world depend on the fish and shellfish in our oceans.

PTEROPODS

The pteropod, or "sea butterfly," is a tiny sea creature about the size of a small pea. Pteropods are eaten by organisms ranging in size from tiny krill to whales and are a major food source for North Pacific juvenile salmon. When a pteropod's shell is placed in sea water with pH and carbonate levels projected for the year 2100, the shell slowly dissolves after 45 days.

SHELLFISH

In recent years, there have been near total failures of developing oysters in both aquaculture facilities and natural ecosystems on the West Coast. These larval oyster failures appear to be correlated with naturally occurring upwelling events that bring low pH waters undersaturated in aragonite as well as other water quality changes to nearshore environments. Lower pH values occur naturally on the West Coast during upwelling events, but recent observations indicate that anthropogenic [human-caused] CO_2 is contributing to seasonal undersaturation. Low pH may be a factor in the current oyster reproductive failure; however, more research is needed to disentangle potential acidification effects from other risk factors, such as episodic freshwater inflow, pathogen increases, or low dissolved oxygen. It is premature to conclude that acidification is responsible for the recent oyster failures, but acidification is a potential factor in the current crisis to this $100 million a year industry, prompting new collaborations of research on ocean acidification and potential biological impacts.

CORAL

Many marine organisms that produce calcium carbonate shells or skeletons are negatively impacted by increasing CO_2 levels and decreasing pH in seawater. For example, increasing ocean acidification has been shown to significantly reduce the ability of reef-building corals to produce their skeletons. In a recent paper, coral biologists reported that ocean acidification could compromise the successful fertilization, larval settlement and survivorship of Elkhorn coral, an endangered species. These research results suggest that ocean acidification could severely impact the ability of coral reefs to recover from disturbance. Other research indicates that, by the end of this century, coral reefs may erode faster than they can be rebuilt. This could compromise the long-term viability of these ecosystems and perhaps impact the estimated one million species that depend on coral reef habitat. For more information on the impact of ocean acidification on coral, see NOAA's Coral Reef Watch website.

Ocean Acidification: An Emerging Global Problem

Ocean acidification is an emerging global problem. Over the last decade, there has been much focus in the ocean science community on studying the potential impacts of ocean acidification. Since sustained efforts to monitor ocean acidification worldwide are only beginning, it is currently impossible to predict exactly how ocean acidification impacts will cascade throughout the marine food chain and affect the overall structure of marine ecosystems. With the pace of ocean acidification accelerating, scientists, resource managers, and policymakers recognize the urgent need to strengthen the science as a basis for sound decision making and action.

Attack of the Invasive Species!

James T. Carlton

Species have been moving around the planet on the Ocean for as long as there have been floating objects to ride on, but now the problem of invasive species has become an acute international issue. The loudest voice trying to bring awareness to the danger of invasive species has been that of James T. Carlton, who brought the problem to light in 1993 with an article in the leading journal Science, *"Ecological Roulette: The Global Transport of Non-indigenous Marine Organisms." Carlton first published the following piece, which summarizes the ongoing threat of invasive species, in 1992. He updated it for this collection.*

In addition to the creatures Carlton mentions here, the list of damaging invasive species introduced from the Ocean is long. The sea lamprey, which came from the Atlantic Ocean via the Saint Lawrence Seaway, is an enormous eel with a suction-cup mouth ringed with sharp teeth, which attaches to desirable species such as lake trout and sucks out their viscera, earning its designation as the "vampire of the Great Lakes." The hideous northern snakehead fish from China, which moves between bodies of water by using its limb-like front fins to crawl across dry land and can survive for long periods out of the water, is spreading across eastern North America. The lionfish is an exquisite-looking creature native to Asian waters, but it is voracious in its appetite for the tiny fluorescent fish that live symbiotically on the coral reefs it has invaded in the Caribbean Sea, and its feathery, ruffled fins are tipped with lethally poisonous spines, which frustrate potential predators. As a result, lionfish have no predators, and, as you read this, they are becoming the dominant species on the dying reefs of Florida, the Bahamas, and the Caribbean.

The catastrophic Japanese tsunami of March 2011 was an unprecedented event for invasive species. It resulted from an earthquake registering 9.0 on the Richter Scale, generating waves that peaked at 130 feet near the epicenter. The tsunami carried far, far more human-made debris out to sea than any event in world history, with shocking ramifications for invasive species, pollution, navigation, international relations, and the fisheries, among many other concerns. The aftermath of the tsunami, specifically the impact of JTMD (Japanese tsunami and marine debris), is clearly under the radar of the general public, despite the troubling implications of this ongoing disaster. James T. Carlton, whose research on JTMD was the cover story of Science *magazine on September 29, 2017, composed the summary of the subject that appears below under the heading "JTMD" as an original contribution for this collection.*

After sixty-four days at sea, the ship *Arbella*, having departed Yarmouth on the Isle of Wight, anchored off Cape Ann, Massachusetts, in June 1630. On board were perhaps 100,000 colonists: somewhat more than 100 men, women, and children; an assortment of livestock, plants, rats, and mice; seeds, insects, snails, and other organisms mixed in with the ship's ballast; and tens of thousands of organisms living in a rich community of marine fouling and boring organisms attached to, and burrowing in, the bottom of the wooden hull. Today, these immigrant species would be recognized as part of a cosmopolitan harbor and port biota created by centuries of maritime exploration, colonization, and commerce.

The *Arbella* followed the general route of many vessels that had been coming to North America from Europe for centuries. Slowly, one European marine species after another appeared on New England's shores, and all along the Atlantic seaboard. So old and numerous were sailing voyages, extending back to the tenth-century Norse explorations, and so recent are our first biological investigations (few being available before the mid-nineteenth century), that it remains difficult both to know when a particular species first arrived in this early era and to grasp a complete understanding of what species existed on America's shores before European contact.

One of the most famous European colonists of New England shores is the common periwinkle snail, *Littorina littorea*, a species so characteristic of the Atlantic coast that many people are surprised to learn that it is not native. In the 1840s this snail was discovered in eastern Canada in regions that had already been well explored for their marine mollusks. Whether introduced accidentally (among ballast rocks) or intentionally imported and released (being at the time one of western Europe's cheapest and most popular seafoods) we do not yet know.

Once it arrived, the European rocky shore periwinkle moved steadily south. By the 1860s it had reached the Gulf of Maine, by the early 1870s Cape Cod, by the late 1870s Long Island Sound, and by the 1880s New Jersey. This snail quickly became one of the most dominant intertidal species from Newfoundland to the mid-Atlantic. Occurring in densities of thousands of snails per square meter, *Littorina littorea* appears to have had a profound effect on the distribution and abundance of many species of animals and plants— effectively removing much of their favored seaweed food, competing with other species, affecting marsh development, providing a new and extraordinarily abundant shell resource for native hermit crabs, and having many other impacts.

Another early colonist was the European green shore crab, *Carcinus maenas*, being introduced on Long Island by the early 1800s. It is difficult to imag-

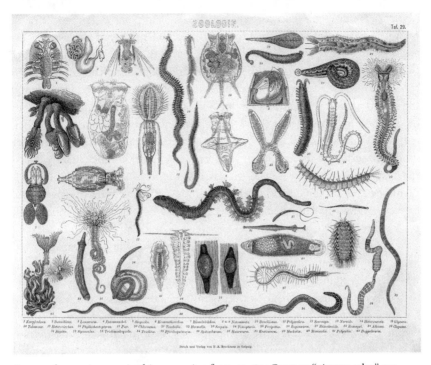

Among the species seen in this engraving from an 1855 German "picture atlas" are
the carp louse, the sea canker, the horse leech, and the double worm. According to
James T. Carlton, "A few of the animals in the 1855 engraving would be found on ships'
hulls—all as fouling organisms, but none as borers. [Number 4 is the goose barnacle;
5 is the balanid cirripedia; and the three species of polychaete worm are 13, 21, and 23.]
Just two barnacles . . . the rest 'worms,' in the mid-nineteenth-century sense, and thus
including a wide variety of terrestrial, freshwater, and marine free-living and parasitic
species." Engraver unknown, from *Zoologie*, edited by Carl Vogt, in *Bilder-Atlas: Ikonographische Encyklopädie der Wissenschaften und Künste [Picture-Atlas: Iconographic Encyclopedia of the Arts and Sciences]*, 2nd ed., vol. 2 (Leipzig: F. A. Brockhaus, 1875). Courtesy of
the Roorda/Doyle Collection.

ine New England shores without this ubiquitous and characteristic species.
As with the European periwinkle, one could hardly imagine a more successful invader, or one that could predictably cause such extensive environmental
change. Green crabs are omnivorous: they crush and remove barnacles from
rocks, dig for clams, and attack and remove hermit crabs from their shells.
They eat worms, other crustaceans, algae, and organic debris. They live on
exposed rocky shores and in quiet backwaters, marshes, and estuaries. They
can live far up rivers where there is the slightest salt, and offshore in coastal
waters. Successful invaders are often habitat generalists—characteristics not
only of green crabs but of backyard weeds as well.

　　While ships carried the green crab—a species with potentially great propensity to snuggle deep inside old shipworm burrows—around the world

(the occasional specimen was found in the 1800s in ports in Panama, Brazil, Hawai'i, and India), it is typical to find that colonists do not successfully establish everywhere they are released. But it is perhaps not surprising to find that the two greatest regions of successful colonization of the green crab in the 1800s outside of Europe were the Atlantic shores of North America and the shores of eastern Australia around Sydney. The world voyages of *Carcinus* did not resume, for reasons that are unclear, until the 1980s and 1990s, when it appeared in Japan and South America—and San Francisco Bay, where, for food, it found an abundant supply of worms and clams, almost all introduced species themselves from New England or Asia.

By the end of the eighteenth century ships—effectively marine biological conveyer belts—had touched most shores of the world. By the mid-nineteenth century, accompanied by global events such as the California and Australia gold rushes, and the establishment of commercial networks to transport humans, grain, guano, lumber, ore, and innumerable other cargoes, the world was virtually itching with shipping activity. Indeed, hundreds of ships made their way, for example, from New England, Europe, South America, Australia, New Zealand, China, Japan, and Hawai'i to San Francisco Bay and other Pacific Coast ports between 1849 and the 1850s, producing, in marine biological terms, one of the greatest movements of marine life in the history of human endeavor. By 1853, the common New England barnacle *Amphibalanus improvisus* had colonized the harbor of San Francisco, more successful than many of the human colonists that had accompanied this barnacle's parental stocks.

Ships today do not typically carry the vast hull-fouling communities they once did. Twenty-first-century vessels, moving at speeds of 25 knots or more, sweep away many of the species that Sir Francis Drake may have carried around the world on the bottom of the *Golden Hinde* in the 1590s at 4 or 5 knots, or what a clipper ship carried around Cape Horn to (or from) California at 10 or 12 knots in the 1850s. Further changing the composition of ships' fouling communities has been the application of extremely effective antifouling paints, typically copper based, that inhibit the settlement of marine organisms such as sea squirts, sponges, barnacles, mussels, seaweeds, and most other species (although some species have already evolved tolerance to some of these antifouling compounds). Finally, handsome and rich fouling communities on vessel bottoms develop best when ships remain dockside or at anchor for many weeks or even months. While longer port residencies were more typical of ship behavior centuries ago, a container ship today may put into New York at 0700 and be away by 1400, hardly enough time for serious barnacle or seaweed colonization.

The bottom line is, however, that the bottom line is not entirely clean. Some hull areas may remain unpainted, or paint may be worn away. In 1957 the Asian green seaweed *Codium fragile fragile* (an unusual trinomial Latin name amid a sea of binomials) appeared in New York, about the same time as the launch of the *Sputnik*, leading some to draw a correlation to a Russian plot. A *Codium* colony may grow to a meter long and a half-meter in diameter and develop into dense, arborescent meadows, at times impacting scallop fisheries. Introduced as a ship-fouling organism from Europe (where it had colonized by the turn of the nineteenth century after an earlier introduction from Japan), *Codium*, or dead man's fingers, is now an abundant fouling species from Canada to the mid-Atlantic.

Less than two decades later, in the early 1970s, the Asian sea squirt *Styela clava* appeared in New England. Typically 15 centimeters tall, *Styela* is a warty, leathery animal attached by a narrow stalk to the substrate, be it a piling or boat hull. It is now another major fouling organism along the Atlantic seaboard. It too was introduced via ship hull fouling from Europe, where it first appeared during the Korean War.

If we pull up a mooring in Long Island Sound today, the dominant organisms may be entirely introduced species. Long, luxurious stands of *Codium* intermingle with the brown tubular sea squirt *Styela*, and these in turn are coated with brilliant orange colonies of the Asian sea squirt *Botrylloides violaceus*, another 1970s arrival. Hauled out of the water, the attached marine life on a buoy may then present a theater of dense, waving, arching, Spielbergian creatures: these are the 2–3-centimeter-long *Caprella mutica*, a small spiny Asian species arriving in the 1990s, again having first colonized European shores. Known as skeleton shrimp (although not shrimp at all, but rather crustaceans known as amphipods), these carnivores now occur in extraordinary densities blanketing docks and pontoons.

While ships today may carry fewer fouling organisms on their hulls, they have remained one of the greatest conveyors of marine life around the world. Modern oceangoing vessels can carry thousands to millions of gallons of seawater in their ballast tanks or floodable cargo holds. Thousands of ships around the world inhale ballast water every hour, moving that water—and all of the marine life in it—days or weeks later to another harbor somewhere else in the world. Large ports may be inoculated with millions of gallons per day of foreign marine organisms, a potentially daunting new wave of potential invasions. Cargo ships have been found to have hundreds of species of animals and plants in their ballast tanks at voyage's end.

Since the opening of the Saint Lawrence Seaway in 1959, even the Great Lakes have been exposed to ballast-mediated invasions. As a result of ballast water release, the European freshwater zebra mussels *Dreissena polymorpha* and *Dreissena bugensis* appeared in the 1980s in the Great Lakes (and have since spread widely through North America). Once found largely only in the drainages of the Black and Caspian seas, zebra mussels spread across the face of western Europe in the nineteenth century during the days of canal building. Their size (typically just a couple of centimeters) belies their impact:

these bivalves are major fouling organisms, occurring by the hundreds of millions as they clog water intake screens and water pipes, coat vessel hulls and marina floats, and cover beaches with deep piles of sharp broken shells. In the same era, a plethora of European species followed zebra mussels into the Great Lakes, including several species of carnivorous fish and spiny water fleas.

In a sort of unintentional international trade arrangement, North America then exported, in ballast water, the comb jellyfish *Mnemiopsis leidyi* to Europe. Russian biological oceanographers reported in the late 1980s and early 1990s that *Mnemiopsis* populations, first detected in the Black Sea, could be measured in terms of hundreds of millions of tons of standing stock. Comb jellies are voracious consumers of zooplankton (including larval fish); plankton and fish populations soon declined dramatically in the Black Sea.

New invasions also began to crop up at the same time on marine shores around North America. The Chinese clam *Corbula amurensis* appeared in 1988 in San Francisco Bay and within a few years were counted in the tens of thousands per square meter. The Japanese shore crab *Hemigrapsus sanguineus* also appeared in 1988—a good year, apparently, for invasions—in New Jersey, and within a few years made its way up to New England. It is now the most abundant intertidal crab along Connecticut and Massachusetts seashores.

On the land, we are perhaps more used to the idea of introduced species: we are surrounded by them in our cities and farms. Most of our common crops, the plants that transformed much of the face of North America, have come from other continents. An empty lot in Boston, or New York, or Los Angeles, or Seattle, is more likely to be home to nonnative weeds, earthworms, insects, spiders, snails, and slugs than to native species. And so it is in our urbanized estuaries and shores and lakes as well, where human activities reaching back many centuries and actively continuing today have homogenized some of the world's coastal marine biota.

Among the wave of new invasions that arrived on North American shores in the last half of the twentieth century, it was zebra mussels that became a poster child for nonnative aquatic species, due to their estimated potential economic impact. In a little over two years after their discovery, reflecting rarely registered legislative speed, the US Congress passed the Nonindigenous Aquatic Nuisance Prevention and Control of 1990. Acronymless, the law became known as the Zebra Mussel Act, or the Ballast Water Act. This law sought to plant the seeds to reduce future invasions by ballast water, management and regulatory strategies that are still evolving nearly thirty years after zebra mussels were first found in the Great Lakes.

New nonnatives continue to appear. More goods move around the world, almost all by ship, than ever before, and hitchhikers are an inevitable part of expanding trade globalization. The World Wide Web, in just over two decades, has established a fluid means—a bioweb—for shipping uncountable species inter- and intranationally. The live seafood market, mariculture industries, and the immense aquarium hobby industry also form global conveyor belts, in no small part moved by airplane. Driven by phenomena and processes seeded long ago, marine life continues to flow along an expanding network of maritime highways, be they oceanic or aerial.

JTMD

In an intersection of natural disasters, oceanographic processes, and human use of coastal zones, the great east Japan earthquake and tsunami of March 11, 2011, created a rare phenomenon: a huge pulse of whole or fragmented materials that was ejected from the Tōhoku coast of northeastern Honshu into the Pacific Ocean and which began to float toward North America and the Hawaiian Islands.[1] The material that departed Japan consisted of an unknown amount of marine debris—buoys, floats, totes, pallets, crates, vessels, home construction wood, and an endless array of other articles, ranging from refrigerators and propane tanks to booms and fisheries gear. Aboard this debris were hundreds of species of Japanese marine life that successfully rafted across the ocean and landed on beaches and rocky shores, and occasionally drifted into bays and estuaries. The sui generis nature of this phenomenon revealed a common myth that debris with Japanese marine life washes ashore regularly on American coasts. In contrast, so uncommon are these events that no examples had previously been recorded in the scientific, historical, or marine policy literature prior to the first Japanese tsunami marine debris coming ashore in the first half of 2012 in the eastern Pacific. The perception that Japanese life was a regular arrival arises in part from confusion with Japanese glass fishing floats, which do come ashore, but support native marine life (such as the pelagic gooseneck barnacle *Lepas*) from the high seas, not from Asian coastal shores. Similarly, prehistoric rafting across vast ocean basins, such as the North Pacific Ocean, would presumably have consisted of natural wood, such as coastal trees, which, like building wood, is susceptible to comparatively rapid bioerosion: marine clams, known as shipworms or teredos, burrow in and destroy drifting wood. In contrast, humans have fundamentally altered the nature of ocean rafting by introducing into the ocean nonbiodegradable materials made of various forms of plastic—polyvinyl chloride, polystyrene, fiberglass, and so on—providing marine life with long-term mini-vessels by which to traverse the oceans for years, much longer than natural materials would typically survive. In turn, prior mega-tsunamis, long ago, interacted with coastal communities that produced far less anthropogenic debris. The interaction of the largest recorded earthquake in modern Japanese history (which led to the tragic loss of over 18,000 people) with an intensely developed coastline produced a unique debris pulse that transported marine life across the ocean for years, including many species

Teredo navalis was a terror for mariners on the Ocean in wooden ships. The tiny shipworm bored into hulls, causing leaks. In the 1730s, the population mushroomed in the Netherlands, moving from watercraft to the wooden frames of dikes; the damage they caused threatened to destroy the nation's sea defenses and flood much of the land. The solution was to replace the wooden construction elements with stone. Since then, shipworms have expanded their global range as a result of water pollution and climate change, and continue to ravage wooden harbor infrastructure around the world.

The engraving's caption reads, "Three Pieces of Oaken wood from the Pilings on the Sea-Dike, drawn from life so as to show how it is pierced through by the Worms."

Jan Ruyter, *Delen paalwerk aangetast door paalwormen*, engraving, 1731–33. From the Rijksmuseum, Amsterdam, the Netherlands.

not previously known from ships' hulls or ballast water. Whether new invasions result from these events awaits longer-term studies.

A few examples of discrete pieces of JTMD illustrate the scale and diversity of its mind-boggling mass. The huge tsunami waves that inundated the port of Misawa, close to the earthquake epicenter, tore out and carried to sea four massive floating concrete docks from the harbor, each weighing 188 tons, each 7 feet high, 19 feet long, and 66 feet wide. These unsinkable structures went adrift in the Pacific Ocean, caught the prevailing current, and floated east. On June 5, 2012, fifteen months after the disaster, one of the docks came ashore at Agate Beach, Oregon, where it became an instant tourist attraction. It was covered with hundreds of hitchhiking marine organisms, with hundreds more of them nestled in every nook and cranny of the monolith. James Carlton and his team of experts examined them, identifying scores of different invasive species among the passengers: urchins, oysters, mussels, sponges, crabs, sea stars, anemones, barnacles, tunicates, and more. In

The tsunami swept large vessels far out to sea, such as this battered ship from the Japanese fishing fleet; the North Pacific Gyre caught them up and carried them to North America. More than one hundred feet in length, the ghostly ship was spotted drifting off the Oregon coast, a virtual ark for invasive species. Photograph by US Coast Guard Air Station Kodiak, 2012.

mid-December 2012, a second dock washed ashore on a stretch of ruggedly remote coastline in Grays Harbor, Washington, which made it difficult for Carlton and his team to reach it. When they did, they found the same situation: hundreds of individual organisms from scores of different invasive species had come ashore on the wayward dock. The third dock later made an appearance near Hawai'i, where an enterprising fishing crew encountered it and kept it secret until they had caught several thousand pounds of mahi-mahi fish, which congregate underneath floating objects. They even took videos of each other walking around on the dock in their fishing boots. But by the time they reported it to the Coast Guard, the dock had continued on its way and has not been spotted since. The whereabouts of the fourth dock are also unknown. What is certain is that it would ruin the day of any vessel that collided with one of these low-floating obstacles.

The tsunami also swept untold thousands of boats of all sizes out to sea. Among the largest was a 164-foot ghost ship of a fishing boat, which floated without a soul aboard for more than a year before nearing the coast of Canada, where the navy sank it as a navigational hazard. Among the smallest was the 20-foot *Sai-shou-maru*, which beached itself at Long Beach, Washington, two years and eleven days after the earthquake. The vast majority of Japanese tsunami small craft capsize at some point and arrive upside down, but the *Sai-shou-maru* managed to stay upright, arriving with a miniature aquarium in its partially submerged hull. It had become home to more than thirty species of plants and animals native to the warm waters and coral reefs near Japan, including five striped beakfish, which had grown to be juveniles while floating across the Pacific for two years. One of the beakfish went on to find a home at the Seaside Aquarium in Seaside, Oregon, where it is known as the Tsunami Fish and is still a leading attraction there. Another fish unique to the warm western Pacific is the banded knifejaw, one of which completed a tsunami-caused trip across the ocean in April 2015, arriving along with twenty yellowtail jack fish, all trapped in the derelict hull of half a shipwreck, a 50-foot fiberglass commercial fishing boat that had split in two. Fishermen near Newport, Oregon, spotted the wreck, barely afloat and covered with fouling organisms, and marine biologists from the Newport Aquarium and the Hatfield Marine Science Center arranged for it to be towed into a bay close by, rather than to come ashore, where it could spill oil and introduce invasive species. The scientists removed the fish from the wreck (which then went to the city dump), and put them in quarantine for several months. On March 11, 2016, the five-year anniversary of the Japanese tsunami, the castaway fish from the catastrophe went on exhibit at the Newport Aquarium.

Note

1. An estimated 22 million tons of JTMD.

The First Dead Zone

Various Authors

The Gulf of Mexico dead zone seems to be the first of many future dead zones in the Ocean. In these barren areas, the water has become severely deprived of oxygen, which makes it uninhabitable for most species of animals and plants.

The causes for the dead zone lie far inland, and the culprit is chemical fertilizer. Fertilizers in many forms flow over the vast fields of corn, wheat, and soybeans that blanket the watershed of the Mississippi River; across the thousands of golf courses, sports fields, and landscaped areas of midwestern towns; and onto innumerable grass lawns, the tidy icon of American suburbia. Rainstorms wash away much of it, which then flows into tributaries of every description on its way to the Ocean, where all water wants to go, if it ever gets the chance. There, all of that nitrogen and other nutrients have no terrestrial crops or grass to nourish, so algae eats it, and grows, and eats more, and grows more, until green clouds form underwater, called algae blooms. This slimy biomass absorbs oxygen from its watery environment, leaving none for fish, shellfish, and multicelled plant life, which then die en masse. The undersea desert that results is called a dead zone.

The University of Michigan posted the following news release, which summarizes the phenomenon, on June 13, 2013. The post on the website of Gulf Restoration Network updated the situation as of June 25, 2015, closing with "a dire update." An even more dire update comes from 2019, when massive midwestern flooding led to massive algae blooms in the Gulf, which closed every beach in Mississippi.

Down the Mississippi to the Gulf of Mexico

UNIVERSITY OF MICHIGAN

Spring floods across the Midwest are expected to contribute to a very large and potentially record-setting 2013 Gulf of Mexico "dead zone," according to a University of Michigan ecologist [Jim Erickson] and colleagues [Ben Sherman, NOAA; Jon Campbell, US Geological Survey; and Amy Pelsinski, University of Maryland] who released their annual forecast today, along with one for the Chesapeake Bay.

The Gulf forecast, one of two announced by the National Oceanic and Atmospheric Administration, calls for an oxygen-depleted, or hypoxic, region of between 7,286 and 8,561 square miles, which would place it among the 10 largest on record.

The low end of the forecast range is well above the long-term average and would be roughly equivalent to the size of Connecticut, Rhode Island and the District of Columbia combined. The upper end would exceed the largest ever reported (8,481 square miles in 2002) and would be comparable in size to New Jersey.

Farmland runoff containing fertilizers and livestock waste, some of it from as far away as the Corn Belt, is the main source of the nitrogen and phosphorus that cause the annual Gulf of Mexico hypoxic zone. In its 2001 and 2008 action plans, the Mississippi River/Gulf of Mexico Watershed Nutrient Task Force, a coalition of federal, state and tribal agencies, set the goal of reducing the five-year running average area extent of the Gulf hypoxic zone to 5,000 square kilometers (1,950 square miles) by 2015.

Little progress has been made toward that goal. Since 1995, the Gulf dead zone has averaged 5,960 square miles, an area roughly the size of Connecticut.

"The size of the Gulf dead zone goes up and down depending on that particular year's weather patterns. But the bottom line is that we will never reach the action plan's goal of 1,950 square miles until more serious actions are taken to reduce the loss of Midwest fertilizers to the Mississippi River system, regardless of the weather," said U-M aquatic ecologist Donald Scavia, director of the Graham Sustainability Institute, who contributes to both the Gulf and Chesapeake Bay forecasts. . . .

The forecast calls for a mid-summer hypoxic zone of 1.46 cubic miles, a mid-summer anoxic zone of 0.26 to 0.38 cubic miles, and a summer average hypoxia of 1.108 cubic miles, all at the low end of previously recorded dead zones. Last year, the mid-summer hypoxic zone was 1.45 cubic miles. . . .

The forecasts are based on nutrient runoff and river-and-stream data from the U.S. Geological Survey, which are then fed into computer models developed with funding from NOAA's National Centers for Coastal Ocean Science.

"Monitoring the health and vitality of our nation's oceans, waterways and watersheds is critical as we work to preserve and protect coastal ecosystems," said Kathryn Sullivan, acting undersecretary of commerce for oceans and atmosphere and acting NOAA administrator. "These ecological forecasts are good examples of the critical environmental intelligence products and tools that help shape a healthier coast, one that is so inextricably linked to the vitality of our communities and our livelihoods."

Floods inundated much of the Midwest this spring. Several states, including Minnesota, Wisconsin, Illinois and Iowa, had spring seasons that ranked among the 10 wettest on record. Iowa had its wettest spring on record, with 17.61 inches of precipitation, according to the National Climatic Data Center.

Nutrient-rich runoff from those farming states ends up in the Mississippi River and eventually makes its way to the Gulf. The amount of nitrogen entering the Gulf of Mexico each spring has increased by about 300 percent since the 1960s, mainly due to increased agricultural runoff.

According to U.S. Geological Survey estimates, 153,000 metric tons of nutrients flowed down the Mississippi and Atchafalaya rivers to the northern Gulf in May 2013, an increase of 94,900 metric tons over last year's drought-reduced 58,100 metric tons. The 2013 input is 16 percent higher than the average nutrient load estimated over the past 34 years.

In the Gulf and the Chesapeake Bay, the nutrient-rich waters fuel explosive algae blooms. When the algae die and sink, bottom-dwelling bacteria decompose the organic matter, consuming oxygen in the process. The result is a low-oxygen (hypoxic) or oxygen-free (anoxic) region in the bottom and near-bottom waters: the dead zone.

Fish and shellfish either leave the oxygen-depleted waters or die, resulting in losses to commercial and sports fisheries. In the Gulf, the dockside value of commercial fisheries was $629 million in 2009, and nearly 3 million recreational anglers contributed more than $1 billion to the region's economy. . . .

A Dire Update

MATT ROTA

Scientists recently released their predictions of the size of this year's Gulf Dead Zone. They predict that the Dead Zone will be approximately 5,500 square miles, or the size of Connecticut. This is approximately the size of last year's Dead Zone (5,052 square miles) and almost three times the goal of the Dead Zone Task Force.

The most recent Dead Zone Action Plan called for a 45% reduction of Dead Zone–causing pollution in the Mississippi River and set a goal of reducing the size of the Dead Zone to 1,930 square miles by 2015. Needless to say, we blew through that goal without any real success. So the EPA and Task Force just said "oops" and just moved the goal posts. Now the goal is to make the same reductions by 2035, still with no real description how that will happen or what consequences the states may face if they don't meet those goals.

One of the items the EPA and states have put forward is that most of them have developed "Nutrient Reduction Strategies," most of which have no goals or timelines (which was pointed out by the EPA Inspector General). Without a real change in how we allow the discharge of nitrogen and phosphorus pollution into our environment, we are worried that once 2035 rolls around, the goal posts will once again be moved, and the Gulf and those that depend on it will be the ones to suffer.

The First Trash Vortex

Charles Moore

A debris field the size of Texas has formed in the center of the North Pacific Ocean. Called the Great Pacific Garbage Patch, it is composed mainly of microscopic Styrofoam particles and tiny pieces of degraded plastic. The millions of pounds of garbage in the patch are stuck in the clockwise gyre that swirls endlessly in the vast North Pacific basin, leading to the coinage of a new term: "trash vortex." The garbage field is growing, going nowhere, and taking the shape of things to come. Since the sudden influx of millions of tons of Japanese tsunami and marine debris in March 2011, a second trash vortex has formed in the western Pacific Ocean. A three-year study published in March 2017 showed that the original garbage patch had grown to cover 1.6 million square miles, double the size of Texas, triple that of France, and sixteen times greater than previous estimates. Of the estimated 80,000 metric tons of trash afloat there, almost half consists of lost or abandoned fishing nets and longlines, called ghost gear, and about one-fifth is Japanese tsunami marine debris.[1]

Oceanographer Charles Moore first publicized the phenomenon and discussed it in an address to the TED Conference in Long Beach, California, in February 2009. He began his talk by saying, "Let's talk trash!" The following interview with Moore comes from Earth Island Journal: News of the World Environment.

In 1997, Charles Moore—surfer, scientific researcher, and sea captain—was the first to cross upon an enormous stretch of floating plastic debris now called the "Pacific garbage patch." The patch, also described as the "Pacific trash vortex," is an area in the North-Central Pacific where tiny bits of trash, together weighing as much as 100 million tons, have been trapped by the currents of the North Pacific Gyre.

In talking to Captain Moore, it becomes clear that the pollution of our oceans, epitomized by the patch's toxic stew of plastic particles, is actually a land-based problem. To Moore, what drives the market and what runs off the street into our oceans are part of the same problem.

What is it about the ocean that captures you? You are a skilled woodworker as well as a chemist. Of all the things you could work on, why the ocean?

I suppose it's the unspoiled beauty of it, really, more than anything else.

We live in a world without remoteness. The only place where you can get away and be in an unspoiled environment, at least formerly, before the plastic plague hit the ocean, was the sea. It has a kind of a soothing quality.

We're evolved from ocean creatures and our blood is the same salinity as ocean water.

There is something about growing up by the ocean. I grew up on Venice Beach, and to this day sleeping where you can hear the waves is unlike any other place for me—it's just in your blood.

Yeah, I feel the same way. I enjoy the forest and the mountains and lakes, but they don't have the freedom really. You can't see the horizon in the forest.

So how did you become a sailor?

Well, I grew up on the ocean and have been sailing basically since I could swim, which was pretty young. Alamitos Bay [in Long Beach, California] is where I live. I still live in the family home my father purchased years ago here on the bay. There is a dock out in front and that's where my boat is.

Let's start in 1997, when you discovered the Pacific garbage patch. What happened?

In a sense, the discovery really had to wait until 1999, because that's when we actually realized that the area was impacted with our trash to the extent that it is. I was just disturbed when I crossed it in 1997.

1997 was the largest El Niño on record; it had the warmest surface water in the Pacific and it had the largest hurricane ever recorded in the Pacific: Hurricane Linda. The high-pressure zone that characterizes this gyre was extremely large and extremely stable then.

The polypropylene and the polyethylene that make up the majority of floater plastics and consumer plastics are just a little bit lighter than water. So if it's rough they get pushed down under. When it's really calm, all these bits and pieces can float to the surface.

When we crossed back in August of 1997 from Hawai'i to the mainland, we decided to take this shortcut because we had spare fuel. So here we are, crossing this huge calm area, really having 10 knots of wind or less for a week. The discovery for me was not so much "Well, I'm in a garbage patch." It wasn't like an island of trash like people keep wanting to say. It's just that I couldn't survey the surface of the ocean for any period of time while standing on deck without seeing some anthropogenic debris, something that was human in origin, float by. Not necessarily a large something, but just something.

The signs of human civilization are everywhere in the ocean, and especially in these high-pressured gyres.

Could you get a sense then of the magnitude of what you were seeing?

You have to assume, when you're in the ocean, that things are fairly homogenous. You're not going to go for a week through an area and see these bobbing bits and assume they are bobbing only for you. That was my concern. I thought, "Well, look, if I'm seeing this stuff, there's got to be a lot out here beyond this single minute track that our boat is following through this area."

Thinking about it later, I said, "Well, with all this monitoring I'm learning how to do, I should get some kind of a handle on what's out there in the Pacific." So I started investigating ways to do it. I developed a half-inch mesh net that I could stretch between the hulls of the catamaran. Because what I was seeing out there was mostly pieces that were bigger than a half-inch in diameter, and I thought that's what I would go catch. I thought that's what the story was.

About that time, we ended up getting a bag of plastic chips [from the Coast Guard]. We sent [Dr. Curtis Ebbesmeyer, an oceanographer who studies flotsam] half the sample to try to decide where this stuff was coming from. He estimated that [these plastic chips] were broken from larger objects, and that it was such that a one-liter bottle could put enough plastic pieces in the ocean to put one on every square mile of beach in the entire world. He said he thought this stuff was not coming from a barge but was getting spit out from this gyre that was accumulating it.

So plastics go into the ocean from various sources, get broken up through this gyre, and then distributed back out in millions of different pieces?

Yeah, it's basically turning the beaches of the world into plastic. Especially those that are the first to see it in this gyre: the Hawai'ian Archipelago and other islands in the North Pacific. Instead of having sand made out of coral and lava rocks and other rocks and shells, now we are having beaches made out of broken-down plastics.

How do you have a solution when the plastic is coming from everywhere from Los Angeles to Japan?

It doesn't matter whether it is hunger or war or trade, the problems are all global, and that's especially true when it comes to ocean problems because the ocean doesn't obey any geographical boundary. There are no border checkpoints in the ocean, and everything that gets in there is just going to go where the ocean takes it. We can't stop it. There is no law that can mandate where the ocean currents flow. And right now, they are flowing to these accumulation zones and they are using the material that we've provided in our trash.

When we talk about solutions, we have to talk about a global reassessment of a product's utility. Right now, a product is considered useful if it sells in the marketplace. The market drives consumption, and consumption is considered to be the be-all and end-all of utility. If people are buying it, it must be good for something. But that calculus is in need of revision.

The public is not given the information it needs to make good consumer choices. It doesn't know that the plastic carries contaminants that are increasing their body-burden of industrial chemicals; it doesn't know that there is no recycling for these products; it doesn't know that many of these products will not even make it to a landfill—that they will end up in the ocean.

At a certain point, the problem gets so big you can't not re-think the whole system.

Yeah, and that's frankly been an issue for many people for some time. But the proliferation of our waste and the visibility of it—you know, we knew already that there was a problem when we started getting liquid chemicals and airborne chemicals, but they're invisible to the average person—now everyone can see the fact that our plastic waste is everywhere.

It just seems as if there is this whole industry involved in producing fast-track trash for profit. Well, where is the redeeming social value in some of these products? That's what we have to start asking ourselves.

So, would you say then that this is a people problem?

Oh, it's first and foremost a materials problem and a marketing blitz.

You've got this fantastic material, which you know there is no precautionary principle involved at the manufacturer's end. He can experiment with any chemicals he wants to make any kind of effects he wants . . . and he doesn't have to tell you diddly about the chemicals that went into making that.

So first and foremost, it is this wonderful, fantastic material that has so many ways it can be fabricated, and the marketing that pushes it onto the marketplace.

What I say is, we can certainly tell manufacturers some basic ground rules for manufacturing.

The amount of time that people are spending unwrapping things wrapped in plastic and disposing of broken things made out of plastic is cutting into their free time to the point where it's oppressive.

Have you been to Trader Joe's lately? If you buy an apple, it's wrapped in two layers of plastic.

Yeah, every single thing is wrapped in plastic. I mean, each toothpick is wrapped in plastic. What, are they afraid the toothpick is going to pollute the toothpick next to it?

What is the impact of all this trash on the creatures that live in the ocean?

Plastic comes in every size-class and mimics the food for every single trophic level. From the tiniest zooplankton all the way to the largest cetaceans, there is a plastic morsel that looks and acts just like their natural food, or that will get them entangled in it when they are trying to feed naturally.

So it's affecting the entire marine food web. What we are doing in the ocean with the breakdown of plastics into the microscopic, nanoparticle size-classes is carrying on an uncontrolled experiment in toxic drug delivery to every organism in the ocean with zero monitoring and zero controls.

These plastics are not just innocent particles: They are hydrophobic chemical sponges, meaning they repel water but are oil-loving. Plastic is the kind of sponge you would put out in an oil spill, so they are very effective sponges for anything oily. Petroleum-derivative toxics are sticking to these plastics, delivering these toxicants to marine creatures from the very base of the food web to the top of the food web, in addition to killing millions by entanglement.

When plastic is so prevalent that it can fill up a creature's stomach, that turns off the desire to feed, and if an organism doesn't put on fat stores for reproduction and migration, it's going to crash in population.

So plastic washes out to the ocean, all these creatures are eating it, and then some of those creatures come back into our own food system and we eat them?

Not only plastics, but all kinds of petroleum and industrial chemicals are in our serum—that's called our "body-burden." There are about 150 chemicals not known before 1950. They are having effects on children especially, and women's reproductive systems, and in males. One out of four male Mediterranean swordfish are making egg yolks, which is not something that should be happening in a male swordfish. There's this feminization being carried out by a lot of industrial chemicals. These hormone disruptors are having a big effect.

Really, it is an uncontrolled experiment in the release of chemicals into the biosphere that is coming back to haunt us. All our conveniences and all our modern technologies have a downside. We really are on such a treadmill of production of new products, and the population is so accustomed to this treadmill, that they are willing to sacrifice life expectancy and health for the affluence of modern society.

When one out of two Latinas is going to have diabetes, and when one out of every three women is going to have breast cancer, we could be looking at that as a global problem that requires a global solution, but we're not.

Is there any documentation about what happens to a population that is feeding on seafood that has plastic in its system?

It's much easier for scientists to work on animals because of ethical restraints. We do have evidence of contamination in birds from ingesting plastic particles. We know that it is a mechanism for delivering organic contaminants into living tissues. We know that it is invading the entire circulatory system of animal life that is exposed to it.

There is a real possibility that physiological changes are occurring without people even being aware of it.

Do you eat fish?

I do eat fish, especially at sea. On land, you can be a vegetarian because you can grow a lot of vegetables, but about all we can grow out at sea is sprouts.

So we do eat fish, but what we're thinking is that it's better to eat small fish. We actually came up with a recipe called "minnow-strone," which focuses on the idea that we don't want to have top predators that have bio-accumulated all of this stuff on our plates.

You're making me think twice about eating fish.

Well, get it from an area that is fairly free from contamination, like Alaska. Alaskan halibut is good. You can also go for farm-raised stuff where they publicize the fact that they use land-based feed and they don't use pesticides.

What about your personal use of plastic?

For the boat, we've gotten rid of a lot of plastic. Even though plastic is lightweight and doesn't break, we've switched. It's a very gradual process of weaning yourself off these non-degradable, non-recyclable plastics. The only thing we come back to port with is plastic.

Beyond the gyre discovery, what are you working on now?

Well, we are working on the problem that you elucidated, which is the food chain. We've harvested in our trolls, just sort of accidentally along with the plastic, 671 little fish. We opened them up and they had 1,391 pieces of plastic in their stomachs. These are like the sardine or the anchovy out in the deep ocean. They are what feed the rest of the fish, and they're eating plastic. So we're going to start analyzing their tissues and the tissues of other fish that eat these fish, looking at the whole food chain in the ocean to see what the impacts are of plastics. Then on the solutions front, we're working on this new paradigm—liberating us from this rat race of cheap replacements for cheap products that pollute and don't work for very long.

Can you elaborate on what that solutions piece looks like?

It's in its incipient stages. The basic question is: Does this liberate us from our pollution problems, and how does it give us room to experience life without constantly being reminded that we live in an industrial civilization? We need space to develop our own needs and our own desires; without that space, we are just consumers in a cage. The future will have to eliminate products that make you need two or three more products. We want products that are the easiest to recycle, that are the least toxic, and the most cradle-to-cradle in terms of raw materials. I am just beginning to formulate that concept.

What do you see as the future for the oceans?

Well, in the near term, it is going to get worse fast. Our research found 6-to-1 plastic to plankton by weight in 1999. We went back last year and found 46-to-1 plastic to plankton—the weight had gone up, the volume had gone up, the number of pieces had gone up. Every decade, it's getting close to 10 times worse.

It's not looking good in the near term.

What gives you hope?

Well, it's not so much hope as it is a realization that change has occurred historically in the recent past through crises. If we're not making serious re-evaluations of our coastal engineering after Katrina, what will it take?

The idea that the visibility of this pollutant comes home to roost, and people, through our research, learn that it has a very serious dark side;

in addition to the one that they observe in their daily life, simply as an aesthetic problem, it is also this toxic layer that is covering the surface of the ocean. I am hopeful that our research will spur this visible blight to be assessed at a more serious level—to create not only public outcry for change, but also governmental awareness that they must mandate changes in production throughout the world.

Until we get this calculus that takes into account the lifecycle of the product and its true value, and until the public rejects the life of cheap products that don't last, until they get fed up with that . . . that has to change. Given the structure of Madison Avenue and the advertising industry, that's not likely to change. It could be extended indefinitely. So the picture is not bright into the future.

We've got to take the slogan "Yes, we can" seriously. We've got to make space where we can see an alternative because the timid solutions being proposed are just not going to work.

Note

1. Marian Liu, "Great Pacific Garbage Patch Now Three Times the Size of France," CNN, March 23, 2018, https://www.cnn.com/2018/03/23/world/plastic-great-pacific-garbage-patch-intl/index.html.

The Rise of Slime

Jeremy Jackson

Changes in the Ocean are causing havoc for an untold number of species, with populations shifting and numbers plummeting, from the tiniest copepods to the most immense whales. But some organisms are thriving, expanding their ranges, and proliferating wildly. Most of these opportunistic animals are slimy or gelatinous creatures that humans regard as useless at best, and at worst disgusting and dangerous. Jellyfish lead the vanguard in this "rise of slime," as oceanographer Jeremy Jackson has dubbed it. These ephemeral life forms are spreading rapidly around the world, reaching waters where they've never been seen before. The wormlike invertebrates called tunicates or sea squirts now blanket the seafloor in places like Georges Bank, off the coast of Massachusetts, where cod, scallops, and flounder once abounded but now are virtually absent. There is little chance of jellyfish and slimy tunicates filling the dietary niche vacated by fish and shellfish, unless Western palates overcome their customary aversion to phlegmy foods, but the viscous reality of the benthic zone suggests that they will have no choice, if seafood is to remain on the menu.

This summary of Jeremy Jackson's thesis was added to the website of his institutional base, the Scripps Institution of Oceanography, University of California–San Diego, in 2008.

Threats to marine ecosystems from overfishing, pollution and climate change must be addressed to halt downward trends.

Human activities are cumulatively driving the health of the world's oceans down a rapid spiral, and only prompt and wholesale changes will slow or perhaps ultimately reverse the catastrophic problems they are facing.

Such is the prognosis of Jeremy Jackson, a professor of oceanography at Scripps Institution of Oceanography at UC San Diego, in a bold new assessment of the oceans and their ecological health. Publishing his study in the online early edition of the *Proceedings of the National Academy of Sciences (PNAS)*, Jackson believes that human impacts are laying the groundwork for mass extinctions in the oceans on par with vast ecological upheavals of the past.

He cites the synergistic effects of habitat destruction, overfishing, ocean warming, increased acidification and massive nutrient runoff as culprits in a grand transformation of once complex ocean ecosystems. Areas that had

Many slimy species are proliferating in the Ocean's benthic zone, blanketing the seafloor. Sprawling, dense, phlegmy biomasses of tunicates and algae destroy the habitats
of fish and shellfish, overwhelming coral reefs. Higher in the water column, an explosive increase in worldwide jellyfish populations is taking place. Invasive species of
jellyfish with no predators are penetrating into new areas of the warming Ocean. This
photograph shows the alga *Boodlea* smothering the coral reef near Kure Atoll in 2009.
Photograph by Peter Vroom, 2009, from the *Quarterly Bulletin* of the National Oceanographic and Atmospheric Administration's Pacific Islands Fisheries Science Center,
March 2010.

featured intricate marine food webs with large animals are being converted
into simplistic ecosystems dominated by microbes, toxic algal blooms, jellyfish and disease.

Jackson, director of the Scripps Center for Marine Biodiversity and Conservation, has tagged the ongoing transformation as "the rise of slime." The
new paper, "Ecological Extinction and Evolution in the Brave New Ocean," is
a result of Jackson's presentation last December at a biodiversity and extinction colloquium convened by the National Academy of Sciences.

"The purpose of the talk and the paper is to make clear just how dire the
situation is and how rapidly things are getting worse," said Jackson. "It's a lot
like the issue of climate change that we had ignored for so long. If anything,
the situation in the oceans could be worse because we are so close to the
precipice in many ways."

In the assessment, Jackson reviews and synthesizes a range of research
studies on marine ecosystem health, and in particular key studies conducted

since a seminal 2001 study he led analyzing the impacts of historical overfishing. The new study includes overfishing, but expands to include threats from areas such as nutrient runoff that lead to so-called dead zones of low oxygen. He also incorporates increases in ocean warming and acidification resulting from greenhouse gas emissions.

Jackson describes the potently destructive effects when forces combine to degrade ocean health. For example, climate change can exacerbate stresses on the marine environment already brought by overfishing and pollution.

"All of the different kinds of data and methods of analysis point in the same direction of drastic and increasingly rapid degradation of marine ecosystems," Jackson writes in the paper.

During a recent research expedition to Kiritimati, or Christmas Island, Jeremy Jackson and other researchers documented a coral reef overtaken by algae, featuring murky waters and few fish. The researchers say pollution, overfishing, warming waters or some combination of the three are to blame.

Jackson furthers his analysis by constructing a chart of marine ecosystems and their endangered status. Coral reefs, Jackson's primary area of research, are critically endangered and among the most threatened ecosystems; also critically endangered are estuaries and coastal seas, threatened by overfishing and runoff; continental shelves are endangered due to, among other things, losses of fishes and sharks; and the open ocean ecosystem is listed as threatened mainly through losses at the hands of overfishing.

"Just as we say that leatherback turtles are critically endangered, I looked at entire ecosystems as if they were a species," said Jackson. "The reality is that if we want to have coral reefs in the future, we're going to have to behave that way and recognize the magnitude of the response that's necessary to achieve it."

To stop the degradation of the oceans, Jackson identifies overexploitation, pollution and climate change as the three main drivers that must be addressed.

"The challenges of bringing these threats under control are enormously complex and will require fundamental changes in fisheries, agricultural practices and the ways we obtain energy for everything we do," he writes.

"So it's not a happy picture and the only way to deal with it is in segments; the only way to keep one's sanity and try to achieve real success is to carve out sectors of the problem that can be addressed in effective terms and get on it as quickly as possible."

The Tragic Common Home of the Ocean

Pope Francis

Pope Francis clearly communicated his perspective on environmental issues when he chose for his own the name of "the patron saint of ecologists," as he calls Saint Francis of Assisi (1182–1226), when he was elected to the papacy in 2013. His 2015 encyclical "The Tragedy of Our Common Home," with its lyrical introduction evoking Saint Francis, fulfills the promise he implicitly made to everyone who loves nature when he first identified himself as Pope Francis.

"Common" is the most important word in the text. It is an adjective derived from the Old French comun, which entered Middle English by about 1300, meaning "belonging to all." By 1500, "common" had become a noun in English, meaning resources shared by everyone, usually meaning pastureland, but also forests and fishing areas.

"Tragedy" is the most important word missing from the text. In Greek literature, a terrible outcome that can be seen coming in advance was a tragedy. The tragedy of the commons is a concept put forth in 1968 by Garrett Hardin, in an influential (if controversial) article with that title published in Science magazine. Hardin's piece theorizes that people have the tendency to take more than their fair share of things held in common, leading to the exhaustion of otherwise sustainable resources. The United States personifies this greed: with 5 percent of the world's population, we consume nearly a quarter of the energy that the species uses annually. Americans are guilty of what the pope calls "cheerful recklessness."

The best—rather, the worst—example of the tragedy of the commons is unfolding on the Ocean, where more than 90 percent of the fish biomass is already gone. In the pope's long-awaited statement of sanity from a world leader, the clarion call to save the Ocean joins a cacophonous chorus of warning bells from across the globe.

40. Oceans not only contain the bulk of our planet's water supply, but also most of the immense variety of living creatures, many of them still unknown to us and threatened for various reasons. What is more, marine life in rivers, lakes, seas and oceans, which feeds a great part of the world's population, is affected by uncontrolled fishing, leading to a drastic depletion of certain species. Selective forms of fishing which discard much of what they collect continue unabated. Particularly threatened are marine organisms which we tend to overlook, like some forms of plankton; they represent a significant

element in the ocean food chain, and species used for our food ultimately depend on them.

41. In tropical and subtropical seas, we find coral reefs comparable to the great forests on dry land, for they shelter approximately a million species, including fish, crabs, molluscs, sponges and algae. Many of the world's coral reefs are already barren or in a state of constant decline. "Who turned the wonderworld of the seas into underwater cemeteries bereft of colour and life?" This phenomenon is due largely to pollution which reaches the sea as the result of deforestation, agricultural monocultures, industrial waste and destructive fishing methods, especially those using cyanide and dynamite. It is aggravated by the rise in temperature of the oceans. All of this helps us to see that every intervention in nature can have consequences which are not immediately evident, and that certain ways of exploiting resources prove costly in terms of degradation which ultimately reaches the ocean bed itself.

Suggestions for Further Reading

General

Buschman, Rainer F. *Oceans in World History*. New York: McGraw-Hill, 2007.

Butel, Paul. *The Atlantic*. London: Routledge, 2014.

Cusack, Tricia, ed. *Framing the Ocean, 1700 to the Present: Envisaging the Sea as a Social Space*. London: Routledge, 2014.

Freeman, Donald B. *The Pacific*. London: Routledge, 2015.

Gillis, John R. *Fluid Frontiers: New Currents in Marine Environmental History*. Cambridge: White Horse Press, 2015.

Gillis, John R. *Islands in the Mind: How the Human Imagination Created the Atlantic World*. New York: Palgrave Macmillan, 2009.

Labaree, Benjamin, William M. Fowler Jr., Edward W. Sloan, John B. Hattendorf, Jeffrey J. Safford, and Andrew W. German. *America and the Sea: A Maritime History*. Mystic, CT: Mystic Seaport Press, 1998.

McDougall, Walter A. *Let the Sea Make a Noise: A History of the North Atlantic from Magellan to MacArthur*. New York: Basic Books, 1993.

Paine, Lincoln. *The Sea and Civilization: A Maritime History of the World*. New York: Alfred A. Knopf, 2013.

Pearson, Michael. *The Indian Ocean*. London: Routledge, 2003.

Rozwadowski, Helen. *Vast Expanses*, London: Reaktion Press, 2019.

Searchable Sea Literature. Williams-Mystic, the Maritime Studies Program of Williams College and Mystic Seaport. https://sites.williams.edu/searchablesealit/.

Part I. Creation

Dalley, Stephanie, trans. *Myths from Mesopotamia: Creation, the Flood, Gilgamesh and Others*. Oxford: Oxford University Press, 1998.

Erwin, Douglas H., and James W. Valentine. *The Cambrian Explosion: The Construction of Animal Biodiversity*. New York: W. H. Freeman, 2013.

Foster, John. *Cambrian Ocean World: Ancient Sea Life of North America*. Bloomington: University of Indiana Press, 2014.

Gould, Stephen Jay. *Wonderful Life: The Burgess Shale and the Nature of History*. New York: W. W. Norton, 1989.

Morris, Simon Conway. *The Crucible of Creation: The Burgess Shale and the Rise of Animals*. Oxford: Oxford University Press, 1998.

Sproul, Barbara C. *Primal Myths: Creation Myths around the World*. New York: Harper-One, 1979.

Part II. Ancient Seas

Cassan, Lionel. *The Ancient Mariners*. Princeton, NJ: Princeton University Press, 1991.

Cassan, Lionel. *Ships and Seafaring in Ancient Times*. Austin: University of Texas Press, 1994.

Cassan, Lionel. *Travel in the Ancient World*. Baltimore, MD: Johns Hopkins University Press, 1994.

Hourani, George F., and John Carswell. *Arab Seafaring: In the Indian Ocean in Ancient and Medieval Times*. Princeton, NJ: Princeton University Press, 1995.

Rainbird, Paul. *The Archaeology of Islands*. New York: Cambridge University Press, 2007.

Skydsgaard, Jens Erik, and Karen Ascani, eds. *Ancient History Matters*. Rome: L'Erma di Bretschneider, 2002.

Part III. Unknown Waters

Ballard, Robert D. *The Eternal Darkness: A Personal History of Deep-Sea Exploration*. Princeton, NJ: Princeton University Press, 2002.

Cousteau, Jacques Y., with James Dugan. *The Living Sea*. New York: Harper and Row, 1963.

Dreyer, Edward L. *Zheng He: China and the Ocean in the Early Ming Dynasty, 1405–1433*. London: Pearson, 2006.

Gould, Carol Grant. *The Remarkable Life of William Beebe, Explorer and Naturalist*. Washington, DC: Island Press/Shearwater, 2004.

Hohn, Donovan. *Moby-Duck: The True Story of 28,800 Bath Toys Lost at Sea and of the Beachcombers, Oceanographers, Environmentalists, and Fools, Including the Author, Who Went in Search of Them*. New York: Penguin, 2012.

Igler, David. *The Great Ocean: The Pacific World from Captain Cook to the Gold Rush*. Oxford: Oxford University Press, 2013.

Kroll, Gary. *America's Ocean Wilderness: A Cultural History of Twentieth-Century Exploration*. Lawrence: University of Kansas Press, 2008.

Lipman, Andrew. *The Saltwater Frontier: Indians and the Contest for the American Coast*. New Haven, CT: Yale University Press, 2015.

Philbrick, Nathaniel. *Sea of Glory: America's Voyage of Discovery, the U.S. Exploring Expedition, 1838–1842*. New York: Viking, 2002.

Rozwadowski, Helen. *Fathoming the Ocean: The Discovery and Exploration of the Deep Sea*. Cambridge, MA: Belknap–Harvard University Press, 2005.

Williams, Glyndwr. *Arctic Labyrinth: The Quest for the Northwest Passage*. Berkeley: University of California Press, 2010.

Williams, Glyndwr. *The Great South Sea: English Voyages and Encounters, 1570–1750*. New Haven, CT: Yale University Press, 1997.

Williams, Glyndwr. *The Prize of All the Oceans: Anson's Voyage around the World*. New York: Viking, 2000.

Williams, Glyndwr. *Voyages of Delusion: The Search for the Northwest Passage in the Age of Reason*. New York: Harper Collins, 2002.

Part IV. Saltwater Hunt

Bolster, W. Jeffrey. *The Mortal Sea: Fishing the Atlantic in the Age of Sail*. Cambridge, MA: Belknap–Harvard University Press, 2014.

Cushman, Gregory. *Guano and the Opening of the Pacific World: A Global Ecological History*. New York: Cambridge University Press, 2013.

Dorsey, Kurkpatrick. *Whales and Nations: Environmental Diplomacy on the High Seas*. Seattle: University of Washington Press, 2013.

Fegan, Brian. *Fish on Friday: Feasting, Fasting, and the Discovery of the New World*. New York: Basic Books, 2006.

Graham, Burnett D. *The Sounding of the Whale: Science and Cetaceans in the Twentieth Century*. Chicago: University of Chicago Press, 2012.

Greenburg, Paul. *American Catch: The Fight for Our Local Seafood*. New York: Penguin, 2015.

Greenburg, Paul. *Four Fish: The Future of the Last Wild Food*. New York: Penguin, 2010.

McKenzie, Matthew. *Breaking the Banks: Representations and Realities in New England Fisheries, 1866–1966*. Amherst: University of Massachusetts Press, 2019.

Part V. Watery Highways

Brinnin, John Malcolm. *The Sway of the Grand Saloon: A Social History of the North Atlantic*. New York: Delacorte, 1971.

Curtin, Philip D. *Cross-Cultural Trade in World History*. New York: Cambridge University Press, 1984.

Klein, Herbert S. *The Atlantic Slave Trade*. 2nd ed. New York: Cambridge University Press, 2010.

Rediker, Marcus. *The Slave Ship: A Human History*. New York: Penguin, 2008.

Roorda, Eric Paul. *Twain at Sea: The Maritime Writings of Samuel Langhorne Clemens*. Hanover, NH: University Press of New England, 2018.

Sheriff, Abdul. *Dhow Cultures of the Indian Ocean: Cosmopolitanism, Commerce and Islam*. London: C. Hurst, 2014.

Sheriff, Abdul. *The Indian Ocean: Oceanic Connections and the Creation of New Societies*. London: C. Hurst, 2009.

Part VI. Battlefields

Adkins, Roy. *Nelson's Trafalgar: The Battle That Changed the World*. New York: Penguin, 2006.

Buchheim, Lothar-Günther. *Das Boot: The Boat*. 1973. Reprint, London: Cassell Military Classics, 2007.

Crowley, Roger. *Empires of the Sea: The Siege of Malta, the Battle of Lepanto, and the Contest for the Center of the World*. New York: Random House, 2009.

Dimbleby, Jonathan. *The Battle of the Atlantic: How the Allies Won the War*. Oxford: Oxford University Press, 2016.

Glete, Jan. *Warfare at Sea, 1500–1650: Maritime Conflicts and the Transformation of Europe*. London: Routledge, 1999.

Hamblin, Jacob Darwin. *Oceanographers and the Cold War: Disciples of Marine Science.* Seattle: University of Washington Press, 2014.

Hornfischer, John D. *The Fleet at Flood Tide: America at Total War in the Pacific, 1944–1945.* New York: Bantam, 2016.

King, Dean, and John B. Hattendorf, eds. *Every Man Will Do His Duty: An Anthology of Firsthand Accounts from the Age of Nelson, 1793–1814.* New York: Henry Holt, 1997.

Miller, Nathan. *Broadsides: The Age of Fighting Sail, 1775–1815.* New York: Wiley, 2008.

Miller, Nathan. *War at Sea: A Naval History of World War II.* Oxford: Oxford University Press, 1997.

Monsarrat, Nicholas. *The Cruel Sea.* 1951. Reprint, Ithaca, NY: Burford, 2000.

Rodger, N. A. M. *The Command of the Ocean: A Naval History of Britain, 1649–1815.* London: Penguin UK, 2005.

Rodger, N. A. M. *The Safeguard of the Sea: A Naval History of Britain 660–1649.* London: Penguin UK, 2004.

Sondhaus, Lawrence. *The Great War at Sea: A Naval History of the First World War.* New York: Cambridge University Press, 2014.

Symonds, Craig L. *The Battle of Midway.* Oxford: Oxford University Press, 2011.

Symonds, Craig L. *The Civil War at Sea.* New York: Oxford University Press, 2012.

Symonds, Craig L. *World War II at Sea: A Global History.* New York: Oxford University Press, 2018.

Tuchman, Barbara. *The First Salute: A View of the American Revolution.* New York: Ballantine, 1988.

Willis, Sam. *The Struggle for Sea Power: A Naval History of the American Revolution.* New York: W. W. Norton, 2016.

Part VII. Piracy

Anderson, Clare, Niklas Frykman, Lex Heema van Voss, and Marcus Rediker, eds. *Mutiny and Maritime Radicalism in the Age of Revolution: A Global Survey.* New York: Cambridge University Press, 2013.

Antony, Robert J., ed. *Pirates in the Age of Sail.* Norton Documents Readers. New York: W. W. Norton, 2007.

Appleby, John C. *Women and English Piracy, 1540–1720: Partners and Victims of Crime.* Woodridge, UK: Boydell Brewer, 2015.

Bahadur, Jay. *The Pirates of Somalia: Inside Their Hidden World.* New York: Pantheon, 2011.

Croizier, Ralph C. *Koxinga and Chinese Nationalism: History, Myth, and the Hero.* Cambridge, MA: Harvard University Press, 1977.

Davis, Robert. *Christian Slaves, Muslim Masters: White Slavery in the Mediterranean, the Barbary Coast, and Italy, 1500–1800.* New York: Palgrave Macmillan, 2003.

Defoe, Daniel. *A General History of the Pyrates.* Edited by Manuel Schonhorn. Mineola, MN: Dover, 1999.

Dening, Greg. *Mr. Bligh's Bad Language: Passion, Power and Theater on the Bounty.* New York: Cambridge University Press, 1992.

Kelsey, Harry. *Sir Francis Drake: The Queen's Pirate.* New Haven, CT: Yale University Press, 2000.

Lane, Kris. *Pillaging the Empire: Piracy in the Americas, 1500–1750*. Armonk, NY: M. E. Sharpe, 1998.

Pennell, C. R., ed. *Bandits at Sea: A Pirates Reader*. New York: New York University Press, 2001.

Preston, Diana, and Michael Preston. *A Pirate of Exquisite Mind: The Life of William Dampier, Explorer, Naturalist and Buccaneer*. New York: Berkley, 2005.

Rediker, Marcus. *Between the Devil and the Deep Blue Sea: Merchant Seamen, Pirates, and the Anglo-American Maritime World, 1700–1750*. New York: Cambridge University Press, 1987.

Rediker, Marcus. *Villains of All Nations: Atlantic Pirates in the Golden Age*. New York: Beacon, 2004.

Williams, Glyndwr. *Buccaneers, Explorers and Settlers: British Enterprise and Encounters in the Pacific, 1670–1800*. London: Routledge, 2005.

Part VIII. Shipwrecks and Castaways

Franklin, Jonathan. *438 Days: An Extraordinary True Story of Survival at Sea*. New York: Atria, 2015.

Garland, Joseph. *Lone Voyager: The Extraordinary Adventures of Howard Blackburn, Hero Fisherman of Gloucester*. New York: Touchstone, 2000.

Gordon, Stewart. *A History of the World in Sixteen Shipwrecks*. Lebanon, NH: Fore Edge, 2015.

Jünger, Sebastian. *The Perfect Storm: A True Story of Men against the Sea*. New York: W. W. Norton, 1997.

Philbrick, Nathaniel. *In the Heart of the Sea: The Tragedy of the Whaleship Essex*. New York: Viking, 2000.

Willis, Clint, ed. *Rough Water: Stories of Survival from the Sea*. Boston: Da Capo, 1999.

Willis, Sam. *Shipwreck: A History of Disasters at Sea*. London: Quercus, 2015.

Part IX. Inspiration

Crew, Bob. *Sea Poems: A Seafarer Anthology*. Dobbs Ferry, NY: Sheridan House, 2005.

McClatchy, J. D. *Poems of the Sea*. New York: Everyman's Library/Penguin, 2001.

Raban, Jonathan. *The Oxford Book of the Sea*. Oxford: Oxford University Press, 1992.

Part X. Recreation

Davin, Tom, ed. *The Rudder Treasury: A Companion for Lovers of Small Craft*. Dobbs Ferry, NY: Sheridan House, 2003.

Gordinier, Glenn. *Surfing Cold Water*. Stonington, CT: Flat Hammock, 2012.

Laderman, Scott. *Empire in Waves: A Political History of Surfing*. Berkeley: University of California Press, 2014.

Maxtone-Graham, John. *Liners to the Sun*. New York: Macmillan, 1985; revised ed., Dobbs Ferry, NY: Sheridan House, 2000.

Maxtone-Graham, John. *The Only Way to Cross*. New York: Collier, 1972.

Steinburg, Philip E. *The Social Construction of the Ocean.* Cambridge, UK: Cambridge University Press, 2011.

Wallace, David Foster. *A Supposedly Fun Thing I Will Never Do Again: Essays and Arguments.* Boston: Back Bay, 1998.

Part XI. Laboratory

Adamowsky, Natascha. *The Mysterious Science of the Sea, 1775–1943.* London: Routledge, 2015.

Grady, John. *Matthew Fontaine Maury, Father of Oceanography: A Biography, 1806–1873.* Jefferson, NC: McFarland, 2015.

Kunzig, Robert. *Mapping the Deep: The Extraordinary Story of Ocean Science.* New York: W. W. Norton, 2000.

MacLeish, William H. *The Gulf Stream: Encounters with the Blue God.* New York: Houghton Mifflin, 1989.

Plakins Thornton, Tamara. *Nathaniel Bowditch and the Power of Numbers.* Chapel Hill: University of North Carolina Press, 2016.

Reidy, Michael S. *Tides of History: Ocean Science and Her Majesty's Navy.* Chicago: University of Chicago Press, 2008.

Smith, Jason W. *To Master the Boundless Sea: The U.S. Navy, the Marine Environment, and the Cartography of Empire.* Chapel Hill: University of North Carolina Press, 2018.

Ulanski, Stan. *The California Current: A Pacific Ecosystem and Its Fliers, Divers, and Swimmers.* Chapel Hill: University of North Carolina Press, 2016.

Ulanski, Stan. *The Gulf Stream: Tiny Plankton, Giant Bluefin, and the Amazing Story of the Powerful River in the Atlantic.* Chapel Hill: University of North Carolina Press, 2010.

Williams, Glyndwr. *Naturalists at Sea: Scientific Travellers from Dampier to Darwin.* New Haven, CT: Yale University Press, 2013.

Part XII. The Endangered Ocean

Earle, Sylvia. *Sea Change: A Message of the Oceans.* New York: Ballantine, 1996.

Earle, Sylvia. *The World Is Blue: How Our Fate and the Ocean's Are One.* Washington, DC: National Geographic Society, 2010.

Hannigan, John. *The Geopolitics of Deep Oceans.* Cambridge: Polity, 2016.

Jackson, Jeremy, Karen Alexander, and Enrico Sala, eds. *Shifting Baselines: The Past and Future of Ocean Fisheries.* Washington, DC: Island Press, 2011.

Moore, Charles. *Plastic Ocean: How a Sea Captain's Chance Discovery Launched a Determined Quest to Save the Oceans.* New York: Avery, 2011.

Roberts, Callum. *The Ocean of Life: The Fate of Man and the Sea.* New York: Penguin, 2013.

Roberts, Callum. *The Unnatural History of the Sea.* Washington, DC: Island Press, 2008.

Acknowledgment of Copyrights and Sources

Part I. Creation

"The Egyptian Sea of Nun," by anonymous, previously published as "Utterance 503," in *The Pyramid Texts in Translation and Commentary*, vol. 3, translated by Samuel A. B. Mercer (New York: Longman, Green and Company, 1952), 186–87.

"Babylon by the Sea," by anonymous, from *The Babylonian Legends of Creation*, edited and translated by E. A. Wallis Budge (London: British Museum, 1921), 31–32.

"Aphrodite Born from Sea Spray," by Hesiod, from *Hesiod: The Homeric Hymns, Epic Cycle, Homerica*, translated by H. G. Evelyn-White, Loeb Classical Library, vol. 57 (Cambridge, MA: Harvard University Press, 1914), 176–90.

"Izanagi and Izanami, Japanese Sea Gods," by Ō no Yasumaro, translated by Basil Hart Chamberlain, from the *Kojiki* in *The Sacred Books and Early Literature of the East, Volume 8: Japan*, edited by Charles F. Horne (New York: Parke, Austin, and Lipscomb, 1917), 15–16.

"The Pacific Islanders' Angry Ocean God," by Sir George Grey, from *Polynesian Mythology and Ancient Traditional History of the New Zealand Race* (London: John Murray, 1855), 1–9.

"The Hindu Ocean Gods," by Edward Washburn Hopkins, from *Epic Mythology* (Strassburg: Verlag von Karl J. Trübner, 1915), 116–22.

"The Finnish Sea Mother," by anonymous, from *Kalevala: Or the Land of Heroes*, vol. 1, edited by William Forsell Kirby (New York: E. P. Dutton and Company, 1907), 3–9.

"The Sea-Creating, Rainbow-Loving Serpent God of Haiti," by Joseph J. Williams, from *Voodoos and Obeahs: Phases of West India Witchcraft* (New York: Dial Press, 1932), 56–57, 96–105.

"Did Comets Bring Water to Earth?," by Kimberly M. Burtnyk, from EarthSky, June 13, 2012, http://earthsky.org/space/did-comets-bring-water-to-earth. Reprinted courtesy of EarthSky.

"Before the Great Extinctions," by Jean-Bernard Caron, previously published as *The Science of the Burgess Shale* virtual exhibit, Royal Ontario Museum, Parks Canada, Department of Canadian Heritage, Virtual Museum of Canada, 2011, https://burgess-shale.rom.on.ca/en/science/index.php. © Royal Ontario Museum. Used by permission of the Royal Ontario Museum.

Part II. Ancient Seas

"The First Aussies," by Fran Dorey, previously published as "The Spread of People
to Australia," on Australian Museum, October 30, 2015, http://australianmuseum
.net.au/the-spread-of-people-to-australia. Reprinted courtesy of Fran Dorey.

"A New View of the Ainu," by David H. Gremillion, previously published as "Pre
Siberian Human Migration to the Americas: Possible Validation by HTLV-1 Mutation
Analysis," on *Archaeolog* (blog), September 25, 2008, http://web.stanford.edu/dept
/archaeology/cgi-bin/archaeolog/?p=219. Reprinted courtesy of *Archaeolog*.

"The Surfing Chinchorro of Chile": (1) "Pre-Hispanic Cultures in the Atacama Desert:
A Pacific Coast Overview," by Victoria Castro, and (2) "The Chinchorro Culture:
Hunter, Gatherers and Fishers of the Atacama Desert Coast," by Vivien G. Standen
and Bernardo T. Arriaza, both from *The Chinchorro Culture: A Comparative Perspective*,
edited by Nuria Sanz, Bernardo T. Arriaza, and Vivien G. Standen (Arica, Chile:
UNESCO, 2014), 23–24, 40–43.

"Canoes: The World's First—and Simplest, and Most Graceful—Boats," by Eric Paul
Roorda. Written for this volume.

"Pacific Island Open Ocean Navigation," by David Lewis, from *We, the Navigators:
The Ancient Art of Landfinding in the Pacific*, edited by Sir Derek Oulton (Honolulu:
University of Hawaii, 1994), 277–89. Reprinted by permission of University of
Hawaii Press.

"The Earliest Seafarers in the Mediterranean and the Near East," by George F. Bass,
from *A History of Seafaring* (London: Thames and Hudson, 1972), 12–13. © Thames
and Hudson London. Reprinted by kind permission of Thames & Hudson Ltd.,
London.

Part III. Unknown Waters

"Chinese Voyages on the Indian Ocean," by Zheng He, transcribed by Teobaldo Filesi
based on temple stelae inscriptions, from *China and Africa in the Middle Ages*, translated by David Morison (London: Frank Cass, 1972), 57, 59–61. Used by permission
of Taylor & Francis Books UK.

"Arab Voyages on the Indian Ocean," by Paul Lunde, previously published as "The
Navigator Ahmad Ibn Majid," in *Saudi Aramco World* 56, no. 4 (July/August 2005),
45–48.

"No Welcome for Newcomers in New Zealand," by Abel Janszoon Tasman, previously
published as "Captain J. Tasman's Discoveries on the Coast of the South Terra
Incognita," in *An Account of Several Late Voyages and Discoveries* (London: D. Brown,
W. Innys, and T. Ward, 1711), 129–34.

"The Oceanic Captain Kirk," by William Reynolds, from *Voyage to the Southern Ocean:
The Letters of Lieutenant William Reynolds from the U.S. Exploring Expedition, 1838–1842*,
edited by Ann H. Cleaver and E. Jeffrey Stann (Annapolis, MD: Naval Institute
Press, 1988), 127–42.

"A Half Mile Down," by William Beebe, from *Half Mile Down* (New York: Harcourt,
Brace, 1934), 157–74, 219–23.

"Walking on the Seafloor," by Sylvia Earle, from an interview with Krista Tippett,

in KTPP/*The On Being Project*, June 7, 2012, http://www.onbeing.org/program
/oceanographer-sylvia-earle/transcript/4706. Used courtesy of the *On Being* project.

"Descent to the Deepest Deep," by Jamie Condliffe, previously published as "Five Ways
James Cameron Could Have Died on His Mission to the Bottom of the Ocean," on
Gizmodo, March 26, 2012, https://gizmodo.com/5896428/five-ways-james-cameron
-could-have-died-on-his-mission-to-the-bottom-of-the-ocean. Reprinted courtesy
of *Gizmodo*.

"Rubber Duckies Navigate the Northwest Passage," by Eric Paul Roorda. Written for
this volume.

Part IV. Saltwater Hunt

"Basque Whaling in the North Atlantic Ocean," by Alex Aguilar, previously published
as "A Review of Old Basque Whaling and Its Effect on the Right Whales (*Eubalaena
glacialis*) of the North Atlantic," in *Report of the International Whaling Commission* 10
(1986): 191–99. Reprinted courtesy of Alex Aguilar.

"The Tragedy of the Mackerel," by George Brown Goode, Joseph W. Collins, H. E.
Earll, and A. Howard Clark, from *Materials for a History of the Mackerel Fishery*
(Washington, DC: Government Printing Office, 1883), 119–23.

"The Tragedy of the Menhaden," by Genio C. Scott, from *Fishing in American Waters*
(New York: Harper and Brothers, 1875), 326–28.

"The Perils of South Pacific Whaling," by Nelson Cole Haley, from *Whale Hunt:
The Narrative of a Voyage by Nelson Cole Haley, Harpooner in the Ship Charles W. Morgan
1849–1853* (New York: Ives Washburn, 1948), 267–80. Reprinted courtesy of Mystic
Seaport Museum.

"The Collapse of Newfoundland Cod," by Greenpeace, previously published as
"The Collapse of the Canadian Newfoundland Cod Fishery," on Greenpeace, May 8,
2009, http://www.greenpeace.org/international/en/campaigns/oceans/seafood
/understanding-the-problem/overfishing-history/cod-fishery-canadian/. Reprinted
courtesy of Greenpeace Media Library.

"The Death of Coral Reefs," by Bob Stewart, previously published as "Coral Reef
Destruction and Conservation," on Texas A&M University's Department of Oceanography website, https://ocean.tamu.edu/academics/resources/ocean-world
/coral-reefs/coral-reef-destruction-and-conservation/index.html.

Part V. Watery Highways

"The Maritime Silk Road," by anonymous, previously published as "Maritime Silk
Road Museum of Guangdong," on Silk Roads, http://en.unesco.org/silkroad
/silk-road-institutions/maritime-silk-road-museum-guangdong.

"Navigating the Indian Ocean in the 1300s," by Ibn Battuta, from *Reḥla of Ibn Battūta
(India, Maldive Islands and Ceylon)*, 2nd ed., edited and translated by Āghā Mahdī
Ḥusain (Baroda [Vadodara], India: Oriental Institute, 1976), 175–77, 184–86, 189–92,
197, 200–201, 217–18, 225–26.

"The Ocean: Bridge or Moat?," by Benjamin W. Labaree, previously published as
"The Atlantic Paradox," in *The Atlantic World of Robert G. Albion*, edited by Benja-

min W. Labaree (Middletown, CT: Wesleyan University Press, 1975), 195–201, 215–17. © Benjamin W. Labaree. Used by permission of Wesleyan University Press.

"Surviving the Slave Ship," by Olaudah Equiano, from *The Interesting Narrative of the Life of Olaudah Equiano, or Gustavus Vassa, the African, Written by Himself* (London, 1789; reprint, Mineola, NY: Dover Thrift Editions, 1999), 31–35.

"Hating the China Trade," by Frederick Law Olmsted, from *The Papers of Frederick Law Olmsted, Volume 1: The Formative Years, 1822 to 1852*, edited by Charles Capen McLaughlin (Baltimore, MD: Johns Hopkins University Press, 1977), 140–42, 148–49, 151. © 1977 Johns Hopkins University Press. Reprinted with permission of Johns Hopkins University Press.

"About All Kinds of Ships," by Mark Twain, from *The American Claimant and Other Stories and Sketches* (New York: Harpers and Brothers, 1898), 470–87.

"Loving Cape Horn," by Irving Johnson, from *Round the Horn in a Square Rigger* (Springfield, MA: Milton Bradley Company, 1932; reprint, New York: Sea History Press, 1977), 123–24, 127–28, 130–31, 133–43, 148–50.

"'Bitter Strength': The International 'Coolie' Trade," by the Chinese Cuba Commission, from *The Cuba Commission Report: A Hidden History of the Chinese in Cuba, the Original English-Language Text of 1876* (Baltimore, MD: Johns Hopkins University Press, 1993): 32, 36–37, 42–48.

"The Container Ship," by Roz Hamlett, previously published as "Port Newark: How Malcolm McLean Changed the World," on *Portfolio* (blog), April 27, 2016, https: //portfolio.panynj.gov/2016/04/27/port-newarkmalcom-mcleans-box-changes-the -world/. Used courtesy of the Port Authority of New York and New Jersey.

Part VI. Battlefields

"The Epic Galley Battle of the Ancient Sea," by Herodotus, previously published as "The Eighth Book of the History of Herodotus, Entitled Urania," in *The History of Herodotus*, vol. 4, edited by George Rawlinson (London: John Murray, 1860), 328–34.

"The Crest of Islamic Sea Power," by Matthew Merighi, previously published as "Lessons from History: An Ottoman Navy by Any Other Name," on *Center for International Maritime Security* (blog), August 5, 2014, http://cimsec.org/lessons -history-ottoman-navy-name-fight-just-well/12269. Used courtesy of Matthew Merighi.

"Elizabethan England's Plausibly Deniable War in the Pacific Ocean," by Sir Francis Pretty, from *The Famous Voyage of Sir Francis Drake* (London: H. Slater, 1742), 3, 5–14.

"The Iconic Tactic of the Age of Sail," by Major General Godfrey Basil Mundy, from *The Life and Correspondence of the Late Admiral Lord Rodney*, edited by Godfrey Basil Mundy (London: John Murray, 1830), 222–33.

"Captain Marryat's War," by Frederick Marryat, from *Peter Simple* (London: Richard Edward King, 1834), 177–81.

"World War I beneath the Waves," by Baron Edgar von Spiegel von und zu Peckel-sheim, from *The Adventures of the U-202: An Actual Narrative* (New York: Century, 1917), 46–49, 52–57.

"The Far-Flung Battle of Midway," by Office of Naval Intelligence, from *The Japanese*

Story of the Battle of Midway, OPNAV P32-1002 (Washington, DC: United States Navy, 1947), 1–11, 39, 57.

"The Barents Sea, Most Dangerous Waters of World War II," by Jack Bowman, from his personal diary, available at *CONVOY—PQ.17*, http://www.pq17.eclipse.co.uk /convoy_PQ17_July1942.htm.

"The Unfinished Cold War at Sea," by Anatoly Miranovsky, translated by Dmitry Sudakov, previously published as "It Was US and UK That Sank Russia's Kursk Submarine," on *Pravda Report*, August 12, 2016, http://www.pravdareport.com /society/stories/12-08-2016/121163-kursk_submarine-0/. Reprinted courtesy of Pravda.Ru.

"China Returns to the Ocean," by Daniel J. Kostecka, previously published as "Aerospace Power and China's Counterstrike Doctrine in the Near Seas," in *China's Near Seas Combat Capabilities*, edited by Peter Dutton, Andrew S. Erickson, and Ryan Martinson (Newport, RI: Naval War College, China Maritime Studies Institute, February 2014), 57–59.

Part VII. Piracy

"The Sea Peoples," by Shelley Wachsmann, previously published as "To the Sea of the Philistines," in *The Sea Peoples and Their World: A Reassessment*, edited by Eliezer Oren (Philadelphia: University of Pennsylvania Press, 2000), 103–5. Used by permission of the University of Pennsylvania Press.

"Patrick and the Pirates," by John Bagnell Bury, from *The Life of St. Patrick and His Place in History* (London: Macmillan and Company, 1905), 16–27.

"The Pirates of the Mediterranean," by Frederic C. Lane, from *Venice: A Maritime Republic* (Baltimore, MD: Johns Hopkins University Press, 1973), 384–88. © 1973 Johns Hopkins University Press. Reprinted with permission of Johns Hopkins University Press.

"The First Pirate of the Caribbean: Christopher Columbus," by Michele de Cuneo, from *Cartas de particulares a Colón y Relaciones coetáneas*, edited by Juan Gil and Consuelo Varela (Madrid: Alianza Editorial, 1984), 239–42. Correspondence from 1495 originally published as "De novitatibus insularum occeani Hesperii repertarum a don Christoforo Columbo genuensi," in *Raccolta di Documenti e Studi pubblicati dalla R. Commissione colombiana*, part III, vol. 2, edited by Guglielmo Berchet (Rome: Ministero della pubblica istruzione, 1893), 96–107.

"American Sea Rovers," by Alexander Exquemelin, from *The History of the Buccaneers of America* (Boston: Benjamin B. Mussey and Company, 1853), 48–50.

"Born to Be Hanged," by Captain Charles Johnson, from *The Lives and Adventures of Sundry Notorious Pirates* (London: Jonathan Cape, 1921), 67–70.

"The Dutch Pirate Admiral: Piet Hein," by Jan Pieter Heije, previously published as "De Zilvervloot," in *Kun je nog zingen, zing dan mee*, edited by Jan Veldkamp and Klaas de Boer (Groningen: P. Noordhoff, 1906), 46.

"The Chinese Pirate Admiral: Koxinga," by Koxinga, from his letter to Coyett, translated by Donald Keene, in *The Battles of Coxinga: Chikamatsu's Puppet Play, Its Background and Importance*, by Donald Keene and Chikamatsu Monzaemon (London: Taylor's Foreign Press, 1950), 57–59. Reprinted by permission of Donald Keene.

"Song of the Pirate," by José de Espronceda, previously published as "Canción del Pirata" in *El Artista*, edited by Eugenio de Ochoa and Federico de Madrazo (Madrid, 1835), 43–44.

"Somali Pirates Attack a Cruise Ship," by Eric Paul Roorda. Written for this volume.

Part VIII. Shipwrecks and Castaways

"Shipwrecked by Worms, Saved by Canoe: The Last Voyage of Columbus," by Diego Méndez, from "Relación hecha por Diego Méndez de algunos acontecimientos del último viaje del Almirante D. Cristóbal Colón," in *Viajes de Cristóbal Colón*, edited by M. Fernández Navarrete (Madrid: Calpe, 1825), 351–67.

"The Unparalleled Sufferings of John Jea," by John Jea, from *The Life, History, and Unparalleled Sufferings of John Jea, the African Preacher, Compiled and Written by Himself* (Portsea, UK: self-published, 1811), 49–54.

"*Pandora's Box*," by Peter Heywood, correspondence from Peter Heywood to Mrs. Elizabeth Heywood, November 20, 1791, from the *Correspondence of Miss Nessy Heywood during 1790–92* (commonly referred to as "'The Heywood Manuscript'") in the Newberry Library, Chicago, call number VAULT Case MS folio E5.H5078.

"The Real Moby-Dick," by Owen Chase, from *Narrative of the Most Extraordinary and Distressing Shipwreck of the Whale-Ship Essex* (New York: W. B. Gilley, 1821), 24–34, 61–62, 77–78, 108, 115–18, 122–24.

"The Castaway," by Herman Melville, from *Moby-Dick; or, The Whale* (New York: Harper and Brothers, 1851), 458–63.

"Just Keep Rowing . . . !," by William Hale, from *Howard Blackburn: Hero and Fisherman* (Gloucester, MA: Cape Ann Breeze Printing, 1895), 25–51.

"Life of Poon," by anonymous, transcribed from "Poon Lim Honoured," *British Pathé* newsreel, August 11, 1943, http://www.britishpathe.com/video/poon-lim-honoured. Used courtesy of British Pathé.

"A Three-Hour Tour Becomes a Four-Month Ordeal," by anonymous, previously published as "*McClusky* Rescues Mariner Adrift for Nearly Four Months," on the United States Navy website, September 25, 2002, http://www.navy.mil/submit /display.asp?story_id=3736.

Part IX. Inspiration

"The Asian Sea Goddess," by Eric Paul Roorda. Written for this volume.

"The Hajj by Sea," by Hadji Khan and Wilfrid Sparroy, from *With the Pilgrims to Mecca: The Great Pilgrimage of A.H. 1319; A.D. 1902* (New York and London: John Lane, 1905), 82–83, 87–90, 93.

"Durr Freedley's 'Saints of the Sea,'" by anonymous, from *Catalogue of the Memorial Exhibition of Paintings and Drawings by Durr Freedley held at the John Herron Art Museum, Indianapolis, Indiana, 1–27 November 1938*, reprinted in an interpretive brochure at the Chapel by the Sea, memorial chapel at Seamen's Church Institute, Newport, RI. Used courtesy of Seamen's Church Institute.

"Missionary to Micronesia," by Hiram Bingham, from *Story of the Morning Star: The Children's Missionary Vessel* (Boston: American Board Missionary House, 1883), 22–24, 28–30, 33, 42–44, 52–53, 77–78.

"The Voyage," by Johann Wolfgang von Goethe, previously published as "Seefahrt" in *Deutsche Lyrik*, edited by Konrad Schaum (New York: W. W. Norton and Company, 1963), 14–16. Originally published as "G. den 11. September 1776" in *Deutsches Museum* 2 (1777): 267–69.

"The Northern Seas," by William Howitt, from *Sketches of Natural History*, by Mary Howitt (London: Effinghan Wilson, Royal Exchange, 1834), 93–96.

"The World below the Brine," by Walt Whitman, from *Leaves of Grass* (Philadelphia: David McKay, 1883), 206–7.

"Far Off-Shore," by Herman Melville, from *John Marr and Other Sailors: With Some Sea-Pieces* (New York: De Vinne Press, 1888), 86.

"Sea Pictures," by Sir Edward Elgar, drawing on poetry by Roden Noel, Caroline Alice Elgar, Elizabeth Barrett Browning, Richard Garnett, and Adam Lindsey Gordon (London: Boosey & Hawkes, 1899), available from http://www.lieder.net/lieder /assemble_texts.html?SongCycleId=384.

"Voyage to Montevideo," by Dino Campana, previously published as "Viaggio a Montevideo," in *Canti Orfici* (Marradi, Italy: Tipografia F. Ravagli, 1914), 39–40.

"The Ballad of the Seawater," by Federico García Lorca, previously published as "La Balada del agua del mar," in *Libro de Poemas* (Madrid: Imprenta Maroto, 1921).

Part X. Recreation

"Surfing: A Royal Sport," by Jack London, from *The Cruise of the Snark* (London: Mills and Boon, 1911), 82–84.

"The Compleat Angler," by Izaak Walton, from *The Compleat Angler, or The Contemplative Man's Recreation* (London and New York: Cassell and Company, 1909), 91 (song), 44–47, 50–51, originally published, London: T. Maxey for Richard Marriot, 1653.

"Women and Children Next: The Family Goes to Sea," by Lady Anna Brassey, from *A Voyage in the Yacht "Sunbeam": Our Home on the Ocean for Eleven Months* (Chicago: J. W. Henry, 1890), 2–6, 10–11, 36–39, 130–32, 186–87, 192–93, 238–39, 284–89, 333–35, 415, 417–18, 426–28, 445–46, 452–53.

"The First Solo Circumnavigation," by Joshua Slocum, from *Sailing Alone around the World* (New York: Century Company, 1900), 81–82, 180–81, 210–11, 267–69, 272–78.

"The Cruise," by G. B. Barrows, from her personal journal. Miss Barrows Archive, 1899. Courtesy of the Roorda/Doyle Collection.

"The Compleat Goggler," by Guy Gilpatric, from *The Compleat Goggler* (New York: Dodd, Mead and Company, 1934), 2–7, 11.

"Round the World! Journal of a Sailing Voyage—from a Teen's Point of View," by Katrina Bercaw, from her personal journal. Used courtesy of the author.

Part XI. Laboratory

"The Pliny Deep," by Pliny the Elder, from *Pliny's Natural History*, vol. 1, translated by John Bostock and H. T. Riley (London: Henry G. Bohn, 1855), 128–31.

"Leonardo's Notes on the Ocean," by Leonardo da Vinci, from *The Notebooks of Leonardo da Vinci*, vol. 2, edited and translated by Jean Paul Richter (Mineola, NY: Dover Publications, 1970), originally published as *The Literary Works of Leonardo da Vinci* (London: Sampson Low, Marston, Searle and Rivington, 1883), 932–53.

"The Discovery of the Gulf Stream," by Benjamin Franklin, from *Transactions of the American Philosophical Association*, vol. 2 (Philadelphia: American Philosophical Association, 1786), 314–17.

"Celestial Navigation for the People," by Nathaniel Ingersoll Bowditch, from *Memoir of Nathaniel Bowditch* (Boston: C. C. Little and J. Brow, 1840), 27–31, 33–37.

"The Ocean and the Atmosphere," by Matthew Fontaine Maury, from *The Physical Geography of the Sea* (New York: Harper and Brothers, 1855), 345–50.

"Hurrah for the Dredge!," by Edward Forbes, previously published as "The Dredging Song," in *Memoir of Edward Forbes*, by George Wilson and Archibald Geikie (London: Macmillan and Co., 1861), 247.

"Return of the Fossil Fish," by J. L. B. Smith, from *The Search beneath the Sea: The Story of the Coelacanth* (New York: Henry Holt and Company, 1956), 20–21, 23–25, 30.

Part XII. The Endangered Ocean

"Goodbye, Plankton," by William Beebe, from *The Arcturus Adventure: An Account of the New York Zoological Society's First Oceanographic Expedition* (New York: G. P. Putnam and Sons, 1926), 194–201.

"Ocean Acidification," by the National Oceanic and Atmospheric Administration, previously published as "What Is Ocean Acidification?," on PMEL Carbon Program, January 2011, http://www.pmel.noaa.gov/co2/story/What+is+Ocean+Acidification %3F. Used by permission of the National Oceanic and Atmospheric Administration (NOAA), Pacific Marine Environmental Laboratory (PMEL).

"Attack of the Invasive Species!": (1) (an earlier version in a different form) "Blue Immigrants: The Marine Biology of Maritime History," by James T. Carlton, *The Log of Mystic Seaport* 44 (1992): 31–36. (2) "JTMD," by James T. Carlton. Used courtesy of the author.

"The First Dead Zone": (1) "Down the Mississippi to the Gulf of Mexico," by University of Michigan, previously published as "U-M Researcher and Colleagues Predict Possible Record-Setting Gulf of Mexico 'Dead Zone,'" in *Michigan News*, University of Michigan, June 13, 2013, http://www.ns.umich.edu/new/releases/21538-u-m -researcher-and-colleagues-predict-possible-record-setting-gulf-of-mexico-dead -zone-modest-chesapeake-bay-oxygen-starved-zone. Used courtesy of *Michigan News*. (2) "A Dire Update," by Matt Rota, previously published as "Dead Zone Forecasted to Be 'Average,' and That's Not Good," on *Gulf Restoration Network* (blog), June 25, 2015, http://www.healthygulf.org/blog/dead-zone-forecasted -be-average-and-thats-not-good. Used courtesy of Matt Rota.

"The First Trash Vortex," by Charles Moore, previously published as "Conversation: Captain Charles Moore . . . Talks Trash," interview conducted and edited by Neil Greenburg, *Earth Island Journal*, spring 2009, http://www.earthisland.org/journal /index.php/eij/article/charles_moore/. Used courtesy of *Earth Island Journal*.

"The Rise of Slime," by Jeremy Jackson, previously published as "Oceans on the Precipice: Scripps Scientist Warns of Mass Extinctions and 'Rise of Slime,'" on Scripps Institution of Oceanography, UC San Diego, August 13, 2008, https://scripps.ucsd .edu/news/2450. Used courtesy of Scripps Institution of Oceanography.

Index

mammals, marine: dolphin, 359, 395, 467;
manatee, 124; polar bear, 343; porpoise,
134, 395, 407, 429–31; sea lion, 56–57, 93, 306,
359, 423; seal, 93, 121, 124, 145, 359, 361, 381,
404, 431, 467; Steller's sea cow, 124; walrus,
124, 363, 419, 463; whale, 2, 23, 56, 76, 109,
112, 121, 123, 125, 135–45, 183, 313–14, 316–17,
321–22
manatee, 124
Manila Bay, 447
Maoris, 88–92
Maquarie Island, 93
Marathon, Battle of, 208
Mariana Islands, 63, 67, 116, 453
Mariana Trench, 2, 116–17, 453
Marie Galante, 274–75
Marmara, Sea of, 209
Marryat, Frederick, 226–33
Marseilles, France, 342
Marshall Islands, 354–57
Martel, Yann, 331
Massachusetts Bay, 127–29
Mauritius, 89–90, 392, 409
Maury, Matthew Fontaine, 450–54
McLean, Malcolm, 199–201
Meadowcroft Rock Shelter, Pennsylvania,
53–54
Mecca, Saudi Arabia, 75, 153, 155, 172, 342–44
Medina, Saudi Arabia, 155
Mediterranean Sea, 205–13, 253–54, 261, 263,
270–72, 344–45, 348, 351, 392, 415–20, 441,
446, 455, 490
Mehmet II, 210
Melville, Herman, 136–43, 151, 167, 226, 313,
321–24, 333, 364, 421, 432
Méndez de Segura, Diego, 299–300
menhaden, 129–34, 136
Mercer, Samuel A. B., 7
Merighi, Matthew, 210–14
Merry Men of Mey, 297
Messina, 435–36; Strait of, 342, 346
Mexico, 219, 256, 279, 428–30
Mexico, Gulf of, 305, 416, 442–43, 483–85
Micronesia, 63–66, 352–57
Midway, Battle of, 238–44
Minoans, 263–65
Moana, 60
Moby Dick, 136, 167, 313, 321, 421, 424, 430, 432
Mon Lei, 287
Monte Verde, Chile, 50, 54–55
Montevideo, Uruguay, 373–74
Moonlight Battle, 220
Moore, Charles, 486–93
Morant Bay, 413
Morning Star, 352–57

Mundy, Godfrey Basil, 220
Muppet Treasure Island, 283
Murderers Bay, 90–91
Murmansk, Russia, 245, 251
murre, 463
Mycenaeans, 263–65

Nantucket, 167, 442
Naples, 271; Bay of, 366
Natasha, 421–32
National Oceanic and Atmospheric Admin-
istration, 470–72, 483–85
Nelson, Horatio, 220, 226–32
Netherlands, 58, 135, 215, 283–84, 289, 480
Newark, New Jersey, 199–200
New Bedford, Massachusetts, 135, 142, 321
New Caledonia, 68
Newfoundland, 120, 123, 144–47, 251, 325, 330,
443, 445, 474
New York City, 281, 305, 321, 331, 346, 349, 417,
442, 476–78
New York Yacht Club, 377
New Zealand, 14, 60, 88–92, 102, 476
Nile, Battle of the, 232
Niles, Blair, 103
Noël, Roden Berkeley Wriothesley,
366–68
Normandy, 199, 278
North Cape, Norway, 251
northern snakehead fish, 473
North Sea, 190, 297, 385–86
Northwest Passage, 118–19
Norway, 125, 135, 246, 251, 388, 397, 460
Novaya Zemlya, 247, 249
Nuku Hiva, 409

O'Brien, Patrick, 226
oceanography, 450, 456, 494
Office of Naval Intelligence, 238
Olmsted, Frederick Law, 174–79
O'Reilly Island, 118
Ottoman Empire, 210–14
Owens Boats, 431
oyster, 403, 413, 438, 468, 471, 480

Pacific Islanders, 14–18, 60–68, 382
Pacific Ocean, 2–3, 14–15, 17, 19, 49, 52, 55–56,
60–65, 67, 86, 88, 116, 118–20, 124, 135–38,
139, 141, 143, 148, 167, 174, 178, 182, 195, 215,
217, 219, 238–39, 241, 245, 256–59, 287, 313,
321, 331, 333, 335, 352–53, 355, 377, 381–82, 397,
402–3, 409, 416, 425, 429, 453, 463–65, 471,
476, 479–82, 486–88, 493, 495
Paisley Caves, Oregon, 50, 54
Palmer, Nathaniel, 93